British
Parliamentary Papers

CHILDREN'S EMPLOYMENT
COMMISSION

Industrial Revolution
Children's Employment 6

IRISH UNIVERSITY PRESS SERIES

OF

British
Parliamentary Papers

CHILDREN'S EMPLOYMENT
COMMISSION
FIRST REPORT OF THE
COMMISSIONERS
MINES

Industrial Revolution
Children's Employment
6

SHANNON · IRELAND

SBN 7165 0085 X

PUBLISHER'S NOTE

The Irish University Press Series of British Parliamentary Papers is a
facsimile reproduction. The original documents in this volume have
been reproduced by photo-lithography and are unabridged even to
the extent of faithfully retaining the printer's imprint.

The contents of this volume have been printed in their entirety by
Robert Hogg, Printer to the Irish University Press, Shannon, Ireland.

As a result of the arrangement of the documents in subject sets and
of the bringing together in a single book of a number of papers, some
volumes in the Irish University Press Series may include the imprints
of more than one printer.

Irish University Press Shannon Ireland
DUBLIN CORK BELFAST LONDON NEW YORK
Captain T M MacGlinchey Publisher

PRINTED IN IRELAND AT SHANNON
BY ROBERT HOGG PRINTER TO IRISH UNIVERSITY PRESS

REPORTS

FROM

COMMISSIONERS:

ELEVEN VOLUMES.

———

—*(1.)*—

CHILDREN'S EMPLOYMENT

(MINES).

Session

3 February —— *12 August* 1842.

VOL. XV.

1842.

REPORTS FROM COMMISSIONERS:

1842.

ELEVEN VOLUMES:—CONTENTS OF THE

FIRST VOLUME.

N.B.—*THE* Figures *at the* beginning of the line, *correspond with the* Nº *at the* foot *of each* Report; *and the* Figures *at the* end of the line, *refer to the* MS. Paging *of the Volumes arranged for The House of Commons.*

CHILDREN'S EMPLOYMENT:

Children's Employment Commission.

FIRST

REPORT OF THE COMMISSIONERS.

MINES.

Presented to both Houses of Parliament by Command of Her Majesty.

LONDON:

PRINTED BY WILLIAM CLOWES AND SONS, STAMFORD STREET,
FOR HER MAJESTY'S STATIONERY OFFICE.

1842.

CONTENTS.

COMMISSION

(UNDER THE GREAT SEAL)

FOR INQUIRING INTO THE EMPLOYMENT AND CONDITION OF CHILDREN IN MINES AND MANUFACTORIES.

VICTORIA, by the Grace of God, of the United Kingdom of Great Britain and Ireland Queen, Defender of the Faith: To Our trusty and well beloved Thomas Tooke, Esquire, Thomas Southwood Smith, Esquire, Doctor in Medicine, together with Leonard Horner, and Robert John Saunders, Esquires, Two of Our Inspectors of Factories, Greeting:—WHEREAS, an humble Address was presented unto Us by the Knights, Citizens, and Burgesses, and Commissioners of Shires and Burghs in Parliament assembled, humbly beseeching Us that We would be graciously pleased to direct an Inquiry to be made into the Employment of the Children of the Poorer Classes in Mines and Collieries, and the various branches of Trade and Manufacture in which numbers of Children work together, not being included in the provisions of the Acts for regulating the Employment of Children and Young Persons in Mills and Factories, and to collect information as to the ages at which they are employed, the number of hours they are engaged in work, the time allowed each day for meals, and as to the actual state, condition, and treatment of such Children, and as to the effects of such Employment, both with regard to their morals and their bodily health; Now KNOW YE, That We, reposing great trust and confidence in your ability and discretion, have nominated, constituted, and appointed, and do by these presents nominate, constitute, and appoint you, the said Thomas Tooke, Thomas Southwood Smith, together with Leonard Horner and Robert John Saunders, to be Our Commissioners for the purposes aforesaid; And We do hereby enjoin you to obey all directions touching the premises which shall from time to time be given to you, or any two or more of you, by one of our principal Secretaries of State: And for the better discovery of the truth in the premises, We do, by these presents, give and grant to you, or any two or more of you, full power and authority to call before you, or any two or more of you, such persons as you shall judge necessary, by whom you may be the better informed of the truth in the premises, and to inquire of the premises and every part thereof, by all other lawful ways and means whatsoever; And We do hereby also give and grant unto you, or any two or more of you, full power and authority when the same shall appear to be requisite, to administer an oath or oaths to any person or persons whatsoever, to be examined before you, or any two or more of you, touching or concerning the premises; And Our further will and pleasure is, that you Our said Commissioners, or any three of you, do, with as little delay as may be consistent with a due discharge of the duties hereby imposed upon you, Certify to Us, under your hands and seals, or under the hands and seals of any three of you, your several proceedings in the premises; And We further will and command, and by these presents ordain, that this Our Commission shall continue in full force and virtue, and that you, Our said Commissioners, or any two or more of you, shall and may from time to time proceed in the execution thereof, and of every matter and thing therein contained, although the same be not continued, from time to time by adjournment: AND WE HEREBY COMMAND all and singular Our Justices of the Peace, Sheriffs, Mayors, Bailiffs, Constables, Officers, Ministers, and all other Our loving Subjects whatsover, as well within Liberties as without, that they be assistant to you and each of you in the execution of these presents: And for your assistance in the due execution of this Commission, We have made choice of Our trusty and well beloved Joseph Fletcher, Esquire, to be Secretary to this Our Commission, whose services we require you to use from time to time, as occasion may require. In witness whereof, We have caused these our Letters to be made Patent. Witness Ourself at Westminster, the Twentieth day of October, in the Fourth Year of Our Reign.

By Writ of Privy Seal.

EDMUNDS.

LETTER OF INSTRUCTIONS EXTENDING THE TERMS OF THE COMMISSION TO "YOUNG PERSONS."

Whitehall, February 11th, 1841.

GENTLEMEN,

THE QUEEN having been pleased to comply with the prayer of an humble Address presented to Her Majesty, in pursuance of a Resolution of the House of Commons, dated 4th of February, 1841, "That Her Majesty will be graciously " pleased to direct that the Commission appointed in answer to an Address of " this House, on August 4, 1840, for the investigation of certain branches of " Infant Labour, do include within its inquiry the Labour also of Young Persons " designated as such by the provisions of the Factory Act;" I am directed by the Marquess of Normanby to desire that you will include within your inquiry the Labour of Young Persons designated as such by the provisions of the Factory Act accordingly.

I am, Gentlemen,

Your obedient Servant,

(Signed)   F. MAULE.

The Commissioners for inquiring into the Condition
of Children employed in Mines, &c.

CONTENTS OF THE REPORT.

Children's Employment Commission.

FIRST REPORT OF THE COMMISSIONERS.

TO THE QUEEN'S MOST EXCELLENT MAJESTY.

MINES.

1. WE, the Commissioners appointed by Your Majesty to inquire into " The Employment and Condition of the Children of the Poorer Classes in Mines and Collieries, and the various branches of Trade and Manufacture in which numbers of Children work together, not being included in the provisions of the Acts for regulating the Employment of Children in Mills and Factories, and to collect information as to the ages at which they are employed, the number of hours they are engaged in work, the time allowed each day for meals, and as to the actual state, condition, and treatment of such Children, and as to the effects of such Employment, both with regard to their morals and their bodily health," humbly report to Your Majesty, in manner following, our proceedings in the execution of Your Majesty's Commission.

2. The original Commission by which your Majesty was pleased to appoint us to our office was issued on the 20th of October, 1840, and, by its terms, the investigation which we were enjoined to institute was restricted to the employment and condition of CHILDREN; a term which we felt bound to construe in the sense assigned to it in the Factories Regulation Act, and to understand as meaning those who have not completed the thirteenth year of their age.

3. In conformity with this view, the Instructions which we first drew up for the guidance of the Sub-Commissioners were framed with a reference to the employment and condition of CHILDREN only; but subsequently, your Majesty having been pleased, in compliance with the prayer of an Address voted by the House of Commons on the 4th of February, 1841, to issue an order, "that the Commission do include within its inquiry the labour also of YOUNG PERSONS, designated as such by the provisions of the Factory Act," thenceforward we extended the inquiry so as to embrace the employment and condition of the adolescent.

4. Our first concern in the execution of the duty confided to us was to divide the wide field of inquiry to be entered upon, into convenient districts; to assign to each district, from among the Sub-Commissioners appointed by the Secretary of State for the Home Department, the person whose previous knowledge and pursuits, as far as we were enabled to judge of them, seemed best to qualify him for prosecuting the investigation into the main branches of industry carried on in that particular district; to frame Instructions for the guidance of the Sub-Commissioners in the collection and verification of evidence; to construct Tabular Forms to be filled up by the Employers of Children and Young Persons, and to draw up Queries to be answered by them, which might assist the Sub-Commissioners in their personal examinations, and economise their time and labour; and finally, by putting the Employers of labour in possession of the real object of the Commission, to endeavour to obtain their co-operation in its accomplishment.

5. To the Instructions to the Sub-Commissioners which accompany this Report, we beg to refer, as containing an exposition of the view which we entertained of the nature and extent of the Inquiry, of the spirit in which it should be conducted, of the difficulties to be expected in the prosecution of it, and of the degree of success which we ventured to hope might ultimately attend the labours of the Commission.

6. We have the satisfaction of being able to state that in every part of the

country, and in relation to every branch of industry, with very few exceptions, the Employers of Children have afforded to the Sub-Commissioners, in their respective districts, all the facilities for prosecuting their personal investigations which could be desired.

7. We have also to acknowledge the readiness with which many of the Employers of Children have answered the Queries addressed to them, and have filled up the Tabular Forms in the manner required. Had all done so, it would have been in our power to state, with a close approximation to the truth, the actual number of Children and Young Persons employed in the various branches of mining and manufacturing industry in each district, as well as the relative proportion of those under age to the adult workpeople. From the Returns actually received we have been enabled to ascertain, in almost all cases, the relative proportion of Children and Young Persons to the Adult labourers in each district; but only a part of the papers in question having been filled up, we are not enabled to form a probable estimate of the total number of persons under age in the mines and manufactures included in the inquiry, either for the whole of the kingdom, or for any portion of it. It is, however, of considerable importance to have obtained some approximation to the proportion which the labour of Children and Young Persons bears to that of Adults.

8. The Inquiry prescribed by the Commission extending to the whole of the United Kingdom, and embracing all occupations in which Children and Young Persons work together in numbers, not included under the Factories Regulation Act, it was difficult in the outset to make exact subdivisions of this extensive field, and to assign to each Sub-Commissioner a precise district to which his local labours should be devoted. At first, indeed, the real amount of the labour necessary to complete the inquiry being altogether unknown, even the number of assistants whose services would be required could not be determined; and there being no sources from which we could obtain such statistical information as would enable us to form any estimate of the extent of the occupations, and the magnitude and relative situation of the places in which they are carried on, some caution was necessary to avoid a waste of time, labour, and expense on the part of those to whom the local investigations were intrusted.

9. On the completion of the Instructions addressed by the Commissioners to their Assistants, six Sub-Commissioners were appointed by the Secretary of State, near the close of November, 1840, namely—James Mitchell, Esq., LL.D.; John Lawson Kennedy, Esq.; Samuel Swain Scriven, Esq.; Leonard Stewart, Esq., M.D.; Jelinger Cookson Symons, Esq.; and Richard Dugard Grainger, Esq. Immediate occupation was found for these gentlemen respectively in the iron and coal mining districts of South Staffordshire and Shropshire; in the mining and manufacturing districts around Manchester; in the pottery district of North Staffordshire; in the manufacturing districts of the West of England; in the manufacturing districts around Sheffield; and in the midland manufacturing districts of Birmingham, Derby, Nottingham, and Leicester: these being portions of South Britain which could not fail to afford ample field for their labours.

10. Having as yet no Assistants to send to the more northern parts of England, nor to Scotland and Ireland, the Commissioners at the commencement of January, 1841, requested the Secretary of State to increase the number of Sub-Commissioners to twelve. Accordingly, in the course of that month, Thomas Tancred, Esq., was sent to the West of Scotland; Robert Hugh Franks, Esq., to the East of Scotland; Frederick Roper, Esq., to Ireland; William Rayner Wood, Esq., to the northern parts of the West Riding of Yorkshire; John Roby Leifchild, Esq., to the coal-mining districts of North Durham and Northumberland; and Anthony Austin, Esq., to the manufacturing and mining districts in the West and North of Lancashire.

11. Such was the severity of the season in which these gentlemen, as well as the six first appointed, had to commence their labours, that nearly all of them incurred serious indisposition, which in a short time compelled Mr. Wood to give up the task he had undertaken, and from which Mr. Roper never recovered during the whole term of his labours. Mr. Austin, also, towards the close of his labours, suffered severely from indisposition, induced by unusual fatigue; nor will this amount of illness occasion surprise to any one who knows the toilsome nature of the duty of inspecting mines, or who is acquainted with the character of the other places of work which were visited in rapid succession by persons accustomed only to ordinary exposure, and to ordinary changes of temperature.

12. Some delay took place before inquiries could be commenced in North and South Wales. It was deemed essential that the Sub-Commissioners for these important mining districts should be acquainted with the Welsh language, no information collected under this Commission being considered satisfactory unless derived, in part at least, from a personal examination of the Children and Young Persons themselves. The knowledge which we obtained at an early period of the magnitude and importance of several other of the mining and manufacturing districts making it evident that the gentlemen already employed in examining them could not complete their investigations within a moderate space of time, the number of Sub-Commissioners was ultimately increased to twenty.

13. The Sub-Commissioners last appointed, eight in number, at the end of February and early in March were directed to proceed—Thomas Martin, Esq., to the North of Ireland, while the South was left to Mr. Roper; Elijah Waring, Esq., to the Forest of Dean and the South Gloucestershire coal districts; Major Burns to the paper manufactories and other establishments in the South-East of England; Richard Henry Horne, Esq., to the iron manufacturing district of Staffordshire and the contiguous counties; John Michael Fellows, Esq., to the coal-mining districts of Derbyshire and Nottinghamshire; Charles Barham Esq., M.D., to the mining districts of Cornwall and Devonshire; Rhys William Jones, Esq., to the mining districts of South Wales; and Hugh Herbert Jones, Esq., to those of North Wales and its borders.

14. Although nearly all the great fields of Infant Labour were now subjected to inquiry, yet the retirement of Mr. Wood, whose indisposition had prevented him from pursuing his investigations beyond the vicinities of Bradford and Leeds, rendered it necessary to extend Mr. Symons's district so as to comprise the more northern part of the West Riding of Yorkshire, while the remainder of the coal fields of this district were allotted to Mr. Scriven, who had completed his labours in the pottery district of Staffordshire. Dr. Mitchell likewise was requested to extend his inquiries from the coal-fields of South Staffordshire to those of Warwickshire, Leicestershire, and South Durham, and ultimately to the lead-mines of the mountainous region on the borders of Durham, Northumberland, and Cumberland. To Mr. Grainger were made over some investigations in the metropolis which had been commenced by Dr. Mitchell. After returning from the cities of Bath and Bristol, and the mining district of North Somersetshire, Dr. Stewart was requested to visit Norwich; Mr. Franks, after concluding his inquiries in the East of Scotland, was directed to visit the South Wales district, to assist Mr. Rhys William Jones, who had allowed so much delay to interrupt his labours that the Commissioners were anxious as to the success of the investigation in this very important district; and lastly, circumstances arose which rendered it desirable that Mr. Symons should further investigate the state of the coal-mines in Cumberland, and that our Secretary, Mr. Fletcher, should inspect some of the coal-mines in the neighbourhood of Oldham.

15. Before proceeding to the execution of the duty which now devolves upon us, it may be proper to state our own view of that duty. We apprehend that the circumstances under which the present Commission has been appointed are materially different from those under which the Factory and the Hand Loom Weavers Commissions, both of which may be regarded as having some analogy to it, were directed to make their investigations. Committees of the House of Commons, in successive sessions, had already inquired into the condition of persons employed in mills and factories; and the principle of legislative interference in behalf of Children and Young Persons so employed having been decided and acted on by the passing of several Acts of Parliament for their protection, the real object of the Factory Commission was to ascertain the practical efficiency or inefficiency of those Acts; and to devise measures, if any should be proved to be necessary, which might better accomplish the declared purpose of the Legislature. Accordingly, by the terms of the Factory Commission, the Commissioners were enjoined not only to collect information in the manufacturing "districts as to the employment of Children in factories," but "as to the propriety and means of curtailing the hours of their labour, so as to enable Parliament to legislate on the subject during the present session (namely, that of 1833);" not only to investigate the actual state and condition of such Children, and the effects of their employment on their morals and health, but also "to inquire in what respect the laws made for the protection of such Children have been found to be insufficient for such purpose, and what further provisions may be necessary for their protection."

16. In like manner public attention had long been drawn in various ways to the altered condition of hand-loom weavers, and the distress of this large body of operatives being a matter of notoriety and a subject of general sympathy, the Commissioners were enjoined not only " to inquire into the condition of the hand-loom weavers," but "to report whether any, and, if so, what measures can be devised for their relief."

17. But of the condition of persons employed in the mining and manufacturing branches of industry, into which it was the object of the present Commission to make inquiry, little was generally known. It was indeed notorious that in some of these occupations great numbers of Children are employed at very early ages. It was equally notorious that some of these occupations are among the most laborious in which it is the lot of human beings to toil; but no Committee of the House of Commons had instituted inquiry into the actual condition of this class of labourers; no Commission had been issued to investigate that condition; no attempt of any kind had hitherto been made to ascertain the ages at which the Children in question really begin to work, the number of hours during which they labour, the exact nature of their employment, nor the immediate and ultimate effects of such employment on their morals and health. It was natural that less should be known of some of the most important of these occupations, those of the mines especially, than of any other descriptions of labour of equal importance, in which equal numbers are employed, because the operations are wholly removed from ordinary view, the places in which they are carried on are inaccessible excepting to the employers and the employed, and the operations themselves are very peculiar, and have little in common with ordinary labour. Whether the condition of the persons employed in this description of labour, and in the various branches of trade and manufacture included in the present inquiry, be such as to call for legislative interference, and if so whether any practical and efficient legislative measures can be devised for their relief, are questions which can be answered only after that condition shall have been fully and correctly ascertained. The terms of the present Commission are framed with a special reference to the acquisition of such information, the possession of which must necessarily precede sound and successful legislation. Accordingly, while this Commission declares its object to be to cause " An Inquiry to be made into the Employment of the Children of the Poorer Classes in Mines and Collieries, and the various branches of Trade and Manufacture in which numbers of Children work together, not being included in the provisions of the Acts for regulating the Employment of Children and Young Persons in Mills and Factories," the Commissioners are enjoined only " to collect information as to the ages at which the Children are employed, the number of hours they are engaged in work, the time allowed each day for meals, and as to the actual state, condition, and treatment of such Children, and as to the effects of such employment, both with regard to their morals and their bodily health;" the Inquiry being subsequently extended to Young Persons. Thus, by the terms of this Commission, the duty expressly assigned to the Commissioners is that of collecting information. They are not enjoined, as in the case of the Factory Commission, to inquire into " the propriety and means of curtailing the hours of the labour of the Children, so as to enable Parliament to legislate on the subject;" nor, as in the case of the Hand Loom Weavers Commission, " to report whether any, and, if so, what measures can be devised for their relief."

18. Conceiving, therefore, the duty assigned to us to be that of ascertaining the actual employment and the condition arising out of that employment of the persons included in the inquiry, we framed the Instructions to the Sub-Commissioners and the Queries addressed to the Employers of Labour, as well as the Tabular Forms to be filled up by them, as the best means which it was in our power to devise for collecting extensive preliminary information on all the subjects indicated in the Commission, as well as on many collateral matters the investigation of which seemed necessary to the complete elucidation of these subjects; and during the progress of the inquiry our care has been to ensure the correctness of all the information collected, and to guard it from being of a partial or *ex parte* character. Our desire has been to obtain the means of exhibiting a faithful picture of the present physical and moral condition of the juvenile working population employed in the great branches of industry included in the inquiry.

19. We believe the measures taken to accomplish this object have been attended with signal success, and that the Evidence collected by the Sub-Commissioners in their respective districts, and their Reports thereon, which are now complete,

together with the Returns received from the Employers of labour, afford a large mass of information, which has been collected with every precaution to ensure its correctness and impartiality, and which is likely to prove practically useful.

20. However arduous the task, we conceive ourselves bound by the acceptance of our office to endeavour, to the best of our power, to give a digest of the whole matter returned to us, and to exhibit the main results in a condensed and connected form. In the execution of this task we have found it absolutely necessary, at the sacrifice of conciseness, which we have very reluctantly been compelled to disregard, to enter into considerable detail, and frequently to repeat very similar statements, partly because the field of inquiry now explored is not only almost entirely new, but is exceedingly extensive and diversified, and partly because the uniformity of the statements of similar classes of witnesses, under a great diversity of circumstances, and in widely different districts, is itself the most satisfactory evidence of the correctness of the declarations which so coincide; and it seemed worth while to incur some risk of tediousness for the sake of obtaining this evidence of the truth of statements so important as many of those which we have to present.

21. The information returned to us has been derived from different classes of witnesses, such as the proprietors, agents, and managers of works, the children and young persons engaged in different kinds of labour, the adult workpeople, the parents of the children, medical men, teachers, ministers of religion, parochial officers connected with the administration of relief to the poor, police-officers, and magistrates. These witnesses give evidence as to the state of things in their own districts, according to their own observation and experience, and the main body of information collected is derived from personal examinations, in the form of depositions, of these different classes of witnesses.

22. When the mass of evidence thus obtained came to be examined, it soon appeared that similar branches of industry are carried on in different districts, under circumstances sometimes of considerable diversity; that the same classes of witnesses are common to all the districts, and that different classes of witnesses frequently make widely different statements in relation to the same alleged matters of fact. It became, therefore, an object of great importance to classify and dispose the statements of the different classes of witnesses in such a manner as to admit of the ready comparison of those statements one with another. Such a disposition of the evidence would not only facilitate, amidst conflicting statements, the discovery of the truth, but would render its exhibition more easy and more striking. With a view to the accomplishment of this object, however, it was necessary to make a complete analysis of the whole body of evidence; a task which has been undertaken and executed under the conviction that its usefulness would afford a full compensation for the labour.

23. The Commission itself divides the field of inquiry which it prescribes into two portions, namely, Mines and Manufactures. This division, which is a natural one, we have found it convenient to follow. Of labour in the mines much less is known than of labour in manufactories. In the labour of the mines there is much that is peculiar, by which it is distinguished from all other employment; and there is no kind of labour which exerts a more important and a more distinctly appreciable influence over the physical, the intellectual, and the moral condition of those who are employed in it from an early period of life. For all these reasons the mines present the first claim to our attention; and accordingly, following the above-mentioned division, we propose to make labour in the mines, and the processes immediately connected with them, the subject of this our first Report; reserving, as the subject of a second Report, the result of inquiries into the other occupations in which Children and Young Persons are employed in numbers.

24. For some of the reasons assigned, especially on account of the very peculiar nature of the work in the mines, the Commissioners, in order that they might be the better qualified to report on this important branch of the inquiry, thought it desirable that some of their own body should see a few instances of underground labour, and make themselves acquainted with the nature of it, by personal observation—at least as far as regards the employment and condition of the Children and Young Persons. With this view, Dr. Southwood Smith and Mr. Saunders, accompanied by the Sub-Commissioners for these districts, went down into, and personally inspected, several coal-mines in the West Riding of Yorkshire, namely, at Barnsley, Flockton, Elland, and Halifax; and that they might have an opportunity of comparing the condition of such pits as these, in which the seams of coal are in general thin, with the condition of those in which

the seams are the thickest, they also went down into one of the largest coal mines in Leicestershire, and minutely examined the workpeople both of that and of an adjoining mine.

25. The mines of the United Kingdom comprehend mines of coal and ironstone, and of the ores of tin, copper, zinc, and lead; the latter containing some proportion of silver. Though the processes by which the ores are reduced to the state of metal, and by which some of the metals, as iron, for example, are brought into a form convenient for their transportation and general use, may be regarded as manufacturing processes; still these processes are so closely connected with mining operations, both are so generally carried on by the same capitalists, and the workpeople employed in both are so intimately related, being often members of the same families, that it will be convenient to treat of the labour of both under the same general head.

26. The most natural distribution of the subject of labour, as connected with Mines, will be under the several heads of—

> I. COAL MINES.
> II. IRONSTONE MINES AND THE MANUFACTURE OF IRON.
> III. TIN, COPPER, LEAD, AND ZINC MINES, AND THE DRESSING AND SMELTING OF THEIR ORES.

I.—COAL MINES.

27. Of the Mines of the United Kingdom the COAL MINES are by far the most extensive; they employ incomparably the greatest number of Children and Young Persons; and, owing to the great diversities of their locality and geological character, they necessarily require corresponding differences in the modes of working them, which differences exert an important influence on the condition of the workers in general, and of those of tender age in particular.

28. The " Coal Measures," as the geological formations comprising the strata of coal are designated, are variously dispersed in the midland, northern, and western portions of South Britain, and in a broad belt of country which traverses the centre of Scotland, from the shores of Ayrshire to those of the Frith of Forth. There are likewise some coal tracts of far inferior importance in Ireland.

29. These several colliery districts will be brought most perspicuously under notice, by commencing with those in the midland counties of England; next noticing those of its northern counties; thence proceeding to Scotland; and finally returning to Wales and the western counties of England, and subjoining a brief notice of the Irish coal tracts. This is nearly the order in which the results of the local investigations have been gathered in; and it is one as well adapted as any other for the purposes of an analysis of them.

30. The most important of the midland coal tracts, or coal fields, as they are geologically termed, is that of SOUTH STAFFORDSHIRE, which, lying to the west and north of Birmingham, is remarkable for the extent to which its vast beds are worked, as well for the purpose of smelting the iron ores, which are raised from strata interspersed among the coal strata, as for the consumption of the neighbouring populous towns, which are the seat of the metal manufactures, and for an extensive " land sale,"—as the supply of the surrounding country with fuel is frequently designated; the country southward, where canals extend, as far as the Thames, being in great part supplied from this region. The SHROPSHIRE district of Coalbrookdale, lying midway between Wolverhampton and Shrewsbury, though much smaller in extent, is in like manner the seat of great iron works, and is the source of a supply of fuel for a great part of the vale of the Severn, and the country to the west of it, to the borders of Wales. The WARWICKSHIRE coal field occupies a large tract on the north-eastern verge of that county, from Coventry to Tamworth; and the LEICESTERSHIRE coal field surrounds the town of Ashby-de-la-Zouch. The coal of the latter is far more extensively wrought than that of the Warwickshire field; but both being without iron furnaces, their produce is required only for the land sale, which extends southward even through Buckinghamshire to the Thames.

31. In NORTH STAFFORDSHIRE, besides the coal field of the potteries, in which there are extensive ironworks at Kidscrew, there is a smaller tract contiguous to the town of Cheadle. The consumption of the produce of both, however, extends little beyond the northern parts of that county.

32. In the vale of the Trent, between Nottingham and Derby, commences the great coal-field of Derbyshire and Yorkshire, which extends hence northward, and of which the southern, or DERBYSHIRE portion, occupies the eastern side of that county, and extends at one extremity into Nottinghamshire. Besides supplying with fuel a vast surrounding region, especially to the east and south, in the counties of Leicester, Nottingham, and Lincoln, it has a considerable home consumption in iron-works. The northern, or YORKSHIRE portion, which is wholly comprised in the WEST RIDING, has extensive iron-works, and supplies with fuel the whole of Yorkshire, except the coast, and even makes some shipments down the Humber for London.

33. On the opposite side of the mountains which enclose Yorkshire on the west are the great coal-fields of LANCASHIRE, extending southward into the eastern part of CHESHIRE, and worked to an enormous extent for the supply of the manufactures and the manufacturing and commercial population which have congregated in their neighbourhood and upon their surface, although there is no manufacture of iron from native ores.

34. North of this is the CUMBERLAND Coal-field, in which likewise the pits are wrought only for sale, to supply the counties of Cumberland and Westmoreland, and for shipment, chiefly at Whitehaven, to Ireland and the opposite shores of Scotland.

35. Again crossing the mountains to the eastern side of the island, we find a large portion of the counties of Durham and Northumberland occupied by the coal tract, which, of all the districts having pits wrought almost wholly for sale, and only to a very small extent for the manufacture of metals, is by far the most important. It supplies not only the whole of those counties, the North Riding of Yorkshire, and the contiguous Scottish counties, but the whole of the eastern and southern coasts of England as far as Cornwall, including the metropolis itself, and the great south-eastern region, into which the sales of the inland coal-districts do not penetrate, because of the greater cost of land-carriage and the want of canals. The export to foreign parts is likewise very extensive; and the whole region is so important as to have rendered necessary, for the purposes of investigation, its division into two districts ; that of SOUTH DURHAM, south of the river Wear, and that of NORTH DURHAM and NORTHUMBERLAND, comprising the rest of the field.

36. The Coal Districts of the EAST OF SCOTLAND encircle the Frith of Forth in tracts of very irregular form, occupying large portions of the counties of East Lothian, Mid-Lothian, and West Lothian, of Stirlingshire and part of Dumbartonshire, of Clackmannanshire and Perthshire ; and of Fifeshire, in the districts of Dunfermline, Kirkaldy, Cupar, and St. Andrews : the coal of the whole of these districts is extensively wrought, chiefly for land sale to Edinburgh and the surrounding counties, though partly for shipment coastwise, and for the celebrated ironworks of the Carron Company in Stirlingshire.

37. Lanarkshire, Ayrshire, and Renfrewshire comprise nearly the whole of the irregularly scattered coal-fields of the WEST OF SCOTLAND, and their mines have been chiefly wrought, like those of Lancashire, for the supply of the manufactures, and of the great manufacturing and commercial population which have seated themselves upon their surface, or in their vicinity, with Glasgow for a centre; but of late years the district of Airdrie, to the east and south-east of Glasgow, has so rapidly extended its importance in the manufacture of iron from the excellent ores there found, as greatly to have augmented the working of its coal for that purpose also.

38. Returning southward, we find, on the eastern border of NORTH WALES, in the counties of Denbigh and Flint, where they border upon Cheshire, a large coal-field, heretofore possessed of considerable ironworks, which, however, seem now to be sinking before the competition of those in the West of Scotland, and other districts : it still, however, supplies with fuel nearly the whole of North Wales and a large portion of Cheshire and Shropshire.

39. But the greatest coal-basin of the West is that of SOUTH WALES, which, commencing in the politically English county of Monmouth, occupies a considerable portion also of the counties of Glamorgan, Carmarthen, and Pembroke. The internal consumption of its coal in the manufacture of its native ores of iron, and of

COAL MINES.
———

those of copper and tin brought from Cornwall and other parts, is enormous; and besides supplying with fuel the whole of South Wales and its borders, Cornwall, and a considerable part of Somersetshire, it exports large quantities of stone coal, even to London.

40. The FOREST OF DEAN is a singular detached coal field in Gloucestershire, between the confluent rivers Wye and Severn, in which pits are wrought for the manufacture of its excellent iron ores, and for the supply not only of the contiguous parts of Herefordshire and Gloucestershire, but also for a considerable land sale eastward towards Oxford. SOUTH GLOUCESTERSHIRE is, in great part, occupied by a coal field which extends northward from Bristol, and supplies that city and the contiguous country with fuel.

41. It is for a similar land sale that the valuable mines of NORTH SOMERSETSHIRE, on the other side of the Avon, are wrought; the principal being those to the south-west of Bath, which not only supply the contiguous country, but have an extensive sale eastward in Wiltshire and Berkshire.

42. Of the comparatively unimportant coal-fields of IRELAND, the principal are those of Castlecomer in Kilkenny and the Queen's County, where pits are worked for country sale by three proprietors; that near Killenaule, in the county of Tipperary, where there are three pits worked by the Mining Company of Ireland; and that of Dromagh and Dysart, in the county of Cork, where there are pits worked by Messrs. Leader. There are also a few pits at Drumglass and Coal Island, in the county of Tyrone, which, with the Arigna coal pits at the northern extremity of Roscommon, supplying some contiguous iron works, complete the list of the Irish coal mines which are now worked.

43. Besides the important coal fields which we have enumerated, there are in Great Britain some very small coal tracts into which it appeared scarcely necessary to direct special investigation; and, indeed, as we had reason to conclude that few if any Children are employed in them " working together in numbers," they seemed hardly to come within the scope of the present inquiry, as defined by the terms of our Commission.

44. Having defined the geographical limits of the several fields of inquiry to which the examinations of the Sub-Commissioners were directed, it is requisite, in order to present a condensed and connected statement of their results, to adopt a few analytical heads of arrangement, under which the peculiarities exhibited in each district may distinctly appear; and the following will serve for this purpose :—

1.—AGES AT WHICH CHILDREN AND YOUNG PERSONS ARE EMPLOYED IN COAL MINES.

2.—SEX: EMPLOYMENT OF GIRLS AND WOMEN IN COAL MINES.

3.—NUMBER OF CHILDREN AND YOUNG PERSONS EMPLOYED IN COAL MINES.

4.—HIRING OF CHILDREN AND YOUNG PERSONS IN COAL MINES.

5.—STATE OF THE PLACE OF WORK IN COAL MINES.

6.—NATURE OF THE EMPLOYMENT IN COAL MINES.

7.—HOURS OF WORK IN COAL MINES.

8.—NIGHT WORK IN COAL MINES.

9.—MEAL HOURS IN COAL MINES.

10.—HOLIDAYS ALLOWED TO CHILDREN AND YOUNG PERSONS EMPLOYED IN COAL MINES.

11.—TREATMENT OF CHILDREN AND YOUNG PERSONS IN COAL MINES.

12.—ACCIDENTS TO WHICH CHILDREN AND YOUNG PERSONS ARE EXPOSED IN COAL MINES.

13.—WAGES OF CHILDREN AND YOUNG PERSONS IN COAL MINES.

14.—INFLUENCE OF EMPLOYMENT IN COAL MINES ON THE PHYSICAL CONDITION OF CHILDREN AND YOUNG PERSONS.

Under these heads may be comprehended all that relates to the physical condition of the Children and Young Persons employed in mining labour; their moral condition will be considered in our next Report, when we purpose to bring under one view the intellectual, moral, and religious state of the Children and Young Persons employed in all the branches of industry included in this inquiry.

1.—AGES AT WHICH CHILDREN AND YOUNG PERSONS ARE EMPLOYED IN
    COAL MINES.

45. The earliest ages at which Children begin to work in the coal-mines of the
United Kingdom differ materially in different districts, and in the same district in
different mines. In almost all the districts there is some discrepancy in the statements of different classes of witnesses as to this point. With very few exceptions,
the coal owners, the coal viewers, the under-ground stewards, the contractors, or,
as they are called in some districts, " the butties," and the agents and managers,
represent the ages of the Children, when they first begin to work, to be more
advanced than the Children and Young Persons themselves, than many of the
adult workpeople, and than the medical practitioners, the schoolmasters, the clergy-
men, and the magistrates. The truth can be ascertained only by a comparison
with each other of the statements of these different classes of witnesses; and in
order that this comparison may be readily made, we proceed to cite examples of
the statements given by each of these classes of witnesses in the several districts,
and, whenever it can be done, in the words of the witnesses themselves.

46. SOUTH STAFFORDSHIRE.—It is common in this district for Children to   *South*
begin to work in the pits when they are seven years of age, very common when   *Staffordshire.*
they are between seven and eight, and general when they are nine.—

Richard Spooner Cooper, Esq., surgeon, states, that " he has been in practice at Bilston
for 10 years; is the medical attendant to about twenty-six clubs, having amongst them upwards of 2000 members, all of whom, with the exception of about 100, are connected with
the collieries and iron-works. Some children go to work in the collieries as early as seven or
eight; many have met with accidents before they are eight. In the very small collieries,
where a man without capital is endeavouring to get on, and cannot afford the proper means
of working his pit, little children are sent into holes in the mines with baskets to get
coals to bring to the foot of the shaft, and they drag them along on their hands and knees"
(Dr. Mitchell, Evidence, No. 3: App. Pt. I., p. 62, ll. 5, 23). Henry Duignan, superintendent-registrar and
clerk of the Walsall Union, says, " Some of the sons of the colliers themselves go down to
the pit at that age (eight). No sooner are the children at the age of eight or nine but there is
a demand for them" (Ibid. No. 31: p. 75, l. 1).

47. The Sub-Commissioner states, that " the Returns obtained from the ministers
of religion afford overwhelming evidence of the fact that Children in South
Staffordshire are sent to work in the coal-field at the early age of seven or eight,
and that some are even removed from school to be sent into the mines still
earlier." (Dr. Mitchell, Report, § 61: App. Pt. I., p. 8.) In some collieries,
however, although the Children may begin work at the bank, driving the horse
which works the gin, as early as seven, yet they do not go down into the pit until
they are nine. This statement is made by Mr. William Hartell Baylis, agent of
James Loxdale, Esq., who has been employed in mines for the last forty years,
has been in the management of mines for thirty years, and is well acquainted with
the habits of the mining people (Dr. Mitchell, Evidence, No. 7: App. Pt. I.,
p. 65, l. 9).

48. NORTH STAFFORDSHIRE.—Throughout the pottery district the employ-   *North*
ment of the Children in the potteries prevents their being taken into the coal-mines   *Staffordshire.*
while under thirteen years of age; but there are many boys under eighteen employed
under ground (S. Scriven, Esq., Report, §§ 5, 9: App. Pt. II., p. 128). In the
collieries near Cheadle, however, boys commence working under ground at ten years
of age, or even younger (Ibid., Evidence, No. 29: p. 140, l. 33; No. 52: p. 141,
l. 26).

49. SHROPSHIRE.—There is evidence that some Children begin to work in the pits   *Shropshire.*
of the Coalbrook Dale district, as the chief coal-field of this country is called, as
early as six years of age. One instance, indeed, came under the observation of the
Sub-Commissioner, in which a Child two years younger, that is, four years of age,
was regularly taken into the pit by his father. " This remarkable instance became
known to me," says Dr. Mitchell, " when exploring the Hill's Lane Pit, belonging
to the Madeley Wood Company; the ground-bailiff, two charter-masters (the persons who contract to work the mines), and a labouring collier accompanied me.
' I say, Jonas,' said the ground-bailiff to one of the charter-masters, ' there are
very few Children working in this mine; I think we have none under ten or
eleven.' The collier immediately said, ' Sir, my boy is only a little more than four.'

This was a very unseasonable interruption; and all that the ground-bailiff said was, 'Well, I suppose that you take good care of him; you take him down and up when you go yourself' " (Dr. Mitchell, Report, § 264: App. Pt. I., p. 33-4).

50. Mr. William Tranter, agent of the Coalbrook Dale Company, who was requested by Mr. Alfred Darby, one of the partners and managers, to give to the Sub-Commissioner full information, in reply to the questions put to him states, that in his capacity of agent to the company he has occasion to go down into the mines, both of coal and iron; that there are many Children in the mines; and that some are as young as about six, and they are of various ages up to manhood (Dr. Mitchell, Evidence, No. 41: App. Pt. I., p. 79, l. 36).

51. This statement as to the very early age at which Children begin to work in this district is confirmed by Mr. Matthew Webb, a medical gentleman residing at Coal-pit Bank, whose evidence to the fact is given somewhat reluctantly, but whose expression is remarkable: " There are," he says, " *very few under six or seven* who are employed to draw weights with a girdle round the body, and those only where the roof of the pit is so low for short distances as to prevent horses of the smallest size, or asses, from being employed" (Ibid. No. 48: p. 81, l. 67). Another surgeon, who did not wish his name to be published, says, " Children go to the iron and coal works at as early an age as six; at all ages from six to ten" (Ibid. No. 45: p. 81, l. 3).

52. It is added that " the lowness of the roof or thinness of the bed of coal, as stated by Mr. Webb, is no doubt the cause of employing boys instead of horses or asses, which otherwise would be more convenient and cheaper; that at least two-thirds of all the beds of coal in the Coalbrook Dale district are of this thin description; that it cannot but be a matter of regret that any Children as young as six or seven should be so employed, and that nothing but long familiarity with the practice could reconcile the mind to the employment of Children of still higher age at such labour" (Dr. Mitchell, Report, § 267: App. Pt. I., p. 34).

53. WARWICKSHIRE.—There is evidence that some Children begin to work in the pits in this district at the same early age.—

Mr. John Sommers, a surgeon residing at Bedworth, states that "he has been in practice there for nineteen years; that he has had many patients among the colliers, having been surgeon to several of their clubs; that the boys go down to the pits, many at six years of age, many at seven, and at all ages; that they generally begin very young" (Dr. Mitchell, Evidence, No. 68: App. Pt. I., p. 107, l. 24).—And Thomas Arrott, a working collier, says, that " he first went down to the mine at seven years of age, and that there are still at the bank boys of seven years of age" (Ibid. No. 64: p. 105, l. 48).

54. On the other hand:—

Mr. Benjamin Stratton, agent to Charles Newdigate, Esq., and manager of the coal-mines near Nuneaton, affirms, that " there are very few children in the mines under ten years of age, and that those few are such as are brought down by their fathers and relations" (Ibid. No. 62: p. 103, l. 5).—Mr. Thomas Pearson, a butty in the colliery called the Bedworth Charity Colliery, states, that "there are no boys employed in that part of the country under eight years of age, and that at the colliery at which he is employed there is one boy on the bank eight years of age, whose work it is to carry picks to the blacksmith, but that the youngest boy in the pit is better than eleven years of age." (Ibid. No. 63: p. 105, ll. 23, 15).—Thomas Arrott, collier, says, " there are boys of seven or eight employed on the bank to carry picks to the blacksmith. There are none under ten in our pit; and there are very few employed at that age in this county, and cannot be so useful now since engines have been introduced" (Ibid. No. 64: p. 105, l. 54).

55. The correctness of these representations is confirmed by the statement of the Sub-Commissioner, who says that " the number of children in the pits of the Warwickshire Coal-field in proportion to the men is small, as compared with other districts; and for this reason, that the coal is very hard, and comes in large masses, and is placed on the waggons in larger and weightier pieces than boys could manage" (Dr. Mitchell, Report, § 21: App. Pt. I., p. 91).

56. LEICESTERSHIRE.—During the inspection of this district no instance was found of any Child being employed in under-ground work in any colliery under seven years of age. In some of the pits no Child is employed under ten years of age.—

Mr. Stephen Evans, ground-bailiff to the Moira Collieries, belonging to the Marquess of Hastings, says, " Some boys go down into the pit as early as seven or eight, and at all ages after that" (Dr. Mitchell, Evidence, No. 75 : App. Pt. I., p. 110, l. 46). Mr. Michael Parker, ground-bailiff to the Snibson Collieries, says, " Children commence going down into the pits at seven, and at all ages afterwards" (Ibid. No. 77: p. 112, l. 59). Mr. Joseph Dooley, under-ground bailiff of the coal pit at Swadlincote, called Granville Colliery, says, " There is one boy as young as ten ; he is the youngest" (Ibid. No. 76 : p. 112, l. 7). In the Snibson Colliery, according to Mr. Charles Tandy, book-keeper, " The youngest child employed in the pit is ten years of age" (Ibid. No. 79 : p. 113, l. 49). In the Whitwick Colliery, according to Mr. Stenson, engineer and manager, " There are no boys under ten" (Ibid. No. 80 : p. 114, l. 5).

57. The proportion of Children and Young Persons to that of adult workpeople is also in this district remarkably small. The coal here is in very large masses ; it is so heavy that Children are of no use in loading the waggons, and the seam of coal is so thick that there is everywhere ample room even for men : whence, says Mr. Stephen Evans, ground bailiff of the Moira Collieries, " it is more to our advantage to employ persons of greater strength than boys of ten, twelve, or thirteen usually possess." (Ibid. No. 75 : p. 110, l. 59.)

58. The Commissioners, in visiting the Moira Collieries, belonging to the Marquess of Hastings, accompanied by John Thomas Woodhouse, Esq., the mining engineer, who has the direction of them, were struck with the absence of Children, with the great muscular development of the " lads," and the extraordinary size and strength of the men ; and they saw at once the correctness of the statements that Children and boys of ordinary strength could be of no use in moving such immense blocks of coal as are here brought to the foot of the shaft.

59. DERBYSHIRE.—The Sub-Commissioner for this district records several cases in which Children began to work in the mines at five and between five and six years of age.—

Esther Ellis says, " She has two sons at work at Tupton, in North Wingfield parish ; one, now fourteen, has worked for Mr. Chambers at Sibshelf since he was five years old" (J. M. Fellows, Esq., Evidence, No. 400: App., Pt. II., p. 348, l. 4). William Ghent : " Is seven years old ; is sure he has worked two years, or nearly, under Mr. Woodley and Mr. Jessop" (Ibid. No. 195: p. 315, l. 10). John Fisher, fifty-five years old, collier: " Has two sons down the pit, one seven, the other eight. The one seven years old has worked three-quarters of a year, the other was a very little above five years old when he opened and shut the door" (Ibid. No. 154: p. 304, l. 49). Samuel Freeman Pinxton, Pit No. 2, banksman: " He earned 3l., at 3s. per week, before he wore breeches ; he was not six years old. A boy ought not to be allowed to work in a pit before he is twelve, but parents will send them." Note by the Sub-Commissioner :—At this period the butty came and he would say no more (Ibid. No. 300: p. 331, l. 27). Samuel Davis, " Is six years old ; has worked half a year" (Ibid. No. 120: p. 295, l. 47).

60. Many Children begin to work in the coal-pits in this district at six years of age.—

William Slater : " Is six years old ; draws the empty corves with a hook" (Ibid. No. 239 : p. 327, l. 56). Adam Widowson : " Is seven years old ; has worked in a pit one year" (Ibid. No. 140 : p. 300, l. 44). Aram Richardson : " Is seven years old ; works in the soft coal-pit ; has done so for nearly a year" (Ibid. No. 144 : p. 300, l. 66). Joseph Cotton : " Is seven years old ; works for Mr. Woolley : has worked in pits more than half a year" (Ibid. No. 276 : p. 327, l. 45). Joseph Latun : " Is nine years old ; has worked in Hutchby's Pit three years" (Ibid. No. 168 : p. 308, l. 24). Mark Edwards, Coal Aston : " Is nine years old ; has worked in pits above three years" (Ibid. No. 448 : p. 354, l. 5). John Peake : " Is nine years old ; is sure he was only just six when he began to work" (Ibid. No. 226 : p. 319, l. 62). Joseph Robinson : " Is twelve years old ; has worked nearly six years" (Ibid. No. 175 : p. 310, l. 22). John Bell : " Is twelve years old ; has worked five or nearly six years" (Ibid. No. 346 : p. 340, l. 45). Levi Richards : " Is thirteen years of age ; has worked in pits since he was six" (Ibid. No. 167 : p. 308, l. 8).

61. Among many others the following Children, of eight years old and upwards, state that they began work in the pits at seven years of age.—

George Bentley (No. 309). William Lees (No. 344). William Riley (No. 158). William Gascoign (No. 268). Richard Gascoign (No. 270). Stephen Gascoign (No. 307). Richard Haywood (No. 351). William Orrall (No. 157), eleven years old, has worked in pits nearly four years. William Hopkins (No. 368). John Bradder (No. 385). Thomas Siddons (No. 243). Joseph Shooter (No. 299). John Gent (No. 194). George Gee (No. 445). Samuel Farnsworth (No. 337).

62. The numbers are comparatively few in this district who began work in the pits at a later age than eight.

63. WEST RIDING OF YORKSHIRE : SOUTHERN PART.—In the large portion of the great West Riding Coal District, examined by J. C. Symons, Esq., Children begin to work in the pits at the same early ages.

Joseph Ellison, Esq., of Birkenshaw, near Birstall, says, " I have been practically acquainted with collieries nearly all my life. I know it as a fact that a collier now living has taken a child of his own, who was only three years old, into a pit to ' hurry,' and when the child was exhausted it was carried home, stripped, and put to bed. This is a rare occurrence, but I can prove it, if required, by undeniable evidence, to have been a fact" (J. C. Symons, Esq., Evidence, No. 249: App. Pt. I., p. 288, ll. 1, 35).—Another witness, John Ibbertson, aged forty-three, collier, examined at the same place, says, " I have been forty-five years in the pits. I knew a man, called Joseph Cawthrey, who sent a child in at four years old ; and there are many who go to thrust behind at that time, and many go at five and six ; but it is soon enough for them to go at nine or ten. The sooner they go in the sooner their constitutions is mashed up" (Ibid. No. 267 : p. 292, ll. 28—34).

64. It is not uncommon, in this district, even for infants of five years old to be sent daily and regularly into the pits with the adult workers.—

John Hobson, thirteen and a half years old, collier's boy, from the Sheffield Soap Pit, says, " I was five years old when I first went into the pit, and no older" (Ibid. No. 8: p. 228, l. 22). —Ebenezer Healey, aged 13, says, " I went into a pit to help before I was five years old ; I used to thrust" (Ibid. No. 284: p. 295, l. 38).—Alfred Lord, aged 14, examined at Mr. Joshua Smithson's colliery, Alverthorpe, says, " I hurry from the dip; it is hard enough; I should not like it to be much harder; I began to go at five years old" (Ibid. No. 178: p. 274, l. 27). —Mr. William Carter, under-ground steward and manager to Messrs. Micklethwaite and Company, says, " I should say children ought to begin at nine or ten years old; nine is early enough. I went in at five; but it was a sad let down to me in point of education" (Ibid. No. 257: p. 290, l. 40).—Edward Ellis, Esq., surgeon, of Silkstone, says, " I have had twenty-five years' professional experience among colliers. They [the children] go to the pits as early as five very frequently" (Ibid. No. 99: p. 248, ll. 17, 21).—Thomas Rayner, Esq., surgeon, of Birstall, says, " I have had twenty-seven years' practice, and I know of no old colliers. Collier children are taken to the pits at five years of age, both boys and girls" (Ibid. No. 268: p. 292, ll. 49, 51).—The Rev. Richard Morton, sheriff's chaplain, and curate of Dodworth, in the parish of Silkstone, says, " The parents get their children into the pits as soon as they think they can do anything. I have been told that some have gone by the time they have been five years old" (Ibid. No. 169: p. 269, l. 10).

65. The Evidence given by all classes of witnesses proves indubitably that it is very common in this district for Children to begin work in the pits at six years of age.—

John Heely, aged eighteen, at Mr. Stancliffe's Day-Hole Pit, Mirfield, says, " I went to work before I was six; I am sure of this. I hurried with another" (J. C. Symons, Esq., Evidence, No. 271 : App., Pt. I., p. 293, l. 18).—Similar evidence is given by William Firth, between six and seven years old; by Mary Holmes, aged fourteen and a half years; and by Caroline Swallow, aged eight and a half years (Ibid. Nos. 218, 283, and 292).—James Ibbetson, aged about twenty, collier at Mr. Harrison's pit, Gomersal, says, " There are three hurriers here in the pit; two are girls ; they are my sisters; they hurry for me. The oldest is twelve and a half; the youngest is between eight and nine. She has been working ever since she was six years old. They have both hurried together since she was six years old. Sometimes, when I have got my stint I come out, as I have done to-day, and leave them to fill and hurry" (Ibid, No. 263 : p. 291, l. 41). —Matthew Lindley, aged fifty-two, collier in Messrs. Day and Twibell's pit, Barnsley, " Children are sometimes brought to the pits at the age of six years, and are taken out of their beds at four o'clock, and between that and five, throughout the year" (Ibid. No. 109 : p. 250, l. 50).—Mr. John Lawton, surveyor and under-ground steward of Messrs. Travis and Horsfall's Colliery, Barnsley, " Has known children go into the pits at six years old" (Ibid. No. 123 : p. 255, l. 3).—Mr. William Pickard, general steward to Sir John Lister Kaye's Collieries, Denby Grange, " I have been a bottom-steward 44 years. We used trappers till lately, and they used to go and begin as early as six years old. The men will let the children go as soon as ever they are big enough to addle any wages" (Ibid. No. 255: p. 289, l. 29).—Benjamin Mellor, forty-six years old, " I am underground steward to some of Mr. Clarke's pits, and I have the superintendence of above 90 collieries. I have known children go as early as six" (Ibid. No. 101: p. 248, l. 49).—Mr. William Colling, under-ground steward to Messrs. Smith, at Gildersome : " There are some children very fine and strong enough to come in at eight ; others not till nine. We have some that come at six" (Ibid. No. 230: p. 284, l. 30).—Joseph Ellison, Esq., of Birkinshaw, near Birstall : " They generally go to work as early as six years old" (Ibid. No. 249 : p. 288, l. 5).—Henry Briggs, Esq., one of the proprietors of Messrs. Stansfield and Briggs's coal mines, Flockton: " Where they are much distressed, and there are large families, they will go as early as six or seven years old" (Ibid. No. 171 : p. 272, l. 59).—Mr. Crooks, surgeon, Barnsley : " The children commence working as early as the age of six" (Ibid. No. 166 : p. 267, l. 33).—The Rev. Henry Watkins, vicar of Silkstone, and one of Her Majesty's Justices of the Peace : " The children go into the pits when about six years of age" (Ibid. No. 167 : p. 268, l. 3).—The Rev. Francis Maude, incumbent of High Hoyland, near Wentworth, " The boys begin to work between six and seven" (Ibid. No. 168 : p. 268, l. 43).

66. Several of the coal-owners themselves admit, with Mr. Henry Briggs, whose evidence has just been quoted, that it is not uncommon for Children to begin work in the pit at seven years of age.—

John Twibell, Esq., coal-master, Barnsley, says, " My opinion is that young children ought not to be employed at all under ten years of age in coal-pits. We intend directing our attention to this point, with a view to its being a rule in our pit. I am aware that children are worked as young as seven years old in some collieries. I look on this as objectionable, both on the score of education and health" (Ibid. No. 111: p. 251, l. 37). Mr. George Travis, coal master, of the firm of Travis and Horsfall, Barnsley, says, "I believe that children go as early as seven years old to work" (Ibid. No. 84: p. 243, l. 50). Mr. William Bedford, one of the proprietors of Gildersome, Morley, and Drighlington Collieries, says, "There are a deal of children go to the pits between seven and eight years old, and some younger" (Ibid. No. 246: p. 286, l. 55).

67. While the evidence is thus overwhelming, that in this district Children are to be found in the coal mines regularly at work at the ages of five, six, and seven, it is clear, from a careful perusal of the whole of the depositions, that this fact could never have been brought to light by the examination of the coal owners only. It is in general with extreme reluctance that this class of witnesses acknowledge that Children begin to work in the pits even as early as seven years of age. With the few exceptions which have been quoted, the evidence uniformly given by the coal-owners would indicate that they are ignorant of the extremely early ages at which Children may be found working in their mines. The same remark is applicable to the tenor of the evidence given by the under-ground stewards and other agents. Some portion of this discrepancy may arise from the different ages at which individuals in the same district permit Children to enter their pits; but witnesses belonging to both these classes almost all say that eight is the lowest age at which Children begin to work; and they further state that, although some Children may be found working at eight, yet in general they do not begin till nine, and that, in the few cases in which they are admitted into the pit at an earlier age, it is solely out of consideration for the poverty or misfortune of the parent. Several of these witnesses declare that there are no Children in their pits under ten or eleven years of age, and even that younger Children would be of no use to them.

Thus Thomas Wilson, Esq. of the Banks, Silkstone, owner of three collieries, says: "The children are first taken into the mine about the age of eight years" (Ibid. No. 137: p. 258, l. 17). —— Payne, Esq., Wadsley, coal-master, says: "The children are employed generally at nine years old in coal-pits, and sometimes at eight" (Ibid. No. 2: p. 226, l. 15). William Newbould, Esq., owner of Intake Colliery, says that "Children go into his pits to work at nine years of age" (Ibid. No. 15: p. 229, l. 60). John Chambers, Esq., of the firm of Newton, Chambers, and Co., Thorncliffe Iron-works and Colliery, says: "The earliest age at which children go to work in the pits is about nine, but they go more generally at ten" (Ibid. No. 64: p. 238, l. 59).

68. Similar statements are made, among others, by the following under-ground stewards :—

William Wood: "The children begin to go about nine, and from nine to eleven" (Ibid. No. 274 p. 293, l. 56). Benjamin Mellor: "The usual age would be nine or ten" (Ibid. No. 101: p. 248, l. 50). Joseph Cooper: "The youngest children taken into our pits are from ten to eleven years of age" (Ibid. No. 48: p. 236, l. 7). Charles Hawcraft: "We have no hurriers under twelve or thirteen years old, and no child at all much under eleven" (Ibid. No. 98: p. 247, l. 47).

69. The statements thus positively made by the under-ground stewards may be strictly true, as far as regards the individual pits of which they have cognizance. On the other hand, with regard to the coal owners, it must be borne in mind that they seldom or never descend into the pits; that few of them have any personal knowledge, or take any superintendence whatever, of the workpeople; that, therefore, they may be wholly ignorant of the early ages at which Children are employed in their own mines, so that, when they make such declarations as have been cited, they may state only what they really believe to be the truth, though the incorrectness of their evidence is indubitably established by other classes of witnesses.

70. BRADFORD AND LEEDS.—In the vicinities of Bradford and Leeds, in which Mr. Wood made a brief investigation, Children begin to work in the mines at the same early ages as in the Barnsley and Wakefield district.—

William Tidswell, six years old, says: "Does not know what made him come into a pit; came in at five years old" (W. R. Wood, Esq., Evidence, No. 69: App., Part II., p. h 30 l. 41). Mr. Thomas Mackley, surgeon of Wilsden, four miles from Bradford, states that "He himself knew a child employed in the coal-mines at the age of five years and ten months" (Ibid. No. 61: p. h 28, l. 23). Thomas Foster, seven years old, says: "Went in at six years old" (Ibid. No. 67: p. h 30, l. 23). George Ackroyd, nine years old: "Went into pit at six" (Ibid. No. 54: p. h 25, l. 43). John Nuns, eleven years old: "Began at six years old" (Ibid. No. 99: p. h 40, l. 59). William Pickett, twelve years old: "Went into pit at six years old" (Ibid. No. 19: p. h 11, l. 34). James Ellis, thirteen years old: "Began at six years old" (Ibid. No. 100: p. h 41, l. 7). Michael Ashley, Wilsden, fifteen years old: "Went in at six" (Ibid. No. 75: p. h 32, l. 1). Sampson Hillam, sixteen years old : " Went into pit at six years old" (Ibid. No. 37 : p. *h* 18, l. 38).   Among others the following adults say they went into the pits at six years of age :—John Laycock, William Barraclough, and William Ramsden (Ibid. Nos. 25, 26, 94).

71. Many Children, colliers, and under-ground stewards, state that they began work at seven years of age : among others witnesses, Nos. 17, 55, 95, 27, 31, 3, 4, and 5.   But, in general, in this district, as well as in the Barnsley and Wakefield district, the colliery-stewards and the coal-owners represent the usual age at which Children begin to work in the mines to be from eight years old and upwards.

Mr. Isaac Clayton, coal-master, Bradford, says, that " of the number of hands employed by them, better than 200, about one-half are boys ; and that these are of all ages, from eight years old to sixteen" (Ibid. No. 48 : p. *h* 23, ll. 25, 28).   Mr. James Sharp, Bowling, says, that " children begin work in some cases at eight years old, and that they have boys at all ages, from eight to thirteen" (Ibid. No. 36 : p. *h* 18, l. 30).   Mr. Thomas William Embleton, agent and manager of the Middleton Colliery, near Leeds, says, that " children generally enter the mines at about nine years of age.   I found the youngest in our employment did not begin work till he was eight and a half years old.   As a general rule, we never take them till they are about nine years old, unless it be the child of a widow, or something of that sort.   The youngest now in our employment is eight years and ten months old" (Ibid. No. 79 : p. *h* 34, l. 10).   Charles Wailes, bottom-steward, Middleton Colliery, says, that " they very seldom take children into the pits till they are about nine years old ; not unless we are solicited by widows, or something of that sort" (Ibid. No. 80 : p. *h* 34, l. 65).

72. HALIFAX.—In this vicinity, which was assigned to the inquiries of Mr. Scriven, the Children begin work in the coal mines at the same early ages. One case is recorded in which a Child was regularly taken into the pit by his father at three years of age.   " It was made to follow him to the workings, there to hold the candle, and when exhausted with fatigue was cradled upon the coals until his return at night.   It is added that out of thirty Children at present at work in six pits in this district seventeen are between five and nine years of age " (S. S. Scriven, Esq., Report, § 48 : App., Pt. II., p. 65.)—

Joseph Gledhill, banksman, aged forty-eight : " I work now as a banksman.   I have three sons living ; one of them went into the pit with me when he was three years old, and commenced working regularly as a hurrier when he was between five and six ; that was at Flockton.   Another began between four and five, another between five and six." (S. S. Scriven, Esq., Evidence, No. 40 : App. Pt. II., p. 112, l. 36.)

73. It is added, " I overtook upon the road a little gang of hurriers returning to their homes ; many of them were very young, and amongst them one of five years of age " (S. S. Scriven, Esq., Report, § 6 : App. Pt. II., p. 57).—

William Ellis, aged nine, examined in the Byerley Company's Garden Pit, says : " I have hurried ever since I was five years old" (S. S. Scriven, Esq., Evidence, No. 50 : App., Pt. II. p. 116, l. 6).—Hiram Stephenson, aged fifteen, examined in the Powell Pit, says : " I have been hurrier ten years and more ; I began when I was five years, for Ben Man, in both coal and ironstone pits" (Ibid. No. 53 : p. 116, l. 56).—Eli Mitchell (a boy), examined in Mr. James Wilcox's Colliery, Parkbottom, says : " I began to work between five and six, thrusting coals, and then hurried" (Ibid. No. 4 : p. 101, l. 49).—William Dyson, aged fourteen, says : " I am a hurrier for Thomas Ditchforth   I have been employed ever since I was six years old" (Ibid. No. 7 : p. 102, l. 50).—Sally Fletcher, aged eight : " I have worked here short of two years" (Ibid. No. 15 : p. 105, l. 22).—Luke Brook, aged forty-nine : " I am one of the stewards of the Low Moor Company's Colliery.   The pits that come under my superintendence are the Taylor, Stone Park, Highfield Raws Pits, &c.   In these are employed a large number of lads and men.   The ages of the lads vary from six to eighteen" (Ibid. No. 84 : p. 125, l. 42).—Mr. Isaac Clayton, aged fifty-one, agent and principal : " I have known children admitted as hurriers as young as six ; 'tis rare to find them younger ; I consider that too young ; eight would be a better age" (Ibid. No. 49 : p. 115, l. 46).—John Marsden, aged eight and a half, examined in the Low Moor Company's Wikelane Pit : " I have been a hurrier nearly two years in this pit" (Ibid. No. 42 : p. 113, l. 10).—John Sidebottom, aged seven, examined in the Byerley Company's Roundhill Pit : " I have hurried seven months ; I hurry for father" (Ibid. No. 61 : p. 119, l. 31).—Squire Hunt, aged fourteen, examined in the Wilson Pit : " I hurry corves for my father ; I began when I was about six and a half years old" (Ibid. No. 55 . p. 117, l. 26).—James Mitchell, aged twelve, examined in the Bins Bottom Colliery : " I hurry corves for Jim Witley ; have hurried five years well nigh, and thrust about six months afore that" (Ibid. No. 2 : p. 101, l. 21).

74. Among others, the following witnesses, nine years of age and upwards, state that they began work at seven years of age.—

William Jagger, No. 6 ; John Dyson, No. 8 ; John Sutcliff, No. 31 ; John Bell, No. 34 ; Joswell Wells, No. 35 ; Saul Hanson, No. 56 ; Joseph Butterfield, No. 62 ; Jonathan Turner, No. 67.

Mr. James Sharp, steward of Messrs. John Sturge and Company's Collieries, Bowling: COAL MINES. " I am the steward of this company; have been so employed fifteen years; we have now working altogether fifty-four pits. The youngest child employed (Charles Pearson) is seven years *Age* and one month. I have made the returns required of us by the Government, and in doing Halifax. so have examined personally every child, and pledge myself that it has been honestly and faithfully done. There is only one child under eight years old; that I consider early enough; their strength is not equal to the duty before that; that is very young." (Ibid. No. 43: p. 113, ll. 31, 35, 57.)

75. LANCASHIRE AND CHESHIRE.—One case is recorded in which a Child Lancashire and Cheshire. began to work in a coal pit in this district soon after he was four years of age. A. B. at Mr. Roscoe's, Rochdale, states, that " he is eleven years old; that he has been six years in the pits, and that he began to go when he was little more than four years old" (J. L. Kennedy, Esq., Evidence, No. 5: App. Pt. II., p. 201, l. 40). And many cases are recorded in which Children began to work in the pits when they were between five and six years of age, and at six.—

Henry Jones, at Messrs. Clegg's, Pauldin-wood, near Oldham, says, " I am going on six years old, and am the youngest in the pit, excepting Jack Jones" (Ibid. No. 64: p. 226, l. 35). Mr. Roscoe, Rochdale, proprietor of coal mine, says, " I believe that the great body of colliers have begun to work by the time they were five or six years old" (Ibid. No. 2: p. 200, l. 52). William Cooper, aged seven years: " Has worked at Almond's coal-pits twelve months" (Ibid. No. 55: p. 224, l. 21). John Wilde, at Messrs. Swire and Lee's, fourteen years old, says, " I began to work in the pit when I was six years old" (Ibid. No. 14: p. 207, l. 63). William Wilde, at Messrs. Swire and Lee's, eighteen years old: " I went into the pit when I was six years old" (Ibid. No. 17: p. 208, l. 44). James Yates, collier, fourteen years old: " Was about six years old when I first went to work" (Ibid. No. 57: p. 224, l. 41). Mr. John Millington, superintendent: " The children, both boys and girls, generally begin at six years old, or from that to ten" (Ibid. No. 6: p. 202, l. 8). Among others the following adults state that they began work in the pits at six years of age:—Mr. Roscoe, No. 2; Mr. Miller, No. 7; John Wright, No. 13; John Oldham, No. 22).

76. Among the Children who state that they began to work in the pits at seven years of age are the following:—

Ellen Taylor, No. 40; John Clarke, No. 44; A. B., No. 61; John Jones, No. 66; Edward Cope, No. 70. Many adults state that they began to work in the pits at seven years of age. (Ibid. Nos. 26, 162, &c.)

77. The Sub-Commissioner, as the general result of his personal investigation, says: " Of the adult mining population of this district, I am convinced that a very large proportion have commenced work as early as the sixth or seventh year of age" (J. L. Kennedy, Esq., Report, § 3, App. Pt. II., p. 149.)

78. OLDHAM.—In the Collieries in this neighbourhood, on the south eastern Oldham. verge of Lancashire, cases are recorded in which Children have been regularly taken into the pits to work at four, and between four and five, and several at five, and between five and six years of age.—

Joseph Gott, aged fifty-three, Richard Barker, aged forty-six, the former an underlooker, and the last a labouring collier: " A great many goes to pit before they be fit to go. Richard Barker went into the pit at five years old himself, and has in the pits four sons, who all went in under six years of age" (J. Fletcher, Esq., Evidence, Nos. 13 and 14 : App. Pt. II., p. 850, l. 29). James Jones: " Is going in thirteen; has been five years in the pit. Has thrutching for him his little brother, Henry Jones, who is going in six, and has been in the pit three months" (Ibid. No. 25: p. 853, l. 35). John Jones: " Is seven years old; has been in the pit a year or more" (Ibid. No. 23: p. 853, l. 10).

79. It is very common in this district for Children to be sent into the pits when they are between six and seven years of age, and between seven and eight.

John Gordon, aged thirty-four: " Is a miner in the employment of Mr. Abraham Lees, at Stoneywell-lane, near Oldham, and commenced underground work under Messrs. Jones at seven years of age. Thinks there is little difference in the ages at which lads have begun in his childhood and since. His own lads have gone into the pit at from seven to eight years of age; they are three in number, and this is a very common age at which to take them into the pit. Edmund Stanley, also a working collier in the same pit, sent in his boy between six and seven" (Ibid. Nos. 15, 16: p. 850, ll. 55, 59). Joseph Gott: " Is an underlooker in a mountain-mine near Rochdale, where the children will come about seven years old. The parents, who are often weavers, come and beg to thrust their children in, really before they are fit to go" (Ibid. No. 13: p. 850, l. 46).

80. " The most common age for boys to be taken to labour in the coal-mines of this district," states Mr. Fletcher, " is at seven, eight, or nine. But in the 'mountain mines,' or smaller collieries towards the hills, which have only thin strata,

varying in thickness from 18 inches to 2 feet, they will go so early as six, five, or even four years of age; ' some are so young they go in their bed-gowns.' One little fellow whom I endeavoured to question could not even articulate, although his father, between whose legs he hid his little black face as he stood before me, answered for him that he was seven years old (J. Fletcher, Esq., Report, § 10 : App. Pt. II., p. 821).

81. NORTH LANCASHIRE.—In this district, examined by Mr. Austin, the youngest age at which Children are stated to be employed in the coal-mines is seven (A. Austin, Esq., Report, § 4 : App. Pt. II., No. 2, p. 787; No. 8, p. 790; § 5 : No. 1, p. 793; No. 5, p. 795).

82. CUMBERLAND.—One case is recorded in which a Child began to work in the pits in this district between five and six years old, and many state that they began at seven.—

John Daly, aged eight years and nine months, says, " I trail with my brother; I've been more than two years" (J. C. Symons, Esq., Evidence, No. 324 : App., Pt., I. p. 309, l. 9). James Sampson, thirty-four years old, collier, says, " I began at six years old" (Ibid. No. 315 : p. 307, l. 2). John Wynn, No. 323; James Atkinson, No. 328; Jonathan Johnson, 330.

83. The agents and under-ground stewards, however, represent the ages at which Children begin work to be much more advanced.—

Mr. Alvan Penrice, colliery-agent for Henry Curwen, Esq., Workington-hall, says, " The children begin as trappers at about nine, as trailers at about twelve years of age" (Ibid. No. 317, p. 307, l. 24). Joseph Sharp, under-steward at the Broughton-moor collieries, near Newport : " In the thin pits they go as soon as ten years old, perhaps a few at nine" (Ibid. No. 300, p. 303, l. 13). Mr. Dickenson, surgeon, Workington : " Mr. Curwen has given positive orders that no child under ten years of age should go into his pits " (Ibid. No. 334, p. 310, l. 68).

84. As the result of his investigations in this district the Sub-Commissioner states, that " the Children do not begin to work in the Cumberland Collieries so early as in Yorkshire ; for the coal-seams are all of a good thickness ; in the inland collieries they are at least four or five feet thick, and in the sea-coast ones eight, nine, and ten feet thick. Ten years is a common age for Children to begin to work ; and they seldom commence before eight and a half years of age (J. C. Symons, Esq., Report, § 2 : App. Pt. I., p. 299). The Evidence collected by Mr. Martin agrees with this statement (App. Pt. I., pp. 876, 881).

85. SOUTH DURHAM.—In this district Children are sometimes taken down into the pits as early as five years of age, and by no means uncommonly at six.

Anthony Dowson, examined in the presence of his father, William Dowson, says, " I am eighteen years of age the 13th of this month (April). I went down first into the pit when five years old" (Dr. Mitchell, Evidence, No. 101 : App. Pt. I., p. 156, l. 19).—James Vicars, aged fifteen, says, " I first went down nine years ago, being only six years of age. There are boys of six in the pits" (Ibid. No. 100 : p. 155, l. 40).—Thomas Lawton, aged twenty-eight, collier, says, " Some boys go down as early as six, which ought not to be allowed. I think children go down into the pit much too soon. I hope not to be compelled to take my children under twelve years of age ; but necessity compels some men against their inclination" (Ibid. No. 112 : p. 162, l. 33).

86. The returns of the Schedules for 14 collieries in this district, namely, Hetton, North Hetton, South Hetton, East and West Rainton, Pittington, Broomside, Coundon, Tees, Thornley, Sherburn, Great Lumley, Newbottle, Cocken, Painshaw, and St. Helens Auckland, show that out of 235 trappers there are 135 under 10 years of age, and 100 above that age. There is, therefore, a decided majority under 10 (Dr. Mitchell, Report, §§ 70, 71 : App. Pt. I., p. 125).

87. " Though the very Young Children," adds the Sub-Commissioner, " are not many in proportion, there are still such a number as is painful to contemplate, and which the great coal-owners will perhaps now learn for the first time ; and I feel a firm belief that they will do so with sorrow and regret" (Ibid. § 48 : p. 124).

88. NORTH DURHAM and NORTHUMBERLAND.—In these districts many Children begin work in the coal-mines at very early ages. One case is recorded in which a Child was taken into the pit at four years and a half old ; and several at five and between five and six.

Robert Harle, Gosforth Colliery, aged sixteen, says, " Has been down pits eleven and a half years, at this pit and Seghill (J. R. Leifchild, Esq., Evidence, No. 137 : App. Pt. I., p. 597, l. 2).— William Hays, aged fifteen, Gosforth Colliery, says : " Has been down his pit ten years ; went down, therefore, at five years old" (Ibid. No. 134 : p. 596, l. 36).—Thomas Dotching, Wellington

Colliery, on the Tyne : " Calls himself six years old, looks about seven ; has been down the pit half a year" (Ibid. No. 4 : p. 569, l. 59).—Thomas Wigham, St. Laurence Colliery : " Was down this pit when, his mother said, he was between five and six years old, a wee thing of a boy" (Ibid. No. 268 : p. 623, l. 22).—James Smeatim, aged seventeen, putter : " Knows one boy, about five and a half years old, and very little, down the pit ; his name is William Fraser" (Ibid. No. 429 : p. 653, l. 10).—Mr. George Elliot, aged twenty-seven, Monkwearmouth Colliery : " Is the head viewer here and at Washington and Belmont Collieries ; is very much pressed and entreated by parents to take children at a very early age, from six years and upwards. Has known boys of five years of age in some pits. Could give two names and instances of boys of five years of age being employed in pits in the county of Durham. One Robert Pattison, now employed down this pit, is now six years of age, and has been down four months. His father, who was not well off, earnestly requested that he might be taken, but the viewer did not know his age till yesterday, neither does the boy know his own age" (Ibid. No. 367 : p. 642, ll. 33, 45.

89. **Many cases are stated in which Children begin work at six years old.**—

Joshua Stephenson, aged about eight years, says : " He has been down the pit two years and more. Went down the pit [the C pit] before he was six years old."—[Note by the Sub-Commissioner.—This witness is entered in the returns as seven years of age, and as having been in the pits two months ; but John Graham, the heap-keeper, states to me that he believes the boy has been down nearly two years.] (Ibid. No. 38 : p. 575, l. 50).—James Strong, aged seven : " Has been down the pit one year" (Ibid. No. 5 : p. 569, l. 66).—Robert Backworth, going fourteen : " Is a half-marrow ; has been down pits eight years ; went down the Piercy Pit at six years old" (Ibid. No. 84 : p. 582, l. 37).—Thomas Fletcher, aged fourteen, Walker Colliery : " Was putting as a foal when he was six years old at this colliery'' (Ibid. No. 296 : p. 628, l. 34).—John Watson, aged seventeen next June, Cowpen Colliery : " Has been nearly eleven years down this pit, all but ten months ; went down at six years old" (Ibid. No. 239 : p. 617, l. 2).—James Punton, aged fifteen : " Has been down pits nine years about ; was six years and a half old when he went down first" (Ibid. No. 130 : p. 596, l. 10).—Andrew Fairs, aged eighteen, Tyne Main Colliery : " Has been down pits eleven years and a half ; first went down this pit at six years and a half old" (Ibid. No. 303 : p. 630, l. 47).—Joseph Watkin, twenty years of age, collier : " Has been down pits 14 years and two months ; was six years and a half old when he went down West Moor [or Killingworth] Colliery" (Ibid. No. 302 : p. 630, l. 8).—Thomas Carr, forty-five years old, collier : " Some of six years old go down now. Lads six years old can keep doors well enough, and soon learn as well as old persons the ways of a pit. Parents could not keep their children if they were not allowed to go down. It takes more to keep a pitman than anybody : pit-lads eat more than other lads, a vast" (Ibid. No. 241 : p. 618, l. 47).—Ann Mills, thirty-five years old, wife of a collier : " Has three children living ; her husband is a hewer at Blaydon Main Pit. Her son, Matthew Mills, first went to work at six years and four months old, on account of her husband's bad health" (Ibid. No. 260 : p. 621, l. 28.)

T. M. Greenhow, Esq., surgeon, professionally engaged at Walker Colliery, in reply to a series of inquiries proposed to him by the Sub-Commissioner, writes : " Though the condition of the children, in common with that of the entire population connected with the collieries, has been considerably improved of late years, many circumstances connected with their mode of life are of a nature to deserve serious consideration, and certainly admit of material improvement. The most conspicuous of these is the early age at which they are usually employed in the pit. In some collieries this takes place when about six years of age" (Ibid. No. 498 : p. 665, l. 33).—S—— P——, a respectable witness, states, respecting one of the largest and best-conducted collieries—" I have resided here many years, and am well acquainted with the people. I have seen children go down here at six years of age, and have seen them scarcely able to walk, from their tender age and the work ; one I knew [named] altered much for the worse after he had been down three or four months ; he looked much worse" (Ibid. No. 502 : p. 671, l. 11).

90. The Sub-Commissioner says, " I visited the house of the parents of a little boy whom I saw keeping a door down Flatworth Pit, on the 20th of May ; it was about seven o'clock on the Sunday evening, and the boy, Thomas Roker, was in bed asleep. His mother said he was aged about six years and seven months, and that he had been down the pit about a month or six weeks. The boy was at school at three years old, and his father wished to make him a better scholar before he went down. Always puts him to bed early, because he must get up every working morning at three o'clock : and he often rubs his eyes when he is woke, and says he has only just been to sleep. He gets up at 3 A.M., and goes down the pit at 4 o'clock A.M. He gets his dinner directly he comes home, about half-past 4 P.M., or a quarter to 5 P.M., and then he washes himself and goes to bed between six and seven ; so that he will never be up more than two hours from the pit for eating, washing, and playing. When his son gets a little more hardened to the pit, his father means to send him to night-school, and stop an hour off his sleep. Thomas generally goes down the pit in a corf, with a good few boys in it, and sometimes he goes up on his father's knee. It is a dusty pit, but he never complains, though he tells many a queer story of the pit. The pit does not hurt him,

but makes him a little whiter, and perhaps thinner. He was a very fat boy when he was three years old. Johnny Fiddis was younger when he first went down; thinks people send their bairns earlier down the pit than they did." (Ibid. No. 95: p. 585, l. 26).

91. The instances recorded in which Children in this district begin to work at seven, and between seven and eight years of age, are so numerous that it would be tedious to cite them. It is generally admitted by all classes of witnesses that it is a common practice in this district for Children to begin work in the pits at eight, and between eight and nine, years of age; though several witnesses state that they admit no Children into their own pits under nine, and some few that they admit none under ten, eleven, and even twelve.

Nicholas Wood, Esq., viewer of Killingworth, Hetton, and other collieries, says, "Trappers may be said to go to work at a minimum average of eight years" (Ibid. No. 97, p. 587, l. 15).—William Morrison, Esq., of Pelaw-house, Chester-le-Street, surgeon, professionally engaged in the Countess of Durham's collieries, says "I think I am perfectly correct in stating eight years to be the earliest age at which children are employed in the mines" (Ibid. No. 496, p. 662, l. 42). This witness must, of course, be understood to speak only of the mines of which he is himself personally cognisant.—Mr. William Bailey, under-viewer of Hetton Colliery: "Has been here nineteen years; has risen up to his present rank through all gradations of work from a trapper at ten years of age. Has worked at various Tyne collieries. Trappers go down from eight to nine years old, and he has frequently to interfere with parents to prevent them from going earlier: thinks they should never go before nine years old" (Ibid. No. 400, p. 648, l. 66; and p. 649, l. 1).—George Johnson, Esq., viewer of Wellington, Heaton, and Burdon Main Collieries: "Does not allow children under nine or ten years old to be trappers, although a strong desire for earlier employment exists both amongst parents and children" (Ibid. No. 3, p. 567, l. 1).

92. EAST OF SCOTLAND.—It is more common for Children to begin to work in the collieries in the East of Scotland at five and six years of age even than in any part of England.

Jane Peacock, found in the Preston Links Colliery, two miles north of Tranent, could have been only five years old when she first commenced work in the pit (R. H. Franks, Esq., Evidence, No. 181, App. Pt. I., p. 469, l. 33).—Jane Cumming began work at six years of age: "A most interesting girl, labouring under a nervous complaint, and though, from sickness, compelled to remain out of the mines for weeks together, yet as convalescence returned was forced to the pits" (Ibid. No. 181, p. 469, l. 38).—Mr. Francis Grier, manager of the Fordel Colliery, the property of Admiral Sir P. Durham, Bart., of Fordel: "We have 82 young persons and children working below ground. The females begin to assist to draw by the chain from six years of age, and many from six to twelve years of age are employed" (Ibid. No. 361, p. 501, l. 6).—Mr. Henry Chisholm, manager of the Lochgelly, Castle Hill, and Dean Pit Collieries, in the parish of Beath and Auchterarder, in the county of Fife: "At some coal-workings children commence as early as six years of age, and remain below as long as the adults." The same witness adds: "Very young children are not needed, indeed they are never required; and no children ought to be employed under twelve years of age in any mines, as they lose both education and strength by being under ground so early" (Ibid. No. 391, p. 505, ll. 41, 44).

93. These statements as to the early age at which Children commence work in the pits are confirmed by the most abundant evidence derived from examinations of the Children themselves; and it must be borne in mind that many of the youngest of these Children have to carry coals on their backs, from the workings to the surface, up steep ladders, as will be found described under "Nature of Employment."

Margaret Leveston, six years old, coal-bearer, says: "Been down at coal-carrying six weeks; makes 10 to 14 rakes a-day; carries full 56 lbs. of coal in a wooden backit. The work is na guid; it is so very sair" (Ibid. No. 116: p. 458, l. 20).—Robert Seton, eleven years old, coal-putter: "Father took me down when I was six years old, and I have wrought below ever since" (Ibid. No. 80: p. 451, l. 62).—Mary Neilson, ten years old, coal-bearer: "Sister was six years old when she first wrought, and I went down at that age" (Ibid. No. 119: p. 458, l. 62).—Margaret Watson, sixteen years of age, coal-bearer: "I was first taken below to carry coals when I was six years old, and have never been away from the work, except a few evenings in the summer months, when some of us go to Carlops, two miles over the moor, to learn the reading" (Ibid. No. 115: p. 458, l. 4).—Thomas Brown, ten years old, putter: "Wrought below four years;" so that he began work at six years of age (Ibid. No. 189: p. 471, l. 36).—David Neil, nine years old, coal-putter: "I work for a master on mother's account; have done so three years;" so that he began work at six years of age (Ibid. No. 166: p. 466, l. 38).—William Kerr, eleven years old, coal-bearer: "Wrought below five years;" began work therefore at six years of age (Ibid. No. 160: p. 465, l. 46).—David M'Neil, nine years old, putter: "I work wi' Johnnie Scott; done so for three years; father first carried me down;" began work therefore at six years of age (Ibid. No. 173: p. 467, l. 30).

94. It is the common practice in this district for Children to begin work at seven and between seven and eight years of age.—

Grahame Hardie, Esq., managing partner of the Falkirk Iron Company, says: " The boys are taken very young to the work, many not reaching the age of seven and eight years; and many do neither read nor write, or are they likely after beginning to work ever to learn to read or write" (Ibid. No. 252: p. 482, l. 55).—Mr. John Blyth, mining overseer, Edgehead Colliery, says: " I have been under-ground overseer in these mines eight years, and have witnessed with regret the early ages colliers take their children below ground. The masters have no control over the colliers; or, rather, they never interfere with the customs of the colliers themselves. Children of seven and eight years of age are repeatedly taken below, and then all hope of instruction ends" (Ibid. No. 104: p. 456, l. 20).—Rev. William Parlane, M.A., minister of the United Associated Church, Tranent: " I have known children often removed from school to coal-mines as early as seven years of age; afterwards they sometimes return a few months in the evenings. Children of amiable temper and conduct at seven years of age often return next season from the collieries greatly corrupted, and, as an old teacher says, with most *hellish dispositions.* Children ought not to be taken from school under twelve or fourteen years of age" (Ibid. No. 178, p. 468, l. 41).

The following also began work at seven years of age:—David Naysmith (No. 6); David Brown (No. 21); Betsy Sharp (No. 135); Mayday Lumsden (No. 201); Grace Cook (No. 365).

95. Many proprietors, managers, agents, and other officers manifest the utmost indifference as to the age at which Children are employed in their works. Their opinions and feelings on the matter are fairly represented by John James Cadell, Esq., proprietor, who says, " No regulation exists here for the prevention of Children working below. I think the parents are the best judges when to take their Children below for assistance" (Ibid. No. 216: p. 476, l. 29).

96. But there are proprietors and managers who perceive the evil of very young Children working in the pits, and who take some pains to prevent it. —

Mr. Adam Begg, lessee of the Lumphinnins Colliery, says: " I do not employ any male or female in my colliery under fourteen years of age" (Ibid. No. 395: p. 506, l. 12).—Mr. Thomas Bishop, mining overseer and manager of Sir William Baillie's mines at Polkemmet, says: " Boys never descend till ten years of age, and that is much too early, as they are not strong enough for the labour. Coal-working being sore heavy labour, **lads** of fourteen years of age, if strong, are more fitted, and are enabled to form themselves **well, as** also to become better workers" (Ibid. No. 202: p. 474, l. 12).—Mr. Andrew Stirling, overseer of the Banknock Colliery, states: " Mr. Wilson, the proprietor, some time since, tried to exclude boys under twelve years of age; but the men rebelled, and the order was obliged to be cancelled" (Ibid. No. 267: p. 485, l. 28).—" I do not allow," says Mr. John Robertson, manager of the Plean and Auchinbowie Collieries, in the parish of St. Ninian's, Stirlingshire, " children to go below under twelve years of age, even if they are forward, unless it be necessary for the subsistence of some widowed mother, or very large family" (Ibid. No. 282: p. 488, l. 12).—John Craich, Esq., says: " Very young children are not allowed to be wrought; some few exceptions exist, as children of widows, or where the families are very large" (Ibid. No. 291: p. 489, l. 50).—Mr. James Marshall, jun., taxman, says: " Few lads are taken down earlier than twelve, unless the parent be destitute, or the mother is a widow; then any amount a boy, a mere infant, can earn is more than double or treble what she would get by applying to a kirk-session" (Ibid. No. 274: p. 486, l. 37).—Mr. William Ballingall, agent to the proprietors of the Balgonie and Balbirnie Collieries, says: " It has not been the practice of the proprietors of these collieries to employ very young persons at the coal for many years. At Balgonie or Thornton Colliery only six boys are employed, not one under eleven years of age. At Balbirnie men only are employed, the nature of the work requiring full strength" (Ibid. No. 420: p. 510, l. 48).

97. But these instances of care on the part of proprietors and managers to keep Children under ten or twelve years old out of the pits are among the exceptions to the general rule. The prevailing tenor of the evidence establishes the correctness of the statement of Mr. David Graham, lessee, that " colliers begin to work at very early ages in this part (Ibid. No. 424: p. 511, l. 25);" and many of the persons whose offices bring them into immediate contact with the Children, express themselves in the language of Mr. Andrew Wilson, coal-grieve: " It is much to be regretted that such young ones are forced to labour in mines about this part of Fife, as few are fitted to do so before fourteen or fifteen years of age" (Ibid. No. 336: p. 496, l. 32). Moreover, in most of the coal districts in the East of Scotland, the proportion of persons under age to the adult workpeople, and the proportion of those under thirteen to those under eighteen years of age, is remarkably large.

98. West of Scotland.—In the collieries in this part of the country, according to Peter Nielson, collier, " the boys that keep the trap-doors are between " six and seven years of age" (T. Tancred, Esq., Evidence, No. 2, App. Pt. I., p. 356, l. 5); but most of the witnesses state that the Children in this district

generally begin work in the pits at eight years of age. "Children are taken down at a very early age, often when eight years old, and even earlier. The rules very general amongst the colliers for stinting or limiting each other's earnings have an effect in promoting the employment of younger Children than would otherwise be taken below ground. The general rule is that a man shall not earn above from 3s. 6d. to 4s. a-day; consequently, whatever quantity of coal delivered at the pit bottom is paid by the employer 3s. 6d. or 4s.—this is fixed by the men as a man's 'darg,' or day's work. No collier is allowed to deliver more than this, though the employer were willing to pay him for it. If, however, a man has children, they can draw this coal for him, and thus enable him to get through his 'darg' in a shorter time, and with less labour than if he had to draw them himself. When the child comes to about ten years old, he is considered by the colliers as a 'quarter man,' sometimes called a 'quarter bain,' or 'ben.' The employment of such a child entitles a man to deliver a quarter more coals above a man's 'darg,' and thus, instead of 4s., to earn 5s. a-day. At twelve or thirteen a child is a half man, and at sixteen or seventeen a three-quarter man, and may then use a pick and hew coal for himself. A child of ten would be of very little or no use alone; but as the fact of his being in the pit enables his father to earn more than he otherwise could, he is induced not only to take him down, but to bring down another younger, of nine or so, to help him in drawing the whirley." (T. Tancred, Esq., Report, § 28, 29: App., Pt. I., p. 317.)

99. NORTH WALES.—From the evidence collected in this district it appears that, although there are cases in which Children begin to work in the coal-pits at five or six years of age, yet that these cases are very rare; but it is not uncommon for them to begin work on the bank at six years old, and it is common for them to go down into the pits at seven.

Mr. Thomas Harrison, aged sixty-six, mining agent: "Many Children are employed in the mines in this district on the surface, and the age at which they usually begin to work is from six to ten" (H. H. Jones, Esq., Evidence, No. 195: App., Pt. II., p. 464, l. 71).—Mr. Richard Wood, general manager of the British Iron Company's coal and iron works, "He has been long used to large works, and the management of men and children working together in numbers in iron and coal works. The collier children begin to go into the pits some as early as seven years old" (Ibid. No. 1: p. 377, ll. 7, 18).—Mr. Charles Harrison, manager of the Cwd Talwr and Leeswood Coal and Iron Works, "He has been accustomed to coal and iron works all his life; children often begin to work in the pits at seven years old" (Ibid. No. 74: p. 398, l. 46).—Mr. Thomas Williams, Rhosmedre: "He was born and bred in the parish of Ruabon, and knows all the works in it; those [parents] that can keep their children at school will not let them go till they are twelve years old; few can keep them so long; they therefore generally go at ten, but very often at seven" (Ibid. No. 42: p. 388, ll. 17, 25.)

100. Many Young Persons and Children state that they themselves began work in the pits at seven years of age; among others the witnesses Nos. 24, 104, 105, 134. About an equal number say that they began work at eight years of age, and from eight to nine; but the great majority state that they did not begin underground labour before they were eleven, twelve, and upwards.

101. The general tenor of the evidence collected in this district corroborates the statement that, "If the seam of coal be thin, as, for instance, from two to three feet, Children even as young as six years are taken, but I met with only a very few instances where Children commenced work in the coal and ironstone pits at such an age. Seven is by no means an uncommon age in the Ruabon district where the seams are thin; nine and ten, however, are the ages at which the great majority begin to go into the pits" (H. H. Jones, Esq., Report, § 10: App. Pt. II., p. 366).

102. SOUTH WALES.—It is widely different in the coal-field of South Wales and the contiguous English county of Monmouth, in which more cases are recorded of the employment of Children in the pits at very early ages than in any other district. From the evidence of several witnesses it appears that it is no very unusual thing for Children in this district to be taken into the pits as early as four years of age.—

Joseph Richards, aged seven, collier, Buttery Hatch Colliery, parish of Mynyodduslluyn, county of Monmouth, says: "Has been down three years and a half." [Steward said he was sure the boy had been down at least three years.] (R. H. Franks, Esq., Evidence, No. 199: App. Pt. II., p. 535, l. 8).—William Richards, aged seven and a half, Buttery Hatch Colliery:

" I been down about three years. When I first went down I couldn't keep my eyes open ; I don't fall asleep now ; I smokes my pipe ; smokes half a quartern a-week." [This little fellow was intelligent and good-humoured ; his cap was furnished with the usual collier candlestick, and his pipe was stuck familiarly in his button-hole.] (Ibid. No. 193 : p. 534, ll. 28, 32).— William Skidmore, aged eight, collier : " Dont know how old I am ; father thinks he is eight years ; doesn't know when first went to work, it is so long since." [The steward here stated he was certain the boy had been down four years.] (Ibid. No. 198 : p. 535, l. 2).—William Smith, ten years old, collier : " Worked below four years and a half ; works with father and brother ; brother is seven years old, and has assisted father three years." Ibid. No. 201 : p. 535, l. 17.)—William Richards, aged 12, coal-cutter : " Works with his father. Has been at work ever since he was four years old. Was taken to work by his father, because times were poor, and he was worth an extra tram." [A tram or dram is the privilege of a cart of coal as additional work.] (Ibid. No. 131 : p. 525, l. 32).—Mr. Frederick Evans, clerk and accountant for the Dowlais Collieries : " I have known instances of a father carrying his child of four years old on his back to the work, and keeping him with him in the stall all day for the purpose of obtaining an additional tram allowed him. Children are generally brought to work about six years old" (R. W. Jones, Esq., Evidence, No. 121 : App. Pt. II., p. 646, l. 31).—Mr. Samuel Jones, cashier and clerk, Waterloo Colliery, parish of Mynyoddusllwyn, Monmouthshire : " When work is dull, the fathers carry the boys below when four or five years old' (R. H. Franks, Esq., Evidence, No. 207 : App. Pt. II., p. 536, l. 31).—Mr. Hananiel Morgan, agent to Sir Thomas Phillips and Company, occupiers, Court y Bella, parish of Mynyoddusllwyn : " Many young boys are taken into the mines as soon as they can stand on their legs" (Ibid. No. 227 : p. 538, l. 48).—Mr. William Jenkins, under agent to the Gellgan Collieries, says : " Children are taken down as soon as they can crawl" (Ibid. No. 137 : p. 526, l. 33).

103. It is by no means uncommon in this district for children to be taken into the pits at five years of age, and at five years and a half.—

Susan Reece, six years old, Plymouth Works, Merthyr Tydvil : " Been below six or eight months" (Ibid. No. 48 : p. 513, l. 16).—Morgan Jenkins, six years old, Taff Vale, parish of Eglwysilan, Glamorganshire : " Began to work four months since" (Ibid. No. 67 : p. 516, l. 42).—David Watkins, six years old : " Been down three months" (Ibid. No. 367 : p. 561, l. 58).—Mary Davis, near seven years old : " A very pretty little girl, who was fast asleep under a piece of rock near the air-door below ground. Her lamp had gone out for want of oil ; and, upon waking her, she said the rats, or some one, had run away with her bread and cheese, so she went to sleep. The overman who was with me thought she was not so old, though he felt sure she had been below near eighteen months" (Ibid. No. 46 : p. 513, l. 5).—Josiah Jenkins, seven years old : " Has been down eighteen months" (Ibid. No. 200 : p. 535, l. 11).—Moses Williams, seven years old : " Father carried me down eighteen months since : he brings me in the morning, and I return with him at night" (Ibid. No. 219 : p. 538, l. 9).—Thomas Lewis, nine years old : " Been four years among the minerals" (Ibid. No. 175 : p. 532, l. 9).—Jeremiah Jeremiah, ten years old, collier : " Has been five years at work" (Ibid. No. 195 : p. 534, l. 49).—William Smith, ten years old, collier : " Worked below four years and a half" (Ibid. No. 201 : p. 535, l. 16.)—William Freeman, eleven years old, collier : " Been working at coal six years" (Ibid. No. 197 : p. 534, l. 60).—Enoch Williams, thirteen years old, haulier : " Thinks father took him to work when five years old" (Ibid. No. 306 : p. 551, l. 6).—Griffith George, fourteen years old, haulier : " We have one, David Rosser, who is only five years old" (Ibid. No. 287 : p. 548, l. 7).—William Brockwier, door-keeper, 30th April : " I shall be seven years old the 1st of August. I keep this door. I have been here ten months" (R. W. Jones, Esq., Evidence, No. 22 : App. Pt. II., p. 605, l. 39).— Mr. Richard Andrews, overseer : " Colliers take their children to work below ground at very early ages. There is one little fellow, by name John Davis, helping his father, who is certainly not more than five years old. It is not unfrequent for colliers now to take them down even in petticoats to claim a tram" (R. H. Franks, Esq., Evidence, No. 152 : App. Pt. II., p. 528, l. 55).—Mr. Thomas Josephs, mineral agent of the Plymouth Works, Merthyr Tydvil, says, " Children are employed as air-door keepers at five years of age" (Ibid. No. 30 : p. 510, l. 40).—Mr. William James, agent, says, " You may see children taken down at five years of age" (Ibid. No. 260 : p. 544, l. 25).—Mrs. Mary Lewis says, " My youngest son, Lewis, was taken down at five years and three months old, and has been down ever since" (Ibid. No. 217 : p. 537, l. 55).—Mr. John Hoare, cashier of the Cwymbuchan Works, parish of Michaelston, Glamorganshire : " Our collier people take their children down to early and laborious employment, and mere infants open and shut the air-doors" (Ibid. No. 335 : p. 556, l. 61).—Mr. William Strange, medica. assistant, Llanvalon, says, " They [the people] certainly had a bad practice here of taking children down as soon as they can creep about ; many as early as five years of age" (Ibid. No. 157 : p. 529, l. 38).

104. The Sub-Commissioner says, " In the returns of the Pentyrch Collieries I find one child, John Thomas, aged five years and seven months, who has been a picker of scattered mine for his father, a miner, seven months, for which he received 2s. a-week ; and one, Edward Milward, aged six years, who has been an assistant to his father, a collier, for two months" (R. H. Franks, Esq., Report, § 6, App. Pt. II., p. 471).

105. Among others the following witnesses state that they themselves began work in the pits at six years of age :—

Among those examined by R. W. Jones, Esq., Richard Painter, No. 43 ; David and William Thomas, No. 52 ; and John Thomas, No. 141 ; and among those examined by R. H. Franks,

Esq., John Thomas, No. 318; Richard Hutton, No. 221; Henry George, No. 228; Richard Richards, No. 145; Morgan Kenneth, No. 181; John Evans, No. 222; John Jones, No. 271; John Thomas, No. 147; Thomas Jenkins, No. 229; John Price, No. 307; George Roberts, No. 231; David Tyler, No. 248; Joseph Roberts, No. 230; William Williams, No. 176; John Reece, No. 177; Charles Pascal, No. 224; Joseph Head, No. 226; John Richard, No. 162; John Hughes, No. 235; John Jones, No. 233; and John Treasure, No. 257.

William David, foreman to the Cwynrhondda Colliery, parish of Llantwert, Glamorganshire: " Many fathers take their children to work very early, to their great injury. I was taken as early as six years myself, and, for want of time, have never been able to learn the English. [Mrs. Davis, the wife of the proprietor of the colliery, who was present, further observed, that the practice of the colliers in that part, of taking down their children so early as five or six years of age, on an idle excuse of looking after their tools and assisting them, was much to be deprecated.]   (Ibid. No. 127, p. 525, ll. 3—10.)

106. The correctness of these statements is borne out by other classes of witnesses, even by some of the coal-owners, among others by Lewis Thomas, Esq., proprietor of several collieries in the counties of Glamorgan and Monmouth, who says: " It is a practice for fathers to carry their children to the mines on their backs at very early ages. Young colliers begin work at six years of age" (Ibid. No. 286: p. 547, l. 45).

Mr. John Millward, constable in the parish of Merthyr Tydvil: " Boys are taken to work sometimes st six years old. I have seen fathers carry their sons on their backs at this age, particularly to the collieries" (Ibid. No. 96: p. 637, l. 12).—Mr. Abraham Rowlands, surgeon to the Nantiglio and Beaufort Works: " The children go to the works very young—about seven or eight years old—girls and boys the same" (Ibid. No. 47: p. 621, l. 23).

107. It is the common practice in this district for Children to be devoted to the labour of the coal-pit at seven years of age, as is proved indubitably by the testimony of witnesses so numerous that it would be tedious to enumerate them.

108. The Sub-Commissioner says in his Report: " You will find in the evidence a sufficient number of instances to enable you to appreciate the very early age at which it is the practice to take Children down to work in the mines, and that it can scarcely be said to be an uncommon occurrence for a Child to work at the early age of five years and a half."   (R. H. Franks, Esq., Report, § 4: App. Pt. II., p. 471.)   From the cases cited, it is clear that the Sub-Commissioner has in this instance under-stated the results of the evidence which he has collected.

109. FOREST OF DEAN.—In this district cases are recorded in which Children began to work in the coal-mines as early as six years of age, but they are comparatively few, the more usual age being from seven to eight.

See Evidence of Mr. David Gethin, clerk to the Parkend Coal Works (E. Waring, Esq., Evidence, No. 9: App. Pt. II., p. 16, l. 8.); and of Thomas Batten, Esq., surgeon, Coleford (Ibid. No. 36, p. 24, l. 14).

110. SOUTH GLOUCESTERSHIRE.—In this district also cases are recorded in which Children began to work in the coal-mines at six years of age and between six and seven. " The youngest boy I have heard of is George Woodington, who has been working as a door-boy one year, though he is now only seven years and a half old. This infantine labourer has never been taught his letters, but attends a place of worship with his father. I went to the mouth of *Easton Pit* to see the colliers come up after work, and saw the urchin of seven years and a half emerge from the *hutch* with his father, his white cheeks strongly contrasting with the coal-dust smeared over them; he had his candle stuck in front of his cap like all the rest. The poor little fellow answered my questions cheerfully, and seemed quite naturalised to his doleful vocation. There was something at once grotesque and revolting in the *workmanlike* demeanour of " this pigmy collier. His father assured me he had been with him in the pit for 12 months" (E. Waring, Esq., Report, § 81: App. Pt. II., p. 37; and Evidence, No. 58: p. 42, l. 7.)

111. Many of the proprietors and managers in this district state, however, that no Children are admitted into their coal-mines under eight or nine years of age.—See Evidence of Mr. Joseph Staley (Ibid. No. 49: p. 39, l. 29). The general tenor of the evidence given by the different classes of witnesses examined in this district is, that Children commence underground labour at nine years of age.

112. NORTH SOMERSETSHIRE.—The managers and proprietors state that the earliest age at which Children are taken into the coal-pits in this district is eight, but that the usual age is ten; although there is abundant evidence, derived from

the Children themselves and the adult colliers, that many begin to work in the pits between six and seven.

Mr. John Smith, acting partner at the Hewish and Writhlington Coal-works, near Radstock, says, " The boys do not commonly begin before ten, but there are some of only eight years of age" (Dr. Stewart, Evidence, No. 11 : App. Pt. II., p. 52, l. 66).—Mr. Moses Reynolds, Bedminster Colliery, near Bristol, says, "He has been thirty years employed in managing the under-ground work of the Bedminster Collieries : for the last twenty years he has been sole manager and bailiff. The smallest boys are usually eight or ten years old" (Ibid. No. 2: p. 49, l. 29).—Mr. William Asham, Crandoun Coal-works, near Radstock : " Has been thirty-four years manager of the Crandoun Coal-works. The youngest boy now employed is ten years old" (Ibid. No. 10 : p. 52, l. 44).—Mr. Charles Asham, Radstock, near Bath : " The boys are taken into the Coal-works at about eight years old by their parents, but not before this age at all regularly. They are occasionally taken in, as a matter of curiosity, when quite young; but since he has had the management of the works no child has been employed before eight years old" (Ibid. No. 9 : p. 51, l. 39).

113. Yet it is stated by Mr. William Brice, clerk and manager of the Coal-Barton and Vobster Collieries, near Frome, that among 100 hands of all descriptions employed in the coal-works at Coal-Barton, " there are some at seven and under" (Ibid. No. 7, p. 50, l. 48); and many of the adult colliers state that they themselves began work between six and seven, and at seven years of age.

114. IRELAND.—In the coal-mines in the South of Ireland, no Children at all were found. All the underground work, which, in the coal-mines of England, Scotland, and Wales, is done by Young Children, appears in Ireland to be done by Young Persons between the ages of thirteen and eighteen. The Sub-Commissioner in reporting on the Dromagh and Dysart Collieries, in the county of Cork, says :— " There are in the Dromagh pits upwards of 200 people employed, but no Children. I examined a good number of the Young Persons, and found their statements generally concurring. All the Young Persons between thirteen and eighteen years of age, and indeed many more who are older, are employed underground as ' hurries,' pushing the loaded waggons along the railways from the workings to the foot of the shafts; this, and filling the waggons and buckets, are their only employments" (Frederick Roper, Esq., Report, No. 6, § 2, 3: App. Pt. I., p. 868).

115. In the Collieries in the County of Tipperary no Children are employed in underground work, excepting a few young boys as trappers. " I first visited Mardyke Colliery, which is the nearest to Killenaule, and where the agent for them all, Mr. Robert Nicolson, resides. Mr. Nicolson stated that they had a few young boys who were employed underground, merely opening and shutting the doors after the waggons had passed through, in order to keep the fresh air in its regular course round the mine; that for the other work, as ' hurries,' they required strong able young men of from about eighteen years old and upwards. At the Sleive Ardagh Colliery, which is about six miles distant, but under the same management and direction, there are about twenty young men under eighteen years of age employed, but no Children. There also were two or three little boys employed as at the other pit, opening and shutting the doors, after the waggons had passed. In this neighbourhood, between the two principal pits of the company, there is a very extensive colliery, called the Coolbrook, belonging to —— Langley, Esq., which I visited. Mr. Nasmyth, the agent, told me they did not employ Children —that they were of no use ; they required strong able lads of seventeen or eighteen years old to do their work, of whom about 30 were employed. There are about 400 people employed at this pit" (Ibid., No. 8, § 1, 2, 4, 8, 9, 10: pp. 871, 872).

116. Of the Coal Field on the borders of Kilkenny and Queen's County he
says, " I inspected about a dozen of the different shafts, worked by contractors, and found none but men employed; indeed, I was informed that none but strong, able young men would be of any use in the pits, the labour being severe; I did not see any apparently under eighteen years of age. I went down into two of the pits and saw the people at their different work, all of whom were strong, able men ; even the ' hurries,' who draw the coals to the foot of the shaft, were mostly strong young men" (Ibid. No. 9, § 3, 4: p. 872).

117. At the small collieries of Drumglass and Coal Island, in the county of Tyrone, examined by T. Martin, Esq., Young People appear to be employed as early as eight and nine years of age. (T. Martin, Esq., Evidence, App. Pt. I.: p. 884, ll. 5 and 62.)

Coal Mines.
—
Age.

118. In concluding the subject of age, it is right to observe that many of the adult workpeople in almost all the districts state that they themselves began work in the pits at the same early ages; and this is constantly assigned as one reason why the colliers now so frequently take their own children down when they are mere infants; but there is also evidence that in some districts it is the practice at present to take children into the coal mines at earlier ages than at any former period.   This appears from the evidence collected by Mr. Fletcher to be the case in Lancashire. " Parents," say the underlookers, "come and beg to thrust their Children in, really before they are fit to go;" and Mr. Fletcher states that the " chief agent of the largest mining company here, having his attention drawn to the subject by the increased number of minor accidents in the pits, has become convinced that parents are pushing their Children into colliery employment at an earlier age, because of the legal restriction from sending them to the neighbouring factories, in which they would be exposed to far less hardship and hazard" (J. Fletcher, Esq., Report, § 10: App. Pt. II., p. 821).

2.—Sex: Employment of Girls and Women in Coal Mines.

1. *Districts in which Girls and Women are Employed Underground.*

Sex: Districts in which girls and women are employed underground.
—

119. In England, exclusive of Wales, it is only in some of the colliery districts of Yorkshire and Lancashire that female Children of tender age and young and adult women are allowed to descend into the coal mines and regularly to perform the same kinds of underground work, and to work for the same number of hours, as boys and men; but in the East of Scotland their employment in the pits is general; and in South Wales it is not uncommon.

West Riding of Yorkshire.

120. West Riding of Yorkshire: Southern Part.—In many of the collieries in this district, as far as relates to the underground employment, there is no distinction of sex, but the labour is distributed indifferently among both sexes, excepting that it is comparatively rare for the women to hew or get the coals, although there are numerous instances in which they regularly perform even this work.   In great numbers of the coal-pits in this district the men work in a state of perfect nakedness, and are in this state assisted in their labour by females of all ages, from girls of six years old to women of twenty-one, these females being themselves quite naked down to the waist.

121. "Girls," says the Sub-Commissioner, "regularly perform all the various offices of trapping, hurrying, filling, riddling, tipping, and occasionally getting, just as they are performed by boys.   One of the most disgusting sights I have ever seen was that of young females, dressed like boys in trousers, crawling on all fours, with belts round their waists and chains passing between their legs, at day pits at Hunshelf Bank, and in many small pits near Holmfrith and New Mills: it exists also in several other places.   I visited the Hunshelf Colliery on the 18th of January: it is a day pit; that is, there is no shaft or descent; the gate or entrance is at the side of a bank, and nearly horizontal.   The gate was not more than a yard high, and in some places not above 2 feet.   When I arrived at the board or workings of the pit I found at one of the side-boards down a narrow passage a girl of fourteen years of age, in boy's clothes, picking down the coal with the regular pick used by the men.   She was half sitting half lying at her work, and said she found it tired her very much, and 'of course she didn't like it.'   The place where she was at work was not 2 feet high.   Further on were men at work lying on their sides and getting.   No less than six girls out of 18 men and children are employed in this pit.   Whilst I was in the pit the Rev. Mr. Bruce, of Wadsley, and the Rev. Mr. Nelson, of Rotherham, who accompanied me, and remained outside, saw another girl of ten years of age, also dressed in boy's clothes, who was employed in hurrying, and these gentlemen saw her at work.   She was a nice-looking little child, but of course as black as a tinker, and with a little necklace round her throat.   In two other pits in the Huddersfield Union I have seen the same sight.   In one near New Mills, the chain, passing high up between the legs of two of these girls, had worn large holes in their trousers; and any sight more disgustingly indecent or revolting can scarcely be imagined than these girls at work—no brothel can beat it. On descending Messrs. Hopwood's pit at Barnsley, I found assembled round the

fire a group of men, boys, and girls, some of whom were of the age of puberty, the girls as well as the boys stark naked down to the waist, their hair bound up with a tight cap, and trousers supported by their hips. (At Silkstone and at Flockton they work in their shifts and trousers.) Their sex was recognisable only by their breasts, and some little difficulty occasionally arose in pointing out to me which were girls and which were boys, and which caused a good deal of laughing and joking. In the Flockton and Thornhill pits the system is even more indecent; for though the girls are clothed, at least three-fourths of the men for whom they 'hurry' work *stark naked*, or with a flannel waistcoat only, and in this state they assist one another to fill the corves 18 or 20 times a-day: I have seen this done myself frequently" (J. C. Symons, Esq., Report, § 111, et seq : App., Pt. I., pp. 181, 182).

122. Evidence to the same effect is given by all classes of witnesses in this district :—

Thomas Dunn, Esq., of the firm of Hounsfield, Wilson, Dunn, and Jeffcock, chief manager, says: "Girls are worked naked down to their waist, the same as men" (J. C. Symons, Esq., Evidence, No. 1 : App., Pt. I., p. 226, l. 9).—Mr. Thomas Peace, of the firm of Webster and Peace, Hunshelf Bank Coal-Works, says : "There are as many girls as boys employed about here" (Ibid. No. 33 : p. 233, l. 20).—Mr. Charles Locke, coal-master and agent at Snafethorpe, near Wakefield : "Girls make better hurriers than boys; the boys are often stripped all but a shirt" (Ibid. No. 172 : p. 273, l. 40).—John Thorneley, Esq., one of Her Majesty's justices of the peace for the county of York : "The system of having females to work in coal-pits prevails generally in this neighbourhood" (Ibid. No. 96 : p. 246, l. 44).—William Bowden, underground steward to Messrs. Hounsfield, Dunn, and Co., at the Soaphouse Colliery, Sheffield : "In Silkstone Pits, believes women and girls work dressed as men, and often naked down to the waist, just the same as men and boys. Decency is disregarded" (Ibid. No. 3 : p. 227, l. 16).—Mr. William Hopwood, agent of Barnsley New Colliery : "In most of the pits round Barnsley girls are employed in trapping and in hurrying : they do the same work as the boys" (Ibid. No. 80 : p. 243, l. 17).—Martin Gomersal, underground steward at Barnsley Colliery: "It is common for girls to hurry in this neighbourhood. I never saw a woman get here, but I have at Silkstone. I have seen two women work like men there" (Ibid. No. 97 : p. 247, l. 29).—William Pickard, general steward to Sir John Lister Lister Kaye's Collieries : "I have known a married woman hurrying for a man who worked stark naked, and not any kin to her" (Ibid. No. 255 : p. 289, l. 59).

Edward Newman, Esq., solicitor : "I have been an inhabitant of Barnsley for eighteen years, and been in the constant habit of seeing the colliers and children passing to and from their work. At Silkstone there are a great many girls who work in the pits, and I have seen them washing themselves naked much below the waist as I passed their doors, and whilst they are doing this they will be talking and chatting with any men who happen to be there with the utmost unconcern; and men, young and old, would be washing in the same place at the same time. They dress so well after their work, and on Sundays, that it is impossible to recognise them. They wear earrings even whilst they work, and I have seen them with them nearly two inches long. There is a great deal of slang and loud talk between the lads and girls as they pass along the streets ; and I conceive that they would behave far more decorously were it not for the dress and the disguise it affords. I have never heard similar language pass between men and girls respectably dressed in Barnsley. Their dress, when they come out of the pit, is a kind of skull-cap which hides all the hair, trousers without stockings, and thick wooden clogs; their waists are covered" (Ibid. No. 108 : p. 250, l. 25).—Mr. Crooks, surgeon, Barnsley : "Girls are employed in the pits as well as boys, and when they have a little relaxation all congregate together, and no one in particular to overlook them (Ibid. No. 166 : p. 267, l. 46).

William Frood, collier : "Some of the men work quite naked, but very few; most work like me, with a flannel shirt and nothing else on" (Ibid. No. 191 : p. 276, l. 16).—Anne Hague, turned of thirteen : "Sarah Monhouse 'gets' as well as hurries; she gets and hurries eight corves a-day" (Ibid. No. 39 : p. 234, l. 23).—Rebecca Hough, aged fourteen, examined whilst getting in the same pit: "I am a regular hurrier; I am used to help the getter. I often do it three or four times a-week. I help to fill and riddle, and then I hurry the corves down to the Bullstake. I find the hurrying the hardest work. It is because I don't do much at getting that it tires me less" (Ibid. No. 136 a : p. 257, l. 49).—Margaret Westwood, aged fourteen and a half, examined whilst hurrying and eating in Messrs. Stansfield's and Briggs's Emryod Pit, Flockton : "I hurry for Charles Littlewood. I am let to him. He is no kin to me; he works stark naked; he has no waistcoat on, nor nothing" (Ibid. No. 192 : p. 276, l. 25).—Mary Holmes, aged fourteen and a half, Meal Hill, Hepworth : "I always hurry as you saw me, with a belt round my waist and the chain through my legs. I hurry so in the board-gates. I always wear lad's clothes. The trousers don't get torn at all" (Ibid. No. 283 : p. 295, l. 22).—Ebenezer Healey, aged thirteen : "There are girls that hurry in the same way, with belt and chain. Our breeches are often torn between the legs with the chain. The girls' breeches are torn as often as ours; they are torn many a time, and when they are going along we can see them all between the legs naked; I have often; and that girl, Mary Holmes, was so to-day; she denies it, but it is true for all that" (Ibid. No. 284 : p. 295, l. 41).—See also witnesses, Nos. 101, 119, 171, 194, 202.

Coal Mines.

Sex: Districts in
which girls and wo-
men are employed
underground.

West Riding of
Yorkshire.

123. To the general correctness of these statements the Commissioners them-selves can bear testimony; for in the coal-pits examined by them both at Barnsley and at Flockton, they saw many girls performing precisely the same work as the boys, the girls dressed in the manner described, and some of them as old as fifteen or eighteen assisting, and often brought by their work into personal contact with men perfectly naked.

124. BRADFORD AND LEEDS.—It is stated by the Sub-Commissioner that "it is not the custom of the district to employ female children in mining operations;" yet it appears from the evidence of Mr. Thomas Mackley, surgeon, Wilsden, four miles from Bradford, that there are "coal-mines lying rather apart from the gene-ral coal and iron mines of the Bradford district, in which girls are employed, and that in these pits the men work perfectly naked" (R. W. Wood, Esq., Evidence, No. 61: App. Pt. II, p. h 28, ll. 3, 12). It appears also from the evidence of William Green, colliery steward of the Low-Moor Iron-Works, that some girls are employed in the pits even there:—"Not generally; some few; never many in this country; more formerly than now, but it never was common in this country to employ girls" (W. R. Wood, Esq., Evidence, No. 3: App. Pt. II., p. h 5, l. 60).

Charles Hardy, Esq., proprietor, Low-Moor, in answer to the question whether any girls are employed underground in his mines, answers: "I find upon inquiry that we have two, but I was not aware of the fact before, and it is quite contrary to our rules. Upon inquiry into the case, I find that they were allowed to go in by the pit steward at the particular request of their mother. They will not be allowed to remain there. The mother, I find, had worked in a pit herself till the time she was married. (Ibid. No. 1, p. h3, l. 14).

125. HALIFAX.—In this neighbourhood girls from five years old and upwards regularly perform the same work as boys. It is stated by the Sub-Commissioner that there is no distinction whatever between the boys and girls in their coming up the shaft and going down; in their mode of hurrying or thrusting; in the weights of corves; in the distance they are hurried; in wages or dress; that the girls asso-ciate and labour with men who are in a state of nakedness, and that they have themselves no other garment than a ragged shift, or, in the absence of that, a pair of broken trousers, to cover their persons.

Susan Pitchforth, aged eleven, Elland: "I have worked in this pit going two years. I have one sister going of fourteen, and she works with me in the pit. I am a thruster" (S. S. Scriven, Esq., Evidence, No. 10: App. Pt. II., p. 103, l. 60; p. 104, l. 2).—"This child," says the Sub-Commissioner, "stood shivering before me from cold. The rags that hung about her waist were once called a shift, which was as black as the coal she thrust, and saturated with water—the drippings of the roof and shaft. During my examination of her, the banksman, whom I had left in the pit, came to the public-house and wanted to take her away, because, as he expressed himself, it was not decent that she should be exposed to us" (Ibid. p. 104, l. 8).—Patience Kershaw, aged seventeen: "I hurry in the clothes I have now got on—trousers and ragged jacket; the bald place upon my head is made by thrusting the corves; the getters that I work for are naked except their caps; they pull off all their clothes; all the men are naked" (Ibid. No. 26: p. 108, l. 8).—Mary Barrett, aged fourteen: "I work always without stockings, or shoes, or trousers; I wear nothing but my shift; I have to go up to the headings with the men; they are all naked there; I am got well used to that, and don't care now much about it; I was afraid at first, and did not like it" (Ibid. No. 72: p. 122, l. 54).—See also witnesses Nos. 66, 73, et seq.

126. LANCASHIRE AND CHESHIRE.—In the greater portion of the Lancashire coal fields it is the general custom for girls and women to be employed in the ordinary work of the mines; and an unusually large proportion appear to be so employed in the mines about Wigan, Blackrod, Worsley, Hulton, Clifton, Outwood, Bolton. Lure, St. Helen's, and Prescot.

Henry Eaton, Ringley Bridge, Bolton, surveyor of coal-mines: "I have been sixteen years and upwards connected with coal-mines, and I have been in almost all the pits in the neighbourhood of Bolton, Bury, Ratcliff, Lure, and Rochdale. There are women in all the pits in those neighbourhoods. I cannot say in which pits there are the most employed; they are em-ployed in all; they are used as drawers" (J. L. Kennedy, Esq., Evidence, No. 18: App. Pt. II., p. 208, l. 56).—John Millington, superintendent of the collieries of Mr. Ashton at Hyde: "They [the women, whilst at work] wear a pair of drawers which come down nearly to the knees, and some women a small handkerchief about their necks; but I have seen many a one with her breasts hanging out. The girls are not a bit ashamed amongst their own pit set; it is the same as if they were one family" (Ibid. No. 6: p. 202, l. 26).—Mr. Miller, underlooker at Mr. Woodley's, near Staleybridge, states that "one reason why women are used so frequently as drawers in the coal-pits is, that a girl of 20 will work for 2s. a-day or less, and a man of that age would want 3s. 6d.: it makes little difference to the coal-master, he pays the same whoever does the work; some would say he got his coal cheaper, but I am not of that opinion; the only difference is that the collier can spend 1*s.* to 1*s.* 6*d.* more at the alehouse, and very often the woman helps him to spend it. Not one woman in a hundred ever becomes a coal-getter, and that is one of the reasons the men prefer them" (Ibid. No. 7: p. 203, l. 12).—Mr. Joseph Hatherton, underlooker at Messrs. Foster's, Ringley-bridge, states that " He has four children in the pits, two girls and two boys. Comes from the neighbourhood of St. Helen's; many women and children are employed in the pits there—many a hundred; the drawers are all women or children there. The girls go down into the pits as soon as the boys, every bit—at eight or nine years old; mine went into them at that time" (Ibid. No. 23: p. 213, ll. 4, 19).

Benjamin Berry, aged twenty-four, collier, at Mr. Lancaster's, Patricroft, near Worsley, says: " The employment of women in the pits in this district is general; I have worked with many a score. When I worked last at Nightingale's they had more women than men. They make far better drawers than lads; they are more steady. When a lad gets to be half, he is all for getting coal; but a lass never expects to be a coal-getter, and that keeps her steady to her work" (Ibid. No. 27: p. 215, l. 29).—Peter Gaskell, collier, at Mr. Lancaster's, near Worsley: " Prefers women to boys as drawers; they are better to manage, and keep the time better; they will fight and shriek and do everything but let anybody pass them; and they never get to be coal-getters, that is another good thing" (Ibid. No. 29: p. 217, l. 25).—Betty Harris, aged thirty-seven, drawer in a coal-pit, Little Bolton: " I have a belt round my waist, and a chain passing between my legs, and I go on my hands and feet. The road is very steep, and we have to hold by a rope, and, when there is no rope, by anything we can catch hold of. There are six women and about six boys and girls in the pit I work in: it is very hard work for a woman. The pit is very wet where I work, and the water comes over our clog-tops always, and I have seen it up to my thighs: it rains in at the roof terribly; my clothes are wet through almost all day long. I never was ill in my life but when I was lying-in. My cousin looks after my children in the day-time. I am very tired when I get home at night; I fall asleep sometimes before I get washed. I am not so strong as I was, and cannot stand my work so well as I used to do. I have drawn till I have had the skin off me; the belt and chain is worse when we are in the family way. My feller [husband] has beaten me many a time for not being ready. I were not used to it at first, and he had little patience: I have known many a man beat his drawer" (Ibid. No. 90: p. 230, l. 64).—Mary Glover, aged thirty-eight, at Messrs. Foster's, Ringley-bridge: " I went into a coal-pit when I was seven years old, and began by being a drawer. I never worked much in the pit when I was in the family way, but since I gave up having children I have begun again a bit. I wear a shift and a pair of trousers when at work. I always will have a good pair of trousers. I have had many a two-pence given me by the boatmen on the canal to show my breeches. I never saw women work naked, but I have seen men work without breeches in the neighbourhood of Bolton. I remember seeing a man who worked stark naked" (Ibid. No. 26: p. 214, l. 31).

William Cooper, aged seven years, thrutcher, at Almond's: " There are about twenty wenches, drawers, in the pit I work in. They are nigh naked; they wear trousers; they have no other clothes except loose shifts" (Ibid. No. 55: p. 224, l. 32).—Robert Hunt, underlooker to Messrs. Foster, Outwood: " It is quite true that women work in the pits when they are in the family way. My last wife worked in a pit from ten years old; and once she worked all day in the pits, and was put to bed at night. That woman you saw in the pit was in the family way [alluding to a person I had seen in the pit]. I cannot say that my wife's health suffered by her working in the pits; she worked in the pits till she was 30. She had four children; two were born alive, but they died afterwards, and two were still-born" (Ibid. No. 19: p. 209, l. 42.)—William Royle, engineer at Mr. Lancaster's, Patricroft: " His wife was in the family way while she was working in the pits: she has had one child, but it is dead. She had a fall in the pits; she was hooking on to her tub, and she missed her hold and fell backwards, and the doctors said that it was that which had hurt her; she had a very bad time" (Ibid. No. 28: p. 216, l. 46).—Betty Harris, drawer in a coal-pit, Little Bolton: " I worked at drawing when I was in the family way. I know a woman who has gone home and washed herself, taken to her bed, been delivered of a child, and gone to work again under the week" (Ibid. No. 90: p. 230, l. 62).—Betty Wardle: " I have worked in a pit since I was six years old. I have had four children, two of them were born while I worked in the pits. I worked in the pits whilst I was in the family way. I had a child born in the pits, and I brought it up the pit-shaft in my skirt; it was born the day after I were married—that makes me to know" (Ibid. Report, § 102: App. Pt. II., p. 163).—Mary Hardman, Outwood, near Leven: " I am thirty-eight years old. I went into the pit when I was seven years old. I am a married woman, and was married whilst I worked in the coal-pits. I have had either three or four children born the same day that I have been at work, and I have gone back to my work nine or ten days after I lay down almost always. Four out of the eight were still-born. I have seen women working in the pits whilst they were in the family way many a time" (Ibid. Evidence, No. 25: App. Pt. II., p. 214, l. 16).

127. NORTH LANCASHIRE.—Throughout the whole of the district examined by A. Austin, Esq., girls and women are regularly employed in the under-ground work of the coal-mines, just as boys and men (Report and Evidence of A. Austin, Esq., App. Pt. II., p. 788, et passim).

128. EAST OF SCOTLAND.—In SCOTLAND the employment of girls and women

COAL MINES.

Sex: *Districts in which girls and women are employed underground.*

East of Scotland.

in the ordinary under-ground work of the coal-pits is even more extensive than in any part of England : but this practice is confined chiefly to the Collieries in the East of Scotland. Of the employment of girls and women in the coal-mines in the East of Scotland, the Sub-Commissioner says, " It will now become a more painful duty to give a particular description of the employment of Children and Young Persons in those departments in which their labour is used, and in which females are, equally with males, employed at very tender years. The *coal-bearers* are women and children employed to carry coal on their backs in un-railed roads with burdens varying from ¾ cwt. to 3 cwt. It is revolting to humanity to reflect upon the barbarous and cruel slavery which this degrading labour constitutes ; a labour which happily has long since been abolished in England, and in the greater part of Scotland, and I believe is only to be found in the Lothians, the remnant of the slavery of a degraded age" (R. H. Franks, Esq., Report, § 10—12 : App. Pt. I., p. 383). The preceding evidence shows how much the Sub-Commissioner is mistaken in supposing that the employment of women in this kind of labour is peculiar to Scotland and to the Lothians, and that the practice does not prevail in England.

129. " To this subject Lord Dundonald is said to have called public indignation so early as the year 1793 ; and, in 1808, Robert Bald, Esq., of Edinburgh, again, in a manly appeal on the same subject, endeavoured, as he himself expresses it, 'to bring into view the state and condition of a class of women in society whose peculiar situation was but little known to the world ;' and after describing the system as ' severe, slavish, and oppressive in the highest degree,' characterised that condition as one 'which renders their existence the most weary of all the pilgrimages of this journey through life' (Ibid. § 13 : p. 384).

130. " The workings in the narrow seams are sometimes 100 to 200 yards from the main roads ; so that the females have to crawl backwards and forwards with their small carts in seams in many cases not exceeding 22 to 28 inches in height. The danger and difficulties of dragging on roads dipping from 1 foot in 3 to 1 foot in 6 may be more easily conceived than explained ; and the state which females are in after pulling like horses through these holes—their perspiration, exhaustion, and tears very frequently—it is painful in the extreme even to witness ; yet, when the work is done, they return to it with a vigour which is surprising, considering how they inwardly hate it. The business of these females is to remove the coals from the hewer, who has picked them from the wall-face, and, placing them either on their backs, which they invariably do when working in edge-seams, or in little carts when on levels, &c., to carry them to the main-road, whence they are conveyed to the pit bottom, where, being emptied into the ascending basket of the shaft, they are wound up by machinery to the pit's mouth, where they lie heaped for further distribution. (Ibid. § 8 : p. 383.)

131. " Now, when the nature of this horrible labour is taken into consideration, its extreme severity, its regular duration of from 12 to 14 hours daily, the damp, heated, and unwholesome atmosphere of a coal-mine, and the tender age and sex of the workers—a picture is presented of deadly physical oppression and systematic slavery, of which I conscientiously believe no one unacquainted with such facts would credit the existence in the British dominions.

132. " The evidence of boys, who are comparatively few, engaged in the same labour, will be found, in most particulars, to be of similar character. To this labour, which is at once so repulsive and severe, the girls are invariably set at an earlier age than boys are to their peculiar labour, from a notion very generally entertained amongst the parents themselves, that girls are more acute and capable of making themselves useful at an earlier age than boys" (Ibid. § 26—28 : p. 387).

133. The statements of all classes of witnesses concur in showing that the labour to which these female workers are subjected is unexampled in severity and most revolting in its nature, but more especially the statements of the girls and young women themselves.

Mary Neilson, ten years old, coal-bearer : " When sister Margaret, who is nine years old, works, we make 10 to 15 rakes each ; when she is away I am forced to make 20. Sister was six years old when she first wrought, and I went down at that age. I carry half a load now ; half a load is 1 cwt., and it is no easy work ; it often causes me to fall asleep below when there is nothing to gang with" (R. H. Franks, Esq., Evidence, No. 119 : App. Pt. I., p. 458, l. 61).—Janet Cumming, eleven years old, bears coals : " I carry the large bits of coal from the wall-face to the pit bottom, and the small pieces called chows in a creel ; the weight is usually a hundredweight; does not know how many pounds there are in the hundredweight, but it is some work to carry; it takes three journeys to fill a tub of 4 cwt. The distance varies, as the work is not always on the same wall; sometimes 150 fathoms, whiles 250. The roof is very low; I have to bend my back and legs, and the water comes frequently up to the calves of my legs; has no liking to the work; father makes me like it" (Ibid. No. 1: p. 436, l. 5).—Rebecca Simpson, eleven years old, putter: "Am wrought with sister Agnes; sister draws the carts with ropes and chains, and I push behind; when it is difficult to draw, brother George, who is 14 years old, helps us up the brae; the carts hold 7 cwt., and run them about 200 yards; we run 14 rakes every day we work" (Ibid. No. 260: p. 484, l. 11).—Isabella Read, twelve years old, coal-bearer: "I am wrought with sister and brother, it is very sore work; cannot say how many rakes or journeys I make from pit's bottom to wall-face and back; thinks about 30 or 25 on the average; the distance varies from 100 to 250 fathoms. I carry about 1 cwt. and a quarter on my back; have to stoop much and creep through water, which is frequently up to the calves of my legs. When first down fell frequently asleep while waiting for coal from heat and fatigue. I do not like the work, nor do the lassies, but they are made to like it. When the weather is warm there is difficulty in breathing, and frequently the lights go out" (Ibid. No. 141: p. 439, l. 23).—Agnes Moffatt, seventeen years old, coal-bearer: "Began working at ten years of age; father took sister and I down; he gets our wages. I fill five baskets; the weight is more than 22 cwt.; it takes me 20 journeys. The work is o'er sair for females. It is no uncommon for women to lose their burthen, and drop off the ladder down the dyke below; Margaret M'Neil did a few weeks since, and injured both legs. When the tugs which pass over the forehead break, which they frequently do, it is very dangerous to be under with a load" (Ibid. No. 23: p. 440, l. 46).—Margaret Jaques, seventeen years of age, coal-bearer: "I have been seven years at coal-bearing; it is horrible sore work; it was not my choice, but we do our parents' will. I make 30 rakes a-day, with two cwt. of coal on my creel. It is a guid distance I journey, and very dangerous on parts of the road. The distance fast increases as the coals are cut down" (Ibid. No. 25: p. 441, l. 2).

Helen Reid, sixteen years old, coal-bearer: "I have wrought five years in the mines in this part; my employment is carrying coal. Am frequently worked from four in the morning until six at night. I work night-work week about [alternate weeks]. I then go down at two in the day, and come up at four and six in the morning. I can carry near two cwt. *on* my back. I do not like the work. Two years since the pit closed upon 13 of us, and we were two days without food or light; nearly one day we were up to our chins in water. At last we got to an old shaft, to which we picked our way, and were heard by people watching above. Two months ago I was filling the tubs at the pit bottom, when the gig clicked too early, and the hook caught me by my pit-clothes—the people did not hear my shrieks—my hand had fast grappled the chain, and the great height of the shaft caused me to lose my courage, and I swooned. The banksman could scarcely remove my hand—the deadly grasp saved my life" (Ibid. No. 26: p. 441, l. 11).—Margaret Drysdale, fifteen years old, coal-putter: "I don't like the work, but mother is dead, and father brought me down; I had no choice. The lasses will tell you they all like the work fine, as they think you are going to take them out of the pits. My employment is to draw the carts. I have harness, or draw-ropes, on like the horses, and pull the carts. Large carts hold 7½ cwt., the smaller 5½ cwt. The roads are wet, and I have to draw the work about 100 fathoms" (Ibid. No. 49: p. 445, l. 16).—Katherine Logan, sixteen years old, coal-putter: "Began to work at coal-carrying more than five years since; works in harness now; draws backwards with face to tubs; the ropes and chains go under my pit-clothes; it is o'er sair work, especially where we crawl" (Ibid. No. 95: p. 454, l. 61).

Janet Duncan, seventeen years old, coal-putter: "Works at putting, and was a coal-bearer at Hen-Muir Pit and New Pencaitland. The carts I push contain three cwt. of coal, being a load and a half; it is very severe work, especially when we have to stay before the tubs, on the braes, to prevent them coming down too fast; they frequently run too quick, and knock us down; when they run over-fast, we fly off the roads and let them go, or we should be crushed. Mary Peacock was severely crushed a fortnight since; is gradually recovering. I have wrought above in harvest-time; it is the only other work that ever I tried my hand at, and having harvested for three seasons, am able to say that the hardest daylight work is infinitely superior to the best of coal-work" (Ibid. No. 130: p. 460, l. 49).—Margaret Harper, thirteen years old, putter: "I work in Hard-hill Mine. We hurry the carts on the railroads by pushing behind; I frequently draw with ropes and chains as the horses do; it is dirty slavish work, and the water quite covers our ankles. I knock my head against the roofs, as they are not so high as I am, and they cause me to stoop, which makes my back ache"—(Ibid. No. 188: p. 471, l. 23).—Ann Harris, fifteen years old, putter: "Heartily hates it; could get no other profitable work, or would not have gone down. It is no woman's work, nor is it good for anybody; am obliged to do the work, as father houks [hews] the coal below" (Ibid. No. 193: p. 472, l. 23).—Ann P. Francis, fourteen years old, putter: "I wheel the carts, which hold 7 cwt. to 8 cwt. coal; it is very ill sort of work, as we have to put four pins in the wheels, to lessen the rapidity of the movement, as the brae is very steep, and the carts often peel my legs [take the skin off]" (Ibid. No. 310: p. 493, l. 3).—Ellspee Thomson, forty years old, coal-bearer: "I wrought all my life, till a stone, 14 months ago, so crushed my leg and right foot, below ground, that I could na' gang. If women did not work below, the children would not go down so soon; and it would be better for them, as they would get more strength and a little learning. Can say, to my own cost, that the bairns are much neglected when both parents work below; for neighbours, if they keep the children, they require as much as women sometimes earn, and neglect them. The oppression of the coal-bearing is such as to injure women in after-life ; and few exist whose legs are not injured, or haunches, before they are thirty years of age" (Ibid. No. 73 : p. 450, 1. 16).

Jane Johnson, aged twenty-nine, draws coal : " I was seven and a half years of age when my uncle first yoked me to the work, as father and mother were dead ; it was at Sheriff-hall, and I carried coal on my back ; I could carry 2 cwt. when fifteen years of age ; but I now feel the weakness upon me from the strains. I have been married near 10 years, and had four children ; have usually wrought till within one or two days of the children's birth. Many women lose their strength early from overwork, and get injured in their backs and legs ; was crushed by a stone some time since, and forced to lose one of my fingers." (Ibid. No. 107 : p. 456, 1. 59). —Jane Peacock Watson, age forty, coal-bearer : " I have wrought in the bowels of the earth 33 years ; have been married 23 years, and had nine children, two dead born ; thinks they were so from the oppressive work ; a vast of women have dead children and false births, which are worse, as they are no able to work after the latter. I have always been obliged to work below till forced to go home to bear the bairn, and so have all the other women. We return as soon as able, never longer than 10 or 12 days ; many less, if they are much needed. It is only horse-work, and ruins the women ; it crushes their haunches, bends their ankles, and makes them old women at forty. Women so soon get weak that they are forced to take the little ones down to relieve them ; even children of six years of age do much to relieve the burthen. Knows it is bad to keep bairns from school, but every little helps" (Ibid. No. 117 : p. 458, 1. 28).—Isabel Hogg, fifty-three years of age, was a coal-bearer : " Been married 37 years ; it was the practice to marry early ; when the coals were all carried on women's backs, men needed us ; from the great sore labour false births are frequent and very dangerous. I have four daughters married, and all work below till they bear their bairns —one is very badly now from working while pregnant, which brought on a miscarriage from which she is not expected to recover. Collier-people suffer much more than others. You must just tell the Queen Victoria that we are guid loyal subjects ; women-people here don't mind work, but they object to horse-work ; and that she would have the blessings of all the Scotch coal-women if she would get them out of the pits, and send them to other labour."— [Mrs. Hogg is one of the most respectable coal-wives in Penston ; her rooms are all well furnished, and the house the cleanest I have seen in East Lothian.] (Ibid. No. 131 : p. 460, 1. 66).

Isabel Wilson, thirty-eight years old, coal-putter : " When women have children thick (fast) they are compelled to take them down early. When on Sir John's work was a carrier of coals, which caused me to miscarry five times from the strains, and was gai ill after each ; last child was born on Saturday morning, and I was at work on the Friday night" (Ibid. No. 134 : p. 461, 1. 42).—Elizabeth M'Neil, thirty-eight years old, coal-putter : " Women think little about working below when with child ; have wrought below myself till last hour and returned 12 or 14 days after. I knew a woman who came up and the child was born in the field next the coal-hill. Women frequently miscarry below and suffer much after ; vast of women are confined before they have time to change themsel" (Ibid. No. 136 : p. 462, 1. 8).— Jane Wood, wife of James Wood, formerly a coal-drawer and bearer : " Worked below more than 30 years. I have two daughters below, who really hate the employment, and often prayed to leave, but we canna do well without them just now. The severe work causes women much trouble ; they frequently have premature births. Jenny M'Donald, a neighbour, was laid idle six months, and William King's wife lately died from miscarriage, and a vast of women suffer from similar causes" (Ibid. No. 149 : p. 464, 1. 7).—Margaret Boxter, fifty years old, coal-hewer : " I hew the coal, have done so since my husband failed in his breath ; he has been off work 12 years. I have a son, daughter, and niece working with me below, and we have sore work to get maintenance. I go down early to hew the coal for my girls to draw ; my son hews also. The work is not fit for women, and men could prevent it were they to labour more regular ; indeed, men about this place don't wish wives to work in mines, but the masters seem to encourage it—at any rate, the masters never interfere to prevent it" (Ibid. No. 208 : p. 475, 1. 2).

134. SOUTH WALES.—The extent to which girls and women are employed in the Coal Mines of South Wales, and the severity of their labour, are shown by the following evidence :—

Hugh Owen, Esq., trustee to Sir John Owen's estate, Landshipping Collieries, county of Pembroke, says : " Females riddle the coals, and wheel above and wind below ; adults can only perform this operation, as it requires great strength" (R. H. Franks, Esq., Evidence, No. 430 : App. Pt. II., p. 575, 1. 2).—Mr. Robert Brough, manager of the Begelly Colliery, stated, that "the women work very hard, both above and below ground. The nature of their employment was severe. They had great strength and patience. Working at the windlasses below ground, wheeling and skreening coals above, formed their usual occupation. Another kind of work women do in common with men is the pouncing, a description of employment peculiar to this county." [Captain Child, one of the proprietors then present, stated that women worked in the mines, and on the banks, harder than the slaves in the West Indies.] (Ibid. No. 431 : p. 575, 1. 43).— Mr. Samuel Singleton, underground steward, Kilgetty Colliery, county of Pembroke : "They (the girls and boys) work hard and regular. Girls and boys do the dramming [dragging carts of coal], and women are worked at windlasses below, and on the bank at wheeling and sorting coal from the culm" (Ibid. No. 432 : p. 576, 1. 10).—Mr. Richard Hare, agent to Kilgetty Colliery : " We employ males and females below ground to draw small waggons. None of the children cut the coal. The work is good hard sort. The weight drawn by girls and boys in the skip (carts) never exceeds 1½ cwt., and the distance they drag varies from two fathoms to 30" (Ibid. No. 433 : p. 576, l. 23).—Mr. P. Kirkhouse, overman to the Cyfarthfa collieries and ironstone mines : " The employment females are put to is the filling and drawing the drams [carts] of coal or ironstone ; it requires great strength. The main-roads are made as easy as the work will allow, by iron rails being run to the ends of the workings ; but this does not alter the nature of the employment, which is certainly unfit for women" (Ibid. No. 2 : p. 503, l. 22).

Susan Reece, six years old, air-door keeper : " Been below six or eight months. Don't much like the work" (Ibid. No. 48 : p. 513, l. 16).—Mary Davis, near seven years old, air-door keeper : " A very pretty little girl, who was fast asleep under a piece of rock near the air-door below ground. Her lamp had gone out for want of oil ; and, upon waking her, she said the rats or some one had run away with her bread and cheese, so she went to sleep. The overs-man, who was with me, thought she was not so old, as he felt sure she had been below near 18 months" (Ibid. No. 46 : p. 513, l. 5).—Elizabeth Williams, aged nine : " Been below ground six months ; assists to fill father's trams ; does not remain under ground more than six or eight hours ; does not like the work at all ; was first taken by father because he could get an extra tram for me ; a good many girls besides me work in the mines, at pushing the trams and tipping" (Ibid. No. 313 : p. 552, l. 47).—Henrietta Frankland, eleven years old, drammer : " When well I draw the drams [carts], which contain 4 to 5 cwt. of coal, from the heads to the main road ; I make 48 to 50 journeys ; sister, who is two years older, works also at dramming ; the work is very hard, and the long hours before the pay-day fatigue us much. The mine is wet where we work, as the water passes through the roof, and the workings are only 30 to 33 inches high." (Ibid. No. 18, p. 505, l. 48.)—Mary Reed, twelve years old, air-door keeper : " Been five years in the Plymouth Mine. Never leaves till the last dram [cart] is drawn past by the horse. Works from six till four and five at night. Has run home very hungry ; runs along the level, or hangs on a cart as it passes. Does not like the work in the dark ; would not mind the daylight work." (Ibid. No. 44 : p. 512, l. 53).—See also witnesses Nos. 314, 315, 317, 321, 437, 439.—Hannah Bowen, sixteen years old, windlass-woman : " Been down two years ; it is good hard work ; work from seven in the morning till three and four in the afternoon, at hauling at the windlass. Can draw up 400 loads of 1½ to 4 cwt. each" (Ibid. No. 422 : p. 573, l. 39).—Ann Thomas, sixteen years old, windlass-woman : " Finds the work very hard ; two women always work the windlass below ground. We wind up 800 loads. Men do not like the winding, it is too hard work for them" (Ibid. No. 440 : p. 577, l. 35).—

135. The same state of things in this district is shown by the evidence collected by R. W. Jones, Esq.—

Richard Painter, aged eighteen, collier, Clydach Collieries and Mines, says : " There are a great many girls working under ground here, keeping doors, and helping the miners and colliers" (R. W. Jones, Esq., Evidence, No. 43 : App. Pt. II., p. 618, l. 34).—Mary Ann Williams, aged thirteen, Ebbw Vale and Sirhowy : " I work the same as the colliers" (Ibid. No. 62 : p. 625, l. 18). —Mr. John Millward, constable : " Girls do the same description of work as boys in the mine, and coal levels, and patches, but not generally under ground, although a great many are employed in filling trams in the levels" (Ibid. No. 96 : p. 637, l. 22).—Mr. Frederick Evans, clerk to the Dowlais Collieries : " Girls are not brought to work at quite so early ages as the boys. Girls generally begin to work about seven years old, and they are few in number in comparison to the boys, probably about one-sixth. In most cases it is the extreme poverty of the parents that compels them to send their young female children to work" (Ibid. No. 121, p. 646, l. 36.)

2. *Moral Effects of the Employment of Girls and Women Underground.*

136. Before quitting the subject of the employment of girls and women in the pits, we should fail in our duty if we did not notice more particularly, as applying to the districts in which women and girls are employed, the evidence of the serious moral injury to which such employment exposes them. All classes of witnesses bear the strongest testimony to the immoral effects of this practice.

137. WEST RIDING OF YORKSHIRE : SOUTHERN PART.—The following may serve as examples of the evidence given on this subject by the several classes of witnesses in this district.—

Matthew Lindley, collier, Day and Twibell's, Barnsley : " I wish the Government would expel all girls and females from mines. I can give proof that they are very immoral, and I am certain that the girls are worse than the men in point of morals, and use far more indecent language. It unbecomes them in every way ; there is not one in ten of them that know how to cut a shirt out or make one, and they learn neither to knit nor sew. I have known myself of a case where a married man and a girl who hurried for him had sexual intercourse often in the bank where he worked" (J. C. Symons, Esq., Evidence, No. 109 : App. Pt. I., p. 251, l. 13).—Mr. George Armitage, aged thirty-six years, Hoyland : " I hardly know how to reprobate the practice sufficiently of girls working in pits ; nothing can be worse. I have no doubt that debauchery is carried on, for which there is every opportunity ; for the girls go constantly, when hurrying, to the men, who work often alone in the bank-faces apart from every one. I think it scarcely possible for girls to remain modest who are in pits, regularly mixing with such company, and hearing such language as they do. I dare venture to say that many of the wives who come from pits know nothing of sewing or any household duty, such as women

COAL MINES.

Sex : Districts in which girls and women are employed underground.

South Wales.

Moral effects of the employment of girls and women underground.

West Riding of Yorkshire.

COAL MINES.

*Sex: Moral Ef-
fects of the employ-
of girls and women
underground.*

West Riding of
Yorkshire.

ought to know—they lose all disposition to learn such things; they are rendered unfit for learning them also by being overworked, and not being trained to the habit of it. I have worked in pits for above ten years, where girls were constantly employed, and I can safely say it is an abominable system. I think that girls ought to be prevented from going into pits, whatever may be the consequence; the effect of preventing them could not be worse than that of letting them be in." (Ibid. No. 138: p. 261, l. 7.)—John Cawthra, collier, Messrs. Wilson's Pit: " I think it is not a good system bringing girls into pits; they get bold. It tends to make the girls have bastards very much in some pits; I know, for instance, at Flockton it leads to immoral conduct" (Ibid. No. 146: p. 264, l. 16).—John Simpkin, collier, Drighlington: " I have worked a great deal where girls were employed in pits. I have had children by them myself, and have frequently had connexion with them in the pits. I am sure that this is the case, especially in pits about Lancashire." [This evidence was given in presence of Mr. William Barber, of the firm of Barber and Haigh, Gildersome, near Leeds.] (Ibid. No. 231: p. 284, l. 45). George Carr, collier, Tankersley: " I make no more money than the colliers at Silkstone, nor so much, but I would be hard put to it before I would bring a lass of mine to the pits—no, not if I was ever so ill put to it. I would live upon one meal a-day sooner. I don't consider it right, no way. I am sure the colliers could do without putting their lasses in the pits. I don't think nought about it, I am sure of it. I have been as hard put to it as any one, and I never found it necessary. It 's a shameful practice" (Ibid. No. 163: p. 266, l. 59).—Thomas Bedford, collier, Drighlington: " If I had 70 votes I would not give one for a lass to come down into pits; it 's attended with bad consequences lasses going to pits. They are exposed to bad things when they are in the pit" (Ibid. No. 233, p. 284, l. 57).—John Hargreave, collier, Thorpe's colliery, Barnsley: " I would not have a lass seen in the pit if I had my will; and nobody will allow them who has any spirit or sense. They can see nought but blackguardism and debauchery. They are best out of pits, are lasses" (Ibid. No. 130: p. 256, l. 47).

At a meeting of above 350 working colliers from the surrounding district, held in the Courthouse, Barnsley, before the Sub-Commissioner, among others the following resolution was passed:—" That the employment of girls in pits is highly injurious to their morals, that it is not proper work for females, and that it is a scandalous practice." (Carried with five dissentients only.) (Ibid. No. 142: p. 262, l. 66).

Mr. John Clarkson Sutcliff, general agent for the Gauber Colliery: " The morals of the girls do suffer from it, from being together along with the lads. They all meet together at the Bull-stake, and it is the same as a rendezvous. The boys and girls meeting together hardens and encourages one another in acts of wickedness, more so than if they were only boys" (Ibid. No. 118: p. 253, l. 43).—Matthew Fountain, under-ground steward at Darton Colliery, belonging to Thomas Wilson, Esq.: " My opinion decidedly is that women and girls ought not to be admitted into pits, though they work as well as the boys. In my belief sexual intercourse does take place, owing to the opportunities, and owing to lads and girls working together, and owing to some of the men working in banks apart, and having girls coming to them to fill the corves, and being alone together. The girls hurry for other men than their relations, and generally prefer it. Altogether it is a very demoralising practice having girls in pits. It is not proper for females at all. The girls are unfitted, by being at pits, from learning to manage families. Many could not make a shirt" (Ibid. No. 119: p. 254, l. 7).— Joseph Ellison, Birkinshaw, near Birstall:—" I know a case of a girl being employed as a hurrier, having been attempted to be ravished frequently by her father-in-law, till at length she could not be got down into the pit. Where girls are employed the immoralities practised are scandalous" (Ibid. No. 249: p. 288, l. 11).—A respectable inhabitant of Silkstone, a female: " I consider it a scandal for girls to work in the pits. I am credibly informed that in some pits scenes pass which are as bad as any house of ill-fame; this I have heard from young men who work in the pit' (Ibid. No. 100: p. 248, l. 38).—Thomas Wilson, Esq., of the Banks, Silkstone, owner of three collieries: " The employment of females of any age in and about the mines is most objectionable, and I should rejoice to see it put an end to; but in the present feeling of the colliers, no individual would succeed in stopping it in a neighbourhood where it prevailed, because the men would immediately go to those pits where their daughters would be employed" (Ibid. No. 137: p. 258, l. 25).

Michael Thomas Sadler, Esq., surgeon, Barnsley: " I strongly disapprove of females being in pits; the female character is totally destroyed by it; their habits and feelings are altogether different; they can neither discharge the duties of wives nor mothers. I see the greatest differences in the homes of those colliers whose wives do not go into the pits in cleanliness and good management. It is a brutalizing practice for women to be in collieries; the effect on their morals is very bad; it would be advisable to prevent females from going into pits" (Ibid. No. 139: p. 261, l. 44).—Mr. Crooks, surgeon, Barnsley: " What seems most revolting is, that girls are employed in the pits as well as boys, and when they have a little relaxation all congregate together, and no one in particular to overlook them; at these times their morals, I fear, are injured " (Ibid. No. 166: p. 267, l. 46).—John Wood Berry, Esq., clerk to the Wakefield Union: " As to the working of girls in pits, I am decidedly of opinion that it is injurious to their morals" (Ibid. No. 198: p. 278, l. 54).—Rev. Oliver Levey Collins, Incumbent of Ossett: " There is a good deal of drunkenness and sensuality. Bastardy is sadly too common; they look on it as a misfortune, and not as a crime" (Ibid. No. 236: p. 285, l. 17).—The Rev. Richard Earnshaw Roberts, incumbent of St. George's, Barnsley: " I think the practice of working females in mines is highly objectionable, physically, intellectually, morally, and spiritually" (Ibid. No. 124: p. 255, l. 61).—John Thorneley, Esq., one of her Majesty's justices of the peace for the county of York: " I consider it to be a most awfully demoralising practice. The youth of both sexes work often in a half-naked state, and the passions are excited before they arrive at puberty. Sexual intercourse decidedly frequently occurs in consequence. Cases of bastardy frequently also occur; and I am decidedly of opinion that women brought up in this way lay aside all modesty, and scarcely know what it is but by name. I sincerely trust that before I die I shall have the satisfaction of seeing it prevented and entirely done away with" (Ibid. No. 96: p. 246, l. 45).

138. The Sub-Commissioner says, " Under no conceivable circumstances is any one sort of employment in collieries proper for females. The practice is flagrantly disgraceful to a Christian as well as to a civilised country. From the guarded evidence of Mr. Clarke, who states that it is ' not suitable work for girls,' to the indignant resolution of the collected body of the colliers themselves, that it is a ' scandalous practice,' I found scarcely an exception to the general reprobation of this revolting abomination" (J. C. Symons, Esq., Report, § 119, 227: App. Pt. I., pp. 182, 196).

139. BRADFORD AND LEEDS.—-The Sub-Commissioner for this district states that he has made, through various channels, minute and particular inquiries into the effect of the employment of females during Childhood in preventing them from forming the domestic habits usually acquired by women in their station, and in rendering them less fit than those whose early years have not been spent in labour for performing the duties of wives and mothers, and he reports that the " result of these inquiries is, in every case, to show that the employment of female Children and Young Persons in labour, to the degree which at present prevails, has the effect of preventing them from acquiring the most ordinary and necessary knowledge of domestic management and family economy; that the young females in general, even where presenting the most tidy and respectable personal appearance before marriage, are nearly ignorant of the arts of baking and cooking, and, generally speaking, entirely so of the use of the needle;* that when they come to marry, the wife possesses not the knowledge to enable her to give to her husband the common comforts of a home; that the husband, even if previously well-disposed, is hence often led to seek at the public-house that cheerfulness and physical comfort which his own fire-side does not afford,† whence all the evils of drunkenness in many cases grow up; that the Children, quite apart from any evils which the altered conduct of the father may bring upon them, but solely from the bad training of the mother, are brought up in no habits of order and comfort, but are habituated from their youth to all the evils of a disorderly and ill-regulated family, and must give birth to a still worse state of things in a succeeding generation; that under these accumulated evils the wife and the mother is perhaps herself the most acute sufferer from the consequences of her own defective education. Such are the evils which the evidence ‡ I have taken appears to establish as the result of the temptations offered by the present high rates of wages for the employment of female labour. From this source a fearful deterioration of the moral and physical condition of our working population is rapidly taking place" (W. R. Wood, Esq., Report, § 56, 57: App. Pt. II., p. H 10).

140. HALIFAX.—The practice is not so common in this district, and is highly reprobated by all classes of witnesses.—

Mr. James Sharp, underground steward, Bowling Company : " We have no girls in the establishment, we would not allow of it by any means; it would be wrong to do so, because they would have to mix with the men often naked; it is in fact not their labour, and ought to be entirely prohibited" (S. S. Scriven, Esq., Evidence, No. 43 : App., Pt. II., p. 113, l. 54).—Mr. Isaac Clayton, coal owner, Bowling Colliery : " We have no girls in our immediate neighbourhood. As a principal I say that it is not prudent to employ them. I would not do so; it is not fit for them; it is disgusting, and it subjects them to many evils" (Ibid. No. 49 : p. 115, l. 61).—Mr. Brook, coal-owner, Norwood Green : " We have no girls, because I would not have them—it is not their duty; I have worked in pits when there were girls, but I thought 'twas not decent; they were fourteen and sixteen years old; I have seen such indecencies and improprieties as to determine me never to give my consent to their being where I am again; you know what lads and lasses at fourteen and fifteen will do in such places; I therefore leave you to judge that their conduct is of the worst kind" (Ibid. No. 32 : p. 110, l. 8).—Mr. Emmet, coal owner, Norwood Green : " Has no girls in his pits; nor does he think it proper to have them, because it is indecent and immoral" (Ibid. No. 36 : p. 111, l. 23).—See also witnesses, Nos. 7, 10, 16, 26, 40, 79, 80, 83.

---

* Evidence of Rev. Joshua Fawcett, M.A. (No. 34.) Evidence of C. H. Dawson, Esq. (No. 35.) Evidence of Henry Leah, Esq. (No. 59.)

† Evidence of Rev. Joshua Fawcett, M.A. (No. 34.)

‡ (Evidence of Charles Hardy, Esq., Magistrate of the West Riding of Yorkshire.) (Evidence of the Rev. Joshua Fawcett, M.A.) (Evidence of Henry Leah, Esq.) (Evidence of A. Muir, Esq., surgeon, Bradford.)

141. LANCASHIRE.—Similar effects are stated to result from the employment of girls and women in the coal mines of this district. The evidence, says the Sub-Commissioner, all tends to the following conclusions :—" First. That the employment itself is, from its peculiar severity, unsuited to the physical condition of females, and especially to those of them who are mothers.—Secondly. That, from the nature of the work below ground, it tends more or less to demoralise and brutalise the females employed.—Thirdly. That their employment below ground prevents their attention to the performance of domestic duties, as diminishing their competency for the proper care and training of their children.—And Fourthly. That for these pernicious effects there appear to be no countervailing advantages to the people employed, or to the public.

142. " There is a growing feeling throughout this district generally against the employment of females in the mines. The trustees of the late Duke of Bridge-water have now excluded married women from the mines belonging to that trust, and girls are not now allowed to enter the pits under twelve years of age. Mr. Peace, the agent for Lord Balcarras, near Wigan, stated to me that his lordship was anxious to discontinue the employment of females in his collieries in the neigh-bourhood of Haigh, Aspul, and Blackrod ; but that the system had been carried on for so many years, and there were so many females employed in them, that it would be impossible to dispense with them on a sudden. Mr. Hilton, near Wigan, stated to me that he should be glad to discontinue the employment of females in his mines, but that it had always been a custom for the men to find their own drawers, and that the masters did not interfere. He mentioned to me that the day before I visited the colliery there had been a disturbance arising from a col-lier having neglected his wife to ' take up ' with a young girl who drew for him in the pits. Violent changes are always to be avoided, but I think it will appear that a stand should be made against this pernicious system" (J. L. Kennedy, Esq., Report, § 105 et seq.: App. Pt. II., p. 164).

143. The statements made by all classes of witnesses as to the general character and conduct of the young women in the coal mines of this district are precisely similar to those which have been given relative to Yorkshire. (See Nos. 2, 6, 26, 27, 92, 98, 100, 102, 103, 104, &c.) Similar statements are made by several witnesses examined by Mr. Fletcher (See Evidence, Nos. 3, 4, 7, 15, 40).

144. EAST OF SCOTLAND.—The Sub-Commissioner states that the employment of females in the mines of this district is universally conceived to be so degrading that all other classes of operatives refuse intermarriage with the daughters of colliers who are wrought in the pits; that it is a labour totally disproportioned to the female strength and sex ; that it is altogether unnecessary ; and that it is wholly inconsistent with the proper discharge of the maternal duties, and with the decent proprieties of domestic life. From the evidence he has collected it appears that in the cases in which the proprietors of coal mines have excluded females from their pits a rapid and great improvement has taken place in the condition of the collier families, and that the measure, however reluctantly submitted to in the first instance, has given entire satisfaction to all classes. For example :—

Mr. John Wright, manager of the Rosewell and Barley Dean Coal-Mines, the property of J. B. W. Ramsay, Esq., says, " It is now four years since the practice of employing females and very young children ceased in these mines, and I have evidenced the advantage of the change religiously, morally, and socially. In these works, since the discharge of women, marriages have been formed with greater care, and more appropriately : few now marry till twenty-three or twenty-four, and we have not had a bastard child since the disemployment of females. On the old system men married more from the advantage their physical strength might procure them, than any degree of affection. Men labour here regularly, and average eleven to twelve days in the fortnight, whereas, when they depended on their wives and children, they rarely wrought nine days in the same period." (R. H. Franks, Esq., Evidence, No. 79 : App. Pt. I., p. 451, l. 43).

145. There has also been for some time past an absolute exclusion of girls and women from the Dalkeith collieries of the Duke of Buccleugh, by express order of his Grace ; and Mr. James Wright, the manager, who had witnessed the beneficial effects of their exclusion from Mr. Ramsay's collieries, says:—

" Where women carry coal on their backs they are more frequently chosen for their strength than for any aptitude for domestic duties; they are often bad wives. The very nature of the employment is degrading, as females are wrought only where no men can be induced to draw or work—in one word, they are mere beasts of burden. I feel confident that the exclusion of females will be followed by a most beneficial result both to the coal-owners, as it must be to

COAL MINES.

*Sex: Moral effects
of the employment
of girls and women
underground.*

East of Scotland.

the colliers' moral and physical condition, and that of their families; and that it will force the alteration of the economy of the mines. Owners will be compelled to alter their system; they will ventilate better, make better roads, and so change the system as to enable men who now work only three or four days a-week to discover their own interest in regularly employing themselves. Since young children and females have been excluded from his Grace's mines, we have never had occasion to increase the price of coal." (Ibid. No. 28 : p. 442, l. 3).

Mr. Alexander Maxton, manager of the Arniston Colliery, says :—" The two primary evils in many Scotch collieries are—1st. The employment of women of any age underground. 2nd. The taking to the mines young boys. The effects of the first are want of comfortable homes, the females being absent all day, and a certain demoralizing effect invariably produced by women subjected to labour in a manner quite unsuited to their sex. The effects of the second are the total neglect of ordinary education, and from the extreme youth of the boys (many under eight years of age) their bodies are quite unable to stand coal working without injuring in some degree their constitutions. Women ought therefore be entirely disused underground, and no boys ought to be permitted to go below under twelve years of age; these have been the rules in this colliery for some time past, and already the good effects are being felt; the houses of the workmen are clean and comfortable, the children are well looked after by their mothers, the young women are going out to service, and the whole workpeople have a better moral aspect. Colliers prior to our regulations migrated in proportion one-fourth, now not one-tenth." (Ibid. No. 86 : p. 453, ll. 8, 30).

146. The evidence further shows that the colliers themselves are fully sensible of the importance of such regulations to their own well-being and to that of their families.—

Joseph Fraser, aged thirty-seven, collier, Dalkeith Collieries, says, " The employment very much unfits them [women] for the performance of mothers' duties; and they frequently cause men to leave their homes, if homes they may be called, and drink hard; the poor bairns are neglected; for in time the women follow the men, and drink hard also" (Ibid. No. 29 : p. 442, l. 30).—George Smith, collier, East Bryants: " The steady colliers would like females to be kept out of the pits; it is very injurious to the children, and equally so to the men, and few other trades associate with us on that account" (Ibid. No. 43 : p. 444, l. 30).—Andrew Salton, aged thirty-nine, Rosewell and Barley Dean, Lasswade, coal-hewer : " I consider it a great boon to keep the women away from the mines. Miners require comforts and good homes as well as other men" (Ibid. No. 81 : p. 452, l. 11).—Henry Naysmith, sixty-five years of age, Rosewell and Barley Dean, coal hewer: " Most of the colliers here are pleased at the masters keeping the women out; sensible men prefer their wives at home instead of their carrying like brutes" (Ibid. No. 83 : p. 452, l. 36).—Thomas Hynd, forty-nine years of age, coal-hewer : " When Mr. Maxton first issued the order, many men and families left; but many have returned, for they find, now the roads are improved, and the output not limited, they can earn as much money, and get better homes. Many of the females have gone to service, and prefer it; and now they know the advantage fully approve the rules" (Ibid. No. 88 : p. 453, l. 53).

3. *Districts in which Girls and Women are not employed Underground.*

*Sex: Districts in
which girls and wo-
men are not employ-
ed underground.*

South
Staffordshire.

147. In some of the most important of the coal-fields of England no female Child and no young or adult woman is employed in any mining operation.

148. SOUTH STAFFORDSHIRE.—It is stated by all classes of witnesses that no girl or woman is employed in underground work in any coal-pit in the whole of the South Staffordshire coal-field; and no case was found by the Sub-Commissioner in the whole of his progress through this district impugning the truth of this statement. But although no girls or women are employed in the underground work of the colliery in this district, yet it is not uncommon for them to be occupied on the surface in certain descriptions of work connected with the coal-pits.

149. " Many girls are employed under the designation of bankswomen. They stand on the bank near the mouth of the shaft, and when a skip comes up, and the slide is thrust forward, and the skip is let down upon it, they unhook it and push it forward, and then empty out the coals. They also hang an empty skip to the chain, and when the slide is withdrawn it is let down the shaft." It is added: " On the banks of the canals in Staffordshire are seen many girls engaged in loading the boats with coals. These girls are substantially though coarsely clothed, and the head and neck more particularly protected from the cold. The work is laborious, but not beyond their strength. The clothing is obviously such that a girl cannot continue to wear it after going home. She therefore lays it aside and washes herself, and puts on more agreeable clothing for the rest of the day : the coarseness of the clothing, which prevents it from being worn after work is over, is an advantage" (Dr. Mitchell, Report, § 101-103 : App. Pt. I., pp. 11, 12).

150. NORTH STAFFORDSHIRE.—There is no mention of employment of girls or women in the pits of either the Potteries or the Cheadle district.

151. SHROPSHIRE.—In this district no girls or women are employed in any kind of undergound labour in the coal-mines, but a considerable number are engaged in preparing the iron ore on the bank, an employment to be noticed hereafter in the account of the Iron-Mines (Dr. Mitchell, Evidence, No. 38: App. Pt. I., p. 78, l. 13).

152. WARWICKSHIRE.—In this district no girls or women are employed in underground work in the coal-mines. Mr. Thomas Pearson, butty of the colliery called the Bedworth Charity Colliery, in answer to the question, " Are any young women or girls employed in the collieries?" says, " None in this part;" and this is the uniform statement of the persons examined on this subject (Dr. Mitchell's Evidence, No. 63: App. Pt. I., p. 105, l. 42).

153. LEICESTERSHIRE.—In the Ashby-de-la-Zouch district no females are employed in any kind of work connected with the collieries, either above or below ground. In answer to the question, " Are any women or girls employed about the pit?" the answer in this district uniformly is, " None whatever; no women are employed about the collieries in this part" (Ibid. No. 75, p. 111, l. 51; and No. 87, p. 118, l. 23).

154. DERBYSHIRE.—All classes of witnesses concur in bearing the same testimony to the exclusion of girls and women from the pits in the Derbyshire Coal-Field. " No females are employed in the pits in these districts." " No girls in the pits, nor did he ever know any" (J. M. Fellows, Esq., Evidence, Nos. 84, 176, 142, 221: App. Pt. I. p. 287 *et seq*.).

155. OLDHAM.—In the Coal-Field in the neighbourhood of Oldham no females are employed in any kind of underground work. Mr. Fletcher reports, " There is a peculiarity in this south-eastern district which distinguishes it from the rest of the Lancashire coal-fields. No females of any age are employed in underground labour; the men unite in a dislike to their being brought into circumstances so disgusting, although their employment is common within a few miles of Manchester, on the other side; and the only man who, coming from that side, has been known to take his wife into the pit, was compelled to leave the district; the men said they would leave work if he continued." All classes of witnesses are uniform and decided in making this statement (J. Fletcher, Esq., Report, § 5: App. Pt. II., p. 820; and Evidence, No. 3, p. 841, and No. 7, p. 846).

156. CUMBERLAND.—In the coal mines of this district girls and women are now excluded from underground work, except in one old colliery belonging to the Earl of Lonsdale (J. C. Symons, Esq., Report, § 25: App. Pt. I., p. 302).

157. DURHAM AND NORTHUMBERLAND.—From the mines of this vast coal-field there is the same absolute exclusion of all female workers.—" No women are employed below in the pits or on the bank in the South Durham collieries." " We have no females, and I do not believe there is a case of females being employed in the collieries either of Durham or Northumberland" (Dr. Mitchell, Evidence, No. 88: App. Pt. I., p. 148, l. 18; and No. 89, p. 149, l. 15).

158. WEST OF SCOTLAND.—In the collieries in this district the employment of girls and women in the coal pits, though not absolutely unknown, is yet extremely rare (T. Tancred, Esq., Report, § 30: App. Pt. I., p. 318).

159. NORTH WALES.—Though in some part of this district girls and women are employed in particular kinds of work at the surface, no female of any age is allowed to descend into the mines for the purpose of engaging in underground labour. The uniform evidence given by the witnesses examined in this district is in conformity with the statement of Mr. Richard Wood, General Manager of the British Iron Company's Coal and Iron Works, Denbighshire, who says: " Girls and women never go below the surface in this or in any of the works in this district" (H. H. Jones, Esq., Evidence, No. 1: App. Pt. II., p. 377, l. 38). The personal investigations of the Sub-Commissioner satisfied him of the general correctness of this representation. " I have," he says, " great satisfaction in reporting, though girls find work at the pit mouth, that they never go underground; such a practice has not yet found its way into the northern parts of the princi-

pality. The number who work on the surface is comparatively few, and the custom of employing females at all is confined to the district around Wrexham. At each pit two females are placed to assist in *banking* the coal, and, where there is no steam-engine or horse-whimsey, also in turning the winding-barrel, by which the coal and ironstone are brought to the surface. In most cases the females employed exceed the age of eighteen; as strength is required there are but few under that age, and rarely any to be found under eighteen. There is nothing in the employment of banking coal which is repugnant to the feelings; and the manner, conduct, and dress of the females so engaged appear respectable and decorous" (H. H. Jones, Esq., Report, § 5, 6: App., Pt. II., p. 365).

160. FOREST OF DEAN.—In the Coal Fields of the West of England the employment of females in the coal mines is extremely rare. " The employment of females in mines and collieries is happily almost unknown in the Forest: one instance only of a female employed in filling the waggons came under my notice; so that I encountered no such repulsive objects there as the degraded and almost unsexed beings I have often beheld, with mingled horror and compassion, among the iron and coal works of South Wales" (Elijah Waring, Esq., Report, § 17: App., Pt. II., p. 2).

161. SOUTH GLOUCESTERSHIRE.—In this district no female Child and no woman of any age is employed in the coal mines in any kind of under-ground work. " Female labour is altogether dispensed with in the coal works of this district, though a few amazons yet practise the vocation of coal carriers, on their own account, from the pits into the city or suburbs, rivalling the men in strength of sinew and vigour of lungs" (Ibid. § 92: p. 38).

162. NORTH SOMERSETSHIRE.—" I have to remark of the whole of this district," says the Sub-Commissioner, "that no females are employed in actually working or conveying the coal, or indeed in any operation under ground." (Dr. Stewart, Report, § 3: App., Pt. II., p. 47.) In conformity with this statement, the declarations uniformly made by all classes of witnesses examined in this district are :—" There are no girls or women at work in the coal-pit." " There are never any girls here, nor in all this neighbourhood." " There are no women or girls employed in these mines" (Dr. Stewart, Evidence, No. 2: App., Pt. II., p. 49, l. 57; No. 7, p. 50, l. 46; No. 9, p. 51, l. 39).

163. IRELAND.—In none of the collieries in the Coal Fields of Ireland was a single instance found of a female Child, or indeed a female of any age, being employed in the coal mines in any kind of underground work. In the Dromagh and Dysart Collieries, in the county of Cork, no females of any age are employed" (F. Roper, Esq., Report, No. 6, § 2: App. Pt. I., p. 868).

3.—NUMBER OF CHILDREN AND YOUNG PERSONS EMPLOYED IN COAL-MINES.

164. Among the subjects which it has appeared desirable to determine with as close an approximation to the truth as might be practicable is the actual number of Children and Young Persons employed in the various branches of industry included in the inquiry; and the Tables constructed with a view to obtain this information would have afforded it in a very satisfactory form had they been generally and faithfully filled up. Though we had no authority to compel the Employers of labour to whom these Tables were addressed to make the Returns in the manner desired, still it seemed reasonable to suppose that the proprietors of works would not in general refuse to take the trouble required to fill up the papers in question, seeing the valuable information which such Returns would obviously enable us to present on some of the branches of industry the most intimately connected with our national prosperity.

165. From many of the districts, and in relation to most of the great branches of industry, a sufficient number of these Returns has been received, not indeed to enable us to estimate the aggregate number of Children and Young Persons employed, but to afford us the means of determining the *proportion* of the non-adult to the adult workpeople. It is true that these Returns are the statements of the Employers themselves as to the numbers and ages of the persons in their employment; but the Sub-Commissioners in their respective districts, to whom these Returns as they were received by us were uniformly sent, were enabled by personal

COAL MINES.

Sex: Districts in which girls and women are not employed underground.

North Wales.

Forest of Dean.

South Gloucestershire.

North Somersetshire.

Ireland.

Number.

COAL MINES.
Number.

examinations on the spot to verify their general fidelity.   It is, however, worthy of observation that, as it was the highest class of employers generally who made these Returns, they exhibit a less proportion of the younger hands than the average, and perhaps also a less proportion of females in those districts in which females are employed under ground.

166. The information to be derived from this source will appear in the clearest light, and the comparison between one district and another will be most readily made, by arranging the results in a tabular form.   Table No. 1 refers to the Coal Fields of England, from which a sufficient number of Returns have been received to justify the conclusion that they afford a near approximation to the truth.   Table No. 2 refers in the same manner to the Coal Fields in the East of Scotland; No. 3, to those in the West of Scotland; and No. 4, to those in South Wales. It must be borne in mind that these Tables are not intended to show the actual number of persons employed, but only the proportion which each class and sex bears to the whole number of the workpeople employed underground, for which purpose it is assumed that 1000 males are so employed in each district.

TABLE No. I.—ENGLAND.

DISTRICTS.	Adults.		13 to 18.		Under 13.		Total of Children and Young Persons to 1000 adult Males.	Proportion of Children and Young Persons in the whole Number employed.	Proportion of Children in the whole Number under 18.
	Males.	Fem.	Males.	Fem.	Males.	Fem.			
Leicestershire . . .	1000	..	227	..	180	..	407	Two-sevenths.	Much more than one-third.
Derbyshire	1000	..	240	..	167	..	407	Two-sevenths.	Much more than one-third.
Yorkshire	1000	22	352	36	246	41	675	Upwards of one-third.	Much more than one-third.
Lancashire	1000	86	352	79	195	27	653	Upwards of one-third.	Upwards of one-third.
South Durham . . .	1000	..	226	..	184	..	410	Two-sevenths.	Much more than one-third.
Northumberland and North Durham .	1000	..	266	..	186	..	452	Nearly one-third.	Much more than one-third.

TABLE No. II.—EAST OF SCOTLAND.

DISTRICTS.	Adults.		13 to 18.		Under 13.		Total of Children and Young Persons to 1000 adult Males.	Proportion of Children and Young Persons in the whole Number employed.	Proportion of Children in the whole Number under 18.
	Males.	Fem.	Males.	Fem.	Males.	Fem.			
Mid Lothian . . .	1000	333	307	184	131	52	674	One-third.	Little more than one-fourth.
East Lothian . . .	1000	338	332	296	164	103	895	Two-fifths.	Not one-third.
West Lothian . . .	1000	192	289	154	180	109	732	Nearly two-fifths.	Much more than one-third.
Stirlingshire	1000	228	283	129	184	107	703	Approaching two-fifths.	Much more than one-third.
Clackmannanshire .	1000	202	246	213	142	87	688	Upwards of one-third.	One-third.
Fifeshire	1000	184	243	109	100	34	486	Nearly three-tenths.	Approaching one-third.

TABLE No. III.—WEST OF SCOTLAND.

	Adults.		13 to 18.		Under 13.		Total of Children and Young Persons to 1000 adult Males.	Proportion of Children and Young Persons in the whole Number employed.	Proportion of Children in the whole Number under 18.
	Males.	Fem.	Males.	Fem.	Males.	Fem.			
Various Mines . . .	1000	..	223	..	99	..	322	Not one-fourth.	Not one-third.

TABLE No. IV.—WALES.

DISTRICTS.	Adults.		13 to 18.		Under 13.		Total of Children and Young Persons to 1000 adult Males.	Proportion of Children and Young Persons in the whole Number employed.	Proportion of Children in the whole Number under 18.
	Males.	Fem.	Males.	Fem.	Males.	Fem.			
Monmouthshire . .	1000	..	302	..	154	..	456	Nearly one-third.	One-third.
Glamorganshire . .	1000	19	239	19	157	12	427	Approaching one-third.	Much more than one-third.
Pembrokeshire . . .	1000	424	366	119	196	19	700	One-third.	More than one-third.

England.

167. From the first of these tables it appears that in England, in three out of six of the districts, namely, in Yorkshire, Lancashire, and Northumberland and North Durham, the proportion of Young Persons to adults is about one-third; in the other three districts, namely, in Leicestershire, Derbyshire, and South Durham, it is two-sevenths.

168. From the second table it appears that in one district in Scotland, namely, East Lothian, the proportion of Young Persons to adults is nearly one-half, and that in the other districts it varies from one-third to two-fifths; while the proportion of |Children to Young Persons in all the districts, excepting Mid Lothian and East Lothian, is one-third and upwards.

169. On the other hand it appears from the third table that in the West of Scotland the proportion of Young Persons to adults is under one-fourth, and that the proportion of Children to Young Persons is under one-third.

170. From the fourth table it appears that in one of the districts of South Wales, Pembrokeshire, the proportion of Young Persons to adults is two-fifths; and in the two other districts, Glamorganshire and Monmouthshire, it is nearly one-third; while in all these districts the proportion of Children to Young Persons is much more than one-third.

171. In the districts in which women and girls are employed in under-ground labour, the proportion of adult women to adult men, and of young women and female Children to young men and male Children varies in different districts, as appears from the following table:—

Proportion (nearly) of Females to adult Males, and of Females under age to Males under age.

DISTRICTS.	Adults.	From 13 to 18.	Under 13.
Yorkshire	1 to 45	1 to 28	1 to 25
Lancashire	1 to 12	1 to 13	1 to 37
EAST OF SCOTLAND:			
Mid Lothian	1 to 3	1 to $5\frac{1}{2}$	1 to 20
East Lothian	1 to 3	1 to $3\frac{1}{2}$	1 to 10
West Lothian	1 to 5	1 to 7	1 to 10
Stirlingshire	1 to $4\frac{1}{2}$	1 to 8	1 to 10
Clackmannanshire	1 to 5	1 to 5	1 to $11\frac{1}{2}$
Fifeshire	1 to $5\frac{1}{2}$	1 to 10	1 to 30
WALES:			
Glamorganshire	1 to 53	1 to 53	1 to 83
Pembrokeshire	1 to $2\frac{1}{2}$	1 to $8\frac{1}{2}$	1 to 53

4. HIRING OF CHILDREN AND YOUNG PERSONS IN COAL MINES.

172. The mode of hiring the persons employed in coal mines varies in different districts. Sometimes the proprietors enter into a contract with certain persons, variously designated as butties or charter-masters, who engage to get the coal and bring it to the foot of the shaft at a certain rate; and these contractors hire all the persons required to work the pits. Sometimes the proprietor himself engages all the workpeople, and sets persons over them to see that they perform their duty; but in other cases the proprietor contracts with the chief workmen, who hire every one who is employed in getting the coal and bringing it to the foot of the shaft.

173. SOUTH STAFFORDSHIRE.—In this district the first of these systems is in universal use, the contractors or butties engaging to do all the work of the mine as far as is necessary to bring the coal to the foot of the shaft; but the proprietor erects the steam-engine, pays the engine-man and the people who raise the coals on the bank, and finds what is termed "the drawing power" (Dr. Mitchell, Report, § 14-16: App. Pt. I., p. 2).

174. SHROPSHIRE.—In this district both the coal and iron mines are worked on the same system as in Staffordshire, contracts being entered into with individuals who hire the subordinate labourers, men and boys; the contractors being here usually called charter masters (Ibid. § 296 et seq.: App. Pt. I., p. 38).

175. WARWICKSHIRE.—In this district the same practice prevails of working the coal mines by butties, at a certain charter for every ton of coals.

176. ASHBY-DE-LA-ZOUCH.—The system of butties is here somewhat modified. A certain number of holers or hewers unite together, and amongst them undertake to work the pit. They hire the other men and boys, and when the reckoning-day comes they pay them their wages, and settle for all the usual charges which fall to the butties, and then the surplus belongs to the partnership, and is divided amongst them. In this way a man who merely as a workman would be earning only about 18*s.* a-week may get 28*s.* or 30*s.* a-week.

177. DERBYSHIRE.—The coal mines in this district are wrought by butties, who hire all the workpeople.

178. WEST RIDING OF YORKSHIRE.—In this district the system of hiring is widely different. The hewers or getters generally undertake to deliver the coals at the foot of the shaft at a fixed rate, employing their own assistants to convey the coals from the workings to the shaft. It is in this occupation of conveying the coals from the workings to the shaft that by far the largest proportion of the whole body of Children are employed, and consequently this system of working the coal mines renders these Children entirely the servants of the colliers. The youngest Children, however, those whose duty it is to attend to the air-doors, are commonly hired by the proprietors" (J. C. Symons, Esq., Report, § 190 et seq.: App. Pt. I., p. 191. See also W. R. Wood, Esq., Report, § 26: App. Pt. II., p. H 5).

179. LANCASHIRE AND CHESHIRE.—In this district also the great body of the Children employed are hired by the colliers for whom they work (J. L. Kennedy, Esq., Report, § 238 et seq.: App. Pt. II., p. 180. See also A. Austin, Esq., Report, § 15: App. Pt. II., p. 803).

180. OLDHAM.—The whole of the young drawers, waggoners, and thrutchers are employed by the adults whom they assist; and it is only the few engaged as air-door tenters, jiggers, hookers-on, engineers, and carters that are hired by the master (J. Fletcher, Esq., Report, § 42: App. Pt. II., p. 826).

181. CUMBERLAND.—The hiring of the Children and Young Persons in this district is sometimes by the owner's agent, and sometimes by the labouring colliers (T. Martin, Esq., Evidence, No. 1: App. Pt. I., p. 876, l. 50; and No. 15: p. 878, l. 61).

182. DURHAM AND NORTHUMBERLAND.—In the coal mines of this vast coal district all descriptions of workpeople whatever, whether employed under ground or on the bank, are in the service of the Company or of the individual occupier of the coal mine, and are accordingly placed under the orders of officers of higher and lower degree, who direct their labour and keep them at their duty. For an account of these officers, and of the viewers, under-viewers, overmen, and deputy-overmen, see Dr. Mitchell's Report, § 71 et seq.: App. Pt. I., p. 9. The hiring of the hewers, putters, and generally of the drivers, is by the year. There is a bond signed by them specifying the conditions; the substance being that they are to do the work of the pit, and be subject to certain forfeitures or penalties for their neglect of duty. The masters on the other hand are bound to pay a certain fixed price for the work performed; and if the hewers are not employed at all, or are only partially employed, the masters are bound to advance them at the end of every fortnight a fixed sum for their maintenance (See Dr. Mitchell, Report, § 192: App. Pt. I., p. 141; and J. R. Leifchild, Esq., Report, § 153: App. Pt. I., pp. 536—9).

183. EAST OF SCOTLAND.—In some of the coal fields in this district the workpeople enter into a contract to work the different seams of coal at specified prices for one year; but in general they are not restrained by any agreement beyond two weeks (R. H. Franks, Esq., Report, § 39 et seq.: App. Pt. I., p. 390).

184. WEST OF SCOTLAND.—In this district the drawers to colliers are generally their own Children or younger brothers or sisters, and are paid by the adults whom they assist; but the air-door Children, horse-drivers, and engine-boys, as in other districts, are hired by the proprietor (T. Tancred, Esq., Report, § 83: App. Pt. I., p. 336).

185. NORTH WALES.—In the collieries in this district the Children and Young Persons are hired by the contractors whom they assist (H. H. Jones, Esq., Report, § 33: App. Pt. II., p. 369).

186. SOUTH WALES.—Here the usual mode of hiring is by the month. " The collier boy is, to all intents and purposes, the property of his father (as to wages) until he attains the age of seventeen years, or marries; his father receives his wages, whether he be an air-door boy of five years of age or a haulier of fifteen" (R. H. Franks, Esq., Report, § 58: App. Pt. II., p. 482).

Apprenticeship to Labour in Coal Mines.

187. There is one mode of engaging the labour of Children and Young Persons in coal mines, peculiar to a few districts, which deserves particular notice, viz., that by

apprenticeship. The district in which the practice of employing apprentices is most in use is South Staffordshire ; it was formerly common in Shropshire, but is now discontinued ; it is still common in Yorkshire, Lancashire, and the West of Scotland : in all the other districts it appears to be unknown.

188. SOUTH STAFFORDSHIRE.—In this district the Sub-Commissioner states that the number of Children and Young Persons working in the mines as apprentices is exceedingly numerous ; that these apprentices are paupers or orphans, and are wholly in the power of the butties; that such is the demand for this class of children by the butties that there are scarcely any boys in the Union Workhouses of Walsall, Wolverhampton, Dudley, and Stourbridge ; that these boys are sent on trial to the butties between the ages of eight and nine, and at nine are bound as apprentices for twelve years, that is, to the age of twenty-one years complete ; that, notwithstanding this long apprenticeship, there is nothing whatever in the coal-mines to learn beyond a little dexterity, readily acquired by short practice ; and that even in the mines of Cornwall, where much skill and judgment is required, there are no apprentices, while in the coal mines of South Staffordshire the orphan whom necessity has driven into a workhouse is made to labour in the mines until the age of twenty-one, solely for the benefit of another (Dr. Mitchell, Report, § 159 : App. Pt. I., p. 19).

Mr. William Grove, mine-agent to James Loxdale, Esq., gives the following evidence : " There are more that 200, probably 300, apprentices belonging to the collieries in this town of Bilston at this moment. One man has five now in his house. Within the last twenty-five years he has had more than forty apprentices. When I first became a butty I had thirteen men and six boys, and I have had twenty-four men and ten boys. Sometimes the apprentices are forced to go where other boys would not go" (Dr. Mitchell, Evidence, No. 5 : App. Pt. I., p. 64, ll. 67, 41, 44).—William Hartell Baylis, agent of James Loxdale, Esq., says, " The men will send a boy where they do not go themselves, and some have their limbs broken and others lose their lives. Some parishes will not let the butties have their pauper children as apprentices" (Ibid. No. 7: p. 65, l. 33).—John Greaves, a collier, states : " The boys are not used so bad as they were. It is the butties' apprentices who are worst used. These lads are made to go where other men will not let their own children go. If they will not do it they take them to the magistrates, who commit them to prison. Mr. * * * caused his apprentices to go where another person would not go. I have seen him take up his foot and kick them to make them go" (Ibid. No. 11 : p. 67, l. 62).—Edward Oakley, forty years of age, collier : " I first went down to the pit at eight. I was an apprentice to a butty collier ; I never received any wages till twenty-one ; I served thirteen years' apprenticeship ; I was bound when I first went down ; I think apprenticeship a very bad thing. Butties get apprentices from parishes, and send their own children to learn other trades. The boy would learn his trade just as well if he were not an apprentice ; not a morsel of difference. Sometimes fathers bind their own children, being induced by the present of a suit of clothes, or a watch, or some other enticement. I had thirteen years of it ; it was a hard time. The last part of it I thought veryhard. The butties here in general do very well, and build lots of building. The apprentice can learn nothing. The colliers are very ignorant, being always buried alive in the pits. The butties never put their own sons to be colliers, but send them to learn other businesses" (Ibid. No. 8 : p. 65, l. 50).—John Davenport, clerk of the Union of Ashby-de-la-Zouch : " Have you many boys in the Union-house ?—From nine to sixteen only two, but from two to nine we have twenty-three. Do you bind any of them as apprentices to colliers ? —We bound three last Saturday as apprentices in Staffordshire. I think all the three must have been bound to men who lived in the parish of Darlaston. They were bound before the magistrates to twenty-one. We never bound but one boy to a collier in our own district, but generally to Staffordshire" (Ibid. No. 82 : p. 114, l. 63).—The Rev. H. S. Fletcher, incumbent of Bilston, says :—" Instances sometimes occur when a master takes a parish apprentice and because his rightful protectors are either at a distance or decline further interference, neglects his duty to a serious degree" (Dr. Mitchell, Report, § 162 : App. Pt. I., p. 20).

189. The Sub-Commissioner reports : " At the age of fourteen he (the apprentice) works side by side with other lads who are getting 14s. a-week (the apprentice getting nothing) ; at seventeen or eighteen he is working side by side with freemen, who may go wherever they please, and are earning 20s. or 25s. a-week" (Ibid § 159 : p. 19). " This condition is unfavourable to the acquisition of industrious habits. The young man toils for the benefit of others, and not of himself. It is also most unfavourable for the acquisition of a virtuous, moral, and religious education. No doubt there are some virtuous and conscientious masters, who train up their apprentices as they would train their own children, but very often it is otherwise. In the case of the greater part of mankind, natural affection aids conscience in the discharge of duty towards their offspring, and, however negligent of their own religious duties, they carefully see to their performance by their families ; but the apprentice is not a subject of natural affection ; if, like the ox, he be strong for labour, it is all that the master cares for. The apprentices have not a holiday

COAL MINES.

Hiring.

Apprentices.

South
Staffordshire.

if there be the means of employing them, as the butties must keep them at all events. and have not to pay them wages. Even if 'the bank play,' that is, if the people on the bank do not draw up coals, still the apprentices are sent down into the pits to carry back slack into the gob, or to do other odd work. It is the apprentices who are set to mind the steam-engines and pump up water on Sundays. It is the apprentices who on that day clean the boilers."

190. "On making inquiry of the clerk of the union at Walsall (No. 31), and of the relieving officer at Wolverhampton, what reasons there could be for such a long term of years, the reply was that it was a gain to the masters. The same reason is given by Mr. Grove (No. 5); but other parties besides the butties who work the mines share in the profit. If the butties get cheap labour they can afford to dig the coals or ironstone at a cheaper rate, and thereby the tenants of the mine benefit; but by how much the cheaper they can raise coal and ironstone, the larger royalty they can afford to pay, and thereby the proprietors gain. Hence all parties are interested, and the pauper children suffer. It is easy in reply to such observations to say that the apprentices are well treated. In many cases it may be so, and the instances of exceedingly gross ill usage may be rare, but all this, and more than this, was said by the planters respecting the slaves in the West Indies; but still the country would not be satisfied, and put an end to slavery in the colonies. Now here is a slavery in the middle of England as reprehensible as ever was the slavery in the West Indies, which justice and humanity alike demand should not longer be endured" (Ibid. § 159: p. 19).

Shropshire.

191. SHROPSHIRE.—Of the system in this district of binding apprentices to work in the mines until the age of twenty-one, the Sub-Commissioner reports that "the practice, if not totally unknown, is at any rate exceedingly rare; and witnesses who were examined on this point stated that they had never heard of such a thing. That apprenticeship is very rare is best of all proved from the fact that no applications are made for apprentices to the mines by any of the charter-masters of the district; but charter-masters do come from the county of Stafford, and it is grievous to think that pauper or orphan boys should be delivered into their hands, to be compelled, for their benefit, to work until twenty-one years of age. From the Madeley Union Children have been so bound, under ten years of age, but in the Wellington Union not until some years afterwards. Such is the evidence of the clerks of these Unions. All the charter-masters in Shropshire, of whom inquiry was made, spoke of it with horror, and said it was as bad as the African Slave Trade."

Mr. George Jones, the agent of the Wombridge collieries, gave evidence as follows:—" It was formerly the custom of the butties to take apprentices from distant parishes by indenture for seven years, to work in collieries till twenty-one years of age. The lads were usually thirteen or fourteen. It was unjust, as the youths for three or four years were full-grown men, and were working for the benefit of butties, and getting nothing at all, except sometimes a small gratuity. It was no trade at last, and I put a stop to it in our collieries. I am not aware that apprentices are taken at all into collieries in this county. I should consider it very wicked to allow it"   (Ibid. § 303, 304: p. 38.)

West Riding of
Yorkshire.

192. WEST RIDING OF YORKSHIRE: SOUTHERN PART.—In this district the employment of apprentices is by no means uncommon:—"A very gross case of the unduly early employment of a workhouse Child came under my notice, who was apprenticed to a collier at Thornhill, working in a thin pit before he was quite five years old. The particulars of this case will be found in the depositions which I took from the matron of the workhouse, and Mr. Rayner, the surgeon, who was himself a Guardian at the time" (J. C. Symons, Esq., Report, § 16: App. Pt. I., p. 167).

Thomas Rayner, Esq., surgeon, Birstall: " I am a Guardian for the township of Gomersall, in the Dewsbury Union. When I first attended the Board meetings, I was surprised to find so many applications from miners for apprentices from the Union Workhouse. The answer was, 'Go to the house and select for yourself, and we will bind you the one you select.' In some cases children (boys) have been selected at seven and eight years of age, because they were strong and healthy. Upon inquiry, I found no question had been asked as to the age; and if in a few months the man found the boy was not strong enough (without reference to his age), he brings him back. One instance occurred only on the 24th December, last Thursday, and the boy is again in the Union Workhouse, only seven years of age. I remonstrated with the other guardians on the enormity of binding a boy so young: they told me they had not bound him, nor should they do until he was nine years of age; but is not this the same as binding? This boy's master had five or six in the same way. I am the only surgeon who has ever been a member of the Dewsbury Board of Guardians, and the other members do not like to be interfered with. Now, in such a case, if the child must have had a certificate of fitness before being sent, he never would have been sent. I was astonished that such things could be" (J. C. Symons, Esq., Evidence, No. 180 : App. Pt. I., p. 274, l. 39).

193. In a subsequent examination this witness further states, that the Board of Guardians at Batley apprentice Children without due care to ascertain their age; and that the boy, Thomas Townsend, aged five years, referred to by the Sub-Commissioner, would not have been brought back to the workhouse had not the grandfather interfered and demanded it, and had not the friends of the Child threatened to acquaint the Poor Law Commissioners with the circumstance. Another witness, Joseph Ellison, Esq., of Birkenshaw, in the same neighbourhood, states that the fact is notorious, that when the colliers in this vicinity are in need of hurriers they apply to the Poor Law Guardians for pauper Children. "I have been," he says, "a Guardian myself, and know it to be a fact. They cannot get them elsewhere, on account of the severity of the labour and treatment hurriers experience; and which makes parents prefer any other sort of employment for their children" (Ibid. No. 249 : p. 288, l. 24).

194. HALIFAX.—In this district it is stated that, "a great number of hurriers are apprenticed by the Boards of Guardians from the age of eight years upwards until twenty-one, paying with them a sovereign, to be expended, at the discretion of the master, for clothes, who likewise receives all their hard earnings, as a compensation for board, lodging, and instruction in the art and mystery of hurrying and thrusting. Many of the colliers take two or three at a time, supporting themselves and families out of their labour : as soon as either of them is old enough he is made a getter, and is then worth from 10s. to 15s. a-week" (S. S. Scriven, Esq., Report, § 68 : App. Pt. II. p. 70).

Joseph Barker, of Windy Bank Pit (No. 14) says, "I have three apprentices (two hurriers, the other a ' getter'); they are bound to me until they are twenty-one. I draw what they earn every fortnight, and for that I keep them in meat, drink, and clothing" (Ibid. § 69 : p. 70).—Thomas Moorhouse, collier-boy : " I don't know how old I am; father is dead; I am a chance child; mother is dead also; I don't know how long she has been dead; 'tis better na three years; I began to hurry when I was nine years old for William Greenwood; I was apprenticed to him till I should be twenty-one; my mother apprenticed me; I lived with Greenwood; I don't know how long it was, but it was a goodish while; he was bound to find me in victuals and drink and clothes; I never had enough; he gave me some old clothes to wear, which he bought at the rag-shop; the overseers gave him a sovereign to buy clothes with, but he never laid it out; the overseers bound me out with mother's consent from the township of Southowram; I ran away from him because he lost my indentures, for he served me very bad; he stuck a pick into me twice in my bottom. [Here I made the boy strip, and found a large cicatrix likely to have been occasioned by such an instrument, which must have passed through the glutei muscles, and have stopped only short of the hip-joint : there were twenty other wounds, occasioned by hurrying in low workings, upon and around the spinous processes of the vertebræ, from the sacrum upwards.] He used to hit me with the belt, and mawl or sledge, and fling coals at me; he served me so bad that I left him, and went about to see if I could get a job; I used to sleep in the cabins upon the pit's bank, and in the old pits that had done working; I laid upon the shale all night : I used to get what I could to eat; I eat for a long time the candles that I found in the pits that the colliers left over night; I had nothing else to eat; the rest of the hurriers did not know where I was; when I got out in the morning, I looked about for work, and begged of the people a bit; I got to Bradford after a while, and had a job there for a month while a collier's lad was poorly; when he came back I was obliged to leave; I work now here for John Cawtherly; he took me into his house, and is serving me very well; I hurry for him now, and he finds me in victuals and drink" (S. S. Scriven, Esq., Evidence, No. 58 : App. Pt. II., p. 118, l. 11. See also Witnesses, Nos. 64 and 65).

195. LANCASHIRE.—In regard to the system of apprenticeship in this district, and the treatment which the apprentices sometimes receive, Mr. John Halliwell, the overseer of Oldham, gives the following evidence .—

" Is it customary to bind the pauper children apprentices to colliers in this neighbourhood? Yes, we have bound more parish children apprentices to colliers latterly than to any other trade.—Do they generally turn out well? Some few turn out well, and others do not; I think they do not do well generally, but it is the only way we have of apprenticing them.— Are cases of cruelty to parish apprentices in coal mines common? Yes, we have had a good many cases lately; I was obliged to summon three cases within the last week, where boys had been unmercifully used; two of them were parish children, and one was the child of a widow who was a pauper; they were all bad cases, but one of them had nearly proved fatal.—Can you recollect the particulars of this case? These boys [for they were all supposed to have committed the same offence] had not brought dinners of their own down the pits, and, being hungry, it was supposed they had stolen other boys' dinners which were missing. For this they were punished in the following manner : One of the biggest of the boys, or a young man, got the boy's head between his legs, and each boy in the pit, and there were 18 to 20 of them, inflicted 12 strokes on the boy's rump and loins with a ' cut.' I never saw such a sight in my life; the flesh of the rump and loins was beaten to a jelly in the worst case. The doctor said the boy could not survive; however he did, and is now in a fair way.—Do the boys ever refuse to beat the offender? It came out in the course of the inquiry that it was a rule that any boy who refused to give his strokes is to be served the same way himself.—Do you think these were extraordinary cases? No, I believe it is a general punishment for this offence; for the old men who came forward to give evidence all stated that it had been the custom ever since they could recollect, and seemed to think it was perfectly right and justifiable.—What ages were these boys? The boy who was so very ill used was just 10, and the others would be 12 or 13.—Have you reason to believe that these boys were not properly supplied with food by their masters? Yes, there can be no doubt that they had been neglected. —Is it usual for the magistrates to cancel the indentures of colliers' apprentices? The magistrates have never broken the indentures excepting in one case, and then the boy's master was not to blame. His wife was a drunken woman, and she let the boy go without food, and he certainly was in a very bad state. In cases of cruelty or ill usage the apprentices appeal to me, and I take the cases before the magistrates" (J. L. Kennedy, Esq., Evidence, No. 98: App. Pt. II., p. 233, l. 58).

West of Scotland.

196. WEST OF SCOTLAND.—The system of apprenticeship is not common in this district, but it is not altogether unknown. " In some cases, from the destitution to which the want of a regular relief for the poor subjects families, and particularly orphans or children of widows in Scotland, a collier is enabled to obtain the services of a Child by merely supplying him with food and clothing. It is rare that any formal contract is entered into with these juvenile workers, unless they are apprentices, and even in that case it seems seldom the custom in Scotland to bind them by formal indentures. Legally, I believe, the ordinary contracts made in Scotland with apprentices are binding only for a twelvemonth, regular indentures being considered an embarrassing tie upon both parties, without any equivalent advantage (T. Tancred, Esq., Report, § 83, 85 : App. Pt. I., p. 336).

5.—STATE OF THE PLACE OF WORK IN COAL-MINES.

Place of Work.

197. It is obvious that the effect of labour on the well-being of the labourer must be materially influenced by the nature and condition of the place in which the employment is carried on. The circumstances which mainly influence the salubrity, comfort, and safety of the place of work in coal mines are the thickness of the seam of coal, and the consequent dimensions of the subterranean roadways, together with the ventilation, drainage, and temperature of the mine.

1. *Thickness of the Seam of Coal, and Dimensions of the Subterranean Roadways.*

Thickness of the seam of coal, and dimensions of the subterranean roadways.

198. On the thickness of the seam of coal, more than on any other single circumstance, depend the natural facilities for rendering the coal-mine convenient, considered as a place of work. How greatly those facilities must vary in different districts will be at once apparent when it is considered that the seams of coal at present actually worked in various parts of the kingdom differ from ten inches to ten yards in thickness.

199. When the seam of coal is thick, the roads made for the conveyance of the coal from the workings to the foot of the shaft are always proportionally high. Whenever the seam of coal is thick enough to render it the interest of the owner of the mine to make the main roads and the side roads sufficiently high for a man to stand upright, in this fortunate case the interest of the proprietor and the comfort of the workman coincide. In this comparatively rare case all the operations of the mine, are in general conducted on a scale of great magnitude ; one result of which commonly is that the mine, considered as a place of work, is at least not oppressive to the workpeople; and it is indeed easily, that is, without much expense to the proprietor, provided with all the conveniences and comforts appropriate to mining labour. Little difference will be felt in seams of different thickness, as long as this is not less than from five to six feet ; but then as the thickness of the seam diminishes it rapidly becomes more expensive, in proportion to the quantity of coal to be procured, to make the roads for carrying on the operations of the mine of a convenient height ; and the cost of doing this is materially affected by the nature of the strata both above and below the seam. Supposing the seam to be very thin

and yet the coal to be of excellent quality, and supposing the strata both above and below the seam to be of such a nature that they cannot be removed, so as to make the roof high and the floor even and smooth, without very great expense; in this case the economical working of the mine will require that the roads be made no higher than is absolutely indispensable for getting the coal and conveying it to the foot of the shaft. Now it may be possible to work such a mine with profit, supposing that no expense is incurred beyond what is necessary to obtain barely sufficient space to render it practicable for the miner to carry on his operations; while it may not be possible to work such a mine with profit, due regard being paid to the convenience, or even to the safety and health, of the workpeople. It is conceivable that, in a case such as is here supposed, labourers in a mine may be obliged to carry on their work under circumstances highly oppressive and injurious: whether this be actually the case in any of the coal-mines at present worked in this country, the evidence about to be adduced will show.

200. In order that a more distinct conception may be formed of the real bearing of the facts collected on this subject under the present Commission, it may be proper to state in general terms* that no coal-mine can be worked, with tolerable convenience or comfort to the workpeople, of which the main roads are less than from five to six feet in height, and the side roads two feet and a half. When the roads are six feet high and upwards there is not only ample space for carrying on the general operations of the mine, but the coals can be drawn direct from the workings to the foot of the shaft by the largest horses. When the main roads are four feet and a half high the mine may still be rendered sufficiently convenient for the workpeople, and the coals may be conveyed along these roads to the foot of the shaft by ponies or asses. But when the main ways are under four feet, the coals can no longer be conveyed along these roads by ponies or asses, or even by adult or young men; they can only be conveyed by children. Yet it is in evidence that, in many mines which are at present worked, the main gates are only from twenty-four to thirty inches high, and in some parts of these mines the passages do not exceed eighteen inches in height. In this case not only is the employment of very young Children absolutely indispensable to the working of the mine, but even the youngest Children must necessarily work in a bent position of the body, in the manner hereafter described.

2. *Ventilation.*

201. The best mode of ventilating mines hitherto discovered is that by means of two shafts sunk near each other, perhaps from 12 to 20 yards apart. A stream of air is made to descend one shaft, called the downcast-shaft, and a corresponding stream of air to ascend the other, called the upcast-shaft. The air is set in motion by means of a fire which is kindled in the upcast-shaft. A portion of the air in contact with the fire in this shaft, undergoing the ordinary chemical change which takes place in atmospheric air in the process of combustion, is decomposed: the nitrogen is separated, and the oxygen uniting with the carbon of the fuel forms carbonic-acid gas. Both these gases, as well as the portion of atmospheric air which remains undecomposed, being heated, are expanded, and occupy a proportionally larger space than the same weight of common atmospheric air, and in obedience to the laws of all fluid bodies are borne upwards, consequently a strong current of air ascends this shaft; but if a free communication has been established below between the two shafts, an equal current must at the same time necessarily descend the second shaft to fill up the partial vacuum which has been made in the first.

202. Here then a power is generated capable of forcing a current of fresh air far beyond the distance to which any mine extends. The great generator of this power is the fire, and this power will act with a force and steadiness proportionate to the degree of heat steadily maintained at the bottom of the upcast-shaft.

203. After two shafts have been sunk in a coal-field, the first operation is to establish a communication between them by digging out the coals from the one to the other. The next is to carry forward a mainway from the foot of each shaft, and then to make a road from the extremity of one mainway to the extremity of the other. If a door be now placed in the road which leads directly from the foot of the one shaft to that of the other, the air cannot then pass that way, but must go round along the one mainway across to the other, and thus to the foot of the shaft in which there is the fire, up which shaft the current must ascend.

---

* This must be considered only as a rough estimate, not as assigning the requisite space with positive accuracy within a few inches, more or less.

204. To whatever distance we suppose the mainways, the sideways, and all the other works of the mine to be carried, communications may thus be made between them, and by means of doors properly placed, the circulation of the air may be conducted and guided through them to any extent and in any direction that may be desired. A very simple diagram, showing the principle of these arrangements for ventilation, without the intricacy attaching to a plan of all the ways in an extensive pit, is added in the margin from Mr. Fletcher's Report, § 20 : App. Pt. II. p. 822.

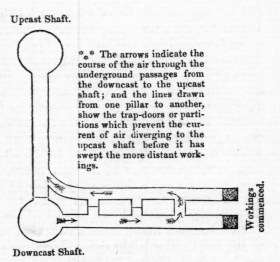

Upcast Shaft.

** The arrows indicate the course of the air through the underground passages from the downcast to the upcast shaft; and the lines drawn from one pillar to another, show the trap-doors or partitions which prevent the current of air diverging to the upcast shaft before it has swept the more distant workings.

Downcast Shaft.

Workings commenced.

205. As the fresh air that descends the downcast-shaft passes along the various roads through which it is directed, it not only affords the means of healthy respiration to the workpeople, but in its course collects and carries with it every heterogeneous matter which it can hold in solution, or which is capable of being mixed with it, which it conveys out of the mine through the upcast-shaft into the air above. The various matters which are thus conveyed out of a coal-mine in this ascending current are atmospheric air, carbonic acid gas, nitrogen gas, carbureted-hydrogen gas, moisture, and animal effluvia.

206. In looking at the plans of large coal-pits there seems to be great perplexity and much ingenuity in the manner in which the air is conducted to the different parts of the mine, but the great principle in all is the very simple one which has now been stated, and at the cost of maintaining a sufficient fire at the foot of the upcast-shaft, and an adequate arrangement for conducting the current of air through the pit, any coal-mine can be perfectly ventilated.

207. Several of the Sub-Commissioners have given detailed descriptions of the different modes of ventilation adopted in their respective districts. (See Dr. Mitchell, Report, § 245, et seq.: App. Pt. I., p. 30; § 101, et seq.: p. 97; § 8, et seq.: p. 120; J. C. Symons, Esq., Report, § 141, et seq.: App. Pt. I., p. 184; J. R. Leifchild, Esq., Report, § 160, et seq.: App. Pt. I., p. 539; J. L. Kennedy, Esq., Report, § 61, et seq.: App. Pt. II., p. 153; J. Fletcher, Esq., Report, § 19, et seq.: App. Pt. II., p. 822).

208. From the evidence it appears that in all the districts there are particular mines in which, often at great expense to the owners, every precaution is taken which intelligence and skill can devise to render the mine healthy and safe; but that there are great numbers of mines in which both ventilation and drainage are grossly neglected, and in which, as a necessary consequence, there is often a frightful destruction of human life.

3. *Drainage.*

Drainage.

209. Next to the due supply of the coal-mine with pure air, which is necessary alike to its salubrity and safety, its healthfulness depends upon its being properly drained. Some pits are naturally very dry; others cannot be made and kept so without constant care and much expense. Various modes are adopted for the drainage of coal-pits, such as bringing the water to the surface in buts worked by machinery, or by successive lifts of pumps, or by collecting the water in a sink or sump at the bottom of one of the shafts, and then drawing it up in buckets by the engine when the engine is not engaged in raising coals; or by sinking a shaft on purpose, in which is placed a series of pumps for raising the water from one lift to another, until from the highest pump of all, which brings the water to the surface, a perpetual stream is made to flow. But without entering into any further account of this, it may suffice to state that, whenever the floor of the pit lies in such a way that the water will flow to the place to which the lowest pump descends, then the pit can be effectually kept dry.

210. In regard to all the conditions which have been described, there is the greatest variety in different coal mines in each district, and a corresponding variety in their character as places of work.

4. *Temperature.*

Temperature.

211. Coal pits are almost always comfortably warm; and in general the deeper they are, the warmer. By proper ventilation the heat can generally be so regulated as to render the temperature unoppressive, and even grateful. When cold in the

main roads the heat is often oppressive in the side gates and at the workings. Oppressive heat may always be regarded as an indication of imperfect ventilation. It is stated that in the mines of the Yorkshire coal fields the thermometer stands in the main roads at from 50° to 60°, in the side roads from 60° to 65°, and at the workings from 64° to 72°. In the deep mines in the northern coal field the temperature is considerably higher. In one of the Hetton pits in South Durham the temperature was found to be 66° at the bottom of the shaft, and 70° in the workings; but in the Monkwearmouth colliery, the deepest in the northern coal field, the average temperature ranges from 78° to 80°, and in some parts of this mine it occasionally rises to 89°.

212. South Staffordshire.—In this coal field the principal seam of coal is 10 yards thick, the roads which are cut out of the coal are seven or eight feet wide and about nine feet high ; and with such a thickness of the seam it would be easy to make the roads of still greater height, were this attended with any advantage ; but a greater height of the roof would increase the danger to the workpeople in case anything should fall out of the roof, from the velocity acquired in descending from so great a height.

213. In this district the coals are brought direct from the workings to the foot of the shaft in cars drawn by horses. A railway is laid along the middle of the road, to make the work easier for the horses. Each horse is conducted by a boy, usually from thirteen to fourteen years of age, who marches at the horse's side, his right hand at the bridle ; and these boys are naked from the waist upwards.

214. In some of the coal mines in which disturbance has been caused by eruptions of basalt, the roads, instead of being uniformly level, are up-hill and down-hill, the risings and depressions being numerous and sudden, and the ascents in some places steeper than Highgate-hill. In such situations horses cannot be employed, the cars are drawn up hill to the foot of the shaft by the jig-chain, and are worked by the steam-engine. Where there is a descent down hill the cars are put in motion by their own gravity, and are kept from going too fast by a chain wound round a cylinder.

215. "In the coal mines of this district the state of the place of work, to persons who have been accustomed to it, is very comfortable. The coal-beds are sufficiently thick to allow abundance of room. The mines are warm and dry. There is a supply of fresh air from ventilation, though less than there easily might be. In conversation with miners, in the whole course of inquiry as to the state of the mines, I never heard a single complaint. The pits are usually of the temperature of a fine summer's day, or, as one of the witnesses expressed, 'it is warm, beautifully warm.' Horses thrive well in the pits. Large, convenient, and comfortable stables are dug out of the coal for them ; they grow fat, and their skins are remarkably smooth and glossy, which is attributed to the warm uniform temperature. The miners in the pit are not exposed to close over-heated air, as in some manufactories ; and in winter escape the miseries of cold, rain, snow, and frost. However unpleasant the coal pits may be to persons who for the first time go down to see them, to those who are used to them they are exceedingly agreeable" (Dr. Mitchell, Report, § 108—110 : App. Pt. I . p. 12).

216. Of the state of a place of work in which the workpeople are capable of pursuing their laborious and dangerous occupation, not only without complaint but with cheerfulness, a vivid picture is presented by the following description of a visit to the Wallbut Pit :—

217. On descending the shaft, " the first step from the skip went above the ancle in water and wet coal-dust, and the second step was like the first. It was of no use then to be on ceremony, and we advanced forward. The water in one place was nearly knee-deep, and through this part we went on a carriage with a skip drawn by a horse. The water everywhere fell from the roof in great drops, like the shower of a thunder-storm, out of the roof of the gateways. The horses had wax cloths spread over them to protect them a little from the rain. The water sometimes fell in spouts. It was stated that all this was merely the drainage of the water which had accumulated for ages in the coal and in the measures (strata) above it ; and that in four or five months, by the time the gateways were completed, the mine would be thoroughly drained, and would be easily kept dry and comfortable with very little pumping. The horses were obedient, the men and boys seemed very cheerful. The holers lay on their sides, with the water covering their lower thighs. There was not a murmur of complaint. There was a long gateway of some hundred yards in length, and other roads coming off at right angles from it, from one to the

COAL MINES.

Place of Work.

Temperature.

South Staffordshire.

Subterranean road-ways.

Drainage.

COAL MINES.

Place of Work.

South
Staffordshire.

Temperature.

other of which airways were drawn which formed the means of ventilation. In one place the gas bubbled up through the water, and when a candle was held to it there was a flash. The horse-road was about eight feet across and eight feet high, and there a railway was laid down. One of the most remarkable things in this pit was the cheerfulness with which men and boys proceeded with their work, seemingly unconscious of there being any hardship in it" (Dr. Mitchell, Report, § 43—48 : App. Pt., I., p. 6).

North
Staffordshire.

218. NORTH STAFFORDSHIRE.—In the Pottery district the seams are of sufficient thickness to permit the employment of horses and ponies to draw the coal along the mainways to the foot of the shaft; and no young Children are employed under-ground. But in the Cheadle district " the seams of coal are not more than from three to four feet thick ; consequently all the main ways are low, with 'shaley' roofs and wet bottoms : no ponies could, therefore, work in them. I descended the Dilhorn Pit, and had to stoop, my hands supporting the body, upon my knees, the whole distance" (S. S. Scriven, Esq., Report, § 2, 9, 15 : Pt. II., pp. 127, 128, 129.)

Shropshire.

*Subterranean road-
ways.*

219. SHROPSHIRE.—Instead of the ample space for carrying on the work of the mines, which the ten-yard seams of Staffordshire afford, the seams are so thin in the Coalbrook Dale district, that there is not above one bed in twelve in which a man can stand upright. Of fifteen pits at present in work, the section of which has been carefully taken, two-thirds of the beds do not exceed three feet ; in three of the pits the beds are above two feet, but do not exceed three feet ; and in four of the pits the beds are under two feet. This may be considered as a fair statement of the thickness of the seams in this district. In general, the best coal is found in the thin seams. Of course, the general system of working must be such as will suit these thin beds, and must be materially different from that of the Staffordshire coal mines.

220. " In the Staffordshire mines it is usual at once to extend the horse-ways from the shafts out to the farthest boundary of the mine, and there to begin working, and gradually to come back to the shafts : the reason is that they are afraid lest the roof of the mine should fall in if they began near the shafts, and they should have to incur the expense of sinking fresh shafts : but in this district, where the roofs are very low, it is comparatively easy to support them, and accordingly they begin near the shafts, and work farther and farther away ; and they extend the horse-way, and lay down the rails, gradually as they proceed. By this method they avoid having capital unnecessarily lying dormant in horse-ways before they are wanted. As the mine advances, other horse-ways are made, so that they may be able conveniently to reach every part ; and then the system of ventilation becomes much more complicated."

221. " In face of the working is laid down a railroad, of which the rails are removable from time to time at pleasure. Upon these rails, which are about 16 inches apart, are placed small carriages, called dans, with wheels only six inches in diameter, and on these low carriages the coals are placed, in order to be wheeled to the horse-way, where they are placed in the carriages which are to be drawn by horses to the foot of the shaft. Many of the beds are exceedingly thin, and hence the space in the workings is so low that the men lie on their sides, and it would be impossible for men to push forward the little carriages or dans, as they could not possibly get room to move easily, and, between fourteen and fifteen years of age, even a boy of ordinary growth becomes inconveniently large. In all beds there are some places where the measures (strata) above and below the coal, approach much nearer to each other than is usually the case, so that beds, which are in most parts 30 inches apart, may become as narrow as 18 inches, and the men employed can barely creep through, and could not by possibility in these places drive the dans half as easily as do the boys."

222. " When the men have moved along the face of a working, and all the coals brought down have been removed, the rails are taken up, and a new railway is made farther on ; and on the ground in face of the working just cleared out, the small coal or slack is pushed back, and all the measure (stratum) taken from above or below the coal is built up also ; and thus the space where the coals were is filled up, and the visiter who comes to look at the mine never sees large empty spaces, but only the horse-ways and the narrow side lanes of the workings. This is done for various reasons : to get rid of the rubbish, which would be an incumbrance ; to support the roof of the pit ; and, for a reason as important as any, that there may not be any room in which a body of carbureted hydrogen gas may accumu-

late and explode. A current of air may also be made to pass through the horse-ways **and** workings, which could not be made to pass through a large wide space" (Dr. Mitchell, Report, §§ 248—252: App. Pt. I., p. 31).

John Anstice, partner in the Madeley Wood Iron Company, thirty years of age : " The coal pits in this district have beds of various thickness, but very many are very shallow, in consequence of which it becomes necessary to employ boys to push the carriages on railing, as it would be impossible in such beds to introduce horses or asses for the purpose. Wherever horses can be employed, it is much more advantageous for the proprietor; and for his own interest, if he had no higher motive, he certainly would not employ boys" (Dr. Mitchell, Evidence, No. 39: App. Pt. I., p. 79, l. 1). Joseph Jones, ground-bailiff to the Madeley Wood Iron Company, aged fifty-eight : "Many of the beds of coal which are worked in Shropshire are very thin, and are under two feet; and oftentimes it happens in beds which are thicker that at particular parts the roof and the bottom may consist of hard rock, and may bend so as to approach nearer to each other, and in such parts as these the mine is very low, though it may not be so generally. There is a large roadway made through the pit, at a heavy expense, where there are carriages drawn by horses; but the coals must be brought from the workings on each side in small carriages, in this district called dans, and horses and asses could not get in or walk along, and the dans are pushed before them on iron rails by boys" (Ibid. No. 44: p. 80, l. 50). William Tranter, agent to the Coalbrook Dale Company : " Some of them (the mines) are two feet in thickness, but there are places to go through at times no more than 18 inches, or perhaps 20 inches. The boys crawl on their hands and knees. The face of the work along which the dans are drawn is made as straight as possible, in order to get out the coal in as good a state as we can" (Ibid. No. 41 : p. 79, l. 41).

223. WARWICKSHIRE.—In this coal field the thickness of the seams is from five to seven feet, a space sufficient to admit of the place in which the miners work being made, without difficulty, perfectly comfortable. In this district also the coal-mines are easily drained, for the seams of coal in general lie on a declivity, and the water readily flows down to the lowest part below the workings. On descending a mine in this district the Sub-Commissioner observes : " We found ourselves when at the foot of the shaft on the side of the hill steeper than the slated roof of a house, the descent being towards the west. The passage through the gate-way or main road was for the most part sufficiently high to admit walking without much stooping." (Dr. Mitchell, Report, § 9, 10 : App. Pt. I., p. 90).

224. LEICESTERSHIRE.—In the Ashby-de-la-Zouch coal field the coal mines are exceedingly comfortable : the beds are of sufficient thickness to enable all persons to work without being forced into a fatiguing or disagreeable position; the mines are perfectly dry, no water being met with below a depth of 100 yards from the surface; and by a powerful ventilation the impure air is rapidly carried off. " On arriving at the foot of the Moira Bath Pit, we had a mile to go before arriving at the place where the miners were at work. The road for the greater part of the way was sufficiently lofty to enable us to walk upright, and even to go bareheaded without fear of being hurt. Every here and there were candles with the ends in clay stuck against the coals forming the sides of the roads. Several boys were engaged in sweeping the railways. There were several faults, and for part of the way the sides of the road and roof were composed entirely of sandstone instead of coal. In some places the road was secured by brick walls on the sides, and also by wood. We met horses and carriages with coals. Generally two horses walked one after the other between the rails, drawing two or more carriages. A lad, almost a man, walked at the head of the first horse, and a boy of ten or twelve at the head of the second. The air was warm in this part of the pit, though in the neighbourhood of the shaft where the air, then about 25° Fahrenheit on the bank, entered, it would be exceedingly cold. The usual system of a moveable railroad, laid along the face of the workings piece after piece as it is wanted, is adopted here.

225. " On returning back the stream of air, which had been in our faces, was now in our backs, and the heat was felt to be oppressive, and coat and waistcoat were laid aside, but notwithstanding, before coming to the foot of the shaft every remaining portion of clothing was wet with perspiration. Happily the cabin, as it is here called, the same as the hovel in Staffordshire, near the mouth of the shaft, with its warm blazing fire, afforded a hospitable protection from the frost and snow.

226. " The heat in this pit is caused by the presence and working of about 80 men and boys, with 30 horses; also by the burning of 100 to 200 candles at a time. The late Mr. Edward Mammatt, in his collection of geological facts respecting the Ashby Coal Field, p. 76, says, 'From the fact that 44° to 46° of Fahrenheit indicates the ordinary heat of water in these mines, it may be inferred that this is the true temperature of the earth at these depths.'

227. " The mine throughout was perfectly dry, and it was stated that no water in

COAL MINES.

Place of Work.

Shropshire.

Subterranean road-ways.

Warwickshire.

Ashby-de-la-Zouch.

Temperature.

Drainage.

that part of the country was met with more than 300 feet below the surface. Water has to be sent down in iron casks for the use of the people who choose to drink it, and for the 30 horses which are there to drag the coals. The salt water which supplies the Moira baths is pumped from a depth of 100 feet lower than the bed of the mine" (Dr. Mitchell, Report, § 88 et seq.: App. Pt. I., pp. 96, 97).

228. From the evidence given by Mr. Woodhouse of Overseal, mining overseer of the Moira Collieries, who has had great experience in the scientific ventilation of coal mines, it appears that a large saving of expense is invariably realised in practice from the adoption of the improved modes of ventilation, because the constant introduction of fresh currents of atmospheric air into the pits, besides being necessary to the health and safety of the workpeople, tends in a remarkable degree to protect the wood-work of the mine, and to keep the roadways dry and in good order. After speaking of the drawbacks from the profits of collieries arising from an imperfect system of ventilation—imperfect as regards the whole quantity of air passed through the workings, but still more imperfect in its distribution, he says— " The improved system adopted in the collieries on the Tyne and the Weare, of dividing the workings into districts, and so obtaining a current of fresh air in every division, may in many cases be adopted at a trifling expense in these counties; and although the extent of the workings in general bears no proportion to those in the collieries in the north, the principle remains the same, and the result would be favourable in a corresponding degree. It may be urged that the immense quantity of gas given out of the coal in the north has called for the improved system there, which is probably the fact; but there are many advantages to be derived from good ventilation beyond the mere prevention of explosion. In pits with a rapid circulation the men respire more freely, the road ways are kept dry and repaired at less expense, and the timber lasts longer *by years*, and therefore it is a matter of strict economy to ensure a good ventilation. The men suffer most materially from working in an impure atmosphere. In some mines the air can scarcely be perceived to move at all, a thick mist or fog pervading the whole pit; which is caused partly from fermentation in the wastes and old works, partly from the lights, and partly from the heat and effluvia from the horses and men. This, with a large proportion of carbonic acid gas, forms an atmosphere that none but colliers who are accustomed to it could endure, but which has the effect of shortening their days." (Ibid. § 101 : App. Pt. I., p. 97).

Joseph Dooley, ground bailiff at Swadlincote, Granville Colliery: "There is a greatly improved plan of ventilation now, and the air-ways are very much larger than formerly. Formerly the air was made to enter, and was conducted through the old workings where it met with foul air, and was brought out in the places where the men were at work, now it is quite the reverse. The fresh air is made to enter and come in the workings where the men are employed, and then it passes into the old workings, carrying with it any foul or dangerous air which it may have met with" (Dr. Mitchell, Evidence, No. 76 : App. Pt. I., p. 112, l. 34).

229. DERBYSHIRE.—In this district the thickness of the seams of coal varies from three to five feet. It is therefore the interest of the proprietors to make the roadways sufficiently high for asses and ponies to draw the coal to the foot of the shaft; in fact, these animals are generally employed for this purpose. Fire-damp is of occasional occurrence, and black-damp very much abounds; nevertheless the whole body of evidence shows that the ventilation in general is exceedingly imperfect. Indeed only a single instance was met with in the whole extent of this district, in which the most efficient mode is adopted, namely, that by two shafts, with a furnace in one. The Sub-Commissioner reports :—" I found the plan of ventilation followed by George Stevenson, Esq., and Company, at Clay Cross, fully answered that gentleman's expectations; it was by sinking two shafts within a few yards of each other, and placing a furnace at the bottom of one, which created a current of air through the whole works in a superior manner to any I had seen before" (J. M. Fellows, Esq., Report, § 30: App. Pt. II., p. 254).

230. The consequences of this imperfect ventilation are, that fatal explosions frequently take place; that the work-people are distressed by the quantity of carbonic acid gas which almost everywhere abounds, and of which they make great complaint; and that the pits are so hot as to add greatly to the fatigue of the labour.

231. But while efficient ventilation is neglected, still less attention is paid to drainage. It is stated by all classes of witnesses that some pits are dry and comfortable, but very many are so wet, that the people have to work all day over their shoes in water, at the same time that the water is constantly dripping upon them from the roof. In other pits, instead of dripping, it constantly "rains," as the people themselves term it, from the roof, so that in a short time after they com-

mence the labour of the day, their clothes are drenched, and in this state, with their feet also in water, they work all day. The Children especially, and in general the younger the age the more painfully this unfavourable state of the place of work is felt, complain bitterly of this, and it must be borne in mind that it is in this district that, according to the evidence, the regular hours of a full day's labour are fourteen, and occasionally sixteen.

Ventilation.

James Davis, aged twenty-seven, holer, Lord Middleton's: " There is not a good ventilation; they are very much put about by the black-damp; are prevented working for a day or two together; never has had the wildfire since he worked there; never use the Davy-lamp; the pit is always tried by a man going with a naked candle; the butties are on the look-out to see all is right" (J. M. Fellows, Esq., Evidence, No. 12: App. Pt. II.., p. 266, l. 57).—Joseph Shelton, aged sixty-four, pitman: " Often black-damp so as to prevent them working for days together. The roof is bad, and often occasions slight accidents. The pit in some places is very hot, owing to the ventilation not being good, and the pit so deep" (Ibid. No. 38: p. 273, l. 20).—John Beasley, pitman, Shipley: " Has frequently experienced the effects of the black-damp, and has known those who have been burnt to death by the wildfire. At Shipley they occasionally use a Davy-lamp, but not regularly. He has within these two years known the pit he works at fired; so that they had to bring up all hands as well as the asses, and close the pit for a week" (Ibid. No. 40: p. 274, l. 55).—Robert Blount, ten years old: " They have no wildfire, but black-damp; it swells their bellies and makes their heads ache" (Ibid. No. 99: p. 290, l. 50).

Drainage.

Thomas Rawling, agent to Mr. Fenton's coal field, Bagthorp: " Worked by asses, men, and boys; dry altogether, so much so, that they have to supply the asses with water" (Ibid. No. 71: p. 283, l. 43).—See also statements of witness Taylor, No. 8; Fletcher, No. 50; Middleton, No. 3; and Bodil, No. 1, as to the dryness of the pits in which they work.

Thomas King, butty at the old pit: " It is dry above; over shoes below" (Ibid. No. 161: p. 306, l. 41).—Vincent Wild, coal-agent, Stoneyford Colliery: " The works are wet both under and over; it is not over shoes under, but 'rains' much over-head, so much so that the boys have to wear flannel; not very hot—if they are still it is cold; no one particularly placed for the purpose of looking after the windways or machinery, but mostly two or three are employed occasionally" (Ibid. No. 45: p. 275, l. 39).—Samuel Richards, aged forty, pitman: " Works for North and Co. at the Flying Nancy Pit; the pit is very wet both over and under; under it is wet to the knees, and the boys are covered with dirt by the asses splashing." (Ibid. No. 166: p. 307, l. 42).—William Ghent: "Is seven years old; is sure he has worked two years: has to work nearly up to his knees in sludge all day; his legs are cold, but other parts very warm. He had rather get coal than head; it is so wet, and he cannot stand up; it makes his neck ache. He is so tired, dirty, and wet, when he gets home, that he undresses, gets his supper, and is glad when he is in bed" (Ibid. No. 195: p. 315, ll. 10, 14.)—Joseph Birkinshaw, eight years old: " He drives between; is wet through directly he gets down." (Ibid. No. 48: p. 276, l. 36).—William Fletcher, nine years old, driver at Underwood: " He is wet quite through in an hour, and has his wet clothes to wear all day" (Ibid. No. 46: p. 276, l. 3).—Joseph Limb, eleven years old: " The pit is wet where he works; it is over his shoe-tops; is standing there all day" (Ibid. No. 68: p. 282, l. 57).—Samuel Elliott, eleven years old, Evans and Co.: " It is very wet in his bank; it rains from the roof; is obliged to wear flannel; it is hot sometimes; the sweat and water are running constantly down his face; is wet through before dinner; he has to sit in his wet things to eat his dinner, and never takes them off until he gets home; there is a cabin, but they never change until they get home" (Ibid. No. 63: p. 281, l. 14). —Joseph Fletcher, aged eleven, driver: " In places the pit is nearly up to his knees in mud and water. Is naked when at work to his breeches" (Ibid. No. 53: p. 277, l. 50).—Joseph Birkinshaw, eight years old, and Samuel Vernon, nine years old, Stoneyford: " These two boys were drawn up from the pit because I insisted upon seeing two of the youngest. After much trouble these two were drawn up for me, and the water actually kept dripping from them and they looked as wretched as drowned rats" (Ibid. Nos. 48, 49: p. 276, l. 40).

Temperature.

Mr. Henry Thorp, agent: " The pits are affected by weather, but are neither too hot or cold. Never knew the workpeople distressed by either" (Ibid. No. 33: p. 272, l. 8).—John Davis, holer, Lord Middleton's: " It is not an unpleasant heat excepting when the black-damp is coming; it is then very 'smothery'" (Ibid. No. 12: p. 267, l. 2).—Samuel Richards, pitman: " It is neither too hot nor too cold except when beans are coming into flower; that's the awkwardest time for a collier" (Ibid. No. 166: p. 307, l. 44.)—Robert Davis, pitman: " The pit in some places is very hot, owing to the ventilation not being good and the pit so deep" (Ibid. No. 39: p. 273, l. 51).—John Beasley, pitman, Shipley: " He has sometimes found the pit 'as hot as a stove'" (Ibid. No. 40: p. 274, l. 9).—Robert Blount, ten years old: " The pit is hot, so that the sweat runs off them" Ibid. No. 99: p. 290, l. 49).—Samuel Elliott, eleven years old: " It is hot sometimes; the sweat and water are running constantly down his face" (Ibid. No. 63: p. 281, l. 15).—John Henshaw, eleven years old: " The pit is hot; it makes them sweat directly they begin to work" (Ibid. No. 135: p. 299, l 17).

232. The general statement of the Sub-Commissioner will be seen to be in strict accordance with this evidence, who says, " I have met with pits where it rained so as to wet the Children to the skin in a few minutes, and at the same time so hot that they could scarcely bear their clothes on to work in, and in this wet state they had to continue fourteen hours, and perhaps had to walk a mile or two at night without changing or drying their clothes." (J. M. Fellows, Esq., Report, § 24: App. Pt. II., p. 254.)

H 2

COAL MINES.

Place of Work.

West Riding of
Yorkshire.

*Subterranean road-
ways.*

233. WEST RIDING OF YORKSHIRE: SOUTHERN PART.—In that part of the Yorkshire coal field, the examination of which was assigned to J. C. Symons, Esq., the thickness of the seams of coal ranges from ten feet to ten inches. The thick seam pits are situated in the neighbourhood of Barnsley, Silkstone, Sheffield, Wakefield, Chapelton, and Elsecar. The thin seam pits are chiefly in the neighbour-hood of Flockton. In the neighbourhood of Barnsley the seams of coal range from nine to ten feet in thickness, and the subterranean roadways are generally about six feet in height. In the neighbourhoods of Silkstone and Sheffield the seams are from five to six feet thick, and the subterranean roadways are commonly about the same height. At Elsecar, near Wentworth, and Rawmarsh, in Lord Fitzwilliam's pits, the seams average five feet and a half, and the roadways are of the same height. In the neighbourhood of Wakefield and Chapelton there are seams three feet thick, and in the mines in which these are worked the roadways are about four feet in height; but in the neighbourhood of Flockton the seams are only from ten to thirty inches in thickness, and in these the height of the main roads varies from twenty-two to thirty-six inches. There are very few collieries working these thin seams in which the main roadways, exceed a yard in height; there are many in which they do not exceed twenty-eight inches, a considerable number in which the greatest height is only twenty-six inches, and some in which it is no more than twenty-two inches. It is obvious that in such collieries all the coal obtained must be conveyed the whole distance from the workings to the foot of the shaft, through a space not greater than that of a common drain. In a space like this it is im-possible either for men or boys to work without great difficulty: the labour of conveying the coal to the shaft can be performed only by young Children, and even these must necessarily work, in a greater or less degree, in a bent posture of the body. It must be borne in mind that, when the main gates are only 28 or 26 inches high, the side gates are often not above 24 or even 22 inches in height. In such a space it is impossible even for the youngest Children to work without an exceedingly constrained posture. Moreover it is in these side gates, in which the height is the smallest, that the ascents and descents, often very considerable, are the steepest; and further, in this part of the mine very frequently no trams are laid down, or if there are any, as they are only placed there temporarily, they are always less evenly laid.

234. In these places, then, the youngest Children must necessarily crawl on their hands and feet; and in this posture they drag after them their loaded corves of coal, without wheels, along roads without trams. It is only the main road which it has been thought worth while, in the instances mentioned by the witness No. 73, to heighten from the thickness of the seam (26 inches) to a yard. Here alone trams are laid down; in what are properly the board-gates no trams are laid, and only the height of the seam itself is left. The same witness adds—" The Children are well tired at night. Not *many* fall ill. They work from seven to five o'clock." They have harder work, and yet work an hour longer than in the ironstone pits (J. C. Symons, Esq., Report, § 98: App. Pt. I., p. 179; and Evidence, No. 73: p. 241, l. 58).

235. Of the state of ventilation in this district the Sub-Commissioner reports:— " I had prepared notes of each different colliery I visited in my district, but I found that a complete and true statement would be more likely to give offence than to do good, and I abandoned the design. I may, however, with truth, state, that venti-lation is not sufficiently attended to for the health and comfort of the workpeople in a majority of cases; whilst in some it is so imperfect that it is positively dangerous. I have seen collieries where fire-damp, or black-damp, prevailed, and where slits for increasing ventilation ought to be cut every ten or a dozen yards, and which are not cut for upwards of fifteen and seventeen. The thin pits are almost always the worst ventilated. As a proof of this I would particularly refer you to the concise reply of Mr. Barber, a proprietor of these pits, in which he states, in reply to query 1st, respecting the provision made for ventilation—' None;—not being necessary.' These are pits where just now Children work all night as well as by day (J. C. Symons, Esq., Report, § 126—134: App. Pt. I., p. 183).

John Thorneley, Esq., one of Her Majesty's justices of the peace for the county of York, says: "Where the ventilation is not sufficiently attended to the health of the children suffers. I have always been of opinion that though Davy's lamp was a valuable discovery, that it has in practice been a curse to the country, for it has enabled colliers to work where they otherwise ought not, and has often superseded a proper renovation of air, and been the cause of the colliers working in an impure atmosphere. Some men left a colliery in the neighbourhood a short time since on the ground that they could not work there with safety, because an air-gate had been stopped to save expense, and which prevented the draft being sufficiently maintained. The men were brought before the bench for absenting themselves from their work; as, however, I was aware of the nature of the case, I reprimanded the masters for thus subjecting the men to the danger of explosion every minute of the day" (J. C. Symons, Esq., Evidence, No. 96 : App. Pt. I., p. 246, l. 53).

236. Very great difference prevails in different collieries in this district in regard to drainage, and the consequent humidity or dryness of the atmosphere of the mine, and the wetness or dryness of the places in which the Children and Young Persons work. Very often where the ventilation is good the drainage is bad. In many collieries in this district the Children work all day long in water and mud, and in some the men actually hew the coals in water. " In very many collieries the ground is extremely wet, and the atmosphere humid, and of an earthy and damp smell. In some collieries both are equally well provided against, and always with the best possible effects on the health and comfort of the workpeople. In a colliery at Mirfield I found the men actually working in water, and in that and many others the Children's feet are never dry. The Mirfield pit was the very worst I ever saw, there being no engine-pump whatever, but merely a handpump to pump the water into a sort of dam to run out again into the gates. This colliery, nevertheless, belongs to a gentleman reputed for benevolence, but who knows nothing of his own pits" (J. C. Symons, Esq., Report, § 124, 125 : App. Pt. I., p. 183).

A collier, aged forty-five, examined at Messrs. Stancliffe's Pit, Mirfield, near Dewsbury : " I was working in water, which was about four inches deep in the bank-face, when you saw me before. It was to dip, and we had no pump but a hand one. I was ordered afterwards to pump the water out, because they heard you were going to come last Wednesday, and I did it. We pump a dam out first where the water runs into, and then lade the water out of the holes into the dam again. The water keeps filling in very fast again, so that we are constantly working in water. We have so much a dozen more for pumping. The banksman told us to work to the rise when they expected you to come, but we wouldn't, and then he swore at me, and said we wanted to be working in the water when you came. But it was the regular thing for us to work down here to dip" (J. C. Symons, Esq., Evidence, No. 277 : App. Pt. I., p. 294, l. 27). —Fanny Drake, aged fifteen, hurrier, Charlesworth's Wood Pit : " It has been a very wet pit before the engine was put up. I have had to hurry up to the calves of my legs in water. It was as bad as this a fortnight at a time ; and this was for half a year last winter ; my feet were skinned, and just as if they were scalded, for the water was bad: it had stood some time ; and I was off my work owing to it, and had a headache and bleeding at my nose" (Ibid. No. 206, p. 280, l. 23).—Mary Margerson, aged sixteen, hurrier, same pit : " The pit is very wet. The water comes up nearly to my calves generally, till they let it off. It is often so for a week together" (Ibid. No. 208 : p. 280, l. 47).—William Pickard, general steward to Sir John Lister, Lister Kaye's, Denby Grange : " The biggest part of the gates are dry. There is some places where the water is over their shoes ; but very few. It is mostly very dry considering. I don't like to see the poor little children dabble in water, if it can be avoided" (Ibid. No. 255 : p. 289, l. 37). —See also witnesses Nos. 219, 220, et seq.

237. In the coal-pits in this district the temperature is seldom oppressive, the thermometer in the main gates generally ranging from 50° to 66° ; and whenever it is higher it is from defective ventilation, which is sometimes the fault of the colliers themselves. " Let a colliery be ever so well provided with the apparatus of ventilation, any one may defeat it by keeping a door open. I was passing through from one bankface to another, through an imperfectly made passage, where men were ' getting,' and was surprised to find the temperature above 70°, although the colliery is one of the best regulated in the country ; on asking the reason the answer was, that the colliers did not like a draft, because it made their candles ' sweal ' (run); and that they kept a door open on purpose to prevent a good current of air !" (J. C. Symons, Esq., Report, § 129, 130 : App. Pt. I., p. 183).

238. BRADFORD AND LEEDS.—The only observation made by Mr. Wood under this head is, " that there is occasionally some dampness in particular parts of the mine" (W. R. Wood, Esq., Report, § 19 : App. Pt. II., p. H 4).

239. HALIFAX.—In this neighbourhood, in the two beds of coal at present worked, called the Hard or Lower and the Soft or Upper bed, the seams vary in thickness from 13 to 27 inches. There are seams which vary from five to eleven inches in thickness, but these are not worked. The thinnest seam at present worked appears to be 13 inches. Generally, however, throughout both the Bradford and the Halifax districts the thickness of the soft-bed seam is 16 inches. The greatest height of the main-roads in this district is 40 inches, and of the side roads 26 inches. Of course with such heights of the main and side roads the necessity of employing Children in conveying the coals the whole distance from the workings to the foot of the shaft is imperative. The distance from the workings to the shaft

COAL MINES.

Place of Work.

West Riding of Yorkshire.

Drainage.

Temperature.

Bradford and Leeds.

Halifax.

Subterranean roadways.

is sometimes very great. " In the Booth Town Pit I walked, crept, and rode 1800 yards to one of the nearest 'faces,' the most distant was 200 further" (S. S. Scriven, Esq., Report, § 36: App. Pt. II., p. 62). In reporting on this district, the Sub-Commissioner adds: " I know but of two gates that will admit of the use of horses (Messrs. Rawson's Swan Bank and the Junction Pit at Low Moor). In some of them I have had to creep upon my hands and knees the whole distance, the height being barely *twenty inches*, and then have gone still lower upon my breast, and crawled like a turtle to get up to the headings. In others I have been more fortunately hurried on a flat board mounted upon four wheels, or in a corve, with my head hanging over the back, and legs over the front of it, in momentary anticipation of getting scalped by the roof, or of meeting with the still more serious infliction of a broken head from a depending rock; whilst in others I have been able to accomplish my journey by stooping" (Ibid. § 33-35: p. 62).

Mr. James Holmes, proprietor of Long Shaw Colliery, Northowram: " Our gates or mainways are generally made a yard high; we cannot make them above or below the seams, because the soil a foot or two above is so loose that it would fall in; as it is we are obliged to prop. We cannot go below the seams because the coals would close in, and the seats or floor rise more than ever; they are so full of water, we are obliged now to remove 80 or 90 rails, every week, and lay them afresh to hurry upon" (S. S. Scriven, Esq., Evidence, No. 47: App. Pt. II., p. 115, l. 14).—Mr. Isaac Clayton, agent and principal; Bradford Union: " I am a surveyor for some proprietors in the neighbourhood, and am pretty well informed of the depths of all the shafts, heights of mainways, length of gates, and other matters relating to mining. The greatest height of our gates is about 3 feet 2 or 3 inches, that is in the better bed; the black-bed gates are not much less, except in the byeways and workings, in which you will find it 2 feet or 26 inches. If the gates are made higher it would occasion the proprietors a great outlay, because the roofs are hard and difficult to get down; if we made them 4 feet high we should have to shut them up altogether, because the coal would not pay for getting; we are therefore under the necessity of employing children instead of horses or men" (Ibid. No. 49: p. 115, l. 38).—See also witnesses Nos. 27, 59, &c.

240. Ventilation in this district is " extremely imperfect," excepting in the mines which belong to the great companies; in these the works are carried on with " system, order, and regularity, and upon a scale of magnitude not to be attained by the small proprietors; their machinery (barring the horse-gins), shafts, roofs, floors, porches, and upcast furnaces are therefore superior to any others that I have met with, either in this or any other district. The currents of air passing through their mines, by this last provision, are so strong that I have had many times a difficulty in opening a door against them—a handkerchief held up in any of the passages would blow out, as in half a gale of wind. It would certainly much surprise me to hear of an explosion in any one of them, except from the extreme negligence of the men in the headings, or from their ignorance, or that of their children, of the principles of the Davy-lamp with which they are provided" (S. S. Scriven, Esq., Report, § 44: App. Pt. II., p. 64).

241. Of the state of the drainage of the pits in this district, even of those belonging to the companies, some conception may be formed from the following notes of the Sub-Commissioner :—

" Messrs. Waterhouse, Lindley, near Huddersfield:—Bottom deep in mire." (S. S. Scriven, Esq., Evidence, No. 9: App. Pt. II., p. 103, l. 44). " Mr. James Wells's Colliery, Norwood Green:—Bottoms wet and undrained; roof rotten." (Ibid. No. 35: p. 111, l. 15). "Low Moor Company's Level Pit:—Bottom in some places near knee-deep in muck and water, full of holes, and most painful to walk, much more to hurry in; so much carbonic gas present that the candles were repeatedly put out" (Ibid. No. 37: p. 111, l. 60). " Low Moor Company's Way House Pit:—Bottom ankle-deep in muck and water; equally rough and uneven as the last." (Ibid. No. 38: p. 112, l. 23). " I descended Mr. Samuel Hall's Engine Pit close by, which is a most dangerous and fearful one, from the circumstance of their working two seams by the same shaft without the slightest protection at the bottom of the first shaft to the mouth of the second. On alighting from a corve in a dark bottom you naturally grope about for a footing and a shelter from falling coal and water. On the platform there is not more than 6 inches of foot-room, so that if I had not exercised the utmost caution a fall into the second shaft would have been inevitable; the banksman refused to descend with me, and gave neither warning nor light—not from wilfulness, but thoughtlessness" (Ibid. No. 82: p. 125, l. 8).

242. LANCASHIRE AND CHESHIRE.—In this district the height of the subterranean roadways," says Mr. Kennedy, " varies from twenty inches to six feet; the greater number being from three feet to three feet six : but in some cases it is not more than twenty inches. In almost all the mines of this district, both carbonic acid gas (choke or black damp) and carbureted hydrogen gas, or fire-damp, are found, but not nearly in the same degree that they exist in mines in Newcastle. I am informed by an experienced coal owner that it would be im-

possible to work the mines of Lancashire with their present inefficient system of ventilation, if they had as much fire-damp to contend against as they have in the mines of the north.   Choke-damp, from its being of greater specific gravity than atmospheric air, occupies the lowest part of the workings ; but as its presence is easily detected by the diminished flame of the candles, it rarely causes much annoyance, though it may be said to be very common in this district.   I have myself seen the air loaded to such a degree with this gas that the candles would scarcely burn when placed near the floor of the mine, a few yards out of the main aircourses" (J. L. Kennedy, Esq., Report, § 58, 59 : App. Pt. II., p. 154).

243. OLDHAM.—In this district, "the depth at which the seams are found varies from a few fathoms to 120 ; the thickness of those which are worked, from eighteen to forty-eight inches ; and their dip, generally to the west of south, from one yard in six to one in two ; there is often a considerable flow of water ; firedamp is troublesome in some of the pits, though not generally ; choke-damp is apt to accumulate in considerable quantities, and when the barometer is low to extend itself considerably through the workings.

244. "The mines in the thin mountain-seams in the higher parts of Oldham and Rochdale parishes are, with few exceptions, worked on a very small scale, and in a very rude manner.   Several, indeed, are entered by 'breast-eyes,' or day-holes, in the hill-side ; and others by ill-constructed pits, with very rude and insecure gearing.   Many have insufficient drainage ; ways so low that only very little boys can work in them, which they do naked, and often in mud and water, dragging sledge-tubs by the girdle and chain, in a ventilation which proves sufficient only because the deleterious gases are almost unknown.   But the greater portion of the coal wrought in the Oldham district is raised by proprietors of larger capital. Each colliery has two or more shafts, perhaps twenty yards from each other ; one, the downcast pit, sunk towards the dip of the strata, for the air to descend, and the other, the upcast pit, towards their rise, for it to return to the surface.   The current is generally quickened by a furnace in the upcast shaft.

245. " The mainways are, in the larger mines, three feet six inches or four feet high, where the young people have to work, and sometimes six inches higher ; but in the narrow seams they are sometimes as little as one foot ten inches, with width enough only for the passage of the tub, a candle stuck in the front of which, or in the drawer's cap, is the sole light in these dark and narrow passages.   These passages are kept on a level by being run across the dip of the strata ; but there are inclined passages from one gallery into another.   Where horses are employed, the ways, by removing portions of the floor or of the roof, according to the material of which they are composed, are made a little higher.   The ends or bays where the getters work are no higher than the thickness of the strata wrought.   The construction of the roadways is various, from the rudest up to the excellent flat railways found in some of the larger mines ; and, what is of still more importance to safety, that of the shafts is unfortunately very various also ; and that of the gearing for effecting ingress and egress, and drawing the coals, scarcely less so" (J. Fletcher, Esq., Report, § 17, 19, 23, 24 : App. Pt. II., p. 822, 283).

According to Andrew Knowles, Esq., colliery proprietor and worker : " Throughout the Lancashire and Cheshire coal field the strata are of such a quality that they emit little fire-damp, and they are so much inclined in their dip, that this gas, which is of lighter specific gravity than the common atmospheric air, easily escapes without any danger, and without any extensive provision of air-doors, trappers, and artificial draughts, which become necessary when the strata pour out more gas, and found in flatter strata.   Not half the mines in this country have any fire-damp whatever ; the consequence is, that the class of children employed in other districts as trappers are here almost unknown.   Is not aware of any mines in which trappers are employed.   The Davy-lamp also is generally dispensed with, except for trying the different workings before the colliers commence their labour.   In mines subject to fire-damp lamps are always provided for trying the state of the mine.   But there is not, perhaps, for 10 miles round here (Little Bolton) one used in working.   There may be a few used in the mines about St. Helen's, and about Wigan, but it is not generally the case in this coal field" (J. Fletcher, Esq., Evidence, No. 1 : App. Pt. II., p. 838, l. 5).

246. NORTH LANCASHIRE.—In this district the seams of coal vary in thickness from eighteen inches to four feet, and the height of the subterranean roadways from thirty-three inches to six feet.   The drainage is often extremely bad.   The evidence given by several of the witnesses is to the following effect : " The place was always knee-deep in water, sometimes it was belly-deep."   " The pit was not above twenty inches seam, and had a foot of water in it ; could hardly keep his head out of water sometimes.   Drew with a belt."   " A terrible wet pit ; the men sit on a board when

they work, and they lade the water out once in half an hour" (A. Austin, Esq., Evidence, No. 3, App. Pt. II., p. 811, l. 46; No. 12, p. 814, l. 23; No. 4, p. 812, l. 2).

Cumberland.

*Subterranean road-
ways.*

*Ventilation and
drainage.*

247. CUMBERLAND.—In this district, in the inland collieries, the seams of coal are at least from four to five feet thick, and in the sea-coast pits from eight to ten feet; and the subterranean roadways are in general of such dimensions that horses are able to go direct to the workings and to draw away the loaded corves. The pits are usually well ventilated, and tolerably dry, Lord Lonsdale's especially (J. C. Symons, Esq., Report, § 21: App. Pt. I., p. 302).

South Durham.

*Subterranean road-
ways.*

248. SOUTH DURHAM.—The coal mines of this district are often most extensive, equalling that which if above ground would be considered farms of the first magnitude. "The manner of cutting out the coals is not the long way, as in the districts already described, by horse-roads and long workings, extending from one horse-way to another, and throwing back the spoil, the top, and the bottom measure (stratum), and the slack as they proceed; but the mode in the northern coal district is to cut out the coals so as to leave great rectangular masses, called pillars, behind them. To take an illustration from a familiar object, imagine a window to be a map or plan of a portion of a Durham coal-field. The wooden partitions between the panes of glass will represent the whole workings, or first workings, from which the coal has been cut. The panes of glass will represent the rectangular masses of coal left behind. The picture is not quite correct, inasmuch as the wooden partitions of a window are not in proportion large enough; but suppose it to be an old-fashioned window, such as we may sometimes see, where the wooden partitions take up one-third of the whole space of the window, then is the picture very near the truth. The whole workings in the coal cross at right angles, like the wooden partitions, and are in extent about one-third of the space, and the rectangular masses of coal occupy the remaining two-thirds. Such in form, and extending many square miles, are the great coal pits of the north.

249. "The pillars vary much in their length and breadth in different collieries, as well as in their distance from each other; but in general they are from 30 yards to 35 yards in length, and from 7 yards to 11 yards in breadth. The object in former times seems to have been to cut as much of the coals as they thought they could do, without letting down the roof by the pillars being crushed by the superincumbent weight, or without the floor being forced up between the pillars, or the pillars themselves being pressed downwards into the strata below. They thus abandoned more than half of the coals, and it is only the increased value of the coals in the present day which has induced the present proprietors to endeavour to cut down and send up what has been left behind" (Dr. Mitchell, Report, § 16, 22: App. Pt. I., p. 121).

250. The seams of coal in this district vary in thickness from two feet to seven feet. According to Mr. Edward Potter, coal-viewer and manager of the South Hetton Colliery, "the principal vein, which runs over the whole of the eastern part of the county of Durham, called the Hutton Vein, is from four to four feet and a half, and there is frequently two feet of coarse coal unfit for market, which is taken up to make horse-roads. The workings are very rarely, if anywhere, under three feet in this county, and by far the greater part of from three to four feet and a half. No seam below from two and a half to three feet in thickness would pay for working in this or the next county" (Ibid. § 147: p. 135).

251. In most pits the top and bottom of the coal consist of shale, or indurated clay, so that a portion of the top or bottom may, without heavy expense, be taken away, if deemed desirable, and sufficient space obtained for the convenient working of the pit. "This state of the mines is the most complete security that young Children are never employed, nor can be profitably employed, to bring the coals from the workings to the horse-ways, because such heavy work can be done far cheaper by strong boys and young men. The putters do not become of too large size for this work at fourteen, and from that age to fifteen, but may continue on to twenty-one, as most of them actually do" (Ibid. § 148: p. 135).

Mr. Thomas Crawford, jun., coal viewer, Little Town and Sherburn: "The seams in this county are not one in a hundred less than three feet in depth; and then when it does so happen there is a part cut away at the top or bottom to make the working three feet thick, which is the lowest we have. Our horse-way is five feet, or five feet six. Four feet is far more usual, and sometimes it is a little more" (Dr. Mitchell, Evidence, No. 88: App. Pt. I., p. 148, l. 12).

Evidence to the same effect is given by Mr. John Wood, manager of Clarence Hetton Colliery (Ibid. No. 90: p. 150, l. 23).

252. Carbureted hydrogen gas abounds so much in the mines of this district that great attention to ventilation is absolutely indispensable. Ventilation is here universally effected by means of the double shaft, or by one great shaft divided into upcast and downcast channels; and a current of air sufficiently powerful to force its way to the remotest parts of these immense mines is created by a furnace in the upcast shaft, which is kept constantly burning, day and night.

Thomas Crawford, jun., coal viewer, Little Town and Sherburn: "There are two shafts in each colliery, by one of which the air descends, and by the other it ascends. There is a great furnace, the entrance to which is forty yards from the foot of the shaft, and the air comes into the shaft at the height of three fathoms. There is the same mode adopted at the other colliery, and it is the usual method in this county. The furnaces are kept constantly burning, day and night, Sunday and all. We have had no explosion since we commenced, seven years ago. We have had no choke-damp; at least we never see it produce any effect" (Ibid. No. 88: p. 148, l. 4).—Edward Potter, coal viewer, South Hetton Colliery: "We have our shafts of 15 feet diameter, and divided into three equal parts at the centre, of course the angle is 120°. In the first working or whole working the men use candles exclusively, and are safe in so doing, as we can guide the air into every working part so as effectually to carry off dangerous gas. But when the men are at pillar-working, that is, removing the pillars, no candles are at all allowed, and the Davy-lamp alone is used; and for this reason, that it would be impossible when so large openings are made, and a vacant space left beyond, for us to secure the men against sudden danger from a large portion of the roof falling in, and throwing a huge flood of gas, and dashing it against the lights. When the stone is very hard, sometimes half an acre, sometimes a whole acre, and even in an extreme case, five acres may be left vacant, and the roof may break and fall down at once" (Ibid. No. 89: p. 149, l. 19).

253. In this district "the mines for the most part are dry; but there are excep-
tions. The place of working is on the whole very satisfactory, and such as persons accustomed to coal mines will consider very comfortable" (Dr. Mitchell, Report, § 145—150: App. Pt. I., pp. 134, 135).

254. NORTH DURHAM and NORTHUMBERLAND.—The seams of coal are here
described to range from 2 feet 6 inches to 5 feet 6 inches in thickness. The thinnest seams at present worked are those of Shilbottle Pit, which are about
2 feet 6 inches in thickness; St. Lawrence colliery, 2 feet 9 inches; Wylam, Walbottle, Sacristan, and Charlaw Pits, where the thinnest seam is 3 feet 2 inches. In most other pits the seams are from 5 to 6 feet thick.

255. It is stated by the coal viewers that, in general, in the narrow seams, the heights of the roads are never less than from 3 feet 4 inches to 4 feet. According to Mr. William Hunter, viewer of Walbottle Colliery, for instance, "Generally the heights are from 3 feet 4 inches to 4 feet. Hewers go in no lower places; wherever the seam is under 3 feet 2 inches high, height is made for the boys, either by taking up the bottom or taking down the top" (J. R. Leifchild, Esq., Evidence, No. 240: App. Pt. I. p. 618. l. 13).—Mr. Matthias Dunn and Mr. Edward Boyd, coal viewers, give similar evidence (Ibid. No. 261: p. 621, l. 44; and No. 495: p. 661, l. 33).

256. These statements may be true of the coal mines of which these gentlemen have the superintendence: nevertheless it appears from the evidence that there are collieries in which some of the roads, at least, are not more than 2 feet or 2 feet 2 inches high, and others in which they are not more than 3 feet high; and great complaint is made by the Young Persons working in these places, of the inconvenience and pain they suffer from the lowness of the roof and want of space to work in.

James Richardson, aged seventeen, putter: "In the Bensham seam they are putting places 2 feet high, and dare not keep their fingers on the tub at the top, else they would get knocked against the roof" (Ibid. No. 272: p. 624, l. 17).—James Richardson, a wasteman, says: "There are places here as long as 200 yards, where the height for the hewers is not more than 26 inches. One north-way is all low places, and perhaps one-third of the colliery is low in the ways" (Ibid. No. 266: p. 623. l. 4).—Mr. Oliver, under-viewer: "At Shilbottle Colliery he has seen boys put coals under a height of 30 inches only. The little lads there, of ten, twelve, thirteen, or fourteen, put the tubs by keeping their hands on the end of the tram, and putting their heads against the tub. The lads wear backskins there to keep their backs from hitting against the roof. There will perhaps be 20 lads doing this. The seam there is 30 inches thick, and they only cut away tops and bottoms for horses and ponies" (Ibid. No. 95: p. 584, l. 63).—William Ritson, going in thirteen, putter: "When he was at Blaydon Main, last year, he was in a place about 30 inches in height, and there he rubbed the skin off his back now and then, when he was putting a corf of 10 pecks by himself. The corf often stuck against the roof there" (Ibid. No. 176: p. 604, l. 64).—Henry Harrison, aged sixteen: "Worked

COAL MINES.

Place of Work.

North Durham
and
Northumberland.

*Subterranean road-
ways.*

at Hebburn four months ago. There he put. The seam was about 30 inches thick; but they made the height about a yard. Very often used to rub the skin off his back there: had a very sore back sometimes" (Ibid. No. 171: p. 603, l. 43).—John Scott, aged sixteen and a half, putter: "The height of the places is about a yard, in some places a bit more. Almost every day he hits his back against the roof. Whiles they may drop down upon their knees." (Ibid. No. 243: p. 619, l. 16).—Robert Crawford, aged sixteen, putter: "Sometimes it rubs the skin off his back. Some have felt so bad as to lie down a few minutes till their backs were less painful. Feel their backs stiff in the morning sometimes" (Ibid. No. 31: p. 574, l. 9).— Peter Rutter, aged fifteen, putter: "Is now putting in low places, and is strained sore at times. The skin of his back is often knocked off. Has now marks on his back where he has hit it yesterday and to-day" [Shows the marks] (Ibid. No. 127: p. 595, l. 51)—Michael Turner, aged fifteen and a half, helper-up: "Some places are low. Many times the skin is rubbed off his back and off his feet. His head works (aches) very often, almost every week. His legs work on (ache) sometimes so that he can hardly trail them" (Ibid. No. 145: p. 598, l. 59).— John Maffin, aged sixteen, putter: "In many places the corf scrapes against the roof. Some-times rubs the skin off his back by rubbing against the sides" (Ibid. No. 141: p. 597, l. 62).—Luke Gray, aged forty-two, hewer: "Many times the skin is off his back [that of the foal] by the corf rubbing it off. Last fortnight his back was skinned almost all the way down by the corf cowping [or falling] upon him, by getting off the tramway. He was off three days from this. He wears a backskin of leather: all the foals do here. The low-seam boys can travel bent very nearly double. They go nearly bent double in walking in general" (Ibid. No. 91: p. 584, l. 19).

Ventilation.

257. It is in this and the adjoining great coal districts that the true principle of ventilating coal mines has been fully developed, and very generally carried into the most complete operation, which the present state of science renders practicable. In this district either the double shaft, or the division of a single shaft into two, is almost universal, and an immense furnace in the upcast shaft, always burning night and day, is the ordinary mode of producing and maintaining the requisite currents of air. The Sub-Commissioner reports:—"As the pits abound in the inflammable gases, it is absolutely essential to adopt the most perfect system of ventilation that can be devised, and on this point the talent and ingenuity of the most eminent colliery viewers appear to have been concentrated. The main and general prin-ciples which have been carried out into their existing detailed system by the im-provements of John Buddle, Esq., and other experienced viewers, may be said to resolve themselves into these four particulars:—1. The downcast shaft. 2. The upcast shaft. 3. The free course for the entrance, transit, and exit of the atmo-spheric air. 4. The rarefying furnace at the bottom of the upcast shaft.

258. "If these four arrangements be complete, the ventilating system may be considered as nearly perfect as possible; but from the additional expense of sinking two shafts in cases of great depth or difficulty, the first two are frequently merged into one, and one shaft is made to answer the purposes of two, by an air-tight wooden division, denominated a 'brattice,' separating the shaft into two or three distinct, often triangular, compartments, one of which serves as a downcast and another as an upcast shaft.

259. "The agent of the ventilation is the difference between the weights of two columns of air, one of which is at the natural temperature, and the other rarefied by the heat of the furnace. The degree of rarefaction being proportionate to the heat, it follows that the efficiency of the ventilation is proportionate to the heat of the upcast shaft; which heat is very variable in different collieries: if there be a steam-engine under ground, the temperature is much increased; and if the mine be one in which gas is largely generated, it is essential to have a larger furnace than common. Thus the mean heat of one upcast shaft has been known to be 146° Fahrenheit, and that of another not more than 80°. Perhaps 90° may be assumed as the average mean temperature (taken half way between the top and bottom) of the Northern upcast shafts.

260. "The ventilating furnace is usually 5 or 6 feet wide, and is placed at some little distance from the bottom of the shaft. It is constantly burning, and repeatedly supplied with coal, and over it the return-air passes by day and by night. If, however, the returns become so impregnated with gases that they would take fire at the furnace, they are in that case conducted by a separate channel (denominated a 'dumb furnace' by Mr. Buddle) into the shaft, above the fiery furnace." (J. R. Leifchild, Esq., Report, § 164—167: App. Pt. I. pp. 539, 540).

Drainage.

261. Drainage, not being so essential to the safety of the coal-mine as ventilation, has been much less attended to in this district, and the wetness of many of the pits is grievously complained of by the workpeople as always increasing the severity of their labour, and often producing positive disease.

Robert Smith, aged seventeen, putter: "Is now in wet places in the high seam; the water

COAL MINES.

Place of Work.

North Durham
and
Northumberland.

Drainage.

is over his ankles in many places. Gets sore feet many times" (J. R. Leifchild, Esq., Evidence, (No. 226 : App. Pt. I. p. 614, 1. 55)'—Cuthbert Todd, aged nineteen, putter: "Some of the places here are wet, over his ankles. Is many times the most part of the day in water, over his ankles; most part of the pit is wet now; this causes a swelling in his face very often: whenever he gets his feet wet is very seldom clear of a swelled face [is suffering now from it]. Has been laid up many days from this, perhaps three or four days in a month sometimes. His head works (aches) very often" (Ibid. No. 229 : p. 615, 1. 27)·—Oswald Gleghorn, aged seventeen, putter: "The wet gave him colds and pains; putting now in a wet place; sometimes over his shoe-tops. May be two or three hours out of the twelve in the water" (Ibid. No. 232 : p. 615, 1. 58).— William Ellison, aged fifteen, putter: "Has had sore feet from the water, which is rather salt, and takes the skin off his feet once or twice in a month" (Ibid. No. 233 : p. 616, 1. 5).— George Faction, aged fourteen, half-marrow: "There is a good deal of stythe in the pit, and it is wet in some places; in one place up to his knees in water, and through this place he passes perhaps 50 or 60 times in a day. Often gets cold from wet, and the water is salt and cankery" (Ibid. No. 267 : p. 623, 1. 14).—Walter Windlow, aged sixteen, putter: "Hebburn was very wet, the wet falling from the roof, and being whiles up to the calf of his leg. This was the C. Pit. Was off work there a year very bad with colds; the water falling on him gave him so stiff a neck, that he could not turn it or go to work" (Ibid. No. 306 : p. 631, 1. 42).

262. No complaint is in general made either of the heat or cold of the coal-mines in this district. The temperature of the great majority of the pits is inoppressive, and that of some agreeable. In an instance in which the degree of heat was taken by the thermometer, namely, in one of the Hetton pits, in South Durham, the temperature was found to be 66° at the bottom of the shaft, and 70° in the workings; the narrowness of this range, a difference of four degrees only between the temperature at the foot of the shaft and in the recesses of the workings, being itself one satisfactory indication of the excellence of the ventilation. There is one coal mine, indeed, in this district, namely, the Monkwearmouth Colliery, remarkable for its extraordinary depth, in which the average temperature ranges from 78° to 80°.

Mr. Elliott, aged twenty, under-viewer, Monkwearmouth Colliery: "The peculiarities of this pit are the extraordinary depth, namely, 265 fathoms to the Bensham seam, 15 fathoms lower being sunk for "standage," or for a reservoir of water. The ordinary time consumed in going down and coming up the shaft is about from two to three minutes respectively. The tub for drawing coals, and also men and boys, is 7 feet high. It holds 105 peck of coals [Newcastle pecks]. The weight of these 105 pecks of coals by themselves is 50 cwt. The shaft produces always, or nearly so, a sensible weight on the drum of his ears when he descends and ascends the upcast shaft, which is always the case; the other division of the brattice being that for the pumping apparatus, and only descended by the engineers, and sometimes the viewer-in-chief, witness's brother."—Mr. George Elliott, aged twenty-seven: "Is the head viewer here, and at Washington, and at Belmont collieries. Has been viewer here about three years. The peculiarities of this pit are its extraordinary depth, and its consequent great heat. The heat of the unbroken coal or mine is at an average of about 78° (Fahrenheit). The extremest heat that he has known or worked in is 89°, being of course increased by the heat of his body, &c., animal heat" (Ibid. Nos. 366, 367: p. 641, 1. 37).

263. In so high a temperature, such labour as that of the colliery must, of course, be extremely oppressive, and in this case a remarkable irritation of the skin is very generally produced.

Alexander Ball, putter: "Is a very hot pit; hotter than Wallsend, Hebburn, or Walker pits. Heat sometimes gives him cold. Puts on a jacket when he comes up the pit. All work quite naked [except the drivers, trappers, and flatmen], with the exception of a front covering of flannel, and shoes" (Ibid. No. 369: p. 643, 1. 42).—George Allen, aged fifteen, driver: "Whiles the salt-water drops from the roof, and the heat together, strikes boils on the boys. The pit is o'er warm; and unless he gets a drink he is whiles sick" (Ibid. No. 371: p. 643, 1. 62). —W. J. Dodd, Esq., surgeon: "Is employed by the owners [of this colliery] for colliery accidents; and also attends in ordinary cases of sickness. Has not observed any peculiar difference in this colliery, excepting the great heat, and consequent thirst, and drinking of water. As to the "boils," when a fresh man comes to the colliery he generally becomes affected by these "boils," most probably from the heat in the first instance, and subsequently they are aggravated by the salt water. The salt water used to pour out in quantities from the dykes and troubles, which are frequently met with in the earlier workings of the pit. The water alluded to is not caustic, but exceedingly irritating. After a time, perhaps two or three months, the men become wholly free from "boils," and remain so ever after. In the first place, the great heat, averaging perhaps about 80° in the working places, affects the vessels and glands of the skin, which leads to the production of the boils, afterwards increased by the falling of the salt water upon them. Evidently the heat must be the chief cause, as these boils are sometimes on parts of the body that could not be reached by the salt water. The thing is more like a carbuncle than a boil. It discharges a little. The "tanner" is a detached portion of cellular substance which is cast off from this carbuncle. These carbuncles appear in succession for a month or two, and then perhaps wholly cease. A little aperient medicine and poultice generally suffice for them; they are very troublesome and irritating for the time they last. Has not heard of their occurring in other pits. The occurrence of these is so distinctive a mark of a fresh man, that witness is well aware of the man

CUAL MINES.

Place of Work.

North Durham
and
Northumberland.

Temperature.

being unaccustomed to the pit from this occurrence. They come more on the hewers and men than the boys. The hewers are more exposed to alterations of temperature, and greater physical exertion and confinement of space, and consequently more likely (from being more heated) to suffer from carbuncles. The hewers work perhaps more naked than others, which exposes them to the salt water, &c. This water is more like the diluted brine of a pickle tub than salt water in common. These carbuncles mostly appear on the legs, from the knee downwards, and on the fore-arm. Out of 12 fresh comers not more than three or four perhaps come to witness for these swellings" (Ibid. No. 385 : p. 645, l. 33).

264. EAST OF SCOTLAND.—The seams of coal here vary in thickness from 13 inches to 22 feet, and the height of the main roads ranges from 3 to 6 feet. "Where the roof is hard—of freestone, for instance, the height is generally 4½ to 6 feet ; when soft, a continual cutting or clearing takes place by a set of men and girls, who *rede* (clear) the roads and ways every night ; otherwise the soft material would soon sink and close up the roads ; and it has occurred that the whole of the roof round the pit-shaft has closed up the shaft. A miraculous escape of thirteen persons from a similar accident occurred in the year 1839 at Edmonstone Colliery, in Mid-Lothian, where the roofs are low and soft, and the long-wall system of taking away the coal is in operation" (R. H. Franks, Esq., Report, § 5 : App. Pt. I., p. 383).

Mr. David Butt, overseer, Dysart Colliery, Fifeshire : "Our coal is 22 feet thick, and we quarry the same from top to bottom ; and horses draw from wall-face to the pit-bottom on main roads trammed with iron ; the lowest horseway is six feet high" (R. H. Franks, Esq., Evidence, No. 419 : App. Pt. I., p. 510, l. 31).— Mr. James A. Naysmith, taxman, Blair Engine Colliery. Perthshire : "The seam of coal being six to seven feet thick upon which I am now working, no very young children need be employed—nor are they at any time necessary (Ibid. No. 326 : p. 495, l. 1).—Mr. James Grier, manager of the mines belonging to the Earl of Elgin, Elgin Colliery, Fifeshire : "The roads in our mines are all railed, and the roofs cut from four and a half to five feet high, but the workings are the same height as the seams of coal, which are three feet eight inches, four, and five feet" (Ibid. No. 339 : p. 497, l. 11).—Mr. David Adams, overseer to the Edmonstone Colliery : "The thickness of the seams is from 32 inches to 5 feet, and the main roads are 42 inches to 5 feet high" (Ibid. No. 27 : p. 441, l. 32).

265. It appears from the evidence that even in the narrow seams the height of the main roads is in general not less than three feet.

Joseph Davison, seventeen years old, coal hewer, Preston Hall Colliery, Cranston : "The seam is only 24 inches, and the road three feet high" (Ibid. No. 105 : p. 456, l. 45).—George Oliver, mining overman, Haugh Lynn Colliery : "The height of the coal varies from 14 to 19 inches. Children draw from the wall-face to the main roads, which are three feet high" (Ibid. No. 113 : p. 457, l.53).—(See also witnesses, Nos. 192, 283, 327, &c.)

266. But though in general the main roads in these collieries are not less than three feet in height, yet it appears that there are coal mines in which the side roads, at least, do not exceed from 22 to 28 inches in height. "The workings in the various seams are sometimes 100 to 200 yards from the main roads ; so that the females have to crawl backwards and forwards with their small carts in seams in many cases not exceeding 22 to 28 inches in height." "The negligence of the under-ground workings corresponds with that above, the roads being carelessly attended to, and the workings very irregularly carried on, so that the oppression of the labour is as much increased by the want of good surveillance as by the irregularity of the workpeople themselves" (R. H. Franks, Esq., Report, § 8 : App. Pt. I., p. 383).

267. In regard to ventilation, the coal-mines in the East of Scotland are in general in a deplorable state. Some of the proprietors say that "every known improvement has been applied to their own mines," and several of the workpeople admit that improvements have lately been introduced ; but the Report of the Sub-Commissioner, and the evidence given by all classes of witnesses, fully justify the opinion expressed on this subject by Matthias Dunn, Esq., viewer of St. Laurence Main and Shield Field Collieries, Northumberland : "Thinks that the main principles of ventilation in many parts of Scotland are ill understood, and as ill practised as understood, to the great danger of the workmen ; they can exist in this state, but minor accidents are constantly happening" (J. R. Leifchild, Esq., Evidence, No. 261 : App. Pt. I., p. 621, l. 50).

Henry Giddes, managing partner, Bannockburn Colliery, Stirlingshire : "As far as the health and safety of our mines are concerned, every known improvement possible to be applied to our mines we have had recourse to. Means are employed to secure the constant operation of currents of air along the wall-faces, and properly constructed air-courses, and furnaces for rarefying the air, are resorted to. Hydrogen gas exists in our mines, and two explosions have taken place within the last two years, but not of a fatal nature. Davy-lamps are used where and when necessary, and are always in overman's charge ready for use" (R. H. Franks, Esq., Evidence, No. 285: p. 489, l. 13). — Similar statements are made by Thomas Bywater, Esq., proprietor (No. 413); Henry Chisholm, manager (No. 391); John Marshall, overman (No. 278); Robert Maxton, manager (No. 318); and others.

On the other hand, David Butt, overseer, Dysart Colliery, Fifeshire, says: "We have no other method of ventilating our pits than by leaving open unemployed shafts" (Ibid. No. 419: p. 510, l. 37).—Mr. John Paton, manager, Largo Ward Colliery, Fifeshire: "The choke-damp gathers below in soft weather, and the small coal below has often taken fire spontaneously, and acted injuriously on the men, but they have always recovered on exposure to the air" (Ibid. No. 421: p. 511, l. 7).—George Oliver, mining overman, Haugh Lynn Colliery: "At times bad air is in the pit, and so it is in all" Ibid. No. 113: p. 457, l. 54).—Janet Cumming, eleven years old: "Bears coals; obliged to scramble out when bad air was in the pit" (Ibid. No. 1: p. 436, l. 12).—Jessy Wright, eleven years old, coal-bearer: "I leave work when bad air is in the pit, which has frequently occurred since I've been here" (Ibid. No. 13: p. 439, l. 11).—Alison Adam, twelve years old, coal-bearer, Edmonstone Colliery, parish of Newton: "Bad air frequently stops my breath" (Ibid. No. 12: p. 439, l. 3).—Isabella Read, twelve years old, coal-bearer: "When the weather is warm there is difficulty in breathing, and frequently the lights go out" (Ibid. No. 14: p. 439, l. 30).—James Wood, twelve years old, coal-hewer, Tranent Colliery: "When bad air is in the pit we are compelled to stop away sometimes for three and four days together" (Ibid. No. 157: p. 465, l. 18).—Margaret Watson, sixteen years of age, coal-bearer: "We often have bad air below, had some a short time since, and lost brother by it; he sunk down, and I tried to draw him out, but the air stopped my breath and I was forced to gang." (Ibid. No. 115: p. 458, l. 15).—See also witnesses Nos. 105, 153, 346, 428, et seq.

268. In general the drainage in this district is quite as bad as the ventilation. "The roads are most commonly wet, but in some places so much so as to come up to the ankles; and where the roofs are soft the drippy and slushy state of the entire chamber is such that none can be said to work in it in a dry condition, and the coarse apparel the labour requires absorbs so much of the drainage of water, as to keep the workmen as thoroughly saturated as if they were working continually in water" (R. H. Franks, Esq., Report, § 7: App. Pt. I., p. 383).

Alexander Gray, ten years old, pump-boy, New Craighall Colliery: "I pump out the water in the under-bottom of the pit to keep the men's rooms dry. I am obliged to pump fast or the water would cover me. I had to run away a few weeks ago, as the water came up so fast that I could not pump at all, and the men were obliged to gang. The water frequently covers my legs and those of the men, when they sit to pick." (R. H. Franks, Esq., Evidence, No. 68: App. Pt. I., p. 449, l. 17).—John Duncan, ten years old, trapper, East and West Bryant's Collieries: "Where I sit is very wet, but I dry myself when I go home" (Ibid. No. 38: p. 443, l. 52).— Thomas Duncan, eleven years old, trapper, East and West Bryant's Collieries: "There is plenty of water in the pit; the part I am in it comes up to my knees" (Ibid. No. 42: p. 444, l. 20).— Robert Thomson, eleven years old, horse-driver, New Craighall Colliery: "The pit is very wet and sair drippie. The women complain of the wet, but they are obliged to like it." (Ibid. No. 69: p. 449, l. 37).—Janet Cumming, eleven years old, bears coals, Sheriff Hall and Somerside Colliery: "The water comes frequently up to the calves of my legs" (Ibid. No. 1: p. 436, l. 9).—Alexander Reid, twelve years old: We often work in slush over our shoe-tops" (Ibid. No. 7: p. 437, l. 43).—Janet Moffat, twelve years old, coal-putter, New Craighall Colliery, parish of Inveresk: "The place of work is very wet and covers my shoe-tops." (Ibid. No. 70: p. 449, l. 50).—John Allen, twelve years old, hewer, Bannockburn Colliery, Stirlingshire: "Works in the Plean Pit, which is full of water; the water having risen above the dip." (Ibid. No. 290: p. 489, l. 41).—Margaret Harper, thirteen years old, putter, Hard Hill Colliery, West Lothian: "It is dirty slavish work, and the water quite covers our ankles" (Ibid. No. 188: p. 471, l. 24).—Margaret Hipps, seventeen years old, putter, Stoney Rigg Colliery, Stirlingshire: "The pavement I drag over is wet, and I am obliged at all times to crawl on hands and feet with my bagie hung to the chain and ropes" (Ibid. No. 233: p. 479, l. 53).—(See also witnesses, Nos. 97, 46, 309). Margaret Chirce, twelve years old, putter, Kipps Colliery, West Lothian: "Father has the dropsy from sitting in wet work" (Ibid. No. 212: p. 475, l. 45).—Alexander Gillespie, twelve years old, hewer, Lochgellie Colliery, Fifeshire: "Father dead, died from dropsy, brought on by sitting in damp work" (Ibid. No. 394: p. 506, l. 2).—Catherine Walter, sixteen years old, putter, Donibristle Colliery, Fifeshire: "Father died some time gone of dropsy, from sitting in damp work and bad air" (Ibid. No. 378: p. 503, l. 18).—Ann Smith, seventeen years old, coal-putter, East and West Bryant's Collieries: "Father died a few years since of cramp in the limbs from sitting in wet work; he was thirty-eight years of age" (Ibid. No. 50: p. 445, l. 33).

269. WEST OF SCOTLAND.—In the coal fields of this district the seams vary in thickness from 12 inches to 14 and 15 feet; and it is stated by the Sub-Commissioner that it is a general rule that colliers have no right to complain if the roads are kept 3 feet high, and they are usually a few inches more than this. Mr. James Allan, manager of the Gowan Colliery, records a striking illustration of the superior efficiency of ventilation with the double shaft and furnace.—

He states that, when depending for ventilation on a single shaft divided by a partition of

COAL MINES.
—
Place of Work.
East of Scotland.
—
Ventilation.

Drainage.

West of Scotland.
—
Subterranean road-ways.

Ventilation.

timber, although "every precaution was taken to prevent an accumulation of the inflammable air, several explosions did take place by which a number of the workmen were burned, and some lives were lost; the employment in consequence was very unsteady, and attended with great expense. In order to remedy this great and growing evil, an additional shaft was sunk (7 feet diameter) at the distance of 12 feet from the original one; new machinery adapted for raising the coals by these two pits was erected; the wooden partition was taken out of the old shaft, and a furnace erected at the bottom of the new one, which is kept constantly burning: the effects of this alteration, as was anticipated, have been the efficient ventilation of the workings, the workmen enjoying comparative safety, and being kept in regular work. All the pits at the colliery are now fitted up upon the same principle, having a partition of solid strata betwixt them in place of a wooden one; the first outlay is considerable, but, after being fitted, becomes a great saving of expense, independent of its other beneficial results" (T. Tancred, Esq., Evidence, No. 3: App. Pt. I., p. 357, l. 52).

270. The Sub-Commissioner adds: "Mr. Houston, of Johnstone Castle, showed me a very simple instrument which he had found very effectual in drawing out impure air from his pits. It was merely a circular fan with vanes like those of a winnowing-machine, only working horizontally in a circular case. This case was fixed air-tight into the mouth of the pit, and being worked by hand was so powerful that its effects extended to the distance of three-quarters of a mile. To show the power it possessed, a part of the pit being on fire, the fan drew the flames and heated air towards it with such force that men were able to approach sufficiently near to erect a wall round the part on fire, and thus to prevent its spreading. Black-damp was also drawn out of a pit where it was applied, so that a man could walk behind it with a lamp, which, if he extended it far enough, would be instantly extinguished, showing exactly where the body of gas was" (T. Tancred, Esq., Report, § 75: App. Pt. I., p. 331).

271. NORTH WALES.—In many of the mines in this district the roads are low and narrow, the air foul, and the places in which the people work dusty, dirty, and damp. The ventilation in general is very imperfect; but the managers of the works state that improvements in ventilation are now beginning to be introduced.

Mr. James Eddy, agent, Aberderfyn Coal Works: "There is inflammable air in the pits. We have done much to improve ventilation, and with good effect. The men use safety-lamps, and every precaution to avoid accidents is used" (H. H. Jones, Esq., Evidence, No. 36: App. Pt. II. p. 384, l. 61).—Daniel Ellis, under-ground agent, Plas Mostyn Colliery, Wrexham: "A good deal of improvement has taken place in the system of working coal. We work it narrower than formerly. When we used to work a greater width more gas was generated, and the danger greater. We have plenty of air now, by good air-ways and shafts: use safety-lamps" (Ibid. No. 52: p. 392, l. 1).

272. SOUTH WALES.—In the Blaenavon and Clydach Iron and Coal Works in the north-eastern angle of the South Wales Mineral Basin, near Abergavenny, the thickness of the seams of coal varies from $2\frac{1}{2}$ feet to $3\frac{1}{2}$ feet. The horse-roads are 5 feet 6 inches to 6 feet high; the roads where horses are not employed, 5 feet, 4 feet, and $3\frac{1}{2}$ feet high. The works are entered in part by shafts, but principally by levels. The head-gear and chains are of the best quality; the workmen need not descend into the mines at all by the chains, as there are footways to go to the bottom of the shafts from the surface. It is not the wish of the employers that any should descend or come up the pits at all by the chains (as there are footways to the workings), only during the time the new pits are being sunk (R. W. Jones, Esq., Report, § 6, 7, 8: App. Pt. II., p. 610). In the Abersychan Coal Works the seam of coal is seven feet thick; and, according to David Rees, aged sixteen, haulier, "The roads are high enough to walk in anywhere" (Evidence, No. 24: App. Pt. II., p. 605, l. 58). In the Coal and Iron Works in the vicinities of Bridgend, Neath, and Swansea, in the county of Glamorgan, according to H. Cooper, clerk to the Cambrian Iron and Spelter Company, "The thickness of the seams of coal varies from 18 inches to 6 feet; and the smallest height of the mainways is 5 feet 6 inches" (R. W. Jones, Esq., Report, § 4: App. Pt. II., p. 666).

In the new iron works of Messrs. Jevans and Company, in the Vale of Neath, according to W. Jevons, Esq., one of the partners, "The beds of coal vary from 3 feet to 18 feet in thickness; the mainways are all high enough for a horse; the coals are drawn out in frames or waggons by horses along the main levels, but boys between thirteen and eighteen years of age are employed to draw (single) such trams from the stalls to the main levels" (R. W. Jones, Esq., Report, § 8, Pt. II., p. 667.)—According to George Crane, Esq., proprietor of the Yniscedwin Works, "The thickness of the seams of ironstone coal varies from 22 inches to 20 feet; but there are not any worked under 3 feet. The lowest mainways are about 5 feet 6 inches high" (Ibid. § 11: p. 668, l. 1),

273. In some of the great works in this district much attention is paid to ventilation; and when any parts of them are ill ventilated, " it is the result of casual circumstances, and the free ventilation is speedily restored and maintained " (R. W. Jones, Esq., Report, § 16: App. Pt. II., p. 583).

According to William Hood, Esq., manager of the Abersychan Works, "Furnaces are sometimes employed to assist the ventilation. This keeps the workings well aired, and is the principle employed at all the pits" (R. W. Jones, Esq., Report: App. Pt. II., p. 590, l. 34).—Samuel Burgess, colliery agent, Pontypool Collieries: " The air is generally good where the boys are put. Our air now is as pure under ground as it can be; we do not use Davy-lamps. Our longest way is more than a mile and a quarter long. We have got it now all through the mountain, and out the other side" (Ibid. No. 8: p. 599, l. 49).

274. But it appears from the Evidence and Report of R. H. Franks, Esq., that in great numbers of coal-mines in this district ventilation is grossly neglected, and that this neglect is in part occasioned by the comparative immunity of these mines from carbureted hydrogen gas. The prevalence of carbonic acid gas, although it undermines the health of the workpeople, does not kill instantaneously like fire-damp. The presence of a quantity of carbonic acid gas sufficient to produce the most injurious effect on the people, may yet not be sufficient absolutely to stop the working of the mine; but the evidence shows that as long as it is possible to go on, as long as a candle will burn, as long, that is, as there is air enough to support the degree of combustion necessary to afford light, the labour is continued. When this noxious gas so far prevails over the quantity of atmospheric air supplied to the workings, that the combustion of a candle can no longer be maintained, then the people leave off work for a few days, and the necessity which compels this temporary cessation of labour under such circumstances is regarded as a hardship by some of the proprietors. " We have carbonic acid gas in the workings," says Morgan Thomas, Esq., Craigyralt Colliery, parish of Eglwysilan, Glamorganshire: " I nearly lost my life once in it. I lost a great deal by bad air preventing the work the summer before last" (R. H. Franks, Esq., Evidence, No. 120: App. Pt. II., p. 523, l. 58). "Air-doors are not necessary," says Mr. Jonathan Isaacs, agent, Top Hill Colliery, Glamorganshire: " *There is no fire-damp*; there is some little choke-damp in this and the other pits in the neighbourhood, and many men suffer from the asthma which it creates at the age of from thirty-five to forty" (Ibid. No. 144: p. 527, l. 63).

275. "There is," says the Sub-Commissioner, " a particular vein of coal, being a red-ash coal, extending from Penwhyn Frank, in the parish of Trevethan, in the county of Monmouth, to Llanvabon Church, in the county of Glamorgan; and from Mammoel, in the parish of Bedwellty, in the county of Monmouth, to Church Farm, in the parish of Mynyodduslwyn, in the same county; to this my attention was more particularly drawn by the fact, elicited in the course of examination in that district, of the frequent stoppages of the works, in consequence of choke-damp; and as the subject is of peculiar interest in the economy of mines and the health of the miners, I subjoin the following communication on the subject, received from Edward Scott Barber, Esq., mineral surveyor of Newport:

" The principal seam at present in work for the supply of the export trade of Newport is a red-ash coal, in which fire-damp is not found. The absence of fire-damp in this vein [the Mynyodduslwyn] has operated very prejudicially throughout the district, by creating a confidence in the minds of the parties engaged, that whatever the state of the ventilation may be, no explosion of fire-damp can possibly occur; consequently the ventilation of the collieries is much neglected. It is a common occurrence for colliers to be obliged to leave their work from not being able to keep their lights in, and, in some cases, when the wind is at an opposite point to the level, the ventilation is so bad as to stop the work; the colliers work as long as they can keep a light in, but the small quantity of air necessary barely to maintain combustion must be a very unhealthy atmosphere for respiration" (R. H. Franks, Esq., Report, § 118: App. Pt. II., p. 489).

276. As the general result of his investigations in this district, the Sub-Commissioner reports: "That labour, in the collieries of the counties of Glamorgan and Pembroke, in South Wales, and of Monmouth in England, is, from want of proper ventilation and economy of mining operations, extremely unwholesome, and productive of diseases which have a manifest tendency either to shorten life or reduce the number of years of useful labour in the mechanic" (Ibid. § 125: p. 491).

277. The collieries in this district appear in general to be dry, excepting in the main-roads, which are often wet and muddy, and many of the workpeople complain

of their feet being constantly wet. Of the Dowlais Collieries it is stated that they are among "the finest in South Wales, and, with the exception of the wet and dirt on the roads, arising from the magnitude of the workings, and the traffic of trams and horses upon them, everything appeared to be in the best working order. From the whole of the Dowlais Collieries I was informed that they raise about 1500 tons of coal per day, the whole of which is consumed in their own gigantic works" (R. W. Jones, Esq., Evidence No. 136: App. Pt. II, p. 649, l. 23.) See witnesses Nos. 14, 25, 53, 184.

278. FOREST OF DEAN.—In this coal field the thickness of the seam of coal varies from two to five feet. In the collieries working the thickest seams, horse-roads are made up to the headings, and the coals are drawn by horses direct from the workings to the foot of the shaft.

Mr. John Trotter Thomas, managing proprietor of coal-works at Howlett's Slade: "In most of our collieries the horseways go up to the headings. The Darby and Mile-end Pits are the only exceptions; where the coal is carted into the horseway. We use no hodding. We work four feet and a half seam" (E. Waring, Esq., Evidence, No. 39: App. Pt. II., p. 26, l. 10).—David Mushet, Esq., proprietor and worker, Bixslade, near Coleford: "The vein of coal averages five feet; in these works there is no hodding" (Ibid. No. 37: p. 25, l. 4).—Mr. Peter Teague, managing partner, Hopewell New Engine and Prosper Pits: "We have no vein in work less than from four to five feet thick" (Ibid. No. 18: p. 19, l. 10).

279. In this district, however, seams of coal are worked not exceeding two feet, and from two feet to two feet ten inches thick.—

Mr. Samuel Barton, aged forty-one, manager of the Tormentor Pit, near Bilson: "Our seam is two feet thick. We work away some of the top to make a better headway for the hodders. Our vein dips a good deal, which gives them easy hauling with the full hods. They have only the empty ones to pull *up*" (Ibid. No. 44: App. Pt. II., p. 28, l. 34)—Mr. Stephen Yemm, manager, Churchaway, Nofold, and Protection Coal Pits, near Bilson: "Work a vein of two feet two inches; use hods drawn by boys through very low-roofed passages" (Ibid. No. 29: p. 22, l. 23).—Mr. John Davis, aged thirty-three, manager of the Haywood Coal Pit near Cinderford: "We work a two-feet-ten-inch vein: we clear a sufficient headway by cutting away the clod at bottom; the roof is sound rock" (Ibid. No. 43: p. 28, l. 9).

280. The lowest height of the roads in these thin-seamed mines is not stated either in the Report or Evidence; but it will be observed that it is said by one of the witnesses (Ibid. No. 29: p. 22, l. 25) that the passages "are very low roofed;" and it is distinctly stated by another witness that in some of the coal-mines in the neighbouring district the roads do not exceed two feet six inches in height. By the same evidence it also appears that there is no real necessity for working in such contracted spaces, since "there is a bed of soft stuff above the coal."

281. On this subject, David Mushet, Esq., expresses a very strong and decided opinion "that there is no necessity for boys being ever obliged to work in such contracted ways as compel them to go on their hands and knees. In *all* cases the rubbish might be so removed from the narrow workings as to give sufficient headway: and the only reason it is not done is the increased expense to the proprietor, and consequent deduction from his profits. The original railway in the old Forest pits was a single pole carried along the middle of the road about eighteen inches from the floor; on this a sliding cart was placed, containing the coal, and the man conveying it had to balance his load whilst he propelled it. The next stage of improvement was laying beech planks on each side, and employing carts with wooden wheels. Has seen the knees and palms of men and boys, who have worked long in narrow seams, perfectly *hoofed* by continued pressure on those parts" (Ibid. No. 37: p. 24, l. 42).

282. In like manner it is stated that "it would be easy for the coal-owners to give the hod-boys more headway—and *reasonable* that they should do so—by clearing out a portion of the rubbish, widening the passage, and stowing away the clod at the sides. This is done in some pits, where the veins are equally shallow, that the boys may not be forced literally to crawl like reptiles through the bowels of the earth" (E. Waring, Esq., Report, § 80: App. Pt. II., p. 7).

283. The mines in this coal field are wholly exempt from carbureted hydrogen gas; and carbonic acid gas is not very prevalent. There is a general concurrence of opinion among the witnesses examined that the ventilation at present is sufficient to obviate danger to the workpeople, and to prevent them from sustaining any material injury from the want of fresh air.—

David Davies, Esq., of Althorp House, Sydney, lessee and worker of the Hopewell and

Miles's Level Collieries, near Coleford : " The pits are well ventilated. Fire-damp is unknown in the Forest, and there is very little choke-damp" (E. Waring, Esq., Evidence, No. 8: App. Pt. II., p. 15, l. 51). —David Mushet, Esq. : " The carbonic acid gas used to be very troublesome when we had a less supply of pure air than now. The recent Act of Parliament, granting powers to sink air-shafts in the Forest enclosures, is likely essentially to benefit the workings" (Ibid. No. 37 : p. 24, l. 50). —See also witnesses Nos. 46, 9, 18, 25.

284. Great attention is paid in this district to the drainage of the coal-mines, by which the roads are kept dry under-foot, while expedients are adopted to protect the workpeople from the drippings of the roofs.

David Mushet, Esq. : " We carry off all our water by drainage, and keep the workings dry under-foot. The men are protected from drippings through the roof, as well as can be done, by iron plates and boards" Ibid. No. 37: p. 25, l. 12).—Mr. Aaron Goold, manager, Bilson : " The pits are quite dry" (Ibid. No. 14 : p. 17, l. 45).—Mr. Peter Teague : " A good deal of water in wet seasons, which is carried off by drainage. The workings are generally quite dry" (Ibid. No. 18 : p. 19, l. 2).—Mr. John Blanch, Futtrill : " One working is wet, the remainder are quite dry : use boards over the wet workings to protect the men (Ibid. No. 25 : p. 21, l. 14). —Mr. John Trotter Thomas, managing proprietor of coal works at Howlett's Slade : " The water is carried off by drainage. The men are protected by plates and boards when working under drippings" (Ibid. No. 39 : p. 26, l. 12).

285. SOUTH GLOUCESTERSHIRE.—In this coal field the seams vary from one foot to six feet in thickness. In the collieries working the thick seams, the main and side roads are sufficiently large to allow all the operations of the mine to be carried on without oppression to the workpeople. But, in some cases, as at Yate Common, the extreme narrowness of the seams altogether precludes adults even from cutting out the coal ; and the work is, therefore, performed by young lads whose size, it is said, " is suited to the contracted space;" the height in some instances being no more than two feet (E. Waring, Esq., Report, § 6 : App. Pt. II., p. 31).

Mr. Joseph Staley, managing partner, Yate Common : " The thickest vein is 2 feet 6 inches, and is worked by the young men : the boys cart through a 2 feet 6 inch passage-way; the young men have 4 feet, there being a bed of soft stuff above the coal to cut away before they come to the roof" (Ibid. Evidence, No. 49 : p. 39, l. 42).—Mr. Samuel Long, underground manager, Hole Lane : " The seams worked are 6 feet and 2 feet 6 inches ; depth of the several shafts are 108, 60, and 34 fathoms ; worked by steam-engines ; running-stages over the pits. The Cowherne Pit requires sixteen hours out of twenty-four pumping to keep dry : the engine is thirty-six-horse power ; that at the deep pit is sixty-four-horse power (Ibid. No. 59 : p. 42, l. 30). —Henry Hewitt, Esq., assistant-manager of coal works at Coal-pit Heath, consisting of eight pits, carried on by Sir John Smyth, Bart., and Co. : " Have very little use for doors in the pits, the workings being so extensively connected with each other that the ventilation is perfect ; not troubled with bad air, being well ventilated everywhere" (Ibid. No. 48 : App. Pt. II., p. 39, l. 15).—Mr. Thomas Waters, managing partner of the coal works at Warmley : " Ventilation good, except when the wind sets against the pit's mouth, when the foul air is troublesome" (Ibid. No. 51 : p. 40, l. 25).—Mr. William Bryant, underground manager, Golden Vale : " Foul air is kept under by ventilation, but is often troublesome. Had one man fall down insensible from it, but was restored on being taken into the fresh air" (Ibid. No. 61 : p. 43, l. 1).—Mr. Charles James, underground manager of the Short-Wood Collieries : " Workings kept middling dry by engine-pump" (Ibid. No. 67 : p. 44, l. 13).—Henry Hewitt, Esq. : " Kept dry by four pumping-engines, two of which are generally sufficient" (Ibid. No. 48 : p. 39, l. 5).—Mr. Joseph Staley, managing partner of coal works at Yate Common : " The workings are quite dry ; a pumping-engine of sixty-horse power is constantly at work when there is water : three or four days a-week is sufficient in summer" (Ibid. No. 49 : p. 39, l. 50).

286. IRELAND.—Of the collieries in Kilkenny and Queen's Counties, it is reported that " The passages are narrow and low, seldom more than three feet high, and often less. In many places there was but just sufficient room for me to crawl. I did not recover from the effects of the severe labour of this underground visit for several days, the muscles of my legs being so painful as almost to prevent my walking." (F. Roper, Esq., Report, § 6 : App. Pt. I., p. 873).

287. At the Drumglass Colliery in the county of Tyrone, " the pit is exposed to the disadvantage of much water coming into it : this is of course raised out, and the working ' is less exposed to noxious gases than it is in most others. We have not had occasion for the safety-lamp yet, there being next to no damp.'" At that of Coal Island, in the same county, " the place is very airy, and is as dry as a clayey bottom will admit of its being, effectual care being taken to keep the pit clear of water. No ' damp' in this mine ; the safety-lamp has never been wanted ; and there is so sufficient a supply of air that ' we have not a single forcing-pump'" T. Martin, Esq., Notes of Evidence, App. Pt. I., p. 884, l. 19 ; p. 885, l. 20).

K

6.—NATURE OF EMPLOYMENT IN COAL MINES.

288. From the widely different conditions under which, as has been shown, coal mines are worked in different districts, the nature of the employment in each must be materially different: it is, therefore, necessary to present a brief account of the various occupations of Children and Young Persons in this branch of industry in each district.

289. SOUTH STAFFORDSHIRE.—Besides adult colliers the persons employed in working the pits in this district consist of air-door boys, fillers, slack-boys, pitchers, pushers, and drivers. The air-door boy, or trapper, commonly the youngest person employed in the mine, has the charge of a door placed in a road, along which horses, men, and boys are constantly passing, but through which it is essential to the ventilation of the mine to prevent the current of air from the downcast shaft from passing, in order that this current may be forced round the other roads and workings of thepit. The duty of the trapper is to open this door for persons who have occasion to pass through it, and then to shut it again as quickly as possible; and on his keeping this door constantly shut, excepting at the moment when persons are passing through it, the safety of the mine, and the lives of the persons employed in it, entirely depend.

290. As the adult colliers, here called holers, gradually undermine the coal and advance backwards perhaps as far as 15 or 16 yards, leaving between the floor and the coal barely sufficient space to admit their own bodies, young persons called fillers crawl after them, push out the larger pieces of coal, and carry them to the carriages, called "skips," in which they are removed. After the young men have carried away the large coal to put it on the skips, boys, called slack-boys, crawl in to rake the small coal and the coal-dust, termed slack, into baskets, and then carry the baskets backwards and throw their contents into the "gobbing," or now empty space from which the coals have been taken. These boys are also employed in cleaning the air-ways.

291. As the process of undergoing proceeds, pillars are left on which the coals are supported; "and when," says the Sub-Commissioner, "it is intended to make a great mass fall down, the miners attack the pillars with prickers, that is, with instruments at the end of long handles, having a sharp point, and at the side a hook or projection, so that the miner may strike with the point and tear away with the hook. After a time the pillar is worked so small that it cracks and yields, and at once down falls a mass of several hundred tons." Then the fillers, and all who are employed in conveying the coal to the shaft, are obliged to work with the utmost vigour. Nothing is now left to support the roof; and as it must be expected to fall soon, every exertion is put forth to remove the coals rapidly; and sometimes for this purpose two sets are employed to work night and day, since the fall of the roof before the removal of the coals would not only cause the loss of the coals, but would also endanger life and limb.

292. The coals in these mines being obtained in very large masses, boys are quite unable to load the skips; this, as has been stated, is the work of the fillers; but the latter are assisted by boys called pitchers, who are useful in pitching the coals in the skips; that is in balancing them or adjusting them so as to build up a load, and in placing the broad iron rings or girdles about them.

293. In the mines in which the seams of coal are too narrow, and the roads too low for horses to go up to the workings, boys, called pushers, commonly from ten to eleven years of age, though some are as old as from seventeen to eighteen, push the carriages either from the workings to the horseways, or the whole distance from the workings to the foot of the shaft. The youngest of the boys employed to drive the horses in these pits are from ten to eleven years of age, but some of them are young men from seventeen to eighteen (Dr. Mitchell, Report, App. Pt. I., § 93—97: p. 11). From this account of the work to be done in the mines of this great coal field, it is obvious that the massiveness of the coal precludes the possibility of the employment of very young Children, except to go errands for the men, or to open and shut doors.

294. NORTH STAFFORDSHIRE.—In the coal districts of Cheadle and the Potteries, boys are employed as trappers, and to drive horses; but the principal labour of youths, for few under thirteen are employed, is in pushing and in drawing the

coals from the workings to the mainways, in carriages called skips, by a harness termed " byats," which consists of a pair of leather straps "over the shoulders, meeting in a broad piece behind, and terminating in a chain and hook—a pair of closed scissors would well illustrate its shape. The corves when loaded weigh from 4 to 5 cwt.; they rest on rails and are mounted on wheels" (S. S. Scriven, Esq., Report, § 9—15: App. Pt. II., p. 128, 129).

Mr. Thomas Holmes, fifty years of age, occupier of Delph House Colliery, Cheadle: " The boys are engaged generally in waggoning, pushing, and pulling; they pull their jacket, waistcoat, and shirt off, and put on a flannel donkin (under flannel jacket), and draw in byats (two pieces of leather over the shoulders, falling down over the back and terminating in a chain and hook), which they attach to the skips or waggons—they work singly, unless one is poorly or weak, then they work in pairs; the heights of our waggon-ways are 4 feet or 4½, so that there is not much stooping in the draw-roads; there is in the workings, where the men work in the flexed position, to which they become so used that, if you see a number together in the highways of a pit, it is ten to one but that they will take it to relieve themselves" (S. S. Scriven, Esq., Evidence, No. 21: App. Pt. II., p. 137, l. 44).— Edward Edwards, forty-one years of age, charter-master, Woodhead Colliery, Cheadle: " The employment of the boys is to push the waggons or skips upon the rail in pairs; if one cannot do it another is put on; the weight comes to about 4 cwt, and the number they draw from the workings to the pit's mouth is 108 or 109 rucks. We have no horse in the pit, the waggon-ways being level; they (the boys) work in their waiscoats, but without coats or shirts, and with a girdle over their shoulders" (Ibid. No. 17: p. 136, l. 36).—John Hammond, fourteen years of age, drawer, Woodhead Colliery, Cheadle: " When I'm in pit I draw coals with a pair of byats over my shoulders that come down my back; all the other boys do the same in the small pits; the passages from the workings to the pit's mouth is 50 yards, and about three-quarters of a yard high; I am obliged to stoop very low to draw the corves on, or should knock my head. I can't always tell how heavy they are; some is little ones, some is big ones; they weigh from one to two cwt." (Ibid. No. 16: p. 136, l. 15.)—Elijah Weston, eleven years of age, pusher, Litley Colliery: " I push waggons down in pit upon rails; the distance from the workings to pit's mouth is two score yards or more; I am obliged to stoop, the waggon-ways are about 4 feet more or less high. When I have done my work I have drawn six rucks a-day, there being 12 corves in a ruck; the weight of every corve with waggon and all is 5½ cwt." (Ibid. No. 29: p. 140, l. 35). See also witnesses Nos. 3, 15, 18, 19, 24, 30, 31.

295. SHROPSHIRE.—In the Coalbrook-dale district the seams of coal are so thin as to afford a striking contrast to the depth of those of South Staffordshire, and in the former district there appear to be no horse-roads up to the workings: there are mines in which horses, and others in which asses, are employed in drawing the coals along the main roads, but in some collieries the coals are pushed by boys and young men, in small carriages called "dans," the whole distance from the workings to the foot of the shaft.

William Tranter, ground-bailiff: " In the coal-mines some boys are employed in bringing the coals in small carriages, called dans, to the horse-road, and others in pitching them into the carriages drawn by the horses. The mines are too low for men to do such work. Some of them are 2 feet in thickness, but there are places to go through at times no more than 18 inches, or perhaps 20 inches. The boys crawl on their hands and knees. The face of the work along which the dans are drawn is made as straight as possible, in order to get out the coal in as good a state as we can. There are no complaints of injury, except when a boy may meet with an accident, and then he leaves off until he gets well. The boys do the work cheerfully, and have no dislike to it. The dans are pushed on rails; it is very low, but the work is not heavy" (Dr. Mitchell, Evidence, No. 41: App. Pt. I. p. 79, l. 38.)

296. When a child has to drag a carriage loaded with coals through a passage "not more than 18 inches in height," some ingenuity is required to get his body and the carriage through this narrow space. " The boys," says Mr. Tranter, " crawl on their hands and knees." But an expedient has been adopted with a view of facilitating this labour, of which the Sub-Commissioner gives the following description: " A girdle is put round the naked waist, to which a chain from the carriage is hooked and passed between the legs, and the boys crawl on their hands and knees, drawing the carriage after them." This is called " Drawing by the Girdle and Chain." " This practice," he adds, " is not totally unknown in South Staffordshire in working some thin seams of coal; and is still more in use in the thin beds of ironstone; but it is not nearly so common as in Shropshire. About thirty years ago it was a very general custom to employ young boys, both in the coal-pits and iron-pits, to draw carriages by this means. The custom is not yet entirely out of use, though the respectable companies have many years discontinued it, and have substituted instead small iron railways, and small carriages called dans, which the boys push before them. All persons who have spoken of the girdles, both in Staffordshire and Shropshire, have described the labour as very severe, and

the girdle as frequently blistering their sides, and occasioning great pain" (Dr. Mitchell, Report, § 276: App. Pt. I., p. 35.)

Mr. William Grove, mine agent to James Loxdale, Esq., now thirty-five years of age, says: " He went down into the pits when he was six years and a half old; he was employed to draw with the girdle under him; there were then no rails or sleepers, and he had to draw the coal or stone to the bottom of the shaft. The work was a hundred degrees more slavish than it is now, and his sides were often cut many times over" (Dr. Mitchell, Evidence, No. 5: App. Pt. I., p. 64, l. 18).—See also Evidence of Mr. John Anstice and Mr. William Tranter, Nos. 39 and 41.

297. " Mr. William Lloyd," continues the Sub-Commissioner, " an old miner who was sent to me to the inn at the Iron Bridge with specimens of coal and iron-stone, on being asked his opinion of the girdle, replied, ' Sir, I can only say of it what the mothers say, it is barbarity! barbarity!' " (Dr. Mitchell, Report, § 279: App. Pt. I., p. 35.)—" All the great companies," he adds, " have made an advance in civilization and have substituted the railroad and the dan for the girdle and chain; but there are still some persons, generally of small capital, who lease a small pit, and instead of a steam-engine use a horse and a gin, and instead of laying down a small railway in their pits, employ boys to drag with the girdle and chain. The examination of the Children shows there is much more of drawing with girdle and chain, in the smaller pits in this district, than what from the evidence of the managers of the large companies we should have supposed. The great cruelty of the system is, when there are no rails laid down in the road, and which poor masters from a difficulty of finding capital are unwilling to provide, whilst rich companies most readily and cheerfully spare no expense which their own interest, as well as humanity towards the workpeople, prompt them to undergo. A perusal of the evidence of the Children will amply show the severe pain which this manner of working inflicts, yet they endure it with great fortitude and resignation. Nevertheless this is no reason why the same means which the humanity and good sense of the larger companies prompt them to adopt should not be adopted by all. That the work can never be accomplished without suffering, there is too much reason to fear, but no means should be spared to render it the least possible" (Ibid. § 280, et seq. p. 35).

James Pearce, twelve years of age: " About a year and a half ago I took to the girdle and chain; I do not like it; it hurts me; it rubs my skin off; I often feel pain. I have often had blisters on my side; but when I was more used to it it would not blister, but it smarted very badly. The chain was made of the same stuff as the rope that goes down the pit. I crawled on hands and feet. I often knocked my back against the top of the pit, and it hurt it very sore. The legs ached very badly. When I came home at night I often sat down to rest me by the way, I was so tired. The work made me look much older than I was. I worked at this drawing with girdle and chain three or four months. I thought that if I kept at this work I should be nothing at all, and I went and worked upon the bank. Many boys draw with girdle and chain now. There is not the railway and the dans. It is like drawing on the roads. I think it is a great hurt to a boy: it must be, to draw the same as a horse draws. A great many boys find that they are unable, and give over drawing with girdle and chain. It is very hard, very hard, sir. If they were to lay down rails, and push the coals on dans, it would be very convenient for the boys, though the expense might not be convenient for the masters" (Dr. Mitchell, Evidence, No. 54: App. Pt. I., p. 84, l. 52).—Thomas Hale, between fourteen and fifteen years of age: " I now draw a dan with a girdle and chain. I do not like it at all: it is hard work. I have marks on my side: it was cut by the girdle. The work is too low for dans: it is only three-quarters high. I never saw any dans pushed; that would be a deal better" (Ibid. No. 51: p. 83, l. 10).—Isaac Tipton, sixteen years of age: " I next went to draw with the girdle and chain. I had a girdle round the middle, and a chain under my legs; it was very hard work. If I had a bit of time in the pit I laid myself down on my back. We had no time unless something was the matter with the engine. Long before night we were so tired that we could hardly walk home sometimes. The girdle often makes blisters. I have had pieces like shillings and half-crowns, with the skin cocking up, all full of water, and when I put on the girdle the blisters would break and the girdle would stick, and next day they would fill again. These blisters give very great pain. There is no railway in the pits in which they use the girdle and chain. In all the pits about this part they use the girdle and chain" (Ibid. No. 53: p. 84, l. 7).—Robert North: " I went into the pit at seven years of age to assist to fill the skips. We cannot stop at what work we like; we are shifted. I drew about twelve months. When I drew by the girdle and chain the skin was broken, and the blood ran down. I durst not say anything. If we said anything, they, the butty, and the reeve who works under him, would take a stick and beat us. Men could not do the work, and they compelled us. I have seen lads of nine drawing with the girdle and chain. I have seen many draw at six; but they were not able to draw the full day out. If they are put to do the work they must do it or be beat" (Ibid. No. 56: p. 85, l. 23).—See also witnesses, Nos. 50, 52, 55, 58, 60.

298. WARWICKSHIRE.—In the Warwickshire coal field the pits are tolerably high, and the girdle and chain are unheard of : boys from ten to eleven years old push the loaded waggons on rails from the workings to the main roadways.

299. LEICESTERSHIRE.—In the Ashby-de-la-Zouch coal field all the roads are of great height, and in general horses or asses draw the coal direct from the workings to the shaft. " The coal is all in large, weighty pieces ; and boys and lads under sixteen are not able to load the waggons. In the Moira Bath Pit there were generally two horses drawing a line of waggons; and a youth walked at the head of the first horse, and a boy of ten, or eleven, or twelve, at the head of the second horse. In the Swadlincote collieries boys are employed in a similar way ; also in placing garlands, or large broad rims of iron, round the lumps of coal in the skips. In the Snibson Collieries the coals are drawn from the workings to the main railways in large baskets holding 7 cwt., placed on carriages. Such baskets are called ' corves.' One boy goes before and draws, and another boy pushes behind. When arrived at the main railway, the baskets are lifted by a crane, and placed on a carriage drawn by a horse or an ass to the foot of the shaft. In the neighbouring colliery of Whitwick boys and lads are not employed in drawing and pushing, as horses and asses are conducted up to the spot where the coals are got in the workings" (Dr. Mitchell, Report, § 116—118 : App. Pt. I., p. 99).

Joseph Dooley, ground-bailiff, Swadlincote: " From ten to sixteen the boys are employed at opening and shutting doors, and sweeping the railways and attending to the horses. The boys assist the men, who fill the skips by placing the garlands, but do not push them forward in any way. The horses come up along the workings to where the skips are loaded, and carry them thence to the foot of the shafts" (Dr. Mitchell, Evidence, No. 76 : App. Pt. I., p. 112, l. 8).—See witnesses Nos. 75 and 77.

300. The Sub-Commissioner reports: " In the course of this inquiry I have not been able to find any instance where machinery was substituted in place of boys in drawing coals from the thin beds of the mines. Some engineers have thought such a thing practicable, and others not." An instance of the employment of animal power in drawing coals from side gates, too shallow to admit boys to labour easily, is worthy of especial notice :—

Mr. Joseph Tomlinson, Alfreton, in Derbyshire: " In Summercoats Pit, formerly, when working in the hard coal, which was a bed 40 yards below the surface, we had a gateway about 4 feet high, sufficiently high for asses to drag the waggons on a railway; and at the corner of the gateway at the side of the workings there was a wheel, around which went a rope, by which the waggons were drawn from the workings down to the gateway. The workings were only 2 feet 7 inches high. It was too little room for boys. We should never think of putting boys to such work : I should consider it inhuman. No such thing would be thought of in this part of the country. We found this mode quite convenient. We every morning shifted the frame in which the wheel was fixed, and the work went on very regularly. We got on fully as quick as when the men drove the carriages before them. An empty carriage was drawn back by a boy without difficulty, and another lad led back the ass to the proper place. It was quite easy and comfortable. The bed got so thin at last that it would be a loss to continue working. In fact, it was a loss at last. We have left off working this bed about a year. It was not until the bed got too thin for the smallest asses we could get that we took to this plan, and we kept to it till the bed got too thin to be worth working at all ' " (Ibid. No. 86 ; p. 117, l. 28).

301. DERBYSHIRE.—In the coal-fields of this county the Sub-Commissioner states that " the youngest children are employed for the first six or twelve months in attending to the wind-doors; at seven years old they ' drive between '—that is, the corve without wheels, with from eight hundredweight to nearly a ton, is drawn the length of the bank (mostly about 200 yards) by three asses. The " between driver " is placed behind the second ass, and has to attend to the two first : the last is driven by the ass lad, who is often not more than twelve years of age. The elder boy wears a dog-belt (identical with the ' belt and chain' already described), but not to draw with continuously, the descent frequently being sufficient, or even more than sufficient, for the corve to run without much drawing : the elder boy walks backwards, and has at the same time to urge the last ass on, and by his belt prevent the corve running against the side of the bank. When the corve reaches the waggon-road it is placed on wheels, and left to the care of two other boys (one perhaps about thirteen, the other eight or nine year old) ; the elder one wears the dog-belt, and occasionally draws by it, or in some pits, when the descent is good, he merely uses the ' crop-stick ;' in returning, the youngest boy goes before the

waggon, and the elder pushes behind.   Until a boy gets accustomed to the dog-belt it frequently produces soreness on the hips, and otherwise injures him." (See Bagthorpe, Nos. 73 and 76; Denby, No. 315; Babbington, No. 150; Watnall, No. 101).

302. " There are mostly one or two boys employed to follow the loader—that is, to place the small coal on the corve, and keep the floor of the bank level, as well as one about twelve years old to assist in hanging the corve on the chain in order that it may be drawn up the shaft.   These, with a boy to assist the banks-man, are I believe the number mostly employed when there is only one bank; when there are two or more banks, as a matter of course the numbers are increased in nearly the same proportion.   The whole of the children in the pit, with the exception of the hanger-on, are working in a stooping posture, and in many pits have not an opportunity of straightening their backs during the day" (J. M. Fellows, Esq., Report, § 20-22: App. Pt. II., p. 253).

John Bostock, seventeen years of age, Babbington : " The belt has often made his hips quite raw " (J. M. Fellows, Esq., Evidence, No. 146: App. Pt. II., p. 301, l. 51).—Charles Booth, nine years old, Smalley, Messrs. Evans, Allen, and Thornley's pits : "Has worked a year; he wears the belt" (Ibid. No. 64: p. 281, l. 30).—William Blount, twelve years old, Messrs. Barber and Co., Beaver : " The waggon-road is upwards of 100 yards; the waggons are drawn by asses, and boys with belts; the lads draw as well as the asses.   There are three waggons, and one ass and one boy to the three " (Ibid. No. 97: p. 290, l. 11).—Thomas Siddons, twelve years old, New Ripley : " Draws by the belt; it hurts him " (Ibid. No. 243: p. 322, l. 7).—William Varley, nearly twelve years old, Creswell's Pit Bagthorpe : " Has worked in Mr. Fenton's pits since he was seven years old; waggons, and draws with the belt; his belt makes him smart again; is sore when he gets home, particularly after a whole day" (Ibid. No. 73: p. 284, l. 9).—Joseph Wilson, twelve years old, same pit : " Has worked three years in a pit; he now goes with the ass, and wears the belt; has done so a year; the belt hurts him; he has sometimes pulled till his hips have hurt him so that he has not known what to do with himself" (Ibid. No. 76: p. 284, l. 40). —Richard Clarke, twelve years old, Messrs. Barber and Walker, Underwood : " The belt chafes him until he is very sore; had rather drive plough or go to school a deal than work as he does" (Ibid. No. 110: p. 293, l. 52).—Evidence to the same effect is given by many young persons and adult colliers.   See Nos. 69, 142, 158, 160, 186, 278, 456.

303. " I wish," says the Sub-Commissioner, " to call the attention of the Board to the pits about Brampton : the seams are so thin that several have only a two-feet headway to all the workings.   The pits are altogether worked by boys; the elder one lies on his side, and in that posture holes and gets the coal; it is then loaded in a barrow or tub, and drawn along the bank to the pit-mouth without wheels, by boys from eight to twelve years of age, on all-fours, with a dog-belt and chain, the passages being very often an inch or two thick in black mud, and are neither ironed nor wooded.   In Mr. Barnes's pit these poor boys have to drag the barrows, with 1 cwt. of coal or slack, 60 times a-day 60 yards, and the empty barrows back, without once straightening their backs, unless they choose to stand under the shaft, and run the risk of having their heads broken by a coal falling" (J. M. Fellows, Esq., Report, § 26: App. Pt. II., p. 254).

Mr. Jonathan Bennet, Brampton : " The seam is two feet; headways, both in banks and waggon-roads, the same; the corves have 1¾ cwt. on each; they are drawn, without wheels or rails, by boys of twelve to fifteen years of age, on all-fours, with a belt; the roads in this pit are wet; the coals are holed, the waggons loaded, and most of the work of the pit done, by children and young men; thinks it might be possible to heighten the headways, but then it would not pay, the seams are so thin" (J. M. Fellows, Esq., Evidence, No. 405 : App. Pt. II., p. 348, ll. 46—54). —John Wright : " Works at Mr. Bainse's pit, Brampton; the corves or barrows are dragged by boys of about twelve years old; have 1¼ cwt. on; they go on all-fours; they—that is, four boys—have to get 40 corves of coal, and 20 of slack, for a day's work; the youngest is only eight years old; he draws the empty corves: if they did not begin by time they could not work these narrow seams; their limbs could not get used to it; he thinks lads like it as well as where there is more room—he knows he did; the pit is quite dry, or else ' it's nasty work;' the pit would not pay to work in any other way" (Ibid. No. 403: p. 348, l. 28).—[Notes by Sub-Commissioner: " No. 1 Wallow Pit is 20 yards deep, seam two feet; two banks, and two barrow or waggon roads; only two-feet headways; both men and boys lie down to work, and creep to draw the corves; the roads are one 60, the other 40 yards long; one or two at once are let down and up; the rope is not thicker than a good well-rope; there is no protection to the shaft-mouth" (Ibid. No. 407: p. 349, l. 9).]—Samuel Hoskin : "Is fourteen years old; has worked four years; he now holes, and is paid by the stint; he also fills; used to draw by belt on all-fours; it is sore work, much harder than what he now does; he is too big for that work now" (Ibid. No. 409: p. 349, l. 23).

304. Of the coal obtained from these thin-seamed pits, in none of which are any of the roads higher than two feet, the Sub-Commissioner says, " I found this said coal was retailed, both in Brampton and Chesterfield, at 3s. per ton.   Out of five

Children I examined (who worked in the Brampton pits), three were not only bow-legged, but their arms were bowed in the same way, and their whole frame appeared far from being well developed" (J. M. Fellows, Esq., Report, § 28, 29 : App., Pt. II., p. 254).

305. WEST RIDING OF YORKSHIRE : SOUTHERN PART.—The chief employ-ment of Children and Young Persons in the coal mines of this district is in attending to the trap-doors, driving the horses along the main-gates, attending to the jenny, and conveying the coals from the bank-faces to the shaft where there are no horses, and to the tram-roads where there are any.

306. " The trappers sit in a little hole scooped out for them in the side of the gates behind each door, where they sit with a string in their hands attached to the door, and pull it open the moment they hear the corves (*i.e.* carriages for conveying the coal) at hand, and the moment it has passed they let the door fall too, which it does of its own weight. If anything impedes the shutting of the door they remove it, or, if unable to do so, run to the nearest man to get him to do it for them. They have nothing else to do ; but, as their office must be performed from the repassing of the first to the passing of the last corve during the day, they are in the pit the whole time it is worked, frequently above 12 hours a-day. They sit, moreover, in the dark, often with a damp floor to stand on, and exposed necessarily to drafts. It is a most painful thing to contemplate the dull dungeon-like life these little creatures are doomed to spend—a life, for the most part, passed in solitude, damp, and darkness. They are allowed no light; but sometimes a good-natured collier will bestow a little bit of candle on them as a treat. On one occa-sion, as I was passing a little trapper, he begged me for a little grease from my candle. I found that the poor child had scooped out a hole in a great stone, and, having obtained a wick, had manufactured a rude sort of lamp ; and that he kept it going as well as he could by begging contributions of melted tallow from the candles of any Samaritan passers by. To be in the dark, in fact, seemed to be the great grievance with all of them. Occasionally, they are so posted as to be near the shaft, where they can sometimes run and enliven themselves with a view of the corves going up with the coals, or, perhaps, occasionally with a bird's-eye peep at the daylight itself; their main amusement is that, however, of seeing the corves pass along the gates at their posts. When we consider the very trifling cost at which these little creatures might be supplied with a light, as is the case in the Cumber-land collieries, there are few things which more strongly indicate the neglect of their comfort than the fact of their being kept in darkness—of all things the most wearisome to a young child" (J. C. Symons, Esq., Report, § 69, 71: App. Pt. I., p. 174).

John Saville, seven years old, collier's boy at the Soap Pit, Sheffield : " I stand and open and shut the door; I'm generally in the dark, and sit me down against the door; I stop 12 hours in the pit ; I never see daylight now, except on Sundays; I fell asleep one day, and a corve ran over my leg and made it smart ; they'd squeeze me against the door if I fall to sleep again" (J. C. Symons, Esq., Evidence, No. 7 : App. Pt. I., p. 228, l. 7).—Sarah Gooder, aged eight years : " I'm a trapper in the Gauber Pit. I have to trap without a light, and I'm scared. I go at four and sometimes half-past three in the morning, and come out at five and half-past, I never go to sleep. Sometimes I sing when I've light, but not in the dark ; I dare not sing then. I don't like being in the pit. I am very sleepy when I go sometimes in the morning" (Ibid. No. 116 : p. 252, l. 67).—James Sanderson, eight years old : " I am a trapper. I sit in the dark all the day, or I run to the bottom of the pit and come back" (Ibid. No. 26 : p. 231, l. 63). —Samuel Hirst, aged nine years and four months, Jump Pit : " I sit by myself. I never have a light. I sit still all day long and never do anything except open and shut the door" (Ibid. No. 45 : p. 235, l. 21).—William Martin, not ten years old, Messrs. Houldsworth's Colliery : " I trap two doors. I never see the daylight except on Sundays" (Ibid. No. 28 : p. 232, l. 18).— See also Witnesses, Nos. 20, 21, 75, 90.

307. " In coal mines in which the seam of coal admits of the gates being high enough, the corves are brought down from the bank-faces to a certain point, whence horses bring six or eight of them together down to the shaft. The drivers are those who drive these horses, and they have by far the best occupation in pits ; it gives them exercise and some degree of variety, and the only work they have is when a corve gets accidentally off the rail, and has to be lifted on again. To facili-this work," says the Sub-Commissioner, " or rather to prevent its occurrence, in Earl Fitzwilliam's collieries there is a second boy who, to use the expression of witness No. 148, acts as footman to the others. There is little work to do as respects the driving, for the horses are perfectly trained to their work; and the boy sits and drives on the front corve whenever they are empty ; he drives back-

wards and forwards all day. There will not be above seven or eight drivers even in a large-sized colliery, except in the Upper and Lower Elsecar and jump-pits belonging to Earl Fitzwilliam, where there are 21 drivers and their assistants, out of 61 young persons in all; this is far above the usual proportion. In Mr. Clarke's collieries, for instance, at Silkstone, there are only 7 horse-drivers out of 144 young persons ; and many pits have none at all. They are not put to drive horses much before they are eleven years old, and it is a matter of accident whether they go to other employment or not before they are fourteen. In the thin coal-pits horses are seldom used. Mr. Ingham's of Thornhill, and one of Messrs. Stansfeld and Briggs, are, I think, the only exceptions I have seen.

308. " It frequently happens that there is a very rapid descent either down a board-gate or occasionally down a main-gate ; or, in large collieries, from one main-gate down to another. In such places a jenny is erected, consisting of a strong pulley, round which a chain passes, to one end of which loaded corves are attached, whilst the other is attached at the bottom of the descent to a train of empty ones, which the weight of the full corves pulls up in its descent, both trains, of course, running on separate lines of rails. It is the duty of the jenny-boys to detach the corves one by one as the horse arrives, and hook them on, called "hanging on," to the descending end of the chain ; and, when they are started, to regulate the speed, by applying a brake or convoy to the chain by means of a lever. The pushing of the corves is rather, but not very, laborious ; and there are varieties and intervals in the work which make it anything but irksome. I found a great muster of these lads at the Elsecar Collieries" (J. C. Symons, Esq., Report, § 80, 81 : App. Pt. I., p. 176).

309. "But the chief employment of Children and Young Persons in the coal mines of this district is to convey the coals in the carriages called corves either from the workings to the horse-ways, or, where the main-roads are not high enough for horses, to the foot of the shaft. The corves are oblong waggons on small wheels of 9 or 12 inches diameter, running on railways, which are laid down in nearly all the gates of every colliery. These corves vary greatly in size, carrying from 2 to 10 cwt. of coal ; but the commonest size in the thicker beds of coal are made to hold 6 cwt. of coal, and weigh about 2 or 2½ cwt. themselves, making a weight of about 8 cwt. in all. The operation of propelling these corves is called ' hurrying,' and, in some places, ' tramming :' it is done by placing both hands on the top rail of the back of the corve, and pushing it forward, running as fast as the degree of inclination of the road or the strength of the hurrier will permit" (Ibid. § 84 : p. 176).

310. In this district girls are almost universally employed as trappers and hurriers in common with boys. The girls employed as hurriers are of all ages, from seven to twenty-one ; they commonly work quite naked down to the waist ; the boys of similar ages who work with them are also naked down to the waist, and both (for the garment is pretty much the same in both) are dressed, as far as they are dressed at all, in a loose pair of trousers, seldom whole in either sex. In many of the collieries, as has been already stated, the adult colliers, whom these girls serve, work perfectly naked.

311. The hurriers, being, as has been stated, hired and paid by the colliers, whose servants they are, must do whatever work is set them by these men, and in whatever time and manner they choose to direct. "The work of the hurrier," observes the Sub-Commissioner, " is not, therefore, as may be readily supposed, confined to the hurrying of the corves backwards and forwards along the gates. When the hurrier arrives with his or her empty corve at the bank-face it has to be filled, and in the north part of my district all the small part of the coal must be riddled (*i. e.* sieved) also : in these operations the hurriers almost invariably assist. In some of the collieries round Sheffield, it is true, there are a few fillers who are, in fact, young getters, learning to get, and who assist the getter, and fill ; but, in the great majority of coal pits in my district, the hurriers help to fill and help to riddle. The filling is performed by shovelling up the smaller coal and throwing it, which is done by the collier, who throws it into the riddle which is held by the hurrier, who then shakes it and throws the coal which remains into the corve. This is equally done by girls where they are employed. These riddles, with the usual quantity of coals thrown into them at once, weigh about 20 lbs. ; they are usually 22 inches in diameter and 3 inches deep. When the corve is nearly filled in this manner it is ' topped' with large coal, which is jointly put on by the collier and by the hurrier with their hands. When the corve is full the hurrier starts and hurries

it down to its destination, and returns back again as soon as possible with an empty corve.

312 ."Sometimes, when the collier has not got sufficient coal by the time the hurrier returns, the hurrier takes the pick with which the coal is hewn and helps to 'get.' By this means the art of getting is usually learnt, and the hurrier by degrees becomes a collier; and at eighteen or nineteen finally leaves off hurrying altogether. Getting is performed first by making a horizontal cut underneath the coal it is intended to get; this is called 'holing;' and as it has to be done low down, the collier is obliged to kneel, and often to lie on one side, in a very constrained posture to work: next, deep vertical cuts are made in order to release the block from either side at given lengths: it is then detached from above by means either of gunpowder or wedges. It is not usual for young persons to perform this work, except as an occasional occupation, and except in the thin-coal pits. Nevertheless, this work is done sufficiently often by older hurriers to justify its being classed as a part of their occasional employment.

313. "The following statement of the actual work done in some of the collieries I visited will give a good idea of the average amount of a hurrier's day's work, as far as mere hurrying goes. In one of Mr. Clark's collieries at Silkstone, where horses are used, the average distance to be hurried each way is 150 yards; the loaded corves weigh 8 cwt. (coal and corf together), and the average day's work is 20 full corves per day. This, both ways, gives an aggregate distance of about three miles and a half per day, half of which distance will be performed pushing 8 cwt. on the descent, and half-pushing about 2 cwt. on the ascent. In Messrs. Traviss and Horsfall's colliery at Worsboro', where no horses are employed, the average distance is 400 yards, the weight of loaded corves 8½ cwt., and the number hurried per day 20; making an aggregate distance of above nine miles. The same statement was made at Messrs. Hopwood and Jackson's colliery, Barnsley, except that the corves weigh there 1½ cwt. less. At Messrs. Thorpe's colliery at Gawber, where horses are employed, the largest corves in the district are used; they weigh, when full, 12½ cwt.: the average journey is 150 yards, and it is made 16 times a-day; giving an aggregate distance of only two miles and two-thirds. In one of the thin-coal pits at Hunshelf Bank, where the corves weigh about 2 cwt. when full, the distance is about 140 yards, and they have 24 to hurry in the day; making a distance of nearly four miles per day" (Ibid. §§ 85—90: p. 177).

Mr. George Traviss, coal master, of the firm of Traviss and Horsfall, Barnsley, depones: " When they are young two hurry together. Our present corves are 6½ cwt. when full, but we are going to make them larger, when they will weigh 9 cwt. The hurriers are paid and employed by the men who get the coal. These men take a bank and are paid by us so much per dozen corves; and they bring their own children, when they have them, or hire others. The hurriers do not generally fill; but when there are two together the elder hurrier may sometimes assist a little to fill" (J. C. Symons, Esq., Evidence, No. 84: App. Pt. I., p. 243, 1. 52).— John Chambers, Esq., of the firm of Newton, Chambers, and Co., Thorncliffe Iron Works and Colliery : " Each bank is placed under the management of a contractor, who is himself a collier. The boys are generally worked pretty hard, but they (the masters) have, however, made regulations to prevent the contractors from overworking the children. The masters always endeavour to lessen the manual labour as much as they can, as well for purposes of economy as to prevent children from working at too early an age" (Ibid. No. 64: p. 238, l. 56).— Henry Briggs, Esq., one of the proprietors of Messrs. Stansfield and Briggs's Coal Mines, Flockton: " The children will hurry themselves a month or two after they come into the pits. The children will have to hurry up hill with loaded corves about one quarter, or rather less, of the whole of the gates, and then they push with their heads. The inclination is one in twenty, and sometimes not so much. The gates vary from 4 feet to 30 inches in height. The children are employed by the men, except the drivers of ponies; the children generally help to fill about here; they help a little to get occasionally; they do this to learn. There are so many stoppages waiting for corves at the shaft or the end of the horse road, that they will amount to an hour and a half on the average for each child each day. The child sometimes riddles, and sometimes fills. The hurriers will hurry 30 corves a-day backwards and forwards, the average distance being about 10,000 yards a-day; this is where there are no horses; where there are horses the distance will be 5000 yards, and the work of the hurriers is far less where there are horses" (Ibid. No. 171: p. 272, l. 69).

Joseph Haigh, forty-three years of age, assistant under-ground steward at New Basset and New Deep Pits, Tinsley Park: "Thinks they can hardly do without boys as little as 10 or 11 in those pits where the seam of coal is only ¾ yard thick. There are a many such pits. Galloways hurry in the main-gates in all their thin coal-pits, but they cannot be used in the board-gates which branch off from the main-gates to the bank-faces, where the men work. If the main-gates were 280 yards in length, the board-gates altogether would be 180 yards in length; the boys have to hurry the whole of these. The horses work a much longer distance than the boys. It would be impossible for the horses to work in the board-gates; for the board-gates are all on the incline, and the corves would come down on the horses' heels in all places. It would be more trouble to the boys to manage the horses for such short distances than to hurry themselves. The horses are not so handy as Christians, and we could not do with them" (Ibid. No. 9: p. 228, l. 51).—George Shaw, aged fifty-nine years: " I am under-ground steward of three coal-pits and three iron-mines, besides nine small iron gin-pits, belonging to the Thorncliffe Company. The undertaker is a collier, and works as such; he contracts to work a bank and produce the coal at so much per ton, which he delivers at the bottom of his own board-gate with his own trammers. There will be 10 or 11 undertakers in a coal-pit in which there are 60 men and boys employed altogether; the undertakers have the entire control of the lads they employ as trammers" (Ibid. No. 67: p. 239, l. 19).—Mr. John Clarkson Sutcliffe, general agent for the Gauber Colliery, belonging to the executors of Mr. Samuel Thorpe: " Each collier works per piece, and delivers the coals he gets at the bull stake, which is the place where the double rails terminate and the horse-gate begins. This point is removed further from the shaft as the workings advance. The men pay for hurrying down to this place themselves; we have no control over the hurriers ourselves except keeping order in the pit. If the men were to overwork the hurriers I should not interfere. I think our corves are heavier than any about here; they will weigh when full 12½ cwt. The journey made each way by the hurrier is 150 yards on the average; they will hurry 20 corves a-day at most, and the average number will be 16. I am certain 16 is the average of the journeys both ways, making 32 backward and forward. They never have to hurry loaded corves up hill. I believe that a girl of 16 can hurry one of these corves very well, and do her day's work with ease. Elizabeth Eggler does hurry alone. We cannot afford to pay the same wages as Lord Fitzwilliam, where you saw men employed to hurry. He gets more for his coal and can afford it better. It is much better for the hurriers to have the larger corf and to go less frequently. When the children are allowed to go in too little they are are certainly tired, and from unfeeling parents this is sometimes the case" (Ibid. No. 118: p. 253, l. 24).—Mr. George Armitage, thirty-six years of age, teacher at Hoyland school: " I am now a teacher at Hoyland school. I was a collier at Silkstone until I was 22 years old. The hurriers are shamefully over-worked in many cases—not in all, but very often. In going up the board-gates they have often to push with their heads, and when the level is dead it is very hard work there. It is the regular business of the hurrier to fill and help to fill, and the slower the collier is the more will the child have to do to help him; in such cases they will often have to fill entirely. I am decidedly of opinion that when trade is good the work of hurriers is generally continuous; but when there are two together, perhaps the little one will have a rest when the big one is filling or riddling" (Ibid. No. 138: p. 260, l. 39).—David Row, collier, Thorp's colliery, Gawber: " I help to fill, and they riddles themselves. They don't top unless they are big, and then perhaps they top to help us. The corves are the heaviest anywhere about. The hurriers have not so oft to go when they are heavy, but they are too heavy for some of them. I'll take this corve which is full, and take it where you can't move it if it stops" (Ibid. No. 133: p. 257, l. 6).—Daniel Crossland, not eighteen years old yet, Silkstone: " I am a hurrier. I am getting to-day, because my brother cannot come. I often get. I cut the top, but my regular work is hurrying. I have cut the top at times ever since I started, and it will be eight years I reckon" (Ibid. No. 135: p. 257, l. 42).

314. " Girls regularly perform all the various offices of trapping, hurrying, filling, riddling, topping, and occasionally getting; just as they are performed by boys. I visited the Hunshelf Colliery. It is a day-pit; that is, there is no shaft or descent; the gate or entrance is at the side of a bank, and nearly horizontal. The gate was not more than a yard high, and in some places not above two feet. The corves are pushed along it on a tram-way a certain distance, and then dragged by the Children. When I arrived at the board or workings of the pit, I found at one of the side-boards down a narrow passage a girl of fourteen years of age, in boy's clothes, picking down the coal with the regular pick used by the men. She was half sitting half lying at her work, and said she found it tired her very much, and ' of course she didn't like it.' The place where she was at work was not two feet high. Further on were men at work lying on their sides and getting. No less than 6 girls out of 18 men and Children are employed in this pit" (J. C. Symons, Esq., Report, §§ 112, 113: App. Pt. I., p. 181).

Rebecca Hough, aged fourteen; examined whilst getting in Messrs. Charlesworth's pit, Silkstone: " I am a regular hurrier; I am used to help the getter; I often do it three or four times a-week. I help to fill and riddle, and then I hurry the corves down to the Bull-stake. It tires me a good deal; I have always enough to do to tire me well at night. I find the hurrying the hardest work; it is because I don't do much at getting that it tires me less" (J. C. Symons, Esq., Evidence, No. 136a: App. Pt. I., p. 257, l. 49).—Ann Fern: " I am a hurrier, and help to fill and riddle. I have been in the pit five years last July. It tires me enough sometimes, and sometimes not. I am up at half-past four and go down at five, and go out at four and sometimes five. I like being in the pit, but I would rather go to service, but I never tried. It's hard work going to pit. I care nothing about where I am. I should be worked hard anywhere, I dare say. I have had my leg broken in pit. I was a trapper. I was poorly with the work when I was at Clarke's pit, for I had to work harder there—often 13 hours" (Ibid. No. 136*b* : p. 258, 1. 2).—Fanny Drake, aged fifteen, Overton, near Wakefield : " I work at Charlesworth's Wood Pit. I hurry by myself; I have hurried to dip side for four or five months. I stop to rest at hole with the getter, and there is none else with us. I don't like it so well ; it's cold, and there is no pan [fire] in the pit. I'd rather be out of pits altogether ; I'd rather wait on my grandmother. I push with my head sometimes ; it makes my head sore sometimes, so that I cannot bear it touched ; it is soft too. I have often had headaches, and colds, and coughs, and sore throats. I work for James Greenwood ; he is no kin to me. I have a singlet and a shift and a petticoat on in the pit ; 1 have had a pair of trousers. The getter I work with wears a flannel waistcoat when he is poorly, but when he is quite well he wears nothing at all. It is about 32 inches high where we hurry, and in some places a yard." [This girl is 4 feet 5½ inches in height, and she looked very healthy.] (Ibid. No. 206 : p. 280, 1. 21).—Mary Margerson, aged sixteen : " I work in a pit above the one where Fanny Drake works. I get muck up generally all the time, and I rest odd times. I hurry alone, to dip. I am quite sure I have nobody to help me. I work for Joseph Lister, who pays me. I find it very heavy work ; I am very tired when I come home. I hurry both muck and coals, and I can't keep count of the number of corves per day. I wear a petticoat and shift, and stays. The man I work for wears nought, he is stark naked. I don't like being in the pit" (Ibid. No. 208 : p. 280, 1. 44).

315. The Sub-Commissioner states that " instances of oppressively hard work performed by young females presented themselves at collieries near Barnsley. The evidence of Elizabeth Day, and of Ann and Elizabeth Eggley, is deserving of especial notice, the more so because I believe both the elder of these witnesses to be respectable and credible, and both gave their evidence with much good feeling and propriety. The work of Elizabeth Day is rendered more severe by her having to hurry part of the way up hill with loaded corves, a very unusual circumstance. The Eggleys are, however, doing the ordinary work of hurriers in their colliery. It is a large, well-ventilated, and well-regulated one, but owing to the size of the corves, which weigh 12½ cwt., it is work very far beyond the strength of females at any age, especially females of sixteen and eighteen years old. After taking the evidence of the two Eggleys I saw them both at their work, and hurried their corves, and also performed the work they had to do at the bank-faces. I can not only corroborate their statements, but have no hesitation in adding that were they galley-slaves their work could not be more oppressive, and I believe would not in all probability be so much so. Elizabeth Eggley, the younger, who is not above fifteen, whilst doing what is called topping the corves, lifted a coal which must have weighed at least a hundred pounds. It measured 30 inches in length, and 10 by 7 in thickness. This she lifted from the ground and placed on the top of the corve, above three feet and a half high. She afterwards lifted a still larger one, which was probably done to show what she could do. The former one was lifted in the ordinary course of her work. This girl was working for her father, who was standing by at the time" (J. C. Symons, Esq., Report, § 117 : App. Pt. I., p. 182).

Elizabeth Day, aged seventeen, working in Messrs. Hopwood's pit at Barnsley : " I have been nearly nine years in the pit. I trapped for two years when I first went, and have hurried ever since. I have hurried for my father until a year ago. I have to help to riddle and fill, and sometimes I have to fill by myself. It is very hard work for me at present. I have to hurry by myself ; I have hurried by myself going fast on three years. Before then I had my sister to hurry with me. I have to hurry up hill with the loaded corves, quite as much up as down, but not many have to hurry up hill with the loaded corve. When I riddle I hold the riddle, and have to shake the slack out of it, and then I throw the rest into the corf. We always hurry in trousers as you saw us to-day when you were in the pit. Generally I work naked down to the waist like the rest ; I had my shift on to-day when I saw you, because I had had to wait, and was cold : but generally the girls hurry naked down to the waist. It is very hard work for us all ; it is harder work than we ought to do a deal. I have been lamed in my ankle, and strained in my back ; it caused a great lump to rise in my ankle-bone once" (J. C. Symons, Esq., Evidence, No. 85 : App. Pt. I., p. 244, 1. 23).—Ann Eggley, hurrier in Messrs. Thorpe's colliery, eighteen years old : " I hurry by myself, and have done so for long. I know the corves are very heavy ; they are the biggest corves anywhere about. The work is far too hard for me ; the sweat runs off me all over sometimes. I am very tired at night. Sometimes when we get home at night we have not power to wash us, and then we go to bed. Sometimes we fall asleep in the chair. Father said last night it was both a shame and a disgrace for girls to work as we do, but there was nought else for us to do. I have tried to get winding to do, but could not. I begun to hurry when I was seven, and I have been hurrying ever since. I have been 11 years in the pit. The girls are always tired. I was poorly twice this winter ; it was with headache. I hurry for Robert Wiggins ; he is not akin to me ; I riddle for him. We all riddle for them except the littlest, when there is two. I am quite sure that we work constantly 12 hours, except on Saturdays. We wear

L 2

trousers and our shifts in the pit, and great big shoes clinkered and nailed. The girls never work naked to the waist in our pit. The men don't insult us in the pit. The conduct of the girls in the pit is good enough sometimes, and sometimes bad enough. The men do not insult the girls with us, but I think they do in some" (Ibid. No. 113: p. 252, l. 16).—Elizabeth Eggley, sixteen years old : " I am sister to the last witness. I hurry in the same pit, and work for my father. I find my work very much too hard for me. I hurry alone ; it tires me in my arms and back most. We go to work between four and five in the morning ; if we are not there by half-past five we are not allowed to go down at all. We come out at four, five, or six at night as it happens. We stop in generally 12 hours, and sometimes longer. We have to hurry only from the bank-face down to the horse-gate and back. I am sure it is very hard work and tires us very much ; it is too hard for girls to do. We sometimes go to sleep before we get to bed" (Ibid. No. 114: p. 252, l. 44).—James Eggley, aged forty-five, same pit as the above : "I have six girls, and only one young boy not old enough to come to the pit. I cannot do without sending my girls to the pit ; the eldest is eighteen and the second sixteen ; they each hurry alone ; it is hard work for them, to be sure, but mine looks well with it. They do complain of being tired sometimes. I don't like their coming down, but I have had one (Ann) at home, and I cannot get any work for her to do ; though I can get nothing, I have tried it. She brings me in 10*s.* per week ; and it is a hard thing to lose it" (Ibid. No. 128: p. 256, l. 20).—Ann Mallender, fifteen years old, Messrs. Hopwood's pit at Barnsley : " I am fifteen years old ; I always dress as you saw me to-day—naked down to the waist, and with trousers on. I work for James Martin, who is no relation, but he is the getter who employs me" (Ibid. No. 86: p. 244, l. 49).—Betty Mallender, of the same colliery : " I was eleven last November ; I always wear trousers, and am naked down to the waist" (Ibid. No. 87: p. 244, l. 64).— Bessy Bailey : " I shall be fifteen next Tuesday. I hurry in the pit you was in this morning ; I always work naked down to the waist, and with trousers on ; and all the girls I know hurry in the same way" (Ibid. No. 88: p.,245, l. 2).—Charles Bailey, aged thirteen years : " I have been in the pit about five years. Sometimes the corves run easy, and other times not ; it tires us much sometimes. We hurry with our trousers on, and naked to the waist ; and sometimes we take our trousers off, and hurry in our shirts. The girls do not take their trousers off, but they are naked down to the waist" (Ibid. No. 91: p. 245, l. 43).—See also witnesses Nos. 10, 42, 73, 97, 101, 123, 134, 203, 255, 368, &c.

316. In the coal-mines in which the seams of coal are thin, the Children almost universally hurry on all-fours with the belt and chain.

George Dyson, coal-owner, Stannington : " The lads hurry with a belt and chain on all-fours. Thirty-eight years ago they had no belts or chains, but used to run along on one hand and feet, and pull the corves with the other hand ; that was much worse for them" (Ibid. No. 83: p. 243, l. 39.) —See witnesses, Nos. 33, 52, 77, 82, et seq.

317. In some parts of this district girls are quite as commonly employed in dragging coals in this manner as boys. "They hurry with a belt and chain, as well as thrust," says Mr. Thomas Peace ; " there are as many girls as boys employed about here." (Ibid. No. 33: p. 233, l. 20).—" One of the most disgusting sights I have ever seen," says the Sub-Commissioner, "was that of young females, dressed like boys in trousers, crawling on all fours, with belts round their waists, and chains passing between their legs, at day pits at Hunshelf Bank, and in many small pits near Holmfirth and New Mills. It exists also in several other places."

318. " Whilst I was in the Hunshelf pit the Rev. Mr. Bruce, of Wadsley, and the Rev. Mr. Nelson, of Rotherham, who accompanied me, and remained outside, saw another girl of ten years of age, also dressed in boy's clothes, who was employed in ' hurrying,' and these gentlemen saw her at work. She was a nice-looking little child, but of course as black as a tinker, and with a little necklace round her throat.

319. " These Children have 24 corves a-day to hurry out of this den, and consequently have 48 times to pass along the gate, which is about the size of a tolerably large drain. I would beg particularly to call your attention to the evidence of the manager of this colliery, No. 33, whose evidence respecting the number of girls employed by him was distinctly disproved by Harriet Morton, No. 38, an intelligent girl, who seemed to feel the degradation of her lot so keenly that it was quite painful to take her evidence.

320. " In two other pits in the Huddersfield Union I have seen the same sight. In one, near New Mills, the chain, passing high up between the legs of two of these girls, had worn large holes in their trousers, and any sight more disgustingly indecent or revolting can scarcely be imagined than these girls at work. No brothel can beat it. I took their evidence afterwards, when they were sent to me washed and dressed, and one of them, at least, was evidently crammed with her evidence" (J. C. Symons, Esq., Report, § 113—116: App. Pt. I., p. 181).

Harriet Morton: "I am nearly fifteen years old, and began to work in Webster's pit when I was going in ten. I've always worked in Webster and Peace's pit; I have hurried all the time; I am the oldest girl there. There are seven regular hurriers, who are girls. There are six boys who hurry. Two of us are employed at each corve both full and empty. When the corve is loaded, one of us is harnessed with a belt round the waist, and a chain comes from the front of the belt and passes betwixt our legs and is hooked on to the corve, and we go along on our hands and feet, on all-fours. I do so myself, and a little boy pushes behind. We wear trousers always as when you saw us" (J. C. Symons, Esq., Evidence, No. 38: App. Pt. I., p. 233, l. 66).—Ann Hague: "I am turned of thirteen years old. I hurry the same as the last girl, in Webster's pit. I draw the corve with a chain and belt. There is a little girl, my sister, who pushes behind. We have 24 corves to go in and out with every day. Sarah Moorhouse 'gets' as well as hurries; she gets and hurries eight corves a-day; I don't like working in the pit so very well; I would rather not do it. Having to pull so hard in the pit makes me poorly sometimes" (Ibid. No. 39: p. 234, l. 16.)—Mary Holmes, aged fourteen and a half, Meal Hill, Hepworth: "I have been eight years working in pits. I have always hurried; I never thrust much. I always hurry as you saw me, with a belt round my waist and the chain through my legs. I hurry so in the board-gates. I always wear lad's clothes. The trousers don't get torn at all. It tires me middling; my back doesn't ache at all, nor my legs. I like being in pit, and don't want to do nought else; I never tried to do anything else. Sometimes I get cold by its being so wet; the wet covers my ankles. I am sure nobody has told me what to say. Sometimes I stop and fill the corves after the getter is gone. I don't know how long I shall stop in the pit. I am sure I would rather be in the pit, where I am thrashed sometimes, and work in the wet, than do anything else" (Ibid. No. 283: p. 295, l. 22).—Ebenezer Healey, aged thirteen: "I went into a pit to help before I was five years old. I used to thrust; I didn't do it long. I hurry now with a belt and chain in the board-gates. There are no rails there. We have to hurry full corves this way, up hill as well as down. I do this myself, and I have 16 runs a-day, for which I have 1s. There are girls that hurry in the same way, with belt and chain. Our breeches are often torn between the legs with the chain. The girls' breeches are torn as often as ours; they are torn many a time, and when they are going along we can see them all between the legs naked; I have often; and that girl, Mary Holmes, was so to-day; she denies it, but it is true for all that" (Ibid. No. 284: p. 295, l. 38).—George Hirst, collier, aged thirty-two, at Messrs. Stansfeld and Briggs's Gin Pit at Low Common, Kirkburton: "The children hurry with belt and chain, the chain passing between their legs; girls and all. It privileges some poor folks to bring their girls to pits, and I have seen many who have made respectable women, and for aught I know useful wives. I don't know that the girls have any more impudence than the other girls that are brought up in other ways. It is true that they all have impudence" (Ibid. No. 294: p. 297, l. 10).

321. BRADFORD AND LEEDS.—According to Mr. Thomas Markley, surgeon, Wilsden, it is the common practice to employ girls in that neighbourhood, and "they have a chain or belt about the waist, which passes between the legs of the female, and is hooked on to the waggon of coals, which they pull from the place where the men work to the bottom of the shaft. I should also add, that the men in the pit work perfectly naked" (W. R. Wood, Esq., Evidence, No. 61: App. Pt. II., p. *h* 28, l. 9). The illustrations extracted below from Mr. Scriven's Report upon a contiguous district are equally applicable to the thin seam mines to which much of the preceding testimony refers.

322. HALIFAX.—In this district, in which, as has been shown, the seams of coal in many of the mines are not more than 14 inches in thickness, and rarely exceed 30, the space at the workings is sometimes too small to allow the adult colliers to carry on their operations even in a stooping posture; they are obliged to work "lying their whole length along the uneven floor, and supporting their heads upon a board or short crutch;" as is shown in the illustrative woodcut at p. 63, in Part II. of the Appendix. When they are able to obtain a little more space, they work "sitting upon one heel balancing their persons by extending the other." In these "low, dark, heated, and dismal chambers they work perfectly naked" (S. S. Scriven, Esq., Report, § 40: Figs. 4, 5, 6: App. Pt. II., pp. 63, 64).

323. The narrowness of the space in which all the operations must be carried on in these mines of course materially influences the labour of the Children and Young Persons. Fortunately but few Children are needed in them as trappers, but those that are employed as in most other districts sit in perfect darkness. "I can never forget," says the Sub-Commissioner, "the first unfortunate creature (of this class) that I met with; it was a boy of about eight years old, who looked at me as I passed through with an expression of countenance the most abject and idiotic— like a thing, a creeping thing peculiar to the place. On approaching and speaking to him he slunk trembling and frightened into a corner, under an impression that I

was about to do him some bodily injury, and from which neither coaxing nor temptations would draw him out" (Ibid. § 87: p. 72).

324. In this district the loaded corves drawn by the hurriers weigh from 2 to 5 cwt.; these carriages are mounted upon four cast-iron wheels of 5 inches in diameter, there being in general no rails from the headings to the main-gates. The Children have to drag these carriages through passages in some cases not more than from 16 to 20 inches in height. Of course to accomplish this the youngest Children must crawl on their hands and feet. To render their labour the more easy the Sub-Commissioner states that " they buckle round their naked persons a broad leather strap, to which is attached in front a ring and about 4 feet of chain terminating in a hook." (Fig. 1.) This illustration of the circumstances of this degrading labour is so much more forcible than any verbal description, that we must claim permission to subjoin it.

Fig. 1.

In passages of somewhat greater height they drag their loads with the belt and chain in the manner represented in Fig. 2.

Fig. 2.

325. " As soon as they enter the main-gates they detach their harness from the corve, change their position by getting behind it, and become ' thrusters.' The venicle is then placed upon the rail, a candle is stuck fast by a piece of wet clay,

and away they run with prodigious celerity to the shaft, pushing the load with their heads and hands. (Fig. 3.)

Fig. 3.

The command they hold over it at every curve and angle, considering the pace, the unevenness of the floors and rails, and the mud, water, and stones, is truly astonishing. The younger Children thrust in pairs" (S. S. Scriven, Esq., Report, §§ 49—52: App. Pt. II., p. 65, 66).

John Marsden, aged eight and a half, Wike-lane Pit: " I hurry a ' dozen and twelve ' corves a day, [that is 20 to the dozen]; my brother Lawrence helps me, and we have to hurry the corves about 200 yards" (S. S. Scriven, Esq., Evidence, No. 42: App. Pt. II., p. 113, l. 14).—Joseph Hellewel, aged ten years, Weigh Pit: " I hurry about 40 corves a-day; they weigh each

Fig. 4.

2¼ cwt.; the distance is three score yards; I hurry by myself; we all hurry by ourselves." (Ibid. No. 57: p. 117, l. 56).—Joseph Barker, aged forty-three, collier, Mr. Stocks' Windybank Pit: " They hurry the corves singly and doubly. The weight of the corves is about 2 cwt.; it is 800 yards from the pit's mouth to the workings; they hurry about 17 corves a-day; as an honest man I think that is too much, but they are bound to do it" (Ibid. No. 14: p. 105, l. 17). —William Dyson, aged fourteen, Messrs. Abraham and Charles Ditchforth, and Clay: "We have but one girl working with us, by name Ann Ambler, who goes down with us upon the clatch harness; she wears her breeches when she goes down, and while at work, and comes up the pit cross-lapped with us in the clatch harness; when she is down she hurries with us in the same way as we do, without shoes or stockings" (Ibid. No. 7: p. 102, l. 59).—See also witnesses Nos. 17, 26, 28, 32, 37, 42, 59, 73.

326. " The sketch given in p. 79 (fig. 4), is intended to represent Ann Ambler and William Dyson, the witness last quoted, hurriers in Messrs. Ditchforth and Clay's colliery at Elland, in the act of being drawn up cross-lapped upon the clatch-iron by a woman. As soon as they arrived at the top the handle was made fast by a bolt drawn from the upright post; the woman then grasped a hand of both at the same time, and by main force brought them to land. The corve on these occasions is detached from the hooks to render the load lighter" (S. S. Scriven, Esq., Report, § 26: App. Pt. II., p. 61).

327. " Girls from five to eighteen perform all the work of boys. There is no distinction whatever in their coming up the shaft or going down—in the mode of hurrying or thrusting—in the weights of corves, or in the distances they are hurried—in wages, or dress. Indeed it is impossible to distinguish, either in the darkness of the gates in which they labour, or in the cabins before the broad light of day, an atom of difference between one sex and the other" (Ibid. § 97, p. 73).

Margaret Gomley, Messrs. Waterhouse, Lindley, near Huddersfield: "I am about nine or going in nine; I have been at work in the pit thrusting corves about a year. There are two other girls working with me. I had rather lake than go into the pit. I had rather set cards than go into the pit."—[Sub-Commissioner: " I descended this pit accompanied by one of the banksmen, and, on alighting at the bottom, found the entrance to the mainway 2 feet 10 inches, and which extended 500 yards. The bottom was deep in mire, and, as I had no corves low enough to convey me to the workings, waited some time under the dripping shaft the arrival of the hurriers, as I had reason to suspect there were some very young children labouring there. At length three girls arrived, with as many boys. It was impossible in the dark to distinguish the sexes. They were all naked excepting their shifts or shirts. Having placed one into the corve, I gave the signal, and ascended. On alighting on the pit's bank I discovered that it was a girl. I could not have believed that I should have found human nature so degraded. Mr. Holroyd, solicitor, and Mr. Brook, surgeon, practising in Stainland, were present, who confessed that, although living within a few miles, they could not have believed that such a system of unchristian cruelty could have existed."] (Ibid. No. 9: p. 103, ll. 27, 40, 44).—Susan Pitchforth, same pit, living at Elland: " I run 24 corves a-day; I cannot come up till I have done them all. I had rather set cards or anything else than work in the pit."—[Sub-Commissioner: " She stood shivering before me from cold. The rag that hung about her waist was once called a shift, which is as black as the coal she thrusts, and saturated with water, the drippings of the roof and shaft. During my examination of her the banksman whom I had left in the pit came to the public-house and wanted to take her away, because, as he expressed himself, it was not decent that she should be (her person) exposed to us; oh, no! it was criminal above ground; and, like the two or three other colliers in the cabin, he became evidently mortified that these deeds of darkness should be brought to light."] (Ibid. No. 10: p. 103, 104, l. 8, 65).—Selina Ambre, aged twelve, Mr. Joseph Stock's Brown Top Pit: " I would rather go to mill than hurry. My uncle could na get a hurrier nowhere, so I had no choice; I was obliged to come for him; I do not like it much; I used to give it up at first, because 'twas so wet at feet; I can run very well by myself. I hurry about 100 yards, 20 corves a-day. We use the belt and chain for about two score yards. I wear breeches and shirt—nothing else" (Ibid. No. 79: p. 124, l. 22).—Esther Craven, aged fourteen, Messrs. Foster and Lassey's, Clewesmore: " I have rued many a time afore now for coming, but I do not now, because I have got used to it; I never think nought about being brayed a bit by the getters" (Ibid. No. 75: p. 123, l. 41).—Mary Barrett, aged fourteen, Messrs. Spencer and Illingsworth's: " I work always without stockings, or shoes, or trousers; I wear nothing but my shift; I have to go up to the headings with the men; they are all naked there; I am got well used to that, and don't care now much about it; I was afraid at first, and did not like it" (Ibid. No. 72: p. 122, l. 54).—Patience Kershaw, aged seventeen, Mr. Joseph Stock's Booth Town Pit, Halifax: " I hurry in the clothes I have now got on, trousers and ragged jacket; the bald place upon my head is made by thrusting the corves; my legs have never swelled, but sisters' did when they went to mill; I hurry the corves a mile and more under ground and back; they weigh 3 cwt.; I hurry 11 a-day; I wear a belt and chain at the workings to get the corves out; the getters that I work for are naked except their caps; they pull off all their clothes; I see them at work when I go up; sometimes they beat me, if I am not quick enough, with their hands; they strike me upon my back; the boys take liberties with me sometimes, they pull me about; I am the only girl in the pit; there are about 20 boys and 15 men; all the men are naked; I would rather work in mill than in coal-pit.—[Sub-Commissioner: "This girl is an ignorant, filthy, ragged, and deplorable-looking object, and such a one as the uncivilised natives of the prairies would be shocked to look upon.]" (Ibid. No. 26: p. 108, l. 8, 17).

328. LANCASHIRE AND CHESHIRE.—The Sub-Commissioner accompanies his account of the occupation of the trappers in this district with the sketch " of an air-door tender in a thin mine in the act of opening an air-door to allow a waggon to pass through." The Child is represented "as sitting on his heels, as is the universal custom of all colliers, young and old, in this district." (See Fig. 5.)

329. " This occupation is one of the most pitiable in a coal-pit, from its extreme monotony. Exertion there is none, nor labour, further than is requisite to open and shut a door. As these little fellows are always the youngest in the pits, I have generally found them very shy, and they have never anything to say for themselves. Their whole time is spent in sitting in the dark for twelve hours, and opening and shutting a door to allow the waggoners to pass. Were it not for the passing and repassing of the waggons it would be equal to solitary confinement of the worst order" (J. L. Kennedy, Esq., Report, § 122: App. Pt. II., p. 166).

330. " But by far the greater number of Children and persons employed in coal-mines are engaged in propelling and drawing tubs laden with coal, from the face to the pit-eye, or the main-levels in those pits where they have horses. This is done by placing the hands on the back of the waggon, and propelling it forward with as great velocity as the inclination of the mine, the state of the road, and the strength of the waggoner admit of. The mines in this district are for the most part laid with rails, and the waggon runs on wheels of various diameters from four to six inches. There are, however, mines throughout the district—namely, Clifton, Bolton, Outwood, Lever, Worsley, Blackrod, and St. Helen's—where the old mode

Fig. 5.

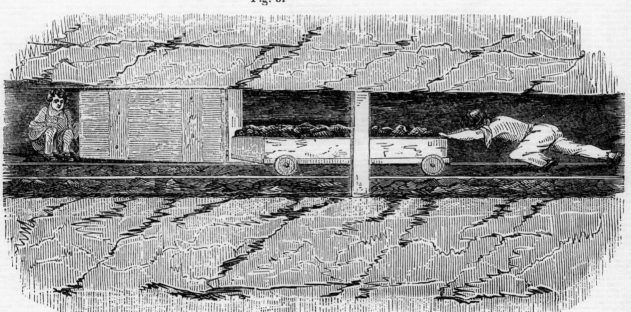

of drawing the baskets or wooden sledges (called in Lancashire 'sleds') is still retained. The drawer is in this case harnessed by means of a chain attached to the 'sled;' the other end of the chain passes between his legs, and fastens in front to a belt round the waist. When thus harnessed, and moving along on his hands and feet, the drawer drags after him the loaded basket; if he is not sufficiently strong he has a helper rather younger than himself, and these latter Children are called in Lancashire 'thrutchers'" (Ibid. § 93: pp. 159, 161). The weight of the loaded tubs or waggons of coal varies in the different mines in this district from 2½ to 9 cwt.; but in those mines where they are drawn on sledges without wheels, the baskets are never more than 3½ to 4 cwt.

331. Figures are given in the Report of the Sub-Commissioner (pages 160—163) illustrating the different modes in which the loaded waggons are propelled in the

thicker seams of coal, this work being performed indiscriminately by girls and boys, and young women and young men. In the thinner seams much younger Children are employed. Fig. 6 represents three young Children hurrying or drawing a loaded waggon of coals. The Child in front " is harnessed by his belt or chain to

Fig. 6.

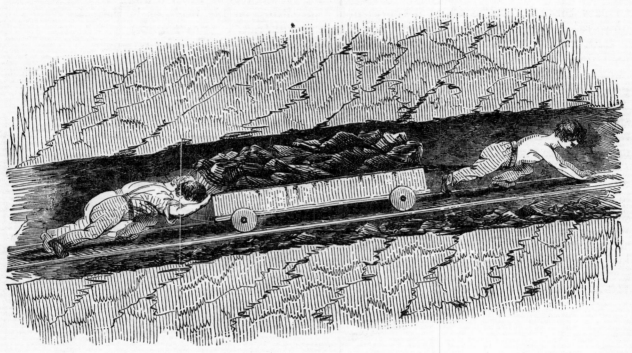

the waggon: the two boys behind are assisting in pushing it forward. Their heads, it will be observed, are brought down to a level with the waggon, and the body almost in a horizontal position. This is done partly to avoid striking the roof, and partly to gain the advantage of the muscular action, which is greatest in that position. It will be observed the boy in front goes on his hands and feet: in that manner the whole weight of his body is in fact supported by the chain attached to the waggon and his feet, and consequently his power of drawing is greater than it would be if he crawled on his knees. These boys, by constantly pushing against the waggons, occasionally rub off the hair from the crowns of their heads so much as to make them almost bald" (Ibid. § 110: pp. 164, 165).

332. The employment of the jigger, or boy who manages the brake on the jig or balance (Fig. 7), consists " in applying the brake so as to stop the frame on which the waggons are carried up and down, at the mouths of the different mines on the gig-brow in succession. I am told that these little boys, for they are generally not more than ten years old, become exceedingly expert, and will stop the machine at the proper place with the greatest precision. These boys are also without light, but as they are in constant communication with the boys at the mouths of the different mines, their occupation is not so monotonous as that of the air-door tenders. As all the tubs which go out of the mines on the gig-brow are carried down by the balance, these boys stay down as long as there are any coals to be sent out, and consequently stay down as long as any person in the pits. This employment may be said to be tedious rather than laborious" (Ibid. § 123: p. 167).

333. " In most of the larger collieries of this district, horses and ponies are used to draw the waggons in the main levels and slant roads. This, however, makes but little difference to the drawers, as they go the shorter distance more frequently." The boys employed to drive the horses and ponies have the most agreeable work in the mine; but they, like the trappers and giggers, must continue their work as long as any other persons are in the pits (Ibid. § 113: p. 165).

334. In this district, as in the Yorkshire coal-mines, the labour of the drawers or hurriers is greatly increased by its being made part of their employment to riddle the coals. " If," says the Sub-Commissioner, " there is only one drawer or waggoner, the collier assists; but I think this operation of riddling the coals and

Fig. 7.

filling the tubs is generally done by the drawers themselves. The smaller pieces are shovelled in first, and the round or larger blocks are placed on the tops. In some mines the operation of riddling is performed at the pit-mouth, or bank : the coals are shot out of the tubs or baskets down a stationary riddle or sieve placed in an inclined position; in this manner the smaller parts fall through the middle, whilst the larger ones slide into the boat or cart underneath, as the case may be " (Ibid. § 96 : p. 161).

Nature of Employment.

Lancashire and Cheshire.

335. In some parts of this district, Young Persons about eighteen years of age are employed in " getting coal," especially in the neighbourhood of Wigan. At Ringley Bridge, near Bolton, young persons not more than eighteen years of age were found thus employed. At Worsley, eighteen is the age at which boys are first allowed to get coal; and they are at that age considered " three-quarters of a man."

Benjamin Berry, aged twenty-four, at Mr. Lancaster's, Patricroft, near Worsley : " It is the custom at Worsley to consider a man as divided into eight parts. When first a boy begins to work, he is considered to be equal to one-eighth part of a man; at ten years he is two-eighths; thirteen, three-eighths; fifteen, one-half; a girl at sixteen, one-half; a boy at eighteen, three-fourths. At this age a boy begins to get coal. Girls and women never get coal, and always remain drawers, and are considered to be equal to half a man." " I have known two drawers, a lad and a lass, one of them three-eighths and the other half, draw 800 yards on the level with rails, each way, ten times without rails; that is, 30,400 yards = 17½ miles nearly. The lad was 17 years old, and the wench would be between 14 and 15" (J. L. Kennedy, Esq., Evidence, No. 27 : App. Pt. II., p. 215, l. 6).—Peter Gaskell, collier at Mr. Lancaster's, near Worsley : " I have known drawers drag 16,000 yards, all on the tub-bottom, but he would be a full drawer; I have known women draw 12,000 yards. Prefers women to boys as drawers; they are better to manage, and keep the time better; they will fight and shriek and do everything but let anybody pass them, and they never get to be coal-getters, that is another good thing" (Ibid. No. 29 ; p. 217, l. 22).—John Millington, superintendent, Mr. T. Ashton's, Hyde : " They have still to work with the belt and chain in the neighbourhood of Worsley, but we never do here" (Ibid. No. 6 : p. 202, l. 24).—Henry Eaton, surveyor, Bolton : " They use the belt and chain in all the pits" (Ibid. No. 18 : p. 208, l. 62).—Henry Jones, at Mr. Clegg's, Pauldin Wood, near Oldham : " Is going in six years old; is a thrutcher; is the youngest in the pit excepting Jack Jones; we are working two shifts of eight hours; we stop noan [none]; we keep worchink [working] all the time" (Ibid. No. 64 : p. 226, l. 35).—William Cooper, aged seven years, Rawlinson's Bridge, near Chorley : " Has worked in a coal-pit twelve months; there are about 20 wenches, drawers, in the pit I work in; they are nigh naked; they wear trousers; they have no other clothes except loose shifts and trousers" (Ibid. No. 55 : p. 224, l. 22, 32).

336. The accompanying sketch (fig. 8) represents a female drawer in Lancashire.

Fig. 8.

Betty Harris, aged thirty-seven, drawer, in a coal-pit at Little Bolton : " I have a belt round my waist, and a chain passing between my legs, and I go on my hands and feet. The road is very steep, and we have to hold by a rope; and, when there is no rope, by anything we can catch hold of. There are six women and about six boys and girls in the pit I work in: it is very hard work for a woman. The pit is very wet where I work, and the water comes over our clog-tops always, and I have seen it up to my thighs : it rains in at the roof terribly; my clothes are wet through almost all day long. I never was ill in my life but when I was lying-in. My cousin looks after my children in the day-time. I am very tired when I get home at night; I fall asleep sometimes before I get washed. I am not so strong as I was, and cannot stand my work so well as I used to do. I have drawn till I have had the skin off me : the belt and chain is worse when we are in the family way. My feller [husband] has beaten me many a time for not being ready. I were not used to it at first, and he had little patience : I have known many a man beat his drawer. I have known men take liberty with the drawers, and some of the women have bastards " (J. L. Kennedy, Esq., Evidence, No. 90: App. Pt. II., p. 230, l. 64).
—Ellen Yates, drawer, Bridgewater Colliery : " Is sixteen years old; draws 180 yards ten or twelve times a-day, sometimes more or sometimes less, just as it happens; draws with the belt and chain; the tubs are not on wheels, we sled 'em [draw them on sledges]" (Ibid. No. 96 : p. 232, l. 49).—Rosa Lucas, nearly eighteen years old, drawer at Mr. Morris's, Lamberhead Green : " What distance did you draw? 23 score yards in length. That is 460 yards each way, or 920 yards? Yes.—How many times had you to draw this distance? 16 and sometimes 18 times. [Taking 16 times, she would have to draw 14,720 yards daily]" (Ibid. No. 92: p. 231, l. 57).—Dinah Bradbury, waggoner at Mr. Evans's, Haydock Colliery : " Draws for two men. *Girl.*—At what age do you intend to turn us out of the pit? Put me down 15 years old. I should like to be turned out.—Do you then not like your present employment?—No, I don't, and I would not go down if I could get anything else to do" (Ibid. No. 73 : p. 229, l. 47, 56).
—Jane Sym, aged twenty-six, waggoner at Mr. Craig's, Blackrod : " I am a drawer; I am a married woman; I work night and day, week about, that is, I work in the day one week and in the night the next; I don't like working in the night shift; it makes me very tired sometimes, and I am ill with it, but I must keep my turn, or ' clem' [go without food]."—[Sub-Commissioner: " This was a delicate and rather interesting-looking young woman; her neatness and cleanliness struck me as remarkable when compared to collier-girls in general; with all this, her appearance denoted great distress, and from what she said I inferred that the misery arose from her husband being a drunkard]" (Ibid. No. 72: p. 229, l. 20).

337. OLDHAM.—" The Children and Young Persons employed in the coal mines of Lancashire, instead of commencing their labours with the 'tenting' of an air-door, usually commence at once with the task of bringing the coal from the place where the getter is at work to the bottom of the pit. In this labour there are great numbers employed ; few horses being taken underground, because the seams are not generally thick, and lie at such moderate depths that it is less expensive to sink new shafts at short distances than to make extensive systems of ways under-ground. In the thin mountain-seams youths begin very early to be getters, work-ing nearly or quite naked, as they lie on their sides. The men in the other mines generally keep on their frieze trousers while at work."

338. The lowest class of employment next to the dreary occupation of the few little trappers is that of the " thrutchers," which " consists in being helper to a ' drawer' or ' waggoner,' who is master or ' butty,' over the ' thrutcher.' He is chiefly employed in ' thrutching,' or thrusting, behind the loaded tubs of coal, with his hands and head, which latter is generally protected by a thick cap, although the thrutcher in the thin-seam mines works in all other respects naked, or nearly so (Nos. 3, 20, 25, 26). In other pits he will keep on his trousers and clogs. The size of the loads which hes has to thrutch varies with the thickness of the seam ; and with the size varies his butty's method of proceeding, which is either as a ' drawer' or a ' waggoner.'

339. " The ' drawers ' are those who use the belt and chain, which is now seldom employed, except in the thinner seams. Their labour consists in loading, with the coals hewn down by the getter, an oblong tub without wheels, measuring 27 inches long by 24 inches wide, and 9 inches high, and containing 3 cwt., or a basket and a half; and dragging this tub on its sledge bottom, by means of a girdle of rough leather passing round the body, and a chain of iron attached to that girdle in front, and hooked to the sledge. The drawer has, with the assistance of his ' thrutcher,' to sledge the tub in this manner from the place of getting to the main-way, generally down, though sometimes up, a ' broo,' brow, or incline, of the same steepness as the inclination of the strata ; in descending which he goes to the front of his tub, where his light is fixed, and, turning his face to it, regulates its mo-tion down the hill, as, proceeding back foremost, he pulls it along by his belt. When he gets to the main-way which will be at various distances, not exceeding forty or fifty yards from his loading-place, he has to leave this tub upon a low truck running on small iron wheels, and then to go and fetch a second, which will complete its load, and with these two to join with his ' thrutcher' in pushing it along the iron railway to the pit bottom, to have the tubs successively hooked on to the drawing-rope. Returning with his tubs empty, he leaves the main-way, first with one, and then with the other tub, to get them loaded, dragging them up the ' broo' by his belt and chain, the latter of which he now passes between his legs, so as to pull, face foremost, on all fours (Nos. 3, 4, 6, 20, 22). In the thin seams this labour has to be performed in ' bays,' leading from the place of getting to the main-ways, of scarcely more than 20 inches in height; and in main-ways of only 2 feet 6 inches and 3 feet high, for the seam itself will be only 18 inches thick (See No. 20, &c.).

340. " ' Waggoning' is the form of ' drawing' the coals which comes into use with the more extensive employment of railways in the thicker seams. Rails are here laid by the miners at the charge of the employer, up to the very spot of getting ; and the tubs, which increase in size from those carrying 3 cwt. to others for 4 cwt., 6 cwt., and 8 cwt., according to the thickness of the seam, are all mounted on their own wheels. The weight of the waggons or tubs will be from $\frac{1}{2}$ cwt. to 2 cwt., in addition to the coal which they carry ; making those of the largest size, when loaded, about half a ton in weight. The ' waggoners' of the larger tubs are youths of seventeen or eighteen, when one person has to manage the whole load ; but younger boys often join two together, to ' make a waggoner,' receiving the pay of one, and dividing it between them, according to their relative ability ; the younger one calling himself a ' thrutcher ' only, and designating the older one his ' butty.' From the place of getting, the loads are pushed by the waggoners with hands and head to the bottom of the pit along the levels ; and where they have to descend from one level into another, this is generally done by a cut at right angles directly with the dip, down the ' broo' or hill which it makes. Here there is a winch and pinion for jigging the waggons down the incline, with a jigger at the top, and a hooker-on at the bottom of the plane, where it is such as to require these. The jiggers and the hookers-on are Children of twelve or thirteen.

Sometimes, however, the descent from one line of level into another is by a diagonal cutting at a smaller angle from the levels, called a slant, down which the waggoners can, and do in some instances, take their waggons without jigging, by their own manual labour; and a very rough process it is, owing to the impetus which so great a weight acquires, notwithstanding the scotching of the wheels. Horses are seldom used (Nos. 4, 6)." (J. Fletcher, Esq., Report, § 31—33: App. Pt. II., p. 824).

341. There is a practice in this district but little known in any other part of England—that " of employing mere Children to manage the engines by which the men as well as the coals are drawn out of the pit. The power of the steam-engine is applied directly, and in the simplest form, to this purpose; and upon the accurate stoppage of the engine, at the exact moment of their appearance at the surface, depends whether the men ascending shall not be wound over the pulley above, and dashed down the shaft again—an event which has here repeatedly occurred" (Ibid. § 25: p. 823).

Mr. John Ogden, chief agent to the Chamber Colliery Company: " Young people are employed as engineers from twelve to twenty years of age. They learn better when young. The company has a regular scale of promotion, of which the engineers themselves are very jealous. They begin at 7*s.* a-week, and get up to 1*l.* It is a very particular job to watch the chains, and stop at the right moment; and if, when a lad is tried at it, he is not a sharp fellow, he is withdrawn from that occupation. As they get older they go to be engineers at factories, where they will get perhaps 30*s.* a-week, in lieu of the 20*s.* which they would alone get here. These collieries are, in fact, a school of engineers for the factories (J. Fletcher, Esq., Evidence, No. 4: App. Pt. II., p. 841, l. 40).—Moses Mills, underlooker at the Hunt-lane Collieries: " Formerly, if a child could but learn to manage the engine, they did not look to what age he was; thinks it has been the case that some might be no more than ten or eleven; they were not so particular as they are now. It is now a rule not to give the management of an engine to any lad under fourteen; may be two months is long enough to learn" (Ibid. No. 35: p. 855, l. 62).— Joseph Gott, aged fifty-three, and Richard Barker, aged forty-six, colliers, coal mine near Rochdale: " Children should not be employed so young as engineers; many a man has been killed by it" (Ibid. Nos. 13 and 14: p. 850, l. 41).—John Gordon, aged thirty-five, and Edmund Stanley, aged thirty-four, miners in the employment of Mr. Abraham Lees, at Stoneywell Lane, near Oldham: " Think that such young boys should not be intrusted, as engineers, with the lives of a lot of men as they are; they are not 'stayable,' and no one under eighteen ought to be intrusted with such a job. This is a general opinion among the men themselves" (Ibid. Nos. 15 and 16: p. 851, l. 37).—Cyrus Taylor, engineer at one of the Slibber Pits, going in thirteen: " Is past thirteen, and has been five weeks next Saturday learning to be engineer at the Slibber Pits, of the company of Messrs. Jones. [Is at this hour by himself winding coals, also one cargo of a boy and three men.] Was working at the bottom, but got two fingers cut off [showing the stumps on the left hand]. Winds men as well as coals. The proper engineer is Samuel Taylor, no relation of his, and who is somewhere about, mending waggons. Samuel Taylor always comes into the engine-house to be with him when he is winding men" (Ibid. No. 38: p. 856, l. 19).—James Woods, engineer at one of the Hunt-lane Pits, going in sixteen: " Has been an engineer about four years. Is now working at the Hunt-lane Collieries, at the Hor-lane Pit. Is busy at his work; is reckoned attentive; in winding has wound over tubs of coals twice; has never wound over men, but was once appointed in place of a lad who wound over three men, and killed them: this was at the Trundley Pit, one of the Chamber-lane Pits, and about two years ago" (Ibid. No. 36: p. 856, l. 3.)—Thomas Whittaker, engineer at one of the Hunt-lane Pits, going in seventeen: " Has been engineer about four years; has wound over coals once or twice; never any men" (Ibid. No. 37: p. 856, l. 11).

342. NORTH LANCASHIRE.—In this district the Sub-Commissioner complains of " the great evil of the want of sufficient height in the 'little coal' mines, and the consequent ungainly position in which Children and Young Persons are compelled to toil and to drag along burthens, which would be as much as they could easily draw even in a more favourable posture."

343. In these mines the use of the belt and chain seems to be universal. "On the hardship of such labour as this I need not dwell: every person of feeling will pity those poor Children whose position in life has caused them to be subject to it. That it does not excite a strong feeling of commiseration in the parents who send their Children at an early age to this work, might surprise any one; but use reconciles them to it; many have been colliers themselves, and see no reason why their Children should not do as their fathers have done before them, forgetting, as age is apt to do, the sufferings they experienced, and remembering only that by this toil they earned their bread, and so must their Children" (A. Austin, Esq., Report, §§ 7-9: App. Pt. II., p. 802). See witnesses Nos. 4, 5, 8, 9, 12, 17.

344. CUMBERLAND.—In this district the height of the coal-seam admits of horses being brought up to the workings; and in all Lord Lonsdale's Collieries, and in the larger mines in general on the coast of Cumberland, the coal is drawn by horses directly from the workings to the shaft. In these coal-mines no Children or Young Persons are employed in trailing, hurrying, or putting. Still the evidence shows that there are mines in which Children are employed as trailers; but these are stated to be chiefly the smaller and inland collieries. In the coal-mines in which trailers are employed the Children have to help to fill and riddle the coals as in the Yorkshire District.

345. Trappers are employed in nearly all the pits, and their work is somewhat augmented by having occasionally two or more doors to attend to, and by having to alter checks, so that the trains may pass along their proper roads at the dividing places. But the chief employment of Children and Young Persons in the coal mines of this district is to drive along the tram-ways the horses which draw the trams of baskets loaded with coal, several of which are hooked together. "The journeys along these tram-ways are greatly lengthened, owing to many of the large collieries being sub-marine. In the William Pit they have 500 acres under the sea, and the distance is 2 miles and a half from the shaft to the extreme part of the workings. There is a stable also under the sea in this immense pit for 45 horses. The shaft is 110 fathoms. A feature exists in this driving employment I have not hitherto seen, and which constitutes the chief labour of the occupation. To prevent the baskets from running down hill and falling on the heels of the horses, it is customary for the driver to place himself as a post between the foremost basket and the buttock of the horse. He places the left shoulder against the horse, the right foot on the rail of the tram, and the right hand on the top of the basket; the left leg being generally supported by the trace. When the train of corves is heavily laden, or the descent very steep, a pole is placed through the hind wheels of the trams, and thus it is in a measure dragged. Nevertheless the work is very toilsome, and, as will be seen by the evidence of the surgeon attending Earl Lonsdale's collieries, accidents sometimes occur by the foot slipping off, and getting struck by part of the wheel or axle. The leaning position in which they stand is not in itself, I think, injurious; but the work strikes one as being palpably unnecessary, and as a barbarous preference of the human body for a mere mechanical process; in which shafts might be, and in some of the inland pits are, used instead. It was indeed stated by one witness, that the use of shafts would be very awkward for the purpose of turning at the foreheads. I believe a very little management would obviate this difficulty" (J. C. Symons, Esq., Report, § 5, 6: App. Pt. I., p. 299). For a further account of the occupations of Trailing and Driving see the statements of witnesses Nos. 301, 302, 303, 310, 312, 315, 318, 320, 324, 325, 328, 329, 332.

346. SOUTH DURHAM.—The juvenile labourers underground, in this district, are the trappers, putters, drivers, helpers-up, trammers, cleavers, switch-boys, and leaders of water, stone, and wood. The three first are the chief classes of hands. The trappers, as in the other districts, sit in solitude and darkness in a hole made in the coal about the size of a common fireplace, in the tram-roads, here called also barrow-roads, because formerly wheelbarrows were used by the persons employed to wheel the coals along these passages.

347. The employment of the putters is to push the trams or sledges, the carriages on which are placed the tubs of coal, along the tram-ways or barrow-ways from the workings to the flats; that is, the place at which the tram-way terminates and the horse-way commences; called flats from the flat plates of coarse cast-iron which are at the termination of the tram-way. The tram-way is generally from 3 to 4 feet in height, so that although the putter must stoop a little in pushing his tram, he need not do so in such a degree as to distort his figure, injure his breathing, or in any way impede his progress. A young man at the flats marks down every tub of coal brought there by a putter. A full day's work performed by the putter is thus estimated. Suppose the distance from the workings to the flats, as measured by the yard-wand of the overman, to be 90 yards, he travels over this space 21 times, pushing a weight of $8\frac{1}{2}$ cwt. (the weight of his tub when full of coals, including the weight of the tub itself), and he travels back the same distance with his empty tub and tram. Moreover he has to assist the hewer in filling his tub; he thus assists 21 times in filling his tub; travels 1890 yards, or 1 mile and

130 yards, with a weight of 8½ cwt. on his tram, and travels back with his tram and empty tub the same distance.

348. In general those who put singly are young men of from sixteen to twenty years of age. But sometimes "two boys, both of them unable singly to put a tram, unite together as partners, and they accomplish the work between them. The work which they perform is put down to their joint account, and they divide the wages between them. Such boys, in the language of the miners, are called half-marrows. After a time, when the boys become sufficiently powerful, each takes to put a tram singly, and immediately enters on a large increase to his income. It sometimes occurs that a youth is not quite able to get through a day's work as a putter by himself, and yet does not want much assistance. In that case a little boy of ten or eleven years of age may be sufficient. The larger youth is called the head man, and the little putter so employed is called a foal. These two classes, the half-marrows and the foals, explain why some of the putters in the lists of the workpeople returned from the collieries are so much younger than the rest, and why their emoluments are so small, as compared to the income of other putters" (Dr. Mitchell, Report, § 139, 140: App. Pt. I., p. 133, 134).

349. The carriage in which the coal is placed after it has been received from the putters, and which is drawn by the horse along the horse-way to the foot of the shaft, is called a rolley. Generally these rolleys are drawn by one horse under the care of a driver, a boy, who sits on the limber beside his horse and is in constant motion throughout the day, without any interval of rest, travelling altogether perhaps 30 miles in the 12 hours.

350. On an equal footing with the drivers, as to emolument, are boys "whose employment is to attend to the switches, and so to place them, where two or more roads in the pit diverge, as that the rolleys may be sent the road by which they are ordered to go. At some openings of two roads a rolley is to be sent by one of the roads, and the next rolley by the other, alternately. There are switches also on the tram-ways or barrow-ways.

351. "Of the same rank and emolument are the boys who sweep the railways of the barrow-ways or tram-ways. The helper-up is a youth who is employed to assist in pushing forward the trams in the pit, in places where there is a steep rising ground. Some helpers-up have a horse ready to be attached to the carriages, and with the horse the youth walks to the top of the incline, and then he unhooks him, and walks with him down the hill to be ready to assist the next who comes up. Some helpers-up are sixteen or seventeen years of age. Some boys are employed in conducting horses with water-carts with water for the men, boys, and horses in the pit. Water is also required to sprinkle the roads, and keep down the dust. In some pits also water collects, which has to be carried away, and the water-leaders have also this business to attend to. The same lads who lead water also bring wood to be used in supporting the roof. Other boys called stone-leaders conduct carts with stones for repairing the roads, and sometimes for building walls along the sides of the road.

352. "Formerly in most of the mines at the flats there stood a crane, by which the corve was hoisted up from the tram and let down upon the rolley. The persons who did this work were boys: it was very severe labour. Now, the more frequent mode is to use tubs instead of corves, and to make the horseway so much lower than the tramway, that the tub may be rolled from the tram into the rolley. This work—the rolling the tubs—is in some pits performed by the drivers; in other pits, the drivers and putters together do it; and there are pits where there are lads who assist in this work, who are also employed to keep the account of the tubs or corves brought by the putters" (Ibid. § 117-123: p. 131).

353. The hewers, the same class of men as in the southern districts are called holers, are in general twenty-one years of age and upwards, and in the northern district it is very rare that any of them are under eighteen, but there are such exceptions.

354. At almost all the collieries in this district an operation is carried on at the surface which "gives employment to great multitudes of children under thirteen, and of young persons between the ages of thirteen and eighteen, namely, that called 'screening the coals,'" which is a plan by which the large coal is separated from the small coal and dust, with a view to exportation by sea either coastwise or to foreign parts. The Sub-Commissioner, who has given a full account of this employment, (see Dr. Mitchell's Report, § 237 et seq., p. 146,) says, "whilst the

coals are lying on the horizontal screen, great numbers of boys are employed as wailers, that is, they wail, or select out the black stones and iron pyrites, commonly called brasses; also, when the coals are shovelled into the railway waggons there are boys in the waggons whose ready glance detects the coal-looking stones and clod, and they remove them from the more marketable commodity" (Ibid. § 241 : p. 146).

355. " Children and Young Persons are much employed in all the labours on the bank. When corves are emptied over the screens, they overturn the little trams on which they have been carried, and oil or grease the axletrees. They overturn the tubs and grease their axletrees; they roll the corves and tubs back to the mouth of the shafts; they move corves or tubs of the coal from which the round coal has been taken; they push, or, as they call it, they put the tubs containing the coal-dust. Sometimes, when a great heap of coals is accumulated on the bank to be ready for a sudden demand, they put the trams on the bank on a temporary railway, in the same manner as is done in the pit. In all these operations the labour is little less, if any, than down in the pit, but the pay is only about half as much" (Ibid. § 252: p. 147). See witnesses, Nos. 88, 100, 105, 107, 108, 109, 110, 111, 112, 116.

356. The girdle and chain are never employed in this district.

357. NORTH DURHAM AND NORTHUMBERLAND.—There is of course little difference in the employment of Children and Young Persons in this and the preceding district, and the names by which the young workers are designated are the same. The minimum weight of the loaded corf pushed by the putters is 5 cwt., and the maximum 10 cwt.; the average weight in the majority of pits being from 6 to 8 cwt. " In order to obtain a fair average of the journeys of putters," says the Sub-Commissioner, who adds the description of their work given by a great number of each class of juvenile hands, " I calculated, by means of the 'renk,' (the gradation of price paid to the putters, according to the distances they put, adjusted by admeasurement every fortnight or oftener), the daily travels of 27 putters at Percy Main Colliery;" the distance was found to be from 8 to 8½ miles per diem; of course the assistants to the putters have to travel the same distance. The putters, in order to equalize for each the distances from the workings to the horseways, which are extremely various, " draw caivils," that is, draw lots for their places once a fortnight, or every morning in some instances (J. R. Leifchild, Esq., Report, § 212: App. Pt. I., p. 544).

According to Nicholas Wood, Esq., viewer of Killingworth, Hetton, and other collieries : " Supposing a lad to put 2 score (40 corves) in a day, at 1*s.* 8*d.* per score, he will have made 40 double trips that day, and each double trip being a distance of 360 yards, he will have travelled over 40 × 360 yards, equalling 14,400 yards, or between 8 and 9 miles. It is the general practice to conduct a tram in the following manner:—1. If one lad puts a tram by himself, he is called a 'tram.' 2. If an old and strong boy, and a young boy together, put a tram, the older boy is called a ' headsman,' and the younger boy a ' foal.' The headsman pays the foal 4*d.* out of every shilling, retaining the 8*d.* for himself. The foal is a servant of the master. 3. If two boys of about equal age and strength together put a tram, they are called ' half-marrows,' and they divide their earnings equally. All these putters are bound to work for 12 hours, and very rarely exceed that time" (J. R. Leifchild, Esq., Evidence, No. 97 : App. Pt. I., p. 586, l. 55).—Ten boys of from fourteen to eighteen years of age : " Are all putters. Two headsmen, five half-marrows, three foals. All down Percy Pit. Headsmen go behind the tram, and push it from the hewers to the crane. A headsman and a half-marrow make up a tram. A foal assists a putter. The foals pull with the soams [a pair of cords from 2 feet 9 inches to 3 feet in length, used by foals and half-marrows for pulling the trams], and sometimes are put upon by the older boys. A lump of leather is sowed on to the backs of the jackets of the half-marrows and foals, because the corf runs against them sometimes when it is going down hill" (Ibid. No. 81 : p. 582, l. 14).—George Johnson, Esq., viewer of Willington, Heaton, and Burdon Main Collieries. on the Tyne : " Putters will never put a full corf beyond a level without a helper up. In addition, it is the true economy of a mine always to put on to level, or as nearly so as possible. The lowest height which boys are compelled to work in is the minimum height of the corf, which is about 3 feet 9 inches in this district. The corf is made to suit the height of the seam, and not, within witness's observation, less than 3 feet 8 or 9 inches. Does not know any instance of putters wearing ' back-skins,' or protection against rubbing their backs. In helping up they go but very short distances. Every nerve and sinew is put into motion in helping up and putting. This labour is only suitable for healthy young men in their very prime. An unhealthy young man could never continue it. He would complain to the viewer, and get easier work. Of course a man having a family of putters is a very desirable man" (Ibid. No. 3 : p. 567, l. 48).—Edward Gregory, turned of thirteen, helper-up, South Shields, or Manor Wallsend Colliery : " Helps up all day down the pit; helps up a heavy place; there are other places steeper; helps up the trams from one bord; used to help up

COAL MINES.

*Nature of
Employment.*

North Durham
and
Northumberland.

from two bords; did so last week. Always helped up from two bords till this week or so; it was harder work then. Used to help up 68 trams in a day then. Each two hewers hewed 34 trams in a day. The men are now in another place, and they hew 28 trams a-day; each pair of hewers hew 28 trams in a day there; hence he has very easy work now for a short time; this will last this week perhaps" (Ibid. No. 351: p. 638, l. 19).

Nicholas Wood, Esq., viewer, Killingworth: "In some cases donkeys assist the putters at very steep places. 'Helpers-up' are boys substituted for these donkeys, and they are much more suitable at slight inclinations, for donkeys are very slow, and are only used at considerable inclinations. At this colliery [Killingworth] they have 13 donkeys in use. There is a practice now in use at Hetton and other collieries of substituting for putters small ponies, drawing a different kind of carriage, and taking the coals direct from the hewers to the shaft bottom" (Ibid. No. 97: p. 586, l. 67).—James Easton, Esq., viewer of Hebburn Fawdon and Wideopen Collieries: "At Wideopen they use entirely ponies for helping up, not donkeys. Hence not any boys are employed for helping up. Only the driver of these Galloways [perhaps 13 hands high] are necessary; no helping up is necessary. In putting at Wideopen the greatest rise is 3 inches to the yard; that is, they put down that inclination a full corve. There are two kinds of putting there. In one the pony brings the weight up the rise to the crane, and the putter puts the empty corf down. In the other case the putter puts the empty corf up the hill and brings it down again when full. In very rare cases, for a short period, a lad may be employed to help up" (Ibid. No. 158: p. 601, l. 6).

Mr. Oliver, under-viewer, Percy Pit: "Has seen boys put coals under a height of 30 inches only. The little lads there [Shilbottle Colliery], of ten, twelve, thirteen, or fourteen, put the tubs by keeping their hands on the end of the tram, and putting their heads against the tub. They roll up their hoggers [or footless stockings], put them in their caps, and place these caps against the tubs, and so make a soft place for leaning their heads against. When these lads get long in the legs they put them to other work, probably men's work, although they do not perform so much work of that kind as men. The lads wear backskins there to keep their backs from hitting against the roof: there will, perhaps, be 20 lads doing this. The seam there is 30 inches thick, and they only cut away tops and bottoms for horses and ponies. In all collieries where it is banky [hilly] the foals wear backskins to keep the skin from rubbing off their backs. The number of foals depends upon the nature of the putting. Dip-putting is putting the full corf up the bank, and rise-putting is fetching the full corf down the bank. This rise-putting is certainly the easier of the two. They will never require boys to put without helpers-up if they have much difficulty in getting away" (Ibid. No. 95: p. 584, l. 63). —Joseph Taylor, going to ten, driver, Heaton Colliery: "Drove for eight months, and is now driving. Gets up every morning at 3 o'clock, except on Saturday morning, when he gets up at 1 A.M., and finishes on Saturday at 1 P.M. Starts work at 4 o'clock A.M. down the pit. Goes down the pit in a corf, about four together; goes a little way in, and gets the candles and puts them in the 'mistress' first; yokes his horse next; yokes it himself without help, no one helps him; then drives the rolleys, three yoked together, holding altogether six corves, to the shaft. The onsetter then puts the chain-hook into the bow of the corf, hooking on two at a time, and then sends them up to bank. Then witness goes in by with the empty corves, and changes his empty corves for full corves at the crane, and then he drives to the onsetter again. This work he does all day" (Ibid. No. 16: p. 571, l. 46).—Evidence to the same effect is given by great numbers of witnesses; among others by Nos. 11, 31, 45, 46, 510, 512, &c.

Luke Gray, aged forty-two, hewer, Percy Main Colliery: "Is a hewer, and has been for 22 years. The labour is too hard for the foal. Many times the skin is off his back by the corf rubbing it off. Last fortnight his back was skinned almost all the way down by the corf crouping [or falling] upon him, by getting off the tramway. He was off three days from this. He wears a back-skin of leather. All the foals do here. The headsman is behind, putting his hand against the roof and against the side. In heavy banks they drag all four wheels of the tram. The boys change places by putting in caivils once a fortnight. Very little boys, of 12 or 13 years of age, put as foals. Foals suffer more than other boys. They are too young, and the work too heavy for them at that age. Men have to leave the colliery sometimes, because their boys are put too young to this work. These boys are wanted, and must be had. They have great need for boys. The extremity of labour is greatest for foals of any boys. The low-seam boys can travel bent very nearly double. They go nearly bent double in walking in general. Has seen boys crying in this office because they were bound to be foals" (Ibid. No. 91: p. 584, l. 2).

George Soulsby, aged sixteen, chalker-on, Walls-end Colliery: "Is called a chalker-on; chalks down all the pit's work. Asks every waggon-driver that passes him as he sits by the rolley way side what crane he comes from; has each crane's name chalked down on a deal board, and against the name he puts down what load of coals is being taken past him. The cranes are named by the boys and men such names as 'Black-horse,' 'Sandgate,' &c. At the end of the day's work the craneman comes, and counts what is chalked down, and puts it in a book, and sends that book to the overman" (Ibid. No. 274: p. 625, l. 42).

358. EAST OF SCOTLAND.—It has been already stated that in this district girls and women are employed equally with males in all the labours of the coal-mines. Indeed it is stated to be a general rule that "girls are invariably set at an earlier age than boys to their peculiar labour from a notion very generally

entertained amongst the parents, that girls are more acute and capable of making themselves useful at an earlier age than boys" (R. H. Franks, Esq., Report, § 28: App. Pt. I., p. 388). The chief employment of Children and Young Persons in the coal mines of this district is in trapping, coal-bearing, putting, pumping, and hewing. In the employment of trapping there is nothing peculiar.

359. The persons employed in coal-bearing are almost always girls and women. Boys are sometimes engaged in the same labour, but that is comparatively rare. The coal-bearers have to carry coal on their backs in unrailed roads with burdens varying from ¾ cwt. to 3 cwt. The Sub-Commissioner represents this labour as " a cruel slaving revolting to humanity;" yet he found engaged in this labour a child, a beautiful girl, only six years old, whose age he ascertained, carrying in the pit ½ cwt. of coals, and regularly making with this load fourteen long and toilsome journeys a-day.

Fig. 9. Fig. 10. Fig. 11

[Trap Staircase.]

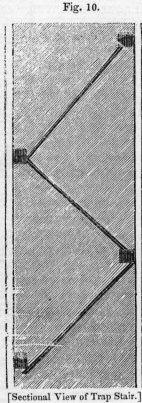

[Sectional View of Trap Stair.]

[Turnpike Stair.]

Margaret Leveston, six years old, coal-bearer : " Been down at coal-carrying six weeks; makes 10 to 14 rakes a-day; carries full 56 lbs. of coal in a wooden backit. The work is na guid; it is so very sair. I work with sister Jesse and mother; dinna ken the time we gang; it is gai dark." [A most interesting child, and perfectly beautiful. I ascertained her age to be six years, 24th May, 1840; she was registered at Inverness.] " (R. H. Franks, Esq., Evidence, No. 116: App. Pt. I., p. 458, l. 20.)—William Burnside, ten years old, coal-bearer, same colliery: " I gang with brother and sister; have done so two months. I can fill one tub in the day : it takes me 17 journeys, as my back gets sore. A tub holds near 5 cwt. I follow sister with bits of coal strapped over my head and back. The work fatigues me muckle" (Ibid. No. 57: p. 447, l. 37).—Ellison Jack, a girl eleven years old, coal-bearer : " I have been working below three years on my father's account; he takes me down at two in the morning, and I come up at one and two next afternoon. I go to bed at six at night to be ready for work next morning ; the part of the pit I bear in the seams are much on the edge. I have to bear my burthen up four traps, or ladders, before I get to the main road which leads to the pit bottom. My task is four to five tubs; each tub holds 4¼ cwt. I fill five tubs in 20 journeys. I have had the strap when I did not do my bidding. Am very glad when my task is wrought, as it sore fatigues" (Ibid. No. 55: p. 446, l. 56).

360. " A brief description of this Child's place of work will better illustrate her evidence. She has first to descend a nine-ladder pit to the first rest, even to which a shaft is sunk, to draw up the baskets or tubs of coals filled by the bearers : she then takes her creel (a basket formed to the back, not unlike a cockle-shell flattened towards the neck, so as to allow lumps of coal to rest on the back of the neck and shoulders), and pursues her journey to the wall-face, or as it is called here, the room of work. She then lays down her basket, into which the coal is rolled, and it is frequently more than one man can do to lift the burden on her

back.   The tugs or straps are placed over the forehead, and the body bent in a semicircular form, in order to stiffen the arch.   Large lumps of coal are then placed on the neck, and she then commences her journey with her burden to the pit bottom, first hanging her lamp to the cloth crossing her head.   In this girl's case she has first to travel about 14 fathoms (84 feet) from wall-face to the first ladder, which is 18 feet high : leaving the first ladder she proceeds along the main road, probably 3 feet 6 inches to 4 feet 6 inches high, to the second ladder, 18 feet high, so on to the third and fourth ladders till she reaches the pit-bottom, where she casts her load, varying from 1 cwt to 1½ cwt., into the tub.   This one journey is designated a rake; the height ascended, and the distance along the roads added together, exceed the height of St. Paul's Cathedral; and it not unfrequently happens that the tugs break, and the load falls upon those females who are following.   However incredible it may be, yet I have taken the evidence of fathers who have ruptured themselves from straining to lift coal on their Children's backs" (Ibid. No. 55 : p. 446, l. 67).   The accompanying sections of the passages (fig. 12) which the coal-bearers (Nos. 13, 14, and 15) have to traverse, will give some idea of the labour of ascending through them with the loads described.

Fig. 12.

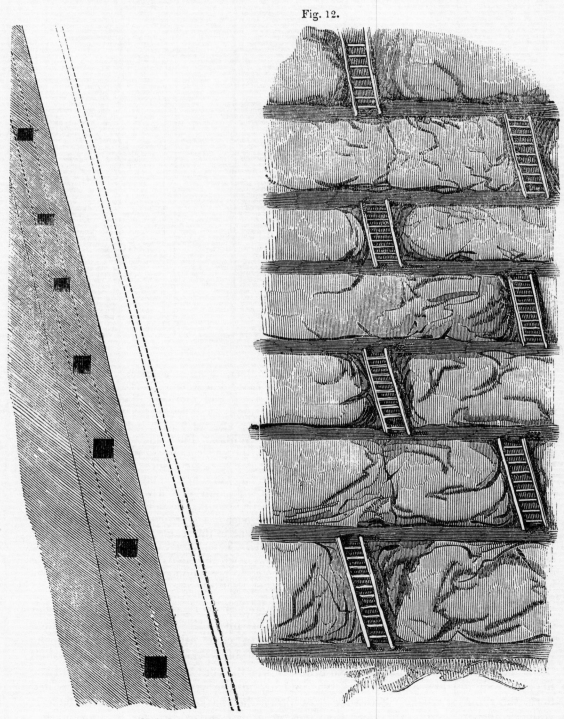

[Rough Section of the working of an Edge Seam in Loanhead.]

Janet Cumming, eleven years old, bears coals: "I gang with the women at five and come up at five at night; work *all night* on Fridays, and come away at twelve in the day. I carry the large bits of coal from the wall-face to the pit-bottom, and the small pieces called chows in a creel. The weight is usually a hundredweight; does not know how many pounds there are in a hundredweight, but it is some weight to carry; it takes three journeys to fill a tub of 4 cwt. The distance varies, as the work is not always on the same wall; sometimes 150 fathoms, whiles 250 fathoms. The roof is very low; I have to bend my back and legs, and the water comes frequently up to the calves of my legs. Has no liking for the work; father makes me like it. Never got hurt, but often obliged to scramble out of the pit when bad air was in" (Ibid. No. 1: p. 436, l. 3). Fig. 14 represents an older girl carrying coals.

Fig. 13.

Isabella Read, twelve years old: "I am wrought with sister and brother; it is very sore work. Cannot say how many rakes or journeys I make from pit-bottom to wall-face and back, thinks about 30 or 25 on the average; distance varies from 100 to 250 fathoms. I carry a hundredweight and a quarter on my back, and am frequently in water up to the calves of my legs. When first down fell frequently asleep while waiting for coal from heat and fatigue. I do not like the work, nor do the lassies, but they are made to like it. When the weather is warm there is difficulty in breathing, and frequently the lights go out" (Ibid. No. 14: p. 439, l. 23). —Agnes Kerr, fifteen years old, coal-bearer, Dryden Colliery: "Was nine years old when commenced carrying coals; carry father's coal; make 18 to 20 journeys a-day; a journey to and fro is about 200 to 250 fathom: have to ascend and descend many ladders; can carry 1½ cwt" (Ibid. No. 65: p. 448, l. 53).—Mary Duncan, sixteen years of age, coal-bearer: "Began to carry coals when twelve years old. Do not like the work, nor do the other women, many of whom have wrought from eight years of age, and know no other. My employment is carrying coals from wall-face to the daylight up the stair-pit. I make 40 to 50 journeys a-day, and can carry 2 cwt. as my burthen. Some females carry 2½ to 3 cwt., but it is overstraining" (Ibid. No. 155: p. 464, l. 60).—Agnes Moffatt, seventeen years of age: "Began working at ten years of age. Works 12 and 14 hours daily. Father took sister and I down; he gets our wages. I fill five baskets; the weight is more than 22 cwt.; it takes me five journeys. The work is o'er sair for females. Had my shoulder knocked out a short time ago, and laid idle some time. It is no uncommon thing for women to lose their burthen [load], and drop off the ladder down the dyke below. (Fig. 15.) Margaret M'Neil did a few weeks since, and injured both legs. When the tugs which pass over the forehead break, which they frequently do, it is very dangerous to be under a load. The lassies hate the work altogether, but they canna run away from it" (Ibid. No. 23: p. 440, l. 46).—Jane Peacock Watson, aged forty, coal-bearer, Bearing Pits, Harlow Muir, Coaly-Burn, Peeblesshire: "I have wrought in the bowels of

Fig. 14.

Fig. 15.

the earth 33 years. Have been married 23 years, and had nine children; six are alive, three died of typhus a few years since; have had two dead born; thinks they were so from the oppressive work: a vast of women have dead children and false births, which are worse, as they are no able to work after" (Ibid. No. 117: p. 458, l. 28).—William Hunter, mining oversman, Arniston Colliery: "I have been 20 years in the works of Robert Dundas, Esq., and had much experience in the manner of drawing coal, as well as the habits and practices of the collier people. Until the last eight months women and lassies were wrought below in these works, when Mr. Alexander Maxton, our manager, issued an order to exclude them from going below, having some months prior given intimation of the same. Women always did the lifting or heavy part of the work, and neither they nor the children were treated like human beings, nor are they where they are employed. Females submit to work in places where no man or even lad could be got to labour in: they work in bad roads, up to their knees in water, in a posture nearly double: they are below till last hour of pregnancy: they have swelled haunches and ankles, and are prematurely brought to the grave, or, what is worse, lingering existence. Many of the daughters of the miners are now at respectable service. I have two who are in families at Leith, and who are much delighted with the change" (Ibid. No. 89: p. 453, l. 59).—Robert Bald, Esq., the eminent coal-viewer, states that, "In surveying the workings of an extensive colliery under ground, a married woman came forward, groaning under an excessive weight of coals, trembling in every nerve, and almost unable to keep her knees from sinking under her. On coming up she said, in a plaintive and melancholy voice, ' Oh, Sir, this is sore, sore, sore work. I wish to God that the first woman who tried to bear coals had broke her back, and none would have tried it again!'" (R. H. Franks, Esq., Report, App. Pt. I., p. 387, note.)

361. At the conclusion of his account of this employment, the Sub-Commissioner reports: "When the nature of this horrible labour is taken into consideration, its extreme severity, its regular duration of from 12 to 14 hours daily, which, once a-week at least, is extended through the whole of the night; the damp, heated, and unwholesome atmosphere in which the work is carried on; the tender age and sex of the workers; when it is considered that such labour is performed not in isolated instances selected to excite compassion, but that it may be truly regarded as the type of the everyday existence of hundreds of our fellow-creatures —a picture is presented of deadly physical oppression and systematic slavery, of which I conscientiously believe no one unacquainted with such facts would credit the existence in the British dominions" (Ibid. § 26: p. 387).

362. The grievous suffering thus inflicted on so many persons of tender age and of the female sex is perpetuated from the coal-owners continuing to work their mines in modes which have become obsolete in all other districts. "A little reflection," says the Sub-Commissioner, "would have prevented a vast deal of unnecessary and painful labour in the working of edge seams in Scotland; for instance, in South Wales (where the stratification is almost vertical), on the sea-coast at Britonferry, and in the Anthracite field in Pembrokeshire, *coal-bearing* as practised in Scotland is entirely unknown. The coal is transported from the different workings by successive windlasses, or balances, working on inclined planes, which plan entirely obviates the necessity of having recourse to the slavish and degrading employment of female labour at present in practice in the collieries in the East of Scotland" (Ibid. § 9: p. 383).

363. The labour in which Children and Young Persons are employed, next in severity to the sore slavery of coal-bearing, is coal-putting, in which we find the sexes more equally distributed. Putters drag or push the carts containing coal, from the coal-wall to the pit-bottom, weight varying from 3 to 10 cwt. Fig. 16 represents the mode of putting in Mid and East Lothian.

Fig. 16.

364. Fig. 17 represents the mode of putting in Fife and Clackmannan Shires.

Fig. 17

365. Fig. 18 represents the mode of putting backwards with the face to the tub.

Fig. 18.

366. The boxes or carriages employed in putting are of two sorts, the hutchie and the slype; the hutchie being an oblong square-sided box with four wheels, which usually runs on a rail; and the slype is a wood-framed box, curved and shod with iron at the bottom, holding from 2¼ to 5 cwt. of coal, adapted to the seams through which it is dragged. The lad or lass is harnessed over the shoulders and back with a strong leathern girth, which behind is furnished with an iron hook, which attaches itself to a chain fastened to the coal-cart or slype, and is thus dragged along. The dresses of these girls are made of coarse hempen stuff, (sacking), fitting close to the figure, the coverings to their heads are of the same material; little or no flannel is used, and their clothing, being of an absorbent nature, frequently gets completely saturated shortly after descending the pit, especially where the roofs are soft (Ibid, § 30: p. 388).

367. Where the seams are narrow and the roofs low, Children and Young Persons of both sexes drag on all-fours, like horses. In these seams the carriages called slypes, already described, are used: Fig. 19. The workings in these narrow

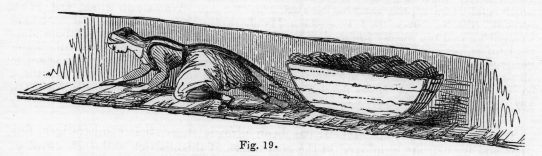

Fig. 19.

seams are from 100 to 200 yards from the main-roads, and the passages through which they have to crawl with their loads do not exceed from 22 to 28 inches in height. "The danger and the difficulties," observes the Sub-Commissioner, "of dragging on roads, dipping from one foot in three to one foot in six, may be more easily conceived than explained; and the state which females are in after pulling like horses through these holes—their perspiration, their exhaustion, and very frequently even their tears, it is painful in the extreme to witness; yet, when the work is done, they return to it with a vigour which is surprising, considering how they inwardly hate it" (Ibid. § 8: App. Pt. I., p. 383).—Of the severity of the labour performed by young women in these pits, the account of her work given by Margaret Hipps (fig. 19) may serve as an example.

Margaret Hipps, seventeen years old, putter, Stoney Rigg Colliery, Stirlingshire: "My employment, after reaching the wall-face, is to fill a bagie, or slype, with 2½ to 3 cwt. of coal. I then hook it on to my chain, and drag it through the seam, which is 26 to 28 inches high, till I get to the main-road—a good distance, probably 200 to 400 yards. The pavement I drag over is wet, and I am obliged at all times to, crawl on hands and feet with my bagie hung to the chain and ropes. (See fig. 19.) It is sad sweating and sore fatiguing work, and frequently maims the women" (R. H. Franks, Esq., Evidence, No. 233: App. Pt. I., p. 479, l. 50).—[Sub-Commissioner: "It is almost incredible that human beings can submit to such employment, crawling on hands and knees, harnessed like horses, over soft slushy floors more difficult than dragging the same weights through our lowest common-sewers, and more difficult in consequence of the inclination, which is frequently one in three to one in six"] (Ibid. l. 61).—See also witnesses, Nos. 102, 231, 236, 262, 362.

368. Another form of severe labour, to which Children of eight years of age and upwards are put, is that of pumping water in the pits.

Alexander Gray, ten years old, below-ground pump-boy, New Craighall Colliery, Inveresk:

" I pump out the water in the under bottom of the pit, to keep the men's rooms dry. I am obliged to pump fast or the water would cover me. I had to run away a few weeks ago, as the water came up so fast that I could no pump at all, and the men were obliged to gang. The water frequently covers my legs, and those of the men when they sit to pick. I have been two years at the pump. I work every day, whether men work or not: no holidays but Sabbath. I go down at three, sometimes five, in the morning; and come up at six and seven at night. I know that I work 12 and 14 hours, as I can tell by the clock " (Ibid. No. 68: p. 449, l. 17). —Janet Murdoch, twelve years old, pumper: " I have wrought in the mines four months. My present employment is to bucket the water and lift [carry] to level face; the work is constant and most wearying, as the place is low I lift in, not being four feet high" (Ibid. No. 242: p. 481, l. 30).

369. Another peculiarity in this district is the early age at which the workers begin to get or hew the coal. It is scarcely to be credited, but the Sub-Commissioner reports, and the Evidence proves, that this labour is performed by male Children from nine years old and upwards.

David Hynde, nine years old, coal-putter and hewer: " Began to work in the bowels of the earth nine months since at this place; was taken down by father and mother, who work below, and so does sister, who is 10 years past" (Ibid. No. 100: p. 455, l. 45).—Walter Cowan, fourteen years old, hewer: " Has been at coal-hewing four years and a half " (Ibid. No. 364: p. 501, l. 37).—Thomas Campbell, ten years old, hewer: " Am learning to hew coal at Dundonald with father" (Ibid. No. 379: p. 503, l. 32).—Robert Bowman, ten years old, hewer: " Am learning to hew the coals with father at Donibristle." (Ibid. No. 376: p. 503, l. 8).—William Russell, ten years old, hewer: " Works with four brothers below; all live together, as mother died in childbed, and father of bad breath some time since; he was only forty years of age, and much afflicted before death " (Ibid. No. 366: p. 501, l. 47).—James Neil, aged ten years, coal-hewer: " Been below eighteen months; the work is gai sore. Place of work is not very dry. I work from four and five in the morning till six and seven at night, and it fatigues me much. Sometimes I change my clothes; not frequent, as it is so late" (Ibid. No. 158: p. 465, l. 27).—Andrew Erskine, fourteen years old, hewer: " Hews coal: has done so four years; works for father" (Ibid. No. 355 a: p. 500, l. 6).—John Allen, twelve years old, hewer: "Wrought full two years; is very much fatigued at times, as most are after hard work. Works in the Plean Pit, which is full of water; the water having risen above the dip. Works with father, and on his account" (Ibid. No. 290: p. 489, l. 40)).—John Hynd, twelve years old, hews coal: " I have wrought on coal two years with mother and father" (Ibid. No. 321: p. 494, l. 20).—William Morris, fourteen years old, hewer: " Began to work 3½ years since; could read and write before going down. Picks the coal at wall-face and draws to main-road, and fills; brother assists to fill; he is same age as self, we are twins; but he is no so stout as I am. Work sometimes on the morning shift, at others the late shift" (Ibid. No. 341: p. 497: l. 57).—See also Nos. 103, 137, 157, 228, 229, 346, 441, &c.

370. WEST OF SCOTLAND.—It has been already stated that comparatively few girls and women are employed in the coal-mines of this district, and their employment in carrying coals on their backs is wholly unknown.—" The practice of employing females in the pit is but very limited in my district, as will be seen by reference to the table given above, not extending at all to the west of Glasgow, and increasing as we approach the east of Lanarkshire and the borders of Linlithgowshire. In these parts, however, it is but of recent introduction, it having been one of the rules of the colliers' union that no females should be allowed under ground. The temptation to employ them arises from their wages being lower than that of males. Nowhere in the West of Scotland, however, do they bear out coal on their backs, as I understand is the case in Fifeshire and the Lothians" (T. Tancred, Esq., Report, § 53: App. Pt. I., p. 324).

371. The chief employment of Children and Young Persons in the coal mines of this district, besides that of trapping, in which latter there is nothing peculiar, is stated to be " in drawing or pushing the loaded whirleys along the tram-roads from the place where the coal is worked out to the bottom of the shaft, where it is hoisted up with its load, and the Children return with an empty one in its place. Up to the age of fourteen or so two Children generally draw together, one pulling by means of leathern loops through which the arms are passed, having a chain from them hooked to the front of the whirley, and the other, a younger one, pushing behind with both hands." The amount of labour to which the drawers are subject " is very different, varying in proportion to the load drawn, the distance, and the number of times it is traversed, the inclination of the road, the state of repair in which the rails or tramways are kept, &c." The corf, or whirley, " is sometimes made of iron, sometimes of wood, but more commonly of wattled hazel-rods secured in a wooden frame, and in all cases running on cast-iron wheels. Its weight when loaded is widely different in different mines, varying from 2½ cwt. the minimum, to 11 cwt. the maximum.

372. "Any one who has seen the Children at work can have no hesitation in saying that the physical exertion necessary in drawing is occasionally considerable. This exertion, however, is by no means continuous. The whirley has to be filled, which is in general chiefly done by the collier with a shovel, and by lifting the larger pieces of coal with his hands. The whirley, being loaded and started on the tramway, runs pretty easily till perchance it gets off the rails at a sudden turn, or where another railway joins in. Then the drawer and his assistant, sometimes called the 'putter,' must put their shoulders to the wheel to lift or drag it upon the rails again. After this they can take a little rest. Once more they start, and perhaps hear a rattling and see a light in the distance; this is another pair of Children trotting along with an empty whirley towards the face of the coal. As there is but one line of rails, the drawer of the loaded carriage halloos to the others to stop, or to turn their whirley off the line. Thus a passage is left for the full one, which proceeds on its way. Now we will suppose they come to a part of the road where there is a slip in the strata, sometimes called 'a trouble.' Here the road rises pretty steeply for a short distance, and now comes the tug of war. The drawer throwing his whole weight upon the chain, and leaning his body so forward that his hands touch the rails, whilst the putter pushes with might and main behind, with many a puff they urge the load to the top of the ascent. Here they sit awhile till they have recovered their wind, after which they soon see the lights dancing about ahead, and hear the hubbub at the pit bottom. Here they have some time to wait their turn, and perhaps eat a part of the food they brought down with them, and pass their jokes with the other drawers. This lasts till the bottomer hooks on their whirley to the engine-rope and returns them an empty one, with which they set off at a run back into the mine, or what they call 'ben.' Thus the drawing, though occasionally hard work, admits of frequent periods of rest and refreshment. It affords a varied exercise to the body and limbs, so that I heard no complaints from the Children of over-fatigue, or of being oppressed by the workmen for whom they draw, who are usually either their father, elder brother, or some relation" (Ibid. § 53 : p. 324).

373. It appears that the practice of employing Children as engineers, so common in Lancashire, is not unknown in the West of Scotland. "I was not a little surprised," says the Sub-Commissioner, "to find that the management of a high-pressure steam-engine, on the proper working of which many lives depend, was not unfrequently intrusted to a mere boy of from twelve to fourteen years of age. In general, indeed, his father was the pit-head man, and from his station could see and communicate with the lad, who acted entirely by his directions; but still it appeared to me a practice full of danger. It should be mentioned that frequently the drainage of the Scotch collieries is all pumped up at one pit, whilst coals and men are raised by small engines for this purpose alone at distinct pits; consequently, every hutch which is raised or lowered requires the engine to be twice stopped to allow of its being hooked on and off, and if this is not done according to the signals given by the pit-head man and bottomer, serious accidents might occur. It is also necessary when men are going up and down to moderate the speed at which the engine works, otherwise they would run the risk of being dashed against the rocky sides of the shaft. The bottomer consequently always calls out 'Men on!' when men are coming up, and it is the duty of the engine manager to regulate the speed accordingly. If too the engine does not stop at the proper moment, the men might be hoisted up and dashed against the pit-head frame, which has sometimes happened. All this requires vigilance and care on the part of the engineer, which can hardly be expected of a boy so young as many employed as such" (Ibid. § 61 : p. 327.)

374. NORTH WALES.—In this district, the "boys in the pits are variously employed, as in keeping the air-doors, filling the waggons, riddling coals, pumping, drawing, hooking on, and driving the horses and asses under ground.

375. "When a child first goes into the pits he is taken down by his father, or some friend who has employment in the work ; he is usually put to keep an air-door, or to some light work. In examining the boys few would own that they felt much fear or distress on entering the pits, and all say they very soon became used and reconciled to their work. They are for the most part the Children of colliers, and from infancy become familiar with the idea of under-ground work, and anxious to go below and begin to work. This wish of course meets with no opposition from parents, who, lured by the wages, are never backward in sending their Children to

the pits as soon as they can get them into employ, so that no sooner is a collier's son able to exert a little muscular force than he becomes an under-ground machine, destitute of the slightest mental cultivation.

376. "Drawing or pushing the coal-waggons, which in North Wales are called pyches, forms the principal employment of Children and Young Persons in the pits. Drawing is performed by means of a chain passing from the pyche between the boy's legs, and fastened to a girdle around his waist; being thus attached to the load he draws it by stooping down, proceeding along 'all-fours.' Some push the pyches from behind, which is done by the hands and forehead. The Children describe it as immaterial to them which method they pursue. In low works, where the seams of coal are very thin, they draw, as they can stoop lower than in the attitude of pushing.

377. "At first the chain in drawing is apt to excoriate the skin, and sometimes causes so much soreness as to oblige the boys to leave off work for a day or two; but no other evil arises from this unnatural and in appearance brutal mode of working boys, and custom soon reconciles and inures them to their wretched fate. The pyches being loaded, they are drawn or pushed, in the manner described, from the workings to the main or horse ways, there to be met by the empty or return pyches.

378. "Where the main-ways are of sufficient height to admit of horses or asses they are employed in drawing the pyches along them to the bottom of the shaft, up which they are brought to the surface either by the engine, horse-whimsey, or turn-barrels worked by men or women on the bank. Where the main-ways are so low as not to admit either horses or asses the boys continue to draw or push the pyches to the bottom of the shaft. There are relays of hands at intervals of 30 or 40 yards. The main-ways are laid with iron rails to facilitate the operation of drawing. The pyches generally contain from 2 cwt. to 4 cwt. of coals. Each has his task to perform; what the men cut the boys must carry off; there is no room in the pits for an accumulation of coal, a due proportion of boys is therefore always employed to prevent a stoppage, which would throw all hands into disorder.

379. "The work of these Children is a grievous subject for reflection and a sad spectacle to behold; they pass the day in working many fathoms under ground, where daylight never enters, and in excavations that will not in many instances admit them to stand in an erect position. The air they breathe is full of dust and noxious gases, and dangers surround them on all sides. Pitable indeed is their condition" (H. H. Jones, Esq., Report, §§ 16—23: App. Pt. II., p. 367).

380. SOUTH WALES.—In this district it is stated that the air-door boy is generally from five to eleven years of age, and that his situation in some of the pits, cold, wet, and not half fed, is exceedingly distressing. It is added that boys called "carters are employed in narrow veins of coal in parts of Monmouthshire; their occupation is to drag the carts or skips of coal from the working to the main roads. In this mode of labour the leather girdle passes round the body, and the chain is, between the legs, attached to the cart, and the lads drag on all-fours, as in fig. 20.

Fig. 20.

381. "In the county of Pembroke the field or bed of coal is what is called anthracite, or stone-coal, and in many workings the angle is so highly inclined as to demand a particular form of labour. Supposing a vein of coal to lie at an angle of 45°, windlasses are fixed at convenient distances on the incline of the vein, by which

means (if the mine is worked by adit or level and *above* the adit) the coal, after being brought from the stalls to the stage of the windlass in carts or skips, is dropped by the chain of the windlass down the incline to the level road, and the empty carts are worked up to the stage on which the windlass is fixed by the opposite chain of the windlass. If, on the contrary, the coal is worked to the dip, the coal is in a similar manner worked *up* to a convenient stage by windlass, and then taken by shaft to the surface. These windlasses are worked by women, and their labour is certainly severe, though only of eight or ten hours' duration.

382. "This mode of working vertical seams, or pitching veins as they are called in Wales, is so decided an improvement on the odious system adopted in Scotland in veins of similar inclination (on which I reported to you some short time since, wherein I described the frightful labour undergone by females in the occupation of coal-bearers), that I can in nowise account for its not having been adopted in that country; I am disposed to believe nothing but strong prejudice can long resist its adoption.

383. "And lest it should be objected that vertical seams in Scotland are found at a much higher angle than 45°, I may state that I have myself visited one anthracite working in the county of Pembroke, the vein of which was at an angle of upwards of 55°, where the system was adopted; indeed no other mode of working pitching veins is practised in South Wales" (R. H. Franks, Esq., Report, §§ 20—24: App. Pt. II., p. 475). Fig. 21 represents the carts or skips of coal descending the incline in a pitching vein to the level road, after their arrival at which they are drawn by horses to the shaft, or to the mouth of a level.

Fig. 21.

384. Fig. 22 represents girls winding coal from the workings in the dip.

Fig. 22.

385. Figs. 23 and 24 (on the following page) present a section of workings in pitching or vertical veins in Pembrokeshire and Glamorganshire.

Fig. 23.—Diagram showing the working of a Pitching Vein in Pembrokeshire, South Wales—angle 55°.

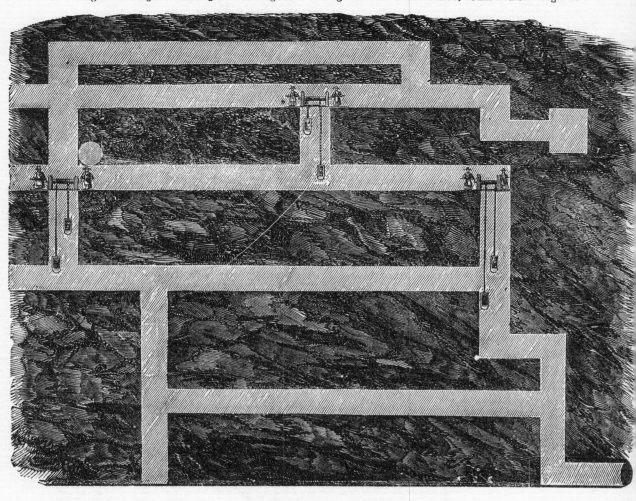

Diagram showing the ordinary working of Pitching or Vertical Veins in Glamorganshire, South Wales—angle 45°.

386. Fig. 25 represents a boy guiding a skip down an incline, angle 45°.

Fig. 25.

387. "The duty of the horse-driver or haulier is to drive the horse and tram, or carriage, from the wall-face, where the colliers are picking the coal, to the mouth of the level. He has to look after his horse, feed him in the day, and take him home at night: his occupation requires great agility in the narrow and low-roofed roads; sometimes he is required to stop his tram suddenly—in an instant he is between the rail and the side of the level, and in almost total darkness slips a sprig between the spokes of his tram-wheel, and is back in his place with amazing dexterity; though it must be confessed, with all his activity, he frequently gets crushed. The haulier is generally from fourteen to seventeen years of age, and his size is a matter of some importance, according to the present height and width of the main roads.

388. "As a class these youths have an appearance of greater health than the rest of the collier population (probably from their being more in the fresh air than the others), with fair animal spirits; and on horseback, going to or returning from work, galloping and scrambling over the field or road, bear the aspect of the most healthy and thoughtless of the collier-boys" (Ibid. §§ 17, 18: pp. 474, 475).

Lewis Wilson, Esq., proprietor, Broad Moor Colliery, Pembrokeshire: "Children and young persons are employed in our mines at hauling and winding up coal. It does not necessarily require young children, but they seek employment, and are put in couples to do what usually one older would be required to do. They work eight hours, and haul in proportion to their ages and wages. The weight of the coal in each tram, drawn up by the windlass in the mainway, is 4 cwt., and the skip drawn by children holds about 1½ cwt. None carry coals on their backs, all are drawn up by windlasses" (R. H. Franks, Esq., Evidence, No. 420: App. Pt. II., p. 572, l. 53, and p. 573, l. 6).—Lewis Thomas, Esq., proprietor: "Children are sometimes employed in pushing the waggons from the workings to the heading or main road. The weight of a dram is from 18 to 25 cwt., and the distance driven along the main road varies from 400 yards to one mile" (Ibid. No. 286: p. 547, l. 48).—Mr. Benjamin Daniel, agent, Yskin Colliery, Glamorgan: "Our mode of working is for boys to cart the coal from the workings down to the main level, horses then drag it from there to the bottom of the bully, the engine then winds it up, and the horses convey it to the incline. We do not use what is commonly called the girdle and chain" (Ibid. No. 324: p. 554, l. 35).—Lionel Brough, Esq., engineer and viewer, Neath: " In one of the Pembrokeshire veins of anthracite, the top and bottom are so excessively bad, that all the timber they can send down the pit is insufficient to keep the ways good enough for horse-roads; they are consequently generally so low and narrow that boys only can tram the coal from the hewers to the bottom of the pit. To say that horse height could not be kept good in this vein would be perhaps a misrepresentation, but it could be only effected at a cost that would deprive the owners of the mine of all profit whatever. Again, in Glamorganshire, there are many veins of coal on the southern side of the basin lying at an angle so highly inclined as entirely to prevent any access of the level trams into the stalls, therefore boys are employed, who bring the coal down in skips, or little carts, to the bottom or mouth of the stall, where a place is prepared to deposit it; after which it is filled into the main trams, which are standing on the level road, and is then removed by horse-power to the mouth of the level, or the bottom of the pit. In some of the thin veins which lie at the angle above alluded to, I can safely say that, but for the aid of boys to perform the carting, these seams would not be worked at all. The employment is by no means more dangerous than other duties which fall to the lot of children under ground" (Ibid. No. 442: p. 578, l. 29).

Mr. David Hill, cashier and clerk, Lansamlet Colliery, Glamorganshire: "The young persons are employed in wheeling coals from the workings to the steam-engine below, which drops the coal down an incline to the bottom of the shaft. The average weight of coal in the barrows is from 2 to 4 cwt." (Ibid. No. 362: p. 560, l. 59).—See also witnesses, Nos. 346, 363, 349, 122, 313).

George Handell Hookey, Esq., part proprietor, Risca Colliery, Monmouthshire: "In working the narrow seams we are compelled to use the labour of children, as men are too large for the works, and from the necessity of the case, lads from eleven to fifteen years of age are employed to draw with the girdle and chain; distances not exceeding 300 yards; the weight drawn from 50 lbs. to 1 cwt.; very young children are of no service to us, as their strength is insufficient; they rarely commence until ten years of age. There is a sick fund for all the workmen" (Ibid. No. 288: p. 548, l. 22).—George Penrose, Esq., proprietor, Gnoll Colliery, Glamorganshire: "The coals are brought from the stalls to the mainway in slypes, drawn by boys with a chain; and the usual age at which boys are used at this work is ten to thirteen; the distance they drag the slype is about 55 yards; the weight of each is about 2 cwt." (Ibid. No. 329: p. 555, l. 26).—William Thomas, thirty-four years old, under-ground over-man, Llanelly Collieries: "'The carters' work with the 'belt and chain,' and two straps over their shoulders; the places where four of them work [in one of the veins] is no more than 2 feet high; they draw in a creeping posture; the distance they draw varies from a few yards, when they begin at the main-road, to 60 or 70 yards; the carts weigh about 5 cwt. when full; they draw them down the slope of the vein, which is very steep; two boys work together; their carts are fastened one each end of a chain, which is as long as the 'top hole' or 'stall' they draw in, the chain passing through a block at the top, and one cart goes up empty while the other comes down full, and the boys go up and down to draw and guide them along; each boy brings out from 15 to 20 carts in a day; they fill and empty as well as draw the carts. The places are tolerably dry, but the boys sometimes wet their backs, and work barefoot" (R. W. Jones, Esq., Evidence, No. 272: App. Pt. II., p. 716, l. 62).

Mr. Richard Hare, agent to Kilgetty Colliery, Pembrokeshire: "We employ males and females below ground to draw small waggons. The vein of our coal is not exceeding two feet in height, and only 12 inches in many parts. None of the children cut the coal. The work is good hard sort, but young people alone can do it, as our mainways do not exceed three feet to three feet six inches in height. Children under ten years of age are of no real use below ground, and a limitation to that age would be of advantage. The weight drawn by girls and boys in the skip [cart] never exceeds 1½ cwt., and the distance they drag varies from 2 fathoms to 30" (R. H. Franks, Esq., Evidence, No. 433: App. Pt. II., p. 576, l. 22—31).—Elias Jones, 14 years old, carter: "I have been down six years; my employment is to cart the coal, and draw with the girdle and chain. [In this mode of labour the girdle passes round the body, and the chain is between the legs attached to the cart, and the lad drags on all-fours. See fig. 20.] The width of the vein I work in varies from 20 inches to three feet, and the distance I cart is about 60 yards. It is very hard work; indeed it is too hard for such lads as we, for we work like little horses. I cart for two colliers, and I load five drams, each weighing 18 cwt." (Ibid. No. 290: p. 548, l. 44).—John William, aged sixteen: "I cart coal in the golden vein; the place is low, I creep on my knees, and often on my belly; I draw with a 'trace and chain,' another boy [Henry Green] 'carts' with me in the same place; the vein pitches, and the place is steep, and we have a chain through a block at the top, and one boy goes up when the other goes down; we fill and empty the carts as well as draw them. It is hard work. We 'cart' out about 40 carts, which makes 20 baskets in a day" (R. W. Jones, Esq., Evidence, No. 274: App. Pt. II., p. 717, l. 62).—William Morgan, aged sixteen: "I 'cart' in the 'fiery vein,' it is more than three feet high; it is easier to cart in than the little vein where John Williams carts; I cart in the same way as he does; the two boys cart about 5¼ carts or 34 baskets in a day" (Ibid. No. 275: p. 718, l. 17).—Ann David, thirteen years old, hauler of skips: "Sister and I haul the skips from the men to where the women wind; it is a good bit away. Boys and girls work together where we work. The time is long, and the work very hard indeed; sad tiring sort, and I feel very glad when over. Works for John Nash, a contractor. Sister and I pull six score skips daily, three score each. The more we draw the more we get. Some draw three score and ten. Cannot say how many three score are, but knows that the men would not pay unless the work was done" (R. H. Franks, Esq., Evidence, No. 436: App. Pt. II., p. 577, l. 1). Sarah Jones, sixteen years old, hauler of skips: "Been working two years and a half. Work the same hours, and on the same kind of work, as the Davids" (Ibid. No. 437: p. 577, l. 18).— Mr. Robert Brough, manager, Begelly Colliery, Pembrokeshire: "The women work very hard, both above and below ground. The nature of their employment was severe. They had great strength and patience. Working at the windlasses below ground, wheeling and skreening coals above, formed their usual occupation" (Ibid. No. 431: p. 575, l. 43).—Hannah Bowen, sixteen years old, windlass-woman, Broad Moor Colliery, Glamorganshire: "Been down two years; earns 3s. a-week; it is good hard work; work from seven in the morning till three or four in the afternoon at hauling at the windlass. Can draw up 400 loads of 1½ to 4 cwt. each" (Ibid. No. 422: p. 573, l. 39).—Ann Thomas, sixteen years old, windlass-woman: "Been at these mines 11 months. Did haul at the windlass before. Find the work very hard, but cannot get any other. Men do not like the winding, it is too hard work for them. We wind up 400 loads. Two women always work the windlass below ground" (Ibid. Nos. 439, 440: p. 577, l. 35).

389. In this district Children begin to hew or get the coal, even at earlier ages than in the East of Scotland, that is, from seven years old and upwards.

Richard Richards, aged seven, *collier*, Top Hill Colliery, parish of Gelligaer, Glamorganshire: "Helps to fill father's coal; sometimes works in stall with father at cutting coal; father gets a dram for me now and then" (Ibid. No. 145: p. 528, l. 12).—Henry George, seven years old, *collier*, Court y Bella and Mammoo Collieries, parish of Mynyodduslwyn, Monmouthshire: "Twelve months below; assists Davy Jones to pick, as father works in the level; works very hard sometimes, and at others goes to sleep" (Ibid. No. 228: p. 539, l. 4).—John Thomas, aged nine, *collier*, Top Hill Colliery, Gelligaer, Glamorganshire: "Been three years below; don't dislike the work now; would like daylight work better" (Ibid. No. 147: p. 528, l. 21).—William Freeman, aged eleven, *collier*, Buttery Hatch Colliery, Mynyodduslwyn, Monmouth: "Been working at coal six years; it is very hard work; I have often got hurt; have had my arm cut open twice with the mandril [the pick]; the rock fell upon father and me; I got much crushed" (Ibid. No. 197: p. 534, l. 60).—Joseph Richards, aged seven, *collier*, Buttery Hatch Colliery, Mynyodduslwyn, Monmouth: "Has been down three years and a half. [Steward said he was sure the boy had been down at least three years]" (Ibid. No. 199: p. 535, l. 8).—Ellis Loydd, aged seven, *collier*, Gilvach Vargoed Colliery, parish of Gelligaer, Glamorgan: "Been 12 months below; father lets me sleep when I am tired; am 12 or 14 hours in the pit; father takes my wages; I don't know what I earn" (Ibid. No. 180: p. 532, l. 51).—Richard Hutton, aged seven, *collier*, Gwrhay and Pen y Van, Mynyodduslwyn, Monmouth: "Has been 12 months at work; thinks the place is 'middling;' is very glad when he gets home. The noise of the shooting used to frighten him; doesn't like it now" (Ibid. No. 221: p. 538, l. 15).—Morgan Kenneth, aged eight, *collier*, Gilvach Vargoed Colliery, Gelligaer, Glamorganshire: "Been down two years; works with father" (Ibid. No. 181: p. 532, l. 55).—Rosser Jenkins, aged eight, *collier*, Gwrhay and Pen y Van, Mynyodduslwyn, Monmouth: "Works with father as often as he works; sometimes works a long time" (Ibid. No. 220: p. 538, l. 12).—John Evans, aged eight, *collier*, Gwrhay and Pen y Van, Mynyodduslyn, Monmouth: "Has been two years below. Father took me down to claim a dram. Has often fallen asleep. Father pulls me up when he wants me" (Ibid. No. 222: p. 538, l. 18).—Thomas Jenkins, ten years old, *collier*, Court y Bella and Mammoo Collieries, Mynyodduslwyn, Monmouth: "Father took me down to claim his dram when I was six years old; have worked below ever since; I work with John Jones now, who pays father 2s. 6d. a-week for my labour. When I fall asleep they shake me up; I work as long as John Jones works, from six morning till six evening, or three morning till five evening" (Ibid. No. 229: p. 539, l. 9).—David Davies, ten years old, *collier*, Rock Colliery, Bedwellty, Monmouth: "Been two years employed at the Rock Colliery cutting coal; earns about 4s. a-week; the work is very hard, and I only get bread and cheese to eat" (Ibid. No. 242: p. 541, l. 56).—See also Nos. 212, 201, 210, 195, 182, 184, 96, 105, 99, 130, 150, &c. &c.

390. FOREST OF DEAN.—In this district the chief employment of Children and Young Persons is "in hodding or carting, according to the mode in which the pit is worked. Hodding varies in the amount of toil required according to the circumstances of the pit, and the construction of the hod in which the coal is drawn into the horseway leading to the bottom of the main shaft. When the passages are high and tolerably level, or inclining downwards, the posture in which the hodder works is not much constrained; and when the hod is mounted on trucks, technically called trollies, a considerable weight is pulled without extraordinary effort. The hods are frequently mounted on slides only, when from 1 cwt. to 1½ cwt. is the ordinary load. The harness by which the boys tug these loads is a convenient apparatus of leather straps for the shoulders and breast, attached by a chain, and they draw the hods much in the same posture as hobblers on a towing-path when tracking a vessel. Where the seams of coal are very thin, and the passages consequently limited to a space just sufficient for working out the coal, the attitude of the hodder is almost prone, and in some instances crawling on hands and knees is indispensable. This is certainly a wretched and slave-like mode of labour. Carting is performed by two lads pushing the coal-waggons out of the stalls into the horseway, the wheels running in iron plates, in fact on a tram-road. In some coal-pits the horseway goes quite up to the stalls" (E. Waring, Esq., Report, § 27—32: App. Pt. II. p. 3).

391. "There is only one other employment for boys in the coal-mines, except occasional jobbing about the roads, and carrying in pit-wood, and that is driving the waggon-horses. In this vocation the driver, or 'jockey-boy,' sits on the front edge of the foremost waggon, immediately behind the horse,—a position of considerable danger, in case of a sudden jolt from a loose plate or other cause; but accidents of this kind are so rare that I did not hear of a single case.

392. "In the collieries at Howlet's Slade I observed a commodious dickey, or moveable seat, attached to the front carriage by strong iron grapnels, being readily unshipped and transferred to another waggon when required. This seat was devised for the safety of the boys, by the considerate managing proprietor, Mr. John Trotter Thomas, of Coleford.

393. "On the whole, I was most impressed with the idea of danger to the heads of

these young charioteers, from their almost constant proximity to the rugged roof of the mine; and so nicely did they adapt their posture to the space above them, that their woollen caps brushed a distinct line of transit along the moist surface of the rock, whenever it was low enough to touch them; showing that another inch of elevation would have seriously endangered their skulls." (Ibid. §§ 36—39: p. 3.) See witnesses, Nos. 16, 29, 31, 43, 46.

394. SOUTH GLOUCESTERSHIRE.—In some of the coal mines in this district the seams of coal are so thin, and the space for working is so small, that adults are not employed in hewing the coal, but the work is performed by young lads, "whose size," says the Sub-Commissioner, "is suited to the contracted space." With reference to the mines in which the seams are the narrowest, he adds: "the coal comes out in blocks of regular thickness, requiring only the clearance of the superincumbent and subjacent clods, so that it is wrought with little labour, and the low stature of the cutters enables them to perform the task with comparative ease." (E. Waring, Esq., Report, §§ 6, 7: App. Pt. II., p. 31).—In Fig. 26 the mode of working with the girdle and chain in this district is represented.

Fig. 26.

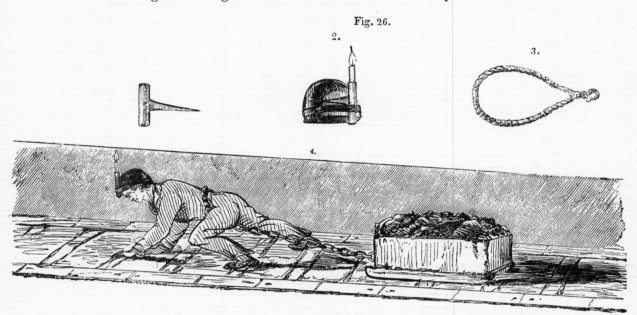

1. The candle-holder: a socket of iron, having a spike at right angles for the convenience of sticking the light in the sides of the pit when stationary. The spike also forms a handle when the light is carried before them.
2. A skull-cap, having a leather band, into which the candle-holder is thrust when the hands are employed in locomotion.
3. The girdle and hook for attaching to the chain.
4. Represents the position of the girdle.

395. In order to bring the whole subject under view, we give the observations of the Sub-Commissioner on this mode of employing Children :—

396. "The mode of tugging tubs with the girdle and chain impressed me so painfully at first, that I was induced to examine closely into its effects on the frame, conceiving it to be a barbarous and unnatural mode of applying muscular power. The results of my investigation, have, nevertheless, been satisfactory as regards the adaptation of the custom to the circumstances which introduced it.

397. "On minute examination I find the direction of the rope girdle is across the lateral dorsal muscles, passing between the crest of the ilium and the great trochanter on each side, then descending in front quite clear of the pubis, so as to pass freely between the thighs, thus pressing but slightly on their superior anterior muscles, in consequence of the inclined position used in tugging. A deliberate comparison of the action of the girdle, in the above position, with that of the shoulder-strap tug used in the Forest of Dean, leads me to a conclusion strongly opposed to my original impression.

398. "The bones principally concerned in resisting the weight of a load thus pulled are those of the pelvis, the ilia, the trochanters, and the thighs and legs, thus presenting a firmer series of bearing points than could be obtained from the shoulder with the spinal vertebræ, curved nearly at right angles with the lower limbs, as they must be in dragging a load through passages not exceeding three feet in height, and often several inches lower. The abdominal muscles also are thus

spared the great strain to which they are subjected in the act of drawing from the shoulder; and I should therefore infer that *hernia* is not likely to be often induced by the mode of labour under consideration. These anatomical facts and deductions appear to corroborate the prevalent opinion of the colliers in favour of the girdle and chain, as giving greater power over the load than the shoulder-strap tug. (See Mr. John Cook's Evidence, No. 31.) The points of traction bear upon the os sacrum, and between the great trochanters and ilia.

399. "The only discoloration arising from constant pressure I invariably found across the loins, which proves the resistance of the load to be principally on the back of the pelvis. Excoriations are commonly produced when the girdle is first used, and many of the boys told me they were obliged to wrap old clothes round the rope at first, to prevent galling, but this effect soon went off. When I conversed on the subject with the under-ground manager of Sir J. Smyth and Co., he aptly compared the boys to young horses, whose shoulders are tender when first broken to the collar. On the same principle, however, that studies the soundness and comfort of a horse by constructing his collar of smooth and elastic materials, it would appear at once benevolent and easy to substitute some less harsh material for the hard twisted rope used by these laborious boys. A pad of stuffed leather might be advantageously connected with the rope by rings fastened on the external side, through which the rope might be tightly reeved, as far as any pressure is produced, and then terminate as at present.

400. "The most frequent course of haulage by the girdle is down an inclined plane, or on a level; but in some cases, as that mentioned at Cowherne Hill (see Evidence, No. 15, also No. 31), the ascending inclination is considerable. On these ascents a wooden ladderway, or plank railroad, is used to facilitate the draft, and strong lads only are employed. Where the ascent from the stalls to the top stage is too steep for tugging, the passages are provincially called *googs*, or *gugs*, and a windlass is employed to haul up the coal to the stage where the boys receive it" (E. Waring, Esq., Report, § 8, 9 : App. Pt. II., p. 32).

401. NORTH SOMERSETSHIRE.—" The youngest Children are generally employed in opening and shutting the doors for ventilation ; but this requires only a limited number. The others assist, as ' pushers,' the youths or men who pull along the carriages of coal, or they help to turn the ' gug-wheel' " (Dr. Stewart, Report, § 4 : App. Pt. II., p. 47).

402. IRELAND.—In the collieries of Ireland a few Children are employed as trappers, but none in pushing or drawing coals from the workings to the shafts. This is invariably done in that country by young men from thirteen to eighteen years of age ; most of them appear to be nearer eighteen than thirteen, and many are still older. Mr. Nicholson, agent of the Mining Company of Ireland, states that " for the work of ' hurries' they require strong able young men of from about eighteen years old and upwards." Mr. Nasmith, agent of the Coalbrook Colliery, county of Tipperary, says, " They employ no Children ; they are of no use : they require strong able lads of seventeen or eighteen years old to do their work." Young People are, in some instances, employed in cleaning the roads and drawing in wood (F. Roper, Esq., Reports and Evidence : App. Pt. I., pp. 868, 871, 872 ; and T. Martin, Esq., pp. 884, 885).

403. Of the collieries in the county of Kilkenny and in Queen's County the Sub-Commissioner reports:—"I visited the five principal establishments and found that no Children or females of any age, and but very few Young Persons, were employed. I inspected about a dozen of the different shafts, worked by contractors, and found none but men employed ; indeed, I was informed that none but strong, able young men would be of any use in the pits, the labour being severe ; I did not see any apparently under eighteen years of age. I went down into two of the pits and saw the people at their different work, all of whom were strong, able men ; even the ' hurries,' who draw the coals to the foot of the shaft, were mostly strong young men, who go along the narrow low passages, of seldom more than three feet high and often less, on their hands and feet, the body stretched out ; they draw the sledges, on which wooden boxes containing the coals are placed, by a girdle round the loins and a long chain fastened to the sledge going between their legs.

404. "It was matter of wonderment to me how these 'hurries,' many of whom w ere stout men upwards of six feet high, could manage to get along these very narrow low passages at such a rate as they do, particularly considering the excessive labour and difficulty I found myself in proceeding along about 130 yards in each of the pits: in many places there was but just sufficient room for me to crawl through. I believe it is customary in the collieries, in many parts of England and Scotland, to employ Children and Young Persons, of both sexes, as 'hurries,' or 'hurriers;' it is therefore worthy of remark that such is not the custom in the south of Ireland, where no females of any age are employed, and but a few young boys, whose sole employment is opening and shutting the doors for the ingress and egress of air. In reply to my numerous inquiries as to why Children were not employed as 'hurries,' I was told, that as labour was so abundant and cheap they would not be troubled with Children; moreover, that, from the laborious nature of the work, even Young Persons, unless nearly as strong and able as men, were of no use. Very many of the Young Persons who worked as 'hurries' complained grievously of the hardness of the work. The reason of this species of labour being so hard, and requiring so much strength, is entirely owing to there being neither tramways nor railways in the collieries, consequently the sledge, on which is the box of coals, has to be drawn along on the surface of the passages, consisting of uneven rock, or more generally soft mud" (F. Roper, Esq., Report, § 2—6: App. Pt. I., p. 872).

Denis Toomey, fourteen years of age, filler, Dromagh Colliery: "I am at work at filling the buckets that go up the shaft with the coal brought in the waggons; I always work at this work; it is hard work; I would not work at it if I could help it; I always work during the day; many of us have to work at night, when the miners are working" (F. Roper, Esq., Evidence, No. 33: App. Pt. I., p. 869, l. 20).—Philip Murphy, seventeen years of age, hurrier, Dromagh Colliery, Cork: "I am employed under ground; I have to fill in the coal as it is got out by the miners into a waggon, and then push it to the bottom of the shaft, and empty the contents and go back again; I have to push the waggon about 100 yards; there is only one of us to each waggon; it is hard work" (Ibid. No. 32: p. 869, l. 4).—Jeremiah Kenelly, seventeen years of age, hurrier, Dromagh Colliery: "I now work at hurrying, which is filling the coals into a waggon and pushing them to the foot of the shaft; I have to push the waggon above 60 yards; it is hard work, and I do not like it; I think the loaded waggon would weigh about 2 cwt. or more (Ibid. No. 34: p. 869, l. 35).

---

7. HOURS OF WORK IN COAL MINES.

405. The hours of work vary considerably in different districts, but universally where there are air-doors to be kept the youngest Children descend into the pits with the first and ascend with the last set of workpeople.

406. SOUTH AND NORTH STAFFORDSHIRE, SHROPSHIRE, WARWICKSHIRE, AND LEICESTERSHIRE.—In all these districts the regular hours of work are uniformly 12, being generally from six in the morning to six at night. From this, however, the time allowed for meals is to be deducted.

407. DERBYSHIRE.—All classes of witnesses concur in stating that in this district some of the Children and Young Persons work 16 hours out of the 24, reckoning from the time they leave their home in the morning until they return to it in the evening.

John Hawkins, eight years of age: "Has worked in Sissons Pit a year and a half; lives a mile from the pit; goes down from five to nine;" that is, this child, eight years old, is employed in the pit at work from five o'clock in the morning to nine at night, a period of 16 hours (J. M. Fellows, Esq., Evidence, No. 108: App. Pt. II., p. 293, l. 10, 11).—John Houghton, nine years old: "Goes down from six to eight—it has been ten;" that is, this child is regularly employed at work in the pits 14 hours and occasionally 16 hours (Ibid. No. 72: p. 283, l. 66, 67).—Ephraim Riley, eleven years old: "Had three miles to walk to the pit; left home at five o'clock, winter and summer, and did not get home again until nine o'clock at night (16 hours); his legs and thighs hurt him so with working so much that he remains in bed on Sunday mornings." (Ibid. No. 29: p. 271, l. 16, 17, 20).—John Chambers, thirteen years old: "Has worked in pits since he was seven; works from six to nine or ten (from 15 to 16 hours). When first he worked in a pit he felt so tired, and his legs, arms, and back ached so much, that his brother has had to help him home many times. He could not go to school on a Sunday morning, he has been so stiff; he felt these pains until about a year since; he now feels tired, but his limbs do not ache as they did" (Ibid. No. 28: p. 271, l. 2, 6, 9). James Creswell, fourteen years old: "Has worked in pits four or five years; goes down at half-past six to nine, has this winter been after ten; half-days half-past six to three or four" (Ibid. No. 315: p. 334, l. 53, 58).—

Elizabeth Gaunt: "They (two of her children) work always from six to eight; has known them often not come home before 12; has been obliged to fetch them from the pit at one o'clock in the morning scores of times; they work there until after 10" (Ibid. No. 363: p. 342, l. 43).—Joseph Cotton: "Is seven years old; works for Mr. Woodley; has worked in pits more than half a year; he leaves home at half-past five, goes down at six, and does not get home again until nine; three-quarters of a day, goes down at six and gets home at seven; half a day from six to half-past three" (Ibid. No. 276: p. 327, l. 45—9).—William Lees: "Is eight years old; has worked above a year; is sure he works from six to nine or half-past eight; three-quarter days from six to after six; half-days from six to two" (Ibid. No. 344: p. 340, l. 29).—Charles Booth: "Is nine years old; has worked a year; works from half-past six to nine or ten" (Ibid. No. 64: p. 281, l. 30).—Joseph Shelton: "Is ten years old; has worked in pits nearly three years; when he works whole days, goes down at five till eight" (Ibid. No. 109: p. 293, l. 26, 27).—Matthew Wilson: "Is eleven years old; has worked in the Hard Pit nearly four years; goes down from five to seven or eight" (Ibid. No. 111: p. 293, l. 59).—Richard Clarke: "Is twelve years old; has worked in a pit five years; goes down at five to eight for a whole day" (Ibid. No. 110: p. 293, l. 39). —Joseph Robinson: "Is twelve years old; has worked nearly six years; they are down from six to nine—they call it eight, but it is oftener nine" (Ibid. No. 175: p. 310, l. 22, 30).—William Ward: "Is fifteen years old; engine-boy; they go down at seven, and if paid for a day, it is nine or ten o'clock before he draws them up" (Ibid. No. 317: p. 335, l. 20, 23).—Thomas Spinks: "Is engine-man to pit No. 2; the children go down at six to eight or nine" (Ibid. No. 171: p. 309, l. 46, 51).—Thomas Gillott: "Is engine-man to the Butterley Company's Hard Coal Pit. They are let down six or ten minutes after six, and for whole days come up between eight and nine, seldom much before nine" (Ibid. No. 180: p. 311, l. 35).—George Wilmot, engine-man: "The children go down at six to eight or nine for a whole day" (Ibid. No. 240: p. 321, l. 48).

408. Among others the following witnesses state that their regular hours of work are from 14 to 14½ hours daily:—

Joseph Birkenshaw, eight years of age, No. 48; John Hant, nine years of age, No. 51; Thomas Lewis, nine years of age, No. 67; William Fletcher, nine years of age, No. 46; William Sissons, nine years of age, No. 114; Joseph Latun, nine years of age, No. 168; Robert Blount, ten years of age, No. 99; Thomas Birkin, ten years of age, No. 78; William Hart, eleven years of age, No. 52; Joseph Fletcher, eleven years of age, No. 53; Joseph Limb, eleven years of age, No. 68; Aaron Chambers, eleven years of age, No. 101; John Henshaw, eleven years of age, No. 135; John Moult, eleven years of age, No. 141; James Webster, thirteen years of age, No. 133; Joseph Fletcher, thirteen and a half, No. 69; Mark Beardsley, fourteen years of age, No. 130; James Robinson, fourteen years of age, No. 169; John Bostock, seventeen years of age, No. 146.

409. These statements of the Children and Young Persons are confirmed by the evidence of the adult working people, among others by the following colliers.—

Wheatley Straw: "They go down at six in the morning and come up at eight in the evening; never work more than 14 hours" (Ibid. No. 22: p. 269, l. 25).—John Beasley: "The boys go down at six in the morning, and has known them kept down until nine or ten, 'until they are almost ready to exhaust;' the children and young persons work the same hours as the men" (Ibid. No. 40: p. 274, l. 30).—John Dakin: "They work from six to eight" (Ibid. No. 56: p. 278, l. 27).—William Fletcher: "They work from six A.M. to eight PM." (Ibid. No. 57: p. 278, l. 59).—Thomas Hughton: "The children are let down from between five and six to eight" (Ibid. No. 79: p. 285, l. 13).—Thomas King: "They work from six to eight" (Ibid. No. 161: p. 306, l. 40).—Thomas King: "They work for whole days from six to eight" (Ibid. No. 162: p. 306, l. 55).—John Fisher: "They go down at six and come up between eight and nine; it has been ten before they get home, about a quarter of a mile distant" (Ibid. No. 154: p. 304, l. 55).

410. Several agents and underground stewards give similar evidence.—

Benjamin Fletcher, coal-agent or ground-bailiff to Francis Newdigate, Esq., West Hallam Coal-works, says: "They are let down from six to eight. He has gone at three o'clock in the morning and worked until ten; he has many and many a time fallen asleep as he was going to work in a morning and fell in the ditches owing to want of sleep" (Ibid. No. 50: p. 276, l. 62).—Thomas Rawling, agent to Mr. Fenton's Coal-field, Bagthorp, says: "The children in both pits go down from six to [stay until] eight" (Ibid. No. 71: p. 283, l. 46).

411. Several parents give similar evidence to that of the witness No. 104, for instance, Ellen Wagstaff, who says she has five Children variously employed; the youngest was not seven years old when he first went to the pits. The whole have worked since they were seven or seven and a half; they have worked from six to eight; from six to two for half-days; she has known them when at full work so tired when they first worked that you could not hear them speak, and they fell asleep before they could eat their suppers; it has grieved her to the heart to see them. Thus it appears that in this district from thirteen to sixteen hours are considered a day's work; from eleven to twelve hours are reckoned three-quarters of a day's work; and eight hours make half a day's work.

COAL MINES.

Hours of Work.

412. The Chesterfield Union presents a contrast to the remaining portion of this district.   The coal owners in that union do not allow the colliers to work more than twelve hours (J. M. Fellows, Esq., Report, § 14 : App. Pt. II., p. 253).

West Riding of Yorkshire.

413. WEST RIDING OF YORKSHIRE : SOUTHERN PART.—In this district many of the coal owners represent the regular hours of work in pits to be only from six to seven per day ; but no manager, agent, or underground steward assigns less than 10, and most of them say it is 11 and upwards, with which latter statement that of the colliers agrees.

At a meeting of above three hundred and fifty working colliers summoned from the surrounding districts, held in the Court-house, Barnsley, the first resolution passed was—" That 11 hours is the usual time collieries are actually worked each day on the average" (J. C. Symons, Esq., Evidence, No. 142 : App. Pt. I., p. 262, l. 55).—The Children themselves state that they work 12 hours, and according to the representation of several of them they are often in the pit 13 hours. —See witnesses, Nos. 19, 23, 24, 25, 28, 31, 32, 56, 59, 60, 136, 149.

414. " The hours of work in thick-seam collieries are usually from 10 to 11 for all persons employed in them, Children as well as adults ; and somewhat shorter where the thinness of the seam increases the severity of the work.   Shorter hours will, in the generality of cases, be owing either to slackness of trade or to some accidental circumstance.   The usual time for commencing work is from five to six in the morning, each man and Child beginning to work as soon as they descend the shaft ; and, as the descent of 100 persons will occupy an hour, the commencement of work will vary with the earliness or lateness of each individual's descent.   The time for leaving off is usually between three and five o'clock" (J. C. Symons, Esq., Report, § 19–21 : App. Pt. I., p. 167.).

Bradford and Leeds.

415. BRADFORD and LEEDS.—In these districts, though there is considerable diversity in different pits, and even in the same pit at different times, so that the regular hours of work are not very definitely fixed, yet, upon the whole, they appear to be under 11 hours per day, and may be said to range from 10 to 11 hours. The usual time for the commencement of work is from six to seven in the morning, and for the termination of it from four to six in the afternoon.   It is true that the same individuals leave off work at a different hour on different days, for there is commonly no general regulation to which the workpeople are required strictly to conform.   In some mines, indeed (for example, in the Low Moor Ironworks and Collieries), it is a rule that all work be peremptorily stopped at six in the evening.   This regulation is strictly enforced, and the object of it is to make the colliers pursue their work with regularity day by day ; and to prevent them from spending whole days, or large portions of days, in idleness, and then working very long on other days to make up lost time.   The strict enforcement of this regulation, in all the pits in which it is insisted on, is attended with a highly beneficial result both to the employers and to the employed (W. R. Wood, Esq., Evidence, Nos. 3, 4, 13, 16, 20, 36, 48, 77, 92, 52, 54, 79, 83, 93, 81 : App. Pt. II.).

Halifax.

416. HALIFAX.—In the collieries in this neighbourhood, according to some of the coal owners and agents, the regular hours of work are only eight or nine ; but the Children and Young Persons in the pits state that they generally work eleven, often twelve, sometimes thirteen hours (S. S. Scriven, Esq., Evidence, Nos. 49, 52, 69, 1, 4, 11, 3, 9, 30, 42, 7, 17 : App. Pt. II.).

Lancashire and Cheshire.

417. LANCASHIRE AND CHESHIRE.—In this district the hours of work are extremely variable, but from five in the morning to five in the afternoon, or from six in the morning to six in the evening, appear to be the usual hours (J. L. Kennedy, Esq., Report, § 207 : App. Pt. II., p. 176.   Evidence, Nos. 22, 8, 9, 45, 46, 37, 49, 54, 58, et seq.).

Oldham.

418. OLDHAM.—"When in full employment, the adult coal-getters work 9, 10, and 11 hours a-day ; and the Children and Young Persons employed in bringing to the pit-bottom the coal which they have hewn, about two hours longer, or 11, 12, and 13 hours, which are sometimes protracted to 14 and 15 (Nos. 6, 7, 10, 11, 15, 16, 20).   When working day-work for the employers, the colliers' hours are 8 ; but when at piece-work, generally 10" (J. Fletcher, Esq., Report, § 36, App. Pt. II., p. 826).

North Lancashire.

419. NORTH LANCASHIRE.—In this district the hours of work vary in different

collieries from 8 to 12 (A. Austin, Esq., Report, § 5: App. Pt. II., pp. 793, 794; and § 6: p. 802).

420. CUMBERLAND.—In this district the regular hours of work are twelve, but very often they are thirteen, and there are cases in which they are extended to fourteen and even to fifteen. "The Children certainly work longer hours in Cumberland than I have found general in Yorkshire. They seem to work twelve hours habitually, and in some of the inland collieries even longer. Owing to the inefficient power of the drawing-engine in one of these collieries belonging to Mr. Westray, the day's work has been extended to fourteen or fifteen hours; but this cannot be considered other than an accidental circumstance. It is, however, by no means uncommon for pits to work thirteen hours a-day without a change of hands" (J. C. Symons, Esq., Report, § 9: App. Pt. I., p. 300). See also Evidence, Nos. 300, 311, 322, 314, 315, 323, 324, 301, 328, 325, 326, 320, 308, 304, 318, 319, 327.

421. SOUTH DURHAM.—In this district the hours of work in all the well-regulated mines are never allowed to exceed twelve. In many of these collieries formerly, and in some collieries still, when the hewers had cut down what was considered their proper quantity, and had departed, the putters, the drivers, and all other persons, were expected to remain until the whole of these coals were brought to the bank, however long it might be, whether thirteen, fourteen, or fifteen, or even more hours. If, therefore, any defect occurred in the engine, or any other cause of delay took place, the people were detained below in consequence. Such is not generally the case now; when the hour comes the sound of "loose" is sent down the shaft, the glad tidings quickly reach the farthest workings, and all come up. But this is true only of the well-regulated mines. There are still in this district collieries in which the hours of work are extremely long.

422. The employers reckon the hours of work from the time when the work actually commences to that when orders are given to stop; but the employed reckon from the time they leave their dwellings until they again return to their houses—that is, they include in the day's labour the time it takes to get to the pit, to descend the shaft, and to reach the place of work in the pit, and in like manner the time spent in the afternoon in getting to the foot of the shaft, and in ascending and going home. Hence, what the masters call twelve hours' work the workpeople call fourteen hours, as they term it, "out of the house."

423. The work of the mines in this district begins at a very early hour. The hewers go down the pits and begin their day's labour at three o'clock, and sometimes even as early as two o'clock; but it is seldom that the Children and Young People descend before four or five o'clock, and there are pits in which they do not commence work until six. At whatever time the work is begun, however, it is always continued for twelve hours at least. An eminent engineer states that in most mines the work is not more than twelve hours; but sometimes the men will complain that they have not been able to get the usual quantity done, and therefore are desirous of longer time, that they may earn the usual amount of wages (Dr. Mitchell, Report, §§ 83, 86: App. Pt. I., pp. 126, 127).—See also Evidence, Nos. 93, 95, 100, 101, 107, 11.

424. NORTH DURHAM and NORTHUMBERLAND.—In these districts the regular hours of work are twelve, being usually from four o'clock in the morning to four o'clock in the afternoon. But the Children and Young Persons often leave their homes for the pit as early as one or two o'clock in the morning; and though they may not be actually at work in the pit longer than twelve hours, yet they are always absent from their homes at least thirteen hours, and commonly more. In some cases, indeed, they are away from home as long even as in the Derbyshire district, namely, sixteen hours daily.

James Strong, aged seven: "Has been down in the pit one year; gets up at three o'clock A.M.; goes down the pit at four o'clock; comes up at four o'clock P.M., sometimes later; does not know how often, but it is very often" (J. R. Leifchild, Esq.,Evidence, No.5: App. Pt. I. p. 569, l. 66).—Thomas Lashley: "Gets up about three o'clock A.M.; goes down the pit at four o'clock; comes up the pit at four o'clock P.M., sometimes five o'clock; gives over work at four o'clock in general, but if the men work a little longer he stops" (Ibid. No. 7: p. 570, l. 11).—George Beresford, going in thirteen: "Gets up at half-past two every morning, because he lives a good way off, at Ouseburn, which is two or three miles off; gets to the pit and goes down at four o'clock. The pit looses at four P.M." (Ibid. No. 34: p. 574, l. 51).—Thomas Smithson, aged eleven: "The caller calls him at half-past two o'clock A.M.; he gets up at three and starts work down the pit at four o'clock; gets home at five o'clock; soon after he washes himself and goes to bed about six or seven o'clock. The caller calls him again at half-past two, and his mother comes to his bedside to wake him. He generally feels sore tired when he comes home" (Ibid. No. 440 : p. 654, l. 55-9).

425. Sixteen drivers from ten to fifteen years of age state that they all work the same hours, from a little before six till about six and after in the evening. Many of them, having some distance to go, do not get home before seven or eight o'clock. It is very often seven before they come up the pit, as they loose the work at half-past six, and some have to walk more than a mile, or two miles sometimes, to the bottom of the shaft, and so it is sometimes seven o'clock before they get up the pit (Ibid. No. 154, p. 599, l. 59). The statements of the overlookers, viewers, and medical men, confirm the correctness of the evidence of the Children and Young Persons.

George Johnson, Esq., viewer of Wellington, Heaton, and Burdon Main Collieries, on the Tyne, says: "The hours of labour are just the same when the demand for coals is great as at other times—that is, in a case where the demand is brisk, the full number of days in a fortnight, 11 days of 12 hours each, is worked; when the demand is dull the number of days is lessened, but the hours of each day's work, 12 hours, remain the same" (Ibid. No. 3 : p. 567, l. 29).—Nicholas Wood, Esq., viewer of Killingworth, Hetton, and other collieries : "The regular hours of work for children are 12 hours down the pit; thinks they would not stay down the pit much longer. It will take something beyond the 12 hours, including the time that is required to reach their place of work from the bottom of the shaft and to return to the shaft bottom. This must, of course, depend on the locality of their work, and in most cases would not exceed half an hour, that is, a quarter of an hour going and a quarter returning. The above is the time they are actually down the pit" (Ibid. No. 97 : p. 586, l. 10).— * * *, deputy overman in a colliery near Newcastle : "They work 12 hours per day, which is the stated time for coals to be drawn out of the pit, which causes them one half-hour more time in the pit at least; and this time on coming and going from work, which is sometimes a good distance, will cause them to be between 13 and 14 hours from home each day" (Ibid. No. 503 : p. 6, 7, l. 48).—William Morrison, Esq., surgeon, professionally engaged in the Countess of Durham's collieries : "Twelve hours are generally the allotted time for the labours of the several persons I have mentioned, and, I may add, 15 hours generally elapses between the time of leaving their homes and returning again" (Ibid. No. 496 : p. 662, l. 59).—R. Elliot, Esq., M.D., Newcastle : "Such children I know to be in the pit about 12 hours at least at each descent; this is about once and a half the length of the men's ' shift.' On ' coming to bank' I have generally found that, child-like, they would play with other children in the village for hours afterwards, to the manifest abridgment of their natural rest; that they would have to be roused at one in the morning, after perhaps not more than six, or even five, hours' sleep—decidedly too short a period for their years—and be sent to work sleepy and fatigued. I have known many accidents occur from their sleeping in the pit, especially by lying on the rails; this may be said to give rise to perhaps a majority of the surgical accidents" (Ibid. No. 499 : p. 668, l. 3).

426. EAST OF SCOTLAND.—According to many of the coal owners, managers, and agents, the regular hours of work in this district are only eight or nine (see Mr. Franks's Evidence, Nos. 331, 364, 418, 440, 447 : App. Pt. I.); but however true this statement may be relative to the particular mines of which these witnesses must be regarded as speaking, it is far indeed from giving a correct representation of the number of hours during which it is usual for the workpeople of the collieries of the East of Scotland to continue their daily labour. There is overwhelming evidence that the labour of the coal pits in this district is often continued, on alternate days at least, for 15, 16, 17, and even 18 hours out of the 24, and great numbers of Children and Young Persons state that 14 hours is the regular and ordinary time during which they daily work in the pits. Some witnesses, indeed, state that they not unfrequently work the whole 24 hours. For example,—

Anne Hamilton, seventeen years old, says: "I have repeatedly wrought the 24 hours, and after two hours of rest and my peas (soup) have returned to the pit and worked another 12 hours" (R. H. Franks, Esq., Evidence, No. 263 : App. Pt. I., p. 484, l. 41).—Catharine Walter, sixteen years old, putter: "Frequently works 18 hours on two shifts—the day 12 hours, night 6 hours; obliged to do so, as mother has five children, and is poor" (Ibid. No. 378 : p. 503, l. 16).—Alexander Simpson, seventeen years old, coal-hewer: "I work 16 hours per day, five and six days in the twelve, and 12 hours the other five" (Ibid. No. 261 : p. 484, l. 20).—Robert Mackay, fourteen years old, coal-hewer: "Works 15 and 16 hours daily three days in the week, and seven to eight hours other three days. The short days are those we prepare the work in, on which days the females who put our work are paid 1s. 6d. per day" (Ibid. No. 243 : p. 481, l. 41).—Ann Waugh, sixteen years old, putter: "Works on the long days 15 and 16 hours: two in the morning till five and six at night. On the lay days [short days] only eight hours" (Ibid. No. 239 : p. 481, l. 4).—William Woods, fourteen years old, coal-hewer: "I gang at three in the morning, and return about six' (Ibid. No. 8 : p. 437, l. 58).

David Guy, seven years old: " I gang at half five [half-past four] in the morning, and come up at half six at night" (Ibid. No. 225: p. 478, l. 20).—William Adams, ten years old: " Works from half six [half-past five] till six and seven at night" (Ibid. No. 253: p. 483, l. 8).—William Morrison, eleven years old: " Works from five in the morning till six and seven at night; do not like such long hours, as have only two rests of twenty minutes each during day" (Ibid. No. 258: p. 483, l. 43).—Andrew Young, eleven years old: " We work from four in the morning till five and six at night; and when on night-work we yoke [commence] at four after-noon, and return six and seven next morning" (Ibid. No. 87: p. 453, l. 39).—Jessie Wright, eleven years old: " Brother and I go down, whether father and mother go down or not. Granny takes charge of the house when we are away. Work from three in the morning till five, whiles later; no certain time of coming up" (Ibid. No. 13: p. 439, l. 13).

David Naysmith, twelve years old: " We work from three in the morning till five" (Ibid. No. 6: p. 437, l. 33).—Emma Bennett, twelve years old, coal-bearer: " Works 12 to 14 hours daily; sometimes all night; does so on Fridays" (Ibid. No. 15: p. 439, l. 37).—Mary Macqueen, twelve years old, coal-bearer: " I go below generally at three in the morning, and return at five or six, and sometimes three in the afternoon" (Ibid. No. 54: p. 446, l. 41).—Robert Dickson, twelve years old, coal-filler: " I never work less than 12 or 14 hours" (Ibid. No. 98: p. 455, l. 26). Elizabeth Dickson, twelve years old: " I am wrought with two brothers and two sisters below; am never wrought less than 12 and 14 hours; week about we work all night" (Ibid. No. 102: p. 455, l. 66).—James Wood, twelve years old: " I go down at five in the morning and come away about seven at night" (Ibid. No. 157: p. 465, l. 18).—Peter Williamson, twelve years old, putter: " Work about 12 and 14 hours, and more when needed." (Ibid. No. 191: p. 471, l. 57).—Andrew Laing, twelve years old: " Works every day 12 to 14 hours" (Ibid. No. 254: p. 483, l. 24). —Robert Fotherington, twelve years old: " We work very long hours, whiles 14 and 15" (Ibid. No. 257: p. 483, l. 39).—Margaret Watson, sixteen years of age: " Most of us work from three in the morning till four or five at night" (Ibid. No. 115: p. 458, l. 7).—Margaret Hipps, seventeen years old, putter: " On short shifts I work from eight in the morning till six at night, on long ones until ten at night" (Ibid. No. 233: p. 479, l. 45).

427. WEST OF SCOTLAND.—In the coal mines in the West of Scotland the re-gular hours of work are from eleven to thirteen; but they are very often protracted to fourteen, and even to sixteen consecutively. It is the practice in this district for the colliers to begin work very early in the morning, generally at four, but often at three, though there are some pits in which the work does not commence till six, but these are comparatively few. It is stated by the Sub-Commissioner that in this district it seems the universal custom to begin work very early in the morning, often by four o'clock, a practice which must increase the hardship of that sort of labour to young children, boys and girls. The collier usually engages not only to hew or pick out the coal, but also to draw it to the bottom of the shaft. In order, therefore, to get coal ready by six o'clock, the time the engine starts to raise it to the surface, when the rule is, " first come first served," the colliers are anxious to get coal picked out in time to supply the engine. The time of ceasing work in the afternoon varies considerably according to the hardness of the coal, the distance it has to be drawn, the demand, and other circumstances. For in-stance, if a large quantity of coal, drawn from considerable distances, is to be raised by one shaft, the drawers must be kept waiting a long time at the pit-bottom till the first comers have sent up their loads before they can return to the face of the coal for another hutchful. In some cases the Children do not go down quite as early as the colliers, though if young it is safer for them to be lowered in the same corf with a man; but in all cases they must remain down as long, if not longer, than the collier, in order to draw the last of his day's work. Consequently, when working full time, the Children will remain down the pit from eleven to thirteen hours consecutively. The same hours apply to the trappers who keep the doors for directing the current of ventilation. On inquiring the reason of the early hour at which colliers commence work, the only explanation I have been able to obtain is, that some sorts of coal deteriorate if stored up at the pit-mouth, so that it is generally sent off to the furnaces, or by carts and canals for shipment or land sale, as soon as raised from the pit. I imagine, however, that habit and custom have more to do with the practice in most cases than any real necessity. The hours of work in collieries are evidently too long, for it is found impossible for men to con-tinue them day after day; and the general custom amongst colliers is not to exceed ten days' work in the fortnight. This is the amount of work stipulated by the regulations of collieries. (T. Tancred, Esq., Report, § 33, 34, 36: App. Pt. I., p. 319, 320; Evidence, Nos. 98, 99, 100, 108, 123, 125, 126, 127, 131, 133, 137.

428. NORTH WALES.—In this district the regular hours of work are twelve, generally from six o'clock in the morning to six o'clock in the evening; but from this is to be deducted the time allowed for meals. There is great uniformity in

the statements of all classes of witnesses as to the regularity with which the colliers in this district begin work in the pits, at six o'clock in the morning, and leave off at six in the evening; but the work is sometimes continued sixteen, and even eighteen hours consecutively. "Occasionally there is work over-hours; but colliers rarely work overtime. Of course when the men remain in the pits beyond the usual time the Children also remain. The hours of work never vary with the seasons; in summer, however, when the demand for coal is not so brisk, it frequently happens that only four or five days' work can be obtained in the week. Casualties, such as the engine being out of repair, or the falling in of the roof of the works now and then, derange the system of work, and render it necessary that the men and boys should work for a day or two a greater number than the usual hours, but these occasions are not of frequent occurrence, and do not entail any lasting hardship, though perhaps two or three days of extended labour may be required" (H. H. Jones, Esq., Report, § 13: App. Pt. II., p. 366; Evidence, Nos. 17, 100, 103, 75, 23, 60, 93, 1, 2, 158).

429. SOUTH WALES.—According to almost all the proprietors and agents, and some of the foremen and managers, the regular hours of work in this district are only from eight to ten hours daily; some of the oversmen, however, state that the day's work is seldom finished in less than eleven or twelve hours; while the Children and Young Persons themselves almost universally declare that they never work less than twelve hours, and many of them state that they occasionally work as long as thirteen, fourteen, fifteen, sixteen, and even eighteen hours. The statements of the Children and Young Persons are in general confirmed by the evidence given by the adult workpeople.

430. The usual hours of work in the collieries in this district are from six in the morning until six in the evening; though there are pits in which the work begins as early as four o'clock in the morning. It is stated by R. H. Franks, Esq., that in the collieries in this district examined by him, "the hours of work are generally from six in the morning until six at night, including the time given to meals; and as in collieries and iron-works the labour of Children and Young Persons accompanies the labour of the adult workmen, their hours of labour are of the same duration as the labour of the men" (R. H. Franks, Esq., Report, § 45: App. Pt. II., p, 480).

431. Of the coal mines in Monmouthshire, more particularly examined by R. W. Jones, Esq., he says, "They mostly commence at six o'clock in the morning, and leave off at six or seven in the evening. They very frequently work two or three hours over-time, which they are induced to do from some accidental circumstances interfering during the day with the despatch of their labours, or when on some occasions a greater quantity of work than usual is required to be done. On these occasions they generally remain at work until the allotted task is done; and at many establishments, when in full work, and when only the day set of hands are employed, the labours of the pits and levels which commenced at six o'clock in the morning are not suspended, three days out of the six, until seven or eight o'clock in the evening" (R. W. Jones, Esq., Report, § 8: App. Pt. II., p. 582; Evidence, Nos. 8, 14, 90, 62, 91, 92, 93, 23, 24, 80, 88; R. H. Franks, Esq., Evidence, Nos. 135, 324, 419, 72, 436, 137, 391, 120, 286, 351, 54, 200, 92, 195, 229, 218, 307, 441, 95, 230, 257, 439.)

432. FOREST OF DEAN.—In this district the regular hours of work are stated not to exceed upon an average eight hours a-day; in some collieries, however, they are always twelve (E. Waring, Esq., Evidence, Nos. 8, 9, 14, 18, 46: App. Pt. II.)

433. SOUTH GLOUCESTERSHIRE.—In this district the regular hours of work are stated to be, as in the Forest of Dean, only from eight to ten hours daily. It is seldom that work commences in the pits before six o'clock in the morning, and in some of the coal mines it does not begin until between six and seven (E. Waring, Esq., Evidence, Nos. 68, 76, 74, 48, 49, 67, 59: App. Pt. II.)

434. NORTH SOMERSETSHIRE.—In some of the coal mines in this district the regular hours of work are only from eight to ten in number; but more often they are from ten to twelve, and occasionally they are prolonged to thirteen. In this district it is the usual practice for the colliers to commence work very early in the morning, often at four o'clock, but in some pits they do not begin work till six, and

in a very few not till between six and seven (See Dr. Stewart, Evidence, Nos. 1, 2, 6, 7, 11, 16, 20, 21, 22: App. Pt. II., p. 49 et seq.).

435. IRELAND.—In some of the Coal Mines of Ireland the regular hours of work are stated to be only eight daily, but in general they are not less than twelve. According to Mr. Naysmith, agent of the Coalbrook Colliery in the county of Tipperary, " the strong able lads of seventeen or eighteen years old, employed to do their work, work from eight to twelve hours." In the other coal mines of the south, as far as they were examined by the Commissioner for this part of the United Kingdom, no mention is made of less than twelve hours' work ; but this includes the time allowed for meals. At the Drumglass Colliery, in the county of Tyrone, the young hands are 10 hours underground ; and at that of Coal Island, in the same county, only seven (F. Roper, Esq., Report, *passim.*—T. Martin, Esq., Evidence, No. 47 : App. Pt. I., p. 884, l. 11 ; and No. 51, p. 885, l. 1).

8. NIGHT WORK IN COAL MINES.

436. In the great majority of the coal fields of the United Kingdom night-work is a part of the ordinary system of colliery labour; the extent to which it is used, and the constancy with which it is practised, being regulated entirely by the demand for coals. There are a few districts, however, in the coal mines in which there is no night-work, properly so called ; that is, none beyond what is absolutely necessary to repair the pit and to put it in order for working during the day.

438. In the following districts night-work is commonly practised, and in some of them the coal mines are regularly worked by night just as they are by day.

437. WARWICKSHIRE.—In this district the coal mines are worked at night when the men are engaged in making a heading up hill, in which case the continuation of the work by night as well as by day is stated to be necessary to prevent the accumulation of gas ; when the heading is so limited in extent as not to allow all the men immediately to work at the same time, in which case a certain number of the hewers work at night, and each man requires a boy or two to be in attendance upon him ; and when there is great demand for coals, says Mr. John Sommers, surgeon, of Bedworth, " they have two turns ; one set works in the day-time, and the other at night. Night-shift and day-shift is what they call it. They work one fortnight in the day-time, and the next fortnight in the night-time" (Dr. Mitchell, Report, § 26: App. Pt. I., p. 91. Evidence, No. 68 : p. 107, l. 56).

439. DERBYSHIRE.—Night-work is practised in some of the pits in this district with double sets of hands, but generally only one or two Young People are engaged all night under ground, whenever there is any work demanding a few hands to be continuously employed.

Mr. John Stafford, agent, Morley-park Foundry, Coal-pits, and Marchay Ripley Coal-pit : " In the soft coal children go down from six P.M. to six A.M." (J. M. Fellows, Esq., Evidence, No. 257: App. Pt. II., p. 324, l. 41).—Henry Thorp, clerk, Shipley Coal-Field, and Pottery of E. M. Mundy, Esq. : " For the last two months at the two Soft Coal-pits had a relay of hands, one set from six A.M. to six P.M., the other from six P.M. to six A.M.; find they do not do so much by night as by day, and they have no time to clear the banks; some of the children who work by night are occasionally changed to day-work. A prohibition of night-work would not injure them" (Ibid. No. 33 : p. 272, l. 14).—Godfrey Hardy : " Is twelve years old; he now goes at six P.M. to six in the morning" (Ibid. No. 34 : p. 272, l. 49).—John Aldred : " Is twelve years old; works at Shipley with his father at night; goes in at six o'clock to four; never works in the days, except Mondays and Saturdays, when he does not work by night. He and his father are left in the pit by themselves all night; had rather work by day; his father ' belts' him so by night" (Ibid. No. 36 : p. 273, l. 2).—David Clark : " Is twelve years old; he is bank-boy by night at Crabtree Pit; he goes at eight P.M. to six A.M. Works five nights a-week; does not like it, being so cold and dark, he had much rather work two hours longer by day" (Ibid., No. 336 : p. 338, l. 65).—Matthew Barnett, aged twelve, Duckmanton : " Every other week he works all night, but not on a Sunday" (Ibid. No. 463 : p. 355, l. 43).—John Beasley, collier, Shipley : " The children are obliged to work in the night if the waggon-road is out of repair, or the water coming on them; it happens sometimes two or three times in the week ; they then go down at six P.M. to six A.M., and have from 10 minutes to half an hour allowed for supper, according to the work they have to do; they mostly ask the children who have been at work the previous day to go down with them, but seldom have to oblige them. When he was a boy he has worked for 36 hours running many a time, and many more besides himself has done so; it is quite impossible for the night-boys to give any alarm in case of wildfire, black-damp, or any other accident; indeed nothing would be known of them until the holers came at three o'clock in the morning; he has known them to get beat and receive no assistance until the engine-man came to his work in the morning; the night-work requires both children and young people" (Ibid. No. 40 : p. 274, 1. 36).

440. BRADFORD and LEEDS.—Although, in the great majority of the coal mines in the Bradford and Leeds coal field, there is no night-work, excepting when some special circumstances render it absolutely indispensable, yet there are collieries in which it is systematically practised. Mr. Thomas William Embleton, manager of the Middleton Colliery, near Leeds, states that they very frequently work during the night, and that this is occasionally the case with other coal-masters in the district. In answer to the question, What are the circumstances under which you do it? this witness replies :—

" One circumstance is this—that in the winter, when the demand for coal is considerable, we cannot work the quantity required during the day-time, owing to the particular state of the works at the time. The number of places at which men can work is so small that it is impossible to get the required quantity of coals within eight hours. We have frequently two and sometimes three sets of men. Another case in which we are obliged to work in the night is in removing the pillars of coal left to support the roof, as if there were an interruption of work for twelve hours the roof would come down, and this coal be buried. Another case is, where there is a constant influx of water, which, if not removed as it comes in during the night as well as the day, would prevent the mine being worked at all. We are also enabled by night-work to prepare coal in the summer for working in winter, and thus give the men and children more regular employment, for in *preparing* that coal the men earn the same wages as in winter, but raise less coal. But we had always rather confine ourselves to day-work, if we can " (W. R. Wood, Esq., Evidence, No. 77 : App. Pt. II., p. *h* 34, l. 43).—William Taylor, nine years old : " Sometimes works in the night; has worked sometimes a week, sometimes a day; does not like it much; had rather work in the day" (Ibid. No. 81 : p. *h* 36, l. 39).—Benjamin Leversedge, thirteen years old : " Sometimes works in the night a week at a time; not oft; does not dislike it, but had rather work in the day ; works less hours when it is night-work, and the same wages" (Ibid. No. 82 : p. *h* 36, l. 56).—John Wood, thirteen years old : " Sometimes works in the night, sometimes a week at once, sometimes a night or two; does not dislike it, but had rather work in the day; night-work does not come very often ; works shorter hours night-work and gets same wages" (Ibid. No. 85: p. *h* 37, l. 33)·—William Sucksmith, aged fourteen years: " Works night-work every other week ; hours for night-work same as day; does not like night-work" (Ibid. No. 7 : p. *h* 8, l. 47).

441. LANCASHIRE AND CHESHIRE.—In the coal fields of these counties it is the usual practice to work at night, more especially in the coal-pits of Staley Bridge, Duckenfield, Ashton, Oldham, Blackrod, Wigan, and Pemberton.

Mr. Miller, underlooker at Mr. Woolley's, near Staley Bridge, says, " We always work night and day; we have a night-shift and a day-shift : in some collieries in Dukinfield they work three shifts; but there, as with us, the waggoners, who are paid day-wages, will only work at two shifts. They work between ten and eleven hours; it will take nearly two hours to change them; as many of the works are a long way in, it will take a man almost an hour to go in and come out from his work; where the leases have been taken on the calculation that they could be worked night and day, I don't think that they could be worked to pay if they were restricted to working in the day only. I should be very glad if night-work could be stopped, but I almost doubt whether it can be done; I have a little boy working at this moment [ten at night]; he went at six o'clock this evening, and he will stop until six to-morrow morning" (J. L. Kennedy, Esq., Evidence, No. 7 : App. Pt. II., p. 203, l. 39).—James Darby, pumper at Mr. Almond's, Lumberhead Green, near Wigan: " I am on the night turn this week. I work at night one week, and in the day the next, week about. When working the night turn I go at five o'clock, and I come out at six in the morning" (Ibid. No. 54 : p. 224, l. 5).—Samuel Rushworth, twelve years old, hurrier, Holebottom: " I work at night every other week; we should work eight-hour shifts, night and day, but we work twelve hours just now" (Ibid. No. 47 : p. 222, l. 42).—Thomas Jackson, between twelve and thirteen years old, thrutcher, Lord Balcarras's, Wigan: " I work at night one week, and in the day the next, in turns" (Ibid. No. 52 : p. 223, l. 49).—Jane Sym, aged twenty-six, waggoner at Mr. Craigg's, Blackrod: " I work night and day week about, that is, I work in the day one week and in the night the next. I work at night from six at night till six in the morning. I don't like working in the night-shift, it makes me very tired sometimes, and I am ill with it, but I must keep my turn or 'clem' [go without food]" (Ibid. No. 72: p. 22 , l. 29).—See witnesses, Nos. 8, 49, 52, 53.

442. OLDHAM.—Night-work is common in the collieries near Oldham, and is felt, by all the witnesses examined in this district, to be a great evil. "When the demand is good the collieries generally are wrought night and day, by alternate sets; the night shift for one week being the day shift for the next (Nos. 4, 7). The young people go down with the men between five and six, or between seven and eight in the morning, or at night, according to their turn, and will not get up again until about the same hours at night or in the morning, although the men will ge-

nerally be out an hour or two earlier (Nos. 4, 7). Some of the collieries are now regularly working double sets; others are not; and the men employed in all are working generally short time, by which the labour of the young people is proportionately reduced, in accordance with regulations among themselves.

443. " In each pit, where there is not a night set regularly at work, there is always, however, one getter, with his waggoner, aided commonly by a thrutcher, during the whole of the night. The drawing-engine, at the top of the shaft, not working during the night, it is needless for more than this one collier to be at work, for his labour alone will suffice to fill the complete set of tubs which the whole of the workmen use during the daytime, when the engine is winding them up loaded and returning them down empty, as fast as they can be brought to the pit-bottom. It is a saving to have all the tubs full, for the engine at once to commence drawing in the morning, while the getters are hewing more. This night-work the men of each pit, and their assistants, take alternately, in addition to their ordinary labour" (J. Fletcher, Esq., Report, § 37, 38 : App. Pt. II., p. 826).

James Taylor, going in eleven years of age : " Used to work at the pit he was last in in the night-shift when it was his master's turn; when he had been working at night could not sleep in the day, not more than two hours, and then he ran a-playing him. Felt when he slept as though he were waggoning, and dreamt that the waggons were all coming on t' butty and him, that the roof was tumbling in on them, or that George Whitehead, his butty, was 'puncing' [kicking or striking] him. He was a wicked lad, and one time wouldn't let him eat his dinner. When he got up to run about th' loan [lane] after t' other lads, he felt queer, and kept shuttin' his 'een and runnin'. He couldn't feel well after watching all t' neet. Could keep awake all night constantly working; for if he stopped work he would go to sleep, and then he would have a clout i' the mouth" (J. Fletcher, Esq., Evidence, No. 10 : App. Pt. II., p. 848, l. 55).—William Dronsfield, going in eighteen years of age : " Worked night-sets in Mr. Wrigley's pits, which are still regularly worked by alternate night and day shifts. Did not like the night-work, nobody does; would liefer work six days than five nights, for the same money. Felt always quite muzzy and sleepy in the night when working" (Ibid. No. 20 : p. 852, l. 26).— Samuel Hall, late book-keeper at Mr. Abraham Lees's colliery ; James Urmson, Edward Taylor, Robert Grimshaw, Benjamin Jackson, Abraham Taylor, colliers, members of the Primitive Methodist congregation, Knot Lane, and the three first members also of the school committee for the management of the Sunday-school there, all say that "One of the most destructive things to the health of the colliers, and of the children working with them, as well as to their well-being in mind, is the night-work to which they are forced. Wish to God that this were put a stop to. The Almighty ordained the night for rest, and not for work. Think it would be a very great 'privilege' to colliers to put a stop to night-work, which would make their habits both of body and mind more healthy. A collier that has been working regularly night and day shifts alternately will not live so long by many years. Object to the system altogether. It would be a grand thing for this country if the night-work were put a stop to. A collier that has been at work in the night cannot sleep in the day, and cannot feel healthily awake the night through. From twelve to two he is chill and drowsy, and the weariness of body which comes from it is dreadful; but the necessities of his family drive him on. The weariness from night-work robs a man even of his religious habits and feelings; and if it have this effect on the men, what must it have on the children? Of those who would go to a night-school, there is only one week in two when they can go ; and it must be a child of very persevering mind that can take up its lessons at intervals in this way. They fall asleep at their work; thence exposure to constant danger, not only to themselves but to others, and they suffer from headaches and other distempers. They are quite dull and sleepy: are all sure that in childhood or manhood the night-work undermines the constitution, and decreases health and strength (Ibid. Nos. 28—33 : p. 855, l. 23).

444. NORTH LANCASHIRE.—In some of the collieries in the North of Lancashire night-work is not uncommon. It is practised, for example, in some of the coal mines in the Burnley and Haslingden Unions, as in the Marsden Lower Pit, parish of Whalley; but in other pits in this same district, as in the Burnley Hill and the Haggate Coal works, there is no night-work; neither does it appear to be practised in the collieries in Blackburn, Over Darwen, and Oswaldtwistle. " Not many of these works carry on their labours at night; where they do so they have regular relays of hands, and the shifts are usually eight hours. But where an occasional call or demand for coal arises, those who do not regularly work at night experience the greatest suffering, for no relays of hands are provided, and the getters will, when paid piece-work, work for many hours together, compelling their drawers, the children, to do the same. And this happens at almost all those works which do not work regularly night or day" (Report and Evidence by A. Austin, Esq., § 6: App. Pt. II., p. 802).

445. CUMBERLAND.—In the Coal Mines of this district it is the general custom to work at night. " In most of Lord Lonsdale's extensive collieries they work

COAL MINES.

Night Work.

Districts in which practised.

Cumberland.

night and day—the shift who work the twelve day-hours one week working thf twelve night-hours the succeeding week, and so on alternately. The appearance o- the adults in these collieries was remarkably pallid and emaciated. I should attri bute this greatly to the system of night-working; and there is a probability that the change from night to day hours operates more unfavourably on the health than it would do were they to work altogether at night. In the latter case habit becomes second nature, and sleep as refreshing is obtained by day as by night. Not so when the animal system is subjected to continual change, no habit is formed, and according to the evidence the rest obtained in the day is very deficient; so much so, as to render the night-work irksome through the inclination for sleep. The wife generally goes to bed by day with her husband, and so do all the family, and the door is often fastened to preserve as much quiet as possible. In some few pits eight-hour shifts are worked" (J. C. Symons, Esq., Report, § 10: App. Pt. I., p. 300).

South Durham.

446. SOUTH DURHAM.—Night-work is rare in this district; but occasionally there springs up a sudden and extraordinary demand for coals, and then the people are employed to do a greater quantity of work. Sometimes on such occasions there may be a day set and a night set, each working ten hours; this is a comparatively rare case, and still more rare is a triple set; though an eminent engineer has stated that he has known such a thing to take place (Dr. Mitchell, Report, § 88: App. Pt. I., p. 127).

Northumberland and North Durham.

447. NORTHUMBERLAND and NORTH DURHAM.—In a large proportion of the coal mines of these districts there is no night-work, yet it is by no means uncommon in some mines in this district, and occasionally boys and young men work in the pits, what is termed double and treble shifts, that is, for 24 or 36 consecutive hours; and some instances are stated of their having worked quadruple shifts, that is, for 48 consecutive hours; a period during which it is scarcely credible that the human frame can sustain such labour.

Nicholas Wood, Esq., viewer of Killingworth, Hetton, and other collieries, says: " In some cases, when the demand is very great, the pits are set to work what is called ' double shifts,' or the entire 24 hours, by two sets of workmen, each 12 hours; but in these cases the boys cannot remain longer than 12 hours" (J. R. Leifchild, Esq., Evidence, No. 97: App. Pt. I., p. 586, l. 29).—Robert Dixon, nine years old: " Works in the night-shift every other fortnight" (Ibid. No. 64: p. 579, l. 65).—George Anderson, eleven years old: " Has worked in the night shift every other fortnight, almost all the year. In the night-shift, went down at four [getting up at three] P.M., and came up at about half-past four in the morning. Was often sleepy. Got his hammers twice [was beaten twice] for being asleep. The putters beat him with their soam-sticks [handles], and hurt him and made him cry, because he did not open the door for them" (Ibid. No. 90: p. 583, l. 53).—John Alexander, fifteen years old: " Works from one o'clock in the morning to one in the afternoon every night. Sometimes goes in on Sunday night. Works six shifts a-week always" (Ibid. No. 212: p. 612, l. 27).—George Taylor, sixteen years old: " Goes regularly to work every night in the week that the pit works, at the Elemore George Pit, at twelve o'clock [at night]; comes up at eight or nine, or ten or twelve o'clock next day" (Ibid. No. 436: p. 653, l. 61).—George Kendall, eighteen years old: " Two or three times has stood 36 hours down the pit. When lads say they stop double shift, they mean generally 36 hours. If, for instance, they are in the day-shift, and are asked to stop for the night-shift, then they stay their own shift next day—their baits being sent down to them. A great quantity of boys are doing this now" (Ibid. No. 105: p. 590, l. 16).—George Foster, sixteen years old: " About a year and a half ago he wrought three shifts at one time; going down at four o'clock one morning, and staying 36 hours without coming up. Was driving for two shifts and helping up for one; stopped about two hours altogether, half an hour or so each shift to get his baits, which were taken down with him the first day, and sent the other two shifts. The overman asked him to stop" (Ibid. No. 35: p. 575, l. 2).—James Richardson, seventeen years old: " About six months ago he worked three shifts following, of 12 hours each shift, and never stopped work more than a few minutes now and then, or came up the pit till he was done. There was then some night-work to do, and the overman asked him to stop, and he could not say no, or else he [the overman] would have frowned on him, and stopped him perhaps of some helpers-up" (Ibid. No. 272: p. 624, l. 33).

George Dryden, between fourteen and fifteen years old: " Last year, at Walbottle Colliery, he worked four shifts following, of 12 hours each, in the new pit. He was up the pit every shift, but never in bed all that time. It happened thus,—he was working in the night-shift, and as some day-shift lads were wanted he stopped for them. Those four shifts were thus managed,—he went down the pit at eight o'clock on the Sunday night, and came up at five on the Monday evening for two hours, and went down again at seven o'clock [P.M.], and came up on Tuesday night at five o'clock [P.M.] This made the four shifts. He went in the regular shift down again on the Wednesday night, and was up at five in the morning, and so he went on. In this night-shift he was about three weeks driving rolleys. The reason he stopped

COAL MINES.

Night Work.

Districts in which practised.

Northumberland
and
North Durham.

the extra shifts [as above described] was because they asked him to stop, and he thought he could do it. Did it for the money, and would like to do it again for the money, although he gave it to his parents. Parents did not force him to stop. Father gave him 1s. that time out of the four shifts' earnings" (Ibid., No. 271: p. 623, l. 64).—John Dixon, fourteen years old: "Last fortnight was down the pit three days and three nights without coming up at all. Got his baits sent him. John Cooper, the overman, told him to stop to drive, because John Short and Thomas Angus were ill. The first day was Thursday. Was down on Thursday morning at four o'clock, and came up on Saturday at four o'clock in the morning. Three other boys stayed down to drive with him; all stopped the same time. Did not feel sleepy. Did not sleep down the pit. Was not tired. Would like to do it again, to get more money. [Seems scarcely to know what induced him to stop.] Is now going to work in the night-shift at Howden Pit." [The evidence of this witness was subsequently confirmed by his father, witness (No. 92: p. 584), who stated that he was always a weakly boy, and that he had driven a good deal in wet places] (Ibid. No. 58: p. 578, l. 44).—See also witnesses, Nos. 118, 129, 135, 138, 191, 192, 302, 304, 36.

448. EAST OF SCOTLAND.—Night-work is very common in the collieries of this district, and the hours of work at night are seldom less than twelve, and usually fourteen.

William Martin, ten years old: "Works on night and day shifts. When on night, goes down at six and seven in the evening, and comes up at ten and eleven next morning. Works the same number of hours when on day-shift" (R. H. Franks, Esq., Evidence, No. 159: App. Pt. I., p. 465, l. 34).—Alexander Fraser, twelve years old: "Sometimes works all night when needed; did so last month; went down at four afternoon, and came up at six in the morning. The work is very sair" (Ibid. No. 31: p. 442, l. 54).—David Burnside, twelve years old: "When I work all night, I gang at five or six in the evening, and return five or six in morning" (Ibid. No. 56: p. 447, l. 25).—Janet Moffat, twelve years old, coal-putter: "Works from six morning till six night; alternate weeks works in the night-shift. Descends at six at night, and returns five or six in morning, as the coals are drawn, whiles later" (Ibid. No. 70: p. 449, l. 42).—Helen Reid, sixteen years old: "I work night-work week about [alternate weeks]. I then go down at two in the day, and come up at four or six in the morning" (Ibid. No. 26: p. 441, l. 13).

449. A few witnesses state that they do not work above eight or ten hours in the night-shift.—(See Nos. 11, 12, 432).

450. NORTH WALES.—In many of the Collieries of North Wales it is also the practice to work at night.

William Griffith, twelve years old, says, "Has worked at night. When a ship was to be loaded in a tide I have worked from six in the morning till one next morning, being nineteen hours, and was only an hour and a half all that time for my meals. On these occasions returned to work the same morning at six, as usual" (H. H. Jones, Esq., Evidence, No. 150: App. Pt. II., p. 435, l. 61).—John Wynne, twelve years old: "Works at night every other week; one week by night and the other week by day. When at night-work I begin at six P.M.; I work till eight, and have half an hour allowed for supper; I then work till one A.M., and rest till three; then work till half-past five, and go home, unless I work overtime" (Ibid. No. 152: p. 436, l. 45).—Henry Dodd, fifteen years old: "Works at night every other week" (Ibid. No. 126: p. 422, l. 35).—William Jones, fifteen years old: "Works day and night every other week. When at night-work we cease working at one and begin again at three; in that time I sleep on the floor in my clothes" (Ibid. No. 154: p. 437, l. 45).

451. SOUTH WALES.—Night-work is not uncommon in the Collieries of South Wales.

Mr. David Hill, cashier and clerk of the Lansamlet Colliery, county of Glamorgan, says: "Our machinery works the whole twenty-four hours, that is to say, is constantly at work. We employ two sets of men and boys" (R. H. Franks, Esq., Evidence, No. 362: App. Pt. II., p. 561, l. 9).—Philip Davis, aged ten, haulier: "Would go to school if the work were not so long; cannot go now as I have to work on the night as well as the day shifts; the night-work is done by gangs who work week about [alternate weeks]" (Ibid. No. 97: p. 521, l. 5).—William Isaac, eleven years old, air-door keeper: "Works frequently at night" (Ibid. No. 103: p. 521, l. 39).—David Davis, aged sixteen, wheeler: "I work twelve hours daily; and it is the practice of the men to change every six months, when those who have been at day-work take the night-shifts, and so change about" (Ibid. No. 363: p. 561, l. 26).

452. FOREST OF DEAN.—In some of the Coal Mines of this district night-work is regularly practised; but the custom of working at night is not general.

Mr. David Gethin, clerk to the Parkend Coal Works, carried on by the Parkend Coal Company: "Night-work occasionally, perhaps ten or twelve times in the year" (E. Waring, Esq., Evidence, No. 9: App. Pt. II., p. 16, l. 10).—Mr. Josiah Marfell, underground manager, Savidge Green: "They are now working day and night, with three sets every twenty-four hours; this is an emergency" (Ibid. No. 46: p. 29, l. 36).—Mr. Aaron Goold, manager of coal works and iron mines at Bilson, carried on by the Parkend Coal Company: "At one of the pits the work is day and night, but there are two sets of men employed" (Ibid. No. 14: p. 17, l. 44).

COAL MINES.

Night Work.

*Districts in which
practised.*

South
Gloucestershire.

453. SOUTH GLOUCESTERSHIRE.—Night-work does not appear to be prevalent in the mines of this coal field. It is indeed stated to be "of rare occurrence, and that it principally arises from the necessity of repairing the roads under ground, at hours when they are not required for the transit of coals" (E. Waring, Esq., Report, § 88 : App. Pt. II. p. 38). See Evidence, Nos. 52, 57, 58, 59, 60, 66, 67, 68.

454. IRELAND.—Night-work is common in some of the Coal Mines of Ireland.—

Dennis Toomey, fourteen years of age, working in the Dromagh Colliery, says, "Many of us have to work at night when the miners are working ; we must work the same time the colliers are working" (F. Roper, Esq., Evidence, No. 33 : App. Pt. I., p. 869, l. 28).—Jeremiah Kenelly, seventeen years of age, says, "We take our turns for our time of work ; when it is my turn for night-work I go down with the night corps about eight o'clock, and come up about five in the morning ; we have none of us any meals during the time we work at night ; I like the day-work best ; every second week we change about from night-work to day-work ; we have just the same kind of work at night-work as day-work" (Ibid. No. 34 : p. 870, l. 4).

*Districts in which
Night Work is not
practised.*

555. The coal fields in which there is no night-work, properly so called, that is, none beyond what is necessary to maintain the colliery in working order, are, South and North Staffordshire, Shropshire, Leicestershire, the greater portion of the West Riding of Yorkshire, West of Scotland, and North Somersetshire (See Dr. Mitchell, Report and Evidence ; J. C. Symons, Esq., and S. S. Scriven, Esq., Reports and Evidence ; and Reports by T. Tancred, Esq., and by Dr. Stewart).

9. MEAL-HOURS IN COAL MINES.

456. Of all the coal districts of Great Britain there are only two in which any regular time is usually set apart for the rest and refreshment of the workpeople during the day, and in which it is the general custom to observe the time so fixed strictly and uniformly. The districts thus distinguished, and in the mines of which there are not only nominal meal-hours, but there is really a cessation of work during the stated time, are those of South Staffordshire and the Forest of Dean. South Staffordshire is also the only district in the United Kingdom in the coal mines of which, as far as appears from the Evidence, any place is provided for the accommodation of the workpeople during their meal-hours ; and this is below ground. In the few coal mines of Ireland hours are set aside for meals, and the hands employed in some of them ascend from the pits to take their food.

457. There are several districts in which the workpeople are nominally allowed a fixed time for meals, namely, those of Warwickshire, Ashby-de-la-Zouch, Derbyshire, Yorkshire, and Lancashire. In some of the coal mines in each of these districts, the full time thus nominally allowed is actually and uniformly taken, but these are comparatively few ; and in all these districts the regular cessation of the work for any period during the working hours may be regarded as an exception to the general practice ; while in the great majority of the coal districts of England, Scotland, and Wales, no regular time whatever is even nominally allowed for meals, but the people take what little food they eat during their long hours of labour when they best can catch a moment to swallow it.

458. With very few exceptions, no time is allowed for breakfast in any of the districts, even in those in which the work commences very early in the morning, as early as five, four, or even three o'clock. It is almost the universal custom among the collier people to take a hasty morning meal before they leave their dwellings, and then to continue their labour without any further refreshment until about noon.. There are exceptions to this, as will be seen, but they are rare.

459. SOUTH STAFFORDSHIRE.—Even in the coal pits of this district no time is allowed for breakfast. The engine does not stop, and the men and boys eat their meal as they can, so as not to interrupt the work. One hour appears to be very regularly allowed for dinner. The engine stops between one and two ; and a little before one the wives and mothers bring to the pit their husbands' and children's dinners bound up in handkerchiefs, which are put into a skip, and sent down the shaft. "The assemblage at dinner," says Dr. Mitchell, "is in a large dining-hall cut out of the coal, and is the most lively, uproarious, and jovial,

that I have ever seen. A quart of ale is then given to the men, and a pint to the boys. The people, after two o'clock, go back to their work" (Dr. Mitchell, Report, § 68: App. Pt. I., p. 9; and Evidence, No. 10, p. 66: and No. 13, p. 68).

460. NORTH STAFFORDSHIRE.—" The meals in the Pottery coal district are taken at no stated periods, nor is there any specified time allotted for eating them; each person having a certain quota of work to do, they are all eager to get it over that they may ascend the sooner" (S. S. Scriven, Esq., Report, § 10: App. Pt. II., p. 128). North Staffordshire.

461. SHROPSHIRE.—In most of the coal pits in the Coalbrookdale District there is generally no regular time for meals: the engine never stops, but the people "manage to relieve each other in their work so as to allow time to sit down by the side of the horse-way, and speedily eat their victuals." In some pits, however, an hour is allowed for dinner; but most of the witnesses say, "We must bite and go on; we eat when we can" (Dr. Mitchell, Evidence, No. 41: App. Pt. I., p. 79; No. 57, p. 86; and No. 61, p. 87). Shropshire.

462. WARWICKSHIRE.—In the coal field of this county, twenty minutes, and sometimes half an hour, is allowed for dinner, to which they have beer, as in South Staffordshire (Ibid. No. 69, p. 107, and No. 74, p. 109). But there are pits (namely, those in which the men work by stint—that is, are paid so much per ton, according to the quantity of coals sent up the shaft) in which no time at all is allowed for meals. The engine never stops, but the people take their food as they can. "The men who work by the stint," say Thomas Arrott and Samuel Shelton, working colliers, "have no time for their meals; but the engine is kept always going until the stint be got down, and then they leave off" (Ibid. No. 64: p. 105, l. 50). Warwickshire.

463. LEICESTERSHIRE.—In some of the collieries of the Ashby-de-la-Zouch Coal Field, half an hour is allowed for dinner, during which time the engine stops, as in the Snibston and the Whitwick Collieries. In others, as in the Ibstock Colliery, half an hour is allowed for breakfast, and an hour for dinner; but there are pits in this district in which no regular time is fixed for meals, but the people take their food when they can, so as not to interrupt the workings. (Dr. Mitchell, Report, § 113, 115: App. Pt. I., pp. 98, 99). Leicestershire.

464. DERBYSHIRE.—In this coal field, the agents, overlookers, and engine-men in general, state that one hour is allowed for meals; and in many of the returns the coal-owners declare that even two hours per day are regularly allowed for meals. The Evidence shows that in some pits a full hour is really allowed for dinner; but in a much greater number the time allowed is only half an hour, and in many it is only twenty minutes, or a quarter of an hour. (See Evidence collected by Mr. Fellows, Nos. 8, 15, 19, 22, 24, 26, 29, 34, 48, 56, 60, 66, &c., App. Pt. II., pp. 265 et seq.) All classes of witnesses, however, concur in stating that in many of the pits no time whatever is allowed for meals. (Ibid. Nos. 38, 82, 88, 106, 107, 118, 134, 142, 209, 276, 278). Derbyshire.

465. The Sub-Commissioner says: " I am sorry to say in many of the Returns the owners state that one or even two hours per day is allowed for meals: by this they prove that neither they nor their agents have taken much interest, at all events on that head, as to the comforts of the Children employed in their pits. I have not met with a single instance where any time was allowed for any meal, excepting dinner, and forty minutes would be a full average allowed for that. At Denby, parts of Eastwood, and other places, the engine is not allowed to stop on whole days; and at very few places when only three-quarters and half-days are worked. (J. M. Fellows, Esq., Report, §§ 15, 16: App. Pt. II., p. 253.)

466. In many of the pits in which a certain time is nominally allowed for dinner, " the butties insist upon the pit being *in order* before they get their dinner—that is, that the corves are filled, and brought into the waggon-road: therefore, supposing these unfortunate boys to have just disposed of their loaded corve when the engine stops, they have to go the whole length of the bank (often 200 or 300 yards) to load, and bring it back to the waggon, by which period nearly the whole of the time allowed is expired" (Ibid. § 17, p. 253).

467. WEST RIDING OF YORKSHIRE: SOUTHERN PART.—Here it is the general practice for the people employed in the collieries to breakfast before they go to the West Riding of Yorkshire.

COAL MINES.

Meal Hours.

West Riding of Yorkshire.

pit: in some few mines a fixed time is set apart for dinner, and is regularly observed; among others this appears to be the case at the Elsecar Collieries, at Chapelton, and at Barnsley; but these are exceptions to the general rule, which is, that in the pits there is no fixed time for meals, or at least none which is strictly and regularly observed. In some pits, while they occasionally stop an hour for dinner, they more often stop only half an hour; but in by far the greater number of cases they scarcely stop a quarter of an hour, and very frequently only a few minutes. (Ibid. Nos. 3, 6, 22, 24, 32, 39, 52, 53, 62, 66, 71, 74, 82, 85, 94, 112, 118.)

Halifax.

468. HALIFAX.—In the collieries in this neighbourhood, as far as regards the Children and Young Persons at least, there is no cessation of work whatever during the whole of the working hours. There are a few pits in which from half an hour to an hour is allowed for dinner, but these are exceedingly rare exceptions to the general rule. (S. S. Scriven, Esq., Nos. 7, 9, 11, 12, 13, 14, 19, 26, 43.)

Bradford and Leeds.

469 BRADFORD AND LEEDS.—All classes of witnesses concur in stating that, in this district, the children in the coal mines have no regular hours for meals, but eat the food which they take with them to the pit as they can, or as they proceed with their work. The Sub-Commissioner reports: "What has been said as to irregularity and absence of uniformity as to hours of work is at least equally applicable with regard to meals. The collier acts, in this respect, just as it pleases him; and the habits of the Child must more or less conform to the habits of the collier. The more general practice of the coal miners is not to cease working for more than a quarter to half an hour. (W. R. Wood, Esq., Report, § 12: App. Pt. II., p. H 3; and Evidence, Nos. 1, 4, 37, 38, 39, 40, 41, 77, 81, 83, pp. *h* 3 et seq.).

Lancashire and Cheshire.

470. LANCASHIRE AND CHESHIRE.—In some few of the coal mines in the districts examined by J. L. Kennedy, Esq., from half an hour to an hour is allowed for dinner, but there is scarcely an instance in which any time is allowed for breakfast; and in the great majority of the pits there is no cessation of the work from morning till night, but the people eat their food as they can, without resting at all, or at any rate only resting a few moments from their labour. " As a general practice, the colliers, Young Persons, and Children, take their first meal before going into the pits in the morning, or, if they take it in the pits, there is no specified time for taking it. The winding-engines generally stop from forty minutes to an hour in the middle of the day, and of the night when there is night-work; and the banksmen, engineers, and hookers-on at the bottom, whose occupations are dependent on the engine, stop at these times for their meals. The pony-drivers also usually stop a short time, as their occupation depends also in some degree on the winding of the baskets. The colliers and drawers, or waggoners, usually keep working, and take their food when it is most convenient to themselves. They are quite independent of the moving power, and are almost invariably paid by the piece. The masters do not generally exercise any control, or specify any particular hours for the colliers or drawers to take their meals" (J. L. Kennedy, Esq., Report, §§ 223, 224: App. Pt. II., p. 178; and Evidence, Nos. 5, 17, 20, 30, 45, 59, 64, 65, 74, pp. 201 et seq.).

Oldham.

471. OLDHAM.—In this neighbourhood " there is only one meal eaten in the pit, which is a dinner, taken down in the morning, or sent down some time in the day. It generally consists, in the case of the Young People, of only bread and butter, or bread and cheese, which they eat as they can snatch an opportunity while at work, or perhaps while waiting to hook on their tubs at the bottom of the shaft (Nos. 4, 10, 25). The desire to get out of the pit again so soon as possible is perhaps a sufficient plea for reducing the time allowed for this meal within such comfortless limits, which are those observed by the men as well as the boys;" but the sacrifice appears to have no actual effect in reducing the hours of labour (J. Fletcher, Esq., Report, § 40: App. Pt. II., p. 826).

North Lancashire.

472. NORTH LANCASHIRE.—No regular time is here allowed for any meal. " The irregularity in the meals is a great addition to the suffering of the Children. In many cases they, the young drawers, are not allowed to stop work, but are compelled to eat their food while they are pushing or drawing their load, and thus derive no benefit or even comfort from it" (A. Austin, Esq., Report, § 10: App. Pt. II., p. 802; Evidence, Nos. 4, 8, 9, 12, 17, pp. 812, et seq).

Cumberland.

473. CUMBERLAND.—No regular hours are here fixed and kept for meals; the

workers generally stop some little time for refreshment about the middle of the day, varying from ten minutes to half an hour, and in some few cases they appear to stop an hour for dinner (J. C. Symons, Esq., Evidence, Nos. 302, 303, 319, 320, 321).

474. SOUTH DURHAM.—In general no regular time is allowed for meals ; each hewer takes his food when it suits himself; the trappers eat and drink when they like; " but the putters who assist to load the corves and push them to the flats, the horse-drivers, and all who are engaged in forwarding the coals to the shaft, keep on their work as if they were engaged in a sea-fight. Rest and provender are never considered as impeding any journey, and we should suppose that matters could be so managed as to keep the engine in full employment, and yet allow the boys in different districts of the pit, one district after another, to sit down to rest and have their meal in peace. Such is the rule in the Dorothea Pit; and this is not the only pit where some time is allowed for refreshment, but it must be owned that these are rare exceptions" (Dr. Mitchell, Report, § 90 : App. Pt. I., p. 127; and Evidence, Nos. 95, 100, 107, 108).

475. NORTH DURHAM AND NORTHUMBERLAND.—Here, as in South Durham, no regular time is set apart for meals; the Children sometimes stop fifteen minutes to eat their " baits," but in many cases they never rest from their work even as long as this for refreshment (J. R. Leifchild, Esq., Evidence, Nos. 3, 97, 145, 355, 401, 403, 440: App. Pt. I., p. 567, et seq.).

476. EAST OF SCOTLAND.—In the Coal Mines in the East of Scotland no time is allowed for meals. The almost uniform statements of the witnesses examined in this district are—"We have no meals below;" "gets no regular meals;" " we have no regular meal-times" (R. H. Franks, Esq., Evidence, Nos. 3, 4, 8, 30, 42, 64, 70, 87, 164: App. Pt. I., p. 436, et seq.). The following witnesses also state that they have porridge or some slight repast sent to them in the pit, but they say nothing about stopping to eat it, and it is evident that they eat it at their work as they can (Ibid. Nos. 5, 97, 98, 100, 102, 138, 145, 204, 264, 296, 299, 301, 426).

477. WEST OF SCOTLAND.—In the Coal Mines of this part of the kingdom no time is allowed for meals. The only collieries in which a regular hour is fixed for meals are the few pits in which " horses are employed below ground to draw the coal to the pit-bottom;" in these a cessation of work occurs in the middle of the day " for the horses to be fed;" but wherever girls and boys are employed to do this work instead of horses, no time is set apart for refreshment; the "drawers" eat while "waiting at the pit-bottom till their turn comes to have their coal hoisted;" the collier eats when it suits him—"the only way in which his work is at all regulated by the coal owner being, that the engine by which the coal is raised to the surface begins to work generally at six o'clock in the morning, and continues to work till the day's out-put is all up;" all the other labourers in the mine eat when they can (T. Tancred, Esq., Evidence, No. 1: App. Pt. I., p. 355, l. 19; No. 3: p. 356, l. 53).

478. NORTH WALES.—In certain mines in the Coal Fields of Denbighshire and Flintshire a fixed time is stated to be generally set apart for meals; but the evidence collected is not sufficient to show whether the practice of allowing an hour and a half for meals is general in the coal mines of this part of the kingdom (H. H. Jones, Esq., Evidence, Nos. 1, 17, 42: App. Pt. II., p. 377, et seq.).

479. SOUTH WALES.—In the Collieries of South Wales and Monmouthshire no regular time is set apart for meals. " The people working in the interior of the mines can scarcely be said to take any meals during the period they are at work— varying from eight to fourteen hours. They get their breakfast before they enter the works, and take with them a small bag of bread and cheese (their almost invariable fare), which they eat at irregular intervals during the day, as the circumstances of their work will allow, and as their appetites invite them ; and on their return from work they get their suppers, or perhaps what may be as correctly called their dinners. In this respect the Children and Young Persons fare precisely the same as the adults, excepting that the latter very frequently get home to their evening meal some hour or two before the former" (R. W. Jones, Esq., Report, § 12: App. Pt. II., p. 582).

COAL MINES.

Meal Hours.

South Wales.

480. All classes of witnesses say that there are no stated meal-times; that the workpeople take their meals as they can, or as the work will allow. The Children say that the bread and cheese which they take with them to their work they eat when they have time. (R. W. Jones, Esq., Evidence.)

481. R. H. Franks, Esq., also states that " the haulier eats his food as he drives his horse along; the little air-door boy takes his meal when he pleases; the collier, who is paid for his work per ton, eats when he chooses, so that in the coal mines of this district there is no cessation of the work for refreshment during any part of the day" (R. H. Franks, Esq., Report, § 49: App. Pt. II., p. 480).—Mr. Richard Andrews, overseer, says: " They are half starved below, as they never can get their meat like other people, and they never grow like other children" (R. H. Franks, Esq., Evidence, No. 152: p. 528, l. 59; see also Nos. 5, 145, &c.).

Forest of Dean.

482. FOREST of DEAN.—In some of the Coal Mines in this district half an hour is allowed for breakfast and an hour for dinner; in others no time is allowed for meals excepting at dinner, and then it is the custom to stop an hour. The Sub-Commissioner states that there is in this district " a great uniformity in the time for meals" (E. Waring, Esq., Report, § 152: App. Pt. II., p. 12; Evidence, Nos. 8, 9).

South Gloucestershire.

483. SOUTH GLOUCESTERSHIRE.—In the mines of this coal field, according to Mr. Samuel Long, under-ground manager of the Hole-Lane Coal Company, only half an hour is allowed for dinner (E. Waring, Esq., Evidence, No. 59: App. Pt. II., p. 42, l. 34).

North Somersetshire.

484. NORTH SOMERSETSHIRE.—In some of the coal mines of North Somersetshire, according to Mr. Moses Reynolds, under-ground manager of the Bedminster Collieries, " they sit down while in the pit to eat something for half an hour in the middle of their work, but do not come up to the open air" (Dr. Stewart, Evidence, No. 2: App. Pt. II., p. 49, l. 35). But in most of the coal mines in this district it does not appear from the Evidence that any regular time is set apart for meals. It is merely stated by the managers that sufficient time is allowed, while the Children in general say that they eat their food in the pit as they can (Ibid. Nos. 7, 9, 11, 20, 21, 22).

Ireland.

485. IRELAND.—In the Coal Mines of Ireland a fixed time appears to be allowed, at least for dinner; and it is stated by one witness that, at the Dromagh mines, the extraordinary time of two hours is allowed for this meal, and that the workpeople ascend the shaft to eat it; a custom, as far as it is prevalent, quite peculiar to this part of the United Kingdom (F. Roper, Esq., Evidence, No. 32: App. Pt. I., p. 869, l. 10).

----

10. HOLIDAYS ALLOWED TO THE CHILDREN AND YOUNG PERSONS EMPLOYED IN COAL MINES.

Holidays.

486. There is no instance in the whole kingdom of rest from colliery labour for a single day or even half a day, the wages going on during the cessation of the work; but in most districts nothing is done in the pits on some of the principal fasts and festivals; and in general the colliers have a considerable portion of idle time, because there is not a sufficient demand for their labour to occupy them every day in the week, winter and summer.

South Staffordshire.

487. SOUTH STAFFORDSHIRE.—In the Coal Mines of this district no work appears to be done on the alternate Mondays—that is, the Monday following the Saturday on which the men are paid. The work of the mines ceases also somewhat sooner than usual on the Saturdays; and there are, moreover, certain " wakes or parochial festivals," which are here universally claimed as holidays (Dr. Mitchell, Evidence, No. 5: App, Pt. I., p. 64, l. 54).

Shropshire.

488. SHROPSHIRE.—The Children and Young Persons in the mines of the Coalbrookdale coal field do not appear to be regularly employed at work every day in the week, not because they have many holidays allowed them, but because there is not a sufficient demand for their labour to occupy their whole time. " The miners are not certain of constant employment. If there be a large stock of coals and

ironstone on hand, they will not be allowed to have 11 or 12 days' work in the fortnight, until the quantity on hand be somewhat reduced. About Christmas last the miners belonging to the Lawley furnace, near Wellington, stated that there was then only nine days' work in the iron mines and ten days' work in the coal mines in the fortnight. They work solely to supply the furnace, and it is not the interest of the proprietors to have a disproportionate amount of capital lying unproductive in coke and ironstone, of which there cannot for some time be any immediate need" (Dr. Mitchell, Report, § 295: App. Pt. I., p. 37; Evidence, No. 39: p. 79, l. 8).

489. WARWICKSHIRE.—For the same reason as in the Shropshire Coal Field, the miners in this district have many days free from labour, particularly during the summer season, when of course there is no great demand for coals. Mr. Thomas Pearson, butty, of the Bedworth Charity Colliery, estimates the actual time employed at little more than one-half. Take the year altogether, he says, the boys in the collieries do not work above half their time, or very little more. " A miner is checked from taking holidays at his own caprice, and thereby putting the set with which he works to inconvenience, by a fine of five shillings for every day which he is absent. As the fine is paid to the fund of the field-club, all have an interest in enforcing the payment of the penalty. But when there is such a matter of universal interest as a prize-fight most go to see it, and it is a day's play. Upon the average there may be five or six such occasions in the course of the summer; but there were, however, only two last summer." (Dr. Mitchell, Report, § 47: App. Pt. I., p. 93; Evidence, No. 65: p. 106, l. 46).

490. LEICESTERSHIRE.—In the Ashby-de-la-Zouch Coal Field, as in the preceding districts, there is not full employment for the workpeople in the coal mines during the whole of the year; so that the Children and Young Persons have a good deal of leisure time, especially in the warm weather of summer, when there is a less demand for coals (Dr. Mitchell, Report, § 131: App. Pt. I., p. 100).

491. DERBYSHIRE.—In the Derbyshire Coal Field the only holidays, properly so called, are Christmas Day, Good Friday, and a day or two at Whitsuntide. (J. M. Fellows, Esq., Report § 37: App. Pt. II., p. 255).

492. WEST RIDING OF YORKSHIRE, SOUTHERN PORTION.—Here it is stated that " collieries are generally but thinly attended directly after pay-day. This occurs sometimes once a-week and sometimes once a-fortnight. The day after is often a half-holiday—sometimes a whole one. At Christmas occasionally the pits stand a day or two, but generally speaking there are no regular holidays. The only time for play or recreation is when they leave off work, and occasionally after they have had their meal and got themselves washed they have time to play. This depends on the time they leave their work and how far they are tired. There are numbers far too much fatigued, but again there are many that are not. I never, however, got many Children to own that they did play on the week-day evening. Sunday I believe to be generally the day for recreation; but in the case of some of the girls working in the pits, they have occasionally to lie in bed on Sundays to rest themselves for Monday's work (J. C. Symons, Esq., Evidence, No. 33, 114, 140). The evidence given by some witnesses, that the Children are cheerful when they get out of the pit, is somewhat akin to evidence that people are cheerful when they get out of prison. It is, however, a very remarkable fact that, excepting in cases of extreme labour, cheerfulness is a characteristic of collier Children" (J. C. Symons, Esq., Report, § 186—189: App. Pt. I., p. 191; Evidence, No. 53).

493. BRADFORD and LEEDS.—Of the Children and Young Persons employed in the coal mines of this neighbourhood the Sub-Commissioner reports:—" Beyond Christmas-day and Good Friday there are no stated holidays. As already mentioned, however, the Children have, on the average, not less than one unoccupied day in the week, besides a fair portion of time for recreation and play in the evenings, and they avail themselves of these opportunities to a considerable extent for engaging in the healthful games of cricket, nor-and-spell, and foot-ball. This they are fortunately enabled to do from the circumstance of there being generally in the neighbourhood of mines a good deal of waste land (W. R. Wood, Esq., Report, § 25: App. Pt. II., p. H 5; Evidence, Nos. 1, 3, 39, 40, 41, 51, 87).

494. Lancashire and Cheshire.—In the Lancashire Coal Field much evil arises to the Children employed in the collieries from the idle time afforded them at the beginning of the week, and the excessive labour imposed on them towards the end of it, in consequence of the irregular manner in which it is the custom for the colliers to carry on their work. " The Monday after the pay is always a holiday; indeed in many collieries it is never expected that they should return to their work on that day (See John Millington's evidence, No. 6); and I am informed by proprietors that many of them will not settle steadily to work before the middle of the week following the pay. In this manner the drawers are kept half employed for two or three days at the beginning of the reckoning (this is the Lancashire way), and towards the end of it they are worked past their strength to make up the lost time. This had arrived at such a pitch at Mr. Harrop's colliery, and the inconvenience of having the boatsmen and banksmen standing idle for two or three days after the pay became so intolerable, that Mr. Harrop devised the plan of only allowing the colliers to send up a certain number of waggons of coal each day; and if the whole number were not sent up one day, that the colliers should not be allowed to make it up by sending an extra quantity the next. In this manner the supply of coal was regulated, much to the convenience of the boatmen and banksmen, and incidentally conferred an act of humanity on the drawers" (J. L. Kennedy, Esq., Report, § 212: App. Pt. II., p. 176).

495. Saturday, in this district, is usually a short day; Sunday and Monday are generally holidays, especially the Mondays after the pay. Of holidays, properly so called, Joseph Hatherton, underlooker at Messrs. Foster's, Ringley Bridge, says: "They have a fortnight at Christmas, a full week at Whitsuntide, three or four days at Ringley Wakes, about the same at Ratcliff Wakes, and at odd times besides. The wages are paid every fortnight; and they are never expected to come on the Monday after pay; an *odd* man may come to keep the roads straight, but that is all; and when they come on a Tuesday they are not fit for their work. Christmas and New-Year's-Day are universal holidays in this district, and generally the wakes or feasts of the different villages, and the races in their respective neighbourhoods—for example, at Worsley, Eccles Wakes, at St. Helen's and Haydock, the Newton Races, the Manchester Races also, which occur during Whitsuntide, attract an immense number of colliers from Clifton, Bolton, Leven, Outwood, Middleton, Worsley, and the whole surrounding district. Taking this into account, and also the time lost during the year from accidents by the colliers for whom they work, I am persuaded that, on the whole, the Children and Young Persons employed in coal mines have more holidays than Children engaged in most other branches of industry" (Ibid. § § 236, 237: App. Pt. II., p. 179).

496. Oldham.—The usual holidays in this neighbourhood are, a day or two at Christmas, New Year's Day, if it be on Monday or Tuesday, two days at Easter, two at Whitsuntide, and two at the wakes; on which occasions the engineers generally leave the engines. But these holidays are not universally taken unless work be slack, when it sometimes happens that the greater portion of the colliers will be doing only three or four days' work in a week, although they may go every day into the pit, and the young people with them. The latter seize with avidity the opportunities which this slackness below, or an hour or two in the evening above, allow to them for play and frolic, not always of a very amicable sort (J. Fletcher, Esq., Report, §41: App. Pt. II., p. 826; Evidence, Nos. 4,14,20, 25).

497. South Durham.—Of holidays in this coal field it is stated that "the Saturday after pay Friday, which occurs once in every fortnight, is a holiday as a matter of course. The miners return to their work on the Monday. There being so many mines opened, and so many miners, that the sale of coals is not sufficient to keep them all at work the whole of their time, there is necessarily a great deal of "play," far more than is agreeable. Holidays with pay going on are very pleasant, but when the rule is, no work no pay, holidays are a subject of complaint if many in number." Holidays of some days at Christmas appear to be universal, but others are of very irregular occurrence (Dr. Mitchell, Report, § 191: App. Pt. I., p. 141 ; Evidence, Nos. 21, 102).

498. North Durham and Northumberland.—Here, according to Nicholas Wood, Esq., viewer of Killingworth, Hilton, and other collieries, " The boys have a fortnight holidays at Christmas and a day on Good Friday, and sometimes Easter

Monday." A statement which is borne out by other witnesses as being of general application in this district (J. R. Leifchild, Esq., Evidence, Nos. 97, 171, 305: App. Pt. I., p. 586, et seq.).

499. EAST OF SCOTLAND.—In the coal mines of this part of the kingdom the idea of a holiday seems never to enter into the minds of the workpeople. The few witnesses who advert to the subject say that they have no holidays but of their own making, and their only regular holiday in the whole year seems to be New-Year's-Day.

500. WEST OF SCOTLAND.—Besides New-Year's-Day, they have, in the West of Scotland, two additional holidays in the year, namely, on the days of the fast or preparation for the sacrament. "These are all the stated holidays which universally prevail; to these may be added another for works in the neighbourhood of Glasgow, viz. the anniversary of the Glasgow Fair. Glasgow Fair, and 'Newrdy,' a con-traction of New-Year's-Day, or 'Hogmanay,' the eve of the New Year, are com-mon epochs from whence Children date their age, the time of their employment, or other particulars. Besides the yearly holidays, colliers seldom work above nine or ten days in the fortnight; and stopping work earlier than usual on Satur-day afternoon is becoming very general in other works comprised in the present Report. For daily recreation and play for the younger hands, alluded to in your instructions, there is not much time" (T. Tancred, Esq., Report, § 80, 81: App. Pt. I., p. 335).

501. NORTH WALES.—In this coal field there appear to be two or three holi-days and as many half holidays in the course of the year.

502. SOUTH WALES.—"There are but few holidays observed at the works in the neighbourhood of Pontypool, and none that I am aware of for the purpose of allowing the Children recreation and play. Every department of the works except-ing the blast furnaces of the iron works are stopped on Sundays and on Christmas Day, and some on Good Friday and on Easter Monday" (R. W. Jones, Esq., Report, § 22, 23: App. Pt. II., p. 583; and Evidence, No. 10: p. 602, l. 12; No. 70: p. 627, l. 4).

503. NORTH SOMERSETSHIRE.—In this district the holidays generally are Christ-mas Day, Good Friday, Easter, and Whitsuntide, and a day or two on club-days (Dr. Stewart, Evidence, Nos. 1, 2, 6, 7, 9, 11).

11.—TREATMENT OF CHILDREN AND YOUNG PERSONS IN COAL MINES.

504. The Treatment of Children and Young Persons employed in Coal-Mines, and the care taken of their health and safety, will be found to differ very materially in different districts, and in different collieries in the same district.

505. In the South Staffordshire, Shropshire, Warwickshire, and Leicestershire coal pits the main body of evidence shows that the Children and Young Persons are not, in general, ill used. The Sub-Commissioner states that they are so much in demand, being able to do many things which could not be done by grown men, on account of their size, that it is in their power to command good treatment. Still, however, even in these districts, there are not wanting cases of rough usage and severe punishment.

John Greaves, collier: "Every boy has to clear away for two men, and if he do not do it they strap him. He dare not say much about it, for fear of their giving him more, and perhaps master turning him off. Most of the men wear a leather strap round them, which they can apply to the boys if need be. The boys are not used so bad as they were" (Dr. Mitchell, Evidence, South Staffordshire, No. 11: App. Pt. I., p. 67, l. 45).—Isaac Tipton, aged 16, Woombridge Col-lieries: "The men did not thump me very often. I was not very bad, only middling. I sometimes deserved it because I would not do as they told me. They sometimes thumped me with the fist and sometimes with the stick; they made marks; I seldom complained unless they gave it me too bad. The butties gave it me sometimes when I neglected to do what I was told. There was nobody to whom I could complain of the butties" (Dr. Mitchell, Evidence, Shropshire, No. 53: App. Pt. I., p. 83, l. 68).—Robert North, Woombridge Collieries: "If

COAL MINES.

Treatment.

South
Staffordshire,
Shropshire,
Warwickshire,
Leicestershire.

they are put to do the work, they must do it or be beat. The butty must not beat big ones. I was beat when I was drawing, and I did not deserve it. I had been ill, and was exhausted, and could not work longer; but the reeve beat me. I complained to the butty. He said that he did not allow a boy to be beat unless he deserved it. He said it was not likely that he could get boys if he let them be beat when they did not deserve it. I was once beat by a man who bullied me to do what was beyond my strength. I said I would not do it, because I could not. The man threw me down, and put out two of my ribs. I had to keep from work eleven months. My father was too quiet to take him before a magistrate" (Ibid. No. 56 : p. 85, l. 40).—Joseph Tomlinson, ground-bailiff, Summercoates: "Boys are much better used every way. The lads are not beat now by the butties, as they once were twenty years ago. The corporals, the same as doggies in Staffordshire, must not ill-use them now" (Dr. Mitchell, Evidence, Leicestershire, No. 86 : App. Pt. I., p. 117, l. 50).

506. DERBYSHIRE.—In this district the treatment of the Children is left entirely either to the butty or to the overlooker, the latter being invested by the master with the same power as the butty, who bargains for, dismisses, and uses the Child just as he pleases. With very few exceptions the proprietors and their agents take no charge whatever of the Children, and neither know nor care how they are treated.

William Willis Bailey, agent to John Ray, Esq., Kilburn : " " He considers the Children belong to the butties—they are paid, engaged, and dismissed by them, and Mr. Ray has nothing to do with them. Mr. Ray has given no orders as to rewards, punishments, or anything further than a notice for fourteen days to be given or taken on leaving" (J. M. Fellows, Esq., Evidence, No. 251 : App. Pt. II., p. 323, l. 39).—William Bettison, ground-bailiff, Merchay Colliery : "He considers the Children are belonging to the butties, and Mr. Woolley has nothing to do with any but the butties themselves. Have no notice excepting the board ordered by the combination for a month's notice on either side in case of leaving ; no orders given as to rewards or punishments" (Ibid. No. 274 : p. 327, l. 18).—Thomas Wilmot, agent to C. V. Hunter, Esq., Ripley : "He does not consider that he or Mr. Hunter has anything to do with the Children. The only notice-board or directions given from the office is, 'That all shall give and take a month's notice' " (Ibid. No. 239 : p. 321, l. 26).—George Staley, agent, Butterly Company : "He has given no orders as to punishments, rewards, or bad language ; if any complaints are made by the children or parents his orders are to refer them to the magistrates" (Ibid. No. 217 : p. 318, l. 10).—Stephen Barton, coal-agent, Babbington : "The firm never interfere as to rewards and punishment ; he has, when he has heard of a child being abused, given the butties a lecture" (Ibid. No. 136 : p. 299, l. 63).—Bradley Mart, colliery clerk, Kirkby Portland : "No directions are given as to rewards or punishments, either for misconduct, swearing, or anything else" (Ibid. No. 170 : p. 309, l. 33).

507. There are exceptions, though extremely rare, to this entire abandonment of the Children to the butties.—

John Hawley Sharpe, agent to Robert Holden, Esq., Denby : "The butties are not allowed either to take on or turn off either man or boy without the consent of Mr. Holden's agent. He considers the Children under Mr. Holden's protection" (Ibid. No. 310 : p. 333, l. 46).

508. The treatment experienced by the Children, in consequence of their being left entirely in the hands of the butties and overlookers, appears from the following evidence.—

Mr. George Haslam, proprietor, Pentridge : "They do not work with butties, have not for sixteen years ; the reason is that the colliers working under the butties had so much difficulty in getting their money, and they worked the men and Children sixteen or eighteen hours per day ; he is sure the Children are much better used, and fewer complaints made by the parents, now than under the old system" (Ibid. No. 322 : p. 336, l. 7).—John Wilders, bailiff to Messrs. Haslam, Pentridge : "Has worked under butties ; thinks the Children are better attended to and better off working directly under masters than butties" (Ibid. No. 323 : p. 336, l. 23). —-Robert Davis, aged nineteen, Shipley : " Mr. Mundy never interferes himself or through his agents as to the rewards or punishments ; the boys get sadly used by the men, who are never called to account" (Ibid. No. 39 : p. 273, l. 56).

509. According to the butties and overlookers no punishment is inflicted on the Children beyond slight chastisement, "with the open hand or a small stick," and the witnesses of this class generally state that the Children employed in the collieries of this district are a happy and contented race.

Thomas Booth, overlooker, Smalley : "No rewards, and very little punishments ; a little slap with the open hand" (Ibid. No. 60 : p. 280, l. 35).—Robert Harrison, overlooker, Eastwood : "The punishments are merely by the hand or small stick, to keep them at work ; and he considers they are full as healthy and happy as their playfellows above ground" (Ibid. No. 82 : p. 286,

l. 24).—Samuel Staley, coal-agent, Butterly Company, Heanor: "He has never had any complaints made to him, and has been at the field six years" (Ibid. No. 176: p. 310, l. 53).

510. The Children and Young Persons themselves, however, make statements widely different.—

William Gent, aged seven, Butterly Park: "The butties beat him so that his mother would not let him go for a day or two" (Ibid. No. 195: p. 315, l. 16).—Jacob Birkin, aged eight, Bagthorpe: "The corporal often beats him, and Gibson has pinched his ears through as well as his brother's" (Ibid. No. 77: p. 284, l. 57).—Joseph Latum, aged nine, Awsworth: "No rewards; the butties sometimes use a stick as thick as a hedge-stake, and hits them over the legs and back and bruises them; they kick them and pull their ears because they do not get the asses on sharp enough. Has known Jonathan Watts, a butty, beat a boy, named Jemmy Robinson, with his fist and stick, pull his ears, and kick him until Robinson's father was obliged to send him home. When the father complained he was told the boy could not get the ass on, and no more notice was taken of it. Other boys have been shamefully used by this man; he struck a boy named Slater with his stick, the boy fell, and he then stamped on him until the boy could scarcely stand; he never told his masters; he said he should not, for he should be only served worse. Slater is near fifteen, Robinson is nearly as old" (Ibid. No. 168: p. 308, l. 31).—George Pollard, aged nine, Strelley: "Is punished every day by Aaron Leadbeater, the man his brother spoke of; he beat him to-day with the ass-stick; his back (which he showed) was marked" (Ibid. No. 116: p. 295, l. 12).—Levi Bradby, aged ten, Kirkby Portland: "Is sometimes beaten by the corporal with the ass-stick, and is pretty well marked; does not like working in pits, being so ill-used by the corporals" (Ibid. No. 174: p. 310, l. 14).—John Bonsor, aged ten, Kirkby Portland: "The corporal thrashes him; he lays on him with the ass-stick and weals him; had rather drive plough or go to school" (Ibid. No. 172: p. 310, l. 2).—Thomas Birkin, aged ten, Bagthorpe: "About half a year since, Thomas Gibson, the loader, nipped him with his nails until he cut quite through the ears; has often nipped his ears both before and since; it was because he could not get on with his asses sharp enough" (Ibid. No. 78: p. 285, l. 1).—Joseph Shelton, aged ten, Underwood: "George Bostock, the loader, who ill-used the others, has beaten him; when he told his father, who has had to threaten him with a summons" (Ibid. No. 109: p. 293, l. 33).—Joseph Robinson, aged twelve, Kirkby Portland: "Has many a time come home with his back covered with weals" (Ibid. No. 175: p. 310, l. 33).—William Bostock, aged twelve, Babbington: "Before he worked under his father he was often beaten with sticks, had his ears and hair pulled and coals thrown at him; as the men take all by the job they use the lads most cruelly. He has heard what his brother has said, and it is true; he has never complained to his masters, but his mother has until it is of no use, and boys who have complained to the magistrates have done no good, as the butties always take the part of the corporals" (Ibid. No. 145: p. 301, l. 9).—William Trace, aged twelve, Bagthorpe: "No rewards; are punished by the corporal with a stick a deal thicker than the ass-stick, and they are pulled up and down by the ears; kicks them and knocks them down merely because they cannot get the asses on fast enough" (Ibid. No. 80: p. 285, l. 46).—Amos Brown, aged thirteen, Heanor: "The corporal thrashes him so much that his mother has threatened to take him before the magistrates" (Ibid. No. 178: p. 311, l. 11).—John Gent, aged thirteen, Butterly Park: "Gets thrashed by the butties with what they can lay their hands on. They set them more than they can do, and then beat them; has been thrashed at Mr. Woolley's pit until the blood has flown out of his side" (Ibid. No. 194: p. 315, l. 5).—James Webster, aged thirteen, Newthorpe: "Is often ill-used by the corporals and bigger boys, both with fists, sticks, and kicks" (Ibid. No. 133: p. 298, l. 51).

James Robinson, aged fourteen, Awsworth: "No rewards, but is often beaten by the corporal Sam Meakin; he beat him last week so that he could not raise his arm; the stick was as thick as two fingers, and a knob at the end; he broke it over him; he was pushing the waggon, and Meakin's son lay in the road all his length, and he not seeing him hurt his leg; he has beaten him before because he has not drawn the corve or start the asses; he has then whealed him all over; he told his father and mother; he had no time to complain to the masters, as the office is shut when they are out of the pits. He worked at Hunt's Pit at Babbington, where he was so beaten that his father on that account took him away; the corporal there has kicked him when he was down, pulled his ears and hair, and threw coals at him; he dare not tell his masters then, or he believes the corporal would have killed him. His brothers, one ten, the other thirteen years old, now work at Hunt's, and are beaten until they can hardly get home, and dare not tell for fear of worse usage, and they and their father losing their work" (Ibid. No. 169: p. 308, l. 55).—Ephraim Riley, aged fifteen, Ilkiston: "He is punished with a stick as described by others, but in no other way; has known boys so abused. Henry Boskett, for instance, was kicked and knocked down and so used that he was obliged altogether to leave the pit; it was the corporal that punished him; he was never called to account for his brutal conduct" (Ibid. No. 27: p. 270, l. 62).—Joseph Aram, aged sixteen, Williamson's Soft Pit: "There are no rewards, but they are often punished until they can scarcely stand. He has to draw as well as guide the corve by the belt; has often to draw hard when the asses tire, and they have to start them again. Has often had his hips ache and smart again when he got home, and it often galls him as the collar does a horse. He is not only punished with a stick, but his ears are pulled, as well as being kicked and bruised by the butties, and those who break the coal out. His brother was so beaten about three or four months since he dare not again go to the pit. He is only nine years old, and drives between; he gets so tired that he cannot get on, and then towards dinner-time, or the end of the day the corporal thrashes him. They may swear, or use what language they please, and are never beat for that. His mother has complained to the masters, who always say they shall not be served so, but they hear no more of it, and are used no better. On other grounds he believes the boys are not used so ill as at Babbington" (Ibid. No. 150: p. 303, l. 15).—John Bostock, aged seventeen, Babbington: "They often get their ears pulled by the corporals, and sometimes they mark their backs; they used, when his father was not with him, to take the burning candlewicks, after the tallow was off, to grease the wheels, light them and burn his arms. His father works in the same pit, and he is now able to do his work, therefore is not so ill used; he has known other lads used so at Ilkiston; he has known his uncle take a boy named William Wright by the ears and knock his head against the wall, because his eyesight was bad and he could not see to do his work so well as the others; he has complained to the butties, but they have always taken the part of the corporal; he has known one boy beaten until he was black and blue; he complained to Messrs. Potter's agent, who then told the butty he would turn him away, and since then the boy has been used better" (Ibid. No. 146: p. 301, l. 30, 40).—William Wright, aged seventeen, Ilkiston: "He last summer worked in the Bath Pit with William and John Bostick; their uncle John was and is now butty at the Bath Pit; he has taken William by his ears and struck his head against the wall; he also about five weeks since struck him (William Wright) over the back several times with the maundrill and hurt him very bad; it was on Saturday, and he was obliged to keep his bed all Sunday; and this was for no other reason than his eyes were not good, and he could not see to do his work so quick as others. He complained to his father, who asked him if he had been saucy to him; he replied he dare not: the man when called to account, altogether denied it; but his father has been told by others it was so, but thought if he had complained to the magistrates he as well as his son would lose their place of work; ' there is many one indeed—many a score beaten until they dare not tell' " (Ibid. No. 20: p. 268, l. 59).

511. These statements of the Children and Young Persons as to the manner in which they are treated in the pits, are too fully confirmed by the evidence of adult workmen.

John Beasley, aged forty-nine, collier, Shipley: " There are no rewards, but when he was a boy they were beaten most unmercifully by the corporals, who were complete blackguards; they mostly used the ass-stick, about as thick as your thumb; they often kicked them, and sometimes used the fist; has seen them throttle the boys, but never so bad but what they soon recovered; has himself been so punished that he was obliged to leave the pit; he has now three children working at Shipley—one sixteen, one fourteen, the other twelve; they are treated much the same as he was, but not so well paid" (Ibid. No. 40: p. 274, l. 12).—John Fisher, collier, aged fifty-five, Greasley: " There are no rewards, but plenty of punishment; they are not particular as to open hand, stick, or fist; they are at times beaten cruelly; he has complained to the masters, and for two or three weeks they have been better used, but it is little use complaining, or both he and his children would be turned off" (Ibid. No. 154: p. 364, l. 62).—Samuel Richards, aged forty, Awsworth: " No rewards excepting the stick, that's all the rewards in pits for little lads. Has within three months seen a boy nine years old beaten by a butty until he wetted his breeches, because he had not come the day before. He has often seen them beat so that they were black and blue; and if the parents were by they dare not say anything, or they would be turned off the ground directly. Has never known the proprietors interfere, ' they only ought to do' " (Ibid. No. 166: p. 307, l. 50).

512. In some few instances the proprietors do interfere, and the evidence shows that there are coal mines in which the treatment of the Children is improved.

Joshua Middleton, collier, aged sixty-seven, Radford: " There are no rewards, but the master will not allow the Children to be ill-treated" (Ibid. No. 3: p. 263, l. 47).—James Davis, collier, aged twenty-seven, Woollaton: " No punishment is allowed on Lord Middleton's coal-fields; they are much better treated here than on other fields, both boys and men" (Ibid. No. 12: p. 267, l. 16).—John Hayne, collier, G. H. Barrow, Esq's., Pit, Staveley: " On Mr. Barrow's fields both men and children are as well treated as at any field. He used to work at Heanor; there and at Shipley and that neighbourhood they are worked and used shameful; ' there's as much difference as heaven and earth' between there and here" (Ibid. No. 440: p. 253, l. 13).—William Wardle, aged forty, Eastwood: " They are seldom beat now—very seldom to what they used to be; indeed there is nothing to complain of on that account. When he was a boy he was beaten bad enough because he could not do more work than he was able; has been beaten till he was black and blue; he was beaten with a stick the asses were beat with, or anything they first got hold of; indeed they used no ceremony on that head; he never saw anything of that kind now" (Ibid. No. 84: p. 287, l. 18).

513. WEST RIDING OF YORKSHIRE, SOUTHERN PART.—Of the treatment of the Children and Young Persons in this district the Sub-Commissioner says :— " Considering the ignorance of the men and their entire control over the Children, their treatment of the Children is highly to their credit. The instances of cruelty and severe beating are very rare. Slight beating constantly occurs; it is unquestionably the means whereby the Children are kept to their work: it is also the mode whereby bad language and misconduct are usually punished. The Children themselves when examined alone constantly bore witness, voluntarily, to

general good treatment; and I am quite sure that, generally speaking, the Children are not much beaten. But it is absurd to assert that corporal punishments are not inflicted: such orders may be given by masters, but they are not attended to. A pleasing instance of kindly feeling is noted by the evidence sent by the Rev. Mr. Blackburne, with respect to their practice of giving each a share to any one Child who happens to be dinnerless. The care taken of the Children when their work is over is that of slightly washing, of feeding, and sending them to bed. I am sure that, generally, they are well cared for by their mothers when they get home. There is not a kinder-hearted set of women living" (J. C. Symons, Esq., Report, §§ 195—197: App. Pt. I., p. 192).

Thomas Wilson, Esq., coal-owner, Silkstone: " It is obvious that in a mine where so many things are going on without the presence of an overlooker, and where accidents of a most fearful nature may arise from the acts of an individual, discipline *must* be maintained at any hazard, for the safety of the miners themselves and the security of the mine, and therefore employers are often obliged to overlook practices which they would gladly see abolished. This is the case with corporal punishments, which it would be unsafe to prohibit publicly; all that can be done is to discourage them privately. I believe they rarely occur, and are not marked by any severity" (J. C. Symons, Esq., Evidence, No. 137: App. Pt. I., p. 258, l. 63).—See also witnesses Nos. 15, 83, and 171.

John Lawton, under-ground steward: " The getters employ their own hurriers, and control them. But if I found a boy ill used I should immediately interfere. Two or three months ago a boy came up and complained to me that he had been beaten. He was disabled from his work for a few days in consequence. I sent for the man out of the pit and reprimanded him. He confessed his fault, and promised not to repeat it, and to pay the boy his wages during the time he was laid up, which he did: and in consequence I let him go down to his work again. Ill usage is not general here, but it used to be. There is a general disposition to be quarrelsome and fractious among the hurriers; and where there is not good management and superintendence there will be ill usage of the less boys by the older" (Ibid. No. 123: p. 255, l. 16).—Joseph Gleadhill, under-ground steward: "The youngest generally gets scolded, and may be now and then a bang, but they are not materially hurt or much ill used; but it is usually the weakest goes to the wall, and the little one often gets blamed" (Ibid. No. 223: p. 283, l. 12).—See also witnesses Nos. 10, 48, 71, 120, 162, 301.

James Ibbitson, collier: " Some hurriers are kept to work with sharp speaking, and sometimes paid with pick-shaft, and anything else the men can lay their hands on" (Ibid. No. 263: p. 291, l. 51).—A Collier, Messrs. Travis, Barnsley: "I don't think boys are much ill treated" (Ibid. No. 94: p. 246, l. 31).—See also witnesses, Nos. 109, 125, 147.

Jonathan Clayton, thirteen years and a half old: " The men don't ill-use us, except we don't suit 'em, then they'll pay us and punch us" (Ibid. No. 6: p. 227, l. 51).—John Hobson, thirteen years and a half old: " They don't use me ill, except when I miss marking the number of the corve, they then give a bit of pick-shaft" (Ibid. No. 8: p. 228, l. 25).—Margaret Westwood, aged fourteen years and a half: " I hurry for Charles Littlewood; I am let to him. He does not use me well. He pays [*i. e.* strikes me] a good deal, but has not lately. He hits me with his hand. Sometimes he hurts me. When we get to pit's bottom we have to wait sometimes for corves, and then he is angry, and that is what he pays me for. I have told my mother, but not my father, of it" (Ibid. No. 192: p. 276, l. 25).—Jonathan Mitchell, aged fifteen, Meal Hill, Hepworth: " When the girls are long on the road they get thrashed the same as us when we do wrong" (Ibid. No. 281: p. 295, l. 14).—Octavius Lee, aged seventeen, Woodthorpe Colliery. " The boys are not ill-used without they do something very wrong" (Ibid. No. 23: p. 231, l. 37).—Charles Hoyle, aged thirteen, Rawmarsh (Barber's Pit): " We don't get beaten so very often, but we do sometimes" (Ibid. No. 78: p. 242, l. 46).—See also witnesses Nos. 19, 102, 103, 153, 167, 231, 235, 265, 283, 284, 289, 331, 381.

514. BRADFORD AND LEEDS.—Of the treatment of the Children and Young Persons in this district the Sub-Commissioner reports:—" I do not find that the exertions of the Children at their work are encouraged or enforced by any severe treatment, nor do I find any serious complaint amongst the Children upon this head. The influences used may be stated to be,—First, the fear of being dismissed, and of consequent punishment from parents. Secondly, very frequent exhortation or reprimand, often delivered in very violent language. Thirdly, but by no means commonly, slight personal chastisement. Upon the last head I made very particular inquiries, but could not learn from the Children whom I examined that it was used commonly, wantonly, or without some valid cause of complaint. It may be observed, in the first place, that the labour is not so severe as to render corporal punishment necessary to enforce attention to it; and secondly, that the parents, though sufficiently inattentive to the interests of their Children at some points, would strongly resent their being beaten. In fact, the Children are in a very independent position; and they, or their parents for them, would change their employers rather than submit to any ill-treatment. It may be observed that, in the largest establishment in the district, the Low Moor Iron Works, the beating of Children is strictly forbidden, and any man guilty of it is discharged, or at

least suspended for a time.   No system of reward for exertion appears to be any-where practised.

515. " With regard to care of the Children after they have finished their daily labour, the subject is in many instances never thought of.   In many others some interest in it is felt by the employers, without producing the slightest practical result.   The only practical measure taken that I am aware of with a view to the welfare of the Children after they have finished their daily labour, is the provision, in one or two cases, of night-schools, which, however, are not attended by more than a most trifling proportion of the Children and Young Persons employed " (W. R. Wood, Esq., Report, §§ 29—31, p. H 6; Evidence, Nos. 3, 4, 6, 13, 14, 22, 37, 38, 39, 40, 41, 50, 51, 55, 57, 56, 67, 71, 68, 83, 84, 87, 88, 89, 90, 96, 97.)

Joseph Butterfield, aged thirteen, Middleton Colliery, near Leeds : " Is sometimes beaten in the pit by his partners, other boys ; men never beat him ; has never seen a man beat a boy" (W. R. Wood, Esq., Evidence, No. 81 : App. Pt. II., p. *h* 36, l. 9).—Ellen Barraclough, Low Moor, thirteen years old : " Is never beaten ; other girls that work are never beaten ; never heard of any girl being beaten.   Boys are beaten sometimes when they won't do as they are telled.   When girls won't do as they are telled they only call 'em" (Ibid. No. 22 : p. *h* 12, l. 49).—Amos Robeyshaw, fourteen years old : " Cries sometimes when t' colliers beat him ; steward wouldn't let him be beat if he knew ; dursn't tell him ; some boys dare" (Ibid. No. 52 : p. *h* 25, l. 22).—William Suck-smith, aged fourteen years : " Is never beaten ; overlooker would turn away any man that beat him ; would not be afraid of telling" (Ibid. No. 7: p. *h* 8, l. 55).—See also witnesses Nos. 13, 22, 37, 38, 39, 40, 50, 51, 84, 87, 88, 89, 90, &c.

Eli Buckley, aged nine : " Is never beaten" (Ibid. No. 57: p. *h* 26, l. 5).—George Hayley, aged ten.   Messrs. Clayton and Co., Rawson, near Bradford : " Is beaten sometimes by the men" (Ibid. No. 55 : p. *h* 25, l. 62).—George Hodshall, eleven years old : " They beat him sometimes ; not oft ; about once a-week ; because they don't *hurry* fast enough.   If he were to tell t' master he would stop their wages for beating him ; but they would *happen* beat him some time else ; would be afraid to tell t' master" (Ibid. No. 41 : p. *h* 20, l. 22).—See also witnesses Nos. 56, 67, 68, 71, 83, 96, 97.

516. HALIFAX.—The Sub-Commissioner for this district found in the coal mines inspected by him, especially in the smaller pits, much harsher treatment of the Children than was found by his colleagues in other portions of the West Riding. " Punishments," he says, " are said never to be allowed ; but how are they pre-vented ?   The colliers work alone in dark and secluded places, at great distances from each other, where they have opportunities of inflicting them when and how they please ; frequent instances have from time to time come under my own obser-vation.   At Mr. Thomas Holmes's Shugden Lane Pit I remember meeting with one of the boys crying very bitterly, and bleeding from a wound in the cheek.   I found out his master at a remote heading, who told me, in a tone of savage defi-ance, ' that the Child was one of the slow ones, who would only move when he saw blood, and that by throwing a piece of coal at him for that purpose, he had accomplished his object, and that he often adopted the like means.' "

Mr. James Sharp, aged forty-five, underground steward : " I sometimes hear of complaints from children and parents of the men ; they use them ill, by flogging them and throwing coals at them, but it is not often, because we have made some severe examples" (S. S. Scriven, Esq., Evidence, No. 43 : App. Pt. II., p. 114, l. 9).—John Bell, aged thirteen : " When they [the men] lake (are idle) we do not—they make us get out the muck in bottom, and get what coals we can, and what we can get we hurry ; if they lake one day, they work longer the next, and make us make it up ; we don't think that is fair, and we tell them so ; they laugh at us for that, and tell us to be sharp ; if we don't, they hit us with the handle of the pick, and throw coals on us : I have been knocked down many times at the Low Moor Company's pit, where I worked before" (Ibid. No. 34 : p. 110, l. 61).—William Dyson, aged fourteen : " I have seen her [his work-mate, Sarah Ambler] thrashed many times ; when she does not please them, they rap her in the face and knock her down ; I repeat I have seen this many times" (Ibid. No. 7 : p. 103, l. 3).—See also witnesses Nos. 58, 74, and 75.

Margaret Gomley, aged nine : " They flog us down in the pit, sometimes with their hand upon my bottom, which hurts me very much ; Thomas Copeland flogs me more than once in a day, which makes me cry" (Ibid. No. 9 : p. 103, l. 36).—William Jagger, aged eleven : " The men serve me out sometimes—they wallop me ; I don't know what for, except 'tis when I don't hurry fast enough" (Ibid. No. 6 : p. 102, l. 39).—Harriet Craven, aged eleven : " What made me cry when you came down was because Ibbotson had been braying [beating] me ; he flung a piece of coal as big as my head at me, and it struck me in my back."—[" In the gate," says the Sub-Commissioner, " I met the deponent, Harriet Craven, crying very bitterly.   She informed me her getter had been beating her very cruelly because she was then about to leave her work (five o'clock) before she had hurried sufficient for his purpose.   Both herself and sister informed me that he was constantly in the habit of ill-treating them ; the several marks upon their persons, which they showed me, were sufficient proofs of it."]—(Ibid. No. 76 : p. 123, l. 45).

517. LANCASHIRE.—" In this district the coal proprietors almost invariably prohibit the colliers from punishing the Children and Young Persons who work for them ; and whenever misconduct of this kind is found out, dismissal of the offending party is the consequence. But from the nature of the employment, and the difficulty of superintendence, cases of punishment and cruelty sometimes happen which never reach the ears of the employers. Cases of gross abuse are, I am persuaded, rare ; but several of a most revolting character have come to my knowledge, and they are so well authenticated by credible eye-witnesses, that it is impossible to refuse them belief." (J. L. Kennedy, Esq., Report, § 259 : App. Pt. II., p. 182.)

Henry Gibson, aged fifteen, Lord Balcarras's, Haigh, near Wigan : " I left them once because they would not give me a pair of clogs, and cousin thrashed me for it.—Did he beat you severely ? Yes, he beat me with a thick stick, and the mark is on my arm now [there was a severe bruise on the boy's right arm], and kicked me with his clogs.—Do you ever see any other boys beaten by their masters in the pits ? Yes, there is a lad called Jonathan Dicks, from St. Helen's workhouse, he gets thrashed very ill. I saw his master beat him with a pick-axe on his legs and arms, and his master cut a great gash in his head with a blow of a pickaxe, and he threw a hundredweight at him and swelled up his eye and made it blue.—Were there any other lads who get them ? Yes, there is another little lad, called Andrew, I don't known his other name ; he is about eight years old ; he is half-clammed, and many a time he comes without any dinner or anything to eat, and we give him some of ours" (J. L. Kennedy, Esq., Evidence, No. 50 : App. Pt. II., p. 223, l. 23).—James Crabtree, aged fifteen, Mr. Dearden's Colliery, near Todmorden : " Do the boys often get beaten ? Yes, sometimes. Old William thrashed a lad to-day ; I heard him skriking [crying], but I don't know which of them it was.—Do they ever thrash the lass ? Not oft" (Ibid. No. 71 : p. 228, l. 68).—Alice Singleton, aged twelve : " Are you ever beaten ? Yes, I get beat sometimes.—What do they beat with ? With a pick-arm, or a belt, or cut, or anything, just as it happens" (Ibid. No. 76 : p. 230, l. 34).—Peter Gaskill, collier, Mr. Lancaster's, near Worsley : " Were you ever beaten whilst you were a drawer ?—I never was much thrashed, but I drew for my brother, and I was lucky ; some men thrash their drawers very much ; I have seen some so ill hurt that they could scarcely go on, and they were obliged to give over drawing.—What do they strike them with ? With a pick-arm, or a belt, or their foot.—Are girls thrashed as boys are ?—Yes, I have seen wenches thrashed very much ; they will thrash a lass as soon as a lad if they don't behave themselves." (Ibid. No. 29 : p. 217, l. 28).—John Oldham, collier, Messrs. Foster's, near Bolton : " Did you ever see the Children cruelly used in the coal-pits ?—Yes, I have ; I never was beaten myself by any master, I was a good one, but I have seen many as has been beaten ; some masters are kind to their drawers, but some are very hasty ; the colliers do not like to be behindhand, and if a drawer is too weak he gets beat : the weakest are always worse off, and get worst beaten ; they have not strength to do the work in time, and the colliers thrash them.—How do they usually punish them ? They lay on them with a belt, a pick-arm, or a *cut* [a notched stick used as an index of the quantity of work done ; one being put into each tub that is sent up], or anything that comes to hand" (Ibid. No. 22 : p. 210, l. 54).—John Bagley, collier : " Were you ever beaten ? Ay, mony a time" (Ibid. No. 30 : p. 217, l. 65).

518. The following evidence shows that there are Children who are never beaten :—

James Jones, aged twelve, Mr. Clegg's, near Oldham : " Are you ever beaten ?—No, they never thrash me" (Ibid. No. 65 : p. 226, l. 57).—Martha Haslam, aged twelve, Messrs. Andrew Knowle's, Clifton : " Are you ever beaten ? No, they never beat me" (Ibid. No. 74 : p. 230, l. 19).—Henry Miller, aged nearly fourteen, Mr. Woolley's, Staley Bridge : " Do the men ever beat you in the pits ?—No, never ; when they are angry they black [blackguard] me" (Ibid. No. 8 : p. 206, l. 11).—See also witnesses Nos. 51, 53, 57, 58, 61, 65, 87, 91.

519. NORTH LANCASHIRE.—" The treatment varies, not only in different pits, but according to the disposition of the man under whom each drawer works. That any harsh usage is contrary to the wish, and even the peremptory orders, of the proprietors or undertakers is certainly the case in almost every pit ; but the colliers are uneducated people, and are usually vicious in temper. In every return from the masters or from the agents of collieries it is stated that no punishments are allowed, and no complaints made, or the parties would be dismissed. Mr. Ashton, the overseer of Blackburn, also states that he has no complaints from the parents of the Children employed in his district. Mr. Hutchinson says he will endeavour to bring me one or two parents who can speak of the ill usage of their Children, but does not know if he can, for there is ' scarcely one as dares.' He did not persuade one to come. What passes under ground in the dark tunnels in which the people work is not known even to the under-ground overlooker ; for the Children dare not complain, and he (the overlooker) can only be in one of the many burrows of which a coal mine consists, and cannot hear what passes in the others (A. Austin, Esq., Report, §§ 16—20 : App. Pt. II., p. 80-34).

Joseph Waring, aged ten, Cheeseden : " At Cheeseden he was badly used. Sometimes when he got his sticks wrong, Billy Bobby Yeates [the man he worked for] got him to the end of the run and beat him with the pick handle. Sometimes he got a stick to lick him with; the pick haum was the worst. Staid half a year there, and then he got ill from being beat. Should not have been ill if he had not been beaten; he was beat because he had not strength to keep his turn; could not draw so much as the others" (A. Austin, Esq., Evidence, No. 4 : App. Pt. II., p. 812, l. 6).—William Forrest, aged fifteen and three quarters : " Sometimes when tired he would stop, and then he was always licked; never spoke before he licked him [with a strap]; did sometimes speak first, and ask what he had been doing; sometimes they would hit us with a pick handle. When he was at George Yates's he was caught in the side with a pick handle by Joseph Eccles, and it knocked him over; he was sick and was obliged to be taken out of the pit; never went to work for three days" (Ibid. No. 3 : p. 811, l. 47).—[Sub-Commissioner—" Mr. Whalley, the relieving-officer, who was present, said that this and the preceding witness were so bad he did not think they would recover; it was owing to the ill usage."]—William Holt, aged eighteen, Red Delf Pit, Over-Darwen, Blackburn : " Has been beat with pick haum, hammer, and lumps of wood; never made any bruises; some as gets their legs broke with it, striking too hard, and [the striker] does not think of it; never seed any, but has heard tell of it; has seen when they gotten an eye knocked out by whizzing stones at them. Does not beat his drawers yet; does not mean to. Some as is great ones does it to some as is not their own" (Ibid. No. 9 : p. 813, l. 43).—John Gallowar, aged fourteen, Park Colliery, near Oswaldtwistle : " Sometimes they [the getters] loses coals, and does not get paid for it, [this is by the drawer putting a wrong stick in,] and then the drawer gets licked; sometimes they hit them with the pickhaum; sometimes they whiz coals after them; has had his head broke with a bit of coal; and had a swelling on his elbow, which kept him a fortnight from work, from a blow of the pickhaum" (Ibid. No. 12 : p. 814, l. 37).

520. OLDHAM.—It is stated by Mr. Fletcher, that in his district when punishments are inflicted they are generally violent; but that the boys are not generally maltreated by the men, notwithstanding the savageness of the cases mentioned by some of the witnesses. (J. Fletcher, Esq., Report, § 48 : App. Pt. II., p. 828.)

Mr. Cornelius Backhouse, head viewer to Messrs. Jones and Co. : " The underlookers interfere when they learn of cases of ill usage of Children by the men. They feel it part of their duty to protect the weak from the strong among those under them, and to preserve decency and order as much as they can in the pit. The abused party will complain to the underlooker, who brings the matter before the head viewer, who has the general management of the pits" (J. Fletcher, Esq., Evidence, No. 5 : App. Pt. II., p. 845, l. 39).—Mr. John Ogden, chief agent of the Chamber Colliery Company : " Put a stop to any ill-treatment of Children in their works, whenever they get to hear of it, by dismissal. Have not had many instances" (Ibid. No. 4 : p. 843, l. 35).—Samuel Walkden, Mr. Wrigley's, Low-Side Mine, near Oldham : " If you ill use a child in our pit, you must take up your tools and be off. The underlooker will allow neither swearing nor fighting. 'Them as is religious would tell the underlooker'" (Ibid. No. 7 : p. 847, l. 21).—James Jones, aged thirteen, Mr. James Clegg's, near Oldham : " Never lick him i' th' pit; some they do; sometimes the lads deserve it" (Ibid. No. 25 ; p. 853, l. 53).—Joseph Wild, chief constable of Oldham : " There have been cases of the maltreatment of Children in collieries brought before the magistrates—perhaps one or two a-year. The maltreatment was always according to barbarous rules among the workers themselves, inflicting punishment on supposed delinquents, generally by holding the head fast between the legs of another, and inflicting each a certain number of blows on the bare posteriors with pieces of wood, called ' cuts,' about a foot long and an inch in diameter, used as tokens to distinguish one man's tubs from another. However the one punished may cry, they stick to him; and in the last case, where a hungry lad had stolen a pit-dinner, they mangled his body seriously. In other cases the injured parties could not work at all for some time. In the case mentioned, the offenders were made to placard the town with an apology, to render some compensation in money to the party, and promise not to follow any such course in future" (Ibid. No. 39 : p. 857, l. 34).

521. Of the savage manner in which the Children are sometimes treated, the following is an example :—

Robert Tweedale, aged fourteen : " The getter he thrutched for was a wicked old fellow, named Charles Hill; once he bit him by the thigh, and lifted him to the roof in his mouth; many a time has he hit him on the side of his head. Worked with him a year, and has been with him four times over. He bit him because he had no' strength to lift the tub on the rails when he came to them in the main-way. Because he could no' work with him ' gradely' [kindly], left him" (Ibid. No. 12 : p. 850, l. 16).

522. SOUTH DURHAM.—" There is no kind of corporal punishment authorised by any of the managers who have been personally examined or who have sent answers to the queries, except in one instance; and they express themselves ignorant of any of the sort existing, or if a rare instance of violence occur, their rule is to send the matter before a magistrate. In all the work done by the younger lads there is in most pits a competition, from there being a greater number desirous of employment than can every day obtain it. It is easy, therefore, to punish an evil doer by diminishing the number of days which he is allowed to work, or by dismissing him altogether" (Dr. Mitchell, Report, § 209 : App. Pt. I., p. 143).

John Wood, Clarence Hetton Colliery, Nicholas Wood and Co. : " No one is allowed to strike any boy or lad. The overman and deputies to the overman in the pit, are not allowed to touch the boys, and the boys are not allowed to strike each other. If they were to do so we should take them to the magistrate; we have done so" (Dr. Mitchell, Evidence, No. 90 : App. Pt. I., p. 150, l. 55).—John Green, aged eleven, Black Boy Pit, near Bishop Auckland : " I never get thumped on the back; I like it nicely" (Ibid. No. 109 : p. 160, l. 38).—William Willis, aged fifteen : " The boys have no other complaint but lang hours, hard work, and little enough money" (Ibid. No. 115 : p. 163, l. 28).—Anthony Dowson, eighteen years of age : "The overman corrects the boys sometimes by a yard wand with which he measures the rank of the putting. The lads deserve it. A man must be master of boys" (Ibid. No. 101 : p. 157, l. 12). —John Vicars, fifteen years of age : " The putters used whiles to beat me. If I was told to clean one place, and was doing it, and another putter told me to clean another place, I could not do both at once, and one of them would hit me; they would hit one a bit to make one sharp" (Ibid. No. 100 : p. 155, l. 44).—William Hardy, aged seventeen : " The men constantly find fault with you, you cannot please them; I often have a battle with some of them. I sometimes lose; I lost one the day before yesterday" (Ibid. No. 110 : p. 160, l. 59).—Robert Storey, aged seventeen: " I was whiles badly used when I was driving by the waggon-way men, the men that repaired the waggon road; I was afraid to complain lest I should be whipped again" (Ibid. No. 114 : p. 162, l. 46).

523. NORTH DURHAM AND NORTHUMBERLAND.—The evidence from this portion of the northern coal field is to the same effect as that collected in South Durham. North Durham and Northumberland.

George Johnson, Esq., viewer : " As to the general treatment of these boys, thinks the parents are very kind, and the owners considerate. Parents do not correct them corporally so much as is necessary. It is impossible that there should be much infliction of brutality or corporal punishment within the care of a tolerably attentive viewer or under-viewer." (J. R. Leif-child, Esq., Evidence, No. 3 : App. Pt. I., p. 567, l. 72).—Mr. W. Bailey, under-viewer, Hetton Colliery : " The overman may hit the boys gently with a bat; but nothing more is allowed. The parents would prefer that the Children should be thrashed rather than fined, and sometimes propose this. The masters are more considerate of them than their parents. Now the parents are noted if any Children behave badly, and the masters dismiss incorrigibles" (Ibid. No. 400 : p. 649, l. 30).—Mr. Stewart, under-viewer, Cox Lodge Colliery : " Now they are only corrected when they stand in need of it. The overman gives them a few strikes with a whip or stick, but not to hurt them at all badly. Boys are not beaten so as to make blood come. The beating is not more than gentle correction" (Ibid. No. 139 : p. 597, l. 38).—Ralph Hardy, aged sixteen, Killingworth Colliery : " Sometimes the big putters or the men may rub [hit] him, but not to hurt" (Ibid. No. 99 : p. 588, l. 65).—Surtis Blackburn, aged seventeen, Heaton Colliery : " Sometimes the overman hits the boys a few bats, but not to hurt them much" (Ibid. No. 29 : p. 573, l. 58).—William Rain, aged seventeen, Clebburn Colliery : " The men whiles rub him, and throw a small piece of coal at him—nothing to hurt" (Ibid. No. 162 : p. 602, l. 18).—See also witnesses, Nos. 35, 73, 77, 123, 124, 145, 148, 171, 238, 264, 270, 272, 274.

Twenty boys taken as they came out of the pit, Walker Colliery : " The boys down the pit are sometimes beaten by the deputies and others with the whip-handles and axe-shaft [handle of the axe]"—See also witnesses, Nos. 57, 61, 75, 151, 166, 299, 355, 372, 456, 479.

524. CUMBERLAND.—The evidence collected in this district shows that the Children and Young Persons are under the protection of the employers, and are in general well treated. Cumberland.

Williamson Peile, Esq., colliery-viewer, Whitehaven : " I have no doubt that the Children are altogether better used, owing to the employer and not the workmen being their master. They get their wages better, and corporal punishments are prevented. No man is allowed to chastise a boy, and it is very seldom done even by the overmen" (J. C. Symons, Esq., Evidence, No. 311 : App. Pt. I., p. 305, l. 35).—Mr. John Percival, agent to Mr. Westray, Cookson Colliery, near Workington : " The men use the Children well; they are most of them the sons of the colliers. I never allow them to be struck" (Ibid. No. 314 : p. 306, l. 60).—Mr. Allen Penrice, agent for Henry Curwen, Esq., Workington : " I am quite sure that the Children are not ill used" (Ibid. No. 317 : p. 307, l. 59).—Joseph Sharp, Broughton Moor Collieries, near Maryport : " They are generally well treated, and they are not overdone" (Ibid. No. 300 : p. 303, l. 19).—Joseph Hodgson, aged fifteen, near Whitehaven : " They used me very well" (Ibid. No. 306 : p. 304, l. 18).—David Saul, aged ten and a half, Broughton Moor Colliery, near Maryport : "They use me well in the pit, and never beat me" (Ibid. No. 303 : p. 303, l. 53).—Jonathan Johnson, aged eleven : " They don't use me well; they welt me when I'm late in; it's not my fault always, because I can't get down sometimes. It's the chicken welts me. James Atkinson [a driver] is the chicken. He made us cry. I complained; but he has not welted me since" (Ibid. No. 330 : p. 310, l. 13).

525. EAST OF SCOTLAND.—The hardships endured by the Young People in the pits of the East of Scotland are such as to preclude the idea of any especial care of them on the part of the employer. East of Scotland.

526. WEST OF SCOTLAND.—In this part of the kingdom, states the Sub-Commissioner, " No inquiries in any town or work which I visited tended to bring West of Scotland.

home either to the masters or men, in any class of works, any systematic tyrannical usage of the boys employed by them.   In all works it is professed to be the duty of the foreman to take care that no violence is offered to the younger hands ; and though an occasional blow may, I have no doubt, be inflicted, the boys being free to leave their employer when they please, the evil cannot amount to anything very great" (T. Tancred, Esq., Report, § 98 : App. Pt. I., p. 344).

527. NORTH WALES.—The Sub-Commissioner for this district states, that he frequently questioned the Children and others whether any cruelty were resorted to, whether blows and kicks were inflicted on them to urge them to the performance of their work, but that he found it was not so.   (H. H. Jones, Esq., Report, § 22. App. Pt. II., p. 367).   A great preponderance of the testimony of all classes of witnesses is to the good treatment which the Young People generally receive.—See witnesses, Nos. 2, 3, 4, 17, 18, 20, 22, 26, 31, 32, 33, 36, 39, 42, 43, 45, 46, 53, 60, 61, 63, 65, 67, 69, 80, 82, 89, 103, 104, 105, 119, 180, &c.   Other witnesses, however, state that the Children are sometimes ill-treated and severely beaten.

Edward Price, aged sixteen, Bont y Cysulty, near Ruabon : " Were the boys in the pits ill-treated when you worked below ground?   Yes, the big boys would thrash the little ones; and the charter-masters often beat the boys.—What for ?   The masters would try to make us draw more than we ought, and if we said anything they would beat us.—If the manager knew that they did so would he allow them?   I don't know; we never made any complaints " (H. H. Jones, Esq., Evidence, No. 118: App. Pt. II., p. 417, l. 36).—John Jones, relieving-officer, Holywell : " Are the boys well-treated?   Yes, by the masters, but the men often ill-treat and thrash them" (Ibid. No. 96 : p. 407, l. 69).—Mr. Edward Williams, clerk of Petty-Sessions, Mold : " Are no complaints ever made by the boys of being ill-treated either by the men in the pits or by masters?   No, but very rarely; though they may be, and I have no doubt often are ill used" (Ibid. No. 86 : p. 403, l. 41).

528. SOUTH GLOUCESTERSHIRE.—" The use of corporal chastisement appears here to be countenanced by many coal proprietors, under the notion that idle or unruly boys cannot be managed without it.   The advocates of this practice, nevertheless, repudiate any cruelty either in the mode or extent of its application ; and though the boys admit that such punishments are inflicted, their most common expressions, when questioned on the point, are merely,—' Sometimes we do get a hiding,' or, ' they do hit us a clump or two now and then.'   I have reason to think the older lads often play the tyrant towards the boys; but when no formal complaint is made it must often be impossible to detect abuses perpetrated in the recesses of a mine " (E. Waring, Esq., Report, § 93 : App. Pt. II., p. 38).

529. NORTH SOMERSETSHIRE.—In this district " there is a decided amendment, as stated on every side, in the conduct of the labourers in collieries towards each other, and in their treatment of the Children under them ; and there is a more strict investigation on the part of the proprietors and of their agents and bailiffs into the discipline and management of all the workpeople.   This improvement, which has taken place in a great measure from dread of exposure and anticipation of legislative interference, gives every hope that still greater good will be effected when these matters shall be fully before the public and proper regulations laid down " (Dr. Stewart, Report, § 7 : App. Pt. II., p. 47).

John Smith, Hewish and Writhlington, Colliery, near Radstock : " There are no instances of cruelty or improper severity exercised towards the Children and Young Persons" (Dr. Stewart, Evidence, No. 11: App. Pt. II., p. 53, l. 21).— Mr. Moses Reynolds, under-ground manager, Bedminster Colliery, near Bristol : " The Young Persons are obliged to come to their work, and are discharged if they do not come regularly; but there is no corporal punishment or severity " (Ibid. No. 2: p. 49, l. 50).—John Gillard, under-ground bailiff, Marsh Pit : " Has never known of any severe or improper punishment of the boys" (Ibid. No. 3: p. 50, l. 17).—Charles Ashman, manager, Radstock coal mine : " With respect to punishment, there is occasionally a strap or two given to the boys by the breakers, who are apt to be kept waiting by them, but there is no undue severity or cruelty exercised towards the boys and young persons.   It is not common to witness any ill-treatment of the children, but on the contrary they are more independent than persons of their age usually are, being rather more in demand in this region than adults" (Ibid. No. 9: p. 52, l. 20).—Mr. Isaac Cox, Nailsea Heath coal works, near Bristol : " They are turned off when they do not work ; but they are never punished by blows. This rule applies to the Children and Young Persons" (Ibid. No. 1: p. 49, l. 18).—Mr. William Brice, clerk to Messrs. Fussel and Company, Coal Barton and Vobster Collieries, Near Frome: " There is no particular punishment of the Children, and no brutal conduct common among the labourers " (Ibid. No. 7: p. 51, l. 10).—William Ashman, aged thirteen, Writhlington, near Radstock : " Has never been punished either by the bailiff or the workmen " (Ibid. No. 16: p. 54, l. 20).—John Pratten, aged sixteen, Writhlington, near Radstock : " Has been very little struck or punished" (Ibid. No. 14 : p. 53, l. 62).—John Milward, aged seventeen, Writhlington, near Radstock : " The carting boys used to beat him, but now they are not allowed to do it " (Ibid. No. 18 : p. 54, l. 37).—Samuel Latchun, aged ten, Writhlington : " Does not himself complain of ill-treatment, but has seen other boys of his own size beaten by the carting boys " (Ibid. No. 24 : p. 55, l. 33).—David Gulliver, aged ten, Writhlington : " Has no punishment or cruelty to complain of " (Ibid. No. 26 : p. 55, l. 46).—George Raikes, aged eleven, Marsh Pit : " Is never struck or punished severely " (Ibid. No. 6 : p. 50, l. 36).—George Gullick, aged eleven, Writhlington : " Has been beaten by the carting boys, but not often. Has been beaten since Christmas, but ' has had no wheal since then' " (Ibid. No. 23 : p. 55, l. 21).

530. IRELAND.—" In all the mines, collieries, and manufactories I have visited in my tour throughout the southern half of Ireland," states Mr. Roper, " I have not observed any instances of ill treatment of the Children or Young Persons therein employed ; on the contrary, I everywhere found them well treated, particularly the Children, as their universal healthy and very cheerful appearance sufficiently indicates" (F. Roper, Esq., Report, § 20 : App. Pt. I., p. 874). The evidence collected by Mr. Martin in the North of Ireland shows the same state of things (T. Martin, Esq., Evidence, Nos. 46, 51 : pp. 884, 885)

13.—ACCIDENTS TO WHICH CHILDREN AND YOUNG PERSONS ARE EXPOSED IN COAL MINES.

531. Every person employed in a coal-mine is from minute to minute exposed to so many sources of danger that " in spite of skill and unremitting attention the risk is constant and imminent." " It is a life," says one of the witnesses, himself a collier, " of great danger both for man and child ; a collier is never safe after he is swung off to be let down the pit."

532. In the year 1835 a Select Committee of the House of Commons was appointed to inquire into accidents in mines, and from their Report it appears that there has been a notable increase in the number of fatal accidents since the introduction of an instrument which was intended and which is unquestionably calculated to lessen them.

533. " If the year 1816," states the Report of this Committee, " is assumed as the period when Sir Humphrey Davy's lamp came into use, a term of 18 years since 1816 and a similar term prior to 1816 being taken, it will be seen, that in the 18 years previous to the introduction of the lamp 447 persons lost their lives in the counties of Durham and Northumberland, whilst in the latter term of 18 years the fatal accidents amounted to 538. To account for this increase, it may be sufficient to observe, that the quantity of coal raised in the said counties has greatly increased ; seams of coal, so fiery as to have lain unwrought, have been approached and worked by the aid of the safety-lamp. Many dangerous mines were successfully carried on, though in a most inflammable state, and without injury to the general health of the people employed in them. Add to this the idea entertained, that on the introduction of that lamp the necessity for former precautions and vigilance in great measure ceased.

534. " These facts led your Committee to a serious part of their inquiry, How are these calamities to be prevented for the future ? They desire fully to recognize the undoubted rights of property, enterprise, and labour. They acknowledge their conviction that the public interest has been served by the opening of the more dangerous mines, and the competition their working has created ; they do not overlook the anxious care alleged to have been maintained to diminish the attendant risk ; but they deem it their duty to state their decided opinion, that the interests of humanity demand consideration, and they would gladly put it to the owners of these mines how far any object of pecuniary interest or personal gain, or even the assumed advantages of public competition, can justify the continued exposure of men and boys in situations where science and mechanical skill have failed in providing anything like adequate protection."

535. The Committee further say :—" It is the bounden duty of owners carefully and constantly to examine into the state of their mines. If this is not personally practicable, they ought to call for written daily reports from their subalterns, of every circumstance and event connected with the proper ventilation of the mine."

536. How far this appeal to humanity and this exhortation to a vigilant attention to the sanatory condition and to the safety of coal mines have been regarded will appear from the evidence now collected. It being obvious that more correct and comprehensive information on the subject of fatal accidents could be obtained from

the public registers of deaths than from any other source, we procured from the office of the Registrar General a list of the deaths described in his annual reports, as deaths by violence, from 55 districts of registration which contain mines, for the year 1838. A classification of these deaths will be found in Appendix, Part II., p. 786.

537. The deaths in mines and on the pit-banks, 349 in number, are as follows :—

Cause of Death.	Under 13 years of age.	13 and not exceeding 18 years of age.	Above 18 years of age.
Fell down the shafts	13	16	31
Fell down the shaft from the rope breaking .	1	..	2
Fell out when ascending	..	..	3
Drawn over the pulley	3	..	3
Fall of stone out of a skip down the shaft . .	1	..	3
Drowned in the mines	3	4	15
Fall of stones, coal, and rubbish in the mines .	14	14	69
Injuries in coal-pits, the nature of which is not specified	6	3	32
Crushed in coal-pits	..	1	1
Explosion of gas	13	18	49
Suffocated by choke-damp	..	2	6
Explosion of gunpowder	..	1	3
By tram-waggons	4	5	12
Total	58	62	229

538. From this table it appears that no less than 60 persons perished in this year from falling down the shafts, of whom 29 were under eighteen years of age and 13 were Children, a result which no one can regard as extraordinary who has considered the evidence relating to the unguarded state of the mouths of the pits in almost all the districts; that 9 persons perished from the breaking of the ropes and from being drawn over the pulley, of which four were Children; that 22 persons perished in the pits from drowning; and that 88 persons perished by the explosion of carbureted hydrogen gas, and from suffocation by carbonic acid gas; so that the number of deaths from the unguarded state of the pit's mouth, the badness of the ropes, the mismanagement of the drawing engine, and the accumulation of water in the mines (91), exceeds the whole of those which happened from the explosive and suffocating gases.

539. It will be observed that in the returns of deaths by violence in the mining districts there are no less than 120 instances in which the cause of death is entered merely as an accident or as an accidental death, but in which no information is given as to the nature of the accident, or how it was occasioned.

540. Several of the Sub-Commissioners, and more especially those for Scotland, in which country there is no coroner, and those for Wales, in which country the duty of the coroner appears to be most imperfectly performed, have earnestly directed our attention to the serious evil arising from the want of a register of accidents; and there will be found to be a perfect coincidence between the opinion expressed by them and that expressed in the Report of the Committee of the House of Commons just referred to; which latter is as follows :—

541. " Here your Committee would observe that, without any disposition to question the zealous and faithful discharge of their important duties by local coroners and juries, it may be expedient to consider how far it is necessary to provide that, at the earliest possible opportunity, information of every accident attended with death to a large number of His Majesty's subjects should be transmitted to the Secretary of State for the Home Department, and that he, or the Chief Justice of England, His Majesty's coroner, should, at his or their discretion, direct the attendance of some fit and proper person or persons, by them to be appointed, to be present at and assist the said coroner and the jury in their investigations. From such a proceeding results the most valuable to humanity and science might be obtained; the aim of justice would be still better secured, and to the public (particularly the relations of the deceased) the verdict would be delivered under the best possible recommendation, and with the highest sanction."

542. The chief accidents to which persons employed in coal mines are exposed

are,—1, falling down the shaft, whether of a pit in work or of one now abandoned; 2, the falling of something on the head while descending or ascending the shaft; 3, the breaking of the rope or chain; 4, the falling of something from the roof of the mine; 5, the being drawn over the pulley and dashed to the ground or precipitated down the shaft from the neglect of the engine-man; 6, being crushed by a mass of coal unexpectedly falling while the hewers are " undergoing;" 7, suffocation by carbonic acid gas; 8, suffocation or burning, or both, from the explosion of carbureted hydrogen gas; 9, drowning from the sudden breaking in of water from old workings; 10, minor accidents from falls in the mine and injuries from the horses and carriages.

543. Of the evidence now collected relative to the frequency and the causes of these accidents in the several coal-fields of the United Kingdom, it would be impossible, within reasonable limits, to give an exhaustive account; all that can be attempted in the present Report is to direct attention to the more important statements; ample details on the subject will be found in the Reports of the Sub-Commissioners, and in the depositions of the witnesses examined by them.

544. South Staffordshire.—In this district the accidents are stated by the Sub-Commissioner to be so frequent that, to judge from the conversation of the people, " we might consider the whole population as engaged in a campaign."

545. " Happily, in 1838, there was in this district no instance of the rope or chain breaking, and the people ascending or descending being precipitated to the bottom. But there was an instance of the chain of a skip breaking, and a miner, aged forty-five, being killed. Several fell out of the skips and were killed. There does not appear to be any sufficient control over the people as to the number going down or up at a time, or such accidents would be of much rarer occurrence. The ages of the persons who fell out of the skips were nine, twelve, fifteen, seventeen, seventeen, twenty-one, twenty-nine, and forty-five. Some deaths were occasioned by lumps of coal or pieces of wood falling down the shaft upon the people. It is not the custom in this district to use an iron umbrella to protect the persons ascending or descending from such accidents.

546. " Of the deaths in the coal-pits by the falling of coals or stone from the roof, explosions of gas, suffocation, or other accidents, altogether 78 in number in 1838, there were 2 of nine years of age, 1 of ten, 3 of eleven, 2 of twelve, 4 of thirteen, 2 of fourteen, 2 of fifteen, and 1 of sixteen. Young and old are equally exposed, but the young have less strength of resistance (Dr. Mitchell, Report, §§ 134—137: App. Pt. I., p. 17.)

547. North Staffordshire.—Accidents from the explosion of carbureted hydrogen gas are common in this district. Describing his visit to one of the pits, the Sub-Commissioner says:—" I was informed by the buttie that wild-fire, as they call it, was not uncommon here, and I too soon heard of a melancholy proof of it, an explosion having occurred only a few days after my visit by which three men were severely burnt and four others killed. There appeared to me to be a great want of precaution in the use of lights, and by their frequent application to crevices in the strata of coal in order to ascertain whether sulphur was really present, as would be indicated by the burning of the jets that issued from them. By the way of amusement the men would sometimes inflate the mouth with a sufficient quantity to produce a stream, by contracting the lips and setting fire to it as from an argand burner, to the great glee of others who looked on." Another practice that ought to be amended is that of allowing more than four persons to descend and ascend together to or from their work. In some of the deep shafts the chains weigh from two to three tons, added to this are the corves and chain-slings, contributing two or three hundredweight more; into these ten, twelve, or fifteen men and boys will leap, to the imminent risk of their lives (S. S. Scriven, Esq., Report, § 3; App. Pt. II., p. 127).

548. Shropshire.—In this district the registers do not so distinctly explain the nature of the fatal accidents as they do in Staffordshire, but enough is stated to show that the causes of death are perfectly similar.

549. Warwickshire.—From the Report and Evidence it appears that there are fewer accidents in this district than in either of the preceding: " Accidents" were uniformly talked of by all the witnesses as comparatively rare: still the life of the miner, in the most favourable circumstances, is full of hazard, and accidents,

though not frequent, do now and then occur even in these collieries" (Dr. Mitchell, Report, § 36 : App. Pt. I., p. 92).

550. LEICESTERSHIRE.—A more systematic care is taken to prevent accidents in this district than in any of the preceding, and with a most successful result. Of the Moira Bath Pit, for example, it is stated that " The wooden posts, or frame-work on which the wheels or pulleys are fixed, over which the rope from the engine runs, and more particularly the great framework which supports the pulley immediately over the shaft, are at this pit most substantial and solid. The rope is made of flat ropes laid side by side, and appeared very secure. Every person going down puts his feet into a loop formed by the lower links of a chain, which will admit his thighs, and will then not permit his body to slip through, and he lays hold of the chain with his hands. There is no risk of a man slipping off the chain, as it might be possible to do in places where it is not so secured round his thighs. Overhead is what is called an umbrella, and it resembles it in form, but it is composed of weighty solid iron, and protects the persons going down or coming up from the stones, pieces of coal, brick, timber, or anything else falling down the shaft. As the depth is 708 feet it is easy to see how much mischief might be done by a body of only very small weight" (Dr. Mitchell, Report, § 85 : App. Pt. I., p. 96).

551. " In answer to the query as to the precaution taken to keep the head-gear, the machinery, and the ropes in good repair, some of the agents reply—' by frequent inspection ;' others, ' by inspection at different times.' But the agent of Messrs. Stephenson and Co. states that he causes this duty to be performed every day ; and the agent of Messrs. Stenson and Co. says that the underground bailiff examines daily the ropes, bull-chains, and tacklers by which the men descend and ascend, and one of the smiths examines the head-gear and machinery daily. Large iron bonnets are provided and used in order to prevent anything from falling on the men descending or coming up the shaft. Such ought to be the system in every mine in the kingdom" (Ibid. § 126, p. 99).

The following is the evidence of Mr. Michael Parker, of the Snibston Collieries :—" How many go down together and come up together? About four men ; and, if all boys, about five or six go. They go in the basket. We have had no accidents in our pits going up and down.—To what do you attribute freedom from accident? To having good tackling, and taking great care. There is a man whose duty it is to see the boys safe in the skips coming up or down, and that there are no more in number than four men, or more than five or six boys. We are particular to have a steady man at the engine.—What precautions do you take against fire-damp and choke-damp? Strong ventilation" (Dr. Mitchell, Evidence, No. 77 : App. Pt. I., p. 113, l. 15).

552. " At the Ibstock Colliery only six are allowed to ascend or descend at a time, and if more go there is a fine of 6d. The solid nature of the coal renders the mines of this district less likely to produce injuries by pieces falling from the roof; also from the moderate height when an injury is inflicted it is less likely to be severe than when a piece of coal has fallen from a great height. Mr. Charles Allsop Dalby, a surgeon in Ashby, who has had much practice amongst the colliers, being asked, ' Have you had much to do with boys? Very little. Sometimes a pinched finger or a pinched foot. There are not half the accidents you would imagine. They still occur sometimes' " (Dr. Mitchell, Report, §§ 128—130 : App. Pt. I., p. 100).

553. DERBYSHIRE.—In this district fatal accidents are extremely frequent, from the imperfect ventilation; from the general neglect of the Davy-lamp; from the unguarded state of the mouths of the pits (" In most of the fields I visited," says the Sub-Commissioner, "the pits were left exposed either for man or beast to fall into"); from the numbers that descend and ascend the shafts at a time ; and from a practice met with occasionally here, as it is common in some other districts, of employing very young Children as engineers to let down and draw up the work-people. " I met with more than one instance of Children only ten years old having the lives of the colliers left to their mercy, and have seen others so inattentive to their duty as to let the corve be drawn over the pulley, and half a ton of coals thrown the distance of a hundred yards or more down the shaft; but notwithstanding these accidents occurring in the immediate neighbourhood, the practice of appointing Children to this responsible post still continues in the most respectable fields. (See Butterley, Nos. 187, 188, and 192; Newlands, No. 198; Swanwick, No. 327, Riddings, Nos. 345, 348) " (J. M. Fellows, Esq., Report, §§ 34—36 : App. Pt. II., p. 255).

John Fisher, aged fifty-five, a collier at Greasley, gives evidence that, " When the wind is in the north they cannot prevent the black-damp, and are obliged to stop the works ; they have time to get off, but it is very dangerous for those that work by night, as the engine is left, and there is no way of giving an alarm ; he and another man and two youths above 18 are working all night, and have to do as well as they can : it makes them very badly, but they get amongst the asses, and can work no more that night. He has not known any serious accident within these two years in the pit, excepting about three months since a youth about 17 years old, it being intensely cold, slipped in the pit, and was killed on the spot ; one of his legs fell from his body ; the pit mouth is not guarded, but if it was is not aware it would have saved him, it was so slippery. The shaft is not laid in lime ; no bonnet, no rope, no Davy-lamp ; eight or nine are let down and up at a time ; thinks there is no business to be above three" (J. M. Fellows, Esq., Evidence, No. 154 : App. Pt. II., p. 304, l. 36).—William Barlow, engine-man of New Birchwood Colliery : " The engine works both Shady and Balguy shafts ; neither of them are laid in lime ; there are cabins and flat ropes to each, but neither bonnets nor Davy-lamps. Balguy is 80 yards deep, Shady 70 ; he lets down and takes up four or five at a time. About three years ago several accidents occurred ; there was a young person fell down the shaft of Balguy, and a very short time afterwards another fell down Shady ; besides these, one man was suffocated, and another killed owing to the bind falling. Six months since a man had his foot crushed by the coal, and has never been able to work since" (Ibid. No. 273 : p. 326, l. 54).—Thomas Stevens, engine-man : " Neither bonnet nor Davy-lamps, although last Saturday, at No. 1, Thomas Stevens was so badly burnt by wild-fire that his life is in great danger ; the flesh of his cheek burnt off, and his body injured ; at the same pit another had his eye blown out by powder" (Ibid. No. 189 : p. 314, l. 14).—Edmund Williamson, engine-boy : " Is fifteen years old ; has had the sole care of an engine since he was ten years old ; at first, for a month or two, his father came to him once or twice a day ; the engine is twelve-horse power, a flat rope, and no chain ; no Davy-lamp or bonnet ; lets up and down two at once" (Ibid. No. 434 : p. 352, l. 45).—John Edwards : " Is eleven years old ; has had the care of the engine a year and a half ; his father is mostly within call ; he often lets the people down ; sometimes his father will be with him ; but not often" (Ibid. No. 449 : p. 354, l. 11).—George Atkin : " Is fourteen years old ; has had the sole charge of the engine for two years and a half ; they go down by a flat rope six at a time" (Ibid. No. 187 : p. 313, l. 62).— Isaac Stevens : " Is just fifteen years old ; has had the sole care of the engine six months ; lets down six at a time ; the company engage him and pay his wages" (Ibid. No. 188 : p. 314, l. 4).— William Rees : " Is fifteen years old ; has had the sole care of the engine to Nos. 2 and 5, Waterloo Field, above a year ; lets down four at a time" (Ibid. No. 192 : p. 314, l. 36).—George Jackson, engine-boy : " Is fourteen years old ; has been sole manager of the engine above a year ; draws up from four to six at once ; the shaft is very bad" (Ibid. No. 198 : p. 315, l. 53).

554. The deaths, the fractured limbs, and the injuries for life, occasioned by the carelessness of these boys, appear in this district to be regarded with the utmost indifference.

John Jackson, overlooker, Morley Park : " Nine weeks ago two men and two boys were descending, when, through the engine-boy being absent, the engine reversed and drew them over the pulley ; one boy about thirteen years of age was killed ; another about eighteen was so much hurt that he lost his arm and is never likely to get well again ; another broke his leg ; the engine-boy is dismissed" (Ibid. No. 258 : p. 325, l. 6).—Mr. John Stafford, agent of the Morley Park Coal Mines, says : " All the shafts are worked by chains and no rope ; have bonnets at all the shafts, but no Davy-lamp ; no accident, excepting Alfred Butler, who was killed 12th February, by he and three others being drawn over the pulley-wheel ; he was aged thirteen. Francis Walker was also much hurt ; has lost his arm. Abraham Stone had his leg broken ; the other escaped unhurt. It was owing to the neglect of the engine-boy, who took his trial at the assizes, but was liberated on consideration of his having been six weeks imprisoned" (Ibid. No. 257 : p. 324, l. 49).

555. The motive for thus employing boys instead of men is merely because boys can be had at less wages.

At Swanwick and Summercotes (W. P. Morewood, Esq.), Charles Mounteney, engine-man : " No bonnet or Davy-lamp ; lets down and up five or six at a time ; no accident at this pit, but at the other to which his engine is attached, but now worked out ; a little more than a year since two lads were much hurt and nearly killed, owing to the carelessness of the engine-boy, who had the care of the engine, and was only fourteen years of age, drawing them over the pulley : the engine-men are obliged to be there before five in the morning, and never home before ten, and the butties only allow 2s. a-day for all these hours, they are therefore obliged often to employ boys" (Ibid. No. 327 : p. 336, l. 49).

556. WEST RIDING OF YORKSHIRE : SOUTHERN PART.—In this district it is reported that " the accidents are so frequent that it is utterly impossible to give anything like a correct statement of all that have happened in each colliery for three years, or even for a much shorter time. Numbers never reach the ears of the employers at all ; and of those that are known to the underground steward, unless they are very serious, he keeps no record. Such statements are easily enough concocted, but must necessarily be imperfect and delusive. If the master

suffered when a child or a man was injured and thrown out of work for one t⁰ ten days, as the case may be, it is probable that some regular register might bᵉ kept of such occurrence, but on the contrary, the collier or the Child are the only sufferers, if the accident be merely a personal one. In many cases it is concealed from the knowledge of the master, especially where carelessness has occasioned a slight explosion, and the master's property has been risked" (J. C. Symons, Esq., Report, § 136: App. Pt. I., p. 184).

557. In some of the pits in this district Davy-lamps have been introduced with beneficial effect, but in others the purpose for which they were intended has been grossly perverted by the ignorance of the men and the avarice of the masters. The men have a dislike to them, because they afford much less light than candles; and as the men are paid generally by the piece, they cannot, with the quantity of light afforded by these lamps, gain the same money in a given time. The men are also unskilful in the use of them.

558. Good ventilation is the only means by which the health of the people can be preserved, and the safety of the mine secured; but in many of the collieries in this district the Davy-lamp is made a substitute for ventilation, and this is carried to such an extent that some well-informed persons are of opinion that on the whole the Davy-lamp has done more harm than good. Among others John Thorneley, Esq., a magistrate of the county of York, in a statement which has been already quoted, expresses a decided opinion to this effect. He does not deny that the Davy-lamp is a valuable discovery; but from facts which have come under his own observation, he thinks " that it has in practice been a curse to the country, because it has enabled colliers to work where they otherwise ought not, and has often superseded a proper renovation of air, and been the cause of the colliers working in an impure atmosphere." Without doubt, unless in practice strict care is taken to secure the proper use of the Davy-lamp it is a dangerous instrument; but experience shows that there is no insuperable difficulty in teaching and enforcing this proper use, and in preventing the abuse of it. It appears in evidence that in well-regulated mines in the Durham and Northumberland Coal-fields a safety-lamp, locked securely, is delivered to every miner; the miner is bound to deliver it back in the same condition; and unless he does so he is punished for his misconduct.

559. It is stated, in relation to black-damp, which is far oftener fatal to health than life, and which, unlike fire-damp, gives warning of its presence by the dim burning, and afterwards by the extinction, of the candles, that no case has come to the knowledge of the Sub-Commissioner in this district of the loss of life immediately arising from it, although in a colliery near Barnsley the work is not unfrequently altogether stopped by it. But he reports that " accidents from the fall of the roof at bank-faces, and occasionally in the bord-gates, are very common. They usually arise from carelessness in not propping up the roof sufficiently often, and in excavating too large a portion unsupported. Next, they arise from the badness of the roof, which usually consists of shale, but which is often shattered by gas, and comes down without much warning. The cases in which men get killed are not unfrequent; those in which they get broken limbs, or are badly bruised, are very frequent; so much so that little note or record is kept of them, at least in my district. (Ibid. § 160, p. 188.) He adds, " I cannot conclude this branch of the subject without expressing in the strongest manner my conviction of the gross negligence of the means of safety prevailing in many collieries. The proprietor of a colliery very rarely visits it at all. (See the Evidence of John Micklethwaite, Esq., No. 121.) The whole management is left to an underground steward, who in all large collieries, where there are more than one pit, appoints a deputy, who becomes the only regular superintendent of the works" (Ibid. § 184, p. 191).

560. BRADFORD and LEEDS.—Explosions of fire-damp, falls of the roof, falling down the shaft, bruises and broken bones with the coal waggons, are stated to be the most common classes of accidents in this vicinity (W. R. Wood, Esq., Report, § 21: App. Pt. II., p. H 4.)

561. HALIFAX.—Of this neighbourhood it is stated, that " the accidents and personal injuries to which they (the workpeople) are subject are consequent upon explosions, falls in coming up and going down the shafts, falling roofs and walls, and from the speed and weight of loaded corves, which, if they happen to be in the way, run over them." After giving the particulars of the deaths from accidents and explosions obtained from the coroner for a period of three years, the Sub-Commissioner observes:—" Here are fifty deaths, and of this number thirty-four

have occurred to Children and Young Persons under sixteen years of age. On the perusal of the verdicts it will be seen that in a large proportion of these cases the fatal results might have been obviated by precaution and care on the part of the proprietors and of the colliers themselves; nor has this neglect subjected the parties guilty of it in any case to that reprehension and punishment which it appears to me might be employed with effect in diminishing their frequency (S. S. Scriven, Esq.. Report, § 79, 80: Nos. 4, 7, 8, 9, 10, 15, 19, 21, 24, 31, 33, 34, 50. App. Pt. II., pp. 71, 72).

562. The imperfection of the machinery for descending and ascending the shats, of which a full account is given at paragraphs 14, *et seq.*, is stated to be the cause of many accidents. Of the three methods described it is stated that the turn-wheel (fig. 3) " is the least expensive, and certainly the most dangerous, as you are, upon all occasions, dependent upon the man, or it may be woman, who works it. It is in fact nothing more or less than a common well-winch, with a fly wheel, without trap-door or stage, conducting-rods, or anything else. In getting on or off the clatch-iron, or corve, in coming up or going down, you are at the mercy of the winder. The unfortunate case of David Pellett, No. 50, page 71, who was drawn over the roller by his own uncle and grandfather, at the time I was pursuing my investigation upon the same ground, just at the moment when their attention was called to a passing funeral, is a painful illustration of their unsafety" (Ibid. § 25, p. 61).

563. LANCASHIRE AND CHESHIRE.—In this district the accidents are stated by one of the Sub-Commissioners to be of " daily occurrence in almost every mine where numbers are employed, and so common that a record of them is seldom kept." Some few of the proprietors, however, have kept such registers, and among others the trustees of the late Duke of Bridgewater.

564. " Many complaints have been made throughout the district of the insufficiency of the ropes, and from what I have seen myself I think there are grounds for them. I saw myself a rope in use at a pit belonging to Mr. Nightingale, near Worsley, which appeared to be in a very dangerous condition. There were iron clamps in many places, and the rope in other parts was much worn. The banksman informed me that the pit was ninety yards deep, and the engine was ninety to a hundred yards from the head-gearing, so that the rope which was in this worn-out condition would have to bear the weight of the tubs, together with the weight of the rope from the head-gear to the tub, which, when at the bottom of the pit, would be the weight of ninety yards of rope.

565. " The grossest cases of mismanagement and neglect of ropes are usually to be found in small mines, when the seam does not lie deep; for in the case of deep mines the expense of winding is very great, and the loss when a breakage takes place falls heavily on the coal owner.

566. " In all the mines I have visited, when the coal field has lain deep, I have remarked that the machinery and gearing have been excellent. Cases have been related to me where a new rope has broken the first day it was put on; of course this is but a rare occasion: to avoid the recurrence of such accidents, perhaps it might be a safe plan to test coal-pit ropes in the same manner that chain-cables are tested, viz. by the hydraulic press.

567, " In some mines it is usual to wind with an endless chain, and this plan is preferred by some coal-owners; there is, however, one disadvantage about a chain, viz. that it gives no warning before it gives way; and in deep mines, when the chain would require to be long, the weight of the material itself would be so great as to render it almost unsafe to use it" (J. L. Kennedy, Esq., Report, §§ 127, 134, 135, 140, 142, 143: App. Pt. II., pp. 168-9).

568. " Many accidents arise from shafts being only cased with brick to the first hard strata. Mr. Kenworthy, of Ashton-under-Lyne, whom I asked to propose some practical measure for the prevention of accidents in coal-mines, makes the following remarks upon this point : ' A great many accidents happen by pieces coming out of the sides of the pit and falling down. I have seen [he proceeds] large portions of rock standing out of the pit side, which have been pushed out by the pressure from above. It is very common to brick the sides only to the beginning of the strata. And the strong currents of air, ascending and descending, decompose the rock, and by-and-by large portions are loosened or detached. . . . I have seen [he continues] great ledges in a pit, where stones and rubbish could lodge, and when anything comes against them they fall down the pit, and probably kill somebody at the pit-eye. When I first began the coal business we had pits which were only bricked to the first strata; and upon one occasion a portion of

the rock gave way, and killed a man. Since that time I have had all the pits cased with brick and mortar, and we have not had a single accident of that kind' (Ibid. §§ 146, 147: p. 169).

569. " I should in this place mention that fatal accidents often occur from pieces of coal falling from the tubs in ascending. The first case in the Table (B) in the Appendix is one of this kind. It is impossible to be too careful in topping the coal in the tubs, so as not to overload them.

570. " The next class of accidents are those arising from the chairs or baskets coming in contact, whilst passing in their ascent and descent, or meeting with obstruction in their passage. There can be no doubt that side-rods are a great preventive of this class of accidents; but great care is necessary in keeping the conductors in order. If they be of iron they should be inspected frequently to see that they do not become so slack as to allow the chairs or sliders to come in contact when passing. I was myself unfortunate enough to witness a fatal accident, when a little boy, of ten years of age, was killed in this manner. The chair which held the tub in which he was standing came in contact with the descending chair; the concussion threw the child out of the tub, and it fell sixty yards down the pit, and was literally dashed to pieces. The same care should be taken daily, if the conductors are of wood; for it occasionally happens that some of the bearers come loose, and obstruct the baskets in their descent.

571. " It will be observed that there are accidents which happen from persons falling out of the baskets, and from the baskets coming unhooked. I need scarcely say that these are all accidents arising from gross inattention, and if proper care were taken they would rarely occur (Ibid. §§ 150, 152, 156, 157: p. 170).

572. " Accidents arising from explosions of fire-damp are by far the most numerous of any which occur in this employment. A glance at Table (B) in the Appendix shows that there have been forty-six cases, in two years, of burns and serious injuries from this cause, four of which proved fatal. The whole body of evidence furnishes examples; and I believe there are few persons who pass their lives in the pits who escape it. Cases such as those related by William Harrison, the relieving officer of the Orrel, Pemberton, and Upholland district, near Wigan, are deplorable in the extreme: 'We have had [says he] as many as twenty-eight people killed at one time by an explosion of fire-damp, and eighteen at another, and often large numbers are killed. They [the colliers] are very reckless. I have been several times foreman of the coroner's jury when inquests have been held: and very often the accidents have happened by the fault of the men themselves, and seldom by that of their employers.' This is certainly the case, for it is quite possible for most serious accidents to happen to great numbers, even with all the requisites for a perfect ventilation, by the carelessness and folly of a single individual. Innumerable instances where this has occurred have been related to me, by leaving air-doors open, by not taking the precaution to ascertain whether fire-damp had collected in the place of work, by walking into fire-damp without a safety-lamp, by taking off the top of the safety-lamp for the purpose of trimming the wick whilst surrounded by fire-damp, which would explode, and being perfectly aware of the effect of so doing; by working with a candle in fire-damp, because the safety-lamp gave a dull light; and, in fact, by every means which ignorance, recklessness, and folly combined, could accomplish (Ibid. §§ 163, 164: p. 171).

573. " The next class of accidents in mines are those which occur from the falling in of the roof. The frequency of them will be observed by a glance at Table (B) in the Appendix. Twenty-two cases of this kind have occurred at Worsley within two years, five cases of which were fatal (Ibid. § 174: p. 172).

574. " The accidents which the drawers are most liable to are those which happen from the waggons running them down in the pit, from the breaking of the chain of the ' gig-brow,' from being caught between the roof of the mine and the coals whilst riding on the waggons in the bottom, from being caught between waggons coming in opposite directions (limbs are frequently fractured from this cause). The drawers of course fall in for their share of those accidents already mentioned; those last may be said to be those to which they are peculiarly liable; these last cases, as well as those previously mentioned, are all more or less the result of carelessness and inattention.

575. " In all the instances which I have met with of accidents occurring in coal-mines, negligence forms an almost invariable element—negligence which is fairly assignable to one or other of the parties concerned in this branch of industry: either negligence on the part of the colliers, whether adults or Children, in neglecting those means of safety which are within their own control; or negligence on

the part of the superintendent, or ultimately of the owners of the mines, in not providing the *means,* or duly regulating those means, of safety which are not within the discretion of any Child or the control of the individual workmen (Ibid. §§ 182, 183 : App. Pt. II., p. 173).

576. " It will, however, be seen that there is a large class of accidents which comes within the control of responsible agents, and which would scarcely be within the control of the colliers, even if they had the discretion. For example; the sufficiency of the winding-ropes, guiders and side-rods, chairs, sliders, casing of the pit sides with brick and mortar, covers over the tubs to prevent coal falling on those ascending and descending in them, and the various other means of security in superior pit-gearing, which, having been adopted in some mines with success, are demonstrably practicable, and no doubt ought to be used in all other similar cases " (Ibid. § 187 : App. Pt. II., p. 173).

577. In addition to all these causes of fatal accidents Mr. Kennedy notices another, which has been already shown to be common in the Derbyshire district, namely, the employment of Young Children as engineers to manage the steam-engines by which the work-people ascend and descend the shafts. " I regret to state," he says, " that in some parts of this district very young and inexperienced boys are employed as engineers. I have myself seen several cases where boys of eleven, twelve, and thirteen years of age have been set to manage the engine throughout this district ; and although they seemed to be tolerably competent to the work, I cannot but think that as this is a post of the greatest responsibility it should only be intrusted to persons of mature age and judgment" (Ibid. §§ 159, 162 : p. 171).

578. O _DHAM.—The evidence collected by Mr. Fletcher, in addition to that quoted in describing the nature of the employment, also places this subject in a striking point of view.

James Warrener, a miner 69 years of age, says: "The worst thing that has ever been brought about against the colliers, is in the masters employing little bits of lads as engineers. The best thing you can do is to look after these engineers, to see that they have men of age and reason to know the value of a man's life. Let any one look and see a child left in care of a man's life, and more the pity. The man who left you just now is a worthy man, but he is overlooker in a colliery, and dare not mention this subject to you. Do you not think that a bad lad, who thought he could thereby play him a day, would not let a misfortune come ?—Really believes it; and therefore, until a man has come to maturity of age, and to know the price of a man's life, he is not to be trusted with the management of an engine. The most encroachment that ever came on collier men in his time has been for Children to manage engines. Is one of the oldest colliers in Oldham, has children and grand-children in the pit, and would like to know them in safety. And if this can be put a stop to, may the Lord send it! Anything (of a boy) that they could teach, and get for the least wages, they would employ, without valuing men's lives. If any man of wisdom and knowledge will go to the pits around, and see the children in charge of the engine, let him see if they are fit to have the care of men's lives. And the children who are taken into the pits are taken at an age when they can know nothing of the danger they go into; and if anything is to be stopped, this ought to be. Is positive that ignorant and bad lads have in this district produced many misfortunes. The steward dare not speak the truth, but himself is not muzzled. The engineers sometimes got killed themselves, from being too little. It is a general complaint among the working colliers that children so young are employed as engineers. They grumble both going in and coming out; but if the men complained they would be turned out of employment, and might work no more. Was once let down himself by a lad whom he had beaten the night before for his carelessness; and he let the tub in which he was go down at such a rate that the wheels were broken, and he saved himself only by running up as much of the loose rope with his hands as he could. No youth ought to have such a charge until he were twenty or twenty-one. But if the masters can get such a duty discharged by a boy to whom they give 5s. or 7s. a-week, it is so much gained to them upon the wages of a man, whom they ought to employ. There are children as engineers who are not thirteen" (J. Fletcher, Esq., Evidence, No. 8 : App. Pt. II., p. 847, l. 39).—John Gordon and Edmund Stanley, miners : " Think that such young boys should not be intrusted, as engineers, with the lives of a lot of men as they are; they are not 'stayable,' and no one under eighteen ought to be intrusted with such a job. This is a general opinion among the men themselves" (Ibid. No. 16 : p. 851, l. 37).

Joseph Byrom, book-keeper to Messrs. Stanley and Schofield, Broadway-lane Colliery: " The engine employed at these works is high-pressure, and managed by an adult; he is upwards of thirty : it is not because the engine is high-pressure that an adult is employed, but because of the danger, in employing young people, that they may wind over the coals and the men. This applies equally to low-pressure as to high-pressure engines. A person under sixteen or eighteen years of age ought not to be at such an occupation at all; judges from his own feelings. The men themselves think little about this or any subject until an accident happens. But they will sometimes turn out against an engineer or banksman who they think does not do his duty. The engineer has 18s. a-week, and his predecessor had 24s.; and these wages are paid entirely for safety, in preference to employing children and young persons, as is the case with other employers. These, if they are to save the cost of safety in wages, ought, at all events, before they employ such very young engineers, to be required to provide some mechanical means of saving from destruction such persons as may be overwound in consequence" (Ibid. No. 34: p. 855, l. 48).

The evidence of Mr. Wild, chief constable of Oldham, is of peculiar importance, on account of his great opportunities of obtaining information, it being his duty to collect evidence for the coroner's inquests. "The neighbourhood of Oldham," he says, "is the most painful to the coroner of this part of the country. There have been a deal of accidents to children and young persons as well as to men, in the mines here, during the last five or six years. But there is a class of accidents of which children employed at coal-works in this neighbourhood are the cause to persons of all ages. These occur in the winding up by the steam-machinery of all persons out of the pit. It is a general system here to employ mere children to tend these engines, and to stop them at the proper moment; and if they be not stopped, the two or three or four or five persons wound up together are thrown over the beam down into the pit again. The inducement to employ these children in circumstances where life and death depend on their momentary attention, is merely that their services can be obtained for perhaps 5*s.* or 7*s.* a-week, instead of the 30*s.* a-week which the proprietors would perhaps have to pay to a man of full years and discretion. There have been people wound over at Oldham Edge, at Werneth, at Chamber-lane, at Robin Hill, at Oldbottom, and on Union Ground here, within the last six or seven years to his recollection. Does not know a case in which children were not the engineers; and though he cannot speak to all of them being such, it was generally the case in these instances. The coroner's juries having to give verdicts in cases where such young people were concerned, and in which to attribute gross neglect would be subjecting them to a charge of manslaughter, have always leaned to the side of extenuation, but have expressed their dissatisfaction with the masters employing children in such a service, and for so indefensible a reason; and on one occasion he was desired by the coroner and jury to go to the master and tell him so. Three or four boys were killed in this way at the Chamber-lane Colliery of Messrs. Jones, two or three years since, by the momentary neglect of a little boy, whom he thinks was only nine years of age, and who he heard, after the worst was over, had turned away from the engine when it was winding up, on his attention being attracted by a mouse on the hearth. In this case a deodand of 100*l.* was levied on the engine, and returned by the coroner to the Court of Exchequer, but it was never recovered from the parties" (Ibid. No. 39: p. 856, l. 31).

579. Mr. Fletcher likewise gives an abstract of a register of all the accidents requiring surgical assistance, occurring in the pits of the largest colliery company at Oldham, during one year: in the course of which there happened to adults 27, of which 2 were fatal; to Young Persons 17, of which 1 was fatal; and to Children 8: making a total of 52. "These accidents have occurred in the pits which, according to the testimony of the colliers themselves, are worked in the most liberal manner known in the district. They consist almost wholly of cuts and contusions received in the rough labour along the roadways, either by portions of the roof falling without warning; by collision with the top, sides, waggons, and rails; or by casualties in the jigbrows and inclines, where the violent exertion and often hazardous position of the waggoners seem to demand some further application of mechanical ingenuity to facilitate the descent" (J. Fletcher, Esq., Report, § 54: App. Pt. II., p. 831).

The evidence of the Chief Constable as to the light in which these casualties are regarded by the colliers themselves is not without its instruction. "It is certainly observable in the case of colliers, that there is a great amount of rude callousness on the subject of accidents among them and their families; they are quite an uneducated set of people, who go to cock-pits, and races, and fights; and many are gamblers and drinkers. In a day or two's time, among such people, even their wives and children seem to have forgotten it. They will say at the time, 'Oh, I am not a bit surprised; I expected it—I expected it;' and it soon passes by. There are so many killed, that it becomes quite customary to expect such things. The chiefest talk is just at the moment, until the body gets home, and then there is no more talk about it. People generally feel, 'Oh, it's only a collier!' There would be more feeling a hundred times if a policeman were to kill a dog in the street. In different neighbourhoods here there would be more bother and talk, is sure there would, about killing a dog than killing a collier. The colliers even amongst themselves say so; so that they learn *which* it is that is killed, that is all they think about it" (J. Fletcher, Esq., Evidence, No. 34: App. Pt. II., p. 857, l. 22).

580. The example of the Chamber and Werneth Company at Oldham, in whose pits there is very little fire-damp, but who not only have lamps for use whenever suspicious appearances present themselves, but distribute to all their men a printed description of the principles of their construction, and of their proper use, is well worthy of imitation (Ibid. No. 4: p. 842, l. 52; and p. 844, l. 15). Their provision of gratuitous medical assistance, their placarded pit regulations, and the description by their agent of the underground government of their pits, are likewise worthy of notice (Ibid. p. 843, l. 12; p. 844, l. 1; and p. 845, l. 5).

581. NORTH LANCASHIRE.—The accidents are few in this district; there is only one mine where fire-damp has been dangerous.

Mr. Bradley, surgeon, states that there has been only one accident from fire-damp within the last 12 months : the man was not killed. Previous to that time there were several accidents, but only one man has been killed ; this was at Dunken Halgh. [From this mine I have no return.] Improvements have been made since ; and it is the fault of the men if they get hurt. The masters here, both printers and colliers, are humane men. Mr. Bradley stated that the man who was hurt, not killed, was amusing himself with lighting the gas as it issued from the fissures by a candle : the quantity must, therefore, generally have been very small. In all the mines I have seen or had any account of the men work by candles, and no necessity exists for the use of the Davy lamp (A. Austin, Esq., Report, § 13, 14 : App. Pt. II., p. 803).

582. CUMBERLAND.—This district has been the scene of numerous and appalling accidents, attended with a fatal result to great numbers of persons. "The accident which occurred in Mr. Curwen's pits near Workington, about two years ago, from an irruption of the sea, was foretold by many. It appears that the seam of coal rose under the sea, so that in working it every step brought the colliers nearer to the water. The salt water is said to have oozed through, and some of the men had heard, or said they heard, the sound of the sea above them. So great was the apprehension, that some of the colliers left their work, and others were only induced to stay by a higher amount of wages. At length the water rushed suddenly in, and though some who were near enough to the entrance escaped, about 40 fell victims, and remain to this hour in the pit. The sea, of course, rapidly filled it, and a black gurgling whirlpool for some time marked the aperture and the entrance of the waters at a considerable distance from the shore. The rush of air expelled by the water was so violent that it blew the hats off of those who stood near" (J. C. Symons, Esq., Report, § 14 : App. Pt. I., p. 300).

Mr. Alvan Penrice, colliery-agent for Henry Curwen, Esq., states : "The sea broke into three of Mr. Curwen's pits, which were under the sea, on the 28th of July, 1837, three years before I had the management ; Ralph Coxton was the manager. They were working the pit out to sea and towards the rise. They were nearly two miles under the sea from the shaft. They were continually getting nearer to the water as the workings were getting further to the rise. It was a report among the men that there was some danger prior to the accident. There is no doubt that the pit was making salt water long before. Had I had the management of the colliery I should certainly not have worked the colliery to anything like the same extent. Some got out. It happened in the night. None were left to tell how it happened, because where it broke in none escaped. The whole of the water had to pass through two drifts about 6 feet square. The bodies were never recovered. The funeral service was read over the pit-top. The place where the water broke in was discernible in the sea by the blackness of the place. It appeared that the hole was about 80 yards by 30. The colliery had been worked for 50 years, and there must have been a large space excavated ; and it was all filled with water in two hours and a half" (J. C. Symons, Esq., Evidence, No. 317 : App. Pt. I., p. 307, l. 45).

583. From the evidence of the Rev. Henry Curwen, son of the proprietor of the Workington Colliery, it appears that higher wages were given to the men to induce them to incur the hazard of working in pits where danger was apprehended. He says—

"There was a report some time before the accident that a sand-feed was apprehended, but I am satisfied that no warning reached Mr. Curwen as to the liability of an irruption of the sea. I never heard of any notice being written or painted up of there being danger in proceeding with the works, and I have been often in the colliery, and must have seen it if it had been there. After the accident had occurred, but not till then, I heard that men had been paid higher wages for working in the pit. The report I heard was that the pit would be lost if we continued working it for three weeks, owing to a sand-feed ; and I spoke to my mother, as to whether my brother should be informed of it ; but it was a mere rumour. Mr. Curwen wishes also to state that Coxton, the steward at the time of the accident, was engaged by him at Mr. Dunn's recommendation, of Newcastle, as a man perfectly capable to take the charge of the colliery, and Mr. Curwen placed implicit confidence in him in consequence" (Ibid. No. 332 : p. 310, l. 44).

584. From the evidence of Mr. William Thornton, underground-steward at the William Pit, it appears that Coxton, the steward, had been distinctly warned of the danger, but instead of listening to the warning he discharged the overman who gave him the caution.

"My uncle, William Thornton, was an overman at the Workington Colliery, and he warned Coxton, the steward, of the probability of the sea breaking in, and was discharged in consequence. I heard before myself that there was danger. We keep 70 fathoms above us, nearly all of sandstone ; 60 fathoms would be safe, but it would of course depend on the nature of the soil" (Ibid. No. 331 : p. 310, l. 30).

585. Another very fatal accident occurred at the John Pit, Harrington, belonging to Mr. Curwen, of which the following is the account given by Thomas Martin, Esq., Sub-Commissioner: "It was in this pit that the calamity of 1838 occurred. On that melancholy event the foreman went down first, but 38 of those whose lives were lost had gone down, and were waiting together till his examination should be announced, when the explosion of fire-damp from his light drove them in an instant into corners of the space about them, jamming them into each other in a mass—instantaneous death. Two men and a boy were at the time in the act of descending, near the pit's mouth; all were driven up into the air, but the boy and one of the men, falling outside, escaped; the other fell into the pit, making, with the foreman, the 40 who perished. Since that memorable day, the foreman and deputy go down by themselves and examine before the workmen come; and 'not so much as a bone,' said Clayburn, 'has been broken since' " (T. Martin, Esq., Evidence, No. 22, App. Pt. I., p. 879: 1. 45).

586. In the year 1839 a similar catastrophe occurred in the William Pit, belonging to Lord Lonsdale, as had occurred in the preceding year in the John Pit, belonging to Mr. Curwen. Of the accident in the William Pit the following account is given by the Sub-Commissioner:—

587. " On the 18th of February, 1839, nine men and twelve boys, who were at work in different parts of the pit, were suffocated (not burnt) by means of an explosion of fire-damp. On the Saturday before, there was no appearance of damp; and the ' waster,' as the person is called whose business it was to examine, had on the Monday morning found all places safe till he came to the last, by which time the people had gone to their work; but going into the last with a boy, who, besides his safety-lamp, had an open candle in his hand, the damp, which had been accumulating since the Saturday, exploded at once. These two were much scorched, but escaped with their lives. The others that were in the pit perished, with the exception of one man, who was recovered. Since last January one man has been killed in this pit, and two or three are not unfrequently killed in it in the course of a year; ' but sometimes we are without losing one.' The more usual cause is the falling of a stone from the roof. Great caution had been observed before, and every possible care appears to be taken now " (Ibid. p. 876, l. 27).

588. In this case not only was the same absurdity repeated of letting the men down into the pit before the " waster" had completed his survey, as produced the catastrophe of the John Pit—the lesson afforded by the latter being wholly disregarded—but there was the further absurdity of the boy carrying a Davy-lamp in the one hand for the sake of safety, and a naked lighted candle in the other, as if for the sake of danger. Beyond this there can be no conceivable thoughtlessness and folly; and when such management is allowed in the mines of two of the most opulent coal-proprietors in the kingdom, we cease to wonder at anything that may take place in mines worked by men equally without capital and science.

589. South Durham.—In considering the gross number of accidents in this district it is necessary to bear in mind that South Durham is now become an important coal district, exporting from two millions to two millions and a half tons of coals, and employing in the collieries both below and above ground, according to the estimate of the Sub-Commissioner, from twelve thousand to fifteen thousand people.

590. In this district the accidents from descending and ascending the shafts, and from falling into pits, are not nearly so numerous as in Staffordshire and Shropshire, notwithstanding the greater number of persons exposed, which is to be attributed to the greater care taken to prevent the heedless approach of strangers, to close up old pits, daily to inspect the tackling, and to regulate the number of the workpeople that descend and ascend at a time. There are likewise fewer killed in this district than in Staffordshire by stones and coals falling from the roof of the mines, which arises from the shallowness of the beds, compared to the ten-yard bed of Staffordshire.

591. On the other hand, the accidents from the explosion of carbureted hydrogen gas are far more frequent and fatal in the northern than in the southern coal-fields. Great care is taken in the northern coal-field to guard against this most destructive agent. The first and most essential expedient is to place an enormous furnace, which is kept burning night and day, at the foot of the up-cast shaft, by which a powerful current of air is made to ascend this shaft, and consequently a corresponding current to descend the down-cast shaft; and carefully to guide this current of air between the

pillars throughout the pit, in order that it may bring with it, and carry up the shaft to the surface, any explosive gas which may have accumulated. The men, when working at cutting out the pillars, and in other places which are supposed to be dangerous, are provided with Davy lamps. The overman goes down every morning, and inspects every part of the workings before the men are allowed to proceed to their work. There are persons called " wastemen," whose duty it is constantly to travel round the " waste," to see that the roof has not fallen in to impede the current of air; and lastly, in the workings there are doors by which, when closed, the air is directed in its proper course, and which, therefore, are only opened when it is necessary to pass through them. Yet, with all these precautions, explosions do take place, and more than one hundred people have been killed at a time. And that such accidents do not take place far more often must be a matter of astonishment to whoever considers that all the expedients devised to secure the safety of the mine, at whatever expense adopted, and with whatever vigilance maintained, may be counteracted by allowing one single trap-door to remain open ; and yet that in all the coal-mines, in all the districts of the United Kingdom, the care of these trap-doors is intrusted to Children of from five to seven or eight years of age, who for the most part sit, excepting at the moments when persons pass through these doors, for twelve hours consecutively in solitude, silence, and darkness.

592. The Sub-Commissioner reports that in all the well-regulated collieries of this district rules are laid down for the purpose of preventing accidents among the workpeople. He says—" In most of the returns which have been obtained from the collieries it is stated, that the utmost vigilance is bestowed to make sure that the machinery and ropes by which persons are let down and are drawn up the shafts of the coal-pits, are in good condition ; and in many of the collieries it is alleged that there is a careful daily inspection by officers whose regular special duty it is. Certainly the inspection ought to be daily, or there is no security that it shall take place when it ought to do so, and accidents might occur from the neglect.

593. " Several of the collieries lay down rules as to the numbers going down and coming up at a time, but it is difficult to ascertain whether these rules are observed or not. Some leave it entirely to the discretion of a banksman at the top of the shaft, and to an onsetter at the bottom. A fixed number should be determined, and no such duty should be left to the discretion of men who will be pressed on all sides to neglect it.

594. " Accidents by falling down the shafts are far less likely to take place in Durham than in the southern districts. The coals are brought up to a platform many feet higher than the level of the surrounding country. No person coming across the coal-field can come near the shaft, unless purposely and intentionally. The shaft is enclosed on three sides, that only being approachable at which they receive the tubs or corves, and there the men are at work. The wooden enclosures of the shafts and the ropes are right before the eye ; trams, tubs are in the way, and no man can approach without abundant warning of his danger. But in the southern coal-fields there is nothing to warn a person of danger. The mouth of the pit is on the same level with the rest of the ground, and the rope or chain presents so small an object to his view, that the straggler may stumble over before he is aware.

595. " The pulleys from which ropes are suspended are far above head, and the tubs and corves swing forwards, and the men are exposed to little danger, though accidents do sometimes happen.

596. " The enclosure of the shafts renders it very unlikely that any coals, or stones, or wood, shall be thrown down the shaft.

597. " The ashlar work employed in building the shafts is more secure than bricks.

598. " In some pits the ropes are of an enormous size. In the South Hetton pit, which is one hundred and eighty fathoms deep, the rope is two hundred and twenty fathoms long, and the weight is about two tons ; the value is about one hundred pounds. Two cages come up at a time, each containing a tub, of which some contain twenty and others thirty pecks, being six or nine hundredweight, and the weight of cage, tubs, and coal may be thirty-five hundredweight.

599. " The rule in respect to the number of people coming up is, that their united weight shall be much less than the usual weight of coals drawn up by the rope.

600. " Some of the cages are entirely open at the top, so that there is nothing whatever to protect the persons descending or ascending from injury from anything which may fall down the shaft upon them. No doubt, from the shafts being lined with stone or iron tubbing, seldom will anything fall out of the wall, but this is no

security from anything falling in from the bank.   The return from one pit states, that a man on the bank takes care that nothing falls into the shaft at such times, but there is not always a man on the watch, and the man whose duty it is to watch cannot be supposed always to be watchful.

601. " Mr. Croudace, agent of the Shincliffe Colliery, says, in answer to a query : ' It is our intention to have an iron canopy placed over the heads of the men attached to the cage by which they descend.'   All the collieries should have such canopy" (Dr. Mitchell, Report, § 175—187 : App. Pt. I., pp. 137, 138).

602. From returns which have been received from nineteen collieries in this district of the fatal accidents thât have occurred within the last two years, it appears that there have been forty-six deaths, that there have been in addition great numbers of minor accidents, and that the trappers, the drivers, and the putters are extremely liable to laceration and fracture of the fingers and limbs. (Ibid. pp. 138—140.)

603. NORTH DURHAM AND NORTHUMBERLAND.—In this district the Sub-Commissioner experienced unusual difficulty in obtaining an approximation to the true number of the accidents.   In general the medical men connected with the collieries either directly refused to give any evidence on the subject, or evaded inquiry : while, at the collieries, the persons whose office and employment rendered them best acquainted with the facts were equally reluctant to afford information.

604. The Sub-Commissioner reports :—" In visiting the majority of the medical gentlemen practising in, or connected with, collieries, I was much disappointed in finding that, with one partial exception, no records of their practice had been preserved ; an omission which, in a district so prolific in every variety of casualty, from a sprain or a burn to a fracture or death, must assuredly appear an unaccountable defect, and the more so as no formidable obstacle exists to furnish a plea for the absence of such records.   Hence the sum of the information that could be obtained from these gentlemen consisted of mere generalisations.

605. " To No. 496, however, I would especially refer as an exception, and as affording medical evidence, which—as the witness has the charge of one of the largest collieries in the whole number, and as they are generally similar in their main features—may be assumed as a fair sample of the opinions of the more enlightened colliery surgeons.

606. " As I could meet with no medical gentleman who had descended the pits and inspected the boys at their labour, I could scarcely expect to collect opinions from them as to its peculiarities, or to trace by their aid minor effects to minor causes.   Nor did they in all cases appear to consider themselves as free to deliver their opinions on special points to an official inquirer, about to make the results of his investigations public, even though all reference to names and localities were suppressed.   For this unwillingness, adequate, and indeed obvious, reasons might be assigned ; and it may be observed that the exceptions (No. 496*, *sub fin.*, and No. 499) are those of gentlemen unconnected with collieries.   All, then, that repeated visits and inquiries (repeated eight times in the case of one surgeon, whose position must have enabled him to state much, but who finally escaped without stating anything) could elicit has been exhibited" (J. R. Leifchild, Esq., Report, § 230, 231 : App. Pt. I., p. 546).

607. From printed documents and private inquiries the Sub-Commissioner has however brought to light a great number of fatal accidents, which have occurred in the collieries of the Tyne and Wear during a long series of years, and which he has arranged in Tables at pp. 547—553 of his Report.   These can be regarded only as examples of the kind of accidents that take place every day ; and nothing can be inferred from those Tables as to the aggregate number of such accidents.   It may be worth while however to state, that, in twenty-six collieries situated north of the River Wear, there occurred during the last two years seventy-four deaths from accidents ; that in sixteen collieries situated south of the River Wear, from the 15th of August, 1839, to March 1841, there occurred sixteen deaths from accidents ; and that no less than forty persons were killed at collieries which the Sub-Commissioner himself visited during the time that he was pursuing his local investigations.   Accidents terminating short of death are seldom or never heard of beyond the place of their occurrence (Ibid. § 233—236 : App. Pt. I., pp. 549, 550).

608. The Sub-Commissioner has incidentally supplied us with remarkable evidence of the fact that very few of the fatal accidents which take place in collieries

come to the knowledge of the public; and that there is not only no public record of them, but that not the slightest notice is taken of them even by the local press. He says:—

609. "The only public notices of the northern colliery accidents in existence are, I believe, contained in a local tract entitled Syke's ' Local Records,' and in the cotemporaneous public newspapers. Both these sources have been carefully waded through, with the kind assistance of James Mather, Esq., of South Shields, from which, and from my personal inquiries of the viewers of the various pits, I am enabled to present, certainly, the completest list of lives lost, during the period in question, that has ever yet appeared in print" (Ibid. § 232: App. Pt. I., p. 547).

610. Then follows a list extending from the year 1799 to 1840, inclusive, comprehending an enumeration of explosions, inundations, suffocation by choke-damp, after-damp, breaking of chains, bursting of boilers, falls, falling of earth, falling of stone from the roof, unhooking of corves, timber falling down the shaft, drowning from old workings, falling down the shaft, and breaking of shaft ropes.

611. From this account it appears that in the year 1838 the deaths by the sevarious casualties were thirteen in number, being two by the fall of stone in Stewart Pit, and eleven by explosion in Wall's End Pit. Such is the statement made as to the deaths by accident in this district during the year in question, after the most careful search for information in the " local records, and in the contemporaneous public newspapers, together with personal inquiries on the spot of the viewers of the various pits." Now the return from the Registrar-General, already quoted, has shown that the deaths which certainly took place about the coal-pits in this district in the year 1838 were seventy-three in number; thus, according to the information to be obtained from the local press, aided by the statements of the coal-viewers of the different pits, who can hardly be supposed to be really ignorant of the facts, the total number of persons killed is only thirteen. By an authentic record it is proved to be at least seventy-three; and it is quite possible that many more are really due to this list, but the entries of which by the local registrars are not sufficiently explicit to enable us to ascertain them with absolute certainty.

612. Of the indifference of the colliery people themselves to these fatal accidents the Sub-Commissioner gives the following remarkable examples:—" Perhaps a collateral proof of the correctness of these suppositions is the slight sensation which casualties seemed to occasion on the spot at the very period of their occurrence. I mention this not as a sign of remissness in precautionary measures, but of the frequency of the occurrences. I was at two collieries on the precise days when, at one a boy was killed in the pit by a fall of stone from the roof, and at the other an inquest was being held on the body of a man who had perished the previous day from the same cause. At neither colliery did I hear of these deaths except by the merest chance in casual conversation, though detained several hours at each. At another pit, I should probably not have heard of the death of five men, very recently, from their falling down the shaft, had I not, from previous information, been led to make distinct inquiries upon the subject (Ibid. § 243, p. 553).

613. EAST OF SCOTLAND.—The Sub-Commissioner complains of the want of all record of accidents in this country, and of the almost total neglect with which this subject has hitherto been regarded: " In the absence of all satisfactory returns on this head," he says, " we have the authority of a medical gentleman well acquainted with the colliery districts, that a week seldom passes without some serious accident occurring in one or more of the collieries, and several persons are killed or die in consequence of accidents every year. These accidents arise from the falling in of the roof, the sudden and unexpected fall of coal before the collier has time to draw back, the rending of ropes, &c.; and this is fearfully confirmed by the witnesses whose evidence I have collected, and who bear testimony to a vast number of individual cases of this sort, but which, of course, are not sufficient to enable us to form any general estimate on the subject. In Scotland there are no coroners to inquire into sudden and violent deaths; and serious accidents of an appalling nature frequently occur, and no notice whatever appears to be taken of them" (R. H. Franks, Esq., Report, § 42, 43: App. Pt. I., p. 393).

614. Of the nature of the fatal accidents that are constantly taking place in this district, and of the manner in which they are regarded by the people, the following statements are given as examples:—

Robert Robinson: " My two sisters were sair horrible crushed by stones falling from the roof; their bowels were forced out, and legs broken' R. H. Franks, Esq., Evidence, No. 144: App. Pt. I.,

p. 463, l. 37).—Mr. Thomas Bishop, overseer to Sir William Baillie's mines at Polkemmet: " Two boys were injured by a stone falling from the roof: one had his leg shattered, and suffered its loss; the other the leg broken, from which he is fast recovering." The same witness adds, " We have no record of accidents; nor is it customary to keep such, not even of accidental and sudden deaths " (Ibid. No. 202 : p. 474, l. 19).—Mary Sneddon : " Brother Robert was killed on the 21st January last : a piece of the roof fell upon his head, and he died instantly. He was brought home, coffined, and buried in Bo'ness kirkyard. No one came to inquire how he was killed : they never do in this place" (Ibid. No. 219 : p. 476, l. 62).—Thomas Walker : " Many accidents here. My father has just had his collar-bone broken ; and the son of William Guy, who was killed nine months gone, got his leg broken by roof falling" (Ibid. No. 228 : p. 478, l. 59).—The evidence of Mr. Marshall, oversman to the Hirse or Netherwood Colliery, states, " Six weeks back a boy [Robert Russell], thirteen years of age, met his death by a hutchie passing over his body and crushing him; he never spoke after; and another [William Blair], twelve years of age, was crushed to death by a falling stone from the roof. Two men were killed within the last two years by the roofs falling. It is not the custom to notice those accidents ; we neither give notice, nor do the friends of the parties. The practice is to bury them a day or two after their decease" (Ibid. No. 278 : p. 487, l. 14).— Robert Jameson, oversman to the Stronne Colliery, says, " Two men were killed [Stirling and King] a short time since by explosion. Stirling had a Davy in his pocket, but descended with his oil lamp lighted, when explosion momentary took place. A short time since four men were drowned by accidentally pricking into an old working. No notice of accidental deaths. They [the deceased] are set home to their friends, and afterwards buried" (Ibid. No. 281 : p. 487, l. 51).—Mr. James Hunter, mining overseer to the Alloa Colliery, Clackmannanshire, states, " That four accidents of a fatal nature have taken place at this colliery, and that when such occur the sheriff sometimes comes down. He did in the last case, after the death of John Patteson, which was occasioned by being overwound at the pit-head. After looking at the ropes, and examining their strength, he walked away, and no further notice was taken. This is the common practice" (Ibid. No. 292 ; p. 490, ll. 9, 15).—A still stronger case occurs in the evidence of Jane Patterson, employed in the Woodlands and Devonside Colliery : " We have [says the witness, a girl of seventeen] no father or mother alive; mother died of consumption, and father was brought home dead a few years since; he was supposed to have been murdered, but no one sought after those who killed him" (Ibid. No. 319 ; p. 494, l. 3).— And Dr. Alison remarks, in reference to this subject : " I am pretty sure about 50 people under my care, and connected with collieries, have lost their lives in consequence of accidents occurring in the works around Tranent; and I do not remember of an investigation having been made by the sheriff in more than one instance" (Report, § 53 : App. Pt. I., p. 394).

615. " With reference to minor accidents, the record of such is scattered over the evidence of nearly all the witnesses ; and from the nature of the labour in which the working-people are employed, it is not to be wondered at that such frequently take place; in truth, it would seem to be almost inseparable from the severe character of the occupation itself; nor is it surprising that no record is kept of this very numerous class ; but where life is lost—where a human being has been suddenly or violently taken off from amongst his fellow-creatures—I certainly was not prepared for the general apathy and indifference which prevails in these districts" (Ibid. § 54 : App. Pt. I., p. 394). See also the evidence of the witnesses, Nos. 23, 26, 51, 65, 102, 106, 113, 144, 153, 219, 261, 279, 329, 373, 419.

616. WEST OF SCOTLAND.—On the part of the medical men of this district, the Sub-Commissioner found the same reluctance to give evidence as has been experienced in some of the English districts. The surgeons alleged that they kept no registers of their patients, and that, even if they had done so, such registers would have contained an account of the wounded only, and would not have comprised the accidents which prove fatal at once, and which, therefore, do not come under surgical care. The Sub-Commissioner reports :—" In every instance where I had an opportunity of seeing surgeons connected with collieries, I made a point of asking for any statistics with which they could furnish me as to the frequency and the nature of the accidents which had occurred in their experience. I was, however, never fortunate enough to obtain any such particulars ; and the want of such suggested to me the propriety of a regulation obliging every public work to make periodical returns of the number and nature of the accidents happening to any of the workers, the result of each case, and the length of time they were kept off their work in consequence.

617. " From the recollections of surgeons, workpeople, and managers, I gathered that serious accidents, even fatal ones, are by no means rare, and lesser ones of constant occurrence, in coal and iron pits. The falling of pieces of the roof, or of masses of coal, are the most frequent sources of accident to the colliers. The drawers often receive hurts from being jammed between whirleys : for instance,

where there is an inclined plane down which loaded whirleys have to travel, unless attention is paid to stopping the wheels properly, the whirley overpowers the children in charge of it, and probably commits some damage before it is stopped. At the pit-bottom, where a crowd of whirleys are always arriving and departing, it must be difficult to escape an occasional disaster. Men are sometimes killed by the fall of pieces of coal upon them from the baskets which are being raised up the shaft, though in general a space is excavated on purpose beneath the roof at the pit-bottom, so that no person need stand in the way of pieces falling as described. The most serious accidents, however, where they occur, are of course the explosions of carbureted hydrogen. I have before remarked that it is never customary in the West of Scotland to work with the Davy-lamp, though in case of suspicion of danger a foreman is sent in the first thing of a morning to explore with one. The only security, however, against this fearful enemy is efficient ventilation.

618. " The state of the law in Scotland with regard to deaths and injuries from accidents seems to me anything but satisfactory. The Procurator-Fiscal, a criminal law-officer, is the only functionary who has authority to investigate cases of sudden death ; and these come under his cognizance, not from the fact of the death having been sudden or violent, but only if there be reasonable suspicion that grounds for a prosecution for manslaughter or murder exist in connection with the case. Hence negligence in respect to dangerous machinery is not subject to that check which the invariable custom of a coroner's inquest in all cases of death by accident imposes upon it in England." (T. Tancred, Esq., Report, § 73—76 : App. Pt. I., pp. 330, 331).

619. From evidence already cited, it is clear that the Sub-Commissioner is in error in supposing that it is the invariable custom in England for the coroner to inquire into the causes of the deaths which occur by accidents in the mining districts.

620. NORTH WALES.—The Sub-Commissioner for this district reports :—" In examining the works, I made it my business to inspect the head-gear and the means of descent into the pits and mines. As may be expected, some works were not so well provided as others ; but the ropes, chains, and other tackle, appeared to me in sufficient order, though I could not help thinking that due precautions against accidents are not always taken, especially in ascending and descending. Both adults and boys seem thoroughly careless and incautious ; and masters and their agents little less so. Rules may be made in each work forbidding more than a certain number of persons to go down or up at the same time, but these rules are not enforced. A proper person ought to be stationed at the mouth of every shaft, whose business it should be to see that all is right, and that every means to prevent accidents are put in force. It may be said that this is the business of the banksmen, but *they* are persons in no authority, and therefore it cannot be expected of them to exercise any." (H. H. Jones, Esq., Report, § 52: App. Pt. II., p. 372).

Mr. Richard Wood, general manager of the British Iron Company's Coal and Iron Works, Denbighshire, gave the following evidence: "Accidents sometimes happen, both in the collieries and in the forges; they frequently occur from the negligence of the persons who are hurt, but every care which can be thought of is used by those in charge or authority to guard against accidents. All the head-gear of the pits and all the machinery are the best that can be procured. An accident occurred last January, whereby six young men lost their lives entirely by negligence: they hooked the pyche, in which they were going to descend, to a chain which had just before received a violent concussion that cracked it; but they did not think of examining it. When they were being lowered into the pit the chain gave way, and they were all killed. Another accident occurred in February, by which four men were killed ; they were charter-masters, and it was their business to examine the rope; this they neglected to do, it gave way, and they fell to the bottom; had they examined it, they would have found that the rope was faulty. There is very great carelessnsss on the part of the men ; they are used to danger, and never think of avoiding it by precaution ; and those whose particular duty it is to examine the head-gear, neglect too frequently to do so, even though they are threatened with punishment" (H. H. Jones, Esq., Evidence, No. 1 : App. Pt. II., p. 377, l. 65).

621. This evidence may be regarded as affording a fair example of the view which is commonly taken of this subject by the coal-proprietors and their agents, whose ordinary custom it is to throw upon the workpeople themselves the whole blame of the accidents that befal them. It is not the duty of the young colliers to examine the chains and inspect the tackling previously to their ascent and descent, nor are they qualified for this office; nor would it be possible for the

workpeople themselves to perform this office every time they go down into the pit and come up from it.   Moreover, in the present case it would probably have required a most acute and practised eye to detect the crack in this broken chain. The same remark is applicable to the four charter-masters, of whom it is said, " it was their business to examine the rope; this they neglected to do; it gave way, and they fell to the bottom."   In well-regulated coal-mines it is not expected that those who are about to descend should stop and inspect the rope, but there is one skilful and trustworthy person, whose office it is constantly to examine the whole of the machinery used in descending and ascending, and to see that it is always in order.

622. SOUTH WALES.—In Glamorganshire and Pembrokeshire the persons connected with the coal mines and the iron works were as unwilling to afford information as to the nature and number of accidents as they have been represented to be in other districts.   The Sub-Commissioner reports :—

623. " I was desirous of ascertaining the whole number of accidents that have happened in the different mines and works which I have personally visited; but it is much to be regretted that an apparent unwillingness to communicate exists amongst those who alone are capable of affording the requisite information.   At present, it should seem, no record whatever is kept of accidents, either by the medical gentleman, who is invariably attached to each work, or in any of the books of the particular firm.

624. " In order, however, that I might be enabled to lay before you such materials as should be sufficient to show the importance of this branch of the inquiry, and the very unsatisfactory and inefficient means afforded of estimating its extent, I have collected, and refer you to the Appendix for, the returns of the district coroners of Glamorganshire and Pembrokeshire ; and have subjoined a list of accidents, with which I have been made acquainted by other means, which have occurred in the various works under my investigation ; to which I beg to refer you as Article (A) in the Appendix.

625. " In perusing the general body of evidence, your attention will have been drawn to the evidence numbered 299 and 260, to the effect that there is a general laxity in the administration of justice, particularly with reference to inquests held in cases of fatal accidents ; and the mode of proceeding is thus described :— ' When a man dies the viewer looks at the body and sends to the coroner ; and, unless a case of suspicion is made out to the coroner, he does not come, but sends an order to the constable to bury ; and frequently the coroner does not attend until there are five or six cases to clear off.'   Or thus, by the other witness :— ' When a death (*i. e.* accidental, or out of the ordinary course of nature) occurs a communication is made with the coroner ; he issues his warrant, and, through the constable, appoints a jury ; and the coroner seldom visits us until there are five or six cases to be disposed of' "   (R. H. Franks, Esq., Report, § 86–89 : App. Pt. II., pp. 485, 486).

626. Not much information relative to accidents has been collected in the Monmouthshire part of this district, but what has been obtained would indicate that fatal accidents are comparatively few.   The Sub-Commissioner reports :—

627. " From the information I have been able to obtain on this head, I find fatal accidents, and even those of any serious importance, comparatively few in this neighbourhood.   I have no precise data to estimate the proportion they bear to the number of persons employed, but I think I should fully calculate their amount if I stated the fatal accidents in the works of this district to be 1 in 1000 per annum, and the serious accidents, permanently maiming or crippling the individuals, 1 in 500 per annum.   Slight acidents, such as burns, cuts, and bruises, are numerous, but as they scarcely come under the notice of the surgeon, no accurate estimate of their proportionate number can be formed.

628. " The fatal accidents mostly occur from explosions of fire-damp (often arising from carelessness) and sudden falls of stone in mines and collieries, and from the falling or slipping of some heavy parts of the machinery or materials on the surface, or upon the numerous railways and ' inclined planes '—and it is from the same causes that the men get maimed or crippled" (R. W. Jones, Esq., Report, §§ 18— 20 : App. Pt. II., p. 583).

629. FOREST OF DEAN.—" Fractures, dislocations, and contusions," states Mr. Waring, " are casualties apparently inseparable from mine-work.   Habituated to dangerous positions, both young and old acquire a heedless disregard of danger,

not more striking to an observer than unconsciously to themselves. It is true that precaution could not always avert accidents; but I have no doubt, from my own observation, as well as the testimony of numerous managers and overlookers, that at least three-fourths of the injuries sustained in collieries might be avoided by the exercise of common prudence. Though there is an unlimited supply of pit-timber, cut into proper lengths, for propping or shoring up the heads of coal during the process of under-cutting them, this simple precaution is continually neglected. Perhaps after a recent death, from the sudden fall of the impending mass, the survivors are more cautious; but the impression soon passes away, and you see the collier, stretched at his full length, cutting away between eight or ten tons of coal, without a single prop, at the risk of its sudden separation by what is termed a *back-crack*, when he knows he must inevitably be crushed to death. If any mode of legislating effectually on such details could be devised, it would be a most philanthropic act that should render the uniform employment of props under coal-headings imperative upon both workmen and masters. Inattention to the state of the winding rope or chain, and the other apparatus for ascending and descending the shaft, is inexcusable on the part of the overlooker; and dangerous places in the roof of the pit are usually palpable enough to any eye accustomed to inspect them. Still fatal accidents have occurred from gross negligence in all these respects; though no recent case of a rope or chain breaking, when men or boys were suspended by it, has come to my knowledge" (E. Waring, Esq., Report, §§ 76—79: App. Pt. II., pp. 6, 7).

630. SOUTH GLOUCESTERSHIRE.—Some of the pits in this district are described as much infested with foul air or choke-damp, and others as having wet ways or wet shafts.

631. " At the Easton Coal Works, the proprietors have caused a commodious ' hutch ' to be constructed of riveted iron plates, in the form of an elliptical dome, with two entrances. In this hutch, seven men, and two or three boys, can go up and down together, snugly protected from the jets of water, as well as from any stone or other substance accidentally falling on them.

632. "This humane and proper accommodation furnishes a praiseworthy contrast to the neglect of everything like attention to the health, safety, and comfort of the colliers, which struck me on visiting another miserably wet pit at Cromhall. There I saw the poor fellows coming up in the coal-tubs, at mid-day, to escape suffocation from bad air in the stalls, smeared with clay, and dripping with shaft-water, from which they protected themselves partially by hanging old sacks over their heads and shoulders. On inquiry, I found they had no other provision for their passage to and from their work.

633. " As a protection to the pit's mouth, the sliding traps, or stages, are much adopted, and appear to be the best contrivances for effectually covering the shaft whilst the coal is landed. The top-man, standing on the sliding stage, has merely to lay hold on the loaded tub as it swings over the pit, and by that action draws the stage, which runs on wheels and iron plates, across the pit's mouth; when the tub is lowered upon it, wheeled off, and replaced by an empty one to go down. Any accident from overreaching is thus effectually prevented.

634. " Stout plaited rope, or hempen strap, is the favourite material for winding, and appears to be much safer than chain; iron being liable to snap in frosty weather, and giving no notice of a flaw to the eye, till it becomes imminently dangerous: whereas the rope gives timely notice of weakness, by showing the ragged end of a broken strand or two. All the most experienced colliers I have conversed with on the subject give the preference to flat rope.

635. " The only fatality involving the lives of boys, that has come to my knowledge, from a defect in the winding apparatus, was caused by the loosening of some wedges between the winding wheel and its shaft, whereby the wheel, running free of the shaft, precipitated two men and three boys to the bottom, with a violence that caused their death. Any recurrence of such a calamity is easily obviated, by using properly constructed machinery, in which it is impossible for the wheel to liberate itself from the shaft unless it breaks in two" (E. Waring, Esq., Report, § 37—41: App. Pt. II., p. 34).

636. NORTH SOMERSETSHIRE.—Accidents here are very numerous (Dr. Stewart, Report, § 8: App. Pt. II., p. 47).

13.—Wages of Children and Young Persons in Coal Mines.

637. The earnings of the Young People employed in coal mines, though they can by no means be called great, when the severity and the circumstances of the labour are considered, are nevertheless such as to form a material addition to the resources of the several families of which they form part, and often to procure for them some advantages which are not attainable among other classes of labourers.

South
Staffordshire.

638. South Staffordshire.—In this district " the wages vary in different pits, and the holers make some 3s. some 4s. a-day" (Dr. Mitchell, Evidence, Nos. 10, 11 : App. Pt. I., p. 67, ll. 14, 49). A collier also has a liberal allowance of coals for his family, and in some places a quart of beer, and in other places two quarts of beer a-day. Boys who drive the horses in the gins have 6d. a-day, and boys opening airdoors in the pits have 6d. or 8d. a-day. These boys are paid by the masters. From certain returns it is found that the wages of boys and young men who load the skips at the ages from thirteen to fourteen are about 12s. a-week, up to ages from seventeen to eighteen, when the wages are about 14s. 6d. The wages of pitchers at the ages from eight to nine are 5s. a-week, gradually rising to ages from fourteen to fifteen, when they are from 7s. 6d. to 8s. a-week. The wages of pushers at the ages of from nine to ten are from 4s. to 5s. a-week, gradually rising to ages from seventeen to eighteen, when the wages are about 15s. a-week. The wages of drivers of horses in the pits at the ages of from ten to eleven are about 5s. a-week, gradually rising to ages from seventeen to eighteen, when the wages are about 14s. a-week (Dr. Mitchell, Report, § 148 *et seq.*: App. Pt. I., p. 18).

North
Staffordshire.

639. North Staffordshire.—A boy's wages vary, according to his age and strength, from 4s. to 8s. and 10s. per week, in the pottery district, where they do not commence labour very early ; and in the Cheadle district they are nearly the same, being described as varying from 8d. to 2s. 6d. per day, according to their strength and age, from ten to eighteen (S. S. Scriven, Esq., Evidence, Nos, 1, 2, 3, 7, 8, 9, 16, 17, 18, 19, 22, 25 : App. P. II., pp. 131—9).

Shropshire.

640. Shropshire.—In the Coalbrookdale districts, " boys from six to seven may earn in the pits 6d. a-day. At nine they may earn 10d. to 1s., according to the work. About twelve a boy gets 1s. 6d. to 1s. 8d., and some as much as 2s. a-day" —(*Tranter*, No. 41.) (Dr. Mitchell, Report, § 297 : App. Pt. I., p. 38). Wages generally in Shropshire are not as high as in Staffordshire by a fifth or a sixth part.

Warwickshire.

641. Warwickshire.—The wages are here much the same as in Shropshire (Dr. Mitchell, Evidence, No. 65 : App. Pt. I., p. 106, l. 43.).

Leicestershire.

642. Leicestershire.—In the Ashby-de-la-Zouch district " a very young Child is paid 8d. a-day. By and bye, when the boy is able to walk with the horses, the wages rise to 1s. 5d. and 1s. 8d. About sixteen the young man gets 2s. a-day, and gradually advances until he arrives at 3s." (Dr. Mitchell, Report, § 132 : App. Pt. I., p. 100).

Derbyshire.

643. Derbyshire.—In this district the wages do not materially differ from those paid in Leicestershire (J. M. Fellows, Esq., Evidence, *passim*).

West Riding of
Yorkshire.

644. West Riding of Yorkshire : Southern Part.—In this part of the kingdom " a trapper earns generally 6d. a-day. The hurriers and others, in the thick-coal pits, at eleven years old will earn about 5s. a-week on the average (though I knew one boy of ten who earns 7s. a-week) ; those of fourteen will earn 8s. ; and those of seventeen 12s. These wages are paid *per week*. The wages of the men vary greatly with their industry and strength ; for young able-bodied men the average will be perhaps 20s. a-week, but many make 25s. In the thin-coal pits wages will be from 10 to 20 per cent. less.

645. " In one colliery (see Evidence No. 314) I found the wages of the adults amounted to 30s. a-week, they being at liberty to work as long as they pleased. I took pains to ascertain the effect of these high wages on their comforts and conduct. I found that they were no better off than those in other places who earned from 20s. to 25s. They drink and live more luxuriously for perhaps two days, and are often ill off for the rest of the week" (J. C. Symons, Esq., Report, § 192 et seq. : App. Pt. I., p. 191).

646. BRADFORD AND LEEDS.—In this neighbourhood " the wages of the Children and Young Persons, upon a general average of the whole of the returns received, are as follows :—

COAL MINES.

Wages.

Bradford and Leeds.

Children.	Number of Children.	Total Amount of Wages per Week.			Average per Week.	
		£.	s.	d.	s.	d.
From 5 to 6 years of age	1	0	2	6	2	6
„ 6 to 7 ditto	8	1	0	0	2	6
„ 7 to 8 ditto	30	4	0	6	2	8
„ 8 to 9 ditto	75	11	6	5	3	0
„ 9 to 10 ditto	123	21	6	0	3	5
„ 10 to 11 ditto	161	32	6	6	4	0
„ 11 to 12 ditto	160	36	16	2	4	7
„ 12 to 13 ditto	191	51	2	9	5	4
	749					
Cases for which the return of wages is omitted	9					
Total	758					

Young Persons.	Number.	Total Amount of Wages per Week.			Average per Week.	
		£.	s.	d.	s.	d.
From 13 to 14 years of age	223	71	3	0	6	4
„ 14 to 15 ditto	196	70	9	0	7	2
„ 15 to 16 ditto	196	76	19	0	7	10
„ 16 to 17 ditto	147	63	9	6	8	7
„ 17 to 18 ditto	141	72	5	3	10	3
	903					
Cases for which the return of wages is omitted	6					
Total	909					

647. "The wages are paid sometimes by the master, more commonly by the adults whom the Children assist. They are paid sometimes to the parents or guardians, somtimes to the Children to be handed over to them, less frequently to the Children for their own account. They are paid occasionally by the piece; more generally by weekly wages (W. R. Wood, Esq., Report, § 28 : App. Pt. II., p. H 5, 6).

648. HALIFAX.—Here, as elsewhere, "the wages of hurriers depend upon their age and aptness. In six pits I selected an equal number of the oldest and youngest, with the view of ascertaining the difference between them, and then recorded the several amounts received by the whole number, and found that it averaged 4s. 8½d. per week, which is received by their parents." See also Table of Wages. (S. S. Scriven, Esq., Report, § 64 : App. Pt. II., p. 67).

Halifax.

649. LANCASHIRE AND CHESHIRE.—In this part of the kingdom, " the best Children will get from 3d. to 8d. per day; and the drawers' earnings will range from 4s. to 15s. a-week, according to their age. The wages in the neighbourhoods of Dukenfield, Staley Bridge, and Ashton, are higher than, I think, in any other part of my district. At Poynton, also, the wages are comparatively high. In the neighbourhood of Worsley and Clifton, where the population is more exclusively occupied in mining, and especially in the former, the wages are much lower.

Lancashire and Cheshire.

650. " Benjamin Berry gives the following account of the wages at Worsley :— ' Were you a drawer? Yes; I was one-eighth.—What does one-eighth mean? It is the custom at Worsley to consider a man as divided into eight parts. When first a boy goes to work he is considered to be equal to one-eighth part of a man, and gets 5s. per month :—

> A boy at 10 years is worth two-eighths, and gets 10s. a-month.
> „ 13 „ „ three-eighths, „ 15s. „
> „ 15 „ „ one-half, „ 20s. „
> A girl at 16 „ „ one-half, „ 20s. „
> A boy at 18 „ „ three-fourths, „ 30s. „

At this age a boy begins to get coal. Girls and women never get coal, and always remain drawers, and are considered to be equal to half a man. These are the present wages at Worsley; I can remember when they were twice as much.'

651. "This statement does not coincide with the returns of the wages in this district, which I have every reason to believe are correct, especially those sent in by the trustees of the late Duke of Bridgewater. The statement is correct in other respects; but there is the greatest difficulty in ascertaining the truth on this point from the colliers, who constantly strive to make it appear that their wages are less than they really are. The wages are certainly lower here than in most parts of the district. A collier will get from 14s. to 16s. per week, and the drawers from 1s. 9d., which is the lowest, to 9s.

652. "There are, however, other circumstances which have to be taken into consideration which tend to equalise the real earnings in the several districts, viz. the rates of house-rent, garden-ground, &c. At Worsley, for example, the smaller cottages and gardens let from 1l. 10s. to 2l. per annum, which is a much lower rate than is paid at Dukenfield. Benjamin Miller, at Dukenfield, states : ' A cottage and a workman's fire will cost 5s. a-week the year round.' When these points and the extra price of milk and vegetable produce are considered, the difference in the wages of the several districts will not be so great, though, after all these allowances are made, the wages in the southern part of this district still stand highest" (J. L. Kennedy, Esq., Report, § 240—249: App. Pt. II., p. 180.)

653. OLDHAM.—The following is an abstract of the average wages paid to the Young People when in full work by the firms in this neighbourhood which have made returns, and under which the best earnings will generally be made :—

Age.	Number returned.	Average Wages when in full Work.	
		s.	d.
7 to 8	3	3	8
8 to 9	11	4	3
9 to 10	20	4	9
10 to 11	32	5	3
11 to 12	36	6	2
12 to 13	47	7	10
13 to 14	55	8	2
14 to 15	44	10	5
15 to 16	48	11	6
16 to 17	37	12	6
17 to 18	31	14	4
	364		

654. A collier reckons his day's work at 5s., but he seldom has six days' work a week: he counts his waggoner's at 3s.; the latter sum being commonly shared with a thrutcher. But those who are now in work are making generally only three days a-week; and the Young People, who can get only the same proportion of work and of pay as the men, have to share the 3s. between two or among three, sometimes equally, but in various proportions, according to their relative ability. In good times they would make about five days a-week (Nos. 4, 7, 10, 11, 14, 15, 16, 20, 21, 25, 27, 28, 29, 30, 31, 32, 33, 37; J. Fletcher, Esq., Report, § 42, 43: App. Pt. II., p. 827).

655. NORTH LANCASHIRE.—In this district, the highest weekly wages of Children under thirteen, returned by employers, is 11s.; the lowest, 1s. 6d.; and the average 6s. 3d.; the highest weekly earnings of Young Persons from thirteen to eighteen, 18s. 8d.; the lowest, 3s.; and the average, 7s. to 10s. (A. Austin, Esq., Report, Table : App. Pt. II., p. 801).

656. CUMBERLAND.—" The wages for both men and children are here very good; they vary from 1s. to 2s. per day for the drivers and trailers, and from 18s. to 25s. per week for the adult colliers" (J. C. Symons, Esq., Report, § 11 : App. Pt. I., p. 300).

657. SOUTH DURHAM.—In this part of the kingdom, though the hewers be not employed at all, or only partially employed, the masters are bound to advance them at the end of every fortnight the sum of 30s. for their maintenance. This is in addition to a house and coals. But when the hewer comes into employment

which yields more than 30*s*. in the fortnight, the surplus above 30*s*. is detained to pay off the sum advanced to him in slack time; which sum, therefore, is to be considered as simply a loan, and not a payment of money due. By this system the miner is always sure of the means of support, with 15*s*. a-week, his house, and firing.

658. "The wages are paid once a fortnight, on the Friday afternoon, the reckoning being made up to the end of the preceeding week. The trappers are paid in by far the greater number of instances 10*d*. a-day, but some are as low as 9*d*. a-day, and some even 8*d*., but very seldom. The drivers are paid 15*d*. a-day, which on full work, being eleven days in the fortnight, is 13*s*. 9*d*. The helpers-up, the cleaners of the tramways, the keepers of the switches, rank with the drivers, and their emoluments vary, but are nearly the same as of the drivers.

659. "The putters are a highly paid class, many of the age of seventeen and eighteen get 40*s*. to 44*s*. in the eleven days of the fortnight, that is, if at that age they are sufficiently vigorous to urge forward a tram singly, and can do it as rapidly as a man in his full strength. If they be not so strong, the wages are less. When two are required to unite to urge forward the tram, the produce of the work is divided between them, either equally, or in a portion beforehand agreed upon.

660. "The lads of the same age with the older drivers and younger putters who assist on the bank in greasing the axletrees of the trams and of the tubs, who push back the empty corves or tubs to the shaft, who assist in wailing, or taking out the bad coals, or push forward the tubs with small coals, coal-dust, or coal as it comes from the pit to a great coal-heap as a store for sudden demand, all these boys are paid considerably less than the boys of the same age who have the courage to go below. This is settled by a law beyond the control of either employer or employed, the law of supply and demand. There is a greater competition to get employment above ground" (Dr. Mitchell, Report, §§ 194, 203—207 : App. Pt. I., pp. 141, 142).

661. NORTH DURHAM AND NORTHUMBERLAND.—" The following is a list of the average wages and earnings of all the principal persons, below the under-viewer, employed in the Tyne and Wear Collieries, taken at the last binding. The evidence will supply the individual varieties, and also the earnings of some few boys whose duties are subsidiary to the main occupations, and who are here omitted for the sake of conciseness.

Overmen	25*s*. to 32*s*.	per Week.
Back Overmen	22*s*. to 25*s*.	,,
Deputies	3*s*. 4*d*. to 3*s*. 9*d*.	per Day.
Principal Wastemen	20*s*. to 30*s*.	per Week.
Ordinary Wasteman	16*s*. to 19*s*.	
Shifters	2*s*. 6*d*. to 3*s*.	per Day.
Rolley-way Men	2*s*. 6*d*. to 3*s*. 4*d*.	,,
Onsetters at Shaft	1¼*d*., 1½*d*., and 2*d*. per Score	,,
Hewers	3*s*. 9*d*. (at Hetton)	,,
Putters for the first 80 Yards, in Collieries with moderate Inclination	} 1*s*. 3*d*. per Score of 21.6 cwt. Tubs or Corves of coals (on the Wear).	

The earnings of putters vary considerably. The averages of the four kinds of putters at Killingworth, on the Tyne, were as follows :—

Trams	2*s*. 6*d*.	per Day.
Headsmen	2*s*. 2*d*.	,,
Half Marrows	1*s*. 10*d*.	,,
Foals	1*s*. 6*d*.	,,
Rolley Drivers	1*s*. 3*d*.	,,
Trappers	10*d*.	,,
Horse-keepers under-ground	14*s*.	,,
Banksmen	2¼*d*. to 3*d*. per Score, or 4*s*.	per Week.
Brakemen	18*s*. to 20*s*.	per Day.
Furnace-men	12*s*. to 14*s*.	per Week.
Plugmen and Firemen	18*s*. to 20*s*., and 14*s*.	,,
Wrights, Foremen	18*s*. to 24*s*.	,,
Do. Common	16*s*. to 19*s*.	,,
Engine-wrights	3*s*. to 3*s*. 4*d*.	per Day.
Blacksmiths, Foreman	20*s*. to 28*s*.	per Week.
Do. Common	17*s*. to 21*s*.	,,
Mason, Foreman	18*s*. to 21*s*.	,,
Do. Common	17*s*. to 19*s*.	,,
Waggonmen	3*d*. to 3½*d*. per Chal. (or 2*s*. 6*d*. and 3*s*. per Day).	
Waggon-wrights	17*s*. to 20*s*.	per Week."

(Report by J. R. Leifchild, Esq., § 149: App. Pt. I., p. 535.)

" There is also various desultory work at the top of the pit, such as taking out stones, carry -

ing the picks, tramming out from skreens, firing the engine, assisting the bankmen, &c.; ages from ten to sixteen years, making from 1s. to 1s. 6d. a-day" (J. R. Leifchild, Esq., Evidence, No. 1: App. Pt. I., p. 563, l. 19).

East of Scotland.

662. EAST OF SCOTLAND.—The following table will present a pretty accurate statement of the late wages in the Lothians, the men averaging nine days' labour per fortnight:—

Year.	Average Weekly Earnings.		Average No. of Days Colliers work.	Amount stopped Weekly at Count Table for Medical Attendance, Burial or Friendly Society.	Amount stopped for Education.	Value of Fire Coal Weekly allowed.	House Rent, and Garden, if any, per week.
	Hewers. s. d.	Putters. s. d.	Days.			s. d.	s. d.
1812	20 0	8 0	..	None.	None.	1 0	0 9
1814	20 0	8 0	5	,,	,,	1 0	0 9
1822	25 0	9 0	5	,,	,,	1 0	0 9
1823	25 0	9 0	5	,,	,,	1 0	0 9
1831	18 0	9 0	5	,,	,,	1 0	0 9
1832	18 0	7 0	5	,,	,,	1 0	0 9
1834	18 0	7 0	5	,,	,,	1 0	0 9
1836	16 0	5 10	5	,,	,,	0 9	0 9
1838	16 0	5 10	5	2d. Medical.	,,	0 9	9d. to 1s.
1840	16 0	5 10	5	2d. ,,	,,	0 9	9d. to 1s.
1841	16 0	5 10	5	2d. ,,	,,	0 9	9d. to 1s.

(R. H. Franks, Esq., Report, § 41: App. Pt. I., p. 391.)

West of Scotland.

663. WEST OF SCOTLAND.—Here, " in some cases," states the Sub-Commissioner, " from the destitution to which the want of a regular relief for the poor subjects families, and particularly orphans or children of widows in Scotland, a collier is enabled to obtain the services of a child by merely supplying him with food and clothing.

664. " The subjoined table will give the information which I have received regarding the points specified under this head in your instructions :—

Classes of Works.	Nature of Employment.	Weekly Earnings.		Whether paid by Day or Piece.	Whether paid by Master or Workmen.
		s. d.	s. d.		
Collieries	Colliers under 18	12 0 to	24 0	Piece-work .	Master.
	Putters and drawers .	4 0	9 0	Generally day	Workmen.
	Trappers .	4 0	..	Day . . .	Master.
	Horse-drivers	3 0	6 0	Day . . .	Master.
	Engine-boys .	6 0	13 0	Day . . .	Master.
Ironstone Mines	Ironstone miners under 18 .	6 0	18 0	Piece . .	Master.
	Female drawers under 18	3 0	12 0	Day . . .	Master.
Iron Works . .	Pig-moulders at blast-furnaces .	2 6	6 0	Day . . .	Workmen.
	Catchers at forge-rolls and heavers-up .	6 0	10 0	Day . . .	Workmen.
	Straighteners and staff-carriers .	5 0	8 0	Day . . .	Workmen.
	Door-drawers .	4 0	6 0	Day . . .	Master.
	Pudlers' underhands under 18 .	8 0	12 6	Day . . .	Workmen.

North Wales.

665. NORTH WALES.—In this part of the kingdom " the amount of wages in the collieries and mines is pretty much on a par; according to capability boys receive from 2s. 6d. to 10s. a-week, and are paid by weekly wages—all of which, or nearly all, the parents receive for food and clothing" (H. H. Jones, Esq., Report, § 33: App. Pt. II., p. 369).

South Wales.

666. SOUTH WALES.—The average of wages in this district differs little from that of North Wales; but there is some variety in different localities (R. H. Franks, Esq., and R. W. Jones, Esq., Evidence, passim).

Forest of Dean.

667. FOREST OF DEAN.—"The average wages of the door boys, who are usually from eight to ten years of age, is 3s. per week. At 'hodding' and 'carting' the

wages vary from 7s. to 18s. per week, according to the age and strength of the lads. The highest rate is rarely earned by lads under eighteen years of age. A stout boy will frequently earn from 12s. to 15s. per week. These rates of wages imply full work, or six days in the week, which the state of trade unfortunately will not always permit" (E. Waring, Esq., Report, §§ 26, 33, 34 : App. Pt. II., p. 3).

668. SOUTH GLOUCESTERSHIRE.—The Sub-Commissioner states that in this district "the current wages of adult colliers are from 18s. to 20s. per week, when in full work. Lads from fourteen to eighteen earn from 7s. to 12s., and boys under thirteen from 2s. to 6s. per week, according to their ages and capabilities. Many of the boys appear to be wretchedly paid for their labour, by the low remuneration of 3d. or 4d. a-day. John Harvey, No. 52, is a case in point" (E. Waring, Esq., Report, § 20: App. Pt. II., p. 2.)

669. NORTH SOMERSETSHIRE.—Here, also, it is noticed that the young people in the collieries are better paid than those in other occupations, "some of them getting 9s., some 12s., and others 13s. 8d. per week" (Dr. Stewart, Evidence, No. 1: App. Pt. II., p. 49, l. 23).

670. IRELAND.—The Young People, generally upwards of thirteen years of age, employed in the collieries in Ireland, get 10d. and 1s. a-day; but the younger and weaker Children, employed at the air doors, and in other lighter labour, only 6d. and 7d. (F. Roper, Esq., and T. Martin, Esq., Evidence, passim : App. Pt. I., p. 869, 884-886).

Truck System.

671. The wages of the labourers of all ages employed in collieries appear in most cases to be paid in the current coin of the realm, at fixed periods, weekly or fortnightly, though sometimes monthly, and occasionally at intervals of six weeks. But in some of the districts, usually the more remote and poor, payment in goods, more or less extensive, and more or less directly, is resorted to by many of the employers. This is especially the case in the West of Scotland. "I have no hesitation in saying," states Mr. Tancred, "that the spirit of the Truck Act, and in some cases its very letter, is most grossly violated in numerous works, by which unfair and illegal profits are made from the hard-earned wages of the workpeople." Pursuing the same subject into detail, he shows the relation between this system and the long intervals at which the wages are paid, and the laws for the arrestment of wages peculiar to Scotland (T. Tancred, Esq., Report, §§ 88-96 : App. Pt. I., p. 337-344).

672. Again, in the South Wales district, it is stated by Mr. Franks, that " in many parts of Glamorganshire and Monmouthshire the wages of the working collier population are very rarely paid in money, but a shop in the neighbourhood, not professedly in the hands of the proprietors of the works, advances goods to the workmen employed in the mine on account of the proprietors; the books of the shop and the books of the colliery are checked on the pay-day at the same office, and the balance, if any, is handed over to the men. It very often happens, however, that the men unfortunately have nothing to receive for months together. It is said by many that the necessaries of life are dearer in these shops by 25 per cent. than in others perhaps five miles off; but whether this is the case or not I cannot decide; but I am convinced that the system adopted has a very pernicious effect on the independent means of subsistence of the labouring population, since there rarely is any balance in the hands of the workmen to apply for the purposes of education. By a reference to the evidence of John Evans, schoolmaster, No. 270, you will see the effect of this. The witness says, ' Nothing can exceed the mischief of the shops ; men will go to the shop and get a pound of sugar, or what not, and take it to the public-house for drink. I frequently myself take goods from the colliers instead of money ; the colliers have no money. I can't do anything else ; I can't express myself sufficiently strongly on this subject. There is very seldom any balance for the working man to receive; they are screwed down to the lowest possible pitch.'

673. " David Edwards, schoolmaster, Blackwood, says, ' I receive my fees sometimes in goods.' The system as at present carried on is much felt by the working people themselves, and is the subject of frequent complaint by them [see the evidence of Mr. John Williams, agent to Mr. Aaron Brain, occupier of

COAL MINES.

Wages.

Forest of Dean.

South Gloucestershire.

North Somersetshire.

Ireland.

Truck System.

Hengoed, and contractor for Place Level Colliery, No. 170, and of John Pickford, collier, No. 171, in the Evidence ; see also the evidence of Howell Lyshon, collier, No. 206] ; and I cannot but consider it highly disadvantageous to the Children as well as the men.   These shops supply food, clothing—in some places articles of luxury, jewellery, &c., and furniture of all sorts" (R. H. Franks, Esq., Report, § 60, 62 : App. Pt. II., p. 482, 483).

674. In North Wales, also, it appears that " the truck system is carried on to a considerable extent.   Wages are settled but once a month ; in the mean time, such as require advances must be content with credit on the shop.   It is now a system to go to the shop, and no one ever insists on cash ; but I know the system is much complained of, and the people would be more contented to have their wages paid in cash" (H. H. Jones, Esq., Evidence, Nos. 42, 43 : App. Pt. II., p. 388, l. 43 ; and p. 389, l. 15).

675. In Derbyshire the evidence collected by Mr. Fellows affords one clear instance of the payment of Children's wages in truck ; the mother of two boys stating that " they are paid once a month, and is quite sure if she wanted any money between times she could not have it otherwise than by a ticket for Horseley's tommy-shop.   Has never been obliged to sell her goods purchased there, but has bought of others ; they sell bacon, cheese, potatoes, flour, bread, groceries, flannels, and worsted.   Twice a year they are paid only once in six weeks ; they then call it the Tommy Fair.   Has known those who had money to go to Belper save 1s. out of 3s. by buying their goods there" (J. M. Fellows, Esq., Evidence, No. 363 : App. Pt. II., p. 342, l. 45).   Another witness in the same neighbourhood says, " They take a ticket from the butties, who are always ready to give it, as they say they receive so much in the shilling for themselves" (Ibid. No. 355 : p. 341, l. 33). Other forms of truck used by the butties in their payment of the labourers, and by the overlookers in the payment of the butties, are thus described by Mr. Fellows :— " In most coal fields the butties are paid every other Saturday night ; at others only once a month, and they are allowed to draw subsistence money weekly.   On the butty receiving the money he appoints the colliers and children to meet him, either at his own or some beer-shop he has an interest in, and generally keeps them waiting until he considers it has answered his purpose well enough, when the landlord produces the change and his bill.   By this stratagem and system the colliers and children are not only compelled to wait, but consider themselves lucky if they get home before midnight ; being moreover driven to the necessity of making all their markets on a Sunday morning.   At some fields the butties are only settled with once a month or six weeks, and no subsistence is allowed them, except from a tommy-shop belonging to the overlooker of the works" (See Riddings, No. 363, and many others.)   (J. M. Fellows, Esq., Report, § 38—40 : App. Pt. II., p. 255).   In Ireland the truck system is in full operation.   The Sub-Commissioner who visited the collieries in Kilkenny and Queen's County, after describing a class of contractors similar to the butties of Derbyshire, adds—" The contractor generally keeps a shop for the sale of tobacco, bread, bacon, herrings, &c., from which his men obtain their supplies on credit till the settling day, when the amount of their bills is deducted from the wages coming to them, thus causing endless disputes, quarrels, and bickerings : many of the poor fellows told me they had seldom any money to take on the settling days.   With the exception of those belonging to the Rushes Colliery Company, who discountenance the practice, nearly all the pits and shafts, of which there are an immense number, are let in this way, but very few of them, comparatively, are worked on the proprietor's own account.   This very bad custom has prevailed so long that several of the proprietors and their agents told me they could not break through it, much as they condemned it as bad for all parties concerned, except the contractor, and that the only way effectually to do away with it would be by sinking new shafts and working them themselves, which some of them are about doing" (F. Roper, Esq., Report, § 13-15 : App. Pt. I., p. 873).

676. It must not, on the other hand, be supposed that the payment of wages in the current coin of the realm necessarily secures to a class of people so improvident as the colliers generally are the advantage of making ready-money purchases, as is well shown by a witness in the Lancashire district, in answer to a question as to the effect of the monthly payment of wages.   " I consider," he says, " that the collier being paid monthly is a great disadvantage both to him and the shopkeeper, for each collier is obliged to go to his shop and have a credit account.   If colliers were prudent, which they very rarely are, it would be necessary for them to have

nearly a month's wages beforehand, in order to go to the best market for their provisions, where they would get the best selection of good articles at the current price; but the shopkeeper will give them credit, sell an inferior article, and demand a higher price. I am sure I am speaking within the mark when I say that buying shop articles on credit they lose 2s. in every 20s. on provisions alone, and the same rule applies to every other article used. I am sure a man would be better off with 16s. wages and paying ready money at the best market, than with 20s. where he must go to the shop and get credit; and it affects the shopkeeper in the same way. With weekly payments, if a customer is behind with his payment, supposing that he makes a bad debt, it is only a week's payment lost to the shopkeeper; but with the monthly customer, when bad debts occur, the loss is four times as great; or if he bring a portion only of the payment at the end of the time the shopkeeper is induced to give further credit in the hope that the debt may be wiped away in the end; and in this way he is frequently disappointed altogether, for the collier often leaves the neighbourhood without paying (J. L. Kennedy, Esq., Evidence, No. 105: App. Pt. II., p. 239, l. 38).

COAL MINES.

Wages—Truck System.

14.—INFLUENCE OF EMPLOYMENT IN COAL MINES ON THE PHYSICAL CONDITION OF CHILDREN AND YOUNG PERSONS.

677. In order to derive from the evidence collected the instruction which it is capable of affording relative to the physical condition of persons employed in coal mines, it will be desirable first of all to bring together the statements made in general terms by various classes of witnesses as to the food, clothing, health, and vigour of the collier population in the several districts, and then to consider more particularly the immediate effects of the excessive labour frequently required from the very young in some districts, and the peculiarities in their actual physical conformation produced by such labour, as indicated by their stature, their muscular development, their diseases, and their comparative longevity.

Physical Condition.

PHYSICAL CONDITION GENERALLY, AS TO FOOD, CLOTHING, HEALTH, AND VIGOUR.

Food, Clothing, Health, and Vigour.

678. SOUTH STAFFORDSHIRE.—All classes of witnesses concur in stating that the collier population of South Staffordshire is in general well fed, well clothed, and in excellent physical condition.

South Staffordshire.

Mr. Samuel Day Fereday, surgeon, of Dudley, says: " There are benefit societies which contract for so much a-head with medical men, and the societies which consist of colliers have a much less ratio of sickness than societies consisting of men of other employments" (Dr. Mitchell, Evidence, No. 2: App. Pt. I., p. 61, l. 34), which this witness accounts for from the superior health of the colliers, from the dryness and agreeable temperature of the mines, and from the colliers being well fed, which keeps up their strength. He adds—" In case of accidents it is remarkable how rapidly the colliers recover. In cases which would be fatal in London and the patients would sink under them, the colliers think nothing of them, and quickly get well. I have known the children of colliers who had a fracture of the thigh able to be down and go about in a month" (Ibid. No. 2: p. 61, l. 54).—Mr. Richard Spooner Cooper: " They are more healthy than men who follow other occupations. From my experience for five years at the Birmingham hospital, I know that the colliers are much more healthy than the workmen of Birmingham. Compound fractures of limb will turn out very well here, which is not frequently the case in Birmingham. A broken leg will heal much sooner, and there is much less risk of permanent injury from any severe accident. When any operation is performed, the patient is much sooner got well" (Ibid. No. 3: p. 62, l. 8).—Mr. Thomas Shorthouse, clerk of the Dudley Union: " The colliers live jovially down in the pits; they keep their families well; not so many applications for relief from colliers as from some other trades; in general the families of colliers are comfortable; the women are strong and hearty; they have always plenty of firing, and you may see them carrying home a cwt. of coals" (Ibid. No. 1: p. 61, l. 15.)

679. Evidence to the same effect is given by all classes of witnesses. (See Nos. 5, 8, 13, 16, 24, 41.)

680. NORTH STAFFORDSHIRE.—In the Cheadle district the Children and Young Persons are stated to be robust and healthy, without personal injury or deformity, and no case was found of murmuring or discontent (S. S. Scriven, Esq., Report, § 14: App. Pt. II., p. 129).

North Staffordshire.

681. SHROPSHIRE.—The medical men assert that the miners of this district, men and boys, are healthy; but there is an extraordinary mortality during infancy and childhood owing to the quantity of gin and opium which is given by the mothers to their children; those who survive are strong, because the weak soon perish (Dr. Mitchell, Report, § 313: App. Pt. I., p. 39; Evidence, Nos. 38, 39, 48).

682. WARWICKSHIRE.—In this district, from the thickness of the seam of coal, the dryness of the mines, and the excellent ventilation, the colliers are under circumstances highly favourable to health; and are a tall, athletic, powerful race of men, continuing their labour to an advanced age, having, as one of the medical witnesses expresses it, lived all their lives " like fighting cocks." Mr. John Craddock, Chairman of the Guardians of the Poor of the Nuneaton District, states, that the applications for relief from colliers are much fewer than from any other class; less than from agricultural labourers or from weavers, and that they keep on working to any age up to sixty, and even to a higher age. (Dr. Mitchell, Evidence, No. 67: App. Pt. I., p. 107, l. 18).

683. LEICESTERSHIRE.—In the Ashby-de-la-Zouch district the state of the coal mines is equally favourable to health and longevity with that of the coal mines of Warwickshire; the colliers are tall, strong, powerful men, but on account of the rocky hardness of the coal, and the great weight of the pieces in which it is got, the labour is extremely severe; and none but the strongest constitutions can bear it long.

684. Mr. Charles Allsopp Dalby, surgeon of the Union at Ashby-de-la-Zouch, states that their health is in general exceedingly good, better than that of agricultural labourers, but that the work of the pit is very laborious, and that many of the colliers are incapable of following their occupation at fifty and others at fifty-five; and Mr. John Davenport, clerk of the Union, says that they have few applications from colliers for relief on account of sickness, although the collier is sooner unfit for work than the agricultural labourer (Dr. Mitchell, Evidence, Nos. 75, 77, 81, 82, 83, 87).

685. DERBYSHIRE.—Of the food, clothing, and physical condition of the collier population of this district the Sub-Commissioner reports:—

686. "Their food, generally speaking, is full as ample and good as those who are labouring above ground; but having to get their meals, one at so early an hour in the morning, often without fire or light, the other in the cold bad air of the pit, after having been in a profuse perspiration, without, as they state, scarcely being able to wipe the mud from their hands—also being so long between their meals, must deprive them of all comfort, if it does not injure their powers of digestion.

687. " Their clothing consists of a coarse flannel shirt or jacket, and trousers mostly of the same material. The jacket is thrown off in most pits, and only used where they are allowed to sit down to their dinner, or on coming out of the pit. As to cleanliness during work, it is impossible; but at the same time I was much pleased at the particularly neat and clean appearance of the collier children I met with at the various Sunday-schools.

688. " Those cottages I visited belonging to the colliers varied very much in different parts of the district; at Ilkistone and its neighbourhood they were decidedly much more neat and comfortable than any of their neighbours who were engaged either in lace-making, stocking-making, or agriculture; but at South Normanton and Kirkby they were the picture of dirt and wretchedness. I observed in all parts, if there was but little furniture, every collier's cottage had a blazing fire; this they get free of any expense, and certainly it is a set-off against some of their deprivations (J. M. Fellows, Esq., Report, §§ 50—55: App. Pt. II., p. 256).

689. " In external appearance I think the Children in the south part of the district are healthy, and (with the exception of those who have worked at a very early age being bow-legged) not ill formed. I have observed that their complexion, although not altogether to be called sickly, is of a sallow hue; this, I suppose, follows as a matter of course from their being nearly deprived of daylight.

690. " Those Children who are employed at the pit mouth, or in farmers' service, are straighter on the legs and better looking than those working under ground. I have noticed the Children who do not work, or have not from an early age worked in pits, are well and better formed than those, if even of the same family, who have worked at an earlier age than twelve years (Ibid. § 45—47, p. 255).

Dr. Blake " considers they are generally as healthy as the labourers above ground, which he attributes to their better diet" (J. M. Fellows, Esq., Evidence, No. 10: App. Pt. II., p. 266, l. 6).—William S. Smith, Esq., surgeon : " As a body, he considers them more healthy than the lower class in the neighbourhood. The cause of this he attributes to their living better, and he always finds a collier child will sooner get the better of an illness than a stocking-maker, as he has better stamina" (Ibid. No. 83: p. 286, l. 57).—See also witnesses Nos. 23, 25, 26, 40, 69, 72, 73, 77, 80, 88, 102, 110, &c.

691. WEST RIDING OF YORKSHIRE : SOUTHERN PART.—In this district the food and clothing of the collier population are in general good. " The Children as well as the adults, have bread and milk, or porridge, to their breakfast ; huge lumps of bread, and often bits of cheese or bacon, or fat, to their luncheon in the pit; a hot meat meal when they come home at five or six, and often porridge, or bread and milk, or tea for supper. See the statement (No. 84) as to the colliers taking nothing but the best quality of articles at shops. Their clothing is generally extremely good. In external appearance the collier Children are decidedly more robust and healthy than any manufacturing Children ; perhaps less so than farm Children, but on the whole they are, excepting where they work in badly-ventilated and ill-regulated collieries, certainly far from unhealthy in appearance. The contrast is most striking between the broad stalwart frame of the swarthy collier, as he stalks home, all grime and muscle, and the puny, pallid, starveling little weaver, with his dirty-white apron and feminine look. There cannot be a stronger proof that it is not muscular exertion which hurts a man" (J. C. Symons, Esq., Report, § 198, 209—213: App. Pt. I., p. 192—194).

Michael Thomas Sadler, Esq., surgeon, Barnsley, says : " The children live well, and look strong" (J. C. Symons, Esq., Evidence, No. 139: App. Pt. I., p. 261, l. 41).—Edwin Ellis, Esq., surgeon, Silkstone : " Taking them as a whole, I am decidedly of opinion that the children who work in pits are more healthy than any other class of children I meet with, much more so than weavers, or even than farm-labourers. I know of no illness that is attendant on their employment. They live better as to food than other classes. They consume a great deal of animal food, milk, and beer or ale" (Ibid. No. 99: p. 248, l. 17).—Mr. Crooks, surgeon, Barnsley : " A more healthy set of children we haven't about us than those who work in coal-pits. I know of no disease incidental to colliers" (Ibid. No. 166: p. 267, l. 16).—See also witnesses Nos. 6, 19, 24, 46, 61, 69, 93, 102, 112, 153, 170, 192, 242, &c.

692. To this representation of the favourable physical condition of the collier population of this exceedingly diversified district there are, however, numerous exceptions ; several witnesses state that some of the Children and Young Persons have never food enough, and their clothing is in many cases described as being wretched, so that it is but too evident that such laborious and exhausting work as has been described does not always bring with it even so much as the reward of sufficient food and raiment.

Joseph Haigh, underground steward, Tinsley Park Collieries : " Thinks the work itself would not hurt them, if they all lived regularly. Many have not proper meals at home. A boy that works ought to have meals every day alike, and regularly, like a horse ; but they are often pinched at the end of the week" (Ibid. No. 9: p. 228, l. 40).—Mr. William Higgett, steward to the Tinsley Park Pits : " Their meals are insufficient with some of them, owing to their belonging to very poor families" (Ibid. No. 10: p. 229, l. 5.)—Mr. Crooks, surgeon, Barnsley : " In my round to-day I rode by a lot of cottages, chiefly occupied by colliers, when I met with a farmer who resides amongst them ; from inquiries I made respecting the condition and management of the children, he said that the greatest part of them went to the pits, and many who had thoughtless parents were badly fed : he stated that he was afraid that some of them were sent to their work without breakfast, and took but little with them and but coarse fare when they returned, though this depended upon their improvident parents ; those who were fortunate enough in having good parents looked well, and went and returned from their work cheerfully and in good spirits : in one family there were two young men who were deformed ; they had lost their mother when children, their father married again to a woman who treated them badly, and as there was a large family they were but ill fed, to which they attributed their deformities" (Ibid. No. 166: p. 267, l. 57).—Mathew Lindley, collier : " They have a little milk or a little coffee and a bit of bread in the morning before they go to the pit, and they will take nothing with them but a little bread and perhaps a little tea, but oftener dry bread than anything else. Their parents cannot often get them more. They do not have meat. The parents do not get wages enough to provide meat for the children. When they come out of the pit at night they may have a little meat or milk porridge, but a bit of dry bread and a sup of milk is the usual supper. The boys do look healthy, it is true, but it is because they are young. The work they get to do is not hard as far as trapping is concerned, but hurrying is very slavish work, and I have known boys go to work all the twelve hours without more than a bit of dry bread to eat" (Ibid. No. 109: p. 250, l. 53).—John Ibbetson, thirteen and a half years old : " I stop at home now, I've no clothes to go in ; I stop in because

COAL MINES.

Physical Condition.

*Food, Clothing,
Health, and Vigour.*

West Riding of
Yorkshire.

I've no clothes to go and lake with other little lads" (Ibid. No. 264 : p. 291, l. 61.)—Thomas Caveney, thirteen years old : " I go to Sunday-school sometimes, but I have no clothes to go in" (Ibid. No. 238 : p. 286, l. 3).

693. The Sub-Commissioner expressly excepts from the account given of the favourable physical condition of the Children in this district those who draw with the girdle and chain; and the medical evidence is decisive as to the great and permanent injury done to the health of the Children who thus work in the thin pits (J. C. Symons, Esq., Report, § 199 : App. Pt. I., p. 193).

Dr. Favell, M.D., of Sheffield, " Is of opinion that where children (especially female children) are harnessed to corves, and where the seam is so low that they are forced to go on their hands and feet, and where the ventilation is also not good, the occupation must necessarily be prejudicial to their health" (J. C. Symons, Esq., Evidence, No. 47 : App. Pt. I., p. 235, l. 64).— Henry Hemingway, Esq., surgeon, Dewsbury : " I have examined the children working in a thin and in a thicker bed of coal, and found projection of the sternum; and sinking in of the spinal column is common in the thin bed, and only in a few instances in the thicker bed of coal" (Ibid. No. 221 : p. 282, l. 42).

694. BRADFORD AND LEEDS.—Of the food, clothing, and general physical condition of the Children and Young Persons in this district, the Sub-Commissioner reports as follows :—" As to food, the number of meals, and the quantity and quality of food at each meal, are perfectly adequate to maintain the health and strength of Children in constant labour. On this head certainly no complaint can be made. Whether the time allowed for eating in the middle of the day is ample, is a point to which I have already adverted under the head of Hours of Work, and on which I do not feel able to speak without hesitation; but I could discover no bad effects resulting from the present practice.

695. " As to clothing, there is considerable difference, according to the habits of the mother of the family, and also, perhaps, according to neighbourhoods, the Children seeming to be on the whole better clothed in those neighbourhoods where there is a larger proportion of the middle and upper classes. The connexion between these two circumstances is, perhaps, to be traced in part to the greater activity in Sunday-school education, which the presence of a large proportion of the middle classes produces; respectability of dress being generally enforced upon the Children who attend Sunday-schools. The larger proportion of Children have two suits of clothes, and are respectably dressed on Sundays. " With regard to clothing in the week-days, there is not the tidiness which could be wished; but I could not discover that the health of the Children at all suffers from insufficiency of clothing.

696. " As to cleanliness, the custom seems universally prevalent, and perfectly established, of a thorough washing upon arrival at home at night, at least of those parts of the body which have been exposed during the day's labour. Cleanliness of person and decency of attire are also enforced upon those who attend Sunday-schools, and attendance there during some period of Childhood is almost universal. Beyond this no encouragement is given to neatness and cleanliness, and the houses of the miners, and the places adjoining them, are, generally speaking, lamentably deficient in these respects. In defence of the miners, however, it may be stated, that much of this is attributable to the generally bad and defective construction of the cottages. It would be a material step towards improvement were the owners of mining property to direct their attention to the construction of a better class of dwellings; nor does there seem to be amongst the operatives, or at least amongst a portion of them, any indisposition to avail themselves of the means of living in better houses, were such means within their reach.

697. " The physical condition of the Children who are the subject of this inquiry is, at the least, equal to the average of other Children in the same neighbourhood. They possess a greater share of spirits and activity, the result, I apprehend, of their employment being active, and of their obtaining, independently of it, a fair share of air and exercise. They are nearly, and in every respect but stature, quite upon a par with Children engaged in agricultural labour, and, judging from appearances, decidedly superior to the neighbouring factory population (R. W. Wood, Esq., Report, § 34—40 : App. Pt. II., p. H 6). See witnesses Nos. 3, 4, 5, 9, 16, 20, 22, 23, 40, 50, 52, 53, 54, 56, 67, 81, &c.

698. HALIFAX.—In this district " the breakfast generally consists of a mess of porridge (oatmeal and hot milk or water), the dinner is almost invariably a flat, thin,

coarse, oaten cake peculiar to the North, or a wheat cake weighing about six ounces, without any other accompaniment save a morsel of salt butter or lard; this they often partially or wholly dispose of before nine, ten, or eleven o'clock, when they feel most hungry, which suffices them until their return home, when they get their suppers, and are said to be satisfied, which I believe to be true, as in very few instances have I heard of any complaints" (S. S. Scriven, Esq., Report, § 63: App. Pt. II., p. 67).

699. Notwithstanding all the injurious influences which are constantly acting on the Children in this district, more especially in the wet, dirty, and ill-ventilated mines, of which, as has been shown, there are so many in this neighbourhood, the Sub-Commissioner reports that the physical condition of the Children is in general good. It has been a source of satisfaction to find that their general health is remarkably good, as out of the many hundreds that have come under my observation I have never met with a solitary case of functional or organic disease as the result of their employment—the opposite condition obtaining in a marked degree, as evidenced by their florid countenances and cheerful dispositions. It has been the practice, and one no less singular than true, for parents unconnected with collieries, whose offspring may have been the victims of constitutional disease, to send them into the pits for 'change of air,' a change, too, that has contributed to the restoration of many, more especially of those suffering from bronchial and pulmonary complaints; and no wonder, since they have been removed from the cold and blighting winds of the moors to a more equal, humid, and genial atmosphere" (Ibid. § 84, 85: p. 72). See witnesses Nos. 2, 3, 6, 11, 12, 13, 14, 15, 17, 18, 19, 22, 23, 25, 29, 53, 86, &c.

700. LANCASHIRE AND CHESHIRE.—Of the physical condition of the collier population in this district the Sub-Commissioner reports as follows :—" As far as I had the opportunity of judging, it appeared to me that the proportion of still-born infants was rather large, and certainly the care bestowed on the Children and the state of the dwellings could not be considered favourable to their healthy growth. The adults are thin and gaunt. One or two colliers, somewhat corpulent, were pointed out to me as remarkable for being corpulent. They have a stooping shambling gait when walking, no doubt acquired from their occupations in the low galleries of the mines. Their complexion, when washed, is pallid, approaching to a dirty yellow; the eye is languid and sometimes inflamed, and the expression of the countenance is listless.

701. "In the women, who drink less and are generally more temperate in their habits than the men, the difference was not striking between the colliers' wives who worked in the mines and those who did not; the chief distinction being that those who worked in the mines had a shambling gait and stoop. I saw several women with clean faces who usually worked in the mines, and their complexions presented a healthy florid appearance. Margaret Winstanley and Dinah Bradbury, whose evidence is given, were instances of this. Those women who worked in the mines appeared to be strong and as well developed as any other women of the labouring casses in the district."

702. " Some of the Children are decently clothed, and, according to their own statements, always have sufficient food; on the other hand, many are in rags and in a disgusting state of dirt, and without enough to eat. The usual food of drawers and colliers in the pits is stated to be " cheese and bread, or bread and butter, and sometimes raisin pasties; they take what they have to eat in their hands, and take a bite now and then; sometimes they carry it till it is as black as a coal" (J. L. Kennedy, Esq., Report, §§ 297, 298, 302: App. Pt. II., p. 188; Evidence, Nos. 28, 32, 49, 50, 57 59,).

Peter Gaskell: " How often do the drawers wash their bodies?—None of the drawers ever wash their bodies; I never wash my body; I let my shirt rub the dirt off, my shirt will show that; I wash my neck and ears and face, of course. Do you think it is usual for the young women to do the same as you do?—I don't think it is usual for the lasses to wash their bodies; my sisters never wash themselves, and seeing is believing; they wash their faces and necks and ears. When a collier is in full dress he has white stockings and low shoes, and very tall shirt-neck, very stiffly starched, and ruffles?—That is very true, Sir, but they never wash their bodies underneath; I know that, and their legs and bodies are as black as your hat." (J. L. Kennedy, Esq. Evidence, No. 29: App. Pt. II. p. 217, l. 45).—— —— Halliwell, parish overseer: " Have you ever noticed the condition of the children as regards the clothing?—Those children are almost invariably badly clothed. As regards cleanliness, can you state as to the condition of he colliers in this district?—Yes, I can safely state that they are generally filthy; there are

COAL MINES.

Physical Condition.

Food, Clothing,
Health, and Vigour.

Lancashire and
Cheshire.

some cases where the parents take pains with the children, but they are very few. The children, and men and women, wash their faces, but that is all. In visiting the houses of the colliers in what condition have you generally found them?—The houses are usually filthy; there is no attention to whitewashing or ventilation; paper and rags are often pasted and stuffed into the broken windows; the beds and bedding are generally poor; they are in the habit of pawning their clothes, and in some instances I have known them pawn the bedding, bed-clothes, and even the coats off their backs, when they have been on the spree" (Ibid. No. 99: p. 234, l. 37).—Mr. Harrison, parish overseer: "In visiting the houses of colliers in what condition have you generally found them? —Very rough, they make rough work in a house; they have very few goods; the beds are often dirty, they must be dirty with the dirt on their bodies. The windows are badly kept, not cleaned, and most of the houses are seldom whitewashed; but there are some exceptions, where colliers keep their houses very decent and clean, and their bedding too" (Ibid. No. 100: p. 235, l. 69). —Mr. Birchall, parish overseer: "Have you ever remarked the clothing of the colliers' children?—There are very few of the children who have any dress but that used by them in the mines; they scarcely ever have any but one suit. Do you think the colliers cleanly in their persons?—No, quite the reverse; they will wash their faces and ears, but I believe that neither the girls or boys ever wash their bodies; you may see a ring round their necks after they have washed them" (Ibid. No. 101: p. 236, l. 66).

North Lancashire.

703. NORTH LANCASHIRE.—Of the physical condition of the collier population in this district the evidence is conflicting; "but the general opinion seems to be that the Children are not unhealthy where well treated. From my own observation I should say that they were generally thin, their cheeks hollow, and of course pale, with a general appearance of weakness" (A. Austin, Esq., Report, §§ 21, 22: App. Pt. II., p. 804).

Oldham.

704. OLDHAM.—" As they (the collier boys) progress towards manhood and middle age they generally lose all traces of florid health, and acquire a wan complexion. The colliery workers who are Children generally, however, present an appearance of robust health. If their parents be among the best conducted they are well fed, and have a change of clothes for the Sunday; cleanliness and comfort character-ising their cottages, which are solidly built. On the other hand, the description given of his own treatment and condition by James Taylor (No. 10) is an example of the privations, physical and moral, to which the Children of ill-conducted parents are subject. The dinner of the colliers taken in the pit must be regarded rather as a lunch, which they devour at any opportunity in the course of their labour; and if this abrogation of the dinner-hour be designed to lessen the time spent under ground, and give increased comfort to the more plentiful evening meal at home, it is the choice of a lesser evil. But the hours of labour appear to be irre-spective of this arrangement" (J. Fletcher, Esq., Report, § 59: App. Pt. II., p. 832).

James Taylor: "Used to take his dinner down with him when he had any, and eat at it as he could, working. Never had anything but butter-cakes [bread and butter] to his dinner. Many a time has gone without both breakfast and dinner altogether, and felt sickly like, and mazy. His mother had now't to give him, because she could na' get now't. Hur said hur had now't for him. Hur said if hur could get a bit for him hur would do, but his father, who was a collier, drank a good deal of his wages. Oftener went to the night-set without his butter-cakes for supper than with them, and felt sickly and mazy then. Was working for David Whitehead, 'an ye know him.' He never axed if he'd come without his butter-cakes, an' he never tou'd him. He ne'er gied him nought. The waggoners, neither, wouldn't gie one another a bit o' butter-cake if they were clamm'd to dead. They work only in their clogs, stockings, trousers, and cap. Has porridge and treacle to breakfast when he has any; bread and butter cakes to dinner, if can get them; and porridge and milk when he comes home; never any potatoes nor any bread, what is in his bread and butter cakes" (J. Fletcher, Esq., Evidence, No. 10: App. Pt. II., p. 848, l. 67).—See also witnesses, Nos. 4, 5, 7, 14, 20, 25.

South Durham.

705. SOUTH DURHAM.—" The medical evidence in this district describes the colliers as a strong healthy race, but the work is laborious and exhausting, and the colliers, though healthy, are not long-lived. The collier Children look well. After their day's work they appear as playful as schoolboys come out of school. They are substantially clothed. Both men and boys on Sundays are dressed exceedingly well. The men generally wear a black suit, and a stranger seeing them would hardly suspect them to be the men whom he had seen coming up from the pits be-grimed with sweat and coal-dust, and as black as negroes. Some of the witnesses in evidence, and all persons in conversation, give the credit to the Wesleyan Me-thodists of having brought about a great change in the respectability of dress and general good behaviour of the miners" (Dr. Mitchell, Report, §§ 212—215: App. Pt. I., p. 143).—See witnesses Nos. 94, 96, 97, 99, 101, 107, 108.

706. NORTH DURHAM AND NORTHUMBERLAND.—The Sub-Commissioner has collected much evidence relative to the food, clothing, health, and general physical condition of the collier population of this district.

707. The proprietors and viewers give such evidence as the following :—

"They [the colliers] live well as to food, and generally eat white bread. Pit people are extravagant in their living. The boys are generally well scrubbed after work, and wash themselves carefully. The parents have great credit in keeping them clean after work hours. The boys are better dressed than most boys of the labouring classes" (J. R. Leifchild, Esq., Evidence, No. 368 : App. Pt. I., p. 643, l. 19).—Mr. William Bailey : "As to luxury, some have flesh meat thrice a-day, and not a few of them twice. Many dress in an extravagant manner on Sundays" (Ibid. No. 400 : p. 649, l. 18).—Mr. Jobling : "The pit people are generally better off than any other labourers ; better fed, better paid, and of a healthy appearance" (Ibid. No. 335 : p. 635, l. 44).—Mr. G. Elliott : "Thinks food is usually sufficient. Will answer for it that white bread of the best flour is commonly used. They do not have much animal food, they say it makes them dry. Plenty of cheese and bacon is consumed, as well as quantities of cold coffee" (Ibid. No. 367, p. 642, l. 74).—Mr. Thomas Clarke : "The lads and boys are generally healthy and full grown, and have quite enough food—bacon, or mutton and bread. There is very little sickness amongst them" (Ibid. No. 159 : p. 601, l. 52).

708. Medical men state as follows :—

William Morrison, Esq., surgeon : "The children of colliers are comfortably and decently clothed ; cleanliness, both in their persons and houses, is a predominant feature in the domestic economy of the female part of this community. The children, although necessarily left much to themselves, and playing much in the dirt, are never sent to bed without ample ablution. Pitmen, of all labouring classes I am acquainted with, enjoy most the pleasure of good living ; their larders abound in potatoes, bacon, fresh meat, sugar, tea, and coffee, of which good things the children as abundantly partake as the parents ; even the sucking infant, to its prejudice, is loaded with as much of the greasy and well-seasoned viands of the table as it will swallow. In this respect the women are foolishly indulgent, and I know no class of persons among whom infantile diseases so much prevail. Durham and Northumberland are not dairy counties, consequently the large population (excepting the *hinds* in the northern part of Northumberland) are very inadequately supplied with milk. Did this wholesome and nutritious beverage more abound, probably the infant population would be more judiciously fed" (Ibid. No. 496 : p. 662, l. 28).

T. M. Greenhow, Esq., surgeon, Newcastle : "Their dwellings are generally pretty well constructed, well warmed, and, from the habit of allowing the doors to remain much open, though very hot from large fires, a circulation of air through them is necessarily maintained. They are warmly clothed and well fed ; frequently very temperate, especially since the introduction amongst them of teetotalism ; and, happily, the nature of their employment renders frequent and thorough ablutions with warm water and soap absolutely necessary. I understand that of late years this wholesome habit has been more diligently attended to than formerly, and with corresponding benefit to health. I am assured that at Walker, where large manufactories of iron and alkali are in the immediate neighbourhood of the colliery, a great contrast is observable in this respect between the colliers and manufacturers, which is greatly in favour of the former. The condition of the skin in relation to health is so important, that could this most wholesome practice of frequent and complete ablution of the person be introduced into manufactories, a great improvement of health would undoubtedly be produced by it. We might very naturally expect that the very unnatural situation in which the children employed in the pits are placed, their exclusion from daylight and the open air, would materially influence their physical health, not only at the time, but would so affect their constitutions as to render them liable to particular forms of disease in after-life. Nevertheless, my experience and observation amongst these people do not lead me to infer that any very pernicious effects result from these circumstances in such numerous instances as to justify anything like a general conclusion. That the health of the boys is for the most part good is frequently shown in a remarkable manner by their favourable recovery from severe wounds and other accidents. In the general condition of the pitmen there are many circumstances which probably tend to counteract any injurious influence which the nature of their employment might otherwise exert over health. Amongst these may be enumerated the warm flannel dresses in which they work ; the thorough washings of the entire person which they practise after the hours of labour, the situation of their houses, and plentiful supply of coals which they enjoy, and the ample means which they generally possess of providing sufficient supplies of wholesome food for their families." (Ibid. No. 498 : p. 665, l. 56).—W. Brown, Esq., surgeon of the Jarrow Colliery : "With regard to their physical condition, I am decidedly of opinion that they are not subject to any disorder resulting from the nature of their employment. It seldom happens that a pitman consults me upon any disorder which may not be imputed to their ridiculous and excessive living, or to the ordinary exciting causes possessed in common by other individuals. Their habitations are generally clean and comfortable ; a too liberal supply of fuel makes them perhaps prodigal of this comfort, and the health of the family is endangered by predisposing to cold. What I have said above applies equally to boys" (Ibid. No. 349 : p. 637, l. 15).

709. Among others the following Young Persons state that they have always sufficient food: See witnesses Nos. 58, 124, 145, 403, 407, 435, 468. The following Children, among others, give the same evidence: Nos. 7, 8, 74, 100, 511, 512.

710. CUMBERLAND.—The Children and Young Persons in this district " present much the same physical phenomena as those of Yorkshire—comparing, of course, those following similar branches of the work. I do not, however, consider the Children, as a body, unhealthy" (J. C. Symons, Esq., Report, § 22: App. Pt. I., p. 302). The viewers state, that " a healthier set never can be seen" (Ibid. No. 311); and the medical men represent the Children as " generally healthy and strong" (Ibid. No. 312). The Children and Young Persons themselves give evidence that they have always abundance of food: " We get plenty to eat, and have bacon every day for dinner; we get mutton or beef on Sundays." (Ibid. No. 309.) " We have bacon every day for dinner, and mutton at week ends." (Ibid. No. 328.) " I always get plenty to eat" (Ibid. No. 324). See also witnesses Nos. 306, 307, 316, 324, &c.

711. EAST OF SCOTLAND.—The Sub-Commissioner reports very unfavourably of the health and strength of the collier population of this district, and assigns the following reasons for their bad physical condition :—" 1st. Because the food taken is too poor in quality and insufficient in quantity to sustain such severe labour, consisting for the most part of oaten cake, oaten bread, or porridge; no butchers' meat ; even the hewers do not enjoy the luxury of common table beer, and the Children invariably drink the water in the pit.—2nd. Because the food, bad in quality and scanty in quantity as it is, is always taken most irregularly, there being no fixed time set apart for meals.—3rd. Because the air of the mines in which the work is carried on, and which the workpeople respire, as well as the air of the houses in which they are crowded, instead of being pure, which is indispensable to convert aliment into nutriment, is loaded with noxious matters.—4th. Because the hours of work are much too long for Children of eight years old and under.—5th. Because the medical evidence shows that this labour is injurious to the bodily frame.

712. " There exists a general want of cleanliness in the habits of the colliers, with exceptions of course; though I believe it is usual for them to wash their faces once in the day after labour, and sometimes the Children follow the same example; but the younger Children, not at work in the pits, present a miserable appearance. The ragged and dirty clothing of the whole family, the flesh of the Children, which seems perfectly innocent of water, and blackened by the general employment, added to the squalid aspect and unwholesome stench of the place, bespeak at one glance a population neglected and abandoned to a course of life which has blunted the commonest perceptions of human comfort. As might be expected, these hovels are infested with vermin, as are the persons of the Children" (R. H. Franks, Esq., Report, § 64 *et seq.*: App. Pt. I., p. 396).

713. The statements in proof of these several positions so abound in every page of the Evidence collected by the Sub-Commissioner, that we deem it useless to refer to particular instances.

714. WEST OF SCOTLAND.—" The labour of Children is often severe for their age, from the early hour at which they rise in the morning, and the physical exertion occasionally necessary in their employment. It appears, however, that from the intervals of rest, amounting in most cases to four or five whole days in a fortnight, and from the more nutritious diet general amongst colliers, as well as from the varied motions of the limbs and body in the sort of employment in which the Children are used, no ill effects to their bodily health or conformation result from colliery labour. In the single instance where a pit is habitually worked at night, the health of the Children seems indeed liable to fail, but I trust the employment of Children in such cases will not be allowed much longer. No deterioration was visible to me in the adult colliers, who are usually I should say rather athletic in appearance; but the hardness of their labour, and the confined air and dust in which they work, are apt to render them asthmatic, as well as to unfit them for labour at an earlier period of life than is the case in other employments. These effects though, I repeat, seem attributable to the nature of their actual employment, and often to their intemperate habits, rather than to the severity of the labour to

which they have been subject in youth, or to the early age at which they began to work."   (T. Tancred, Esq., Report, § 99: App. Pt. I., p. 345).

715. NORTH WALES.—Of the food, clothing, health, and physical condition of the collier population of this district, the Sub-Commissioner reports:—" In comparing the condition of colliers and miners and their Children with agricultural and other labourers, I found they had better wages, that they live better, their houses are better furnished, and their clothing equal if not superior, nor do they work more hours.   Until the years of adolescence, and for some time afterwards, their health and physical condition continue good.

716. " In respect to food I must observe that the diet in Wales is of a lower order than that of England.   Less of animal and more of milk and farinaceous food is used ; but everywhere the Children have a sufficient quantity of nourishing diet, though in quality it may be esteemed inferior.   Children at work in the pits and mines breakfast before they leave home ; their dinner is brought to them by their friends, and consists of bread, butter, potatoes, a little bacon occasionally, with milk or broth.   They have supper at home on their return from work ; most of them have a piece of bread and butter to eat between breakfast and dinner, and between dinner and supper, which is eaten while at work.

717. " Their physical condition is a proof that they have a sufficiency of nutritive food to maintain health and strength, and their food is certainly both in quality and quantity equal to that which Children of their station and neighbourhood have who do no work ; their clothing is in most instances well calculated to their work and station.   The collier boys have thick coarse woollen jackets in common wear ; none whom I examined had less than two suits and three shirts.

718 " As soon as the Children came up I was surprised and pleased to observe the alacrity with which they went to play ; they were quite alive to their amusements, and enjoyed themselves with all the vivacity of youth and health, preferring their games to going home to their food.   When examining Mr. James Jones, the under-ground bailiff at the British Iron Company's Collieries at Ruabon, he, in answer to my question whether the boys were fatigued and wearied by their day's work so that they could not enjoy recreation when it was over, replied in his native tongue, " No, they bound like young goats from their work to their play."   The language was a little figurative, but I found the fact as he stated it.

719. " From personal examination of the Children and Young Persons at many collieries, and from the information I obtained from several medical men of extensive practice amongst the colliers, I am enabled to state that they are by no means an unhealthy class.   I expected to find them suffering under numerous diseases, and martyrs to a thousand accidents ; my surprise, however, was excited by their general good health.   A little peculiarity may be observed in their gait, from the long-continued action and tension of some of the muscles and the relaxation of others, but it is scarcely observable" (H. H. Jones, Esq., Report, §§ 25, 26, 36, 37: App. Pt. II., pp. 368, 369).

720. SOUTH WALES.—In this district " the Children and Young Persons employed in collieries generally take to their work bread and cheese for their meal in the day-time.   A supper is generally provided for the collier's return, of bacon and vegetables most usually, for the colliers rarely eat much fresh meat during the week (R. H. Franks, Esq., Report, § 49: App. Pt. II., p. 480).

721. " In general the Welsh women are remarkable for attention to warm clothing, which they secure for themselves in woollens, flannels, &c.; nor are they less anxious for their husbands and children ; the men and children are always well defended against the general inclemency of the mountain country.   On the return from work it is usual for the workmen and children to be washed; in fact, in lodging-houses it is part of the bargain that the lodger shall be washed every night previous to retiring to rest ; a point which, by the way, is strenuously insisted on by the housekeeper (Ibid. § 51, p. 481).

722. " As affecting the health and comfort of a working population, few subjects are more important than the situation, structure, and drainage of their houses.   The situation of houses inhabited by colliers in the county of Glamorgan is generally on the side of a hill, from the hilly character of the country ; and as the drainage is almost universally neglected, they are much affected by the heavy rains to which South Wales is particularly exposed, and which pour in torrents down the mountain sides.

COAL MINES.
Physical Condition.
Food, Clothing, Health, and Vigour.
North Wales.

South Wales.

Thomas Fellon, Esq., of Blackwood, says—" The houses occupied by the collier population in this neighbourhood are generally built on sloping grounds, where one habitation is above another, and very rarely drained; although it must be obvious, from the side-land situation, that drains are much required." And, continues that gentleman—" There are places occupied by the poorer part of the population that require to be drained; and as there are no public means for carrying off filth, &c., from these places, it must influence fever during different periods of the year. The interior of the cottages is small, comprising generally two rooms on the floor, one of them used as a bed-room : the rooms above are used as bed-rooms, and there is usually a pantry or scullery in the cottage. This district is particularly hilly, and the houses are for the most part scattered; some are built on elevated spots, while others are near the river, where the fog and damp exists to a much greater degree, in which places low and continued fevers, which frequently end in typhus, exist in a much greater degree than in more airy situations' (Ibid. § 119, 120. p. 489).

723. " Indeed it would be very difficult to find many collier communities where the drainage can be said to be good : whole villages labour under similar disadvantages, and the absence of privies, &c., amongst the labouring population manifests a want of appreciation of comfort in domestic arrangements. In the large village of Blackwood there are not 10 privies; and it is the more remarkable where houses are built by the proprietors themselves for the people employed in their collieries and mines that such arrangements are not made: but in a small cluster of houses, called the Land-level Houses, perhaps 25 altogether, which in themselves are well constructed and clean, inhabited by the colliers and other workmen of the Pentyrch Works, there was but *one* privy for the whole community. But perhaps the most miserable hovels inhabited by the working people are to be found in the neighbourhood of the Hirwain Works, and they derive a more comfortless appearance from the barren surface of the plain in which they are situated. Many of these are nothing more than mud-cabins, in many instances a deserted cowshed converted into a human habitation; a rude thatch forms the roof, and, apparently to avoid the storms that sweep along that plain, they are built in every hollow that can be found, where of course they receive the drainage of the surrounding elevations. Hirwain itself, literally the long meadow, is bordered by a lofty range of hills, and is in many parts boggy and full of water. A more cheerless place could scarcely be found in South Wales : even the school which I visited here more resembles a stable than a place for education, and is almost surrounded with a ditch of dirty water " (Ibid. § 122, p. 490.)

724. " From a careful examination of the collected evidence, and from attentive inquiry into the several subjects distinguished in this Report, I submit to you the following points as the result of my investigations :—

725. " That labour in the collieries of the counties of Glamorgan and Pembroke, in South Wales, and of Monmouth in England, is unwholesome, and productive of diseases which have a tendency either to shorten life or reduce the number of years of useful labour in the mechanic.

726. " That the physical health and strength of Children and Young Persons are deteriorated by their employment at the early ages and in the works before enumerated" (Ibid. §§ 124—126, p. 491).

727. From the evidence collected in Monmouthshire it also appears that the men and boys in this district "wash themselves all over every evening; that the diet is plain, nutritive, and plentiful generally; one meal of animal food daily, and a liberal quantity of home-brewed beer; the good wages the Children earn enabling their parents to provide a more generous diet than the other labouring classes can afford; and that the clothing is of a sufficient quantity and proper quality." (R. W. Jones, Esq., Evidence, No. 48: App. Pt. II., p. 622, l. 27).

728. " I have not observed that the physical condition of the Children and Young Persons employed in the works of this district is in any way deteriorated by either the nature or amount of their employment. There may be some cases in which the health of the Children may be affected by their employment, but these cases are few and not one has yet been brought under my notice worthy of comment, and this head I must beg to refer you to the Report of Mr. Edward E. Tucker, the experienced resident surgeon at the British Iron Company's Works (R. W. Jones, Esq., Report, § 37: App. Pt. II., p. 586).

729. " I have not observed, nor have I been able to learn, that any branch of employment at the different works in this district is unfavourable to the health of the Children or Young Persons engaged in it, no cases having been brought under my notice of sickness arising either from the nature or duration of the employment of parties ; on the contrary, all the medical men attached to the works which I

have visited, and with whom I have been enabled to confer on this subject, agree in stating that the Children and Young Persons employed in the works enjoy a greater share of health, and are freer from the epidemics of the neighbourhood, than Children of similar ages not so employed (Ibid. § 14, 15: p. 583).

COAL MINES.

Physical Condition.

Food, Clothing, Health, and vigour.

730. FOREST OF DEAN.—" My observations and inquiries have alike issued in the conviction that the general health and vigour of colliers and miners are nearly on a par with those of other labourers employed under circumstances apparently more favourable to both. The more hale complexion, and fuller development of manly growth, in the latter class are very observable; but in point of ability for enduring fatigue, and in the average duration of life, there is less difference between them and their underground brethren than is commonly supposed.

Forest of Dean.

731. " I could not discover that the health of the Children, even of seven or eight years of age, was materially affected by their daily subhumation of eight or ten hours. Their eyes exhibited no signs of inflammation or weakness; and though pallor of countenance is prevalent, it is by no means universal among them. On the contrary, many of the boys have a robust and even ruddy appearance, after clean water has performed its office on their grim visages. Their general demeanour is cheerful, and they generally profess themselves satisfied with their employment, though always ambitious of advancing to a higher class in the pit, and higher wages. To some lads of more delicate fibre, and active intellect, under-ground labour is confessedly irksome; and I could not but feel a painful sympathy with several of this description, whose hard fate gives them little hope of any change.

732. " A striking proof that the human constitution becomes reconciled to severe trials of its hardihood, is found in the absolute impunity with which some of the hod-boys, in ill-drained pits with narrow galleries, continue dragging their loads, day after day, for eight or ten consecutive hours, on hands and knees, along what is, in fact, a water-drain, though the water may not be more than an inch deep. John Knight (No. 31) is a good illustration of this fact, being a fine hale-looking and stout lad. He declared he never felt any inconvenience from this slavish work, after he had got it over, though the condition of his hands and knees, besmeared with clay and coal-dust, sufficiently indicated the sort of pathway he is doomed to traverse in performing his daily task.

733. " Nothing impressed me more with the idea of vital danger to the health of these laborious Children than the sudden transitions they make from the uniform temperature of the mine to the external atmosphere, under all its variations. They often emerge, bare-chested and bare-throated, in a state of copious perspiration, into an atmosphere many degrees lower than that they have been working in, and never seem to think of any precaution. I have observed them hovering, for a few minutes, about a fire near the pit's mouth, as though sensible of a chill; but they appear neither to apprehend nor experience any ill effects. Probably their practice of diligent ablution, after arriving at their homes, restores the healthy action of the pores, and prevents diseases which might otherwise supervene, even in their hardy constitutions" (E. Waring, Esq., Report, § 53-62: App. Pt. II., p. 5). The Evidence shows that in general the food and clothing of the Children and Young Persons employed in the coal-mines of this district are substantially good. (See witnesses Nos. 9, 10, 17, 39, *et seq.*)

734. SOUTH GLOUCESTERSHIRE.—The physical condition of the collier population in this district is stated to be similar to that of the people employed in the coal-mines of the Forest of Dean. To the evidence which shows that the Children and Young Persons in general are well fed and clothed, there are some painful exceptions, of which the following is an example:—

South Gloucestershire.

John Harvey, thirteen years of age, a carter in Crown Pit (Mr. Waters's): " Gets potatoes and butter, or potatoes fried with bacon, when he goes home from the pit; gets whatever he can catch; is always very hungry after work; seldom has as much as he could eat. Does not go to Sunday-school, because he has no clothes besides what he works in; cannot read; never had a pair of shoes or stockings in his life." Sub-Commissioner: " This boy has evidently been stunted in his growth: I should say more from want of sufficient food than any other cause. He states that he has rarely as much as he wants, and subsequently acknowledged that he had sometimes gone without food for two or three days! He is straight, and not badly proportioned, but has altogether a melancholy and starveling appearance. Mr.

COAL MINES.

Physical Condition.

*Food, Clothing,
Health, and Vigour.*

South
Gloucestershire.

Waters confirmed this boy's statement, on my naming his assertion of having gone without food for two or three days, saying that he learnt the fact too late to obviate such sad privation. It was named to him immediately afterwards, and he knows this poor little fellow did actually work in the pit for three days, without food, for sheer poverty, which should not have happened had he known in time that the boy was so badly off. He has a drunken father, and an improvident mother" (E. Waring, Esq., Evidence, No. 52 : App. Pt. II., p. 40, l. 52).

735. " This lad is a pitiable specimen of a much enduring class of colliery boys, whose subsistence depends on their own exertions, often prematurely stimulated, either from being deprived of their fathers by death, or labouring under the curse of drunken, dissolute, and unfeeling parents, who would apathetically see their Children enslave themselves, rather than contribute to their comfort by a single act of self-denial. These neglected beings turn out in the morning, taking with them a scanty bag of provisions, to be eaten in the bowels of the earth, where they toil out their daily dole of eight or ten hours ; then return to a comfortless home, taking their chance of a good meal, a bad one, or none at all. For a bed they are content with an old coal-sack laid upon straw, or occupy whatever portion they can secure of a family bed, which must suffice for three or four other inmates. Grovelling in their habits, depressed in spirit, and without any stimulus to improvement, these poor boys passively take such work, and wages, as they can most readily obtain ; and if they can satisfy the cravings of hunger, seem to abandon all expectation of anything further, beyond the most sordid covering for their nakedness, and a place of shelter and repose. Some of them will eagerly ask permission to work by night occasionally, as well as by day, for the sake of a small addition to their weekly pittance.

736. " To these victims of ignorance and poverty the Sabbath is a day of wearisome vacuity, or reckless play. An act of worship is nearly as strange to them as to a Hottentot unenlightened by Christianity. Instruction they have no idea of, and, if they had, the want of decent clothing would keep them from mingling with their better provided yoke-fellows at the Sunday-school. This is, indeed, the picture of an extreme case, but it is only too correct an outline which might be filled up with still darker colours in portraying the unhappy class to which Harvey belongs. It will be seen by the evidence that this half-fed and half-clothed lad—stunted in growth, so that his companion in carting, though two years younger than himself, is a full head taller—assists in drawing 2 cwt. of coal a distance of 160 yards in a tub without wheels. I did not ascertain how many tubs are carted by these two boys, one pulling and the other pushing behind, during their day's work ; but, judging from the general practice, I should say from 50 to 60. Even supposing them to be fewer, this is surely hard labour for the poor returns of 5*s*. 6*d*. weekly, that is, 3*s*. to Harvey, and 2*s*. 6*d*. to his helper.

737. " The other boy has a good and careful mother, who feeds him well, and keeps whole garments on his back ; whilst Harvey's father is represented to be a drunkard, and his mother an improvident slattern. The poor little fellow told me he had never in his life possessed a pair of shoes or stockings. There is but too manifest a deficiency in nutritious diet and comfortable clothing, in the case of large families, where few are old enough to earn even the smallest pittance. Still the colliers, as a class, are considered better off than the agricultural labourers ; and I have every reason to believe this to be the fact" (E. Waring, Esq., Report, § 21, *et seq :* App. Pt. II., p. 32).

738. NORTH SOMERSETSHIRE.—" They are, with few exceptions, a strong and robust set of men, and their Children have such a trying ordeal to pass through that, on the Spartan principle, they must either sink under it or become hardy and enduring. They do not, however, long retain their full vigour, and they then exchange from ' coal-breaking,' which is the most trying kind of work, to the ordinary labour of clearing the ' ways' and propping the roofs of the galleries. In some mines where ' firedamp ' prevails their health gets soon broken from the deleterious quality of the air" (Dr. Stewart, Report, § 9 : App. Pt. II., p. 48).

739. IRELAND.—The two Sub-Commissioners who visited Ireland equally testify to the healthy appearance of the Young People connected with the colleries of both the North and the South of Ireland. Their wages, indeed, procure for them better food than is attainable by the very poor population by which they are gene-

rally surrounded.   Mr. Roper's description of the young workers at the Dromagh colliery will serve, with slight variations, for the whole :—" Their appearance was very healthy : they said their work was hard, and that they must live well.   I found they were much in the habit of using bread instead of potatoes, and had meat two or three times a-week.   Cleanliness is a thing not very often met with in Ireland, but these boys I fancy do not wash themselves more than once a-week. It was the dinner-hour when I got there, and not one of them did I see who had washed even his face and hands.   Like most of the miners and colliers I have seen in Ireland, they do not generally change their clothes but once a-week" (F. Roper, Esq., Report, § 5 : App. Pt. I., p. 869.—T. Martin, Esq., Evidence, Nos. 47 and 51 ; Ibid, p. 884, l. 33, and p. 885, l. 33.)

COAL MINES.

Physical Condition

Food, Clothing, Health, and Vigour.

Ireland.

PECULIAR EFFECTS UPON THE PHYSICAL CONDITION OF EARLY EMPLOYMENT IN COAL MINES.

740.   Although the physical condition generally of the persons employed in collieries, as long as they are able to pursue their labour, is thus seen to derive a favourable character from the advantages procured by superior wages, yet the testimony is equally full to the fact that the nature and circumstances of this labour itself have an appreciable effect upon the Children and Young Persons, especially injurious in the many cases in which it is pursued to excess ; and that they entail ultimately grievous diseases, accompanied by an imminent liability to casualties, which shorten the period during which the labour can be continued, or bring it suddenly to a close by premature death.

Peculiarities of Physical Condition.

1.—*Immediate Effects of Overworking.*

741.   In describing the circumstances which mainly influence the character of the labour of Children and Young Persons in coal mines, we have already noticed the feelings of fatigue by which the severity that some of those circumstances give to it is commonly measured.   Some of the Sub-Commissioners, and a large proportion of the witnesses examined by them, describe fatigue beyond the power of healthful endurance merely as the immediate result of these circumstances of severity, wherever they prevail.   Such is the case in North Staffordshire, Oldham, North Lancashire, Cumberland, the West of Scotland, North Wales, South Gloucestershire, and North Somersetshire, and in Ireland.   In other districts they bear express testimony to the ample strength of all classes of the workpeople to bear the labour without fatigue, severe as all colliery labour may in some respects be regarded.   This is especially seen in South Staffordshire (Dr. Mitchell, Evidence, No. 3 : App. Pt. I. p. 62, l. 28) ; Shropshire (Ibid., Report, § 287, p. 36 ; and 313, p. 39 ; Warwickshire (Ibid. Report, § 16, p. 90) ; Leicestershire (Ibid. Evidence, passim) ; and South Durham (Ibid. Report, §§ 212, 215, p. 143 ; Evidence, Nos. 101, 514, 115, &c.).   But there are other districts in which fatigue to the young labourers is described as so common and so severe, as to challenge attention, rather as the result of a general excess of labour, than that of any peculiar form of severity.*

Effects of overworkings.

---

* The feeling of fatigue, when constant and painful, may be regarded as a certain indication that labour is excessive.   All the organs of the animal body are directly or indirectly sentient, and the final cause of their being rendered capable of painful sensation is conceived by physiologists to be, that by means of pain warning may be given when they so deviate from the state of health as to be incapable of the due performance of their functions.   The painful feeling called fatigue is a monitor of this kind.   That health can remain unimpaired, and that the duration of life can reach its natural term, while there is ever present the consciousness of excessive fatigue, is impossible, because by that very feeling the fatigued organs declare that they are worked beyond their strength ; and we learn from experience that, if such an amount of work continue to be exacted from them, they not only become progressively weaker, but sooner or later lapse into a state of positive disease.   Disease may not be the manifest and immediate result : on the contrary, the development of disease may be a somewhat slow process, and the manifestation of it proportionally distant ; but the ultimate production of it is as certain as the production of any physical effect from the operation of its physical cause.   If, then, in great

742. DERBYSHIRE.—In this district, as has been shown, the hours of work are commonly 14, and are sometimes extended to 16 out of the 24, and the mines in general are most imperfectly drained and ventilated. Of the fatigue of such labour, so protracted and carried on in such places of work, the following evidence exhibits a striking picture, and it will be observed that the witnesses of every class, children, young persons, colliers, underground stewards, agents, parents, teachers, and ministers of religion, all concur in making similar statements.

Thomas Straw, aged seven, Ilkiston: "They wouldn't let him sleep in the pit or stand still; he feels very tired when he comes out; gets his tea and goes to bed. Feels tired and sleepy on a Sunday morning; would rather be in bed than go to school" (J. M. Fellows, Esq., Evidence, No. 21: App. Pt. II., p. 269, l. 11).—John Hawkins, aged eight, Underwood: "Is tired and glad to get home; never wants to play" (Ibid. No. 108: p. 293, l. 16).—George Pollard, Strelley: "Feels very tired; his back and shoulders ache; he is always too tired to play" (Ibid. No. 116: p. 295, l. 8).—Thomas Moult, aged nine, Trowell: "They want no play, but go home to bed as soon as they can" (Ibid. No. 15: p. 267, l. 35).—Matthew Carrington, aged nine, Ilkiston: "Is tired, and very seldom goes out of doors" (Ibid. No. 19: p. 268, l. 45).—Robert Blount, aged ten, Eastwood: "He is always too tired to play, and is glad to get to bed; his back and legs ache; he had rather drive plough or go to school than work in a pit" (Ibid. No. 99: p. 290, l. 44). —Joseph Skelton, aged ten, Underwood: "He is very tired, and always glad to get to bed; had much rather work above ground; they dare not then work them so hard" (Ibid. No. 109: p. 293, l. 35).—Aaron Chambers, aged eleven, Watnall: "He never plays from one week to another; he is too tired without play; had rather do any work above ground, it is such hard work" (Ibid. No. 101: p. 291, l. 30).—William Hart, aged eleven, West Hallam: "Has felt so tired, that he was glad to get home, and too tired to play; has felt very stiff and tired on a Sunday" (Ibid. No. 52: p. 277, l. 40).—Joseph Limb, aged eleven, Loscoe: "Never plays when he has done three-quarters of a day's work, he is too tired" (Ibid. No. 68: p. 282, l. 59).—George Riley, twelve years old, Babbington: "At night is so stiff and sore that when he sits down can hardly get up again" (Ibid. No. 147: p. 301, l. 56).—William Watson, aged twelve, Watnall: "Always too tired for play, and glad to get to bed" (Ibid. No. 102: p. 291, l. 54).—William Trance, aged twelve, Bagthorpe: "Is very tired and glad to get home; his arms, legs, and back, all ache" (Ibid. No. 80: p. 285, l. 50).—Stephen Morley, aged twelve, Newthorpe: "Had rather work above ground, the colliers' work is so hard; often is so tired that his limbs ache again" (Ibid. No. 134: p. 299, l. 8).

John Bostock, aged seventeen, Babbington: "Has often been made to work until he was so tired as to lie down on his road home until 12 o'clock, when his mother has come and led him home—has done so many times when he first went to the pits; he has sometimes been so fatigued that he could not eat his dinner, but has been beaten and made to work until night; he never thought of play, was always too anxious to get to bed; is sure this is all true" (Ibid. No. 146: p. 301, l. 33).—John Leadbeater, aged eighteen, Babbington: "Has two miles to go to the pit, and must be there before six, and works until eight; he has often worked all night, and been made by the butties to work as usual the next day; has often been so tired that he has lain in bed all Sunday. He knows no work so bad as that of a pit lad" (Ibid. No. 138: p. 300, l. 16).—Samuel Radford, aged nineteen, New Birchwood: "Has been a week together and never seen daylight, but on a Sunday, and not much then, he was so sleepy" (Ibid. No. 271: p. 326, l. 45).—See also Nos. 51, 53, 195.

743. These statements of the Children are fully confirmed by the evidence of the adult workpeople.—

William Fletcher, aged thirty-three, collier, West Hallam: "Considers the collier's life a very hard one, both for man and boy; the latter full as hard as the former" (Ibid. No. 57: p. 279, l. 17). —John Beasley, collier, aged forty-nine, Shipley: "He has known instances where children have been so overcome with the work as to cause them to go off in a decline; he has seen those who could not get home without their father's assistance, and have fallen asleep before they could be got to bed; has known children of six years old sent to the pit, but thinks there are none at Shipley under seven or eight; in his opinion a boy is too weak to stand the hours even to drive between until he is eight or nine years old; the boys go down at six in the morning, and has known them kept down until nine or ten, until they are 'almost ready to exhaust;' the children and young persons work the same hours as the men; the children are obliged to work in the night if the waggon-road is out of repair, or the water coming on them; it happens sometimes two or three times in the week; they then go down at six P.M. to six A.M., and have from ten minutes to half an hour allowed for supper, according to the work they have to do; they mostly ask the children who have been at work the previous day to go down with them, but seldom have to oblige them; when he was a boy he has worked for 36 hours running many a time, and many more besides himself have done so" (Ibid. No. 40:

numbers of instances, the labour of the coal-mines in its present duration and degree produce throughout the period of Childhood the constant feeling of fatigue, and if this feeling continue, though in a somewhat diminished degree, throughout the period of Adolescence, what, from the known operation of the laws of the animal economy, we should anticipate in Manhood, would be a less perfect development of the growth and stature of the body, a less healthy and vigorous physical constitution, and, as the natural consequence, an appreciable diminution in the duration of life.—T. S. S.

p. 274, l. 23).—William Wardle, aged forty, Eastwood: " There is no doubt colliers are much harder worked than labourers; ' indeed it is the hardest work under heaven' " (Ibid. No. 84 : p. 287, l. 51).—Samuel Richards, aged forty, Awsworth: " There are Sunday Schools when they will go; but when boys have been beaten, knocked about, and covered with sludge all the week, they want to be in bed to rest all day on Sunday" (Ibid. No. 166 : p. 307, l. 58).— William Sellers, operative, aged twenty-two, Butterley Company: " When he first worked in a pit he has been so tired that he has slept as he walked " (Ibid. No. 222 : p. 319, l. 35)).

William Knighton, aged twenty-four, Denby: " He remembers "mony" a time he has dropped asleep with the meat in his mouth through fatigue. It is those butties, they are the very devil; they first impose upon them in one way, then in another" (Ibid. No. 314 : p. 334, l. 42.)— * * * * * *, engine-man, Babbington: " Has, when working whole days, often seen the children lie down on the pit-bank and go to sleep, they were so tired" (Ibid. No. 137 : p. 300, l. 10). —John Attenborough, schoolmaster, Greasley: " Has observed the collier children are more tired and dull than the others, but equally as anxious to learn" (Ibid. No. 153 : p. 304, l. 22).— Ann Birkin: " Is mother to Thomas and Jacob, who work in Messrs. Fenton's pits; they have been so tired after a whole day's work that she has at times had to wash them and lift them into bed" (Ibid. No. 81 : p. 285, l. 59).—Hannah Neale, Butterley Park : " They come home so tired, that they become stiff, and can hardly get to bed. Constantine, the one ten years old, formerly worked in the same pit as his brothers, but about half a year since his toe was cut off by the bind falling; notwithstanding this, the loader made him work until the end of the day, although in the greatest pain. He was out of work more than four months owing to this accident." (Ibid. No. 237 : p. 320, l. 51).—Ellen Wagstaff, Watnall: " Has five children, three at Trough-lane and two at Willow-lane, Greasley; one at Trough-lane is eighteen, one fourteen, one thirteen years of age; and those at Willow-lane are sixteen and nineteen; they are variously employed; the youngest was not seven years old when he first went to the pits. The whole have worked since they were seven or seven and a half; they have worked from six to eight; from six to two for half-days; no meal-time in half-days; she has known them when at full work so tired when they first worked, that you could not hear them speak, and they fell asleep before they could eat their suppers; ' it has grieved her to the heart to see them.' " (Ibid. No. 104 : p. 292, l. 18).—Ann Wilson, Underwood: " Is mother to Richard Clarke and mother-in-law to Matthew Wilson. Has heard what they have said, and believes it to be true; has known when they work whole days they have come home so tired and dirty, that they could scarcely be prevented lying down on the ashes by the fire-side, and could not take their clothes off; has had to do it for them, and take them to the brook to wash them, and has set up most of the night to get their clothes dry. The next morning they have gone to the pit like bears to the stake" (Ibid. No. 112 : p. 294, l. 5).—Hannah Brixton, Babbington : " The butties slave them past anything. Has frequently had them drop asleep as soon as they have got in the house, and complain of their legs and arms aching very bad" (Ibid. No. 149 : p. 302, l. 44).

William Hawley, schoolmaster, Ilkiston " Has certainly perceived those children who work in the pits much more dull and stupid than the others, both at school and chapel; it is his opinion children are sent to work at the pits too young, and it is decidedly too long for children to work from six to eight; he has often to complain of the colliers' children's bad attendance on Sunday mornings, and the reply generally is, they were so tired they overslept themselves" (Ibid. No. 32 : p. 271, l. 47).—Isaac Rowbotham, schoolmaster, West Hallam : " Has observed boys who have been brought up in the free-school, and afterwards worked in a pit, and attended the Sunday-school, read much worse than they formerly did, appear duller, and more tired than other boys, although equally as willing to learn" (Ibid. No. 59 : p. 279, l. 7).— Samuel Brentnall, Kimberley School : " Has been superintendent more than six years; has observed the pit-boys much duller and more stupid at learning; they are very heavy and drowsy, and frequently drop asleep during the service; has observed this more so amongst the younger ones" (Ibid. No. 165 : p. 307, l. 19).—Daniel Hook, schoolmaster, Radford : " Has often observed and mentioned it that the pit-boys are anxious and willing to be taught, but he scarcely ever knew one but what was duller than the other boys in the school, and always appeared more tired and sleepy." [This opinion was agreed to by the other teachers] (Ibid. No. 4 : p. 264, l. 6).—Samuel Morris, schoolmaster, Ilkiston : " Has noticed that they are much more tired than other boys, and do not come before 10; they are also much more apt to sleep during the service than others" (Ibid. No. 30 : p. 271, l. 29).—William Robinson, Sunday-school teacher, Ilkiston : " Has taught the class where the principal part of the collier-boys are; he finds them duller and more tired than the other boys; has often seen even the bigger boys fall to sleep, and is sure they are not so quick as the frame-work knitting boys; they have told him, excepting on a Sunday, they are months without seeing daylight; another reason is, that being so fatigued they do not attend school-hours so well as the other boys; they often tell him they could not awake: he finds they are as willing, but far backwarder than the other boys who are not so old" (Ibid. No. 31 : p. 271, l. 35).—Rev. F. Hewgill, rector, Radford : " He certainly thinks, indeed has noticed, they are more dull than their school-fellows" (Ibid. No. 6 : p. 264, l. 54).—Rev. W. J. Hobson, minister of Trowell : " He has observed they appear more tired, and do not attend so early, and the parents, when applied to, often say they come home so wearied they cannot get them to school in time" (Ibid. No. 11 : p. 266, l. 33).

744. WEST RIDING OF YORKSHIRE.—In this district the coal owners in general, and most of the managers and underground stewards, state that the work is not

particularly severe, and that the Children and Young Persons are not fatigued by it. Some few of the girls and boys themselves say that they like the work, and that it does not fatigue them; a few others state that it tired them at first, but that they have now become used to it, and that it does not fatigue them much; but the great majority say that they are always tired, and the language which many of them use to express their sensations shows that they feel their labour to be extremely oppressive.

Mr. George Traviss, coal master, Barnsley : " I do not think the children are overworked so as to hurt them. They always appear to me to be very cheerful, and run and play about when they come out of the pit in the evening" (J. C. Symons, Esq., Evidence, No. 84 : App. Pt. I., p. 243, l. 55).—Robert C. Clarke, Esq., coal-master, Silkstone : " I think they are not overworked, because I know they will run home when they get out of the pits, and are up to all sorts of mischief and fun" (Ibid. No. 140 : p. 261, l. 67).—William Newbould, Esq., coal master : " They could learn in the evenings if they chose ; they are not too tired with their work to do so" (Ibid. No. 15 : p. 230, l. 6).—Among others the following Children and Young Persons, all of whom are upwards of eleven years of age, and most of them upwards of fourteen, state that they are not fatigued by their work : Witnesses Nos. 213, 301, 302, 307, 316, 318, 319, 326, 327.

745. Some of the coal owners themselves, however, together with their agents and all other classes of witnesses, corroborate the statements of most of the Children and Young Persons, as to the severity of the labour and the great fatigue produced by it.—

John Twibell, Esq., coalmaster, Barnsley : " I am confident that children ought to be prevented from going into pits till ten years old. It has a bad effect on their minds, and tends to cripple their strength" (Ibid. No. 111 : p. 251, l. 50).—Moses Kay, underground steward to Mr. Barber, Rawmarsh : " It is hard work hurrying. They are tired at night" (Ibid. No. 52 : p. 236, l. 45).—Mr. John Clarkson Sutcliffe, agent for the Gauber Colliery, belonging to the executors of Mr. Samuel Thorpe : " When the children are allowed to go in too little, they are certainly tired, and from unfeeling parents this is sometimes the case" (Ibid. No. 118 : p. 253, l. 39).—George Norburn, pit-steward to Mr. Swann of Chapelton : "Very little is learnt in the evening schools ; the boys are wearied and not disposed to go : they would rather, when it's light and fine in the summer time, go out to play when they are not too tired" (Ibid. No. 71 : p. 241, l. 16).—William Froggatt, underground steward, Mr. Swann's colliery, Chapelton : "The children are harder worked in these pits and are well tired at night. Not many fall ill" (Ibid. No. 73 : p. 241, l. 58).

John Rawson, collier, aged forty : "I work at Mr. Sorby's pit, Handsworth. I think children are worked over much sometimes" (Ibid. No. 81 : p. 243, l. 25).—Peter Waring, collier, Billingley : " I never should like my children to go in. They are not beaten, it is the work that hurts them. It is mere slavery, and nothing but it" (Ibid. No. 125 : p. 256, l. 6).—John Hargreave, collier, Thorpe's colliery : " Hurrying is heavy work for children. They ought not to work till they are 12 years old, and then put two together for these heavy corves" (Ibid. No. 130 : p. 256, l. 44).—Mr. Timothy Marshall, collier, aged thirty-five, Darton : " I think the hurrying is what hurts girls, and it is too hard work for their strength. I think that children cannot be educated after they once get to work in pits ; they are both tired and even disinclined to learn when they have done work" (Ibid. No. 141 : p. 262, l. 39).—A collier at Messrs. Traviss's Pit : "The children get but little schooling ; six or seven out of nine or ten know nothing. They never go to night-schools, except some odd ones. When the children get home they cannot go to school, for they have to be up so early in the morning—soon after four—and they cannot do without rest" (Ibid. No. 94 : p. 246, l. 33).—Mr. George Armitage, aged thirty-six, formerly collier at Silkstone, now teacher at Hayland school : " Little can be learnt merely on Sundays, and they are too tired as well as indisposed to go to night-schools. I am decidedly of opinion that when trade is good the work of hurriers is generally continuous ; but when there are two together, perhaps the little one will have a rest when the big one is filling or riddling" (Ibid. No. 138 : p. 261, l. 24).

William Firth, between six and seven years old, Deal Wood Pit, Flockton :—" I hurry with my sister. I don't like to be in pit. I was crying to go out this morning. It tires me a great deal" (Ibid. No. 218 : p. 282, l. 11).—John Wright, hurrier in Thorpe's colliery : " I shall be nine years old next Whitsuntide. It tires me much. It tires my arms. I have been two years in the pit, and have been hurrying all the time. It tires the small of my arms" (Ibid. No. 129 ; p. 256, l. 31).—Daniel Drenchfield : " I am going in ten. I am more tired in the forenoon than at night ; it makes my back ache ; I work all day, the same as the other boy ; I rest me when I go home at night ; I never go to play at night ; I get my supper and go to bed" (Ibid. No. 63 : p. 238, l. 32).—George Glossop, aged twelve : " I help to fill and hurry, and am always tired at night when I've done" (Ibid. No. 50 : p. 236, l. 21).—Martin Stanley : " I tram by myself and find it very hard work. It tires me in my legs and shoulders every day. (Ibid. No. 69 : p. 240, l. 27).—Charles Hoyle : " I was thirteen last January. I work in the thin coal-pit. I find it very hard work. We work at night one week, and in the day the other. It tires me very much sometimes. It tires us most in the legs, especially when we have to go on our hands and feet. I fill as well as hurry" (Ibid. No. 78 : p. 242, l. 41).—Jonathan Clayton, thirteen and a half years old, Soap Work Colliery, Sheffield : " Hurrying is very hard work ; when

I got home at night I was knocked up" (Ibid. No. 6 : p. 227, l. 48).—Andrew Roger, aged seventeen years : " I work for my father, who is an undertaker. I get, and have been getting two years. I find it very hard work indeed ; it tires me very much ; I can hardly get washed of a night till nine o'clock, I am so tired" (Ibid. No. 60: p. 237, l. 49).—[" This witness," says the Sub-Commissioner, " when examined in the evening after his work was over, ached so much with fatigue that he could not stand upright"] (Report, § 109: App. Pt. I., p. 181).—Joseph Reynard, aged nineteen, Mr. Stancliffe's pit, Mirfield : " I began hurrying when I was nine ; I get now ; I cannot hurry because one leg is shorter than another. I have had my hip bad since I was fifteen. I am very tired at night. I worked in a wet place to day. I have worked in places before as wet as I have been in to-day. [I examined Joseph Reynard ; he has had several large abscesses in the thigh from hip-joint disease. The thigh-bone is dislocated from the same cause ; the leg is about three inches shorter ; the spinal column is curved ; two or three of the abscesses are now discharging. No appearance of puberty from all the examinations I made. I should not think him more than eleven or twelve years of age, except from his teeth. I think him quite unfit to follow any occupation, much less the one he now occupies. (Signed) U. Bradbury, surgeon.]"—"This case," says the Sub-Commissioner, " is one reflecting the deepest discredit on his employers" (J. C. Symons, Esq., Evidence, No. 272: App. Pt. I., p. 293, l. 29).—Elizabeth Eggley, sixteen years old : " I find my work very much too hard for me. I hurry alone. It tires me in my arms and back most. I am sure it is very hard work and tires us very much ; it is too hard for girls to do. We sometimes go to sleep before we get to bed" (Ibid, No. 114 : p. 252, l. 44).—Ann Wilson, aged ten and a half, Messrs. Smith's colliery : " Sometimes the work tires us when we have a good bit to do ; it tries me in my back. I hurry by myself. I push with my head " (Ibid. 229 : p. 284, l. 12).—Elizabeth Day, hurrier. Messrs Hopwood's pit, Barnsley : " It is very hard work for us all. It is harder work than we ought to do a deal. I have been lamed in my ankle, and strained in my back" (Ibid. No. 85 : p. 244, l. 33).—Mary Shaw : " I am nineteen years old. I hurry in the pit you were in to-day. I have ever been much tired with my work" (Ibid. No. 123: p. 249, l. 38).—Ann Eggley, hurrier in Messrs. Thorpe's colliery : " The work is far too hard for me ; the sweat runs off me all over sometimes. I'm very tired at night. Sometimes when we get home at night we have not power to wash us, and then we go to bed. Sometimes we fall asleep in the chair. Father said last night it was both a shame and a disgrace for girls to work as we do, but there was nought else for us to do. The girls are always tired" (Ibid. No. 113 : p. 252, l. 17).—Eliza Coats : " I hurry with my brother. It tires me a great deal, and tires my back and arms" (Ibid. No. 115: p. 252, l. 59).—Elizabeth Ibbetson, at Mr. Harrison's Pit, Gomersal : " I don't like being at pit ; its too hard work for us. It tires my legs and arms. I push the corf with my head, and it hurts me, and is sore" (Ibid. No. 266 : p. 292, l. 17).

Margaret Gomley, Lindley Moor, aged nine : " Am very tired" (S. S. Scriven, Esq., Evidence, No. 9 : App. Pt. II., p. 103, l. 34).—James Mitchell, aged twelve, Messrs. Holt and Heblewaite's : " I am very tired when I get home ; 'tis enough to tire a horse, and stooping so much makes it bad" (Ibid. No. 2 : p. 101, l. 32).—William Whittaker, aged sixteen, Swan Bank, Mr. Rawson's colliery : " I am always very tired when I go home" (Ibid. No. 13 : p. 104, l. 55).—George Wilkinson, aged thirteen, Low Moor : " Are you tired now ?—Nay. Were you tired then ?—Yea. What makes the difference ?—I can hurry a deal better now" (W. R. Wood, Esq., Evidence, No. 18 : App. Pt. II., p. h 11, l. 30).—John Stevenson, aged fourteen, Low Moor : " Has worked in a coal-pit eight years, went in at six years old ; used to rue to go in, does not rue now ; was very hard work when he went in, and ' I were nobbud a right little one ; ' was not strong enough when he first went, had better have been a bit bigger ; used to be very tired ; sleeps well, did not when first he went ; ' I waur ill tired' " (Ibid. No. 15 : p. h 10, l. 39).—Jabez Scott, aged fifteen, Bowling Iron Works : " Work is very hard ; sleeps well sometimes, sometimes is very ill tired and cannot sleep so weel" (Ibid. No. 38 : p. h 19, l. 29).—William Sharp, Esq., F.R.S., surgeon, Bradford, states, " That he has for twenty years professionally attended at the Low Moor Iron Works ; that there are occasionally cases of deformity, and also bad cases of scrofula, apparently induced by the boys being too early sent into the pits, by their working beyond their strength, by the constant stooping, and by occasionally working in water" (Ibid. No. 60 : p. h 27, l. 45).

746. LANCASHIRE.—Various witnesses examined by Mr. Kennedy describe their labour as producing great exhaustion :—

Rosa Lucas, aged eighteen, Lamberhead Green : " Do you find it very hard work ?—Yes, it is very hard work for a woman. I have been so tired many a time that I could scarcely wash myself. I could scarcely ever wash myself at night, I was so tired ; and I felt very dull and stiff when I set off in the morning" (J. L. Kennedy, Esq., Evidence, No. 92 : App. Pt. II., p. 231, l. 53).—James Crabtree, aged fifteen, Mr. Dearden's, near Todmorden : " Is it hard work for the lads in winter ?—My brother falls asleep before his supper, and the little lass that helps him is often very tired" (Ibid. No. 71 : p. 229, l. 11).—Peter Gaskell, Mr. Lancaster's, near Worsley : " Has four sisters, and they have all worked in the pits ; one of them works in the pits now ; she sometimes complains of the severity of her work. Three years ago, when they had very hard work, I used to hear her complain of the boils on her back, and her legs were all eaten with the water ; she had to go through water to her work ; she used to go about four or five o'clock in the morning, and stay till three or four in the afternoon, just as she was wanted ; I have known her to be that tired at night that she would go to sleep before she had anything to eat" (Ibid. No. 29 : p. 217, l. 36).

747. NORTH LANCASHIRE.—Mr. Austin, after giving a deplorable picture of the labour of Young Children in the thin-seam mines, illustrates its effects by the

words of the parents of some young workers. " I wish," one of them states, "you could see them come in; they come as tired as dogs, and throw themselves on the ground like dogs (here pointing to the hearthstone before the fire); we cannot get them to bed (A. Austin, Esq., Report, § 11 : App. Pt. II., p. 803).

748. North Durham and Northumberland.—The chief employment of Children and Young Persons in the coal mines of this district, namely, in putting, is very severe; none but those who possess strong constitutions and robust health can bear it without extreme fatigue; and different classes of witnesses state that great numbers of the younger Children are often completely exhausted by the labour, while those more advanced in years say that it deprives them of appetite and produces the constant feeling of sickness. The Sub-Commissioner observes that "the silence of some putters on the oppressiveness of their employment must be considered in connexion with the fact that they possess no standard with which to compare their labour; for in neighbourhoods where the inhabitants are wholly colliery workers, remote from towns, it is probable that the younger boys have never witnessed any other species of juvenile employment. Hence, too, when some reply that their putting is easy, such answers must be received as merely implying that it is easy in comparison with difficult putting; while, in fact, the lightest of that labour requires very considerable exertion. 'Canny' or easy putting being all that a boy can expect, his ideas of hardship are associated only with very laborious putting. A considerable variation, however, of the degrees of difficulty is observable in different collieries, as well from artificial causes as from the natural position of the seams of coal. All collieries situated within half a mile north of the great ninety-fathom dyke, which has intruded itself into the northern depository of fossil fuel, are necessarily subject to 'banky' or hilly putting, as the seam rises from nine or ten inches to the yard, and then dips correspondingly. Their labour (that of the helpers-up) is necessarily severe, as they are only employed in emergencies. Occasionally its severity is productive of painful effects, as in Nos. 145, 457, &c." (J. R. Leifchild, Esq., Report, §§ 52, 53: App. Pt. I., p. 522.)

749. The Sub-Commissioner further states that the youngest of the putters, those called " foals " are greatly to be commiserated; that many of them declared that the severity of their labour was such that they would willingly suffer a proportionate diminution of wages to secure a limitation of the hours of work; that in endeavours temporarily to increase his earnings, the putter is frequently regardless of fatigue, and, were he permitted, would ofttimes only terminate his toil by entire physical exhaustion; yet, notwithstanding that this is so well-known a characteristic of the putter, the agents represent the labour as perfectly voluntary, and, even in cases of double and treble shifts undergone by the same boy, state that the undertaking is quite optional. (Ibid. §§ 56, 57: p. 523.)

Twenty boys at the Walker Colliery: "The 20 witnesses, when questioned collectively, say, that the way is so very dirty, and the pit so warm, that the lads often get tired very soon" (J. R. Leifchild, Esq., Evidence, No. 291: App. Pt. I., p. 627, l. 66)—Nineteen boys, examined together, of various ages, of whom the spokesman was William Holt, seventeen years old, putter: " The bad air, when they are whiles working in the broken, makes them sick. Has felt weak like in his legs at those times. Was weary like. Has gone on working, but very slowly. Many a one has had to come home before getting a fair start, from the bad air and hard work. Hours are too long. Would sooner work less hours and get less money" (Ibid. No. 300: p. 629 l. 1).—Twenty-three witnesses assembled state, "That their work is too hard for them; that they feel sore tired; that some of them constantly throw up their meat from their stomachs; that their heads often work [ache]; the back sometimes; and the legs feel weak" (Ibid. No. 354: p. 639, l. 18).—John Wilkinson, aged thirteen, Piercy Main Colliery: "Was in for a double shift about five weeks ago, and fell asleep about one o'clock P.M., as he was going to lift the limmers off to join the rolleys together, and got himself lamed by the horse turning about and jamming one of his fingers. Split his finger. Was off a week from this accident. Sometimes feels sick down the pit, felt so once or twice last fortnight. Whiles his head works [aches]; and he has pains in his legs as if they were weak. Feels pains in his knees. Thinks the work is hard for foals, more so than for others" (Ibid. No. 60: p. 579, l. 22).—John Middlemas: " Sometimes, but very rarely, they work the whole double-shift; that is, they go down at four o'clock A.M., and do not come up till four o'clock in the day after that, thus stopping down 36 hours, without coming up sometimes; and sometimes they come up for a half-hour, and then go down again. Another worked for 24 hours last week, and never came up at all. Another has stopped down 36 hours without coming up at all twice during last year. When working this double shift, they go to bed directly they come home" (Ibid. No. 98: p. 588, l. 42).—Michael Turner, helper-up, aged fourteen and a half, Gosforth Colliery: " Mostly he puts up hill the full corves. Many times the skin is rubbed off his back and off his feet. His head works [aches] very often, almost every week. His legs work on sometimes so that he can hardly trail them. Is at hard work now, shoving rolleys and hoisting the crane; the former is the hardest work. His back works very often so that he has sometimes to sit down for half a minute or so" (Ibid. No. 145: p. 598, l. 58).—George Short, aged nearly sixteen: "Hoists a crane. His head works [aches] very often, and he feels sickish sometimes, and drowsy sometimes, especally if he sits down. Has always been drowsy since he went there. Twice he has worked three shifts following, of 12 hours each shift; never came up at all during the 36 hours; was sleepy, but had no time to sleep. Has many times worked double shifts, of 19 hours, and he does this now nearly every pay Friday night. A vast of boys work in this shift, 10 or 11, and sometimes more. The boys are very tired and sleepy" (Ibid. No. 191: p. 606, l. 41).—John Maffin, sixteen years old, putter, Gosforth Colliery: "Was strong before he went down pits, but is not so now, from being over-hard wrought, and among bad air" (Ibid. No. 141: p. 598, l. 2).—Robert Hall, seventeen years old, half-marrow, Felling Colliery: "The work of putting makes his arms weak and his legs work all the day; makes his back work. Is putting to the dip now in a heavy place. Each one takes his turn to use 'soams' [the drawing straps]; one pulls with them, and the other shoves behind. Both are equally hard. If it is a very heavy place there are helpers-up, but not so many as they want. Has known one sore strained by putting—John Peel, aged 13; is off now from this. Is healthy in general, but is now and then off from this work" (Ibid. No. 325: p. 634, l. 11).—Michael Richardson, fiteen years old, putter, St. Lawrence Main Colliery: "About three-quarters of a year since he wrought double-shift every other night, or, rather, he worked three times in 11 days for 36 hours a time without coming up the pit. About six months ago he worked three shifts following, of 12 hours each shift, and never stopped work more than a few minutes now and then, or came up the pit till he was done. There was then some night-work to do, and the overman asked him to stop, and he could not say no, or else he [the overman] would have frowned on him and stopped him perhaps of some helpers-up. Thinks the hours for lads ought to be shortened, and does not know whether it would not be better even if their wages were less" (Ibid. No. 270: p. 623, l. 32).—James Glass, eighteen years old, putter, Walbottle: "Puts a tram by himself. Has no helper-up and no assistance. Mostly puts a full tram up. Is putting from a distance now. Mostly the trams are put by one person. Was off work the week before last three days by being sick. Was then putting in the night-shift, and had to go home and give over. Could not work. His head works nearly every day. He is always hitting his head against stone roofs. His arms work very often. Has to stoop a good deal. The weight of his body lies upon his arms when he is putting. The skin is rubbed off his back very often" (Ibid. No. 244: p. 619, l. 27).—Mr. James Anderson, a home missionary, residing in Easington Lane, Hetton-le-Hole, in reply to queries proposed, handed in the following written evidence: "The boys go too soon to work; I have seen boys at work not six years of age, and though their work is not hard, still they have long hours, so that when they come home they are quite spent. I have often seen them lying on the floor fast asleep; then they often fall asleep in the pit, and have been killed. Not long ago a boy fell asleep, lay down on the way, and the waggons killed him. Another boy was killed; it was supposed he had fallen asleep when driving his waggon, and fallen off and was killed" (Ibid. No. 446: p. 655, l. 62).

750. EAST OF SCOTLAND.—From the tender age and sex of the great proportion of the workpeople, the long hours of work, the wretched condition of the pits, and the meagre and unsubstantial food, the degree of fatigue produced by colliery labour in this district is extreme. "The tender and feeble powers of girls and boys of this age (eight years old and under) must be taxed beyond their strength by an uninterrupted labour of twelve hours' average daily—labour called for at irregular periods, sometimes by day and sometimes extending through the whole night. The medical evidence shows that this labour is injurious to the bodily frame; from the exhaustion of their labour they are in most instances too fatigued even to attend their evening-school, should one be found in their neighbourhood; and, after taking a meagre supper of kail and porridge, they are but too glad to seek the ill-provided rest which is to prepare them for the toil of the succeeding day" (R. H. Franks, Esq., Report, § 61: App. Pt. I., p. 395).

Barney Walker, ten years old, Blindwells, St. Germain's, Beving Pit, East Lothian: "Pushes the carts and carries coal; I go down at six in the morning, and go home at seven, when mother sends me to bed, as am so fatigued" (R. H. Franks, Esq., Evidence, No. 161: App. Pt. I., p. 465, l. 54).—Catherine Thompson, eleven years old, putter, Redding Collieries, Stirlingshire: "We both work on father's account, and draw his coal; the hutchies hold 8 cwt., which we have first to fill before we draw; the distance we draw is said to be full 1000 yards. I can scarcely stand after I have been running and pushing all day" (Ibid. No. 226: p. 478, l. 29).—Ellison Jack, a girl, eleven years old, Loanhead Colliery, Mid-Lothian: "My task is four to five tubs; each tub holds 4¼ cwt. I fill five tubs in 20 journeys. Am very glad when my task is wrought, as it sore fatigues" (Ibid. No. 55: p. 446, l. 60).—Jesse Wright, eleven years old, coal-bearer, Edmonstone Colliery, Mid-Lothian: "Don't like the work at all; daylight is better; the 'work is horrible sair.' When mother and father first took me down I was frighted at the place; have got a little used to the work, but it crushes me much. I leave work when bad air is in the pit, which frequently has occurred" (Ibid. No. 13: p. 439, l. 8).—Jane Young, eleven years old: "I am very sore fatigued when home, and have little time to look about me" (Ibid, No. 63 : p. 448, l. 31).—Robert Seton, eleven years old, coal-putter, Rosewell and Barley Dean Collieries, Mid-Lothian : " Father took me down when I was six years old, and I have wrought below ever since. Brother and I draw one waggon, which holds 6 cwt. of coal. The work is as sair as ever laddie put his hand to" (Ibid. No. 80: p. 451, l. 62).—Andrew Young, eleven years of age, coal-putter, Arniston Colliery, Mid-Lothian : " Draws with the ropes and chains ; slype first to the main-road, and then pull to the pit bottom on the railroads ; sometimes I have to slype 100 to 300 fathoms, according to the rooms the men work in ; the wall is far away from level road. We draw as the horses do, only we have no wheels to the slypes, therefore the work is very sore. Boys frequently fall under the slypes, and get much injured. When we descend a brae the practice is to hang on in front, and other laddie to pull behind ; but with the baskets holding 5 cwt. we are frequently overpowered" (Ibid. No. 87: p. 453, l. 32.)—Jane Kerr, twelve years old, coal-bearer, Dryden Colliery, Mid-Lothian : " I work every day. The work is very sair and fatiguing. I would like to go to school, but canna wone [go] owing to sair fatigue" (Ibid. No. 64: p. 448, l. 35).—Elizabeth Selkirk, eleven years old, coal-drawer, Haugh Lynn Colliery, Mid-Lothian : " Works from three in the morning till four and five in the afternoon, and frequently all night. The work is so sore that canna help going to sleep when waiting for the gig to draw. Father is very bad in the breath, so I am wrought with brother. I do not always change mysel, as one o'erfatigued. We have had much trouble [sickness]. My work causes me to stoop double, and when I draw I crawl on all-fours, like the cuddies. [Very sickly emaciated child, subject to severe pains in limbs and bowels, arising no doubt from overwork and want of food. Her parents, with seven children, live in a wretched hovel at Perthhead ; the room not more than 10 feet by 14 ; the furniture consisted of two old bedsteads, nearly destitute of covering, and a few old stools and bits of broken crockery.]" (Ibid. No. 111 : p. 457, l. 32).—David Woddell, eleven years old, picks and draws, Edgehead Colliery, Mid-Lothian : " I work 14 and 15 hours, and work every day except Monday, when I stay up because father does ; sister and I work, and we are very sore wrought just now, as we have night and day work. Father cannot labour much, as he is nearly done in the breath ; I don't know how old he is. Mother is clean done for ; she can hardly breathe, and has not worked for some years" (Ibid. No. 103 : p. 456, l. 11).

James Miller, twelve years old, coal-hewer, Still Colliery, Stirlingshire : "Worked at picking and riddling coal upwards of two years ; does so as often as the state of the pit will allow. Occasionally much wet in the pit, sometimes bad air. Has fallen asleep often ; has na muckle time to do so now, as am over-sore worked" (Ibid. No. 271 : p. 486, l. 7).—David Smith, twelve years old, coal-drawer, Preston Hall Colliery, Mid-Lothian : " Draws in harness ; it is very horrible sore work ; do not like it ; would like daylight work better, drawing is so sair " (Ibid. No. 106: p. 456, l. 48).—Janet Moffatt, twelve years old, putter, New Craighall Colliery, Mid-Lothian : " I draw the carts through the narrow seams. The roads are 24 to 30 inches high ; draw in harness, which passes over my shoulders and back ; the cart is fastened to my chain. The place of work is very wet, and covers my shoe-tops. I pull the waggons, of 4 to 5 cwt., from the men's rooms to the horse-road. We are worse off than the horses, as they draw on iron rails, and we on flat floors" (Ibid. No. 70 : p. 449, l. 48).—William Naysmith, twelve years old, putter, Rosewell and Barley Dean Collieries, Mid-Lothian : " It is very hard, extraordinary hard work. I am now learning to hew the coal" (Ibid. No. 82: p. 452, l. 18).—Archibald Muckle, twelve years old, coal-hewer, Edgehead Colliery, Mid-Lothian : " I go down at four in the morning, and don't come up till six and seven at night : it is very sair work, and am obliged to lie on my side, or stoop, all the time, as the seam is only 24 to 26 inches high. There is much bad air below, and when it rises in our room we shift, and gang to some other part, and leave when the pit is full, as it stops our breath. The pit is very wet, and am compelled to shift mysel when home on that account. Never been to day-school since down : go to the night as often as the labour will allow, am so sore fatigued" (Ibid. No. 97: p. 455, l. 7).—John King, aged twelve years, coal-hewer, Sheriff Hall and Somerside Collieries, Mid-Lothian : " The work takes away the desire for food, as it is o'ersair" (Ibid. No. 4: p. 437, l. 3).—Isabella Read, twelve years old, coal-bearer, Edmonstone Colliery, Mid-Lothian : " Works on mother's account, as father has been dead two years. I am wrought with sister and brother, it is very sore work ; cannot say how many rakes or journeys I make from pit's bottom to wall-face and back, thinks about 30 or 25 on the average ; the distance varies from 100 to 250 fathom. I carry about 1 cwt. and a quarter on my back ; have to stoop much and creep through water, which is frequently up to the calves of my legs. When first down fell frequently asleep while waiting for coal from heat and fatigue. I do not like the work, nor do the lassies, but they are made to like it. When the weather is warm there is difficulty in breathing, and frequently the lights go out" (Ibid. No. 14 : p. 439, l. 22).—George Wright, twelve years old, coal-putter, Blindwell, St. Germain's, Beving Pit, East Lothian : " Works 12 to 14 hours with father. The place I draw in is wet ; the water comes up to my knees. Am much fatigued by the work, which is distressing, being 300 fathoms from coal to pit bottom, and makes me very sick. Never been able to get the knowledge of the letters, as am so sore wrought. [Poor, ignorant, miserable object.]" (Ibid. No. 162 ; p. 466, l. 2).—Catherine Meiklejohn, aged twelve, coal-bearer, Blindwell, St. Germain's, Beving Pit, East Lothian : " I start to work at five in the morning, and lay by at six at night. I bring coal from the wall-face to pit-bottom—large pieces on my back, small in a creel. The distance of my journey about 200 fathoms. It takes me three burthens to fill one tub of 5¼ cwt. My back is very sore at times, but I never lie idle. Would not like to work so long, only father bids me. [A most intelligent, healthy girl. Few men could do one-third the labour this lassie is compelled to perform.]" (Ibid. No. 164: p. 466, l. 19).

William Woods, fourteen years of age, coal-hewer, Sheriff Hall and Somerside Collieries, Mid Lothian : "The sore labour makes me feel very ill and fatigued ; it injures my breath.

[I examined this boy on the Saturday, at a cottage near the pit, and the state of exhaustion he was in can scarcely be imagined]" (Ibid. No. 8: p. 437, l. 58).—John Baxter, aged fifteen years, coal-hewer, Collinshield Collieries, Linlithgowshire: " I work from two in the morning till six at night; done so for five years. My adopted mother puts my coal. The work is gai sore for both of us, but the woman has been a real kind friend to me, as I lost my mother soon after my birth, and my father was murdered seven or eight years ago; he was thrown into the canal, and the murderer was never sought after, as there was no talk about the death, and therefore no inquiry" (Ibid. No. 195: p. 472, l. 38).—Walter Cossar, fifteen years old, coal-putter, Dalkeith Collieries, Mid Lothian: " Could go to night-school, but am aye that wearied that am never fit to gang" (Ibid. No. 34: p. 443, l. 11).—Agnes Kerr, fifteen years old, coal-bearer, Loanhead Colliery, Mid Lothian: " It is sore crushing work: many lassies cry as they bring up their burthens. I canna say that I like the work well; for I am obliged to do it: it is horse-work" (Ibid. No. 65: p. 448, l. 57).—Margaret Drylie, sixteen years old, putter, Elgin Colliery, Fifeshire: " The work is sore straining; was laid by for three months short time since with pains in the limbs, caused by overwork" (Ibid. No. 347: p. 498, l. 45).—Mary Morgan, sixteen years old, putter, Hulheath Colliery, Fifeshire: " As the road is long and the brae awful steep, the sweat drops off like streams of water. The roads are 600 yards and many 900 yards long, and we have to stoop very much. Been idle sometimes with pains in limbs for day or two" (Ibid. No. 359: p. 500, l. 51).—Janet Neilson, sixteen years of age, putter: " Was at service, but left her place as father persuaded her to go below; much prefers service, only suppose father needs my earnings. The work is very, very sair" (Ibid. No. 397: p. 506, l. 32).— Margaret Hipps, seventeen years old, putter, Stoney Rigg Colliery, Stirlingshire: " It is sad sweating and sore fatiguing work, and frequently maims the women" (Ibid. No. 283: p. 479, l. 57). —Agnes Phinn, seventeen years old, coal-bearer, Edmonstone Colliery, Mid Lothian: " The work is most exhausting; were it not for the sake of cleanliness, I should not change my clothes. I seldom gang out, as the work is gai fair slavery" (Ibid. No. 20: p. 440, l. 21).—Edward Bennett, seventeen years old, coal-hewer, Edmonstone Colliery, Mid Lothian: " Coal-carrying knocks the lassies all out of joints" (Ibid. No. 22: p. 440, l. 42).—Agnes Johnson, aged seventeen years, road-redder, New Craighall Colliery, Mid Lothian: " Assists in redding the road in the Tunnel Pit, and works 12 hours. It is very sore work, but I prefer it, as I work on the master's account, and get 14d. a-day. When I work with father he keeps me 15 or 16 hours at coal-carrying, which I hate, as it last year twisted my ankles out of place, and I was idle near 12 months" (Ibid. No. 77: p. 451, l. 19).

John Duncan, fifty-seven years old, coal-hewer, Pencaitland Colliery, East Lothian: " It must be admitted that children are sadly overwrought; have been sorry always when two of my own wrought hard, still I had need of their help, although not nine years of age" (Ibid. No. 152: p. 464, l. 39).—Walter Kerr, collier, aged sixty-two, Tranent Colliery: " Women in order to get home early carry too heavy weights. I know many who have filled tubs of 5 cwt. in two burdens, and brought them 200 fathoms" (Ibid. No. 175: p. 468, l. 3).—Mr. John Thompson, Mining overseer, Tranent Colliery: " Coal-work at best is of an o'er sair kind, and few lads can acquire the knowledge of hewing, or have good strength to put, till fourteen years of age, and even then it depends on their physical strength. Colliers frequently exhaust themselves and children; if regular they would not need the assistance of such quantities of infant labour" (Ibid. No. 176: p. 468, l. 19).

571. SOUTH WALES.—Witnesses in this district also dwell much upon the fatigue of their occupations.—

Solomon Hancock, aged ten, collier, Rock Colliery, Bedwelty, Monmouthshire: "Thinks it is very hard work." (R. H. Franks, Esq., Evidence, No. 245: App. Pt. II., p. 542, l. 4).—John Fuge, aged eleven, pump-boy, Llantwryarde: " The work is very fatiguing and requires sixteen hours' rest" (Ibid. No. 73: p. 517, l. 41).—Joseph and John Neath, twins, aged eleven, Gilvach Vargoed Colliery: " Work very hard indeed; when we rest a little we fall asleep" (Ibid. No. 184: p. 533, l. 5). —Moses Moon, aged eleven: " It is sad, sloppy, hard work" (Ibid. No. 292: p. 548, l. 63)— Henrietta Frankland, eleven years old, drammer: " When well I draw the drams [carts], which contain 4 to 5 cwt. of coal, from the heads to the main road; I make 48 to 50 journeys; sister, who is two years older, works also at dramming; the work is very hard, and the long hours before the pay-day fatigue us much" (Ibid. No. 18: p. 505, l. 48).—John Fuge, aged eleven " I am so very tired at times that I hardly care about eating" (Ibid. No. 67: p. 517, l. 46).—William Davis, aged twelve, collier: " The work is very hard, and I am very fatigued by it." (Ibid. No. 183: p. 532, l. 60).—William Locklas, twelve years old: " Find it very hard work, as the crawling is very fatiguing" (Ibid. No. 438: p. 577, l. 22).—William Williams, aged thirteen, Plas Level Colliery: " Work is very hard; when I first went down used to fall asleep; can't fall asleep now, am kept too close at it" (Ibid. No. 176: p. 532, l. 14).—Joseph Roberts, aged thirteen, collier, Court y Bella and Mamwhale Collieries: " Feels very tired; the work is very hard" (Ibid. No. 230: p. 539, l. 16.)—William Hopkin, aged fourteen, pumper, Llantwitfardye: " The work is very hard; I have no time to rest" (Ibid. No. 76: p. 518, l. 7).—Elias Jones, aged fourteen, carter: " It is very hard work indeed, it is too hard for such lads as we, for we work like little horses" (Ibid. No. 290: p. 548, l. 48).—William Hopkins, aged fourteen, pumper: " The work is very hard; have no time to rest when below, as the water rises very fast, which makes me dislike the work very much, as there is no cessation; it is very wet, although I stand on a stair" (Ibid. No. 76: p. 518, l. 7).—James Bentley, father, Risca Colliery, parish of Machin: " The boys' work in this colliery is extremely hard and very exhausting" (Ibid. No. 293: p. 549, l. 9).—Samuel Jones, cashier and clerk, Waterloo Colliery: " The work is fatiguing for young boys, but the masters have no control over the colliers as to whom they shall take to assist them, and when work is dull the fathers carry the boys below when four or five years old" (Ibid. No. 207: p. 536, l. 30).

752. FOREST OF DEAN.—Instances of fatigue to a destructive excess are mentioned in this coal field also.—

Thomas Batten, Esq., surgeon, Coleford: " Sometimes has known cases of nervous relaxation from an exhaustion of strength in young boys.   Had one case of epilepsy in a boy about thirteen, brought on by too much exertion of the muscles and whole frame; another boy, in the Parkend pits, died of *hemorragia purpurea* (a suffusion of blood under the cuticle) from the same cause.   This boy was not more than seven years of age" (E. Waring, Esq. Evidence, No. 36: App. Pt. II., p. 24, l. 19).—Josiah Marfell, underground manager, Strip-and-at-it Pit. " Thinks some of the boys overwork themselves in their anxiety to earn more money, or to do their work in a shorter time.   When he was a boy between fourteen and eighteen, he often hodded eight tons in a short day, *up* an ascent, and could hardly move when he got home.   Thinks some of the men do, sometimes, put upon the boys rather too much" (Ibid. No. 46: p. 29, l. 39).

2.—*Extraordinary Muscular Development.*

753. One of the most remarkable of the effects produced by colliery labour is an extraordinary development of the muscular system, especially of the muscles about the shoulders, chest, arms, and legs.

754. The fine muscular development of the Children, Young Persons, and Adults in the South Staffordshire, Shropshire, Warwickshire, and Leicestershire districts, and more especially in the two latter, has been already fully described. And a very extraordinary development of some of the muscles of the body has been observed in other districts.   In the West Riding of Yorkshire it is stated " that there is in all cases a strong development of the muscles on each side of the spinal column" (J. C. Symons, Esq., Report, § 201: App. Pt. I., p. 193). And the Sub-Commissioner for the Halifax district states " that the muscles of the children are extraordinarily firm and prominent, especially those of the shoulders, arms, and legs" (S. S. Scriven, Esq., Report, § 49: App. Pt. II., p. 65).

755. The latter was so struck with this extraordinary muscular development, and with some other peculiarities in the external conformation of the hurriers, particularly those in the thin-seam pits, that he measured 220 of these Children and Young Persons, with a view of comparing them with an equal number of persons of the same ages employed in factories, in the potteries of Staffordshire, and in agricultural labour ; and in order to obtain an expression for the differences thus ascertained in these several classes, he calls the Children and Young Persons exhibiting extraordinary muscular development " very muscular ;" those exhibiting decided muscular development, " muscular ;" those exhibiting only an ordinary degree of muscular development, " at par ;" and those exhibiting a less degree of muscular development than common, " below par."   Now, on referring to the tables exhibiting the results, it appears that out of 124 Children and Young Persons in the Low Moor Collieries there are 56 classed as " very muscular ;" 40 as " muscular ;" 27 " at par ;" and only one " below par."   On the other hand, out of 150 Children and Young Persons employed in factories, there is not one classed as " very muscular," only 13 are classed as " muscular," 87 are classed " at par," and 50 " below par ;" while in the potteries out of 150 Children and Young Persons not one is classed as " very muscular," not one even as " muscular," 44 are classed " at par," and 106 " below par."

756. The Sub-Commissioner for Lancashire reports :—" Amongst the Children and Young Persons I remarked that some of the muscles were developed to a degree amounting to deformity ; for example, the muscles of the back and loins stood from the body and appeared almost like a rope passing under the skin."   But in the same paragraph he states that he was struck with the thin and gaunt appearance of the adults, and that their muscular development did not appear as great as might be anticipated from the laborious nature of their employment (J. L. Kennedy, Esq., Report, § 297: App. Pt. II. p. 188).   Mr. Fletcher also states that " the most remarkable personal characteristic of the colliery boys in the neighbourhood of Oldham is their great muscular development about the shoulders and chest" (J. Fletcher, Esq., Report, § 59: App. Pt. II.,p. 832).

757. The collier population of South Durham is represented as a strong and healthy race, possessing great muscular development and power.   And of the

COAL MINES.

*Peculiarities of
Physical Condition.*

*Extraordinary
Muscular
Development.*

great muscular development of the Children employed in the coal mines of Cumberland, among many others are noticed the following instances:—Benjamin Atkinson, aged twelve years and three months: " Measures 4 feet 4½ inches; the spinal column is sunk inwards, the muscles much developed and the breast likewise."—John Holmes, aged eleven years and three months: " Measures 4 feet 4½ inches; immense development of muscle on each side the spine, the whole way from the top to the bottom of the back" (J. C. Symons, Esq., Evidence, No. 321: App. Pt. I., p. 308, l. 37).

3.—*Stunted Growth.*

758. With this great muscular development there is commonly a proportionate diminution of stature. All classes of witnesses state that the colliers as a body, Children, Young Persons, and Adults, are stunted in growth. There are only two exceptions to this in Great Britain, namely, Warwickshire and Leicestershire. It is to be inferred from the statements of the Sub-Commissioner for Ireland that that country forms the third exception for the United Kingdom. Of the uniformity of the statements as to the small stature and the stunted growth of colliers in all other districts, the following may be regarded as examples.—

759. In Shropshire the miners as a body are of small stature; this is abundantly obvious even to a casual observer, and there are many instances of men never exceeding the size of boys (Dr. Mitchell, Report, § 314: App. Pt. I., p. 39). Andrew Blake, Esq., M.D., states of the colliers in Derbyshire, that he has observed that many of them are not so tall as their neighbours in other employments; this, in a degree, he considers is owing to their being worked too young" (J. M. Fellows, Esq., Evidence, No. 10: App. Pt. II., p. 266, l. 10). In the West Riding of Yorkshire, also, there is in stature an " appreciable difference in colliers' Children, manifest at all ages after they have been three years constantly in the pits: there is little malformation, but as Mr. Eliss, a surgeon constantly attending them, admits, they are somewhat stunted in growth and expanded in width" (J. C. Symons, Esq., Report, § 200: App. Pt. I., p. 193).

Henry Hemingway, surgeon, Dewsbury: " I am quite sure that the rule is that children in coal-pits are of a lower stature than others" (J. C. Symons, Esq., Evidence, No. 221: App. Pt. I. p. 282, l. 47).—Thomas Rayner, Esq., surgeon, Birstall: " I account for the stunted growth from the stooping position, which makes them grow laterally, and prevents the cartilaginous substance from expanding" (Ibid. No. 268: p. 292, l. 52).—Henry Moorhouse, surgeon, Huddersfield: " I may state, from my own personal examination of a number of them, that they are much less in stature in proportion to their ages than those working in mills" (Ibid. No. 273: p. 293, l. 49).—Jos. Ellison, Gent., Birstall: " The employment of the children decidedly stunts their growth" (Ibid. No. 249: p. 288, l. 8).

760. Mr. Symons, in Appendix to p. 212 of his Report, has given in detail the names, ages, and measurement, both in stature and in girth of breast, of a great number of farm and colliery Children of both sexes respectively. By taking the first ten collier boys, and the first ten farm boys, of ages between twelve and fourteen, we find that the former measured in the aggregate 44 feet 6 inches in height, and 274½ inches round the breast; while the farm boys measured 47 feet in height, and 272 inches round the breast. By taking the ten first collier girls and farm girls, respectively, between the ages of fourteen and seventeen, we find that the ten collier girls measure 46 feet 4 inches in height, and 293½ inches round the breast; whilst the ten farm girls measure 50 feet 5 inches in height, and 297 inches round the breast; so that in the girls there is a difference in the height of those employed in farms compared with those in collieries of eight and a half per cent. in favour of the former; while between the colliery and farm boys of a somewhat younger age, and before any long period had been spent in the collieries, the difference appears to be five and a half per cent. in favour of the farm Children.

761. In like manner, of 60 Children employed as hurriers in the neighbourhood of Halifax, at the average ages of ten years and nine months, Mr. Scriven states that the average measurement in height was 3 feet $11\frac{3}{10}$ inches, and in circumference 2 feet 3 inches; while of 51 Children of the same age employed in farms, the measurement in height was 4 feet 3 inches, the circumference being the same in both, namely, 2 feet 3 inches. In like manner, of 50 Young Persons of the average of fourteen years and eleven months, the measurement in height was 4 feet 5 inches, and in circumference 2 feet 3 inches; while of 49 Young Persons employed in farms of the average age of fifteen years and six months, the measure-

ment in height was 4 feet 10$\frac{8}{11}$ inches, and in circumference 2 feet 3 inches, being a difference of nearly 6 inches in height in favour of the agricultural labourers.

762. In the district of Bradford and Leeds there is " in stature an appreciable difference, from about the age at which the Children begin to work, between Children employed in mines and Children of the same age and station in the same neighbourhood not so employed ; and this shortness of stature is generally, though to a less degree, visible in the adult " (W. R. Wood, Esq., Report, § 36 : App. Pt. II., p. H 7—Also Evidence, Nos. 60, 75, 76).

763. In Lancashire the Sub-Commissioner reports that " it appeared to him that the average of the colliers are considerably shorter in stature than the agricultural labourers" (J. L. Kennedy, Esq., Report, § 296 : App. Pt. II., p. 188). The evidence collected by the other gentlemen in this district is to the same effect. Mr. Pearson, surgeon to the Dispensary, Wigan, states, with regard to the physical condition of the Children and Young Persons employed in coal-mining, as compared with that of Children in other employments, that they are smaller, and have a stunted appearance, which he attributes to their being employed too early in life (Ibid. § 304 : p. 188) And Mr. Richard Ashton, relieving officer of the Blackburn district, describes the colliers as " a low race, and their appearance is rather decrepit" (A. Austin, Esq., Evidence, No. 1 : App. Pt. II., p. 811, l. 12). See also the remarks by Mr. Fletcher on the vicinity of Oldham, App. Pt. II., § 59, p. 832.

764. " Though some remarkable exceptions have been seen in the counties of Warwick and Leicester, the colliers, as a race of men, in most districts, and in Durham amongst the rest, are not of large stature" (Dr. Mitchell, Report, § 214 : App. Pt. I., p. 143).—George Canney, medical practitioner, Bishop Auckland, states that " they are less in weight and bulk than the generality of men" (Dr. Mitchell, Evidence, No. 97 : App. Pt. I., p. 154, l. 19).

765. Of the collier boys of Durham and Northumberland the Sub-Commissioner reports that an inspection of more than a thousand of these boys convinced him that, " as a class (with many individual exceptions), their stature must be considered as diminished" (J. R. Leifchild, Esq., Report, § 72 : App. Pt. I., p. 525). Nicholas Wood, Esq., viewer of Killingworth, &c., states, that " there is a very general diminution of stature amongst pitmen" (J. R. Leifchild, Esq., Evidence, No. 97 : App. Pt. I., p. 587, l. 39).—Mr. Heath, of Newcastle, surgeon to Killingworth, Gosforth, and Coxlodge Collieries, " Thinks the confinement of Children for twelve hours in a pit is not consistent with ordinary health ; the stature is rather diminished, and there is an absence of colour; they are shortened in stature" (Ibid. No. 497 : p. 665, l. 7).—And J. Brown, Esq., M.D., Sunderland, states that " They are generally stunted in stature, thin, and swarthy" Ibid. No. 504) : p. 672, l. 22).

766. Of the collier population in Cumberland it is stated that " They are in appearance quite as stunted in growth, and present much the same physical phenomena, as those of Yorkshire ; comparing, of course, those following similar branches of the work" (J. C. Symons, Esq., Report, § 22 : App. Pt. I., p. 302).— Thomas Mitchell, Esq., surgeon, Whitehaven, says, " Their stature is partially decreased" (J. C. Symons, Esq., Evidence, No. 312 : App. Pt. I., p. 305, l. 59).

767. Of the deteriorated physical condition of the collier population in the East of Scotland, as shown among other indications by diminished stature, Dr. S. Scott Alison states that " Many of the infants in a collier community are thin, skinny, and wasted, and indicate, by their contracted features and sickly dirty-white or faint-yellowish aspect, their early participation in a deteriorated physical condition From the age of infancy up to the seventh or eight year, much sickliness and general imperfection of physical development is observable The physical condition of the boys and girls engaged in the collieries is much inferior to that of Children of the same years engaged in farming operations, in most trades, or who remain at home unemployed. These Children are, upon the whole, prejudicially affected to a material extent in their growth and development; many of them are short for their years" (R. H. Franks, Esq., Report, App. A, No. 2 : App. Pt. I., p. 410, 411).

768. In North Wales Mr. Samuel Cunnah, manager of the Morton Colliery, Ruabon, states that " He considers early work bad for Children, because he thinks it stops their growth" (H. H. Jones, Esq., Evidence, No. 44 : App. Pt. II., p. 389, l. 61).

769. In South Wales "the testimony of medical gentlemen, and of managers and overseers in various works, in which large numbers of Children as well as adults are employed, proves that the physical health and strength of Children and Young Persons is deteriorated by their employment at the early ages and in the works before enumerated" (R. H. Franks, Esq., Report, § 85: App. Pt. II., p. 485).—Mr. Jonathan Isaacs, agent of the Top Hill Colliery :—" I have noticed that the Children of miners, who are sent to work, do not grow as they ought to do; they get pale in their looks, are weak in their limbs, and any one can distinguish a collier's child from the children of other working people" (R. H. Franks, Esq., Evidence, No. 144: App. Pt. II., p. 528, l. 4).— Mr. P. Kirkhouse, oversman to the Cyfarthfa Collieries and Ironstone Mines, on this point observes—" The infantine ages at which Children are employed cranks [stunts] their growth and injures their constitution" (Ibid. No. 2: p. 503, l. 21).—John Russell, Esq., surgeon to the Dowlais Iron Works : " In stature I believe a difference to exist in the male youth from twelve to sixteen employed in the mines and collieries, compared with those engaged in other work, the former being somewhat stunted; and this difference (under some form or other) seems still perceptible in the adult miners and colliers" (R. W. Jones, Esq., Evidence, No. 102: App. Pt. II., p. 641, l. 28).—Abraham Rowlands, Esq., surgeon to the Nantyglo and Beaufort Works : " The stature of the Children working under ground is generally small, especially those who begin to work very young; although in some cases it does not affect the growth at all" (Ibid. No. 47: p. 621, l. 36).

770. In the Forest of Dean "the colliers who have been habituated, from Childhood, to work in pits where the veins of coal are thin, and the workings consequently contracted, have certainly a remarkably stunted appearance, and the boys are commonly of low stature for their respective ages" (E. Waring, Esq., Report, § 55: App. Pt. II., p. 5).—Mr. Josiah Marfell, agent : "Thinks the colliers and miners, generally, would be taller and better grown men if they had not done so much hard work when young. Thinks the boys in these narrow workings are much stunted in their growth." The Sub-Commissioner adds : " I inquired of a man near the spot, who had a boy in the work, whether he thought the employment injured them; and he replied, in no other way than hindering their growth, which was not equal to that of other boys who work above ground, or in more roomy pits " (E. Waring, Esq., Evidence, No. 46: App. Pt. II., p. 29, l. 44, 55). In South Gloucestershire " the same stunted character of growth is remarkable in those employed at the 'low delf,' or narrow seam collieries, here as in the Forest of Dean " (E. Waring, Esq., Report, § 87: App. Pt. II., p. 38).

4.—*Crippled Gait.*

771. A third result frequently takes place from employment in the coal mines, namely a crippled gait, often connected with positive deformity. This result is of course the most frequent, and in the greatest degree, in those districts in which the working of the mines is carried on under circumstances the least favourable to health, and is therefore little perceptible, or at least little noted, in Warwickshire and Leicestershire, while it is sufficiently apparent in the Staffordshire and Shropshire districts, and forces itself on the attention in the districts of Derbyshire, Yorkshire, Lancashire, and Scotland. In Derbyshire the Children who have worked in the collieries from a very early age are stated to be bow-legged (J. M. Fellows, Esq., Report, § 45: App. Pt. II., p. 255).

772. In the West Riding of Yorkshire, after " they are turned forty-five or fifty they walk home from their work almost like cripples, stiffly stalking along, often leaning on sticks, bearing the visible evidences in their frame and gait of overstrained muscles and overtaxed strength. Where the lowness of the gates induces a very bent posture, I have observed an inward curvature of the spine; and chicken-breasted Children are very common among those who work in low thin coal-mines" (J. C. Symons, Esq., Report, § 110: App. Pt. I., p. 181).

Uriah Bradbury, Esq., surgeon, Mirfield: " Their knees never stand straight like other people's" (J. C. Symons, Esq., Evidence, No. 199: App. Pt. I., p. 279, l. 3).— Henry Hemingway, Esq., surgeon, Dewsbury: " May be distinguished among crowds of people by the bending of the spinal column " (Ibid. No. 221: p. 282, l. 46).—William Sharp, Esq., surgeon, Bradford : "There are occasionally cases of deformity" (W. R. Wood, Esq., Evidence, No. 60: App. Pt. II., p. *h* 27, l. 46).

773. In the Lancashire district, John Bagley, about thirty-nine years of age, collier, Mr. Lancaster's, Patricroft, states, " that the women drawing in pits are generally crooked. Can tell any woman who has been in the pits; they are rarely if ever so straight as other women that stop above ground" (J. L. Kennedy, Esq., Evidence, No. 30 : App. Pt. II., p. 218, l. 6).—Mr. William Gualter, surgeon, of Over Darwen, says, " Has practised as a surgeon 24 years in this neighbourhood. Those who work in collieries at an early age, when they arrive at maturity are generally not so robust as those who work elsewhere ; they are frequently crooked (not distorted), bow-legged, and stooping" (A. Austin, Esq., Evidence, No. 7 : App. Pt. II., p. 812, l. 60).—Betty Duxberry, a woman having Children in the pits, asserts that " Colliers are all crooked and short-legged, not like other men who work above ground ; but there were always colliers and always will be. This young boy turns his feet out and his knees together ; drawing puts them out of shape" (Ibid. No. 17 : p. 815, l. 53).

774. Evidence collected in Durham and Northumberland shows th t the underground labour produces similar effects in that district.—

Nicholas Wood, Esq., viewer of Killingworth, Hetton, and other Collieries : " The children are perhaps a little ill-formed, and the majority of them pale and not robust. Men working in low seams are bent double and bow-legged very often" (J. R. Leifchild, Esq., Evidence, No. 97 : App. Pt. I., p. 587, l. 32).—J. Brown, Esq., M.D. and J.P., Sunderland : " They labour more frequently than other classes of the community under deformity of the lower limbs, especially that variety of it described as being ' in kneed.' This I should ascribe to yielding of the ligaments owing to long standing in the mines in a curved and awkward position" (Ibid. No. 504 : p. 672, l. 22).—Mr. Thomas Greenshaw, surgeon, Walker Colliery : " Their persons are apt to be somewhat bent and cramped. As they advance in life their knees and back frequently exhibit a curved appearance from constant bending at their work" (Ibid. No. 498 : p. 665, l. 50).—W. Morrison, Esq., surgeon of PelawHouse, Chester-le-street, Countess of Durham's Collieries : " The ' outward man' distinguishes a pitman from every other operative. His stature is diminutive, his figure disproportionate and misshapen; his legs being much bowed ; his chest protruding (the thoracic region being unequally developed). His countenance is not less striking than his figure ; his cheeks being generally hollow, his brow overhanging, his cheek bones high, his forehead low and retreating; nor is his appearance healthful ; his habit is tainted with scrofula. I have seen agricultural labourers, blacksmiths, carpenters, and even those among the wan and distressed stocking weavers of Nottinghamshire, to whom the term ' jolly' might not be inaptly applied, but I never saw a 'jolly-looking' pitman. As the germ of this physical degeneration may beformed in the youthful days of the pitman, it is desirable to look for its cause" (Ibid. No. 496 : p. 662, l. 62).

775. Of the colliers in the East of Scotland, Dr. Scott Alison says : " Several become crooked, and the subjects of spinal curvature. Diseases of the spinal column are very common at all ages among individuals employed in collieries. I have attended many persons labouring under the most serious of the diseases which are incident to the spine. Few middle-aged or old colliers are to be seen without curvature of the spine more or less extensive, the result of the unnatural position in which their bodies are retained for hours together when at work. This affection is indicated by general crookedness of the trunk, by stooping, and in general by one shoulder being higher than the other."

776. Of girls and women employed in the collieries of this district, he says : " Several of them are distorted in the spine and pelvis, and suffer considerable difficulty in consequence at the period of parturition ; but where this has not arisen from direct violence, it has been induced by general debility and bad habt of body, induced in infancy or childhood" (R. H. Franks, Esq., Evidence, App. Pt. I., p. 417, 412).

777. Similar evidence is given by the medical men in regard to the South Wales district as to the effect of employment in the coal mines in rendering the Children weak in their limbs and crippled in their gait, " so that any one can distinguish a collier's Child from the Children of other working people" (R. H. Franks, Esq. Report, § 63 *et seq.* : App. Pt. II., p. 484).

5.—*Irritation of the Head, Back, &c.*

778. There are certain minor evils connected with employment in the worst classes of coal mines, which, though not perhaps very serious, are nevertheless the sources of much suffering, such as irritation of the head, feet, back, and skin, together with occasional strains. " The upper parts of their head are always denuded of hair ; their scalps are also thickened and inflamed, sometimes taking on the appearance of *tinea*

capitis, from the pressure and friction which they undergo in the act of pushing the corves forward, although they are mostly defended by a padded cap" (S. S. Scriven, Esq., Report, 83 : App. Pt. II. p. 72). " It is no uncommon thing to see hurriers bald, owing to pushing the corves up steep board-gates with their heads" (J. C. Symons, Esq., Report, § 96 : App. Pt. I., p. 178).

Alexander Muir, Esq., surgeon : " Are there any peculiar diseases to which colliers are subject ?—No, excepting that the hurriers are occasionally affected by a formation of matter upon the forehead, in consequence of their pushing the waggons with the head. To what extent is such formation of matter injurious to the general health ?—It produces considerable local irritation. When the matter is allowed to escape it heals as perfectly as before. Do you conceive this use of the head to be a necessary or unnecessary part of the occupation ?—I should think not necessary. Does it arise from any deficiency of strength, the head being used to supply the place of the arms ?—I should think it does " (W. R. Wood, Esq., Evidence, No. 76 : App. Pt. II., p. *h* 32, 1. 18).—David Swallow, collier, East Moor : " The hair is very often worn off bald, and the part is swollen so that sometimes it is like a bulb filled with spongy matter, so very bad after they have done their day's work, that they cannot bear it touching " (J. C. Symons, Esq., Evidence, No. 197 : App. Pt. I., p. 277, 1. 68).—William Holt : " Some thrutched with their head, because they cannot thrutch enough with their hands alone. Thrutching with the head makes a gathering in the head, and makes them very ill " (A. Austin, Esq., Evidence, No. 9 : App. Pt. II., p. 813, 1. 40).

779. " In running continually over uneven ground without shoes or stockings, particles of coal, dirt, and stone get between the toes, and are prolific sources of irritation and lameness, of which they often complain ; the skin covering the balls of the toes and heels becomes thickened and horny, occasioning a good deal of pain and pustular gathering" (S. S. Scriven, Esq., Report, § 82 : App. Pt. II., p. 72).

James Mitchell : " I have hurt my feet often ; sometimes the coals cut them, and they run matter ; and the corves run o'er 'em when I stand ' agate ;' I an't not always aware o' their coming " (S. S. Scriven, Esq., Evidence, No. 2 : App. Pt. II., p. 101, 1. 33).—Selina Ambler : " I many times hurt my feet and legs with the coals and scale in gate ; sometimes we run corve over them ; my feet have many a time been blooded" (Ibid. No. 79 : p. 124, 1. 28).—See also Nos. 12, 13, 18, 25.—Mrs. Carr : " Has known many foals laid off with sore backs, especially last year and the year before, when the putting was said to be very heavy in the Flatworth Pit. Some foals had to lie off a day or two, to get their backs healed before they could go to work again" (J. R. Liefchild, Esq., Evidence, No. 86 : App. Pt. I., p. 583, 1. 27).—William Jakes : " His back is often skinned ; is now sore and all red, from holding on or back against the corf" (Ibid. No. 201 : p. 610, 1. 52).—George Faction : " In some places he bends quite double, and rubs his back so as to bring the skin off, and whiles to make it bleed, and whiles he is off work. from these things" (Ibid. No. 267 : p. 623, 1. 11).—James Probert, Esq., surgeon : " Chronic pain of the back is a very common complaint amongst colliers arising from overstraining the tendinous muscles, and it is the source of much discomfort to the colliers" (R. H. Franks, Esq., Evidence, No. 31 : App. Pt. II., p. 510, 1. 49).—William Dodd, Esq., surgeon : " As to the ' boils,' when a fresh man comes to the colliery he generally becomes affected by these ' boils,' most probably from the heat in the first instance, and subsequently they are aggravated by the salt water" (J. R. Leifchild, Esq., Evidence, No. 385 : App. Pt. I., p. 645, 1. 35).—James Johnson : " Sometimes, when amongst the salt water, the heat, &c., brings out boils about the size of a hen's egg upon him, about his legs and thighs, and under his arms sometimes. A vast of the boys, men and all, have these boils at times. These boils, perhaps, last a fortnight before they get ripe, and then they burst. A great white thing follows and is called a ' tanner' " (Ibid. No. 375 : p. 644, 1. 48).—Dr. Adams, Glasgow : " An eruption on the skin is very prevalent among colliers" (T. Tancred, Esq., Evidence, No. 9 : App. Pt. I., p. 361, 1. 45).—William Mackenzie : " Had about 20 boils on his back at one time, about two years since. These lasted about three months. He was kept off work about a week. If he touched them against anything they were like death to him. But few of the boys have so many at a time ; many of the boys get two or three at a time. The boys take physic to bring them all out ; then they get rid of them for some time. If the salt water falls upon any part of them that is scotched it burns into the flesh like ; it is like red rust. It almost blinds the boys if it gets into their eyes" (J. R. Liefchild, Esq., Evidence, No. 376 : App. Pt. I., p. 644, 1. 54).

6.—*Diseases.*

780. The evidence shows that employment in coal mines, as now too frequently pursued, produces certain positive diseases, partly the direct result of excessive muscular exertion, and partly the result of such exertion combined with the unhealthy state of the place of work. Loss of appetite, pain in the stomach, nausea and vomiting, are stated in the evidence to be, in some districts, felt by great numbers of persons employed in the labour of the coal-mines. Many of the witnesses make grievous complaints of their suffering from this cause. In the Durham and Northumberland Coal Field, for instance :—

Diseases.

Michael Mikings : " Never has a mind for his victuals; never feels himself hungry."—John Charlton : "Thinks the stythe makes him bad so that he cannot eat his bait, and very often brings it all home with him again, or eats very little of it."—Michael Richardson : "He never has much appetite; and the dust often blacks his victuals. Is always dry and thirsty."—Wilson Beaney : "Has thrown up his victuals often when he came home; thinks the bad air made him do this."—John Thompson : "Very often throws up his food."—Thomas Newton : "Threw up his victuals last night when he came home. Never does so down in the pit, but often does when he comes home."—Moses Clerk : "Throws up his victuals nearly every day at home and down the pit."—Thomas Martin : "Many times feels sick, and feels headach, and throws up his food. Was well before he went down in the pit."—Thomas Fawcett : "Many a night falls sick; and he many times throws up his meat when he is in bed. Sometimes feels bad and sick in the morning."—George Alder : "Has been unwell of late with the hard work. Has felt very sick and very weak all this last week. (Looks very pale and unwell.)"—John Charlton : "Often obliged to give over. Has been off five days in the last month. Each of these days was down in the pit and obliged to come up again."—John Laverick and others : "Many times they fell sick down the pit. Sometimes they have the heartburn; sometimes force up their meat again. Some boys are off a week from being sick; and occasionally they feel pains."—Six Trappers : "Sometimes they feel sick upon going to work in the morning. Sometimes bring up their breakfast from their stomachs again. Different boys at different times do this."—George Short : "It is bad air where he is, and makes him bad; makes small spots come out upon him [small pimples], which he thinks is from the air, and he takes physic to stop them. His head works very often, and he feels sickish sometimes."—Nichol Hudderson : "The pit makes him sick. Has been very bad in his health ever since he went down the pit. Was very healthy before. The heat makes him sick. The sulphur rising up the shaft as he goes down makes his head work. Often so sick that he cannot eat when he gets up, at least he cannot eat very much. About half a year since a boy named John Huggins was very sick down the pit, and wanted to come up, but the keeper would not let him ride [come up], and he died of a fever one week afterwards. [The father of this lad and his brother fully corroborate this statement, and the father says the doctor told him if he (the boy) had not been kept in the pit, he might have been, perhaps, saved. This boy never had anything the matter with him before he went down into the pit]" (J. R. Leifchild, Esq., Evidence, Nos. 156, 169, 270, 83, 110, 142, 143, 374, 194, 364, 135, 100, 101: App. Pt. I., p. 582 *et seq.*)—See also the statements of Witnesses Nos. 315, 327, 351, 359, 360, 361, 362, 363, 365, 377, 381, 382, 384, 430, 434, 454, 455, 457, 464, 465, 466.)

781. Similar statements are made by all classes of witnesses in some of the other districts. Thus in Shropshire,—

A surgeon who did not wish his name to be published : "They are subject to hypertrophy of the heart, no doubt laying the foundation of such disease at the early age of from eight to thirteen years" (Dr. Mitchell, Evidence, No. 45 : App. Pt. I., p. 81, l. 16).—Michael Thomas Sadler, Esq., surgeon, Barnsley : "I have found diseases of the heart in adult colliers, which it struck me arose from violent exertion. I know of no trade about here where the work is harder" (J. C. Symons, Esq., Evidence, No. 139 : App. Pt. I., p. 261, l. 36.)—Mr. Pearson, surgeon to the Dispensary, Wigan : "They are very subject to diseases of the heart" (J. L. Kennedy, Esq., Report, § 304 : App. Pt. II. p. 189).—Dr. William Thompson, Edinburgh : "Workers in coal-mines are exceedingly liable to suffer from irregular action, and ultimately organic disease of the heart" (R. H. Franks, Esq., Evidence : App. Pt. I., p. 409).—S. Scott Alison, Esq., M.D., East Lothian : "I found diseases of the heart very common among colliers at all ages from boyhood up to old age. The most common of them were, inflammation of that organ, and of its covering the pericardium, simple enlargement or hypertrophy, contraction of the auriculo ventricular communications and of the commencement of the aorta. The symptoms were well marked, attended for the most part with increase of the heart's action, the force of its contractions being sensibly augmented, and in many cases, especially those of hypertrophy, much and preternaturally extended over the chest" (Ibid., p. 417).—Thomas Batten, Esq., surgeon, Coleford : "A boy about thirteen years of age in the Parkend Pits died of *hœmorragia purpurea* [a suffusion of blood under the cuticle] brought on by too much exertion of the muscles and whole frame" (E. Waring, Esq., Evidence, No. 36 : App. Pt. II., p. 24, l. 21).

782. To this list of diseases arising from great muscular exertion must be added rupture.

Dr. Favell, Sheffield : "Many of them are ruptured; nor is this by any means uncommon amongst lads—arising, in all probability, from over-exertion" (J. C. Symons, Esq., Evidence, No. 47 : App. Pt. I., p. 236, l. 2).—Mr. Pearson, surgeon to the Dispensary, Wigan : "Colliers are often ruptured, and they often come to me for advice" (J. L. Kennedy, Esq., Report, § 304 : App. Pt. II., p. 189). —Andrew Grey : "Severe ruptures occasioned by lifting coal. Many are ruptured on both sides : I am, and suffer severely, and a vast of men here are also" (R. H. Franks, Esq., Evidence, No. 147 : App. Pt. I., p. 463, l. 61).

783. But employment in the coal-mines produces another series of diseases incomparably more painful and fatal, partly referrible to excessive muscular exertion, and partly to the state of the place of work, that is, to the foul air from imperfect ventilation, and to the wetness from inefficient drainage. Of the diseases of the lungs produced by employment in the coal mines asthma is the most frequent.—

Mr. William Hartell Baylis: "The working of the mines brings on asthma" (Dr. Mitchell, Evidence, No. 7: App. Pt. I., p. 65, l. 31).—A surgeon who does not wish his name to be published: "Most colliers at the age of thirty become asthmatic. There are few attain that age without having the respiratory apparatus disordered" (Ibid. No. 45: p. 81, l. 15).—Mr. George Marcy, clerk to the Wellington Union: "Many applications are made from miners for relief on account of sickness, and chiefly from asthmatic complaints, when arrived at an advanced age. At forty, perhaps, the generality suffer much from asthma. Those who have applied have been first to the medical officer, who has confirmed what they said" (Ibid. No. 46: p. 81, l. 44).

"I met with very few colliers above forty years of age who, if they had not a confirmed asthma, were not suffering from difficult breathing" (J. M. Fellows, Esq., Report, § 57: App. Pt. II., p. 256).—Phœbe Gilbert, Watnall, Messrs. Barber and Walker: "She thinks they are much subject to asthma. Her first husband, who died aged 57, was unable to work on that account for seven years" (J. M. Fellows, Esq., Evidence, No. 105: App. Pt. II., p. 292, l. 46).—William Wardle, collier, forty years of age, Eastwood: "There are some who are asthmatical, and many go double" (Ibid. No. 84: p. 287, l. 40).—Henry Hemingway, Esq., surgeon, Dewsbury: "When children are working where carbonic acid gas prevails, they are rendered more liable to affections of the brain and of the lungs. This acid prevents the blood from its proper decarbonization when it passes from the heart to the lungs. It does not get properly quit of the carbon" (J. C. Symons, Esq., Evidence, No. 221: App. Pt. I., p. 282, l. 38).—Uriah Bradbury, Esq., surgeon, Mirfield: "They suffer from asthma" (Ibid. No. 199: p. 278, l. 58).—J. B. Greenwood, Esq., surgeon, Cleckheaton: "The cases which have come before me professionally have been chiefly affections of the chest and asthma, owing to the damp underfoot, and also to the dust which arises from the working of the coal" (Ibid., No. 200: p. 279, l. 8).—J. Ibbetson, collier, aged fifty-three, Birkenshaw: "I have suffered from asthma, and am regularly knocked up. A collier cannot stand the work regularly. He must stop now and then, or he would be mashed up before any time" (Ibid. No. 267: p. 292, l. 42).

Joseph Barker, collier, aged forty-three, Windybank Pit: "I have a wife and two children, one of them is two-and-twenty years old; he is 'mashed up' [that is, he is asthmatical]; he has been as good a worker as ever worked in a skin" (S. S. Scriven, Esq, Evidence, No. 14: App. Pt. II., p. 104, l. 60).—George Canney, Esq., surgeon, Bishop Auckland: "Do the children suffer from early employment in the pits?—Yes, seven and eight is a very early age, and the constitution must suffer in consequence. It is injurious to be kept in one position so long, and in the dark. They go to bed when they come home, and enjoy very little air. I think there is more than the usual proportion of pulmonary affections" (Dr. Mitchell, Evidence, No. 97: App. Pt. I., p. 154, l. 12).—Dr. Headlam, physician, Newcastle: "Diseases of respiration are more common amongst pitmen than others, distinctly referable to the air in which they work. The air contains a great proportion of carbonic acid gas and carbureted hydrogen; these diseases of the respiratory organs arise from the breathing of these gases, principally the carbonic acid gas" (J. R. Leifchild, Esq., Evidence, No. 499: App. Pt. I., p, 670, l. 11).—Mr. Heath, of Newcastle, surgeon: "More than usually liable to asthma; mostly between thirty and forty years of age. A person always working in the broken would be more liable to asthma. Asthma is of very slow growth, and it is difficult to say when it begins; custom and habit will not diminish the evil effects, but will diminish the sensibility to these evils" (Ibid. No. 497: p. 665, l. 10, 14).—Matthew Blackburn, driver, fifteen years of age, Heaton Colliery: "Has felt shortness of breath. Helps up sometimes, but is bound to drive. Cannot help up sometimes for shortness of breath. His legs often work (ache); his shoulders work sometimes. Working in a wet place" (Ibid. No. 27: p. 573, l. 34).

Dr. S. Scott Alison, East Lothian: "Between the twentieth and the thirtieth year many colliers decline in bodily vigour and become more and more spare; the difficulty of breathing progresses, and they find themselves very desirous of some remission of their labour. This period is fruitful in acute diseases, such as fever, inflammation of lungs and pleura, and many other ailments, the product of over-exertion, exposure to cold and wet, violence, insufficient clothing, intemperance, and foul air. For the first few years chronic bronchitis is usually found alone and unaccompanied by disease of the body of the lungs. The patient suffers more or less difficulty of breathing, which is much affected by changes of the weather and by variations in the weight of the atmosphere; he coughs frequently, and the expectoration is composed, for the most part, of white frothy and yellowish mucous fluid, occasionally containing blackish particles of carbon, the result of the combustion of the lamp, and also of minute coal-dust. At first, and indeed for several years, the patient, for the most part, does not suffer much in his general health, eating heartily, and retaining his muscular strength little impaired in consequence. The disease is rarely, if ever, entirely cured; and if the collier be not carried off by some other lesion in the mean time, this disease ultimately deprives him of life by a slow and lingering process. The difficulty of breathing increases and becomes more or less permanent, the expectoration becomes very abundant, effusion of water takes place in the chest, the feet swell, and the urine is secreted in small quantity, the general health gradually breaks up, and the patient, after reaching premature old age, slips into the grave at a comparatively early period with perfect willingness on his part, and with no surprise on that of his family and friends" (R. H. Franks, Esq., Evidence, App. Pt. I., p. 412, 415: Appendix A).—John Duncan, aged 59, hewer, Pencaitland: "Mining has caused my breath to be affected, and I am, like many more colliers, obliged to hang upon my children for existence. The want of proper ventilation in the pits is the chief cause; no part requires more looking to than East Lothian; the men die off like rotten sheep" (Ibid. No. 150: p. 464, l. 28).—George Hogg, thirty-two years of age, coal-hewer, Pencaitland Colliery: "Unable to labour much now, as am fashed with bad breath: the air below is very bad; until lately no ventilation existed" (Ibid. No. 153: p. 464, l. 46).

COAL MINES.

Peculiarities of Physical Condition.

Diseases.

—See also witnesses Nos. 4, 36, 53, 131, 152, 155, 175, 275, 277, &c.—" The confined air and dust in which they work is apt to render them asthmatic, as well as to unfit them for labour at an earlier period of life than is the case in other employments" (T. Tancred, Esq., Report, § 99 : App. Pt. I., p. 345).—Dr. Adams, Glasgow: " Amongst colliers bronchitis or asthma is very prevalent amongst the older hands" (T. Tancred, Esq., Evidence, No. 9 : App. Pt. I., p. 361, l. 44).

Peter Williams, surgeon, Holiwell, North Wales: " The chief diseases to which they are liable are those of the bronchiæ. Miners and colliers, by the age of forty, generally become affected by chronic bronchitis, and commonly before the age of sixty fall martyrs to the disease. The workmen are, for the most part, very healthy and hardy, until the symptoms of affections of the bronchial tubes show themselves" (H. H. Jones, Esq., Evidence, No. 95 : App. Pt. II., p. 407, l. 8).—Jeremiah Bradley, underground agent, Plaskynaston : " The men are apt to get a tightness of breath, and become unfit for the pits, even before sixty" (Ibid. No. 30 : p. 383, l. 8). —" Amongst colliers in South Wales the diseases most prevalent are chronic diseases of the respiratory organs, especially asthma and bronchitis" (R. H. Franks, Esq., Report, § 64 : App. Pt. II., p. 484).—David Davis, contractor, Gilvachvargoed Colliery, Glamorganshire : " I am of opinion that miners are sooner disabled and off work than other mechanics, for they suffer from shortness of breath long before they leave off work ; shortness of breath may be said to commence about from forty to fifty years of age" R. H. Franks, Esq., Evidence, No. 178 : App. Pt. II., p. 533, l. 32).— Mr. Richard Andrews, overseer, Llancyach, Glamorganshire: " The miners about here are very subject to asthmatic complaints" (Ibid. No. 152 : p. 529, l. 7).—Mr. Frederick Evans, clerk and accountant for the Dowlais Collieries, Monmouthshire : " Asthma is a prevalent disease among colliers" (R. W. Jones, Esq., Evidence, No. 121 : App. Pt. II., p. 646, l. 48).

David Mushet, Esq., Forest of Dean : " The men generally become asthmatic from fifty to fifty-five years of age" (E. Waring, Esq., Evidence, No. 37 : App. Part II., p. 25, l. 3).—" Asthmatic and other bronchial affections are common amongst the more elderly colliers and miners" (E. Waring, Esq., Report, § 72 : App. Pt. II., p. 6).—Mr. William Brice, clerk, Coal Barton and Vobster Collieries, North Somersetshire : " The work requires the full vigour of a man ; and they are ' apt at this place to get asthmatical, from the gas and foul air' " (Dr. Stewart, Evidence, N6. 7 : App. Pt. II., p. 50, l. 49).—James Beacham, coal-breaker, Writhlington, near Radstock : " Many of the miners suffer from ' tight breath' " (Ibid. No. 32 : p. 56, l. 31).

784. Of that disease which is peculiar to colliers, called " black spittle," much evidence is given by many medical witnesses and others :—

Mr. Cooper, surgeon, of Bilston, gives the following account of this malady when it appears in its mildest form : " Frequently it occurs that colliers appear at the offices of medical men complaining of symptoms of general debility, which appear to arise from inhalation of certain gases in the mines (probably an excess of carbonic). These patients present a pallid appearance, are affected with headach (without febrile symptoms) and constriction of the chest, to which may be added dark bronchial expectoration and deficient appetite. Gentle aperients, mild stomachics, and rest from labour above ground, restore them in a week or so, and they are perhaps visited at intervals with a relapse, if the state of the atmosphere or ill ventilation of the mine favour the development of deleterious gas. (Dr. Mitchell, Evidence, No. 3 : App. Pt. I., p. 62, l. 48).

785. In other districts this disease assumes a much more formidable character.—

Dr. Thomson, of Edinburgh, states that, " The workmen in coal-mines occasionally die of an affection of the lungs, accompanied with the expectoration of a large quantity of matter of a deep black colour, this kind of expectoration continuing long after they have, from illness or from choice, abandoned their subterranean employment, and the lungs of such persons are found on examination after death to be most deeply impregnated with black matter. This black deposition may occur to a very considerable extent in the lungs of workers in coal-mines, without being accompanied with any black expectoration or with any phenomena of active disease, and may come to light only after death has been occasioned by causes of a different nature, as by external injuries" (R. H. Franks, Esq., Appendix A, No. 1 : App. Pt. I., p. 409).

Dr. S. Scott Alison : " Spurious melanosis, or the ' black-spit' of colliers, is a disease of pretty frequent occurrence among the older colliers, and among those men who have been employed in cutting and blasting stone dykes in the collieries. The symptoms are emaciation of the whole body, constant shortness and quickness of breath, occasional stitches in the sides, quick pulse, usually upwards of one hundred in the minute, hacking cough day and night, attended by a copious expectoration, for the most part perfectly black, and very much the same as thick blacking in colour and consistence, but occasionally yellowish and mucous, or white and frothy; respiration is cavernous in some parts and dull in others; a wheezing noise is heard in the bronchial passages, from the presence of an inordinate quantity of fluid; the muscles of respiration become very prominent, the neck is shortened, the chest being drawn up, the nostrils are dilated, and the countenance is of an anxious aspect. The strength gradually wasting, the collier who has hitherto continued at his employment finds that he is unable to work six days in the week, and goes under ground perhaps only two or three days in that time; in the course of time he finds an occasional half day's employment as much as he can manage, and when only a few weeks' or months' journey from the grave, ultimately takes a final leave of his labour. This disease is never cured, and if the unhappy victim of an unwholesome occupation is not hurried off by some more acute disease, or by violence, it invariably ends in the death of the sufferer. Several colliers have died of this disease under my care" (Ibid. Appendix A, No. 2 : App. Pt. I., p. 415, 416).

Dr. Makellar, Pencaitland, East Lothian : " The most serious and fatal disease which I have been called to treat, connected with colliers, is carbonaceous infiltration into the substance of the lungs. It is a disease which has long been overlooked, on account of the unwillingness which formerly existed amongst that class of people to allow examination of the body after death; but of late such a prejudice has in a great measure been removed. From the nature of Pencaitland Coal-works, the seams of coal being thin when compared with other coal-pits, mining operations are carried on with difficulty, and in such a situation there is a deficiency in the supply of atmospheric air, thereby causing difficulty of breathing, and consequently the inhalation of the carbon which the lungs in expiration throw off, and also any carbonaceous substances floating in this impure atmosphere. I consider the pulmonary diseases of coal-miners to be excited chiefly by two causes, viz. first, by running stone-mines with the use of gunpowder; and secondly, coal-mining in an atmosphere charged with lamp smoke and the *carbon* exhaled from the lungs. All who are engaged at coal-pits here are either employed as coal or stone miners, and the peculiar disease to which both parties are liable varies considerably according to the employment." (Ibid. Appendix A. No. 3: p. 422). See also witnesses Nos. 7, 44, 122, 144, 146. For a full account of this disease, see Reports of Drs. Alison, Thomson, Makellar, and Reid, in the Appendix to the Sub-Commissioner's Report for the East of Scotland.

Coal Mines.

Peculiarities of Physical Condition.

Diseases.

786. Dr. Makellar gives the following remarkable evidence as to the efficacy of ventilation in obviating the production of this disease :—

" The only effectual remedy for this disease is a free admission of pure air, and to be so applied as to remove the confined smoke both as to stone-mining and coal-mining, and also the introduction of some other mode of lighting such pits than by oil. I know many coal-pits where there is no *black-spit*, nor was it ever known, and on examination I find that there is and ever has been in them a free circulation of air. For example, the Penston Coal-works, which joins Pencaitland, has ever been free of this disease, but many of the Penston colliers on coming to work at Pencaitland Pit have been seized with, and died of, the disease. Penston has always good air, while it is quite the contrary at Pencaitland" (Ibid. Appendix A, No. 3: App. Pt. I., p. 422).

787. Other diseases produced by employment in coal mines, less fatal, but scarcely less painful, are rheumatism and inflammation of the joints.

788. Mr. William Hartell Baylis states that working in the cold and wet often brings on rheumatism. More suffer from this than from any other complaint" (Dr. Mitchell, Evidence, No. 7: App. Pt. I., p. 65, l. 31). Asthma and rheumatism, which are so prevalent in other districts, are very rare in Warwickshire and Leicestershire. (Dr. Mitchell's Reports *in loco*.) But in Derbyshire "rheumatism is very general; I believe you will scarcely meet a collier, and ask him what he thinks of the weather, but he will in reply say, ' Why, his back or shoulders have or have not pained him so much as usual' " (J. M. Fellows, Esq., Report, § 58: App. Pt. II., p. 256).

789. Mr. George Tweddell, surgeon, Houghton-le-Spring, South Durham, says, in answer to the question—Are the miners much subject to rheumatism?— "Not particularly so. Our mines are dry; but there is one mine which is wet, where the men often complain from rheumatism" (Dr. Mitchell, Evidence, No. 99: App. Pt. I., p. 155, l. 8). Similar evidence is given by the medical and other witnesses in all the districts. Wherever the mines are not properly drained, and are therefore wet and cold, the workpeople are invariably afflicted with rheumatism, and with painful diseases of the glands.

790. The Sub-Commissioner for the Forest of Dean gives the following account of a painful disease of the joints, common in that district: " The men employed in cutting down the coal are subject to inflammation of the *bursæ*, both in the knees and elbows, from the constant pressure and friction on these joints, in their working postures. Where the seams are several feet thick, they begin by kneeling and cutting away the exterior portion of the base. They proceed, undermining, till they are obliged to lie down on their sides, in order to work beneath the mass, as far as the arm can urge the pick, for the purpose of bringing down a good head of coal. In this last posture the elbow forms a pivot, resting on the ground, on which the arm of the workman oscillates as he plies his sharp pick. It is easy to comprehend how this action, combined with pressure, should affect the delicate cellular membrane of the joint, and bring on the disease indicated. The thin seams of coal are, necessarily, altogether worked in a horizontal posture " (E. Waring, Esq., Report, §§ 63—66: App. Pt. II., pp. 5, 6).

7.—*Premature Old Age and Death.*

791. An employment often pursued under circumstances which bring with them so many and such formidable diseases, must prematurely exhaust the strength of ordinary constitutions; and the evidence collected in almost all the districts proves that too often the collier is a disabled man, with the marks of old age upon him, when other men have scarcely passed beyond their prime.

Premature Old Age and Death.

792. The evidence shows that in South Staffordshire and Shropshire many colliers are incapable of following their occupation after they are forty years of age; others continue at their work up to fifty, which is stated by several of the witnesses to be about the general average.   Mr. Marcy, clerk to the Wellington Union, Salop, states "That about forty the greater part of the colliers may be considered as disabled and regular old men, as much as some are at eighty" (Dr. Mitchell, Evidence, No. 46: App. Pt. I., p. 81, l. 47).

793. Even in Warwickshire and Leicestershire, in which the physical condition of the colliers is better than in any other districts, Mr. Michael Parker, ground-bailiff of the Snibson Collieries, states " That some of the men are knocked up at forty-five and fifty, and that fifty may be the average, which early exhaustion of the physical strength he attributes to the severe labour and the bad air" (Ibid. No. 77: p. 113, l. 6).—Mr. Dalby, surgeon of the Union of Ashby-de-la-Zouch, says, "The work in the pit is very laborious, and some are unable for it as early as fifty, others at fifty-five, and some at sixty : I should say the greater part about fifty-five" (Ibid. No. 81 : p.114, l. 22).—And Mr. Davenport, clerk of the Union of Ashby-de-la-Zouch, gives a higher average, and says, " That a collier may wear from sixty-five to seventy, while an agricultural labourer may wear from seventy to seventy-five" (Ibid. No. 82: p. 114, l. 61).

794. Of Derbyshire the Sub-Commissioner reports :—" I have not perceived that look of premature old age, so general amongst colliers, *until they are forty years of age,* excepting in the loaders, who evidently appear so *at twenty-eight or thirty ;* and this I think must arise from the hardness of their labour in having such great weights to lift, and breathing a worse atmosphere than any other in the pit" (J. M. Fellows, Esq., Report, § 49: App. Pt. II., p. 256).—Phœbe Gilbert states : " The loaders are, as the saying is, ' old men before they are young ones' " (J. M. Fellows, Esq., Evidence, No. 105: p. 292, l. 48).—Dr. Blake says: " He has also noticed that when a collier has worked from a Child, and becomes forty, he looks much older than those of the same age above ground" (Ibid. No. 10: p. 266, l. 8).

795. In Yorkshire " the collier of fifty is usually an aged man ; he looks over-strained and stiffened by labour" (J. C. Symons, Esq., Report, § 209: App. Pt. I., p. 193).—" But whilst both the child and the adult miner appear to enjoy excellent health, and to be remarkably free from disease, it nevertheless appears that their labour, at least that of the adult miner, is, in its general result, and in the extent to which it is pursued, of a character more severe than the constitution is properly able to bear. It is rare that a collier is able to follow his calling beyond the age of from forty to fifty, and then, unless he be fortunate enough to obtain some easier occupation, he sinks into a state of helpless dependence.   Better habits with regard to temperance might diminish, but would not remove this evil, and the existence of this fact, in despite of the general healthiness of the collier population, gives rise to the question whether, apart from all considerations of mental and moral improvement, a fatal mistake is not at present committed in employing Children of tender years to the extent that their strength will bear, instead of giving opportunity by short hours of labour for the fuller and more perfect physical development which would better fit them to go through the severe labour of their after-life"   (R. W. Wood, Esq., Report, § 42: App. Pt. II., p. H 7).

796. In the Coal Fields of North Durham and Northumberland Dr. Elliott states ' That premature old age in appearance is common ; men of thirty-five or forty years may often be taken for ten years older than they really are" (J. R. Leif-child, Esq., Evidence, No. 499 : App. Pt. I., p. 668, l. 44).—Mr. Thomas Green-how, surgeon, Walker Colliery, North Durham, says: "They have an aged aspect somewhat early in life" (Ibid. No. 498: p. 665, l. 52).

797. Of the effect of employment in the coal mines of the East of Scotland in producing an early and irreparable deterioration of the physical condition, the Sub-Commissioner thus reports :—" In a state of society such as has been described, the condition of the Children may be easily imagined, and its baneful influence on the health cannot well be exaggerated ; and I am informed by very competent authorities that six months' labour in the mines is sufficient to effect a very visible change in the physical condition of the Children: and indeed it is scarcely possible to conceive of circumstances more calculated to sow the seeds of future disease, and, to borrow the language of the Instructions, to prevent the organs from being fully developed, to enfeeble and disorder their functions, and to subject the whole system to injury which cannot be repaired at any subsequent

stage of life" (R. H. Franks, Esq., Report, § 68 : App. Pt. I., p. 396). In the West of Scotland, Dr. Thompson, Ayr, says : " A collier at fifty generally has the appearance of a man ten years older than he is " (T. Tancred, Esq., Evidence, No. 34 : App. Pt. I., p. 371, l. 58).

798. The Sub-Commissioner for North Wales reports :—"They fail in health and strength early in life : at thirty a miner begins to look wan and emaciated, and so does a collier at forty : while the farming labourer continues robust and hearty" (H. H. Jones, Esq., Report, § 83 : App. Pt. II., p. 375).—John Jones, relieving officer for the Holywell district, states : " Though the Children and Young Persons employed in these works are healthy, still it is observable that they soon get to look old, and they often become asthmatic before they are forty" (H. H. Jones, Esq., Evidence, No. 96 : App. Pt. II., p. 407, l. 51).

799. In the Forest of Dean, Thomas Marsh, Esq., surgeon, Coleford, states that " Colliers usually become old men at fifty to fifty-five years of age" (E. Waring, Esq , Evidence, No. 38 : App. Pt. II., p. 25, l. 57). In North Somersetshire, William Brice, clerk and manager, says : " There are very few at work who are above fifty years of age " (Dr. Stewart, Evidence, No. 7 : App. Pt. II., p. 50, l. 48).

800. Early death is the natural consequence of the premature decrepitude thus described to those whom ever imminent casualties have not brought to the grave during the years of their vigour. The medical Evidence shows that even in South Staffordshire and Shropshire comparatively few miners attain their fifty-first year. In Warwickshire and Leicestershire it is not uncommon for the men to follow their occupation ten years longer ; but all classes of witnesses in the other districts uniformly state that it is rare to see an old collier.

801. In Derbyshire ; William Wardle " Does not think colliers live so long as those above ground ; very few live to be sixty" (J. M. Fellows, Esq., Evidence, No. 84 : App. Pt. II., p. 287, l. 38). In Yorkshire, " Colliers have harder work than any other class of workmen, and the length of time they work, as well as the intense exertion they undergo, added to the frequent unhealthiness of the atmosphere, decidedly tend to shorten their lives " (J. C. Symons, Esq., Report, § 110 : App. Pt. I., p. 181).—Henry Hemingway, Esq., surgeon, Dewsbury, states, " I only know one old collier" (J. C. Symons, Esq., Evidence, No. 221 : App. Pt. I., p. 282, l. 45).—Thomas Rayner, Esq., surgeon, Birstall, says, " I have had 27 years' practice, and I know of no old colliers—their extreme term of life is from fifty-six to sixty years of age " (Ibid. No. 268 : p. 292, l. 51). In Lancashire, states Mr. Kennedy, " it appeared to me that the number of aged men was much smaller than in other occupations" (J. L. Kennedy, Esq., Report, § 299 : App. Pt. II., p. 188).

802. After stating that the colliers of South Durham are a strong and healthy race, Dr. Mitchell adds :—"The work, however, is laborious and exhausting, and the colliers though healthy are not long-lived" (Dr. Mitchell, Report, § 212 : App. Pt. I., p. 143).—John Wetherell Hays, clerk of the Union, Durham, states, " That the colliers are not long-lived ; that they live well and live fast" (Dr. Mitchell, Evidence, No. 96 : App. Pt. I., p. 153, l. 57) ; And George Canney, medical practitioner, Bishop Auckland, says : "They are generally short-lived" (Ibid. No. 97 : p. 153, l. 64).

803. The Sub-Commissioner for the East of Scotland reports, that after a careful consideration of all the sources of information which could assist him in the object of his inquiry, he arrives at the following conclusion : " That the labour in the coal mines in the Lothian and River Forth districts of Scotland is most severe, and that its severity is in many cases increased by the want of proper attention to the economy of mining operations ; whence those operations, as at present carried on, are extremely unwholesome and productive of diseases which have a manifest tendency to shorten life" (R. H. Franks, Esq., Report, § 121 : App. Pt. I., p. 408).—Mr. Walter Jarvie, manager to Mr. Cadell, of Banton, states that " In the small village of Banton there are nearly 40 widows ; and as the Children work always on parents' behalf, it prevents them having recourse to the kirk-session for relief" (R. H. Franks, Esq., Evidence, No. 273 : App. Pt. I., p. 486, l. 25).—Elspee Thomson says, " Most of the men begin to complain at thirty to thirty-five years of age, and drop off before they get the length of forty" (Ibid. No. 73 : p. 450, l. 31).—Henry Naysmith, sixty-five years of age, collier, who says he has wrought upwards of 50 years, adds that "he has

been off work near 10 years, and is much afflicted with shortness of breath : it is the bane of the colliers, and few men live to my age" (Ibid. No. 83 : p. 452, l. 29).

804. In North Wales, "It is said but few colliers come to the age of sixty, and still fewer miners. This I believe to be the fact, though I met with many, both miners and colliers, who had attained the age of sixty, yet they were few compared with the number employed in these branches of industry" (H. H. Jones, Esq., Report, § 84 : App. Pt. II., p. 375).—Mr. John Jones, relieving-officer for the Holywell district : " Thinks they are not as long-lived as agriculturists" (H. H. Jones, Esq., Evidence, No. 96 : App. Pt. II., p. 407, l 53).—James Jones, overman, Cyfarthfa Works, states " That the colliers are generally very healthy and strong up to the age of forty or fifty ; they then often have a difficulty of breathing, and they die at younger ages than agricultural labourers or handi-craftsmen" (Ibid. No. 2 : p. 378, l. 35).—Mr. John Hughes, assistant under-ground agent, says, " They do not appear to live long after fifty or sixty years old" (Ibid. No. 3 : p. 379, l. 34).

805. In South Wales the Sub-Commissioner reports that he " has not been able to ascertain for want of sufficient data the average duration of a collier's life in the counties either of Glamorgan or Monmouth, but it is admitted that such average duration is less than that of a common labourer. In the county of Pembroke, however, James Bowen, Esq., surgeon, Narbeth, in that county, informs me— ' The average life of a collier is about forty ; they rarely attain forty-five years of age ; and in the entire population of *Begelly* and *East Williamson*, being 1163, forming, strictly speaking, a mining population, there are not six colliers of sixty years of age.'

806. " The Rev. Richard Buckby, rector of Begelly, in answer to one of the Queries in the Educational Paper of the Central Board, writes—' The foul air of the mines seriously affects the lungs of the Children and Young Persons employed therein, and shortens the term of life. In a population of 1000 there are not six colliers sixty years of age.'" (R. H. Franks, Esq., Report, §§ 67, 68 : App. Pt. II., p. 484). In North Somersetshire, Mr. William Bryce, clerk and manager, Coal-Barton, states that they " Commonly get broken in their health about forty or forty-five years of age, and then are not a long-lived race." (Dr. Stewart, Evidence, No. 7 : App. Pt. II., p. 51, l. 14.)

807. From a consideration of the whole of the preceding evidence it appears that persons employed in coal mines in general acquire a preternatural develop-ment of the muscles, especially about the arms, shoulders, chest, and back ; that for some time they are capable of prodigious muscular exertion ; that in a few years their strength diminishes, and many lose their robust appearance ; that these then become pallid, stunted in growth, short of breath, sometimes thin, and often crooked and crippled, and that, in addition to several minor ailments, which, how-ever, occasion no inconsiderable suffering, they are peculiarly subject to certain mortal diseases, the direct result of their employment, and of the state of the place in which they work.*

---

* After this review of the ascertained effects on health and life of employment in coal mines, under the circumstances in which it is at present carried on, a brief account of the mode in which these results are produced, as far as a knowledge of the laws of the animal economy enables us to afford it, may not be without interest.

From the period of birth to that of adult age, two processes are constantly taking place in the human body : one a process of consolidation, by which the proportion of the solids to the fluids in-creases, and the soft and tender structures gradually acquire density and firmness; and the other a process of augmentation, by which the several organs progressively increase in bulk. By the conjoint operation of these two processes, which comprise the essential conditions of growth, all the organs of the body are successively brought from their rudimentary state in infancy to their state of full perfec-tion in adult age. Of these stages of growth, which are marked by definite and peculiar characters, known to every one, and which are commonly called epochs of life, namely, infancy, childhood, boy-hood, girlhood, and adolescence, the first, or the period of infancy, extends from birth to the com-pletion of the first dentition, that is, about the end of the second year. The second, or the period of childhood, extends from the completion of the first to the completion of the second dentition, that is, from the second to the seventh or eighth year. The third, or the period of boyhood and girlhood, extends from the seventh or eighth year, to the epoch of commencing puberty, that is, in this climate, from the twelfth to the fourteenth year. The fourth, or the period of adolescence, extends from the commencement of puberty to adult age, that is, to the twentieth year for females, and the twenty-fourth for males.

In childhood all the organs are merely in the course of development, not one being complete in

II.--IRONSTONE MINES AND THE MANUFACTURE OF IRON.

1. Ironstone Mines.

808. Most of the circumstances connected with the working of iron-stone mines are similar to those which have been so fully detailed relative to coal mines; it will, therefore, be necessary here to advert only to the differences.

IRONSTONE
MINES.

---

structure, or mature in function; and this is more especially the case with the osseous, the nervous, and the muscular systems, on the full development of which the future health, strength, and intelligence wholly depend. The consolidation and augmentation of these systems, the object of every vital process which is now carried on, are accomplished chiefly by the nutritive organs, all of which, during this stage of growth, are in most active operation; and if from any cause the function of these organs is interrupted at this epoch, the injury inflicted is irreparable.

The external physical agents which are essential to the vital process of nutrition are food, air, and light; the two former supplying the materials that are employed in the process, while the latter exercises a modifying influence upon the process itself, which is shown by experience to be as important in the animal as it is in the vegetable body. But supposing these agents to be afforded in abundance, and supposing at the same time the digestive organs to be sound and active, so that sufficient nutriment is formed, it is obvious that the nutritive process may be interrupted, and the growth of the body impeded, by any causes which unduly abstract this nutriment from the system, or which give an undue proportion of it to some one part at the expense of the other parts. One of the most powerful means of rapidly expending the nutriment of the system is great and permanently sustained muscular exertion, the consequent exhaustion being in exact proportion to the degree in which the exertion is carried beyond the natural strength, and the measure of this excess being, as has been shown, the degree of fatigue induced. Even in the adult, who has only to maintain the tone and strength of muscles already fully developed, there is no more powerful cause of exhaustion than great and continuous muscular exertion, but when such exertion is exacted while the muscles are merely in the process of growth, it must be still more exhausting, because the muscles, as all other organs, are weak in proportion to their immaturity; and it must at the same time impede the process of growth, because the nutriment, instead of being applied to the development of the structures, is expended in sustaining this muscular exertion.

One evidence that great and continuous muscular exertion during the period of childhood acts injuriously on the body, and the more injuriously the younger the age, is afforded by that very effect which, at first view, might seem to indicate that it is innoxious, namely, the preternatural muscular development which it produces. Such a disproportionate muscular development, instead of being an indication of sound and robust health, is really a proof that the general system is starved by the over-nourishment of this one particular part of it; and that the system is weakened, not strengthened, by this undue expenditure of its nutriment upon the muscles, is shown by the evidence now collected, which proves indubitably that the body in general is stunted in its growth, that it is peculiarly prone to disease, and that it prematurely decays and perishes.

In estimating the influence on the physical constitution of great muscular exertion constantly exacted during the period of childhood, one further result of it deserves especial notice, namely, the retardation of the epoch of "puberty." Attention was first drawn to this result during the examination, by one of the Commissioners, of some Young Persons at a thin-seam coal-pit in Yorkshire, in which the work was particularly laborious, and the pit more than commonly wet and dirty. The Young Persons who came under observation were stated to be of various ages, from fourteen to eighteen, and one case was nineteen. On a careful examination of them, the Commissioner found that, with the exception of the teeth, which had developed naturally, there was not present a single sign of puberty. The same was subsequently found to be the case with great numbers of Young Persons examined specially with reference to this point, in many pits in the neighbourhoods of Wakefield and Halifax; and a similar retardation, though not in so great a degree, was observed in girls.

This effect of early labour will not be deemed of slight importance when it is considered that the determination of a due supply of blood to the organs to be developed at this epoch (which in the employment in question is abstracted from them, and spent upon the muscles) is essential to the maturity of the body, while the natural development of those organs imparts to the system an excitement which is essential to the completion of the growth of all the others, and more especially to the perfection of the organisation of the nervous system in general, and of the brain in particular—the last organ to acquire its mature growth, the seat and source of all the higher capacities and powers of the human being.

The positive diseases produced by the employment in question are of a peculiar and specific nature, partly the direct result of violent exertion long continued, such as disease of the heart, hæmorrhage, and rupture; and partly of the imperfect ventilation and drainage of the place of work, such as disease of the lungs, joints, and glands. In consequence of imperfect ventilation, the air of coal mines, which is commonly breathed during 12 out of the 24 hours, does not contain sufficient oxygen to decarbonise the blood: hence the blood becomes overcharged with that noxious ingredient (carbon). from which

IRONSTONE
MINES.

809. The characteristic differences between the ironstone mines and the coal mines, as far as those differences influence the manner of working the former, are the following :—

810. 1. In the ironstone mines the beds are, for the most part, thin, generally from two to three feet, a little more or less. In many of these pits the ore is in thin bands of two or three inches in width, and very often two thin beds lie near each other, with a stratum of indurated clay beneath them. The miners have only the space between the bands to work in ; or if they clear away some space more, it is the smallest possible, on account of the expense. The ironstone found in the form of rounded boulders is distributed through strata of clay, or of clay and sand ; and in this case more room is usually afforded for work.

811. 2. The ironstone mines are generally much more wet and cold than the coal-mines, and are proportionally more productive of those diseases which have been shown to be produced by wet and cold.

812. 3. In consequence of the thinness of the beds, horses and asses cannot be employed in bringing the ironstone from the workings to the foot of the shaft, and consequently a proportionately greater number of Children and Young Persons are required for this purpose. As, however, the ironstone is heavy, very young Children are altogether unable to perform the work, and are, therefore, not employed.

813. 4. The shallowness of the ironstone-mines renders it more difficult to ventilate them properly, and consequently they are not only generally more wet, but are also less abundantly supplied with pure air than the coal-mines ; hence pulmonary diseases are still more frequent and severe even than in the coal-mines, and rheumatism, inflammation of the joints, and scrofulous disease of the glands far more common.

South Staffordshire.

814. SOUTH STAFFORDSHIRE.—There are no means of forming an estimate of the proportion between the number of people in the ironstone pits, and the coal pits in this district ; but, according to Mr. Hartell Baylis, agent to James Loxdale, Esq.,—" The proportion of men to boys in the ironstone pits is about 100 men to 70 boys, while in the coal-pits the proportion is 100 men to 30 boys." The Sub-Commissioner states, that in ironstone pits the work is laborious, and very young Children would be of little or no use ; and that some of these boys are as young as from ten to eleven, but that others are as old as from seventeen to eighteen. (Dr. Mitchell, Report, § 64, 66: App. Pt. I., p. 8 ; and Evidence, No. 7: App. Pt. I., p. 65, l. 41.)

815. In this district no females are employed in any kind of under-ground work in the ironstone pits ; but many girls are employed on the bank " in picking out the ironstone boulders from the measures (useless material of the stratum) in which they are contained." (Ibid., Report, § 105: p. 12.)

Shropshire.

816. SHROPSHIRE.—The great difference between the ironstone mines of

---

it is the main purpose of the function of respiration to purify it, and therefore cannot supply the organs with their natural pabulum and stimulus. For the same space of time, not pure atmospheric air, but atmospheric air loaded with deleterious gases, is unceasingly in contact with the lungs, by which these delicate structures are kept in a state of constant irritation, and their organisation ultimately destroyed ; and, in great numbers of instances, these grievous effects are enhanced and hastened by exposure to damp and cold, by which inflammations and other painful affections are produced and maintained in the muscles, ligaments, and joints. The final result is, that by the combined operation of these various causes, the organic structures are worn out, and the vital powers exhausted, sooner than under the ordinary conditions of human life.

The transition from one stage of growth, or one epoch of life, into another, marks a corresponding advancement in the completion of the physical organisation, and the consequent acquisition of an increased capacity for usefulness and enjoyment. Under the ordinary circumstances of human life, this transition, up to the period of adult age, takes place with so much uniformity and precision that it is rare to find any one of these epochs anticipated or postponed by a single year. The vast mass of evidence which has now been brought under view proves indubitably that, by the employment of children at the very tender ages at which they commonly commence work in the coal mines, the growth of the body is retarded, and the period of childhood, properly so called, proportionally prolonged ; while the same evidence shows that the period intervening between adult age and decrepitude—that is, the period during which the physical, the intellectual, and the moral powers of the human being are in full vigour—is abridged. It follows therefore that, at least in great numbers of instances, if not in general, employment in the coal mines, as that employment is at present carried on, protracts the period of childhood, shortens the period of manhood, and anticipates the period of old age, decrepitude, and death.—T. S. S.

Staffordshire and Shropshire, is, that whereas in the former county the seams of coal are thick, and the seams of ironstone thin; in Shropshire it is the reverse, the seams of coal being thin, and those of ironstone thick. One consequence of this difference is, that Children and Young Persons are not so much required in the ironstone-pits of Shropshire, as in those of Staffordshire; accordingly, the Sub-Commissioner states that "the persons employed about the iron mines is not a third of the number of those employed about the coal mines." (Dr. Mitchell, Report, § 330 : App. Pt. I., p. 41.) And of the persons employed, according to Mr. Tranter, agent to the Coalbrook Dale Company, " there is not so large a proportion of boys, and the reason is that the mines are in general higher, and consequently there is room for men, for small horses and donkeys, and in some of them for large horses" (Ibid., Evidence, No. 41 : App. Pt. I., p. 79, 1. 68),

817. In this district no females are employed in any kind of under-ground work in the ironstone-mines, but great numbers of girls and young women are employed on the bank in breaking up the pieces of clod and gathering out the "pennystone," as the most abundant ironstone in Shropshire is called. (Ibid., Report, § 332 : App. Pt. I., p. 41 ; and Evidence, Nos. 15, 58, 78.)

818. DERBYSHIRE.—Some particulars are given in the evidence collected by the Sub-Commissioner relative to the ironstone mines of this district, from which it appears that very few Children and Young Persons are employed in them. (J. M. Fellows, Esq., Evidence, Nos. 196, 198, 201, 340, 365. See also pages 324, 315.) No females are employed in any kind of under-ground work in the ironstone pits of this district, but girls are occasionally, though seldom, employed about the mines at the surface.

819. YORKSHIRE.—The Sub-Commissioners for this district make no distinction in their Reports between the ironstone mines and the coal mines, excepting Mr. Wood, who states that it is the custom in the Low-Moor ironstone mines to stop an hour regularly for dinner, while in the coal mines in this district this is not generally the case.

820. EAST OF SCOTLAND.—In this district girls at very early ages, and women of all ages, are sent down into the ironstone-pits to work, just as they are in the coal-pits ; and all classes of witnesses bear testimony to the extreme severity of the labour. Mr. John Reid, contractor of the Crofthead ironstone pits, Whitburn, Linlithgowshire, says : " The work being of a heavy kind, weak or very young persons are useless, and only create confusion. We cannot prevent men taking down children, though we do not sanction or approve of it. I am of opinion that no children should be employed under fourteen years of age." (R. H. Franks, Esq., Evidence, No. 196 : App. Pt. I., p. 472, 1. 52.

821. Mr. Thomas Stevenson, overseer of the mines worked by the Shotts Company at Green Burn, and the under-ground workings at Shotts, in the county of Lanark, states that " Parents will take their young ones below, and do so at the early age of eight years. There appears a desire amongst the men to keep the females out, and many who keep their wives at home object to the conduct of others who continue the bad practice. The employment is very fatiguing, and unfit for women ; still many married ones continue to labour while pregnant, and do so as long as they dare venture to keep from home. It would be of great advantage to the people themselves, and no injury to masters, to keep boys out of mines till they had good strength for the work, and had got well educated ; the work is heavy, and requires both strength and skill. I would not permit my own sons to work until they were of full age and strength " (Ibid. No. 199 : p. 473, 1. 36).

822. The workpeople of the long-established Carron Company have grown up in their service, but many of their ironstone-pits are wrought by contractors, who engage what people they please. Joseph Dawson, Esq., manager of the Carron Company's coal and ironstone mines, parishes of Falkirk, Larbert, and Bothkenner, Stirlingshire: " In the Carron collieries and ironstone pits the miners and many of their wives and children have wrought all their lives, and very few changes take place. Every reasonable thing that

IRONSTONE
MINES.

East of Scotland.

can conduce to their comfort and accommodation is granted, and no dispute of any importance has taken place amongst our colliers and miners for some years" (Ibid. No. 238 : p. 480, l. 34).

823. All the witnesses agree as to the fatiguing nature of the work in the ironstone-pits of this district.   (Nos. 315, 317, 340, *et seq.*)

West of Scotland.

824. WEST OF SCOTLAND.—The Sub-Commissioner furnishes the following table as an example of such particulars as could be collected with regard to the ironstone mines of this district (T. Tancred, Esq., Report, § 30 : App. Pt. I., p. 319) :—

IRONSTONE MINES.

Name of Mines, and of Owner or Lessee.	Number of Seams worked; Thickness and Depth of each.	Number of People employed.			Whether Females are employed; and Age at which Children begin to work.	Gross Weight of Loaded Corf; and Distance drawn.	Power of Engines.
		Adults.	13 to 18.	Below 13.			
Whiterigg, W. Dixon, Esq., New Monkland Parish.	Seam, 10 to 13 inches. Wild coal, 8 in. Working places, 22 in. high. Main-way, 3½ feet.	251	39	19	4 females; 1 child at 8 years, others at 9.	11 cwt. Drawn by women and adult males.	153 horses.
Staurigg Plaw-yards, Cairn Hill, Raivyards, Coatdye, New Monkland Parish, W. Baird and Co.	..	Not stated.	132	82	13 females; boys begin from 9 to 10 years old.	,.	..
Shotts, Chas. Baird and Co., Shotts Parish.	Coal, 2 ft. 6 in., 6 ft. 9 in. Blaes and ironstone, 1 ft. Depth, 16 to 28 fath.	240	41	32	49 females; children begin to work about 9 years old.	5 cwt. 200 fathoms furthest. Drawn by females.	1 engine 50, and 2 gins.

825. From this table it appears that at Whiterigg women are employed in the ironstone pit to draw loaded corves weighing 11 cwt., and that in an ironstone pit at Shotts women commonly draw 5 cwt. different distances, the furthest being 200 fathoms. "The labour of the ironstone miners is often worse than that of colliers. I have seen them at work in a space of from twenty-two inches to two feet high, where even when seated a man could not keep his neck straight, and to get into the place where he was at work was no easy matter. The management of his heavy tools in such a confined space must be very fatiguing. Two men take between them fourteen yards of the band of stone, and make their own walls of the roof which comes down when the stone is extracted, leaving a road six feet wide to each space of fourteen yards. The drawing in the ironstone-pits is never done by Children, being too heavy for them. It is often, however, very improperly made the work of women, and in other cases migratory Irishmen commence working under ground by engaging as drawers of ironstone, being the business easiest learned" (Ibid., § 60 : p. 327).

North Wales.

826. NORTH WALES.—No distinction is made between the employment in ironstone mines and collieries in this district, and therefore the Report of the Sub-Commissioner must be regarded as equally applicable to both. No women or girls are employed under ground.

South Wales.

827. SOUTH WALES.—In this district it is the custom to send Children into the ironstone-mines at the same early ages as into the coal-mines, and girls and women are employed in the former just as in the latter, with the sam unhappy results.   As an example of the evidence given on this suject we may cite that of Mr. P. Kirkhouse, overman to the Cyfarthfa collieries and ironstone mines, Glamorganshire:—" As far as memory will permit, I should say the number of children and young persons working below ground in the Cyfarthfa mines amounts to 400: out of the number, 50 may be females.   The youngest are employed at the air-doors, and are taken below at very infantine ages, which cranks [stunts] their growth and injures their constitution, as well as keeping them in a state of ignorance of a very deplorable kind.   The employment females are put to is the filling and drawing the drams [carts] of coal or

ironstone : it requires great strength.   The main-roads are made as easy as the
work will allow, by iron rails being run to the ends of the workings ; but this
does not alter the nature of the employment, which is certainly unfit for women,
and totally deprives them, by the liberty it gives, of getting after-employ at labour
of domestic kind.

828. FOREST OF DEAN.—The difference between the employment in the
ironstone mines and that in the coal mines of this district is thus described :
" The principal difference between the modes of juvenile labour in the coal
pits and iron mines, is in the conveyance of the ore out of the narrow workings,
which is done in baskets or boxes, placed on '*billies*,' a kind of saddle strapped
to the shoulders.   The *billy* was originally an accredited Forest measure
(*vide* Mr. Mushet's Evidence, No. 37).   It now carries from 1 cwt. to $1\frac{1}{2}$ cwt.
The former is the usual load, and a boy of thirteen will manage this, after
another has assisted in lifting it to his back.   The iron ore usually running in
ascending diagonal veins, often at an angle of sixty degrees, greatly facilitates
this mode of conveyance, by giving the boys a descending path to the place
where they deposit their loads.   Where the nature of the passage will admit,
the ore is conveyed to the horse-way in wheelbarrows.   Young boys, of from
eight to ten years of age, are sometimes employed in picking stones out of the
ore before it leaves the mine ; but very few are employed at so early an age,
except in the small mines carried on by working-men on their own account.
There is something very remarkable in the distribution of the iron ore among
the limestone which forms its matrix.   It lies in '*churns*,' or '*pockets*,' as
the miners term these deposits ; and as these are cut away, natural pillars
and arches of limestone are left, supporting the roof in a variety of grotesque
forms and combinations.   The contents of the '*churns*' vary both in quality
and quantity, which produces a picturesque irregularity in the mine-works,
strongly contrasting with the even courses of the coal strata.   In the Upper
Oakwood Level, carried on by the Cinderford Iron Company, a number of
young lads were pursuing their labours at the sides of a remarkably preci-
pitous gallery, which I was told ran up through the superincumbent hill
quite to the surface.   An immense heap of pulverescent ore, said to be of
superior quality, was collected in the tipping-place, at the foot of this steep,
which forms an admirable ventilator for the mine.   Just on one side of this
long and narrow vein, a vast mass of ore was excavating, leaving a lofty dome
of magnificent dimensions overhead.   Great advantages must have been derived, by the labouring miners, from the introduction of capital in the various
branches connected with their trade ; the old method of raising ore being
incomparably more tedious, as well as more laborious, from the absence of
levels, or other facilities for the work, unattainable without considerable cost.
I visited some of the more primitive iron mines, called *scowles*, still worked
on a small scale, near the village of Bream.   The entrances to some of these
grubbing places are more like rabbit-burrows, or fox-earths, than the mouth
of a mine.   An insignificant aperture, generally beneath a crop of limestone
rock, admits the miner, who descends, almost perpendicularly, either by
notches cut in the rock, or wooden pegs driven into the soil, taking with him
a light ladder, by which, at some stages in his progress, he lets himself down
to his working place.   The ore from these little mines is carried to the surface in billies, on the backs of young boys, who crawl along the galleries and
climb into daylight with the address and activity of monkeys.   These concerns are now carried on solely, on a small scale, by old free miners, assisted
by their own families, some of whom perform this toilsome work at the too
early age of six years" (E. Waring, Esq., Report, § 41 *et seq.:* App. Pt. II.
p. 4, 5).

829. Some of the ironstone pits in this district are dry and well ventilated,
but others are stated by witnesses to be very wet and imperfectly ventilated.
(See Witnesses Nos. 15, 27, 28; 45, 49).   No girls or women are employed
in them in any kind of under-ground work.

2. Iron Works.

830. An elaborate account is given by the Sub-Commissioner for South Staffordshire and Shropshire, of all the operations that are carried on in the iron works, from the first to the last: the making of coke—the calcining of ironstone—the blasting in the furnace—the casting of iron—the refining of iron—the changing of crude iron into wrought iron by the process of puddling, and by the forge-hammer and the puddle-rolls—and lastly the passing of iron through the rolling-mills. As the account of these operations is concise and clear, we do not conceive that it can be advantageously abridged. For the description of these operations, given *seriatim*, see Dr. Mitchell's Report, App. Pt. I., pp. 44—53; and for the account of the several operations given by the Witnesses, see Dr. Mitchell's Evidence, App. Pt. I., pp. 69—74. Some of these operations are also noticed in the Reports of the Sub-Commissioners for Scotland and South Wales. See the Report of T. Tancred, Esq., App. Pt. I., pp. 328—330; and R. H. Franks, Esq., App. Pt. II., pp. 475—479.

831. Some of the Commissioners have themselves visited several of the iron districts, and have witnessed most of the operations, so that they can bear their own testimony to the general faithfulness of the descriptions.

832. In connexion with the blast furnaces, many Children are employed in building up heaps of coals, to be burnt into coke, on the field adjoining the furnaces.

833. Children and Young Persons are also employed in building up the heaps of ironstone and coal preparatory to the process of calcination.

834. Children and Young Persons also break the limestone into small pieces, preparatory to its being thrown into the blast-furnaces.

835. These operations are carried on in the day-time, under the direction of grown persons, who often contract to do the work, and pay the Children and Young Persons who assist them.

836. The work is not necessarily laborious or exhausting; it is carried on in the open air; and there is no evidence that any of the operations are oppressive or injurious.

837. Many Children and Young Persons, of both sexes, are employed in the more immediate attendance on the blast furnace.

838. Some fill boxes or barrows with coke, for cold-blast furnaces, or with coal for the hot-blast furnaces, and often fill for the hot-blast furnaces boxes or barrows both of coal and coke.

839. Some are employed filling boxes or barrows with calcined ironstone, and riddling the small ironstone from the dirt and dust mixed up with it.

840. Some fill the boxes or barrows with broken limestone.

841. None of these operations are above the strength of the persons employed, and are conducted in the open air.

842. These materials are carried to the furnaces by grown men, sometimes they are wheeled up, and in the larger furnaces they are drawn up by machinery. In the case of some of the smaller furnaces young men and boys assist the adults in the performance of this labour.

843. The operations of the blast furnace must go on by night as well as by day, and there must be two sets of people, and the Children and Young Persons must work at night as well as the adults. It is the universal practice for one set to work one week during the day, and the same set to work the following week during the night. As long as blast furnaces are in operation at all, there appears to be no means of avoiding this night work.

Working of Furnaces on Sundays.

Working of Furnaces on Sundays.

844. For the same reasons that the furnaces are kept working during the night, they are also kept in work during the Sunday; so that they work unceasingly every hour of the week, and the Sunday is made the day of what is called the double turn; that is, the workpeople who had been at work from six o'clock on the Sunday morning, instead of leaving the furnace at six o'clock on Sunday afternoon, as on ordinary days, continue at work until six o'clock the next morning;

thus the Sunday, instead of being a day of rest, is made the day during which the labour continues twenty-four hours in succession. In order to mitigate the great severity of labour continued unremittingly for this long period, and to avoid the privation of the workpeople, on every alternate Sunday, of the day of rest, efforts have been made by several of the iron-masters in all the districts to dispense with the attendance of the people employed at the furnaces during a certain number of hours on the Sunday. The evidence proves indubitably that those efforts have been attended with complete success in every one of the iron districts, though it has been more difficult to ensure success in some districts than in others.

Mr. John Anstice, partner in the Madeley Wood Iron Works, states that—" The Company .began, about twenty-five years ago, to allow the people employed about their furnaces to discontinue labour for certain hours on the Sundays, and have so continued to do ever since. The usual number of hours during which the works stand is from six to eight ; being from nine or ten to four or five ; the time being longer or shorter, according as the state of the furnaces will allow. We have found most decidedly that we have not sustained any loss by so doing ; but, on the contrary, it does good, because there is more care required before the stand commenced to see that the furnaces are in good order, and that care is of great benefit. We would willingly give more time if the nature of the manufacture could admit of it ; but if the furnace stops longer the heat abates, and there then is an inclination in the material in the furnace to set and become stiff and cloggy. The men feel the stand a great comfort, and greatly prefer it. The stand takes place during the double turn, which is a greater relief, as there are only sixteen or eighteen hours' labour instead of twenty-four." (Dr. Mitchell, Evidence, No. 39 : App. Pt. I., p. 78, l. 62).

Mr. Alfred Darby, a partner, and one of the managers of the Coalbrookdale Company, gives the following evidence of their experience on this subject : " About a dozen years ago the Coalbrookdale Company, knowing that the Madeley Wood Iron Company had discontinued blowing their iron-furnaces for certain hours of the Sunday, determined to try what could be done in the same way, and adopted the practice, which has been continued ever since, of letting the furnaces stand every Sunday from ten in the morning to four in the afternoon. They are not sensible that any loss has been sustained thereby, excepting that during such time no iron is made, and the capital employed in the furnace department is for such time unproductive. They would willingly extend the time of cessation from labour on Sundays longer, if they could safely do so ; but this they fear they cannot. The furnaces would in such case become too much cooled, and great injury would arise. As a proof of this, it often happens, when an accident occurs to the engine by which the furnaces are stopped for several hours (say eight to twenty hours), that it takes several days to recover before they come to as good and efficient a working state as previously : and during this time they not only produce a less quantity, but with a greater consumption of coal. The coal used at these works is not of the best quality ; but experience only would show whether with the very best coal the blast-furnaces might stand longer than six hours" (Ibid, No. 40 : p. 79, l. 19).

Mr. George Lane, who superintends the furnaces at Horsehays, belonging to the Coalbrookdale Company, gives the following account : " For these twelve years past the furnaces have stood six hours on the Sundays, and sometimes a little longer. No injury arises if the furnace be at the time in a good working state ; but if not in a good working state, or if it was to stand too long, the iron would be thick and hard, and would fall into the hearth and set ; that is, it would congeal and pass from a fluid into a solid state, and, consequently, when the time came for tapping the furnace to let out the melted iron, it would be necessary to make the opening higher up to let out the fluid iron, and it would be, perhaps, three weeks before all the congealed iron came off by little and little, and cleared the furnace. If the furnace were to stand for ten or twelve hours, at the end of that time it would not be in so good a state, it would not make so good iron, and it would be at greater expense ; there would be more fuel consumed, and there would be more labour and less iron, and that not so good in quality. When an accident happened by which the furnace was stopped twenty-four hours, it was from a week to nine days before the furnace was set right. . . . Has known a case where, from an accident, the furnace has stopped eight hours, the furnace was not in good working order after it commenced, and it was not right until the third day. He has frequently known the furnaces in worse condition from stopping the usual six hours on Sundays" (Ibid. No. 42 : p. 80, l. 5).

845. The furnaces of Mr. Botfield, in this part of Shropshire, stop about the same number of hours as those of the Coalbrookdale and of the Madeley Wood Companies.

Mr. Thomas Onions, the manager, states : " We sustain no material injury by the furnaces standing on a Sunday, only the loss of the quantity of iron that would be made in that time, or that of a few hours more before the furnaces regain the same intensity of heat they had before they stood, and the iron a little deteriorated" (Dr. Mitchell, Report, § 449 : App. Pt. I., p. 55).

846. " In the end of last December the men at the Lawley furnace in the same district made bitter complaint of the hardship which they sustained in not having the rest of the sabbath-day. Very happily for them, I found in May last that the proprietors had determined to stand on the Sundays, and had commenced doing so

the Sunday before I was there. The other companies in this district have not suspended their furnaces on Sundays" (Ibid. § 450, 451 : p. 55).

847. Dr. Mitchell enters into a critical examination of the reasons assigned by the partners and agents of these companies why the example that has been set them has not been followed; and he appears to us to have succeeded in proving their fallacy (Ibid. § 452, *et seq.*: p. 55). In South Staffordshire, " About two years ago great exertions had been made by many of the iron masters, aided by the influence of the clergy, to have all the blast furnaces to stand for a certain number of hours; and at a numerous meeting it was decided by a majority that the experiment should be universally tried. The decisions of such meetings have, however, only a moral influence, and have no legal power. Accordingly, some did not comply with the recommendation at all, and after the time the greater part resumed the working on Sundays, alleging that the experiment had proved a failure. Altogether about one-third of the furnaces stand on Sundays (Ibid. § 458 : p. 56).

848. In Monmouthshire and South Wales the evidence collected by William Rhys Jones, Esq., shows that the Sunday is observed by the iron-masters and their people in these districts in the same way as in Staffordshire; some suspending their furnaces for a certain number of hours on the Sunday, and some going on as on other days, and giving the same reasons as in Staffordshire for so doing, the chief of which is the diminished make of iron, and the disorder occasioned to the furnaces. The furnaces of the Dowlais Iron Works, which are the largest in the kingdom, and belong to Sir John Josiah Guest and Co., are suspended for several hours every Sunday, with the best effect, and without any diminution in the make of iron. The furnaces are purposely brought by Sunday morning into a good state for stopping. The arguments so frequently urged by the iron-masters who do not stop their furnaces, that they suffer loss when an accident to the steam-engine, or any other cause, obliges them to stop, is not really applicable to the subject in question, because those accidental stoppages seldom occur when the furnaces are in the best state for stopping; but the evidence above quoted shows that they may by anticipation be brought into such a good state, that the gain may upon the whole be greater than the loss.

Mr. Daniel James, aged 45, master founder: " The furnaces are stopped from seven o'clock to four on Sundays, excepting only when a furnace may be out of order: it does not happen perhaps once in a year that we have a furnace blowing of a Sunday; but we have at present one out of order, and we have been obliged to blow it for the last five Sundays, but shall stop it next Sunday. We stop the furnaces after the morning tapping at seven o'clock, and cease to blow until four o'clock in the afternoon, when the engine is again set at work, and the men come on; sometimes the men have a little more work for about two hours in clearing the hearth, tap-holes, and tuyeres, when the furnaces are not in good order; but when the furnaces are in good order, there is no extra work or trouble. We have been in the practice of stopping the blast-furnaces on Sundays for the last ten years without any deviation, and make from the furnaces more iron in the year than we did before we commenced to stop. I cannot account for this circumstance, but such is the fact" (R. W. Jones, Esq., Evidence, No. 104 : App. Pt. II., p. 642, l. 17.

Rees Lewis, aged 41, under furnace-manager at the new Iron furnaces: " We stop the iron-furnaces every Sunday, the same as they do at the old Dowlais works. The engine stops about half past seven o'clock in the morning, when the men go off, and the next turn comes on at two o'clock, and works until six o'clock on Monday morning, when the men who went off about eight o'clock on Sunday morning come on again, and then they change regularly every twelve hours during the week. Sometimes, when the tuyeres or dams are out of order, some of the men remain on a Sunday morning to repair them; and about once a fortnight, or sometimes once a month, they pack the blowing cylinder, which is two hours' work for about four men. They are ordered by the company to stop every Sunday at eight o'clock in the morning, and to blow again at two o'clock in the afternoon; but they are seldom able to get the engine ready before four o'clock, as the engineers have generally something to do to her; the stoppage therefore is for about eight hours. There are from twenty-four to thirty persons working about the four Ivor furnaces in a turn; and by stopping on the Sunday both turns have either the morning or evening of that day to themselves. I do not find that the iron is much affected by stopping the furnaces for eight hours once a-week. The first tapping after it may be a little cold and hard, but the second tapping is generally as usual. The furnaces here are blown with hot blast. They lose a certain portion of their make by stopping, but I do not know that the decrease is much at the week's end" (Ibid. p. 642, l. 54).

At Pennydawan Works in Glamorganshire, Mr. Hugh Morgan, furnace master : " The furnaces work on Sundays the same as on other days, but no other part of the works. The long turn is from six o'clock on Sunday morning to six o'clock on Monday morning for the children as well as the men. I never tried to stop the furnaces on Sundays; if we stopped we should lose iron, because our blast is weak. When we do stop to repair the engines, from three to eight hours, we find the iron alter—it gets white and hard. We have two furnaces blown with ' hot blast;' it would not be so difficult to stop them. Their ' pillar of blast' at the Dowlais works is stronger than ours, and they are in consequence better able to stop their furnaces on Sundays. The limestone girls do not work on Sundays, or those emptying coal : the persons we have employed on Sundays are six furnace-keepers, six fillers, six cinder-fillers, six girls filling coals, three or four helpers, four boys at the hot-blast stoves, and three at the engines" (Ibid. No. 148: p. 653, l. 59).—Mr. Benjamin Martin, mineral agent: "Every department of the works is suspended on Sundays except the blast-furnaces. We have not tried to suspend them, but when we stop them for some hours, from accidents, we have some trouble in starting again. The men prefer changing the turn by working twenty-four hours to working only six hours. Sunday is the day of the double shift at the blast-furnaces. The long turn begins at six o'clock on Sunday morning and ends at six o'clock on Monday morning" (Ibid. No. 147: p. 653, l. 11).

George Crane, Esq., the proprietor of Yniscedwyn Iron Works in Glamorganshire, gives the following statement: " Our blast-furnaces are not stopped on Sundays; we have made the attempt this year, but the furnaces were disordered by this attempt. We tried for six or eight Sundays, determined to suspend the workings for twelve hours, but we were obliged to give up the attempt; on the last occasion the furnaces (from the effect of taking the blast off) cooled so much that they were nearly gobbed up. Sometimes in a favourable state a furnace might not suffer seriously by taking the blast off, at other times it might be very seriously injured. I have known instances when, from the accidental breaking of a part of the engine, the operation of the blast-furnaces has been suspended only for six hours, and that the effect has not been recovered for six or eight days. When we did stop, we are very apprehensive that few of the men did avail themselves of the opportunity of going to a place of worship. Sunday is the day of the double-shift : no part of the works except the furnaces is in operation on Sunday" (R. W. Jones, Esq., Report, § 11: App. Pt. II., p. 669).

849. There is a singular contrast between this evidence about the furnaces getting out of order and that of the furnace-manager at these same works.

Rees Davies, aged 38 : " I am furnace-manager (at Yniscedwyn); I have been here for four years to last January. We have two blast-furnaces at work here now, and another just going to be blown in. One of our furnaces is worked with stone-coal alone, and the other with stone-coal and coke ; we use hot blast to both. About twelve months ago we stopped our furnaces on Sundays for a period of eight or ten weeks ; we stopped from eight o'clock to three; we did not tap before we stopped; we tapped on Saturday nights, and stopped with the hearth full. We blew at three, and tapped about six or seven o'clock on Sunday evening, and then we did not tap again until ten instead of six o'clock, on Monday morning. The iron from the ' cast' on Sunday evening was as good as usual, when the furnace was in order; it was not at all whiter, or worse, nor from the next cast on Monday morning. We gave up the practice of stopping in consequence of one of our furnaces getting out of order ; the ' tuyers' got strong, and we were obliged to blow it on Sunday ; and, not liking to work the engine for one furnace alone, we blew the two furnaces. And the next Sunday it happened that we put another furnace into blast, and we were consequently obliged to blow it ; and from that time we have continued to blow on every Sunday. We have stopped, by accident for twelve and fourteen hours, and we have afterwards blown on without much hinderance or hurt. We stopped about five weeks ago for eleven hours to pack the piston of the engine, and found not the least inconvenience in blowing on again. We always stop for eight or nine hours when we ' pack,' as there is always some repairs wanted the same time. We pack the steam-cylinder every five or six weeks ; the blast cylinder is not packed more than once in two or three years. I do not think that there would be any difficulty in stopping a furnace with stone-coal for eight or nine hours, or perhaps for ten or twelve hours, on Sundays ; but we have not had much experience in this practice yet. Not one of the furnaces which we stopped on Sunday was worked at the time entirely with stone-coal ; but we have stopped the furnace worked entirely with stone-coal, when we packed the steam-cylinder, as long as the others were stopped on Sundays, that is for ten or eleven hours, without hurt. We make good grey iron in our furnaces, principally ' Nos. 2 and 3,' and sometimes ' No. 1.' The quality of the iron is not altered by stopping. I do not think that the stopping of the furnaces at Merthyr hurts the furnaces ; perhaps when they are making forge-iron, and the furnaces are working hot, the stopping of them for a few hours would be a benefit to them. A furnace might be prepared for stopping the blast for some hours by attending to the charges for a short time before ; but it would, perhaps, be attended with some loss in the make, particularly when working on foundry-iron" (R. W. Jones, Esq., Evidence, No. 201: App. Pt. II., p. 675, l. 9).

III.—TIN, COPPER, LEAD, AND ZINC MINES, AND THE DRESSING AND SMELTING OF THEIR ORES.

850. The employment of Children and Young Persons in the Mines of Tin, Copper, Lead, and Zinc, has little in common with their employment in Mines of Coal and Iron, on account of the different physical circumstances

in which the ores of these metals are found, and the peculiar operations required to separate them from the worthless materials with which they are combined.

851. Instead of forming beds more or less horizontal, and in regular alternation with strata of which the material is for the most part readily removed by the tools of the workmen, these ores are found in veins which variously approach a vertical position, in the hard rocks of the primary formations, or in the scarcely less solid lower beds of the carboniferous system.

852. The ores of tin are found only in the CORNISH District, in granitic and slaty rocks, of various structure, which are interspersed occasionally with masses of trap, and extend from Dartmoor, in Devonshire, to the Land's End, in Cornwall. This district is also the most productive in copper ores of any in the British Islands, and contains, moreover, mines of manganese, of iron, and of lead, the ores of which latter often contain a portion of silver, which is worth extracting from the baser metal. Of the various mines of this district, those of tin, copper, and lead present the characteristic features of its mining labour, and employ at least nineteen-twentieths of the young people engaged in it. The ores here obtained are smelted chiefly in South Wales, being shipped to Swansea for the convenience of fuel; but in the other principal mining districts the ores are smelted near the place of their excavation.

853. The elevated district of mountain limestone, intermingled with various strata of gritstone and shale, which occupies the borders of Northumberland, Durham, and Cumberland, and of which ALSTON MOOR may be considered as the capital, is the only other part of England in which metallic veins are now extensively wrought: these are exclusively of lead, containing a proportion of silver, which is commonly worth extracting. The veins in the mountain limestone of Derbyshire are now nearly exhausted.

854. In Wales, the Plinlimmon District, composed of various qualities of slate, was formerly much celebrated for its metallic products, but is now of inferior importance, and has not been subjected to any special investigation under the terms of the present Commission. In the neighbourhood of Snowdon the scattered mines are also of inferior importance. But the mines in the mountain limestone of FLINTSHIRE present an important group of works, into which the inquiry has been extended.

855. In Scotland the principal metallic veins that have yet been worked are still those in the clay slate mountains in the neighbourhood of LEADHILLS, on the borders of Lanarkshire and Dumfries-shire, although trials are also making in various parts of Galloway, and one of them, at Carsephairn, is on a considerable scale.

856. In IRELAND, in the slate and limestone rocks of the most mountainous districts, and generally near the sea-coast, there are scattered some mines of copper and lead, but chiefly of copper, for the most part in the counties of Wicklow, Wexford, Waterford, Cork, Kerry, Tipperary, Down, and Armagh.

857. Most of the regions in which the metallic veins occur, are thus seen to be hilly or mountainous. The South Western and the Flintshire Districts are the least elevated; the loftiest hills in the former rarely exceeding 1,000 feet above the level of the sea, while the greater number of them range from 500 to 700, and the plains at their bases are in general but from 100 to 200 feet above high water. This circumstance materially affects the comfort of the Children and Young Persons employed in working the mines.

PECULIARITIES IN THE LABOUR OF CHILDREN AND YOUNG PERSONS CONNECTED WITH MINES OF TIN, COPPER, LEAD, AND ZINC.

858. Unlike colliery labour, which has for its object merely to raise a mineral substance, capable of being hewn, to be used in the condition in which it is dug, that connected with the mines in metallic veins embraces not only the slow and difficult excavation of the ores from hard rocks, accomplished only by the constant aid of gunpowder, but likewise the "dressing" of the ores, or the mechanical separation of the metallic as much as possible from all extraneous substances, and the "smelting" of them into metal in its marketable form.

859. "The great body of the miners under ground," states Dr. Barham,

in regard to the South-Western District, and his terms will apply equally to the rest, " are employed in excavating the rock, whether for the sinking of shafts, the driving of levels, or the removing the veins of ore. These operations require, in most of the mines, the almost constant application of the explosive force of gunpowder. The greatest part of the work consequently consists in ' beating the borer;' that is, driving an iron cylinder terminating in a wedge-shaped point, by blows with a heavy hammer (mallet), whilst it is turned by another hand. The necessity or advantage of making the hole in a particular direction, often constrains the miner to assume every variety of posture in carrying on this work ; at times he is even compelled to lie on his side for this purpose. When the rock has been bored to a sufficient depth, the charged is introduced, and rammed down with a ' tamping-iron,' a particular clay being used for wadding, and a certain length of safety-fuse keeping up the communication with the powder ; fire is applied to this, and the miners retire till the explosion has taken place. After the blasting, the ' pick' comes into requisition, for the removal of the partially separated and angular pieces of rock. In soft ground the use of gunpowder is only occasionally required." (Dr. Barham, Report, § 62–64 : App. Pt. I., p. 747).

860. This slow and laborious process, it is obvious, can produce, in the course of a day, no such quantity of available ores to be brought to the surface, after their separation from the contiguous masses, as to afford underground employment in their removal for such large classes of Children and Young Persons as are employed in the mines of the softer rocks of mineral fuel, in waggoning the hewn coals to the main-ways, or to the bottom of the shafts, or in conveying them by levels and ladders to the surface. The number of Children and Young Persons employed in underground labour in the metallic mines is therefore small.

861. On the other hand, the labour of " dressing" the ores for the furnace is so exclusively theirs throughout the kingdom, that it employs the great body of the Young People connected with these mines ; and being an out-door labour on the surface, differs in all its circumstances from the underground work of the Children in coal mines.

862. In the "smelting" department, indeed, except in the copper works in the neighbourhoods of Swansea and Holywell, Young Persons are scarcely at all employed, until Youths of seventeen or eighteen, when they are taken generally from the labour of dressing the ores, to commence working with the adult smelters, with a view to make the furnace-work their future trade.

863. The effects of these circumstances in dividing the Children and Young Persons into distinct classes, according to the occupations which they pursue, will be best estimated by anticipating a statement of the numbers employed in each of them.

NUMBER OF CHILDREN AND YOUNG PERSONS EMPLOYED IN EACH DEPARTMENT OF LABOUR CONNECTED WITH MINES OF TIN, COPPER, LEAD, AND ZINC.

864. CORNISH DISTRICT.—The total number of persons employed in the mines of Cornwall is estimated at from 28,000 to 30,000; and in the mines of Devonshire, at about 1,500. From Returns received from certain mines in this district, in answer to a form of queries, it appears that out of 24,995 persons there are adult males, 15,500; adult females, 2,700; Young Persons (males) from thirteen to eighteen, 2,720; Young Persons (females) 1,740; Children (males) under thirteen, 1,639; females, 696; making the total number of Children and Young Persons, out of the number returned, 6,795 (Dr. Barham, Report, § 109,110: App. Pt. I., p. 764,765). The following Abstract from Returns received from certain mines in this district shows the proportions engaged in under-ground and in surface labour at each year of age.—

Cornish District.

TABLE showing the Number and the Ages of the Children and Young Persons employed in certain Mines.

Number, &c., according to the Returns made on the Tabular Forms.

Districts.	7 to 8 Males Under ground	7 to 8 Males Surface	7 to 8 Females	8 to 9 M U	8 to 9 M S	8 to 9 F	9 to 10 M U	9 to 10 M S	9 to 10 F	10 to 11 M U	10 to 11 M S	10 to 11 F	11 to 12 M U	11 to 12 M S	11 to 12 F	12 to 13 M U	12 to 13 M S	12 to 13 F	13 to 14 M U	13 to 14 M S	13 to 14 F
Cornwall, Western District.	..	1	..	..	9	..	2	31	..	5	59	1	13	75	4	19	70	8	22	65	13
Cornwall, Central (Part I.)	..	2	1	..	26	6	..	71	16	1	110	27	1	131	40	8	147	79	21	130	108
District (Part II.)	1	2	1	..	20	6	2	61	21	8	80	35	14	124	81	28	130	111	70	115	116
Cornwall, Eastern District.	..	..	..	..	8	..	..	27	2	1	51	8	3	41	24	5	77	32	3	73	46
Devonshire	..	1	..	..	6	..	2	12	3	..	27	4	6	28	13	9	27	8	8	31	16
Totals	1	6	2	..	69	12	6	202	42	15	327	75	37	399	162	69	451	238	124	414	299
	7						208			342			436			520			538		

Districts.	14 to 15 M U	14 to 15 M S	14 to 15 F	15 to 16 M U	15 to 16 M S	15 to 16 F	16 to 17 M U	16 to 17 M S	16 to 17 F	17 to 18 M U	17 to 18 M S	17 to 18 F	Total under 13 M U	Total under 13 M S	Total under 13 F	Total 13 to 18 M U	Total 13 to 18 M S	Total 13 to 18 F	Total of Children and young Persons M U	M S	F
Cornwall, Western District.	41	61	15	31	42	25	48	38	28	42	21	34	39	246	13	184	227	115	223	473	128
Cornwall, Central (Part I.)	30	119	84	40	89	122	36	48	96	42	25	117	10	488	168	167	406	522	177	894	690
District (Part II.)	78	103	114	105	77	120	101	47	118	113	41	120	53	417	255	167	362	587	520	779	1002
Cornwall, Eastern District.	4	81	55	12	57	57	28	29	48	11	29	55	9	204	66	58	269	261	67	473	465
Devonshire	20	28	15	6	37	23	14	23	18	12	12	18	17	101	33	60	131	90	50	232	191
Totals	173	392	283	194	302	347	227	185	208	220	128	344	128	1456	535	636	1395	1585	1064	2851	2120
	565			496			412			348			1584			2331			3915		

(Dr. Barham's Report, App. Pt. I. p. 770.)

MINES OF TIN, COPPER, LEAD, AND ZINC.

Alston Moor District.

865. ALSTON MOOR DISTRICT.—The total number of persons employed in the lead mines of this district is estimated by the Sub-Commissioners at upwards of 5,000. Of these 2,061 are returned as employed by Colonel Beaumont. Of this number those under thirteen years of age are 182; those between thirteen and eighteen are 250. Out of this number of Children and Young Persons (432), there are employed under-ground only fifty-three, of which seven only are under thirteen. If the Children and Young Persons employed under-ground be in the same proportion throughout this district, there will be but eighteen under thirteen, and 115 from thirteen to eighteen years of age. When the frost sets in, however, in the winter, there is a cessation from washing ores for three or four months; and most of the men and bigger boys go and work in the mines. (Dr. Mitchell, Report, § 35: App. Pt. II., p. 725.) The London Lead Company does not allow the boys under fourteen to go into the mines in winter, but makes them go to school; a rule which is relaxed only in the case of the Children of widows or persons having large families (Dr. Mitchell, Evidence, No. 3: App. Pt. II., p. 757, l. 3).

Derbyshire.

866. DERBYSHIRE.—No Children appear to be employed under-ground in the metallic mines of this district, excepting a few near Bonsall, where the very poor people who work the mines in this vicinity occasionally take their own Children to work with them. There are, however, some employed in the neighbourhood of Crick in washing ores. (J. M. Fellows, Esq., Report and Evidence, Appendix, Pt. II., pp. 259, 360—363.)

Scotland.

867. LEADHILLS.—The total number of persons employed in the Leadhills district is about 400, of whom very few begin to work underground under eighteen years of age. Nearly all the Children and Young Persons employed about these mines are occupied on the surface in washing the ores (J. Fletcher, Esq., Report, §§ 3, 8: App. Pt. II., p. 882, 883).

North Wales.

868. NORTH WALES.—In like manner very few Children and Young Persons descend into the lead mines in this district; they are almost all employed on the surface in breaking, picking, and washing the ore so as to prepare it for the smelters (H. H. Jones, Esq., Report, § 11: App. Pt. II., p. 366).

869. IRELAND.—In Ireland adult labour is so cheap and abundant, that Children and Young Persons are employed in far less proportion than in Great Britain. The following numbers are approximations to accuracy.—

County.	Mines.	Total of Work-people.	Employment of Children and Young Persons.
Wicklow .	Avoca Copper and Sulphur Mines; Glenmahee and Lugenaue Lead Mines; and the Gold Washings.	2,150	No children, and few of the young men under eighteen.
Wexford .	Caime Lead Mine	127	7 boys under thirteen; 20 from thirteen to eighteen; and 26 girls between those ages.
Waterford .	Knockmahon Copper Mines .	1,100	Children employed, though not liked; young persons also, though number not stated.
Cork . .	Cusheen Copper Mine, near Skull	120	None.
	Allihies Copper Mine . . .	800	Young persons employed, but few children.
	Rooska Lead Mine	20	None.
Tipperary .	Lackamore Copper Mine . .	200	Young persons and children employed.
Down . .	Newton Ards Lead Mine . .	..	10 young persons and 22 children.
Armagh .	Curryhughs Lead Mine . .	..	8 boys and 8 girls under eighteen.

Among upwards of 4,500 hands employed in connexion with these mines, the proportion under eighteen is seen to be very small, and of these scarcely any are under ground. The number of adult females is likewise small. The Children formerly employed at the copper mines of Avoca have lost their employment through the hands at those mines being all engaged in the raising of a sulphurous material, since the commencement of difficulties in the sulphur trade with Sicily (F. Roper, Esq., Report, App. Pt. I., pp. 855, 858, 862, 863, 865, 867, 868, 870).

870. From these statements will be seen the propriety of regarding each branch of labour connected with the mines of tin, &c., separate from the rest, in the order of the processes themselves: viz., 1. Underground Labour in the Mines; 2. Surface Labour in Dressing the Ores; and 3. Labour in Works for Smelting the Ores.

I. UNDERGROUND LABOUR IN MINES OF TIN, COPPER, LEAD, AND ZINC.

1.—*Age, Sex, and Number of the Children and Young Persons employed Under Ground.*

871. The small proportion of Children employed under ground has just been described; and the employment of girls or women in any kind of underground work in these mines is altogether unknown in any part of the kingdom, nor is there any record of their ever having been so employed.

872. CORNISH DISTRICT.—In the whole of the evidence collected in this district, there is no example of a Child having been found in any of the mines under eight years of age. Below this age Children are not taken into these mines, nor do they begin work at the surface until they are at least seven years of age. Richard Lanyon, Esq., surgeon, who has been in practice in the neighbourhood of Cramborne ten years, and his father before him for forty-five years, and who contracts to give surgical attendance annually to between 2,000 and 3,000 miners, says,—" The age at which Children begin to work at surface is about seven very commonly, and the usual age at which boys begin to work under ground is from eight to twelve. Has not known very many as early as eight; from ten to twelve is the most frequent age" (Dr. Barham, Evidence, No. 56: App. Pt. I., p. 834, 1. 44).

UNDERGROUND
LABOUR IN
MINES OF TIN,
COPPER, LEAD, AND
ZINC.
*Age, Sex, and
Number,*

———

Cornish District.

873. " From the whole of the evidence collected, it appears that the most usual age at which boys go to work at these mines is from eight to ten, and that they go under-ground at twelve very commonly, if they are strong and well-grown" (Dr. Barham, Report, § 117: App. Pt. I., p. 771). And " The opinion of the best-informed persons (he adds) is, that Children are now employed at the mines at an earlier age than they formerly were" (Ibid. § 118: App. Pt. I., p. 771).

Mr. Joseph Jennings, one of the principal agents superintending the working of the Tresavean Mine, in answer to the question—" Do you know of any change having taken place of late years in the ages at which Children generally begin to work at the mines?" says,—" If any difference exists, the Children are younger now than formerly. In the course of a month we send back many, thinking them too small for the work, being from seven to eight or nine; they are brought by the mothers, who complain that they cannot get bread for them." (Dr. Barham, Evidence, No. 8: App. Pt. I., p. 823, l. 64).—Mr. Thomas Moyle, under-ground agent at Trevascus, says: " I think they [the Children] did not go to work so early formerly, and that a younger set are employed at the same work. They also seem to me to be smaller of their age, and the men, as well, are smaller, I think" (Ibid. No. 48: p. 831, l. 55).—Richard Thomas, fifty-five years old, miner, examined at the Charlestown Mines, says: "Went to work at surface at ten years of age, and went under-ground almost immediately. It was not usual at that time for boys to go under-ground at so early an age, but he had an uncle who was a captain in the mine, and who put him into the place. He considered it a favour to go under-ground. He believes that the boys in his early days did not generally work under-ground as young as they do now" (Ibid., No. 99: p. 851, l. 19).—Richard Lanyon, Esq., surgeon, says: " My impression is, that they [the Children] are put to work at an earlier age than they were formerly" (Ibid., No. 56: p. 834, l. 46).

874. From the Returns it appears, that out of 3,915 boys under eighteen employed in connexion with these mines, 1,064, or little more than one-fourth, are at work under-ground, and that of these only 128 are under thirteen years of age, the remaining 936 being between thirteen and eighteen.

875. ALSTON MOOR DISTRICT.—The proportion of Children working all the year round in the mines in this district also is very small; only eighteen are reported as under thirteen, while 115 are from thirteen to eighteen.

876. LEADHILLS.—Youths are generally eighteen years of age before they are engaged in under-ground work. (J. Fletcher, Esq., Evidence; Thomas Weir, No. 46: p. 868).

877. FLINTSHIRE.—The Sub-Commissioner states that the whole number of boys employed in under-ground work in all the lead mines of this district does not amount to sixty, and they are met with only in a few mines near Holywell, where the workings are deep and extensive, the chief employment of these boys being to pump air into different parts of the mine (H. H. Jones, Esq., Report, § 27: p. 368).

878. IRELAND.—In the mines of this country there is scarcely an instance of a Child being employed in any kind of under-ground work, and even the young men do not generally enter the mines until approaching adult age.

879. The number of Children and Young Persons employed under ground is thus seen to be so small in all the districts, except those of Cornwall and Alston Moor, that it is unnecessary to enter into detail concerning more than these two.

2.—*Hiring of Children and Young Persons for Underground Labour.*

880. CORNISH DISTRICT.—In this district the Sub-Commissioner reports that " the boys under ground are employed for the most part by the men (Evidence, p. 824, l. 38; p. 833, l. 26), and are usually engaged for the same term as they; but in particular situations, when their services are only occasionally required, they are passed from one party to another (Evidence, p. 833, l. 64), and at times exchange under-ground for surface work (Evidence, p. 853, l. 3). In some departments, as in the sump and pit work, a few boys are employed by the owners. In all cases the arrangement is made between the boys and the employers, without the intervention of any third party; and no conditions at all oppressive to the former are annexed. Those employed by the owners are paid in the same manner as the surface boys, once a-month; and such is usually, and should always be, the case with regard to those em

ployed by the men. Some irregularity of payment does, however, not unfrequently arise, generally from the poverty of the men, and the interference of the managers is then required" (Dr. Barham, Report, § 189, p. 786.)

881. But when the boys are so far advanced in their under-ground labour as to be able to take a turn at "beating the borer," they are commonly associated in partnership with the men, or, as it is termed, are " taken into concern." The miner's work is done almost universally by the piece. He " contracts to excavate the rock in a certain situation, at so much per solid fathom,—this is denominated ' tut-work ;' or he undertakes to excavate the vein, and to fit the ore for the market, at the price of so much in the pound of the sum for which the ore is sold; this is called ' tribute.' Each place of work (pitch) requires a certain number of men and boys, determined by the agent; the partnership between the individuals being entirely voluntary. The contract is commonly good from one setting-day to another, or for two months; but longer terms are often given, where the work to be done is known to be of very equable value" (Ibid, § 65, 67, 69: pp. 747, 748).

882. The boys are usually reckoned in " the first place as ' part of a man,' that is, as holding ' a half,' or three-quarters of the share allotted to each man. To this system no inconsiderable portion of the evil inflicted by mining labour, both on the adult and on the boy, may be traced. To be ' taken into concern' is a sort of promotion for the boy, and this is an inducement, concurring with the more urgent one of pecuniary advantage, leading the father to make his son a co-partner with himself at the earliest opportunity. But the other partners will not be satisfied unless work is done by every member of the firm equivalent to the proportion of profit he is to receive; the father and the son both feel this, and the young energies of the one are willingly tasked to the utmost, whilst the other makes good by extra toil what is still deficient in the amount of work executed. The boy, under these circumstances, is likewise equally exposed with the men to the most impure air and to risk of accident (Ibid. § 163: p. 780).

883. " It may be confidently stated, that no hiring of Children or Young Persons takes place in the mines of the West of England to which they are not voluntary parties. The advance of money to parents on the credit of the future labour of their children is totally unknown. No system of apprenticeship is practised anywhere, and the obligation of giving a month's notice of the intention to quit a mine is the most stringent condition by which the labourer is in any instance bound (Evidence. p. 841, 1. 44.) It may be further remarked, that a great deal of protective influence is, generally speaking, exercised by the managers of mines, with respect to the regularity and the convenient mode of payment of the wages of the Young People.

884. " Evidence may be seen (Ibid. p. 821, 1. 25; p. 830, 1. 28; p. 847, 1. 49; p. 849, 1. 52) of the rarity of disagreements between employers and the younger class of labourers, with regard to hiring or wages. The testimony of the magistrates is equally satisfactory (Dr. Barham, Report, § 191—193: App. Pt. I., pp. 786—788).

885. Alston Moor District.—In this district the Sub-Commissioner reports :—" Some of the boys and Young Persons under eighteen working in the mines are hired and paid by the masters, as those who work the machines, that is, the fanners, to force in air; and those who drive the horses. But most of them, all those who engage in the work which is properly called mining, are hired and paid by the partnerships whom they serve, and some few, but then only an exception to the general rule, are admitted into partnership with the men" (Dr. Mitchell, Report, § 203: App. Pt. II., p. 743).

886. These partnerships are described in detail in the Report of the Sub-Commissioner (II., 743–5), and resemble those in the Cornish District, of which every particular is given by Dr. Barham (App. Pt. I., pp. 747–52).

3.—State of the Place of Work Underground.

887. Cornish District.—In this district the *lodes* or metalliferous veins have an average direction of four degrees south of due west, with a dip of about 60 or 70 degrees from the horizon, four out of the six towards the nearest mass of granite. On the whole, they are tolerably straight, both

Underground Labour in Mines of Tin, Copper, Lead, and Zinc.

Hiring.

Cornish District.

Alston Moor District.

Place of Work.

Cornish District.

UNDERGROUND
LABOUR IN
MINES OF TIN,
COPPER, LEAD, AND
ZINC.

Place of Work.

Cornish District.

in direction and inclination; and their width averages about three feet and a half, though in this respect there are great irregularities, from a mere line to 40 and 50 feet, and sometimes more.

888. " The composition of the *lodes* is as variable as the nature of the rocks through which they pass. By far the greatest part of them is, however, earthy matter, of the nature of the contiguous rock, but also containing large quantities of quartz. These ingredients are sometimes in separate veins, but for the most part they are mixed without regularity or order, and through them the metallic ores are dispersed; sometimes very thickly, or in large irregular lumps, connected with each other by small veins of ore; in other cases the ore is very sparingly sprinkled through the whole of the earthy matter of the vein, and in some rare instances the ore forms the larger part of its contents. The masses of ore in the *lodes* usually dip from the granite, and the deepest parts of the mines are therefore in general farthest from where that rock appears at the surface" (Dr. Barham, Report, § 13 : App. Pt. I., p. 732).

889. " It is a prevailing and apparently well-founded opinion among practical miners that the *lodes* are usually most productive near the junction of the granite and slate rocks. Accordingly the mines, instead of being irregularly distributed over the face of the country, are clustered together near the lines of these junctions, and the heaps of worthless rubbish separated from the ores may be traced in such situations for considerable distances on the lines of the chief *lodes*, rising in some cases amid rich fields, and destroying the vegetation ' like streams of lava from a volcano' (Ibid. § 19 : p. 733).

890. " When it is known or is thought probable that a lode which will repay the cost of working exists in a particular locality, the usual course of proceeding is to sink a shaft vertically to a certain depth in the first place. In so doing the lode may be met with, or as it is termed ' cut.' If this is not the case, a gallery, or ' level,' is excavated (driven) at right angles to the shaft, in the assumed direction of the lode, and continued till it is reached. In either case, when the lode is reached, a level is driven horizontally along its course, and the miner then works upwards and removes it from above. It must depend on the thickness of the vein, and also in some measure on its inclination, whether it is necessary to excavate any of the adjoining rock, and to what extent. Meantime, the shaft being sunk still deeper, another gallery or level is carried along the vein or lode, usually about ten fathoms below the former one, and the metalliferous stone intervening between the two levels is subsequently removed. This process is repeated again and again; and as the workings become more extensive in length, additional shafts become necessary in that direction. Horse and water power are employed for effecting the earlier operations, but the steam-engine is soon requisite in most of these mines, and as they increase in depth and extent, more powerful machinery is needed to raise the excavated rock and the water. Shorter shafts, called *winzes*, are also formed at intervals between the levels, chiefly for the purpose of ventilation. It is clear that in proportion to the dip or inclination of the vein there will be an advance in a horizontal direction, as the depth of the workings increases; and this may also render necessary communications from the lower levels to the surface more direct than can be furnished by the shafts originally adapted to the shallower ones.

891. " At a very early stage of this progress a separation is established between the shafts by which the men pass to and from their work and those in which machinery is employed. This separation is in the first place effected by the boarded division of a single shaft, and subsequently by the devoting distinct shafts to these distinct purposes. Excepting the occasional raising of men and boys in buckets through short distances, ladders are the universal means of ascent and descent in these mines. Many of the shorter shafts (winzes) are provided with ladders, so that the course taken by the miner is commonly not one of continuous descent and ascent, but varied by his traversing at different intervals a considerable length of horizontal galleries" (Ibid. § 23—25: p. 734).

892. A reference to the sections given by Dr. Barham (I., p. 734), will render intelligible at once his description of the method of working metalliferous veins, which, in all its main features, is the same that is pursued throughout the kingdom.

Dimensions of the Levels.

893. CORNISH DISTRICT.—The levels are in general of good height and of commodious breadth; five, six, and seven feet in height, and from two to four feet in width are common dimensions. "The statement made in the answers from the United Mines of the relatively larger dimensions of the levels in the more recent than in the older workings is true of the mines generally, and especially of those which have been carried to a great depth.

894. "The natural conditions of these shafts and levels, supposing no one to have been in them for some time, are darkness, and an air more condensed than that on the surface, and a temperature higher in proportion to the depth. There is no reason to believe that any gas, except carbonic acid, is generated from the strata or veins in these mines. Where they have been carried beneath beds of alluvium which are periodically submerged, some of the inflammable compounds of hydrogen are at times emitted. Instances of this kind are mentioned in the Evidence (p. 851, l. 28; p. 852, l. 7)." (Dr. Barham, Report, § 27, 28: App. Pt. I., p. 736.)

Ventilation.

895. CORNISH DISTRICT.—"In proportion as a mine increases in depth, the importance of ventilation increases, and it becomes at the same time more difficult to effect it thoroughly. As far down as the adit level there is usually a free perflation, and it is only in an 'end,' a cul-de-sac remote from the shaft, that the air can be materially impure. Farther down, as no horizontal communication with the surface can exist, the interchange of ascending and descending currents of air affords the only natural supply; and by making the levels of large size, and establishing free communication between them by the short levels, called winzes, aëration (considered sufficient) is effected even in the deepest mine in Cornwall, without the use of air machines. In fact, those which have been hitherto commonly adopted are much more advantageously applied in the shallower mines or parts of mines." (Ibid. § 30, 31: p. 738). To ventilate ends not relieved by winzes, resort is had to air cylinders, a current being forced through wooden pipes, and to falls of water from one level to another.

896. An analysis of eighteen samples of the air from different places in which the men are employed, shows an average composition of oxygen 17·067, carbonic acid 0·85, and nitrogen 82·848. The Sub-Commissioner states, "that in one instance the quantity of oxygen was reduced to 14·51, and in another the quantity of carbonic acid was raised to 0·23. These results exhibit a lessening in the proportion of the vital ingredient of the air from its usual percentage 21, and an increase in a directly noxious ingredient, carbonic acid gas, from 0·05, its ordinary amount, calculated to produce effects sufficiently injurious to those who, for hours together, inhale such a fluid. But the proportion of deleterious gases occasionally present where the miner must labour (whether of sulphuretted hydrogen and sulphurous acid, which are very rapidly absorbed by the water lying in the levels, or of carbonic acid, which accumulates, like water, where there is no drainage), is much greater than that detected in the analyses here reported. It is then that the distinctly poisonous effects of these agents are produced, and loss of life, either at once or more remotely, has often been the consequence. Carbonaceous particles from the candles and from blasting, and mineral-dust from the working of the strata or veins, are also suspended in the air which the miner inspires, and give a peculiar character to his expectoration: copper has even been detected by analysis in notable quantity in such air (Ibid. § 30: p. 738).

897. "No method hitherto introduced is adequate to maintaining the air in the places in which the miners work in anything like a state of purity; and even in those parts in which ventilation keeps up a fair supply of fresh air, there is in almost all mines a constant smoke after the first blasting in the morning; so that the shafts and galleries are not unlike chimneys, often sending out a visible column at the surface. The smoke is sometimes so thick (Evidence, No. 1: App. Pt. I., p. 822, l. 3) that the miner can with difficulty see his hand.

898. "From the nature of the case, the most advanced point of the excavation

UNDERGROUND
LABOUR IN
MINES OF TIN,
COPPER, LEAD, AND
ZINC.

Place of Work.
—
Ventilation.
—

Alston Moor
District.

must be a cul-de-sac, and it will often be impossible to establish any communication with parts above or below.   Hence it is that almost every miner in the deeper mines is at times exposed to what he himself designates ' poor air,' by which he means air so impure as to affect him in a noxious way distinctly perceived by him at the time.   Of the less marked degrees of impurity he makes no account.   Of the deficiency of oxygen, the excess of carbonic acid, the presence of sulphurous acid or sulphuretted hydrogen, he is not aware, and of smoke, however dense, he seldom takes any notice." (Ibid. § 32, 33: pp. 738, 739).

899. ALSTON MOOR DISTRICT.—At his place of work, however remote, says the Sub-Commissioner for this district, the under-ground labourer has no air except what comes from the level by which he has entered.   There is nothing to make a current.   Yet some levels in this district are half a mile in length, some a mile, and one called the First Force Level is nearly five miles in length.   In such a situation " only slowly, and very slowly, can the air about him, merely by the effect of a difference of temperature, wind its way upwards, and make room for other air which may penetrate to take its place.

900. " Means may be taken to diminish an evil which cannot be removed. Sometimes a body of air may be forced in by a fall of a stream of water from the top surface of the hill.   An opening is made for it to descend down to the level, which it does with great violence, driving a body of air before it, and then it runs out along the bottom of the level from the mine.   Fig. 7 in the diagram will show how this is done; *a* is the stream of water descending, and *b* is the level extending to where the miners are at work.

901. " Machines, or fanners, are also used, being worked by boys, and the air is carried along pipes to places to which it would otherwise only very slowly penetrate.   Forcing-pumps are also employed to force forward the air in a similar way.   Sometimes a supply of fresh air may be got by running a second level from the air into the hill, and making a communication.   In that case the air may be put in action, and may enter at one level and go out by the other.   Sometimes a shaft may be carried up to the open air, or let down from the open air into the level; and when that is done a current of air may be effected.   Whatever is within the range of such current, of course, is well ventilated.

902. " Such things, however, are not the general rule.   In most mines there are not two levels communicating with the open air, neither can there be shafts from the open air down to the levels.   Where nature does not interpose a physical impossibility, there is what is equally powerful—the dread of expense.   The sum required to sink a shaft or to run a level may be so great that the mine is not worth it.   The proprietor would rather discontinue working it than submit to the burthen; and the men, Young Persons, and boys, having no other means of existence, are eager to be allowed to work at the mine such as it is" (Dr. Mitchell, Report, § 51, 56: App. Pt. II., pp. 727, 728).

Drainage.

903. CORNISH DISTRICT.—" Every mine," says Dr. Barham, " is more or less *wet*.   It constitutes a receptacle for the waters permeating the strata through which it passes.   The *adit* is the drain through which a great part of the water lying above its level, and a great part of that raised by machinery, is discharged.   One or more of the deepest shafts are appropriated as wells, and from these the water is raised by steam power—a preliminary process involving the greatest difficulty and outlay connected with the working of many mines.   The quantity of water in one mine differs exceedingly from that in another—partly in relation to the nature of the strata: thus mines in slate are generally wetter than those in granite.   But a greater difference is artificially produced by the multiplication of mines in a district; the whole of its waters being thus distributed among many wells instead of a few, and the pumping being thus rendered less onerous to each" (Dr. Barham, Report, § 34: p. 739).

Temperature.

904. CORNISH DISTRICT.—The natural temperature of the mines in the South Western district increases so rapidly, that at the depth of 200 fathoms

from the surface it varies from 81·2 degrees to 85·6 degrees Fahrenheit. When the work is in progress, there is, of course, a rapid exchange of oxygen for carbonic acid, by means of the respiration of the miners and the burning of the candles; and when the blasting takes place, the gases generated by the explosion of gunpowder are diffused, and a thick smoke fills the shaft.

UNDERGROUND
LABOUR IN
MINES OF TIN,
COPPER, LEAD, AND
ZINC.

Place of Work.

*Mode of Ascent
and Descent.*

Cornish District.

Mode of Ascent and Descent.

905. CORNISH DISTRICT.—Ladders are the universal means of ascent and descent in these mines. There are a few instances of veins emerging at the surface, and being inclined at such an angle that they have been followed and excavated without much other footway than steps cut in the rock; but these are merely exceptions. The ladders vary in different mines, and sometimes in different parts of the same mine, from two and a half to ten fathoms in length, and from a direction nearly vertical to an inclination of two feet six inches, or even more, in the fathom. The distance between the levels being generally ten fathoms, or sixty feet, a single ladder very often reached in former times from one to the other. Some of these ladders are still found (Evidence, p. 848, 1. 35), but they are rare (Evidence, p. 821, 1. 20). The most usual length at present is from four to five fathoms.

906. " In the perpendicular shafts the inclination is commonly such that the ladder may nearly traverse the breadth of the shaft. From 18 to 21 inches in the fathom is the inclination which experience has determined to be the most calculated to facilitate the progress of the miner; being that which enables him to stand upright in the ladder, with the leg clear from the stave above, so that the effort is divided between the upper and lower extremities (Evidence, p. 824, 1. 49; and Mr. Henwood's letter, Appendix A). The inclination of the ladders is, however, in many cases determined by that of the veins, and when the underlie is great, the footway will be at times much further removed from the perpendicular (Evidence, p. 821, 1. 7).

907. " The distance of the staves in these ladders is very generally one foot from the upper surface of one to the same point in the next. In some old ladders they were as much as 14 inches apart (Evidence, p. 824, 1. 50). But the results of the trials made of shorter intervals will tend to produce a gradual change in that direction. It will be seen in the evidence that at Tresavean (p. 824, 1. 46), at Trethellan (p. 821, 1. 11), and (Mr. Henwood's letter, Appendix A) at Wheal Mary, the distance of ten inches has been adopted with very important effect in facilitating the climbing: so that one-fourth of the labour is estimated to be saved; and even men who had been obliged to relinquish work in the lower levels have been able to resume it.

908. " The staves are most usually of wood; iron is in many instances preferred; in others it is said to become both slippery and jagged from the corrosive action of water impregnated with salts of other metals, chiefly copper.

909. " Each ladder usually terminates on a platform (sollar), an opening (man-hole) in which leads to the ladder below. This is generally so situated that the ladders are parallel to each other. ⋆In a few instances there is, in addition to this platform, a penthouse placed between the back of the ladder and the walls of the shaft, so that it covers the passage to the ladder below, and prevents the risk of the descending miner falling more than a few feet, supposing the ladder to be from four to five fathoms in length,—and the much greater risk of the falling of anything from above upon those who are below (Evidence, p. 851, 1. 63). A contrivance of similar intention is adopted in some mines—that of placing trap-doors over the man-holes, and making it a rule for the last man of a party to close them (Return for Boscean Mine). It is clear that more is here trusted to the carefulness of the miner than in the former method; the closing of these trap-doors must also, it is conceived, cause a serious obstruction to ventilation" (Dr. Barham, Report, § 36—41: App. Pt. I., p. 739, 740).

910. By a communication made to the Commissioners since his Report was printed, Dr. Barham informs us that the experiment of lowering and raising the miners by machinery has been for the first time tried in Cornwall, at the great copper mine Tresavean in Gwennap. The method adopted has been very little varied from that long in use in the mines in the

UNDERGROUND
LABOUR IN
MINES OF TIN,
COPPER, LEAD, AND
ZINC.

Place of Work.

*Mode of Ascent
and Descent.*

Cornish District.

Hartz in Germany, being that of two parallel rods, with stages projecting from them at intervals of about 12 feet, of a convenient size for one man to stand upon. One rod being made to descend while the other ascends, the miner steps from his stage or platform on one rod to that which he finds opposite to it on the other rod, and by this alternate change he is conveyed up or down the shaft without any other exertion. The moving power to which the rods are attached is at present a water wheel. This experiment, which has been perfectly successful, has been carried into effect by the spirited and benevolent exertions of the principal lords and adventurers of Tresavean, stimulated and aided by the Polytechnic Society.

Alston Moor
District.

911. ALSTON MOOR DISTRICT.—Into the lead mines of this district, the entrance is pretty generally by means of levels driven into the hills of this elevated region. In some mines, says the Sub-Commissioner, "there is much work in the first level which is driven, but frequently it is necessary to ascend upwards, and make another level, and this is effected by drilling and blasting out the rock by gunpowder, and placing scaffolding by which the miners may climb up to their work. It is easier to work upwards than to work downwards, because in working upwards all the dust and broken pieces fall down, whereas, in working downwards, they accumulate at the bottom, and it is troublesome to remove them. The miners in their upward work make a small landing-place, and go from one stage to another, so that they may be able to place ladders or pieces of wood from side to side, and be afterwards able to climb up, and have halting places at short distances all the way. When arrived at the height thought best to fall in with the veins, they move forward horizontally, or in a line parallel to the first level which was driven in from the air. It may be necessary to work upwards a second time, and form another flight of ladders, and then, after getting to a certain height, again to move forward farther into the mountain, in a line parallel to the preceding two, and it may be several times repeated.

912. "In like manner it may be expedient to follow the vein downwards, by sinking from one stage to another an opening for ladders, or flights of steps, to go down perhaps 18 to 20 fathoms, or 108 to 120 feet. Then they may run an opening forward horizontally, or parallel to the first level, and after a time they may have to descend again, as much as before, and then move forward, and so on several times, perhaps four, five, or six times, until the place of working may be 500 or 600 feet lower down than the first level" (Dr. Mitchell, Report, § 49, 50: App. Pt. II., p. 727).

*Nature of
Employment.*

Cornish District.

4.—*Nature of the Employment Underground.*

913. CORNISH DISTRICT.—Of the chief under-ground employments of the Children and Young Persons in the mines of this district, the Sub-Commissioner gives the following account:—" Working air-machines, where they are used, is perhaps the first work at which boys are employed. The ordinary machine is a sort of hydraulic bellows, consisting of two boxes or cisterns, one moving inverted within the other, which is filled with water. The moving power is applied at the end of a lever, very much like the handle of a common pump, and by the raising of the inner cistern, the impure air is drawn in, to be expelled from its upper part when it is depressed, by a proper arrangement of valves and pipes. The work of the boy is not very hard in itself, but statements will be found in the Evidence (p. 853, l. 11, 22, 46; p. 854, l. 38), of the occasional extension of the impurity of the air to the place in which the machine stands, so that he is sometimes affected by it, suffering chiefly in the head and stomach.

914. "Another employment of the younger boys under ground, is that designated as 'hauling tackle,' which implies working a windlass for the raising (in an iron-bucket) of the ground, in proportion as it is excavated in the sinking of any pit, but chiefly of the communications or winzes between the levels. A good deal of labour is involved in this occupation, but the air is not usually very impure in the upper level in which the windlass is placed. (Evidence, p. 825, l. 38).

915. "But the work which employs the greater part of the younger boys under ground is what is termed by them 'rulling,' that is, rolling or wheeling

UNDERGROUND
LABOUR IN
MINES OF TIN,
COPPER, LEAD, AND
ZINC.

*Nature of
Employment.*

Cornish District.

barrows, loaded with the ground removed, from the place where it has been excavated to that from which it is to be taken to the surface. This occupation is always laborious (Evidence, p. 825, 1. 6; p. 834, 1. 4); but the degree in which it is so varies with the distance traversed, which may be 10 or 100 fathoms, with the roughness and dryness of the ground, the temperature and purity of the air, as well as with the weight of the barrow, which, where older boys are associated at this work with younger ones, is often filled by the former to an extent more adapted to their own powers than to those of their comrades (Evidence, p. 834, 1. 16).

916. " Exposure to a very impure air is generally limited, in this employment, to the time occupied in filling the barrows at the place where the men are working; but its effects are often distinctly marked, as described in the Evidence, (p. 836, 1. 59, 64). The boys are often allowed to leave, at the end of six hours' barrow-work, where it is continuous, that period being considered equivalent to eight hours of other labour: if the stuff has been cleared away, they are not even detained so long. The period at which iron rails are laid down varies in different cases, in accordance chiefly with the apparent occasion for the more permanent use of a particular line of communication. Whenever it is done, tram-waggons are substituted for wheelbarrows, and most commonly, men for boys (Evidence, p. 825, 1. 13). The ore and rubbish are raised to the surface in a large iron bucket called the 'kibble;' a few boys are employed in assisting the men to fill it, which is hard work (Evidence, p. 823, 1. 60), but performed for the most part where there is good ventilation."

917. " The work in which boys are in the first instance engaged, altogether in the same locality with the adult miner, is that of holding and turning ' the borer' while it is beaten.

918. " After the blasting, the 'pick' comes into requisition, for the removal of the partially separated and angular pieces of rock. In soft ground, the use of gunpowder is only occasionally required. The exposure to impure air is the chief evil connected with this employment, but it is an evil of the greatest magnitude. A light description of work connected with blasting, in which, conjointly, with rendering any little assistance needed by the miners, very young boys are sometimes employed, is the pulverising and otherwise preparing the clay used for 'tamping'—plugging the holes before the charge is fired (Evidence, p. 847, 1. 41).

919. " Taking a turn at 'beating the borer' comes next in the succession of employment. This work occasions, perhaps, more direct injury than any other, from the general severity of the labour, and from the sudden strains and over-reaching, which can only be avoided by a greater exercise of caution than is likely to be permanently maintained. The miners themselves frequently date the commencement of ill health from some hurt received whilst engaged in this work (Evidence, p. 827, 1. 23). The mischief arising from the labour itself is greatly aggravated by the noxious qualities of the air in which it is carried on, being often necessarily that of the extremity of the cul-de-sac in which the most advanced excavations are in progress.

920. " In the consideration of the nature of the employment of under-ground miners of every age, the mode of *descent* and *ascent* must be included as a constituent item. The labour of climbing ladders is always intrinsically great (Evidence, p. 834, 1. 15), and the distance traversed even by the youngest boy is, with very few exceptions, several hundred feet, whilst in many instances it is from one to two thousand. The cheerfulness with which the boys climb the ladders is not to be taken as proof that they are not injured by the exertion. The inclination to muscular activity is so strong in early life, that it is in this, as in more entirely voluntary feats of strength or agility, expended lavishly. Rest and sleep seem to restore the powers completely; and unless some distinct injury occurs, it is left to the feeble and ill-developed frame of the youth—to the slow inroads of disease of the heart and lungs, or to premature decrepitude—to testify what have been the consequences of the early exhaustion of vital power, and of the fixing of the bones and muscles in a rigid position at a period when nature intended them to be still plastic (Evidence, p. 835, 1. 5). But the injurious effects are very often alike distinctly and rapidly produced. Examples of their nature may be found in the Evidence (p. 840, 1. 20; p. 854, 1. 40) " (Dr. Barham, Report, § 157—164: App. Pt. I., p. 779).

UNDERGROUND
LABOUR IN
MINES OF TIN,
COPPER, LEAD, AND
ZINC.

*Nature of
Employment.*

Cornish District.

921. " The state of the place of work, no less than the nature of the employment, is rendered more unfavourable by this premature association in the labour of the men. The spot in which they are working is that in which all the causes of impurity in the air are most concentrated in their action, and least checked by ventilation; being that in which the space is most narrow,— where men and candles are consuming the most oxygen, and giving out the greatest quantity of deleterious matter,—where the powder-smoke and the gases generated in blasting are the least diluted; and, lastly, it is the most remote from any shaft or winze, and, consequently, from any current of air. The levels are now much more spacious than they formerly were (Evidence, p. 851, l. 60), and no greater improvement than this in the state of the place of work could have been introduced; but, supposing that they were in all cases six or seven feet high, by four or five wide, which is very far from being the case, still the tributer (working man), in following the lode, will often avoid the labour of excavation at the cost of the greatest inconvenience from the narrowness of the passage in which he works; and at times will pursue his labour lying on his side in so contracted a space that, if he drops his tool, he is obliged to retreat to some distance, in order that he may turn himself round, so as to recover it. In such places, the boy who is ' in concern' must lend a hand; and, indeed, his smaller size and greater suppleness will often lead to his being employed in preference, under analogous circumstances, where his strength is sufficient for the duty required. It is however, generally considered that the tut workman is even more exposed than the tributer to poor air, being employed in driving the levels, the extremities of which can have no lateral communication for the passage of air, and the boy who is in partnership with him must incur the same risk of suffering from the poisonous agent" (Ibid. § 173: p. 782).

922. " As an example of the division of Labour among the Boys under ground, the Ages and Employment of those in the Levant Mine may be stated:—

	Ages.									Total.
	9	10	11	12	13	14	15	16	17	
Tramming . . .	..	..	..	1	1	2	..	..	..	4
Rolling . . .	..	1	2	5	6	8	3	3	2	30
Tending men . .	1	4	..	3	..	5	2	3	1	19
Breaking ground .	..	..	..	..	..	..	1	5	12	18

(Dr. Barham's Report, I., p. 778.)

923. ALSTON MOOR DISTRICT.—The employment of the few Children and Young Persons who go under ground in this district appears to consist chiefly in assisting the adult miners, by turning the drill or borer while they are striking it, preparatory to inserting a charge of gunpowder ; and by shovelling the rubbish out of the way   (Evidence of John Robinson, No. 5). Others are engaged in working the fanners which force down the air; and in driving the horses in the carts which bring the lead ore out of the levels into which it is let down from the workings above ; or in urging those which turn the whimseys that raise the ore into the levels from the workings beneath. (Dr. Mitchell, Report, § 58: App. Pt. II., p. 728). " In mines where there is bad air, however," states Mr. Jacob Crawhall, " the boys are of little use, and cannot stand it, and it is thought best not to have them," *i. e.*, where the carbonic acid gas is in such proportion as to " break the wind" (Ibid. No. 6.: App. Pt. II., p. 759, l. 61).

5.—*Hours of Work Underground.*

924. CORNISH DISTRICT.—In this district the regular hours of work are, under certain circumstances, six in number, but generally they are eight; and if the relays of workpeople " relieve each other at the place of work, as is usually the case in the more considerable mines, the eight-hour term of labour is, in fact, raised to nine or ten, according to the depth, as the descent into the deepest parts of some of the mines (nearly 300 fathoms) is calculated

UNDERGROUND
LABOUR IN
MINES OF TIN,
COPPER, LEAD, AND
ZINC.

Hours of Work.
——
Cornish District.

to occupy about forty minutes, and the ascent twice as long. Where parties relieve each other at the end of six hours, it is always done 'in place,' so that the work is uninterruptedly continued. The old miners generally state that this practice of relieving 'in place' in the case of the eight-hour course is an innovation, the practice in their younger days being to relieve at surface, one party going down when the other came up (Dr. Barham, Evidence, Richard Thomas, No. 99: p. 851, l. 36). It is also stated that six-hour courses were formerly the most usual.

925. " But the duration of labour underground is often much more prolonged by the voluntary act of the miners themselves, in working overtime— 'double stem,' or 'double core,' as they term it. This is done, either for the sake of profit, where the contract turns out favourably to the takers, and it is wished to make the most of it within the term for which it holds good (Ibid. No. 48: p. 832, l. 15); or to supply the place of a comrade who is prevented from being at his post. In deep and hot places the miner commonly finds the regular course of work quite as much as he can endure (Evidence, p. 825, l. 66); though even there some of the more robust will at times continue to labour for twelve or sixteen hours, but it is in less exhausting situations that this is more frequently done. Mr. Thomas Moyle states, in his evidence (Ibid. p. 832, l. 5), that when young he had stayed down three turns of twelve hours each successively, with only a brief interval between them, during which he came to the surface and took some food, and that others did the same. The consequent exhaustion prevented him from sleeping when his labour terminated.

926. " No example of such excessive perseverance in toil has presented itself in the course of the present inquiry; but the working 'double stem' is stated as the frequent practice of several of the boys examined (Evidence, p. 825, l. 40). At No. 63 (Evidence, p. 836, l. 68), an instance is mentioned of a boy working five 'double stems' in the preceding week, &c. By the boys this is most commonly done as an act of kindness to a comrade, to prevent his losing his place, as he probably would do if the men were obliged to supply it by a stranger (Evidence, p. 853, l. 34). In other cases they work overtime for the sake of gaining something for themselves, as it is usual to allow them for pocket-money what they earn at these extra times (Ibid. 35). (Dr. Barham, Report, § 127, 128: App. Pt. I., p. 772).

927. " The most frequent arrangement of the time of under-ground work is the division of the twenty-four hours into three 'courses' of eight hours each, with three relays, so that the place of work is never unoccupied. In this case the relays usually succeed each other at six A.M., two P.M., and ten P.M. In other mines, or parts of mines, in which, from the nature of the ground, the work can be rapidly performed, or where from impurity of air or other cause labour of longer duration cannot be borne, each party works only six hours, and there are four relays of men. They then relieve each other at six and twelve of the day and night; this is usually the case in the 'sump,' the bottom of the engine-shaft, in every mine. It is the practice of the miners to make a weekly exchange in their turns of work, so that an equal amount of night-work may fall to each. Another very frequent division is that of two relays, omitting the one commencing at ten at night; and in some cases, where less constant attendance is needed, one party only is employed in a particular place, and the work is then generally taken from seven or eight in the morning till about four in the afternoon.

928. " Whatever arrangement is adopted by the miners the boys are included in it, and continue at work during the same time, except that six hours of the harder work of wheeling barrows is sometimes equivalent to eight hours lighter work, and that they are now and then allowed to go up before the men, if the stuff which they have been employed in removing has been cleared away (Evidence, p. 828, l. 32; p. 832, l. 2; p. 833, l. 16). The night-work is taken by the boys equally with the men (Evidence, p. 853, l. 6, 36, 49), where boys are employed at all by the party; but they are perhaps more regularly required in those places in which the men themselves do not work through the night.

929. " From one to three hours may be added to the duration of labour for the walk to and from the mine. The distance of the miner's house is sometimes six or seven miles; but a walk of from two to four miles (Evidence, p. 845,

UNDERGROUND
LABOUR IN
MINES OF TIN,
COPPER, LEAD, AND
ZINC.

Hours of Work.

Cornish District.

1. 6, 24) is very commonly the commencement and conclusion of the day's work of the younger part of those employed.

930. "Speaking generally, it may be stated that no work is done by Children or Young Persons in these mines on the Sunday; the only exception being the employment of a few in watching the stamps. This is chiefly necessary where water-power is used. Some notice is taken of this Sunday-work in the Evidence (p. 833, l. 20). The total amount is very inconsiderable." (Dr. Barham, Report, § 124-130: App. Pt. I., pp. 772-773).

Alston Moor
District.

931. ALSTON MOOR DISTRICT. — In this district the Sub-Commissioner reports,—" The number of hours a-day of work in the mines is eight, and for five days in the week. Occasionally the miners may choose to work longer, more particularly if they 'fall in with a canny bit of ore;' but it is very seldom. They have to come from home and return back, sometimes to a great distance, which makes the hours 'out of the house,' as is the phrase in the coal districts, considerably more. Some begin at six and leave off at two, some at seven and leave off at three.

932. " There are mines where the men work double shifts, that is, one set goes in to work when the other set comes away: and in some mines there are three shifts working one after another for the whole twenty-four hours. It is thought to be better for the health when the work can be got done in the day-time" (Dr. Mitchell, Report, § 33: App. Pt. II., p. 725).

6.—*Meal Hours Underground.*

Meal Hours.

Cornish District.

933. CORNISH DISTRICT.—In this district the Sub-Commissioner reports that "the under-ground labourers, whether adults or boys, take their food when they choose. The practice is now universal of taking some food with them when they descend, and those who work during the mid-day hours generally make a substantial meal at about the usual dinner-time; others make use of some lighter 'crowst,' and reserve themselves for their principal sustenance after their return to their homes" (Dr. Barham, Report, § 133: App. Pt. I., p. 773).

Alston Moor
District.

934. ALSTON MOOR DISTRICT.—In this district " the pickmen, young men, and boys, take a hasty meal when they can. Some allow themselves a certain length of time, and have what they intend to be a regular hour; but often there is not a watch amongst the partnership, and they must guess the time when to sit down by the state of their appetite; they must, in like manner, guess in the best way they can when their eight hours are up" (Dr. Mitchell, Report, § 39: App. Pt. II., p. 725. Evidence, Nos. 8 and 9: p. 761, l. 8; p. 762, l. 22).

7.—*Holidays allowed to the Children and Young Persons employed Underground.*

Holidays

Cornish District.

935. CORNISH DISTRICT.—As a general rule no holidays are allowed in the mines of this district, except Christmas-day and Good Friday; but the boys who work underground have usually more time at their disposal than those who work on the surface. This time "is often occupied in giving assistance in whatever is to be done at home; often in carrying water, or helping to cultivate the garden or the little farm. It is not so easy to judge of their disposition to engage in sports as of that of the surface boys, as they are not often collected together in numbers. The risks, increased demand for the exercise of intelligence, and perhaps the higher wages connected with under-ground mining, appear to give them more thoughtfulness of expression and demeanour, and contribute, with the unhealthiness of their occupation, to make them look older than they really are. But in this there is no approach to depression of spirits, and there is no reason to doubt that they join very cheerfully in play suitable to their years when occasion offers" (Dr. Barham, Report, § 180—184: App. Pt. I., p. 783).

Alston Moor
District.

936. ALSTON MOOR DISTRICT.—" In this district the miners work five days in the week, and have from Friday evening till Monday morning every week in the year. Men employed in driving a level work three days long shifts, each day of 12 hours, then rest on the Sabbath, and then work other three

EMPLOYMENT OF CHILDREN.   219

UNDERGROUND
LABOUR IN
MINES OF TIN,
COPPER, LEAD, AND
ZINC.

days. They have now seven days to recruit their strength. This violent
working, notwithstanding the long rest, cannot be otherwise than injurious.
It is, however, only occasionally that such work is going on" (Dr. Mitchell,
Report, § 200 : App. Pt. II., p. 743).

8.—*Treatment of the Children and Young Persons employed Underground.*

937. CORNISH DISTRICT.—The boys employed under ground by the men are
subject to be ' spaled ' (fined) when they are absent from their posts at the
regular hours; but the fine seldom much exceeds what is necessary to be paid
for the procuring a substitute (Evidence, p. 848, l. 52; p. 850, l. 32).   If the
boy or his friends think it too heavy, application is made to the managers, and
justice is done; but no interference is exercised between the men and their
boys, except in extreme cases (Ibid. p. 848, l. 38).   In some cases the fines
are credited to the adventurers (owners), so that no gain can arise to the men
from the infliction.

938. " On the whole, the concurrent testimony of all the agents, and other
well-informed parties, to whom inquiries have been directed, goes to show that
not only is no corporal punishment or other ill-usage inflicted by the men on the
boys employed by them under ground, nor any tyranny exercised (Ibid.
p. 834, l. 70); but that there is a very general consideration, on the part of
the men, of the age and powers of their young fellow-labourers, and a disposition to relieve them from any excess of toil, even at the expense of
increased exertion of their own.   The very frequent association in work of
children with their parents or near relatives contributes to the promotion of
this generous and manly feeling" (Ibid, p. 847, l. 44); (Dr. Barham, Report,
§ 196, 197: App. Pt. I., p. 789).

939. ALSTON MOOR DISTRICT.—The Sub-Commissioner for this district
states, that the London Lead Company extend to the Children under ground
the regard which they show in various modes for the welfare of all the people
in their employment (Dr. Mitchell, Report, § § 237, 254: App. Pt. II.,
p. 748—750).

9.—*Accidents to which Children and Young Persons are exposed in the Under-ground Labour.*

940. CORNISH DISTRICT.—By returns obtained from certain mines employing a male population of 12,409, there appear to have been in these mines 75
fatal accidents, of which, however, no less than 70 were amongst adults.   Of
these, 25 were from falling, 26 from the ground falling, and the remainder from
accidents connected with the machinery; but it is stated that " many injuries,
though not immediately fatal, ultimately occasion the death of the sufferers; a
great number of individuals in the mining districts are permanently disabled by
such contingencies for mining labour, and many for any mode of gaining a liveli-
hood.   Loss of sight has been one of the most frequent injuries of this kind.

941. " A marked diminution of the accidents from ' blasting' has followed the
introduction of safety-fuse for firing the powder.   The destruction of the eyes,
noticed above, originated chiefly in accidents from this cause; and the prevention of
the condition of helplessness thus induced is a benefit only less important than the
saving of life.

942. " Underground, the boys (especially before they are taken ' into concern ')
are not much exposed to injury from blasting—one of the causes of accidents
among adults.   They are proportionally more exposed to falling down shafts or
winzes, both in consequence of boyish carelessness, and from their passing more
frequently in the neighbourhood of these pits in their usual employment of wheeling
barrows (Evidence, p. 826, l. 11; p. 834, l. 59).   In many cases of such accidents,
the candle has in all probability been extinguished (Evidence, p. 853, l. 35).   In
climbing the ladders, the comparative deficiency of muscular power, and the liability to its sudden failure, belonging to their early age, have doubtless occasioned
the ' falling away' of boys where men would have been safe (Evidence, p. 854,
l. 55).   Many accidents have happened to miners from the sudden loss of self-
possession occasioned either by the apprehension of danger or by the shock produced by the witnessing some awful catastrophe.   It can hardly be doubted that
boys under similar circumstances would be more vividly and dangerously impressed.

UNDERGROUND
LABOUR IN
MINES OF TIN,
COPPER, LEAD, AND
ZINC.

Accidents.

Cornish District.

Some individuals have, by such occurrences, been deterred from following the occupation of under-ground mining (Evidence, p. 829, l. 41). In other cases, the fright is succeeded by severe, and not seldom fatal, disease of the brain, which is described by Mr. Lanyon as happening chiefly to young subjects.

943. " A great number of accidents, though for the most part slight, occur in almost every mine. No record exists by which the proportion can be ascertained in which such accidents befall Children and Young Persons.

944. " It is, however, almost superfluous to adduce specific proof of what may be directly inferred from the nature of the human constitution, that, where carelessness and exhaustion are the two chief causes of accidents, they must happen in larger proportion, other circumstances being the same, where there is most carelessness and most weakness,—in other terms, more frequently among boys than among men" (Dr. Barham, Report, § 177—179 : App. Pt. I., p. 783).

945. ALSTON MOOR DISTRICT.—In this part of the kingdom, " accidents from the explosion of hydrogen gas are not common in the lead mines, especially where the levels and workings are in limestone. But there are very different strata, even where the lead is chiefly found in limestone. There are beds containing iron-stone and iron pyrites from which hydrogen gas makes its escape, and explosions are far from being unknown. Several were mentioned to me by which men had been scorched, but none which had been known to be fatal. Such things are very rare. Choke-damp, or carbonic acid gas, is much more frequent, but is seldom fatal. In Weardale, according to a return obtained from the Registrar-General, there were killed in 1838 one man, aged forty-two, by fall of earth in the mines ; and six, aged fifteen, eighteen, twenty-nine, thirty-three, thirty-three, and forty-two, by fall of stones and roof. In Alston parish, between the 1st of July, 1837, and 30th June, 1841, one man, aged twenty-two, was killed by fall of stone ; two men, aged forty-four and fifty-four, were killed by fall of stones ; and one man, aged twenty-six, by an explosion. An explosion by the gunpowder going off when a man is within the reach of danger may arise from gross carelessness on the part of the man himself, or it may be attributable to the master. Sometimes the squibs and matches are carelessly made, and the explosion may take place before the man is sufficiently out of the way. Sometimes an explosion takes place from a spark struck from the rock by the pricker or the driver. Even in limestone rocks there are siliceous particles, and I have seen abundance of sparks struck from the picks and from the spades" (Dr. Mitchell, Report, § 191-195: p. 742, 743) ; Evidence, Nos. 6, 9, 21, 26.)

10.—*Wages of Children and Young Persons employed Underground.*

946. CORNISH DISTRICT.—" The men being paid once in two months only, a certain advance is made under the name of ' subsist' (subsistence money), which is intended in the first place to enable them to pay the boys (Evidence, p. 833, l. 27). If this is not done, the manager generally pays them himself, and deducts the amount from what is due to the men, besides in many cases depriving them of the whole or part of their ' subsist' for some time. This guardianship of the rights of the boys is even taken up by the managers of other mines, when a miner has left a mine and gone to another without paying the wages of the boys employed by him at the first. The Evidence (p. 821, l. 25 ; p. 841, l. 41) will illustrate these points. Where the boys under ground work over-time (double core) it is usual for them to be allowed the disposal of these extra earnings, as in the case of those at the surface (Evidence, p. 832, l. 13). The wages under ground are much higher than at surface for boys of the same age, as will appear by comparing the following table of wages paid for under-ground labour with that of the wages paid for surface labour at the same mines" (Dr. Barham, Report, § 189, 190: App. Pt. I., p. 786).

TABLE 20.—Showing the Rates of Wages in Mines of different Metals in the several Districts.

Names of Mines.	No. of Boys Employed.	Ages.		Wages.		Districts and Metals.
		Oldest.	Youngest.	Highest.	Lowest.	
		Yrs. Mths.	Yrs. Mths.	s. d.	s. d.	
Boscaswell Downs .	16	16 2	11 0	6 3	3 0	⎫ Western District,
Levant	70	17 10	9 1	13 6	2 6	⎬ Copper.
St. Ives Consols . .	15	17 11	12 5	7 6	7 3	⎭
Godolphin . . .	38	17 6	12 6	10 0	3 0	⎧ Central District,
British Silver, Lead,⎱ &c. ⎰	8	17 6	13 6	7 6	5 0	⎨ S.W., Copper and ⎩ Lead.
East Wheal Crofty .	33	17 6	12 6	10 0	3 6	⎫ Central District,
United Mines . .	113	17 6	11 6	12 0	2 0	⎬ Middle, Copper.
Wheal Jewell. . .	32	17 2	11 2	8 0	3 6	⎭
Hallenbeagle . . .	62	15 1	7 5	7 0	1 6	⎫ Central District,
Polberou Consols . .	16	17 6	10 6	12 6	2 4½	⎬ N.E., Copper.
Wheal Budnick . .	14	17 6	13 6	15 0	3 9	⎭
Cornubian . . .	7	17 6	12 6	10 0	3 9	Lead Mine, ditto.
Polgooth	12	17 6	11 6	9 6	2 6	Eastern District.
Wheal Friendship,⎱ Devon . . . .⎰	62	17 10	9 5	10 6	2 6	Copper.
Wheal Betsy, Devon.	12	17 6	12 6	9 0	5 0	Lead.

947. " The money received is in all these cases handed over to the parent by the younger boys, and they generally continue to do so beyond the age of eighteen. In some cases, where the boy's earnings are large, he pays a portion of them only in return for his board and lodging (Evidence, p. 848, l. 47); and in a few instances the paternal roof is quitted altogether. (Evidence, p. 829, l. 30; p. 832, l. 68.) Ibid., § 191, p. 786.

948. ALSTON MOOR DISTRICT.—" There is a difference in the earnings of boys working in the mines. Some begin at 9d. a-day, at the age of 14, and gradually get on to 1s. a-day, and some more, even as high as 1s. 6d. a-day, until eighteen years of age, when it is usual to admit the youth of full strength into a partnership" (Dr. Mitchell, Report, App. Pt. II., pp. 746, 747).

Alston Moor District.

949. " If his father or brother be already working in the mine, his advance to be a partner is much facilitated. He then gets his subsistence-money, or lent-money, at the beginning of every month, and has his chance of receiving an additional sum at the end of the year, if the mine shall have been fortunate" (Ibid., § 218, p. 745.)

See also Witnesses, Nos. 7, 9, 11, 15, 18.

11.—*Influence of the Employment Underground on the Physical Condition.*

Physical Condition.

950. CORNISH DISTRICT.—" When the boys in this district exchange surface for underground work, they speedily lose the freshness of complexion in the first place, and gradually become for the most part sallow and sickly in hue (Evidence, p. 830, l. 66; p. 848, l. 31; p. 849, l. 49; p. 850, l. 45). This change is often, but not at all uniformly, associated with distinct unhealthiness, but it is no doubt connected with an impeded progress of development. No sort of deformity arises from their occupation. A very slight forward stoop is gradually acquired, and a rather long and cautious step, arising out of the habit of climbing, and of feeling the way among dark and dangerous places (Dr. Barham, Report, § 201: App. Pt. I., p. 790).

Cornish District.

951. " The influence of the solar rays, as constituting one of the modifiers of the nutrition of the body, is proportionally most important at the periods of life when that nutrition is most active. The same principle applies to the supply of the vital constituent of the air, only with greater force, as air is more indispensable to the completion of nutrition than light. The more directly poisonous gases and irritant particles diffused through the air are really more pernicious to the immature than to the adult, though they are apparently less so. The irritability of the nervous system of the young animal takes alarm on the first impression of hurtful agents, and the freedom

UNDERGROUND
LABOUR IN
MINES OF TIN,
COPPER, LEAD, AND
ZINC.

Physical Condition.

Cornish District.

of the secreting functions generally causes their complete elimination at the expense only of some temporarily increased action. But besides that this process, after being several times repeated, each time with less facility than before, is exchanged at last for inflammation or hemorrhage, the whole development of the body is arrested, whilst organs, whose healthy actions are essential to its nourishment, are occupied in resisting agents threatening direct injury to their structure. The result is that, when the usual age of maturity is attained at all, the maturity of a healthy and well-balanced constitution is rarely attained (Ibid. p. 831, l. 56; p. 834, l. 11-66; p. 835, l. 16). The mischief will be in this respect nearly proportional to the earliness of employment: and that it is so, the evidence collected for the present inquiry is abundantly sufficient to prove. The depositions at p. 829, l. 53-66; p. 830, l. 6; p. 841, l. 69; p. 843, l. 40; p. 848, l. 31; p. 852, l. 49; p. 853, l. 7, may be adduced as some of the more pointed statements of facts, which are illustrated by a very large proportion of the examinations.

952. " To put out of sight the frequent production of well-marked disease, the pallid complexion indicates clearly enough that the oxygenation of the blood is imperfect, and that the nutritive processes are interfered with, which is further proved on the large scale by the inferior development of the men as a body to that of the women (Evidence, p. 830, l. 67); (Dr. Barham, Report, § 171, 172, p. 781, 782).

953. " Under ground the boys take with them fare more or less substantial, according to the part of the day in which their 'course' of labour falls. But they always make use of some food whilst they are below, and this is justly considered one of the most beneficial changes which have occurred in the habitual practices of the miners (Evidence, p. 826, l. 14; p. 834, l. 1). The appetite is not always very keen in the hot and impure air with which they are surrounded, and sometimes very little of the food taken down is eaten there (Evidence, p. 853, l. 23, 45). Butchers' meat is only combined in very small proportion with the different articles mentioned above, especially for the children. Beef is very little used; mutton is more common, but pork is the meat most largely employed for this as for all other purposes among the mining population (Evidence, p. 821, l. 43)" (Dr. Barham, Report, § 207: App. Pt. I., p. 790).

954. " The boys, like the men, when they go under ground, substitute for their ordinary apparel a loose woollen dress, thick shoes without stockings, and a strong hat with a convex crown, usually weighing from one to two pounds, and affording efficient protection to the head from falling bodies and blows, on which the candle is for the most part placed, inserted into a lump of wet clay. In very hot places the miners often throw off the greater part of the clothing of the body, and work almost in a state of nudity. On their return to the surface the under-ground garments are hung in a building appropriated to that use, called the ' dry' or ' drying-house,' and the ordinary dress is resumed. The habit of wearing flannel next the skin is prevalent among the miners, and the boys working under ground are commonly provided with it. Their surface attire is very decent, and generally kept in pretty good repair. As they advance in age, a similar inclination to that manifested by their companions of the other sex to smartness of dress is developed; though it cannot usually be much indulged within the age to which this inquiry refers" (Ibid., § 213: p. 792).

955. " In a few mines, under the benevolent auspices lately referred to, the access to them, from the shafts by which the miner ascends, is by shallow levels terminating, by means of a short footway, in the interior of these buildings, so that the miner, when he comes to the surface, issues at once into a warm air without any exposure. In the changing-houses themselves, the degree in which accommodation is furnished for drying the clothes, and enabling the miner to change his dress without running the risk of chill, is very various. Some of the most perfect are described in the Evidence (p. 838, l. 54; p. 839, l. 39).

956. " Closely associated with these arrangements is the provision of warm water for cleansing the surface before the dress is changed. The quantity of water heated in condensing the steam—the great moving power in these mines

UNDERGROUND
LABOUR IN
MINES OF TIN,
COPPER, LEAD, AND
ZINC.

Physical Condition.

Cornish District.

—causes a ready access to this article, so essentially beneficial when the frame is exhausted, and the skin coated with mineral dirt; but in the greater number of the mines it is allowed to escape without being collected in any reservoir where the men might effectually avail themselves of it.   The excellent contrivance for this purpose at North Roskear is described in the Evidence (p. 839, l. 44)" (Dr. Barham, Report, § 60, 61: App. Pt. I., p. 747).

957. The evidence shows that when a boy, inheriting from nature a sound and vigorous frame, and does not begin to work in the mines until seventeen or eighteen years of age, he is able to pursue his occupation with comparative impunity.   (Evidence attached to Dr. Barham's Report, I., p. 839, l. 56, 66; p. 838, l. 59; p. 841, l. 69; p. 828, l. 17; p. 829, l. 51; p. 831, l. 14; p. 836, l. 59.)   But in general the same physical deterioration is produced by employment in these mines, as has been so fully shown to result from early labour in coal-mines.   "When," says the Sub-Commissioner, "a boy, originally, perhaps, inclined to consumptive disease, having often a declining father (Evidence, p. 843, l. 55; p. 831, l. 9), sometimes left as the principal stay to a widowed mother with a large family (Evidence, p. 831, l. 32; p. 840, l. 24; p. 846, l. 62), obtains at 10 or 11 years of age a place under ground, he works with spirit for some years, but he expends the whole capital of his constitution.   He cannot give up his place whilst he can possibly do the work, for the necessities of his home render any exercise of parental authority rarely required to urge him forwards.   He cannot get the kind of nourishment, or enough of it, to support his strength under exhausting labour, still less to give full materials for the development of the frame in its just proportions.   The result is that he falls a victim either to acute disease, often produced by the rapid transitions of temperature occurring to every miner, or to consumption pursuing rather a rapid course, and frequently preceded by hemoptysis.   This is a statement of facts which have repeatedly fallen under my own notice; similar ones may be seen in Evidence (p. 828, l. 18; p. 835, l. 45).

958. " Where there is more power of resistance in the original constitution, the effects of the excess of labour, deleterious and exhausting agencies, and deficient nutriment, will be evidenced chiefly in a stunting of growth and a general feebleness (Evidence, p. 824, l. 62).   In these cases life is often prolonged, and the occupation of mining continued for many years, though the labour is always felt more or less oppressive (Evidence, Nos. 16 and 17), and is generally interrupted by attacks of illness; but such men have always the appearance of being older than they really are, and from 35 to 45 years of age they are often completely broken down, and at that period of life frequently fall into the slower and more characteristic form of consumption common among miners, and do, I am well convinced, contribute very much indeed to swell the list of premature deaths by which the average life of the miner is rendered so much shorter than that of his agricultural neighbour.

959. " Various forms of unhealthy action occur among the boys working under ground, whether as preludes of the early termination of life, or concomitants of the defective development noticed above, or as affecting those on whom they operate as timely warnings to quit the occupation altogether, or those whose more robust constitutions, or more favourable circumstances, enable them to resume it without permanent detriment."

960. From the Report of the Sub-Commissioner, there appears to be a striking analogy between the positive diseases produced by employment in the mines of this district, and the maladies which have been shown to result from early employment in coal-mines.

961. The Sub-Commissioner reports that " Disordered action of the heart, sometimes connected with hypertrophy, or with the changes consequent on rheumatism, but more commonly without structural mischief, is a frequent occurrence.   It is often associated with derangement of the functions of digestion, and both classes of symptoms may have been occasioned by exposure to ' poor air.'   But I have seen several cases in which the palpitation appeared to have resulted purely from repeated over-exertion of the organ; and in some of these there was reason to believe that the food was very insufficient.   That weakness, and correspondent irritability, were the conditions under which this unnatural action took place, was further shown by the perfect success of a treat-

UNDERGROUND
LABOUR IN
MINES OF TIN,
COPPER, LEAD, AND
ZINC.

Physical Condition.

Cornish District.

ment essentially tonic.* Instances of affections of the heart, varying in character as above detailed, may be found (Evidence, p. 840, l. 18, 27 ; p. 841, l. 69).

962. " Affections of the organs of respiration are frequent, and are either of the acute inflammatory nature, to which sudden transitions of temperature will give rise, and consequently most common among those who work in the shallower mines, or parts of mines, and where the air and water is cold (Evidence, p. 835, l. 55 ; p. 828, l. 11 ; p. 840, l. 16) ; or they are of a more chronic form, apparently connected with the repeated inhalation of noxious gases and particles of matter, and, perhaps, with over-distention of the ramifications of the air-tubes and cells. Where inflammation is not produced, a more abundant secretion from the surfaces to which those noxious agents are applied, is the protection and mode of elimination furnished by nature, but this secretion being associated with an increased flow of blood to those surfaces, the reiterated call for the one renders the other almost continually necessary. The consequences are, an engorged and thickened state of the linings of the air-tubes, and a contraction of their bore, leading to forced dilatation afterwards in the course of violent respiratory efforts. Instances of such dyspnœa may be found (Evidence, p. 827, l. 46 ; p. 848, l. 17 ; p. 853, l. 58). It is probably an engorgement of the above description, affecting the larynx and trachea, which produces the hoarseness very commonly noticeable among these boys, examples of which occur in the Evidence (p. 843, l. 57; p. 853, l. 39; p. 854, l. 1).

963. " The affections of the digestive organs chiefly met with among the boys working under ground are disorders of the stomach, connected with the inhalation of ' poor air,' and seeming to be merely secondary to the influence of this air upon the brain. Pain in the head, becoming intense on stooping, giddiness proceeding sometimes to loss of consciousness, failure of muscular power, are described by miners of all ages as effects of this deleterious agent (Evidence, p. 854, l. 61 ; p. 852, l. 50 ; p. 853, l. 8, 22) ; but the greater irritability of the young subject seems to occasion the sympathetic affection of the stomach, shown by loss of appetite, nausea, or vomiting (Evidence, p. 853, l. 11, 23, 45). The powers of digestion are usually recovered in these cases very readily on the return to a pure air. It is at a later period of adolescence, approaching the limit of this inquiry, that more permanent dyspepsia often occurs (Evidence, p. 835, l. 20), arising mainly, I believe, from the general feebleness induced by premature under-ground labour, partly perhaps from repetition of the more transient disturbance just now spoken of, and increased by coarseness of fare, and at times by the use of tobacco, which is often commenced at about this age.

964. " No other forms of sickness can be said to be at all prevalent among this class of boys. From diseases of the skin it has even been supposed that they enjoy something approaching to immunity; and though I have met with too many cases, even within the last few months, to accede to that opinion, it seems probable that the free action of the skin, promoted by under-ground labour, does tend to preserve it from eruption.

965. " Excluding the effects of accidents, no surgical disease whatever occurs among these more frequently than among other labouring boys. They are, indeed, remarkably exempt from distortion and from hernia. The defective development, spoken of more than once, applies to the body as a whole, and not obviously to one part more than another; certainly it is not localised to the extent of causing deformity " (Dr. Barham, Report, § 225–232, App. Pt. I., p. 795–97).

966. ALSTON MOOR DISTRICT.—The miners in this district are constantly exposed while at work to a highly deleterious air, of which James F. W. Johnston, Esq., F.R.S., of the University of Durham, gives the following account :—" In the lead mines in general the most abundant, and, I believe, the most deleterious gaseous *exhalation* is carbonic acid. This is particularly injurious in the dead-work, or drifts, where there is no ventilation. It comes out sometimes in distinct jets from the sides of the passages and chambers, but more frequently it escapes from the rock in numerous places, and in quan-

---

* It will be seen, on reference to Evidence, p. 825, l. 59, that of seven boys examined very soon after their coming to the surface on the conclusion of their day's work, the pulse in all but one proved the exhaustion of the muscular power of the heart, produced by the circumstances of their labour.

UNDERGROUND
LABOUR IN
MINES OF TIN,
COPPER, LEAD, AND
ZINC.
___
Physical Condition.
___
Alston Moor
District.

tities too small to be easily observed at each place of escape. The deleterious effect of this acid is heightened by that of the gases which are formed during the combustion of the gunpowder employed in blasting. These fumes float long in the atmosphere, especially of the longer drifts, and, to a stranger coming immediately from the purer air, render the air almost irrespirable. In the air by which the miner is surrounded there float also continually minute particles of ore and other stony materials, which contribute, in no little degree, to the production of those distressing complaints by which the latter years of a miner are almost always rendered miserable, and the lives of all shortened many years." (Dr. Mitchell, Report, § 160: p. 739.)

967. George Arnison, Esq., surgeon to the workpeople employed by the London Company, says,—" Although the ventilation of the mines is, with few exceptions, good and efficient, much superior to what it was some thirty years ago, yet even in those parts of the mine where it is the best, and where there is neither a deficiency or vitiation of the air, the miners are continually respiring, whilst at work in the mine, an air (however good in other respects) highly charged with minute particles of dust, smoke, and other effluvia, arising from their constant operation with the pick, the jumper, &c., and the frequent explosions of gunpowder used in blasting the mine.

968. " The miners," he continues, " generally speaking, are healthy and robust in early life, and do not exhibit any striking indications of their health being impaired by the nature of their employment before they reach the age of thirty. From that to forty their peculiar complaint imperceptibly steals upon them, and at the latter age they are generally affected with a degree of constriction in the chest, and difficulty of breathing, attended with increased embarrassment on ascending a hill or using any extra exertion. Few old miners are exempt from this dyspnœa, which, instead of regarding in a serious light, they look upon as a matter of course, and numbers of them continue their employment for many years after, suffering in a partial degree in this way. Some few individuals continue their work in the lead mines to the verge of seventy years, but they constitute a comparatively small number who are enabled to continue that employment even to the age of sixty; very many of them, I might say the majority of them, being permanently disabled at fifty, very frequently at forty, or from that to fifty. The habitual dyspnœa becomes seriously aggravated, so that the miner is no longer able to pursue his employment" (Dr. Mitchell, Evidence, No. 1: App. Pt. II., p. 755, l. 12.)

969. " After the first shot goes off," says John Robinson, a working miner, " we have the reek about us all day" (Dr. Mitchell, Report, § 159: App. Pt. II., p. 739).—" A man, by inhaling the powder-smoke and effluvia of the mine, injures his lungs. There is the perspiration off the men as well which hurts them. There is a great quantity of sulphur in the spar, and the miner inhales it. There is arsenic combined in the stuff" (Ibid., § 156: p. 738).— "What between the powder-reek and the want of fresh air," says another miner, " we have sometimes great difficulty of breathing" (Ibid., § 158: p. 739).

970. " All the evidence of the miners themselves and of the medical men," says Dr. Mitchell, " agrees in proving that the lives of the miners are shortened by the nature of their employment; yet I met with an agent of a large mining establishment who boldly asserted that the miners lived even beyond the average duration of life, and in proof of his assertion produced a paper drawn up by a surgeon, showing that the miners connected with his mine who have died for the 28 years past had averaged, one with another, 51½ years.

971. " As persons do not become miners until nineteen years of age, the above result, if correct, would show that the chance of life to a miner entering on the employment at nineteen was 32½ years. This will no doubt appear a long period, but it falls short of the probable duration of life, as ascertained by the Swedish tables, which, for men of nineteen, is 38$\frac{88}{100}$, or upwards of seven years longer than the average given by this surgeon of the miners. The Swedish tables are generally considered as more applicable to the body of the working people than any other which we possess, and give a shorter probable duration of life than tables formed from select bodies of men, as the government annuitants, or persons whose lives are insured in the Equitable Life Office.

972. " Having no means of testing the authenticity of the data for the table

UNDERGROUND
LABOUR IN
MINES OF TIN,
COPPER, LEAD, AND
ZINC.

Physical Condition.

Alston Moor
District.

formed by the surgeon, I thought it expedient to consult the public register of the deaths for the district of Alston Moor for the last four years, from July 1, 1837, to June 30, 1841, being the whole period for which it has been kept. I found there the deaths of 79 persons entered as miners, but as four of them are under nineteen, and they probably were not regularly working in the mines, I omit them; and I find that the 75 miners who died above eighteen had amongst them lived the aggregate number of years 3,389, being on the average forty-five years; from which nineteen, the time of commencing their labours, being deducted, gives us twenty-six as the average duration of the life of a miner after commencing his profession. This is six years and a half less than the time in the table formed by the surgeon, and it is nearly fourteen years less than the time ascertained by the experience of the males of the whole kingdom of Sweden.

973. " Out of the 75 deaths the cause of death stated in 37 cases was consumption. There were also six cases of death from asthma, also a disease of the lungs. Considering it of importance that the truth as to the age of miners at death should be fully ascertained, and the value of the evidence of the medical men and miners rigorously tested, returns were obtained from the office of the Registrar-General in London of the deaths of the miners for the four years from July 1, 1837, to June 30, 1841, from the parishes of Allendale, in Northumberland; from the parish of Stanhope, including the chapelry of St. John's Weardale, in the county of Durham; and the parish of Middleton, in Teesdale, in the same county. From these returns the following results were obtained:—

974. " In Allendale, during the four years, there were the deaths of 79 miners of nineteen years of age and upwards, and their aggregate ages amount to 3802 years, making the average age at death 48⅑⅒. This is more favourable than in Alston Moor, but falls short of the number of years given by the surgeon, and greatly short of the Swedish tables for the probability of life of persons of nineteen. The number of deaths from consumption is 36, and from asthma 2; together 38" (Ibid., §§ 264—270: p. 751).—" In the parish of Stanhope, including the chapelry of St. John's Weardale, the number of deaths of the miners of nineteen years and upwards was 129, and their aggregate ages come to 6383 years, giving an average of 49⁴⁹⁄₁₂₉ years. The number of deaths from consumption is 64, and from asthma 6; making together 70" (Ibid., §§ 272, 273, p. 752).—See also Evidence, Witnesses Nos. 1, 2, 5, 6, 7, 8, 17, 21, 26.

975. " At Middleton-in-Teesdale the number of deaths of miners nineteen years of age and upwards in four years is 57, and the aggregate ages make 2693 years, giving an average of 47¼⅟. The deaths from consumption are 19, and from asthma 13; making together 32 deaths from diseases of the lungs, out of 57 deaths altogether" (Ibid., § 276: p. 752).

976. " The evidence of the medical men and of the miners is fully borne out from the authentic registers of the districts; and it is to be observed that the Young Persons who go into the mines to begin the profession of a miner have survived the dangers of childhood and boyhood, and are probably in almost every case in at least an average state of health, or they would not likely undertake so laborious an employment. The average expectation of life in the table formed from the experience of the capital of the county of Cumberland, and commonly called the Carlisle Table, is, for persons of nineteen years of age, 42¹⁷⁄₁₀₀ years; that is to say, the average age at which they die is sixty-one years, and far exceeds that of the miners of the fine, healthy, upland vales of the lead country" (Ibid., § 278: p. 752).

*Limited
Employment.*

Derbyshire.

12.—*Limited Underground Employment of Children and Young Persons in the less important Mining Districts.*

977. DERBYSHIRE.—The principal mines now worked in Derbyshire are the lead mines in the manor of Crich, which employ under ground no Children, and few Young Persons (J. M. Fellows, Esq., Report, § 93: App. Pt. II., p. 259). The Young Persons employed under ground approach adult age, and they work only six hours a-day (J. M. Fellows, Esq, Evidence, No. 495: App. Pt. II., p. 360, l. 25; and No. 509, p. 361, l. 50).

978. At Bonsall there are many lead mines, which, however, are worked only by poor people on a very small scale. Few employ Children or Young Persons, but those who are taken into the mines "are very badly off; for instance, Job Bunting, a miner, works himself, with his two sons, and they have scarcely a rag to cover them. Job Bunting, jun., is eleven years old; has worked four years; works from seven to six, with half an hour for breakfast and one hour for dinner; comes home to his meals; went three years to free school; now goes neither to church, chapel, or school" (See ibid., and the Witnesses Nos. 519, 520: App. Pt. II., p. 363, 1. 40).

UNDERGROUND LABOUR IN MINES OF TIN, COPPER, LEAD, AND ZINC.
—
Limited Employment.

Derbyshire.

979. LEADHILLS.—Although Children are early employed in washing the ore, yet none descend into the mines at an early age, and even very few Young Persons are employed under ground before the age of eighteen. Dr. James Martin, a native and resident of Leadhills, gives the following account of the influence of this employment on health and longevity :— " Finds that the people generally, through exposure to the winds and rains of the mountains, are liable to rheumatism, and to inflammatory affections of the throat and chest, perhaps in the same degree as the shepherds on the hills. The children employed in the washing are peculiarly exposed to colds, and one is now occasionally spitting blood. The miners too, though no deleterious gases are generated in the mines, or escape into them from natural passages, as in Durham and Northumberland, yet by long continuance under ground, in galleries damp, ill-ventilated, and loaded with the fumes of the gunpowder, and the broken particles of stone, become liable to difficulty of breathing, arising from chronic affections of the chest. As a general rule, the difficulty of breathing creeps upon a miner towards the close of life, and helps to break him up sooner than occurs with the population generally; and the effect is exhibited in the much greater number of widows than widowers, the women living perhaps to the full average" (J. Fletcher, Esq., Evidence, No. 47: App Pt. II., p. 870, l. 22).

Scotland.

980. NORTH WALES.—" The boys employed at the lead mines in the Flintshire district very rarely find employment below the surface. Mining requires strength; and until eighteen or twenty years of age few engage in underground work. Where the ventilation is bad, young lads about twelve years old are occasionally employed in pumping air in different parts of the mine; and as the men work by night, so the boys who pump are also employed at night; each set pumps twelve hours, with only short intervals for meals. The whole number of boys engaged in this work is but small; probably in all the lead-mines in Flintshire it does not amount to sixty, perhaps it may be under fifty, and to be met with only in a few mines near Holywell, where the workings are deep and extensive." The access to these mines is exclusively by ladders, the ascent of which produces the severest exhaustion (H. H. Jones, Esq., Report, § 27 : App. Pt. II., p. 368).

North Wales.

981. Abundant testimony is given by the witnesses examined by the Sub-Commissioner that under-ground employment in the mines of this district produces the same deleterious effects as in the South-Western and the Alston Moor Districts. Of the positive diseases induced, those of the respiratory organs are the most prominent, all of which are classed by the miners themselves under the name of asthma. In this district these diseases are felt in a painful degree as early as the age of twenty-five, and they gradually increase between this age and thirty-five. The uniform statement is that these maladies always terminate in a comparatively early death.

2.—SURFACE LABOUR IN DRESSING THE ORES OF TIN, COPPER, LEAD, AND ZINC.

1. *Ages, Sex, and Number of the Children and Young Persons employea on the Surface in Dressing Ores.*

982. The CORNISH DISTRICT is the only one in which female labour takes any important part in this branch of industry.

983. At a preceding page (206) is given a tabular statement of the numbers, age, and sex of those returned as employed at the mines of the Cornish District, on the surface as well as under ground; and in Dr. Barham's Report (App. Pt. I.,

SURFACE LABOUR IN DRESSING THE ORES OF TIN, COPPER, LEAD, AND ZINC.
—
Age, Sex, and Number.

Surface Labour
in Dressing
the Ores of Tin,
Copper, Lead, and
Zinc.

*Age, Sex, and
Number.*

Cornish District.

p. 766-770) will be found the numbers employed at each of the several mines, arranged geographically, nearly as they follow each other from west to east. Of the Children and Young Persons employed at surface labour in this district he thus reports :—

984. "The proportion of females, and especially of female children, is materially less in the Western District of Cornwall (Table 11) than in the others. The returns are in this point in accordance with direct observation and inquiry.

985. "The existing state of the employment of Children and Young Persons in the mines of the West of England, as inferred from the returns, is that the boys begin to work at the surface between eight and nine, and the girls between nine and ten. Some few commence in each case a year or two before (Dr. Barham, Report, §§ 113, 114 : App. Pt. I., p. 765).

986. "It will be seen that a large number of boys are returned as working at the surface between nine and ten years of age, and that this reaches its maximum between twelve and thirteen : afterwards it gradually lessens, whilst the number employed under ground steadily increases. The girls, on the other hand, are not very numerous until they are more than eleven years old, and their number goes on increasing till they reach sixteen, when it remains stationary. The total number of females above eighteen years of age is rather greater than that of those below eighteen" (Ibid. § 116 : p. 765).

987. "The opinion of the best-informed persons is, that Children are now employed at the mines at an earlier age than they formerly were. (Evidence, p. 851, l. 30.) The more necessitous condition of parents is the cause generally assigned for this change. (Evidence, p. 830, l. 60 ; p. 831, l. 9, 55 ; p. 834, l. 47 ; p. 848, l. 34.) The increased difficulty of obtaining relief under the New Poor Law has also been mentioned as occasioning a greater necessity for the employment of the younger Children. (Evidence, p. 823, l. 64.) The introduction of machinery for the performing of particular operations, previously executed by manual labour, has generally tended to the substitution of younger hands for those before employed" (Ibid. § 118 : p. 771).

988. **Alston Moor District.**—" A very few young women, between thirteen and eighteen years of age, are employed in the dressing of lead ores in this district. The reason generally given for not employing women was, that they considered it was work not fit for women. Certainly the labour is not too severe for women, but it must be admitted that the exposure to the weather is so great an evil that it is neither fit for men, women, nor Children. A more definite reason was given by Mr. Parmley, of Stanhope : ' We do not think it suitable to the modesty and delicacy of the sex to be so much associated in labour with boys. The discontinuance of the employment of girls is all but universal in Weardale, and in all our company's mines everywhere it is so.' The working-men in Teesdale say : ' We think in this place that it is very improper that girls should be allowed to work at washing ore. It is worse than Indian slavery. It is not suitable for girls to have to work along with grown boys, and to hear what the boys may say to them' " (Dr. Mitchell, Report, §§ 228, 229 : App. Pt. II., p. 747 ; Evidence, Nos. 21, 22, and 23).

989. "As to the age when Children first begin to work in washing the ore, there are a few and but very rare instances between eight and nine : the greater part begin between nine and ten. In the mines of the London Lead Company the rule is to admit Children at twelve years complete, but in practice they are allowed to begin to work in their twelfth year. The importunity and poverty of the parents, particularly of widows, procure this relaxation of the strict rule.

990. "The Returns show the above to be ages for the commencement of labour, and the same appears from all the evidence, and was confirmed by personal inspection of many of the washing-floors where the Children were employed. Children under nine are seldom so strong as to be of any use whatever, which is the best security against their being employed. There are no apprentices at any description of work" (Ibid. §§ 30, 31 : p. 725).—See also the evidence of John Parmley, agent (No. 3 : App. Pt. II., p. 756, l. 65) ; of Jacob Crawhall, (No. 6 : p. 759, l. 18), Joseph Collingwood (No. 16 : p. 763, l. 64), and Joseph Walton (No. 24 : p. 765, l. 56), miners ; that of Joseph Fleming (No. 10 : p. 762, l. 43), Ralph Elliott, (No. 15 : p. 763, l. 53), Hall Robinson (No. 19 : p. 764, l. 56), Joseph Collingwood (No. 20 : p. 764, l. 68), Matthew Dowson (No. 25 : p. 766, l. 20), and William Salkeld (No. 31: p. 768, l. 49), youths employed at washing ; and finally that

of William Whitfield (No. 33: p. 769, l. 34), and Robert Hetherington (No. 35: p. 769, l. 61), Children similarly employed.

991. LEADHILLS.—Here about one-fifth of the total number of hands are boys employed in the washing of the lead ores, which they commence generally at nine or ten years of age, and sometimes earlier (J. Fletcher, Esq., Report, § 8 : App. Pt. II., p. 862; and Evidence, No. 43: App. Pt. II., p. 866).

992. NORTH WALES.—The usual age at which Children commence work at the surface labour of the Flintshire mines is ten, though sometimes a year or more earlier or later. Some go to work as early as six, seven, and eight years of age. It is almost exclusively boys who are so employed. (H. H. Jones, Esq., Evidence, No. 136: App. Part II., p. 426, l. 48; No. 140: p. 429, l. 9; No. 189: p. 459, l. 9; No. 148: p. 434, l. 54; No. 179, p. 453, l. 4; No. 195: p. 464, l. 71; No. 198: p. 467, l. 31; No. 197: p. 466, l. 28; No. 194: p. 463, l. 41; No. 196: p. 465, l. 40; No. 143: p. 430, l. 66; No. 146: p. 433, l. 28; No. 137: p. 427, l. 40; No. 141: p. 430, l. 2; No. 155: p. 438, l. 14; No. 163: p. 442, l. 45; No. 166: p. 443, l. 50; No. 165: p. 443, l. 18).

993. IRELAND.—The proportion of Children employed in this as in many other branches of labour in Ireland is less than in Great Britain, through the greater cheapness of adult labour. Girls, however, are employed as well as boys. The Children and Young Persons are nearly all at the surface ; some cobbing, or breaking the ores with a hammer of a size to be received into the crushing machine, and others at the divers operations of washing. Boys sometimes commence work so early as seven or eight years of age (F. Roper, Esq., Evidence, No. 13: App. Pt. I., p. 864, l. 10 ; and T. Martin, Esq., Evidence, No. 28 : App. Pt. 1., p. 881, l. 26), but generally not until ten, eleven, or later; and girls not until eleven, twelve, and upwards. (See Evidence collected by F. Roper, Esq., Nos. 2, 5, 6, 7, 8, 9, 10, 11, 12, 14, 19, 22, 23, 24, 25, 27, 28, 29, 30, 31, 35, 36, 37, 38, 39 ; and by T. Martin, Esq., No. 28.) Indeed the managing agent at the Knockmahon Copper Mines objects to the trouble which the Children give as almost counterbalancing the value of their labour ; alleging that they are most irregular in their attendance, and will not come when the weather is unfavourable, although they work under good wooden sheds. (F. Roper, Esq., Report, § 5 : App. Pt. I., p. 862).

2.—*Hiring of Children and Young Persons employed on the Surface in Dressing Ores.*

994. CORNISH DISTRICT.—" The first introduction of a Child to mining labour in the Cornish districts," says the Sub-Commissioner, " usually consists in its being brought by the parent with a request for work ; or, if the father is employed, he is probably allowed to put a child into any opening which may occur. The first wages are generally 2d. or 3d. a-day. Afterwards there is not usually any intervention of the parents in the agreements or in the receipt of wages for their children. In different mines, and with respect to different work in the same mines, there is much variety as to the performance of work on the owners' account, or by tribute contract ; but the persons employed are paid in all cases virtually by the owners: the rate of wages is also nearly fixed, and the fluctuations which do arise are not dependent on any special arrangement between the contractor and the labourer. A gradual advance of wages, according to the practice of the mine or district, takes effect as age and skill increase. Much is also done by piecework, and the payment in that case is generally calculated on such a scale as to give the daily wages usual for persons of the same age and ability. In the ordinary course of business the labourer is not allowed to earn more than a certain sum in the day, and is expected to employ the whole day in earning that sum (Evidence, p. 846, l. 18). On particular occasions, however, and more in some mines than in others, a certain amount of piece-work is allowed to be completed as expeditiously as is compatible with its being done well, and the labourers are then free to go. In some cases they are afterwards at liberty to undertake fresh piecework, and thus to earn higher wages (Dr. Barham, Report, § 185: App. Pt. I., p. 784).

SURFACE LABOUR
IN DRESSING
THE ORES OF TIN,
COPPER, LEAD, AND
ZINC.

Hiring.

Cornish District.

995. "It may be confidently stated that no hiring of Children or Young Persons takes place in the mines of the West of England to which they are not voluntary parties. The advance of money to parents on the credit of the future labour of their Children is totally unknown. No system of apprenticeship is practised anywhere, and the obligation of giving a month's notice of the intention to quit a mine is the most stringent condition by which the labourer is in any instance bound (Dr. Barham, Evidence, p. 841, l. 44). It may be further remarked, that a great deal of protective influence is, generally speaking, exercised by the managers of mines with respect to the regularity and convenient mode of payment of the wages of the young people" (Ibid. witnesses No. 1, p. 821, l. 25; No. 41, p. 830, l. 28; No. 93, p. 847, l. 49; No. 97, p. 849, l. 52. Ibid. § 191-2: p. 786).

996. Of the rarity of disagreements between employers and the younger class of labourers with regard to hiring and wages, see Dr. Barham, Report, §§ 192-3: App. Pt. I., p. 784-8).

Alston Moor
District.

997. ALSTON MOOR DISTRICT.—The Sub-Commissioner states that in this district "some companies hire the Boys and Young Persons and pay them themselves, and set men over them to see that they do their work. This is the case with the London Lead Company. But at most mines the custom is to contract at so much per bing of dressed ore, and the contractor engages and pays the people who work for him. A man may have 10 under him, or he may have 40; there is no rule" (Dr. Mitchell, Report, § 227: App. Pt. II., p. 746). No apprentices are employed in this district on the surface, any more than in under-ground work (Ibid. § 234: p. 748).

Scotland.

998. LEADHILLS.—In this neighbourhood the Children are hired and paid by the master, and work under the inspection of a superintendent (J. Fletcher, Esq., Evidence, No. 43: App. Pt. II., p. 866, l. 66).

North Wales.

999. NORTH WALES.—The work of preparing the ore for the process of smelting in this district is usually contracted for, and the contractor hires the boys, and pays them by the day (H. H. Jones, Esq., Report, § 30: App. Pt. II., p. 369).

Ireland.

1000. IRELAND.—In this district the Children are sometimes employed by the mining companies, and sometimes by contractors for the labour under them; a difference which appears to be without effect on the amount of their earnings (Evidence collected by Mr. Roper, *passim*).

Place of Work.

3.—*Place of Work on the Surface for Dressing the Ores.*

Cornish District.

1001. CORNISH DISTRICT.—Of the mines of the West of England, the Sub-Commissioner reports, that "they are situated in places for the most part remote, and always separate from towns, and the only permanent dwellers within their precincts are the few individuals having charge of the counting-houses. Consequently no contamination of air such as results from the assemblage of human habitations can arise. On the surface, the evils which do exist are connected either with a defective shelter from the elements, or with impregnations or effluvia occurring in the processes employed.

1002. "A large proportion of the mines are located in very exposed situations,— on the bleak sides of hills, many hundred feet above the sea,—and often open to the stormy north-west wind as it comes fresh from the ocean. The climate is a rainy and cloudy one, and high winds are very prevalent. Where the arrangements are the best, the shelter provided, which consists of sheds chiefly formed by planks, is barely sufficient (Evidence, p. 846, l. 6) to protect those within. The buildings which are the most perfectly walled in are usually occupied by those engaged in 'cobbing' and 'bucking;' for the 'jiggers' the sheds are open at the front, and of course less effectually defensive; whilst the 'pickers' have only a roof overhead, and are therefore nearly open to the wind, which often brings the rain along with it. (Some evidence on these particulars may be seen at p. 845, l. 15.) Those employed in 'framing' or 'recking' are generally furnished with sheds open in front. This is a description of the best appointed accommodation. In many mines, those especially which are of small or recent working, the provision of shelter is very inferior, and quite inadequate to the effecting what should be its design.

1003. "Much of the work which succeeds the stamping of the ore, such as buddling, trunking, wheeling slimes, &c., is performed in the open air; and this is likewise

Surface Labour in Dressing the Ores of Tin, Copper, Lead, and Zinc.

Place of Work.

Cornish District.

the case with the first separation and breaking of the stuff raised, by riddling, spalling, &c. In these occupations, all that can be done to obviate the inclemencies of the sky is to run under a shed when the rain is violent, and to the 'dry' or the smith's shop for warmth when the cold is severe,—indulgences usually permitted during a short time. Those stamping-mills which are at a distance from the mines to which they belong, or are altogether distinct concerns, are generally provided with very little shelter indeed, and being usually placed in deep valleys (where water-power can be most advantageously employed), they are likewise within reach of any malaria which may be generated there. These observations apply also to the greater part of stream-works.

1004. "The impregnation of the water with mineral substances, commonly called 'mundic-water' by the miners, causes sometimes a sort of poisoning where there is any abrasion of skin, of which instances are given in the Evidence (p. 822, l. 65; p. 827, l. 50); and at times the vapour arising from such water, when it is warm, is said to produce injurious effects. (Evidence, p. 835, l. 67.)

1005. "With this slight exception, no effluvia of injurious tendency can be said to be diffused in the air of the places in which any of the surface operations in these mines are carried on. The arsenical fumes emitted from the calcining furnace, respecting the mischievous effects of which some evidence will be found (at p. 841, l. 28), are now carefully collected in flues of great length, in which the poison is precipitated. The furnaces employ very few hands, and these are chiefly adults; neither is their exposure to heat or effluvia at all materially detrimental. Mention has already been made of the mischief occasioned by the dust produced in the crushing-mill. It is rare that more than one or two boys are engaged in this work.

1006. "It appears then that the surface-work in these mines is, with scarcely an exception, carried on under a condition the opposite of defective ventilation; and it cannot reasonably be doubted that the constant exposure to a cool and rapidly-renewed air lessens very greatly the susceptibility of the frame to affections more directly produced by cold and wet, whilst it enables the system to support without exhaustion labour of much longer continuance than can be endured where the supply of oxygen is deficient, and the temperature high" (Dr. Barham, Report, §§ 165, 170: App. Pt. I., p. 780, 781).

1007. Alston Moor District.—Here the Young People employed at the washing complain of the hardship they endure from exposure to all the severities of the cold wind and rain of this mountainous region. In general, the statements they make are similar to the evidence given by Thomas Davidson, aged sixteen, ore-washer, who says :—" We sometimes get wet as early as eight o'clock; it would be a vast deal better if we could go under some place during the rain, and keep ourselves dry, than stand wet all day. We do not complain of anything else" (Dr. Mitchell, Evidence, No. 34: App. Pt. II., p. 769, l. 57).

1008. "The proprietors," adds the Sub-Commissioner, "might mitigate considerably the hardships of the employment, and might do so at a very slight expense. At the washing-place, a mile lower down than Coalcleugh, in West Allendale, the agent of Mr. Beaumont has erected some sheds under which this work may be done. In other washing-floors I saw one or two such sheds; but in general, and with exceedingly few exceptions, it may be asserted that this work is done in the open air, with nothing to shelter the poor lads from the cold and freezing blast; and nothing to shelter them from heavy thunder-storms and continued rain, or from excessive heat on some days in summer, which may be succeeded by cold. An exceedingly small sum, not worthy of so much as being named, from the profits of a great company or rich proprietor, would be sufficient to defray the cost of such sheds; and it is to be hoped that the agents of Mr. Beaumont and of the London Lead Company will persevere until all this is accomplished, and the smaller companies will be compelled to imitate their good example.

1009. "The London Lead Company has at some of its floors what the witnesses called fleaks, which are large boards nailed together forming a wall of timber, which may be moved about from one spot to another, and so placed that the boys working at washing may be protected from the direct violence of the wind and tempest of rain. But this is no protection when the rain falls directly downwards, and is a very imperfect protection under any circumstances.

1010. "No doubt the space on which are the sieves, the buddles, and dolly-tubs is very considerable, but the expense of erecting sheds to screen the Children from

SURFACE LABOUR
IN DRESSING
THE ORES OF TIN,
COPPER, LEAD, AND
ZINC.

Place of Work.

Alston Moor
District.

the rain could be no object. I was informed that the London Lead Company had lately taken this subject into consideration, and it is to be hoped of such a company that their decision will be as honourable to themselves as it will be humane towards the Children who depend upon them for subsistence" (Dr. Mitchell, Report, §§ 93—96 : App. Pt. II., pp. 731, 732).

1012. The Boys and Young Persons engaged in washing the ore, it is stated, are substantially clothed, and must be sufficiently warm so long as their clothes are not soaked by the rain from above. Their feet are well protected by clogs. The soles consist of wood, say three-quarters of an inch thick, with iron all round the edges, and doubled down to come a short way beneath the sole : there is iron also on the heels. The upper part consists of very thick leather, which comes up about the ankles (Ibid. § 89 : App. Pt. II., p. 732.)

1013. LEADHILLS.—In this district the same complaint is made by the Young People employed in breaking, washing, and scumming the ore, of their great exposure to wet and cold. The work is stated to be easy and healthy in itself, but the exposure to weather is sometimes very severe. There is no overhead shelter whatever, and the obstacle against providing it is, that the consequent obstruction of the light would prevent a ready distinction between the ore and the material of the matrix from which it is broken ; the *grey* ores being here very common. There seems to be no objection to providing each worker with a sort of narrow upright box, with a roof slanting backward, such as the stonemasons use, and which would exclude no light (J. Fletcher, Esq., Evidence, No. 43, App. Pt. II., p. 866, l. 43).

1014. NORTH WALES.—The exposure in this district is equally great, and is alike complained of as a hardship. (H. H. Jones, Esq., Evidence, No. 146: App. Pt. II., p. 433, l. 67). "'The work, as I saw it performed in summer," states the Sub-Commissioner, " appeared rather agreeable than otherwise ; but being in the open air, and entirely connected with water, so that the hands and arms are always wet, and the feet very often so, it must in winter be a cheerless occupation, and likely to produce bad health. In this, as in many other works, habit must do a great deal, as, from all the testimony I could collect, these boys are a healthy class ; and in those works which I inspected in the summer they were as healthy, if not as robust, a set of lads as I ever saw, and this notwithstanding the tendency to constipation from the particles of lead-ore which they must occasionally swallow when at work, or which are taken up by the absorbents from the external parts of the body, where much dust laden with lead must necessarily lodge during the time of work" (H. H. Jones, Esq., Report, § 29 : App. Pt. II., p. 368).

1015. IRELAND.—The washing-grounds of the Irish mines present no peculiarities of character. Sheds are provided in some few instances ; but generally there is a complete exposure to the weather, against which there is much complaint (F. Roper, Esq., Evidence, *passim*).

4.—*Nature of the Employment on the Surface in Dressing Ores.*

1016. CORNISH DISTRICT.—After describing the several qualities of ore raised in the Cornish district, and premising that it is only the tin-ores that are generally subjected to a process of " stamping" into small particles by mechanical power, the Sub-Commissioner describes the surface labour of the Children and Young Persons in the " dressing" of the copper and other ores, which consists of various processes for separating the valuable from the worthless portions of the matter sent up by the miners. These processes of " dressing" are the last to which the ores are subjected in the district in which they are raised, it being found economical to ship them to South Wales to be smelted, as a back freight for the vessels which bring supplies of coal for the working of the steam-engines employed to raise water and ore from the mines. " In the preparation or 'dressing' of copper ores, the first step is the separation of the larger pieces raised from the smaller by a sieve called a ' riddle,' or ' griddle.' When this has been done the process of ' picking' the valuable portions of the latter from the worthless succeeds, and this is the work in which female Children are first employed, while some of the youngest boys are engaged in ' washing up,' or cleansing the stones previously to this selection ; this is usually done in wooden troughs, through which

SURFACE LABOUR
IN DRESSING
THE ORES OF TIN,
COPPER, LEAD, AND
ZINC.

*Nature of
Employment.*

Cornish District.

a stream of water flows, immediately in front of the ' pickers ' " (Evidence, p. 822 l. 22).

1016. " These little girls are seated, or half reclining on a table, and a small heap of the mineral being thrown before them, they select and put into a basket, or otherwise separate, the valuable pieces, and throw back the others into what are called the ' boxes,' whence they are wheeled by boys to a large heap, which is again subjected to examination. This ' picking ' is carried on under a shed (hutch) which is open on both sides, for the convenience of the washing in front, and of the carrying away the rejected portion at the back.

1017. " This work is in itself but little laborious; but there is much exposure to cold from the openness of the sheds and the wetness of the mineral, and the posture is constrained, the lower limbs having little or no exercise. The sufferings from cold and its effects are accordingly much complained of, but not so much as the exposed situations of many of the mines would lead one to expect. The ' washing-up,' which is generally effected by the agitation of a sieve under water, occasioning a strain on the back, often causes pain there, and the feet are very frequently wet during the greater part of the day.

1018. " The ' riddling ' which has been mentioned as the first process of separation of the larger from the smaller pieces of ore, is usually performed by girls of sixteen years old or more. The very large masses are broken or ' ragged ' by men. Those somewhat smaller are ' spalled,' by stout girls of the age above mentioned, with long-handled hammers, much in the way in which the larger pieces of stone are broken for the repair of roads. The ' riddling ' and ' spalling ' are performed in the open air. The labour is in both cases considerable; its occasional effects may be learned from the Evidence (p. 845, l. 56; p. 846, l. 12; p. 852, l. 33).

1019. " The fragments are next taken to be ' cobbed.' This process is performed by girls, generally above fifteen, who are seated a little above the ground, with an iron anvil at their side. They break the stones with a short-handled hammer to about the size usual in the repair of roads, rejecting as they proceed the worthless and the very inferior parts. The feet and legs of the cobbers are often buried in a heap of these broken pieces of ore, which, being cold, and frequently wet, produce a chilling effect, not unconnected, I believe, with ailments of common occurrence among these girls (Evidence, p. 828, l. 1; p. 846, ll. 6, 16.) To obviate this burying, a screen is in many instances interposed between the legs and the anvil.

1020. " The stones of ore are now taken to be bruised or ' bucked,' where the further reduction of size is not effected by the mill called a ' crusher ' or ' grinder,' which is now employed in the pulverising of probably a full half of the copper-ores raised. The manual process of ' bucking ' consists in pulverising, by a sort of combined movement of percussion and trituration, the pieces of ore already reduced to the weight of an ounce or two, being chiefly those brought from the cobbers. This is done with a broad square hammer, two or three pounds in weight, which is worked sometimes with both hands, sometimes with one only, whilst the other is employed in sweeping the ore within convenient range. The bucker stands by a sort of counter, having iron anvils let into it an intervals. The pulverised ore is allowed to fall on the ground, from which it is afterwards swept up, and measured into barrows, for each of which a certain price is paid.

1021. " This ' bucking,' which is always performed by girls, is considered to be about the hardest work in which they are regularly engaged. The great assiduity commonly exhibited by them, which is indeed necessary to the earning of 10*d.* or 1*s.* a-day (Evidence, p. 826, l. 61), is no doubt followed by a good deal of exhaustion. The less robust are usually obliged to relinquish this work after a short time (Evidence, p. 831, l. 38): and many apparently strong girls are unable to continue at it. Pain in the side and back is the most frequent complaint; giddiness and faintness now and then occur (Evidence, p. 828, l. 47). The ' cobbing ' and ' bucking ' are usually carried on in similar, often in the same, sheds, pretty well protected, for the most part, from wet and wind. The richer portions of the ores of lead are likewise reduced in size to the necessary extent by these processes.

1022. " The substitute for this method of pulverising copper-ores is the crushing-mill. This consists of two parallel cylinders of iron, placed nearly in contact, one of which is made to revolve whilst the other is fixed so as only to yield to great pressure. The stones of ore thrown in from above are ground between these rollers, and a cylindrical sieve is placed beneath, which, being inclined at an angle of about 45°, and turning on its axis, allows the particles which have been suffi-

SURFACE LABOUR
IN DRESSING
THE ORES OF TIN,
COPPER, LEAD, AND
ZINC.

*Nature of
Employment.*

Cornish District.

ciently pulverised to pass through its holes, whilst the larger pieces fall out at the bottom, and are returned to the mill. The working of this machine is attended with the suspension in the air of a great quantity of mineral dust, often of a very suffocating nature when inhaled even cursorily, but producing serious ill effects when the lungs are exposed to it during many successive days. (Evidence illustrative of these effects may be found at I., p. 822, l. 5; p. 852, l. 6; p. 853, l. 57.) The ores are wetted for the purpose of lessening the escape of this dust, and the consequent loss. The extent of evil arising to the persons employed about this mill, among whom there are generally, if not always, some boys, is in a great measure dependent on the continuity with which it is worked. When a very powerful machine is moved by steam, a day or two in the week may be time enough to grind all the ores requiring this process in a particular mine, whilst in another, where water-power is used, and the quantity of ores great, the 'crushers' will be almost constantly at work.

1023. " A further separation of the more valuable part of the pulverised ore from that which is less so is effected by the process called 'jigging,' which consists in keeping the whole of the mineral particles suspended in water for a time sufficient to allow of the subsidence of the more ponderous portion. This is done by the agitation of the water in a sieve, in which the broken ore is placed. The more finely pulverised part passes through the interstices of the sieve, and the heavier pieces of larger size occupy the bottom of it, and are sufficiently separated to admit of the light and worthless stone being removed from the top with a piece of wood. The agitation of the water was formerly always produced by hand-labour, and this is still the case very extensively. Boys are commonly employed at this work, which is perhaps more fatiguing and injurious than any other performed on the surface (Evidence, p. 846, l. 39); and it falls on the young or undersized, as the stooping posture can hardly be maintained except by those whose stature is short. The 'jigger' is obliged to bend forwards over the water, across which he generally strides, and to shake the sieve (usually a foot and a half or two feet in diameter) beneath the surface of the water. When the separation of the several portions of the mineral is judged to be effected, the sieve is lifted out of the water, and the refuse is removed. Pains in the back and limbs (Evidence, p. 827, l. 14), and headache, are represented as the earlier effects of this employment, and more serious consequences, bringing up blood in particular, are stated to be the not unusual results of its long continuance (Evidence, p. 821, l. 32). Most of the evil appears to be obviated by a system of relays, which is adopted in many mines.

1024. " Machinery has, however, superseded, in a large proportion of the more considerable works, the worst parts of this process. Two methods are in use in different mines, by one of which a succession of sieves are kept in motion under water by means of a connexion with a water-wheel or steam-engine, and in the other the water itself, in which a number of the sieves are immersed, is kept in a state of agitation by the motion of a body in the centre. Whichever of these contrivances is adopted, the only manual operations required are the supply of the mineral and the removal of the worthless portion from the surface. Girls are quite capable of doing this, and are consequently often employed for the purpose. Pain in the back is sometimes complained of even under these arrangements (Evidence, p. 853, l. 61, and p. 854, l. 8).

1025. " The inferior portion of the copper-ores, from which the metalliferous particles cannot be extracted by the methods described, is subjected to the stamping-mill, as are almost all the ores of tin. The mineral is reduced by the action of these heavy hammers to a fine powder, which is carried by a stream of water through the perforations in a set of plates of iron surrounding the boxes in which the stamps work. A series of washings of this powder succeeds, the principle of all of which is the carrying off the lighter particles by a current of water of graduated power, and allowing the more ponderous to remain and subside.

1026. " The number of these washings, amounting in some tin-mines to about 100, from first to last, causes the employment of a large number of boys and girls. The operations called 'trunking,' 'buddling,' &c., chiefly fall to the lot of the former, together with the clearing out of the 'slime' pits, in which the mineral mud is collected, and wheeling this slime to different parts for further dressing; all of which is rather dirty work, and carried on for the most part under the open sky. The more delicate manipulations are chiefly intrusted to females. Among these what is called 'framing' in some districts, and 'recking' or 'racking' in others, employs a great number. In this the girl stands at the side of a very

SURFACE LABOUR IN DRESSING THE ORES OF TIN, COPPER, LEAD, AND ZINC.

Nature of Employment.

Cornish District.

shallow wooden frame, inclined at a moderate angle, and open at the foot; at the head of this, on a ledge more or less raised above it, a portion of the metalliferous mud is extended, and, being divided by a light rake, a gentle stream of water is allowed to find its way through it, and to carry it gradually to the frame below. By a skilful direction of the current, the lighter portion is carried off at the bottom, and the heavier is then thrown beneath the frame, by tilting it into a vertical direction upon the pivot on which it hangs, and throwing some water with the shovel upon its surface, to wash off any portions which might adhere to it. This is light work (Evidence, p. 852, l. 33, 41), although it may be irksome from the constant standing. Some injurious effects have been imputed, in certain mines in which hot water is used, to the rapid transition from a sort of vapour-bath (to which the girls are especially exposed whilst the frame is raised) to the chill of a wintry air, conjoined perhaps with wet feet (Evidence, p. 842, l. 42). 'Buddling' is a coarser kind of 'framing;' 'trunking' consists in flapping a portion of the staniferous mud from one reservoir called a 'cover,' over a partition, into another called a 'hutch.' This was done formerly, and is so still in some small concerns, by the agitation of the water by single shovels; but it is now generally effected by the raising of a long handle attached to an axis on which a row of blades acting as shovels is fixed, and this axis is in some cases moved by machinery.

1027. " The tin-ores, after these successive cleanings, are removed to the calcining furnace, and afterwards are subjected to several further washings. In some of these the girls sit within and at the lower part of a long wooden trough, and direct the gentle current of water with a light brush or feather over the surface of the ore. This is perhaps an occupation involving less muscular exercise than any other department of mining labour. The following examples of mines of different metals and in different districts will serve to illustrate the distribution as to sex and age of the Children and Young Persons among the several branches of surface labour.—(Table, p. 236.)

1028. " An additional number of hands, of females especially, is employed in many mines at the time of ' sampling,' that is finally preparing and dividing the ores for sale, which occurs at intervals of a fortnight, a month, or two months (Evidence, p. 833, l. 28). This division of the ores into separate parcels presents some peculiarities in the labour of the females, and constitutes an animated scene in the larger mines (Evidence, p. 831, l. 40). The general heap, containing, perhaps, some hundred tons, is surrounded by a number of pairs of girls with hand-barrows, which are filled from the edge of the heap by a party stationed round, in a regular succession, dictated by a girl appointed to the post. The barrows are then carried off rapidly, and emptied as the germs of a certain number of distinct parcels; and to each of these a barrowful is added in regular order, so that the total number in every one is the same. This business is attended with some bustle and hilarity. Those who fill the barrows exchange places after a time with those who carry them. The latter have, during their turn, by far the harder work. Indeed, carrying barrows (usually about 1½ cwt.), whether on this occasion or in the ordinary course of work, when it is part of the business of the girls who break the ores, and of the boys associated with the 'pickers,' and those employed at the 'slime' pits, is hard work, and is often complained of as causing pain in various parts, and not unfrequently occasioning more permanent injury from sudden strains or falls." (Evidence, p. 826, l. 45; p. 831, l. 28; p. 845, ll. 14, 50; p. 846, l. 60. Dr. Barham, Report, §§ 143-156: App. Pt. I., pp. 775, 779).

1029. ALSTON MOOR DISTRICT.—The " dressing" of the lead-ores raised in this district resembles that of the harder sort of Cornish ores subjected to the process of " stamping," and requires a constant supply of running water. It is, therefore, liable to interruption by frost, and when the frost has permanently set in this branch of labour is discontinued altogether until the spring. It is also liable to be interrupted in dry weather, in places where water is not abundant.

1030. " In former days," says the Sub-Commissioner, " the washing of the ore was a very simple and rude operation. It was placed on a buddle, or space of ground, made a few inches lower down than the other ground, and in extent not much larger than the door of a house, and with a gentle declivity, so that water coming at one end might slowly flow over the stony bottom to the other. The water carried off the loose dirt or clay, or pulverized stone. The solid pieces of ore were broken by a rude instrument called a bucker, which is not yet entirely out of use. This instrument consists of a flat piece of iron about the size of a man's

SURFACE LABOUR IN DRESSING THE ORES OF TIN, COPPER, LEAD, AND ZINC.

Nature of Employment.

TABLE showing the several Employments of the Children and Young Persons at the Surface in certain Mines of Copper, Tin, and Lead, in different Districts; distinguishing the Ages and the Sex of the Individuals.

PROCESSES	Sex	Copper Mines — Western District — Levant				Copper Mines — Central District — United Mines				Copper Mines — Eastern District — Fowey Consols				Tin Mines — Central District — Wheal Vor				Tin Mines — Eastern District — Charlestown Mines				Lead Mines — Central District — East Wheal Rose				Total				REMARKS
		Un.10	to 13	to 15	to 18	Un.10	to 13	to 15	to 18	Un.10	to 13	to 15	to 18	Un.10	to 13	to 15	to 18	Un.10	to 13	to 15	to 18	Un.10	to 13	to 15	to 18	Un.10	to 13	to 15	to 18	
Riddling, or Gridling	M																														Riddling and spalling are often performed by the same person, and the return must be taken in that sense.
	F											4	23															4	23	
Picking	M		2	3	5		32	11	10		23	30	7										6	10	3	6	6	67	47	30	
	F																														
Spalling	M										2	8	15								8							2	8	23	See remark on riddling.
	F																														
Cobbing	M										1	3	4													3		1	3	7	Cobbing and bucking, and some other operations, are often united in the returns under the head of dressing or separating ores. This is the case at the Cornubian, where there are under this description—61 males from 10 to 13, 9 from 13 to 15, and 3 from 15 to 18; and 1 female from 10 to 13, 4 from 13 to 15, and 5 from 15 to 18. In East Wheal Rose, in like manner, there are under this designation—of females, 1 from 10 to 13, 1 from 13 to 15, and 7 from 15 to 18.
	F																														
Bucking	M																														
	F							2	29								3												2	32	
Jigging	M					2	17	9	5	2	20	33	43	27	75	10	5								14	7	2	37	56	55	
	F									6	36	6	1	1	9	17	8		9	19	15						33	11	16	6	
Trunking Slimes	M	7																									5	5	1		
	F									4	29	20	13														5	63	62	36	
Buddling, & serving buddle	M																	8	18	19	15	2	4	1					1	1	
	F			6												1	2										3	25	27	13	
Tying, and tending tyers	M									3	17	10	7														8	18	6		
	F																						3	6	6		1	17	25	37	
Framing, or recking	M																					4	3	2	1	5	21	27	30	
	F														18	25	29	8	17	6											
Rolling, or wheeling barrows																															This is also a frequent occupation conjointly with buddling, trunking, &c.

SURFACE LABOUR
IN DRESSING
THE ORES OF TIN,
COPPER, LEAD, AND
ZINC.

*Nature of
Employment.*

Alston Moor
District.

open hand : at the back of it is a broad ring, through which is thrust a piece of wood for a handle. The boy takes this instrument in his hand, and, striking the ore with it, breaks it into pieces, by which means the water is able to carry off the earthy matter and leave the metal behind. The large pieces of lead thus separated from extraneous matter are carried away in a state fit for the smelting-mill. Other pieces are put on a sieve, as will hereafter be described.

1031. "In small concerns in the distant fells, which will not afford the expense of machinery, and where also there may be but a small supply of water, this mode is still in use. A few persons may also be seen employed in ths way as auxiliary to washing establishments, working at buddles along the side of a gill, taking advantage of the little streams of water which flow down after a heavy fall of rain.

1032. "It is obvious that in this mode of washing many small particles of lead must be carried away, and although this is in part obviated by the water falling into pits, and there depositing and leaving much of the lead, still a portion is carried off and for ever lost.

1033. "About 40 years ago crushing-mills were introduced, and other improvements have since been made, by which the lead is separated from earthy matter at much less expense, and also a greater proportion of the lead is obtained." (Dr. Mitchell, Report, §§ 68-71: App. Pt. II., p. 729).

1034. After the pieces of pure ore and of absolute refuse have been sorted out on a grate supplied with a feeder of water, in the process called "grating," the remainder, called the "bouse-ore," is passed through the two fluted cylinders of the crushing-mill, working into each other, and turned by a stream of water, as more fully described by Dr. Mitchell, together with the other machinery employed.

1035. "From the pits below the crushing-mill the broken ore is drawn up to the chat-mill, on the right-hand side, by means of iron buckets on an endless chain, much in the same way as we see, on a larger scale, the ballast dragged up into the barges from the bottom of the river Thames. Every bucket on arriving at the top discharges its load upon a grating, by the bars of which the larger pieces are retained, and are passed again through the crushing-mill, or sent to the stamping-mill. The smaller pieces are made to pass the three pair of chat-rolls, which are exactly on the same plan with the crushing-rolls, only being on a smaller scale, and adapted for ore of a smaller size.

1036. "As the crushed ore comes down from the chat-mill a boy stirs it, and much is disentangled, and much of the small lead, with dirt adhering to it, is carried by the stream of water to pits lower down.

1037. "The stamping-mill is used for breaking the hard refractory pieces of ore which resist the rollers of the crushing-mill and chat-mill" (Dr. Mitchell, Report, §§ 79-81 : App. Pt. II., p. 730, 731).

1038. "After the ore has come from the chat-mill, and the smaller portion has been carried off by water, it is taken up and put into a sieve to undergo the process technically called hutching. The sieve is made of iron wire, and it is let into a box which is full of water. From the stalks or chains of the sieve proceeds a long lever, which rests upon a fulcrum, and at the end of the lever stands a boy who places his two hands above his head, and pulls the end of the lever down to him, and lets it up again a few inches, and in consequence, the sieve with the ore upon it is raised up and down with agitated motion in the water in the box. The boy keeps on doing this for some time. The effect of this motion on the sieve is, that much of the very small lead or dust falls through the sieve, and sinks to the bottom of the box, and is called smiddum ; and then, of that portion which remains above the sieve, the lead, being the heaviest part, works down to the lowest place next the wires of the sieve. Immediately above the lead are the larger pieces of stone, with portions of ore, which are called chats ; and above the chats are lighter bits of stone, called cuttings.

1039. "The cuttings are removed off by a limp, which is a broad piece of iron, and is given to the cutting cleaners, and is again put into a sieve and treated as before, and the chats are sent back to the chat-mill to be again ground.

1040. "It has already been stated that when the ore was laid on the grating the smaller portions were carried through the bars to a pit below by the stream of water. Part of this matter carried into the pit below is sludge, or slime, which is carried farther down the stream to pits, in which it settles ; but there is another portion much too large and weighty to be thus carried off. This portion is taken up out of the pits, and is put on the sieves, and is hutched ; that is, it is jerked or tossed up and down on the sieve in the water, by the boy pulling at the end of the

Surface Labour in Dressing the Ores of Tin, Copper, Lead and Zinc.

Nature of Employment.

Alston Moor District.

lever, and when sufficiently well hutched the stony matter is carried off by the limp, and the clean ore lying at the bottom is taken to the bingstead.

1041. " The smiddum is taken from the bottom of the boxes in which the sieves were agitated, and it is removed to a running buddle. This is a space of ground with a stone floor made a little lower than the ground about it, and with a little declivity, and over which water is made to run very gently. Upon the upper end of this buddle the smiddum or ore from the boxes is put, and the water is let in upon it. The washing-boys and young persons stir this smiddum with an instrument called a colrake, and the water carries away much dirt, and the little fragments of stone called cuttings, and the lighter ore, both called smiddum-tails, are brought to the lower end of the buddle, whilst the weightier ore is left at the upper end. Thus the two are separated, and the weightier ore is removed to the bingstead.

1042. " It will appear a necessary consequence to every one who has paid attention to the description of the preceding operations, the grating and crushing of the ore under the action of water, that a great quantity of finely pulverized earthy matter must have been produced, and much lead in the form of minute detached particles must have been brought away in company with the pulverized matter, and carried down the stream with the water. Now there are pits one after the other into which the water is made to flow, and in which the water deposits all this matter, which is merely mechanically diffused through it. This composes a mass more or less stiff, and that portion of it which is coarse, and contains larger grains of lead, has been called sludge, and the matter consisting of smaller and finer particles has been called slime.

1043. " It would be tedious and of little utility to give a minute account of the labours of the Children and Young Persons in the treatment of the sludge and slime, in extracting from the earthy matter as many as possible of the particles of the metal. It is put into trunks and agitated with water; it is laid on the floors of the buddles, and streams of water pass over it and through it; and it is stirred and rubbed against the bottom of the buddles, whilst the water is flowing over it; the object being to separate the lead and send the water off down the stream with the clayey matter diffused through it. The last process of all is to put the slime into the dolly-tub. By means of a handle the board in the tub is turned round and round, and agitates the slime: the lead comes to the bottom of the tub, and the worthless matter above it is taken away. After all that can be done to get all the lead from the ore, many particles are carried down in the muddy water of the river, or burn, and no man allows himself or his cattle for many miles below a washing-place to take the poisonous draught" (Ibid. §§ 83, 88: App. Pt. II., p. 731, 732.)

1044. Leadhills.—In the Leadhills district the employment of the children in washing the ores resembles that of the lead-washers in the Alston Moor district.

1045. " The adult miners who raise the ore first sort out the pieces containing metal from the stony refuse which is unavoidably brought up with it; and those pieces are next put through the crushing-mill, fed by a boy sitting in a little box, assisted by several others bringing the ore in little waggons. The broken materials are then put in the sieves, jolted in a long trough of water, at which a number of boys stand in a row, attending the sieves and " skumming" away the lighter matter, while the very smallest particles escape with the water. The bits of metallic ore left in the bottom of the sieves, being thus separated, are placed in distinct heaps ready for smelting; and according to the smelted produce the several sets of men who raised each heap are paid.

1046. " The refuse materials put aside by the men themselves as waste are subjected to the same process as the rough ores, since they are found to contain a proportion of lead sufficient to pay the proprietors for this labour; and the water which brings away all the smallest particles from the sieves is made to deposit, in a succession of little wooden troughs on the ground, all that portion of them which is marked as lead-ore by its greater specific gravity, while the rest flows away in a poisonous impurity of the water.

1047. " The great disadvantages of this employment to the young people engaged in it are the constant dabbling in the cold water, from which the feet are not always protected, and the exposure to the mountain storms and pitiless winds without any shelter whatever" (J. Fletcher, Esq., Report, §§ 10-12: App. Pt. II., p. 862, 863; Evidence, No. 46: p. 866, l. 10).

1048. NORTH WALES.—In this district the Sub-Commissioner states "that it is in preparing ore for the smelters that boys are so extensively employed at the mines, and their work is all performed on the surface in the open air. Formerly the boys used to break the lumps into small fragments by means of hammers ; the dust arising from this operation was in part inhaled by them, and produced bad effects, as it tended to induce constipation of the bowels and a peculiar kind of colic, and.laid the foundation of many constitutional diseases. At present there are few works in which the ore is not broken by machinery, an improvement which lessens labour and reduces the chances of ill health. When broken, the ore is conveyed by boys to the washing-pits and tubs, and by other boys it undergoes several washings through riddles ; the parts which contain no metal go off with the water ; the lead, on account of its specific gravity, sinks to the bottom of the sieve, and by means of these washings is soon fitted for the smelters" (H. H. Jones, Esq., Report, § 28 : App. Pt. II., p. 368 ; Evidence, No. 136 : p. 426, l. 44, &c.

1049. IRELAND.—The processes at the Irish mines are precisely similar (see Reports by Mr. Roper, App. Pt. I., p. 855 *et seq. passim*).

5.—*Hours of Work on the Surface in Dressing Ores.*

1050. CORNISH DISTRICT.—The Sub-Commissioner states that the " usual length of the working-day for the surface labourers in the mines of this district is ten hours in summer and about nine in winter. Work begins at seven in the morning in summer, and with daylight in winter, and it concludes at five, half-past five, or six, or when it grows dusk. Half an hour, three quarters, or a whole hour, is allowed for dinner in different districts, and in one instance two hours. A short interval is, in a few cases only, permitted about ten A.M.

1051. " The hours of labour are often shortened, when the nature of the work admits of its being done by the piece, by the setting of tasks, which can very commonly be completed two or three hours before the regular time of closing. In some instances the Young People continue to work on their own account afterwards, but this is not the most common practice (Evidence, App. Pt. I., p. 824, l. 25; p. 833, l. 10; p. 854, l. 9, 18).

1052. " On the other hand, the hours of work are often prolonged until seven or eight in the evening; and in some cases work is begun an hour earlier than usual in the mornings as well. This working at extra hours is commonly required when the ore is about to be prepared and arranged for sale, which is termed 'sampling.' This occurs in some mines only once in two months, whilst in others it is done twice in the month. In some mines it is the practice to employ a number of extra hands at these times, and these being employed by different mines in succession, there is little or no occasion for working beyond the regular hours. But in other cases, and that in some of the largest mines, where the same hands are almost constantly employed, the larger amount of work must be performed by their increased exertions (Evidence, App. Pt. I., p. 824, l. 30; p. 833, l. 13; p. 845, l. 1).

1053. " In these cases the day is sometimes disposed of as follows :—A boy or girl, from nine to twelve years old, is obliged to rise at about four o'clock in the morning, gets a hasty breakfast, and after a walk of an hour or more—three or four miles—reaches the mine at six. Work is continued till twelve, without intermission or refreshment, save what may be got by stealth. Half an hour is then employed in taking dinner. The child then works without interruption till eight; gets home, after repeating the walk of the morning, and may have had supper, and get to bed about ten. It is chiefly the younger children who are called upon to begin their work at six o'clock, the process on which they are engaged being preparatory for the others. According to the statement of some of the children at a great mine in which this system is followed, they are employed in this way about a third of each month in the summer (Evidence, App. Pt. I., p. 845, l. 22; p. 846, l. 5, 33).

1054. " In some other mines a system is followed for the performance of an extra quantity of work, which overtasks still more the powers of the child, though it is not imposed on so great a number, nor continued so long. The boys are in these cases employed in preparing the ore for sale, from seven in the morning of one day till two in the afternoon of the following, working through the whole night. (*See* Evidence, p. 852, l. 19.) In the former instance (120) the extra time is allowed, and is either paid for according to the number of hours, or it is made up to the Children at some less busy time (Evidence, p. 845, l. 31) in the form of a holiday,

SURFACE LABOUR IN DRESSING THE ORES OF TIN, COPPER, LEAD, AND ZINC.

Nature of Employment.

North Wales.

Ireland.

Hours of Work.

Cornish District.

SURFACE LABOUR
IN DRESSING
THE ORES OF TIN,
COPPER, LEAD, AND
ZINC

Hours of Work.

Cornish District.

no deduction being taken from their wages.   In the latter arrangement, a separate payment is made, and being generally given as pocket-money to the boy, he is not at all disinclined to this increase of fatigue (Evidence *ubi supra*).   Other occasions arise in which the boys are kept at work during the whole night for the despatch of business (Evidence, p. 846, l. 30); but they are not frequent.   With these exceptions, Children and Young Persons are not employed at night on the surface" (Dr. Barham, Report, §§ 119—123: App. Pt. I., p. 771).

Alston Moor
District.

1055. ALSTON MOOR DISTRICT.—In this district the regular hours of work are stated to be twelve, out of which one is allowed for dinner (Dr. Mitchell, Evidence, App. Pt. II.; John Walton, No. 37, p. 770, l. 57; William Whitfield, No. 33, p. 769, l. 35; Anthony Johnson (J. R. Leifchild, Esq., Evidence, App. Pt. I.), No. 516, p. 682, l. 43; W. C. Arnison, Esq., surgeon, No. 525, p. 684, l. 40; and others.—" At washing the lead ore the usual time is from seven to six, with an hour for dinner.   Very often some extra hours are employed during the five days of the week, in consideration of which the washers are allowed to go home so much sooner on Saturdays.   Sometimes when time has been lost in summer, for want of water, and at last rain falls and water becomes plentiful, the washers will come early and stop late, to make up a little for lost time.

1056. "The people of every mine do as they like, but in general the hours are from seven to six, and one hour for dinner; and no one witness has ever made complaint of too long hours at work.   No doubt the desire to get what money they can reconciles all parties to make exertions which, but for the money, they would describe as much too severe and beyond their strength.   The washers begin their work sometimes as early as the end of February, but frost may come on, and then the water will no longer separate the dirt from the ore, and they must discontinue.   In this cold upland country they are not secure against interruption even in the beginning of April, and if strong frost take place they must stop.   In the short days the Children and Young People work from daylight to dark.   When the hard winter frosts set in the washing is necessarily stopped, but in soft winters at some places they may go on till near Christmas.   But, in general, it may be said that there is a cessation from washing from three to four months every winter, and most of the men and bigger boys go and work in the mines" (Dr. Mitchell, Report, §§ 34, 35: App. Pt. II., p. 725).

1057. The evidence of the Young People at the Allenhead's Mines shows that their labour is sometimes protracted till midnight in summer, generally in attendance at the grinding-mill (J. R. Leifchild, Esq., Evidence, App. Pt. I., p. 682, 684).

Scotland.

1058. LEADHILLS.—In this district they commence work at seven in the morning, and leave work at six at night, with one, two, or three days a-week an extra hour, sometimes an hour and a half, and on occasions as much as three hours,—once a-month perhaps, hardly that.   For this overwork they are paid extra.   The time during which, however, the works are suspended by severe weather—by the absolute freezing of the water, which alone stops them—is sometimes three or four months in the year.   On the average the time of work is forty-two weeks in the year.   The regular number of hours' work per day is ten, except on Saturday, when it is only five, the work being closed at twelve o'clock.   Over-work may extend the time three or four hours per week more.   (J. Fletcher, Esq., Evidence, No. 43, App. Pt. II., p. 866, l. 35).

North Wales.

1059. NORTH WALES.—In this district the regular hours of work are ten and eleven daily, from six or seven A.M. to six P.M., with an hour for dinner, and sometimes half an hour for breakfast.   In winter, however, the work is no longer than the daylight.   But in summer there is commonly occasion for a quarter of a day of overwork for a day or two in each month, when the labour is continued to eight and nine o'clock (H. H. Jones, Esq., Evidence, App. Pt. II., No. 142, p. 430, l. 57; No. 147, p. 434, l. 7; No. 136, p. 427, l. 1; No. 172, p. 447, l. 22; No. 140, p. 429, l. 13; No. 148, p. 434, l. 56; No. 178, p. 451, l. 69; &c. &c.).

Jane Davies states, that they work about ten hours a-day, and sometimes they work more, for which they get extra pay; they are quite healthy, and never appear to be tired, or to think the work too much; they come home about seven o'clock, and in summer, after they eat, they go to the field to weed and hoe the potatoes, and they do other little jobs about the house; in winter evenings they go to bed early (Ibid., No. 144: p. 431, l. 62.)—But other witnesses give their opinion that ten and eleven hours' work is too much (Ibid. No. 158: p. 439, l. 38).

1060. IRELAND.—In this country the regular hours of work appear to be the same as in England, from six to six in summer, with an hour for dinner and half an hour for breakfast (F. Roper, Esq., Evidence, Nos. 2, 3, 5, 7, 8, 12, App. Pt. I.).—At Kenmare, however, only three quarters of an hour are allowed for meals (Ibid. § 3: p. 867).—At Newton Ards the same, but the hour of commencing is seven (T. Martin, Esq., Evidence, No. 28: App. Pt. I., p. 881, l. 33). Overwork is common in summer.

SURFACE LABOUR IN DRESSING THE ORES OF TIN, COPPER, LEAD, AND ZINC.

Hours of Work.

Ireland.

6.—*Meal Hours of the Children and Young Persons employed on the Surface in Dressing Ores.*

1061. CORNISH DISTRICT.—The Sub-Commissioner states, that in this district " dinner is the only meal for which time is usually allowed. Twelve o'clock is universally the time of leaving work for this purpose. In winter, half an hour is the interval, almost without exception; in summer this is still maintained in some mines; but more usually an extension of time is granted, sometimes to three quarters of an hour, sometimes to an hour, and in a few cases even to two hours. In a few places some minutes are allowed about ten o'clock in the morning, when a sort of lunch, called 'crowst,' consisting of a portion of the intended dinner, is taken (Evidence, p. 826, l. 22; p. 843, l. 9; p. 844, l. 22; p. 845, l. 29); but this is by no means frequent. A corner of the pasty is more usually eaten as occasion offers.

1062. " There is generally but little provision for comfort in taking dinner. In some of the larger mines sheds are appropriated to this purpose, and furnished in winter with sufficient firing; but more frequently recourse is had to the smith's shop, or to the 'dry,' the place in which the miners' clothes are dried when the sheds in which the work is carried on, and where dinner is usually eaten, are too cold for the purpose. In the warmer season groups are often formed on some bank or field in the neighbourhood, where the meal is taken. In all cases there is little or no mixing of the sexes at their meal. The younger boys very often eat their pasties almost by snatches, and make the most of the time at some game. The proportion is very small of those who go to their homes to dinner, even when the distance might admit of their doing so; in such cases their food is often brought warm from their homes, and, where several members of a family are employed, they unite at their meal. Preparatory washing or change of dress is seldom practised. There is no work going on during the time allowed for dinner which requires the attention of the Young People. The shortness of the time is complained of, by the females especially, where they are limited to half an hour" (Dr. Barham, Report, §§ 131, 132: App. Pt. I., p. 773).

1063. ALSTON MOOR DISTRICT.—In this district "the Children and Young People employed in washing lead ore take an hour for dinner, from twelve to one. They sit where they can, very seldom having any other covering over them than the canopy of heaven. During the dinner all the machinery stops, and in places where the water requires to be accumulated in a dam the sluice is shut, and the water is preserved. On the Saturday the meal is taken an hour earlier at most of the washing-places" (Dr. Mitchell, Report, §§ 37, 38: App. Pt. II., p. 725; Evidence, No. 9: p. 761).

1064. The hours allowed for meals in Scotland, North Wales, and Ireland have been already stated under the preceding head.

7.—*Holidays allowed to Children and Young Persons employed on the Surface in Dressing Ores.*

1065. CORNISH DISTRICT.—" As a general rule, no holidays are allowed in the mines in the West of England but Christmas Day and Good Friday (Evidence, p. 832, l. 47). In some few cases the day of the parish feast is added to these (Evidence, p. 850, l. 27); but in by far the greater number the attendance at this is so contrived as not to occasion any loss of time at the mine (Evidence, p. 841, l. 33). In one mine (Levant) an old custom of having six holidays in the year still obtains (Evidence, p. 848, l. 28). A few hours may be given on some other festivals, as stated (Evidence, p. 845, l. 52) with respect to the Consols.

1066. "On Saturdays, work is closed in many mines about an hour earlier than

SURFACE LABOUR
IN DRESSING
THE ORES OF TIN,
COPPER, LEAD, AND
ZINC.

Holidays.

Cornish District.

usual; and generally, about once a-month (on pay and setting days), little, if any, work is done after dinner. The setting of piece-work (tasks) causes on the whole a more important abatement of the duration of labour than the more professed holidays; but this does not apply to any great extent to those mines, commonly the largest, in which the work is much pushed.

1067. "The most material suspension of the working of the Children and Young Persons at the mines arises either from their voluntary or involuntary irregularity of attendance. In many cases there is not constant employment to be obtained, in many it is left very much to the choice of the labourer to come to the mine or not; in others, again, illness, or some more urgent call elsewhere, interrupts the regularity of attendance, and substitutes are sometimes provided when business or pleasure causes the absence of the young people from the mine, and it is yet necessary for them to make good their place or to lose it. These particulars have respect to those employed at surface—under ground, substitutes are almost always provided." The average attendance at the mine, and the number of days of work in the year, are illustrated by Dr. Barham, in returns of the total earnings of young people as compared to what those earnings would have been had they been fully employed (I., p. 785), and the following statement of Mr. Francis, the principal agent of the United Mines, gives analogous results :—

" The gettings of six girls of the largest class for the last twelve months was 9*l*. 6*s*. each, or 15*s*. 6*d*. per month; and their wages, if constantly employed, would have been 18*s*. 6*d*. per month each.

" The gettings of six girls of the smaller class, for the same time, was 4*l*. 15*s*. each, or 7*s*. 11*d*. per month; and their wages, if constantly employed, would have been 8*s*. 6*d*. per month each.

" The gettings of six boys employed at the surface in preparing the ores for the same time was 6*l*. 5*s*. each, or 10*s*. 5*d*. per month; and their wages, if constantly employed, would have been 12*s*. per month each."

1068. "The air of the Children and Young Persons employed at the surface is cheerful and alert, and a disposition to make the most of the intervals of labour in sports of different kinds is generally evinced. Even when labour is excessively prolonged, it is rare to perceive any external sign that the flow of youthful spirits has been dried up." (Dr. Barham, Report, §§ 180-3 : App. Pt. I., p. 783.)

Alston Moor
District.

1069. ALSTON MOOR DISTRICT.—" The washers of lead-ore," says the Sub-Commissioner, " get away at twelve or one on Saturdays. These unfortunate Young Persons and Boys have but too many holidays forced upon them by the inclemency of the weather, as in most places where they work there is no protection whatever, and in the best places the protection is exceedingly imperfect. Altogether a washer is prevented from working above 21 or 22 days in the month, and he works at washing from eight to nine months in the year. In the winter-time, when the washing becomes impossible, many of the young persons go to work in the mines and the young boys go to school." (Dr. Mitchell, Report, § 201 : App. Pt. II., p. 743.)

Scotland.

1070. LEADHILLS.—Besides the blank days of bad weather, the holidays are the day before and part of the day after the sacrament day, Christmas and New Year's days, and those of the two fairs. (J. Fletcher, Esq., Evidence App. Pt. II., p. 866, l. 64.)

North Wales.

1071. NORTH WALES.—In this district the Sub-Commissioner states that there are no stated and fixed holidays, though the boys often take a holiday; and on occasions of public rejoicings the works are usually stopped. (H. H. Jones, Esq., Report, § 32 : App. Pt. II., p. 369.)

Ireland.

1072. IRELAND.—In this part of the kingdom the holidays are sometimes very numerous. (J. Martin, Esq., Evidence, App. Pt. I., p. 883, l. 30.)

8.—*Treatment and Care of the Children and Young Persons employed on the Surface in Dressing Ores.*

Treatment.

Cornish District.

1073. CORNISH DISTRICT.—Of the Treatment and Care of the Children and Young Persons employed on the surface in this district, the Sub-Commissioner reports—" Very little is done in the way either of reward or punishment. The more rapid advancement of the diligent and skilful, and the giving them an opportunity of leaving work earlier than usual, and at times of earning a trifle for themselves, by the setting of tasks, are the only encouragements to exertion at all extensively employed. In a few mines, of which Wheal Vor is the most important, a premium is given to those girls who have attended at their work without interruption during the whole month. In the mine mentioned, 1s. is the monthly reward for the first-class girls employed at ' framing,' and 6d. that of the second class." (Evidence, p. 841, l. 20.)

1074. " The superintendence of the agents is the only ordinary check on indolence or misconduct. Absence from work without leave (Evidence, p. 847, l. 52), and some particular offences, are punished by ' spaling' (fine), differing in amount in different mines, but always moderate. Where these, or the reprimand of the agent, are ineffectual, dismissal is the only ulterior measure. Corporal punishment may be said to be never inflicted. In fact, as there is no system of apprenticeship, any such punishment would be illegal, and it would certainly be resented by recourse to legal process on the part of the friends (Dr. Barham, Report, §§ 194-5 : App. Pt. I., p. 788).

1075. " The mutual relations between the managers of mines and the Children and Young Persons employed under them may be said to terminate when the work of the day is closed. A large proportion of the mines are situated at a distance of several miles from the dwellings of both these parties, and no connexion between them could be well maintained except at the mines. The mining district between Redruth and Camborne is the most favourably situated for the continuing such relations beyond the limits of the places of work, and a beneficial influence arising from this continuance is more perceptible there than elsewhere. What is chiefly exhibited is, however, rather a regard by the general body of proprietors and managers of mines for the benefit of the general body of mining labourers than a special attention to the individuals employed by themselves. Cases of gross misconduct out of the mine are generally brought under the animadversion of the agents, and reprimand or dismissal will follow" (Evidence, p. 850, l. 34).—(Ibid. § 198 : App. Pt. I., p. 789).

1076. ALSTON MOOR DISTRICT.—The Sub-Commissioner states that the treatment and care which the London Lead Company bestow on the whole of the workpeople employed in their mines, and on their wives and families, is worthy of the imitation of all employers of large bodies of workmen. The means taken by this company to improve the condition and elevate the character of their workpeople deserve attentive perusal (Dr. Mitchell, Report, App. Pt. II., § 237, p. 748 ; § 259, p. 750 ; Evidence, No. 4, p. 757, l. 60; No. 24, p. 765, l. 65).

1077. LEADHILLS.—No complaint was made in this district of the treatment of the Children (J. Fletcher, Esq., Evidence, App. Pt. II., No. 43, p. 867, l. 1 ; No. 44, p. 867, l. 55).

1078. NORTH WALES.—" I particularly inquired," says the Sub-Commissioner for this district, " into the treatment of these boys when at work, and from others as well as from themselves I heard no complaints nor found any instances of cruelty or oppression. The mining agents all say that they allow of no personal chastisement being inflicted on the boys. My observation of them while they were at work and while under my inspection leads me to believe they are well treated ; and though they work about ten hours a-day, and in summer twelve or thirteen hours, that they are not oppressed or much fatigued : when they left off work they appeared fresh and lively, and engaged in play with animation and joy" (H. H. Jones, Esq., Report, § 30: App. Pt. II., p. 369). " One overlooker says he is obliged to thrash the boys, but the parents do not complain of him" (H. H. Jones, Esq., Evidence, No. 184 : App. Pt. II., p. 456, l. 8).

1079. IRELAND.—The performance of a day's work is enforced by the fear of dismissal, and this is all the care taken by the employer. (T. Martin, Esq., Evidence, No. 28 : App. Pt. I., p. 881, l. 63 ; and No. 42, p. 883, l. 36).

9.—Accidents to which Children and Young Persons are exposed on the Surface in Dressing Ores.

1080. CORNISH DISTRICT.—" The surface operations," observes Dr. Barham, of the Cornish district, " are very free from occasions of accident; and such as do occur are for the most part slight, arising from strains or falls, or casual blows

---

Margin notes:

SURFACE LABOUR IN DRESSING THE ORES OF TIN, COPPER, LEAD, AND ZINC.

Treatment.

Cornish District.

Alston Moor District.

Scotland.

North Wales.

Ireland.

Accidents.

Cornish District.

SURFACE LABOUR IN DRESSING THE ORES OF TIN, COPPER, LEAD, AND ZINC.

Accidents.

Cornish District.

with the tools. The machinery used for 'jigging,' the only department in which Young People are employed in any number, is not at all of a dangerous sort. Very few boys are employed about the steam-engines, but injuries have arisen to some of them. In the St. Agnes District Register is entered the case of an engineer of the age of 15, whose death is recorded as being accidentally caused in Wheal Kitty, and at Evidence, p. 835, l. 35, will be found another instance of a less serious character. The *crushing-mill* has also occasioned some fatal accidents, though likewise employing very few boys. These latter cases may be said to have been entirely attributable to the heedlessness natural to boys; the nature and position of the machinery being such as to involve no risk whatever where the most common caution is used. This juvenile imprudence is still more evident in the case of an accident which occurred at Wheal Vor, where one boy was killed and another seriously injured by the falling on them of a heap of 'slime' (mud from the stamps), which they were employed in wheeling to another part, and which they undermined (with the view probably of facilitating their work) in so incautious a way as to bring it down on their own heads" (Dr. Barham, Evidence, No. 75: App. Pt. I., p. 841, l. 26).

Alston Moor District.

1081. ALSTON MOOR DISTRICT.—The surface operations in this district are, in like manner, so little liable to accident, that this subject is deemed unworthy of express notice by Dr. Mitchell.

Scotland.

1082. LEADHILLS.—The only place where there is exposure to serious accident is in feeding the crushing-mill, into which the feeder has been drawn in several instances in the North of England; but no accident, except the hurting of two fingers by a cog-wheel shaking one of the troughs, has occurred here (J. Fletcher, Esq., Evidence, No. 43: App. Pt. II., p. 866, l. 60).

North Wales.

1083. NORTH WALES.—" Boys engaged at the lead-mines of Flintshire," says the Sub-Commissioner, "are not much in the way of accidents, and in appearance and physical strength are inferior to no set of working lads" (H. H. Jones, Esq., Report, § 31: App. Pt. II., p. 369).

Ireland.

1084. IRELAND.—An accident to a girl from the stamping-machine at the Knockmahon mines is mentioned by Mr. Roper; but accidents in the washing-grounds can seldom occur (F. Roper, Esq., Evidence, No. 21: App. Pt. I., p. 865, l. 31. T. Martin, Esq., Evidence, No. 28: App. Pt. I., p. 881, l. 53; No. 42, p. 883, l. 27).

10.—*Wages of Children and Young Persons employed on the Surface in Dressing Ores.*

Wages.

Cornish District.

1085. CORNISH DISTRICT.—" The surface labourers are paid monthly, at the counting-house of the mine (Evidence, p. 833, l. 23). This is done with very great regularity at almost all the mines. A party of five or six boys or girls is generally represented by one, who receives the money for all, and distribution is afterwards made. Much care is now generally taken to pay them with such a proportion of silver as may enable them to make the division without having recourse to the shop or public-house for change (Evidence, p. 830, l. 49; p. 841, l. 36; p. 845, l. 7). This system is not, however, yet carried so far as it ought to be (Evidence, p. 848, l. 50), and in some instances is very little attended to. When the surface labourers are employed by the tributers, the wages are still for the most part paid by the owners; or, if not, care is taken that they are regularly paid (Evidence, p. 850, l. 30).

1086. " The wages are paid over to the parents by their children. Now and then, in consequence of the amount not being so great as was expected, the former will inquire at the mine how much was received by the latter (Evidence, p. 848, l. 43); but usually the children take to their homes the full amount which has been paid to them. The payment for the extra work, spoken of above, is in many districts the perquisite of the children, and is kept by them as pocket-money, when not absolutely needed by the parents (Evidence, p. 836, l. 16).

1087. " The following table will show the highest and lowest wages given in different mines to Children and Young Persons employed at the surface, together with the corresponding ages (Dr. Barham, Report, §§ 186-89: App. Pt. I., p. 786):—

Table showing the Rates of Wages in the Mines of different Metals in the several Districts, distinguishing the Sexes, and the extreme Ages.

Names of Mines.	No. of Boys employed.	SURFACE.				No. of Girls employed.					Districts.
		Ages.		Wages.			Ages.		Wages.		
		Oldest.	Youngest.	Highest.	Lowest.		Oldest.	Youngest.	Highest.	Lowest.	
		Yrs. Ms.	Yrs. Ms.	s. d.	s. d.		Yrs. Ms.	Yrs. Mo.	s. d.	s. d.	
Boscaswell Downs	19	16 2	8 6	6 0	1 9	..	..	..	..	..	} Western.
Levant	33	17 10	10 0	8 9	2 6	25	17 8	12 4	6 0	2 6	
St Ives Consols	45	17 0	5 0	7 6	1 3	9	17 3	13 1	4 6	2 6	} Central S. W.
Godolphin	59	17 6	9 0	6 3	1 0	24	17 0	10 0	4 0	1 6	
British Silver, Lead, &c.	26	17 6	9 0	7 6	1 3	16	17 6	9 0	3 6	1 6	} Central Middle.
East Wheal Crofty	56	15 0	8 0	9 6	1 3	43	17 4	8 0	4 0	2 0	
United Mines	89	17 4	10 1	5 5	1 3	69	17 11	9 1	4 3	1 9	
Wheal Jewell	17	17 1	9 2	4 3	1 3	19	17 1	9 11	4 3	1 6	
Hallenbeagle	17	16 8	9 9	3 9	1 6	55	17 9	9 11	4 6	1 6	} Central N.
Polberou Consols	81	17 0	8 0	6 9	0 9	35	17 0	10 0	4 0	1 0	
Wheal Budnick	40	17 8	9 3	9 0	0 9	32	17 9	10 7	4 0	0 9	
Cornubian	16	16 0	11 0	5 0	2 3	10	16 6	11 0	4 0	2 6	Lead Mine ditto.
Polgooth	50	17 0	9 10	4 6	1 0	7	16 11	14 1	3 6	1 9	Eastern District.
Wheal Friendship, Devon	87	17 7	8 0	10 0	1 0	55	17 9	9 6	4 6	1 6	Copper.
Wheal Betsey, Devon	44	16 10	7 0	7 6	1 0	9	16 0	9 0	4 0	1 6	Lead.

1088 " The money received is in all these cases handed over to the parent by the younger boys, and they generally continue to do so beyond the age of eighteen. In some cases, where the boy's earnings are large, he pays a portion of them only in return for his board and lodging (Evidence, p. 848, l. 47) ; and in a few instances the paternal roof is quitted altogether (Evidence, p. 829, l. 30; p. 832, l. 68; Dr. Barham's Report § 191: App. Pt. I. p. 786.)

SURFACE LABOUR IN DRESSING THE ORES OF TIN, COPPER, LEAD, AND ZINC.

Wages.

1089. ALSTON MOOR DISTRICT.—" When Children go to wash ore at nine years of age the usual wages are 4d. or 5d. a-day, and it is customary to advance the Child a penny a day for every additional year of his life. Some years there is a rise of 1½d. or 2d. a-day.

Alston Moor District.

1090. " Some grown men work in the washing, and perform those operations which require strength and skill. They earn 2s. and 2s. 6d. a-day. Some of the overlookers may get 1s. or 2s. a-week more" (Dr. Mitchell, Report, § 219, 20: App. Pt. II., p. 745).

1091. The weekly wages paid to the Young People employed at washing in the mines of T. W. Beaumont, Esq., are stated in detail by Dr. Mitchell (Ibid. § 231-4: p. 747-8). No apprentices are employed in this district on the surface anymore than in underground work. (See also the evidence of Joseph Collingwood, No. 16; Joseph Eddy, No. 39; Stephen Collingwood, No. 12; Ralph Elliott, No. 15; John Appleby, No. 18; Joseph Collingwood, No. 20; Matthew Dawson, No. 25; William Davidson, No. 30, &c.)

1092. LEADHILLS.—In this district the wages of the young workers are, according to their ages and qualifications, 16d., 10d., 9d., 7d., 6d., 5d., 4d., and 3d. per day, to which a trifle for overwork has to be added at the end of the week (J. Fletcher, Esq., Evidence, No. 43: App. Pt. II., p. 866, l. 66).

Scotland.

1093. NORTH WALES.—The young workers in this district get about 2s. a-week at first, but the wages increase as the boys get used to the work; at twelve they will earn from 3s. to 4s. 6d. a-week; and at sixteen, 7s. 6d. or 8s. a-week. Nearly all is paid over to the parents (Evidence, No. 184: p. 455, l. 67. See also No. 189, p. 459, l. 35; No. 148, p. 434, l. 61; No. 179, p. 453, l. 4; No. 195, p. 464, l. 5; No. 139, p. 428, l. 41; No. 150, p. 435, l. 70; No. 154, p. 437, l. 42; No. 166, p. 443, l. 51; No. 170, p. 445, l. 68; &c.)

North Wales.

1094. IRELAND.—The wages of the young workers in this part of the kingdom vary from 3½d. to 8d. per day, but the greater number are making only 4d. or 5d. (Evidence collected by F. Roper, Esq., Nos. 2, 3, 5, 7, 12, 14, 15, 20, 22, 23, 24, 25, 27, 30, 35, 36, 37, 39.) At the latter price, indeed, the services of men may be had in some of the mining localities (See also the Evidence collected by T. Martin, Esq., App. Pt. I., p. 881-3).

Ireland.

11.—*Influence on the Physical Condition of Surface Employment in Dressing Ores.*

Physical Condition.

1095. SOUTH-WESTERN DISTRICT.—" A strong line of demarcation," says the Sub-Commissioner, " must be drawn between the Children and Young Persons

South-Western District.

Surface Labour
in Dressing
the Ores of Tin,
Copper, Lead, and
Zinc.

Physical Condition.

South-Western
District.

employed at the surface and those employed under ground in the mines of the Cornish district, in respect to certain points in their physical condition.

1096. " The *external appearance* of the Children and Young Persons employed at the surface, taken as a class, is that of robust health. The complexion is generally florid, the person well formed, the expression alert and cheerful (Evidence, p. 830, l. 58). Among the girls as they approach towards womanhood there is an inclination to *embonpoint*, and many of them possess a considerable share of personal beauty; in the central district perhaps most remarkably, the features being often handsome. The greater part of the boys are drafted off to under-ground work before the frame is at all fully developed, but they are generally healthy and well-formed as long as they continue at the surface. The abundant supply of fresh air, and the variety of muscular movement, are the main causes of their healthiness and their freedom from deformity respectively. (Dr. Barham's, Report, §§ 199, 200: App Pt. I. p. 789.)

1097. " In *stature*, the difference which exists between those employed in mines, and others, is as regards the females in favour of the former, as has been partly stated already. The use of hammers tends perhaps to the production of some fulness of bust. In a former part of this report the weights of the men in different mines are given, and their stature is spoken of. The tendency of under-ground labour is to check the nutrition of the body, as has been already explained, and the degree of stunting produced will be proportionate to the earliness of the period of growth at which that labour is begun. Those who go under ground when very young often acquire, after a short time, the countenance of much older boys, whilst their size is below the average at their real age; their figures are also more set and angular than is natural in early life.

1098. " The *food* brought to the mines by the Children and Young Persons is for the most part sufficient in quantity for the one meal usually taken by them there, and perhaps for a slight refection between breakfast and dinner. It is coarse in its quality and mode of preparation, and from these causes does not always afford sufficient nutriment (Evidence, p. 821, l. 45; p. 845, l. 53). The hoggans and pasties are described in the Evidence, p. 821, l. 51.

1099. " The Children of both sexes seem to get on very well with this diet. It is chiefly among the females a few years older that dyspeptic affections are frequent. Stews and fish and potatoes mixed together, and sent warm from their homes, are most common in the western districts (Evidence, p. 841, ll. 1, 23; p. 847, l. 37; p. 848, l. 27). The Children appear to find half an hour long enough to take their dinners (Evidence, p. 826, l. 26; p. 836, l. 21), and usually to get a little play as well. The older females complain sometimes that it is too short (Evidence, p. 846, l. 3; p. 851, l. 44).

1100. " The extent of accommodation afforded for warming the food varies much in different mines. The most ample provision is that of ovens for the purpose (Evidence, p. 836, l. 34), but this is unusual. In other instances, as at Fowey Consols, the long iron cylinder, heated by a fire at one end, used for heating the shed in which the meal is taken, serves also to warm the latter. In many places recourse must be had to the house in which the miners' clothes are dried (Evidence, p. 845, l. 34), to the boilers of the steam-engines, or to the smith's shop, to effect this object. In some instances, as at the Fowey Consols, where ovens are kept in the neighbourhood, those who wish to get their pasties effectually warmed, are able to have it done at the charge of a penny a-week.

1101. " Cold water is most commonly the only drink to be obtained, and that is not always very abundant, being sometimes brought from a considerable distance, and distributed in limited quantities (Evidence, p. 845, l. 36). In a few mines there are facilities for obtaining hot water, or even a cup of tea, usually an infusion of indigenous herbs (Evidence, p. 836, l. 35. Ibid. §§ 202—207: App. Pt. I., p. 790).

1102. " The food obtained by the Children and Young Persons at their homes varies very much in quality and abundance with the circumstances of the families. It is too frequently scanty (Evidence, p. 830, ll. 9, 18) as well as innutritious, and is usually very coarsely prepared (Evidence, p. 835, l. 27). Breakfast before going to work in the morning, and supper after their return, are the regular meals for those employed at the surface (Evidence, p. 822, ll. 28, 38, 54; p. 823, ll. 13, 45; p. 845, l. 55. The under-ground boys generally get some food when they reach their homes, at whatever hour that may be: at night some cold potatoes or bread will probably be all that can be obtained. (Appendix A.)

1103. " Where the family is large and very poor it will often happen that the earn-

ings of the Young Persons of either sex will be disposed of in providing absolute
necessaries for the whole party, so that no difference is made in the amount of
nourishment afforded to those employed in hard labour and the younger Children
not yet able to work (Evidence, p. 825, l. 29 ; p. 828, l. 52). Such circumstances
frequently induce the young men to seek a separate residence at the age of seventeen or eighteen ; and the medical man will often be consulted by females who are
feeling the ill effects of being so situated, suffering from painful dyspeptic affections,
arising chiefly from their not having sustenance at all calculated to give them strength
for their laborious life, and seeking a delusive comfort from the stimulus of tea,
which is largely used by all females of the working classes in the West of England. A further cause of the scantiness of their fare will be noticed presently.

SURFACE LABOUR
IN DRESSING
THE ORES OF TIN,
COPPER, LEAD, AND
ZINC.

Physical Condition.

South-Western
District.

1104. " Speaking generally, the *clothing* of the Children and Young Persons employed in these mines is good and sufficient. Among the females a great deal of
attention is paid to dress, increasing with their approach to womanhood ; but even
the younger girls are usually furnished with very decent attire by their friends
(Evidence, p. 850, l. 15). The occupations of the females not being usually very
dirty, the ordinary dress, or one only slightly varied, is worn at the mine ; additional protection is, however, given to the lower part of the legs by wrapping them
in woollen bands in the winter, and often in cotton ones in the summer. A certain
smartness is noticeable in the bonnets, and in the manner of wearing them ; they are
generally small in the winter, and thrown rather back on the head, chiefly made of
some lively-coloured material in some districts, and of straw in others ; whilst in
summer they are commonly large, straight, and projecting, with a long loose border,
such as may afford effectual shelter from the sun. A rather amusing degree of concern for the preservation of the complexion is exhibited by some, who envelop their
faces and throats with handkerchiefs, so as to present something of an invalided
appearance.

1105. " On Sundays, and on any holiday occasion, apparel of a showy and often
expensive description is commonly worn. Girls under the age of eighteen have
not often money at their disposal for any great outlay in this line ; but, without any
disposition to underrate the value of a regard for personal appearance in the article
of dress, as an evidence of self-respect, the writer is obliged to notice the existence
of what may fairly be called a passion for dress, as very extensively diffused among
the young women connected with the mines in every district (Evidence, p. 832,
l. 69). As a medical man, he has often had cases brought under his notice in
which he has been satisfied that disordered health has been mainly induced by coarse
and scanty nourishment, whilst the patients have presented themselves in dresses
only to be procured at very considerable cost. The same love of display is shown
in the wearing of thin shoes and stockings during weather in which they are very un-
suitable, causing a dangerous transition from the thick shoes usually worn by them,
and the legs rolled up in woollen bands just now described. There is reason to
believe that the provision of warm inner garments for the colder season is by no
means correspondent with the outlay on those external ones which may serve to increase the personal attraction of the wearers. Some of the girls are liable to get
wet, especially in the feet, in their employments ; and all are so in coming to the
mines. No provision is ever made there for a change of shoes or stockings under
these circumstances, and the liability to injurious chill is consequently great, particularly to those (a large majority of the whole class) whose labour gives little or
no exercise to the lower limbs. (Evidence, p. 845, l. 18.)

1106. " The work of a large proportion of the boys employed at the surface exposes them to wet and dirt ; and, however wet or dirty they may be, the same
clothes are worn from the time they rise in the morning until bed-time at night ;
and it is well if they are effectually dried before they are put on again on the following day (Evidence, p. 823, l. 10). The clothing is generally sound and sufficiently
decent for labouring boys, and a good protection against cold and wet is commonly
furnished in thick woollen frocks (Evidence, p. 850, l. 53), worn outside during
the winter. The whole body, moreover, is brought into pretty active exercise in
most of their occupations (Ibid. §§ 208-213 : App. Pt. I., p. 790-2).

1107. " *Cleanliness* of person and dress will almost attend as a natural concomi-
tant of that regard to appearance which has been noticed as exhibited by both sexes
—it is accordingly *the rule* among the Children as well as the Young Persons. Of
the latter, the greater part employed on the surface are females. Their work is
not usually very dirty, and even when engaged about it they preserve a very

SURFACE LABOUR
IN DRESSING
THE ORES OF TIN,
COPPER, LEAD, AND
ZINC.

Physical Condition.

South-Western
District.

cleanly appearance. At other times their fresh and clear skin, and well-washed clothing, correspond with the smartness of the articles themselves of their attire. The younger girls are neither equally well clothed nor equally clean; and the work of the greater number (picking) exposes them more to wet and dirt. Still there is generally, even here, a degree of neatness, proving the disposition to do as well as circumstances permit. The little boys are most extensively employed in the midst of mineral mud, but they generally get rid of a great deal of it when their work is over. More might certainly be done in respect of these, both as to person and clothing. Still it is exceedingly rare to meet with an example of squalid filthiness in any member of a miner's family (Ibid. § 214: App. Pt. I., p. 792).

1108. "The generally healthy condition of the Children and Young Persons employed at the surface in these mines has been already noticed. In the principal mining districts comparatively few individuals belonging to families of the poorer class remain unconnected with mining labour during the period of life with which this inquiry is concerned. It is therefore difficult to ascertain whether the *amount of sickness* is greater or less among those working at the surface than among those remaining at home or otherwise employed. The concurrent testimony of medical men, mine agents, and other well-informed parties, is to the effect that no young people are more healthy (Evidence, p. 830, l. 57; p. 835, l. 2; p. 848, l. 56; p. 850, l. 42.) By one medical deponent a comparison is drawn (Evidence, p. 835, l. 9) between the mining and manufacturing girls, to the advantage of the former. Evidence may also be seen that the exchange of the occupation of straw-bonnet making (p. 823, l. 22) and of domestic service (p. 852, l. 41) for surface-labour at a mine, may be positively beneficial to the health. The opinions of other medical men in different districts, equally favourable, may be seen in the Appendix (F).

1109. "On the other hand, a certain amount of sickness is distinctly produced by the work itself, or its attendant circumstances. Many instances of this have been referred to in treating of the particular branches of employment. The depositions of the patients examined furnish many other examples. One of the surgeons of Wheal Vor Mine confirms the statement given in the Evidence (p. 842, l. 42) of the frequency of certain disorders in that mine. (See his answers to queries, Appendix F. Ibid., §§ 216-17: App. Pt. I., p. 792.)

1110. "It seems probable that the ruddiness of hue imparted by constant exposure to fresh air, may give to these boys and girls an appearance of health to a certain extent deceptive. Moreover, as their ailments are, for the most part, of rather acute character, they prevent those who are suffering from them from coming to work, and thus the appearance of the whole body is not rendered less healthy by the admixture of many individuals labouring under disease: but some of these acute disorders prove rapidly fatal, and a greater number pass into incurable structural changes.

1111. "But whatever be the ultimate influence on the average duration of life produced by these surface operations, it is certain that no kind of surgical disease beyond the results of accident is occasioned by them. It would be difficult to find anywhere a class of girls and young women more free from malformation, distortion, or infirmity. The whole body is exceedingly well and equably developed, the muscular movements easy, and the step firm and elastic (Ibid., §§ 219-20: App. Pt. I., p. 793).

1112. "Neither is there any prevalence of medical diseases, acute or chronic. Fever, whether epidemic or sporadic, is infrequent, and, when generally diffused through their neighbourhood, does not affect the Young People employed on mines in any greater proportion than others. Scrofula is not common among this class, atrophy is very rare. There is reason to believe that consumption is more frequent than in non-mining districts; whether it is more frequent among those members of miners' families who are engaged in surface-labour at the mines than among those members who are not so employed, must for the present, as has been before remarked, remain in doubt." (Ibid. § 221: App. Pt. I., p. 793.)

1113. Additional light is thrown upon the physical condition of the whole population in the South-Western Mining Districts by the Tables at pp. 740, 741, 742, 743, 793, and 794 of Dr. Barham's Report. The undersized appearance of the men is remarked by Dr. Mitchell in the Lead Mining District of Alston Moor, as well as by Dr. Barham in the Cornish District.

1114. ALSTON MOOR DISTRICT.—The Sub-Commissioner states, that "the boys at the washing-floors in this district looked well, and seemed to go through their work with great spirit.

1115. "At the national school at Stanhope are about fifty boys and fifty girls; they manifested the usual animation of Children in their march to church, and their countenances announced mental activity and intellect.

1116. "The same observation might be made of the Children of both sexes at the schools supported by the London Lead Company at Nenthead, in Alston Moor, and at Middleton, in Teesdale. In the clothing of the Children economy was evidently the first consideration, and substantial strength was more thought of than ornament; but altogether their clothing seemed quite sufficient.

1117. "The medical witnesses state that the Children are not subject to any particular diseases; so also state the workmen themselves. If any country be favourable to health, we may say so of this.

1118. "Intimately connected with the physical condition is the diet and lodging. As to the diet, it will appear, from the evidence of the witnesses, that it consists much more of vegetable food than amongst the miners of the coal districts. Beer is not nearly so much drunk. In the parish of Hunstonworth, which is seven miles long and three broad, and in which are the works of the Derwent Company, there is not a single beer-shop or public-house of any sort. A miner in the lead-mines, as some of the witnesses have observed, does not require so much food as in the coal-mines, and this arises from want of ventilation to procure him an appetite; and so much the worse.

1119. "The houses of the miners are substantial and well whitewashed, but the furniture is nothing like so valuable as the furniture of the miner in the coal districts; the wages will not afford it" (Dr. Mitchell, Report, §§ 257-62: App. Pt. II., p. 750. Evidence, Nos. 2, 25, 31-33, 40, 42).

1120. We have already noticed the injurious effects of the places called "Lodging Shops," common in some parts of this district, which contain Young Persons as well as adults, and the close, crowded, filthy, and poisonous condition of which would be beyond all belief but for the evidence by which the faithfulness of the picture that has been drawn of them is established. (Dr. Mitchell, Report, § 164: App. Pt. II., p. 740; § 187, p. 742. Evidence, Nos. 38, 39.)

1121. In a room 18 feet in length and about 15 feet in breadth were found "on one side of the room three beds each 6 feet long by about 4½ feet wide, the three beds extending the length of the room; then there were three other beds on the other side; and at the farther end was a seventh bed, extending from the one line of beds to the other. Immediately over these seven beds, and supported on posts, were seven other beds, placed exactly in the same way. The person who slept in each of the six beds next the wall of the upper tier could raise his head only a very little way, on account of the roof. Each of these fourteen beds was intended for two persons, when only few men were employed at the mine, but they might be made to receive three men each; and, in case of need, a boy might lie across at their feet. There was no opening of any sort to let out the foul air. Yet from thirty to forty persons might have to sleep there; the men perspiring from their work, and inhaling the small dust from their clothes floating in clouds. The beds were stuffed with chaff. There were blankets, but no sheets. Though the beds had not been occupied for the three preceding nights the smell was to me utterly intolerable. What the place must be in the summer's nights is, happily for those who have never felt it, utterly inconceivable. The medical men are best able to give a judgment on these matters, but, for my own part, I cannot but believe that these lodging-houses are more destructive than the air of the mines. I should think it no hardship to have to remain 24 hours in a mine, but I should be terrified at being ordered to be shut up a quarter of an hour in the bed-room of a lodging-shop."

1122. LEADHILLS.—In this district the food of the Children is generally oatmeal porridge, butter-milk, and oatmeal cake for breakfast and supper, and for dinner, potatoes with a little butter or milk; scarcely ever flesh meat. The parents are all very poor, and some of the children are poorly clad for their exposed labour, with their clothes and clogs worn out, and too often with bare feet.

1123. "I entered," says Mr. Fletcher, "many of the miners' cottages, in which the principal apartment serves for both bed-room, sitting-room, and kitchen; an arrangement inimical to neatness and cleanliness, and the advantages of which can be appreciated only by bearing in mind the wretched climate and the cost of fuel.

SURFACE LABOUR
IN DRESSING
THE ORES OF TIN,
COPPER, LEAD, AND
ZINC.

Physical Condition.

Alston Moor
District.

Scotland.

SURFACE LABOUR
IN DRESSING
THE ORES OF TIN,
COPPER, LEAD, AND
ZINC.

Physical Condition.

Scotland.

The entrance to these cottages is generally by narrow folding-doors opening into a little sunken porch, communicating with an outer chamber of varying size, used generally for stores of turf, potatoes, &c. Two contiguous beds, sunk into closets, usually occupy the side of the living-room opposite the fire; and in the most comfortable of these rooms are respectable presses, tables, shelves, &c. But others exhibited the extreme of destitution, with floors of earth, beds of heath, and an utter want of bed-clothes. Scarcely any were without books, of which the most modern were productions of the Scottish popular press, and the older, the Scriptures, and some books of divinity of the past century.

1124. "So small is the consumption of animal food at Leadhills, that the butcher who used to be in the place has left it; and when a sheep is killed it falls by a general conspiracy of the principal inhabitants, who bespeak the several portions of it from the man who kills, and who, I was told, might otherwise ' eat it himsel'.' The old men complain that advanced prices, with which their wages have by no means kept pace, prevent their getting meat and butter as they did when a sheep sold for 4s. and butter for 4d. per lb. Scots. But for this deprivation they have been partly compensated by the increased use of milk, as they have reclaimed additional meadow plots for their cows from the sides of the hills around them. Mr. Weir, overseer of the underground works, describes their principal food to be oatmeal (No. 46), and his account of the prevalent mode of living was confirmed by other witnesses, part of whose testimony on this subject is annexed (Nos. 43, 44). It is the habit to dress very decently on holidays.

1125. "The effects resulting to health from mining labour, as here conducted, are by no means favourable. The results are summed up in Dr. Martin's Medico-Statistical Report (No. 47), with which the common opinion of the older inhabitants agrees (No. 46). The children are cleanly for the style of cottage life which prevails generally in North Britain." (J. Fletcher, Esq., Report, App. Pt. II., §§ 15, 17, p. 863; and No. 44, p. 867, l. 5, l. 58.)

1126. NORTH WALES.—The Sub-Commissioner for this district reports:—"The physical condition of the boys is very satisfactory. It is observed that the Welsh in stature do not come up to the standard of the English and Scotch; the observation may be founded on fact and accounted for by the little intermixture of foreign blood, which, till of late years, took place in the principality, at least in the northern parts. The distinctive character which has almost up to the present time been preserved in Wales is likely very soon to be lost. The increase of works, the improved state of the roads, and the general introduction of steam-vessels, have tended to bring into Wales an immense influx of English, Scotch, and Irish, persons of all ranks, who intermarry with the Welsh families. In the course of my inspection I cannot say I met with any appreciable difference in the stature of the Welsh boys. Those employed in the pits and at the mines were at least equal in personal appearance and stature to the children of the same age and station in the same neighbourhood not put to any such labour.

1127. " In respect to food I must observe that the diet in Wales is of a lower order than that of England. Less of animal and more of milk and farinaceous food is used; but everywhere the children have a sufficient quantity of nourishing diet, though in quality it may be esteemed inferior. Children at work in the pits and mines breakfast before they leave home; their dinner is brought to them by their friends, and consists of bread, butter, potatoes, a little bacon occasionally, with milk or broth. They have supper at home on their return from work; most of them have a piece of bread and butter to eat between breakfast and dinner, and between dinner and supper, which is eaten while at work.

1128. "Their physical condition is a proof that they have a sufficiency of nutritive food to maintain health and strength, and their food is certainly both in quality and quantity equal to that which children of their station and neighbourhood have who do no work; their clothing is in most instances well calculated to their work and station. At neither the pit nor the mines is it usual for the children to have a change of clothing to put on after work; it may not be requisite in the pits, but at the mines, where they work in the open air in all sorts of weather, a change would be desirable, especially as the working clothes must be loaded with the dust of lead-ore.

1129. "It is difficult to say whether the amount of sickness amongst these Children be greater than amongst the children of the poorer classes employed or remaining at home unemployed, as I found but few who were not employed in the pits or at the lead-mines; those so employed are a healthy class, and evidently suffer nothing from the nature of their work, with the exception of the liability to the peculiar state of the bowels which the children employed in picking and washing the lead-ore are occasionally subject to. It is, however, easily removed by aperients, and is rarely dangerous, as is proved by the evidence of the medical men in Mold and Holywell, who also prove that the surgical diseases prevalent among the Children in question are only such as are caused by accident, as burns, bruises, dislocations, and fractures, and that hernia, distortion of the spine or joints, or any other maladies to which human nature is liable, are no more common than amongst other children not so employed. Nor are acute medical diseases found to prevail more amongst Children in the mines and pits than others. Mr. Roberts, surgeon, at Ruabon, states that fever, when once in a collier's house, generally runs through the family; and in crowded villages through all the families. He attributes this to no peculiarity brought on by the nature of their work, but to the smallness of their cottages, the want of due ventilation, the total neglect of external cleanliness and drainage, the cottage floors being on a level with the ground, and the pig-sty and dunghill close to the door. The medical men allege that the colliers and miners bear the usual means of cure, such as bleeding and depletion in inflammatory diseases, and amputation when necessary, as well as others differently employed." (H. H. Jones, Esq., Report, §§ 35-8: App. Pt. II., p. 369-70.)

Surface Labour in Dressing the Ores of Tin, Copper, Lead, and Zinc.
——
Physical Condition.
——
North Wales.

1130 IRELAND.—The appearance of the Young People at work on the surface in this district is described as being generally that of robust health, although they are without shoes or stockings, commonly without any change of clothes, get only two meals of potatoes a-day, with sometimes a little butter-milk, and inhabit the wretched cabins which shelter a teeming population even on the sides of the poorest and remotest mountains. (Reports and Evidence from F. Roper, Esq., *passim*, and from T. Martin, Esq., App. Pt. II., No. 28, p. 881, l. 66; No. 42, p. 883, l. 391.)

Ireland.

12.—*Surface Employment of Children and Young Persons in washing Ores in the less important Mining Districts.*

1131. DERBYSHIRE.—The Young People employed in dressing lead ores in the neighbourhood of Crich in Derbyshire are too few, and their labour so precisely similar to that of the washers in the Alston Moor District, to demand notice, beyond the few words of the Sub-Commissioner in referring to his evidence:— "Several," he says, "are employed in dressing the ore, that is, washing it after it has been ground, and passing it through riddles or sieves. They work eleven hours, but out of that time are allowed half an hour for breakfast and half an hour for dinner. They are paid weekly in cash, and seldom work overtime; if they do, they are paid for it according to their weekly wages. The places of work are open sheds, but there are cabins with fires, to which they can retire for their meals, or, if they prefer it, they may go home to them. I did not hear of a single accident, nor do I conceive that any could occur. They have the same holidays as at the collieries, with the addition of the miner's festival on May Day. In external appearance these young people are robust and well formed; and in every respect they are a much healthier and apparently happier body of Children than those employed in the neighbouring collieries. They are full as well clothed as other labouring Children; and, considering the nature of their employment, they are cleanly." (J. M. Fellows, Esq., Report, §§ 95-104: App. Pt. II., p. 259. Evidence, pp. 360-64.)

Labour in connexion with less important Mines.
——
Derbyshire.

1132. ECTON MINES.—At the Ecton lead, copper, and zinc mines, belonging to the Duke of Devonshire, in the parish of Whitoon, near Leek, there are seventeen Children and Young People employed in the dressing of ores, of whom a favourable account is given (S. S. Scriven, Esq., Report and Evidence, App. Pt. II., pp. 129, 134).

North Staffordshire.

3. LABOUR IN WORKS FOR SMELTING THE ORES OF TIN, COPPER, LEAD, AND ZINC.

1133. In the lead districts, in which the ores are generally smelted near the spot where they are raised, no Children are employed in the smelting department, and even the Young Persons who follow this occupation commonly approach adult age before they commence the work; few are found under eighteen years of age, and none under sixteen, unless it be a boy or two employed to wheel in materials. The whole of the circumstances of this branch of labour, in the Alston Moor district,

Labour in Works for Smelting Ores of Tin, Copper, Lead, and Zinc.

are described in detail by Dr. Mitchell (Report, App. Pt. II., p. 733-40); in the Lead Hills neighbourhood, by Mr. Fletcher (Report and Evidence, App. Pt. II., p. 862, § 7; No. 45, p. 867, l. 69; and No. 47, p. 870, l. 21; and in North Wales, by Mr. H. H. Jones (App. Pt. II., p. 434-45). It here remains only for us to notice the smelting processes as connected with the ores of Cornwall when brought to SOUTH WALES, especially those of copper; for the metal derived from those of tin becomes at once the subject of a considerable manufacture, the employment of Children and Young Persons in which will demand express notice in our second Report.

1.—*Age, Sex, and Number of the Children and Young Persons employed in Copper Works in South Wales.*

Age, Sex, and Number.

South Wales.

1134. It has been already stated that the copper ores of Cornwall are shipped to the coal district of South Wales to be smelted. The following abstract from returns made by six different copper works in this district will show the number of the Children and Young Persons employed in these works, and the proportion of the boys and girls : —

Total Number of Children and Young Persons.		Name of the Works.	Adults.		Young Persons.		Children.		Total.	
M.	F.		M.	F.	M.	F.	M.	F.	M.	F.
40	..	Middle Bank Copper-works .	240	..	27	..	13	..	280	..
54	2	White Rock ditto . . .	196	4	34	1	20	1	250	6
133	38	Hafod ditto	345	45	92	38	41	..	478	83
87	7	Morfa ditto	484	5	74	6	13	1	571	12
51	1	Llanelly Copper-works . .	230	3	30	1	21	..	281	4
21	..	Cambrian Copper-works .	110	..	13	..	8	..	131	..
386	48		1605	57	270	46	116	2	1901	105
434									2096	

1135. From this table it appears that of the total number of work-people employed, the proportion of Children and Young Persons is only one-sixth; and that of these, the proportion of girls is not more than one in ten; the Hafod works alone employing any considerable number. The common age at which Children commence labour in these works is from nine to ten. (R. W. Jones, Esq., Evidence, Nos. 223, 224, 230, 232, 234, 238, 241: App. Pt. II.)

2.—*Nature of the Employment in Copper Works.*

Nature of Employment.

1136. The different occupations of the Children and Young Persons in the copper-works is thus described:—"The youngest boys are employed to 'pickle' the copper sheets after they have been rolled. The sheets weigh from 4 lbs. to 12 lbs. each. The boys take the sheets in their hands and dip them into a copper pan filled with the 'pickle' or liquor; they then put them at the front of a furnace, and a man puts them into the furnace and takes them out again when hot with tongs, and dips them into clear water, and lays them on the ground at the side of the water-pit; the boys then take them and put them up to the front of the furnace to dry. Two boys are employed at each pickling-furnace; there are two pickling-furnaces; each furnace pickles about two tons of copper sheets, which are thus handled by the two boys in a day when in full work. The pickling-furnaces are near together, and in the same building as the mill, just behind 'the rolls.' The oldest boys are employed behind the rolls; their employment is to receive the metal in 'tongs' as it comes through the rolls, and return it over the rolls back to the 'roller-men,' who bring it in the first instance from the furnace-men to the rolls; when the plates or sheets are heavy four boys are employed together, but when the sheets are light one boy does it." (Ibid. No. 245: App. Pt. II., p. 688, l. 31).

1137. "The hardest work to which the boys are put is working ' the calciners' [the furnaces in which the copper-ore is first calcined]. They are mostly worked by boys from thirteen to sixteen years old: their turn continues for twenty-four hours, and they are obliged to tend the furnace every two hours; they can sleep for an hour, perhaps two or three times in the night. They work six turns or 'watches'

LABOUR IN WORKS
FOR SMELTING
ORES OF TIN,
COPPER, LEAD, AND
ZINC.

*Nature of
Employment.*

South Wales.

one week and eight the other, and get 2*s.* 2*d.* for each double watch of twenty-four hours.

1138. " Next to the calciners the hardest work is wheeling coal and ashes to and from the smelting-furnaces. This is mostly done by girls from thirteen to eighteen years old. They begin their work at six in the morning, and if they can finish wheeling enough for their furnace they leave from three to four in the afternoon, but some stay as late as six or after. They get about 5*s.* per week. The time they work each day is determined by the quantity of work they do ; when what is required is done they leave. No girls work at night, nor boys but those at the calciners. They [the boys at the calciners] also work every other Sunday, and some girls that are wheeling ore to them do the same.

1139, "The youngest boys and girls are employed to wheel the coal and ashes for the furnaces which are worked by their fathers ; and the most of the Children employed are the Children of the workmen, or those who have worked here.

1140. " We don't consider that the children are over-worked here, but we don't think it is a fit place for girls to work at, as it unfits them for all other work ; we should not like to bring our daughters up in the works." (Ibid. No. 219, App. Pt. II., p. 683, l. 27.)

3.—*Hours of Work in Copper Works.*

1041. In the rolling-mills the regular hours of work are fourteen, namely, from six in the morning to eight at night ; over-work is not reckoned until past nine, after which hour the labour is sometimes continued to eleven, and even twelve o'clock. (Ibid. App. Pt. II., Nos. 245-6 *et seq.*) In some rolling-mills night-work is common, a night-set of boys and men succeeding to the day-set. (Ibid. No. 239, App. Pt. II., p. 686, l. 43.)

1142. " There is a peculiarity in the hours of work, as practised by the men and boys who attend the smelting and calcining furnaces in copper-works, which is seldom found in other works. These persons continue on duty for twenty-four hours, working (as described by some of the boys whom I examined at the Havod) ' from six o'clock one morning to six o'clock the next morning,' and sleeping in the works near the furnaces during the night, for three or four ' spells' of an hour each, being awakened at stated periods to attend the furnaces, by a watchman employed for that purpose ; and once a fortnight, in order to change the ' turn,' or days of working, some of these persons work what they call the ' long watch,' or from Saturday morning to Monday morning, being forty-eight hours, which period they have on the alternate fortnight for rest and recreation.

1143. " This system would seem extremely laborious and fatiguing, but the nature of the work being such as to allow them to have three or four hours' sleep during the night, and to have every other day to themselves, the men generally prefer it to any other regulation of the hours of working ; some, however, are often inclined to mitigate the fatigue of the ' long watch,' particularly the boys, on which occasions there is always a ' spare hand ' ready to relieve them on the ' night watch,' on receiving the pay for the time he is so engaged." (R. W. Jones, Esq., Report, §§ 13, 14 : p. 680.)

4.—*Working of Copper Calcining Furnaces on Sundays.*

1144. This mode of working the calcining furnaces has led to the practice of keeping them in work on Sundays as well as on other days, as the blast furnaces are in some of the iron works of this same district, and in the South Staffordshire and Shropshire districts. But the practice of working the calcining furnaces on Sundays is not universal in this district ; the Sub-Commissioner stating that there are many works in which these furnaces are kept during the Sundays on what is called "deadfire ;" and expressing it as his opinion, that there is no necessity for the employment of any Children or Young Persons on those days. He reports on this subject as follows :—

1145. " The above-mentioned mode of working makes it necessary for the furnace-men (the calciner-men in particular) to be at work all day on the Sunday once a fortnight, and some on every Sunday ; but at many works all the furnaces, including the calciners, are on Sundays suspended from *active operations,* and simply kept on ' deadfire,' as it is termed, attended only by watchmen, one of whom generally serves two or more of such fires, until the hands resume their regular work on the Sunday night or Monday morning.

LABOUR IN WORKS
FOR SMELTING
ORES OF TIN,
COPPER, LEAD, AND
ZINC.

*Working of Copper
Calcining Furnaces
on Sundays.*

South Wales.

1146. " In my own opinion very little is actually required to be done on Sunday in order to keep the copper-works in action, and none, of necessity, on the parts of *Children, Young Persons, or Females*.   I regret, however, that it will be observed, from the evidence I have collected, that Sunday-labour is practised at some works to a considerable extent, and that several young persons of both sexes are allowed to work every Sunday, ' the same as on other days, until three or four o'clock in the afternoon,' by which they are precluded from attending the Sunday-schools, and are ' often too tired' on the Sunday afternoon to attend public worship at either church or chapel" (Ibid. App. Pt. II., §§ 13, 15, and 17 : p. 680).

5.—*Meal Hours in Copper Works.*

Meal Hours.

1147. An hour and a half is allowed out of each day in the rolling mills for meals. Tea is very commonly brought to the works, and taken as occasion may offer. (Ibid. *passim.*)

6.—*Wages of Children and Young Persons in Copper Works.*

Wages.

1148. The following are the wages commonly obtained in the copper works, per week :—

	s.	d.	s.	d.
Boys from thirteen to eighteen . .	3	6 to	10	0
Girls from thirteen to eighteen . .	3	0 to	7	6
Children (girls and boys) . . .	3	0 to	5	0

(R. W. Jones, Esq., Evidence, Nos. 220, 221, 222, 223, 224, 227, 234, 237, 238, 240, 241, 242, 245, 246.)

7.—*Physical Condition of Children and Young Persons in Copper Works.*

Physical Condition.

1149. Notwithstanding the deleterious effects of the copper-smoke upon vegetable and animal life, as above described, the inhalation of it does not appear to operate prejudicially upon human health, as will be observed by the testimony of the work-people and agents who reside around the works, and of the medical gentlemen of the neighbourhood.   Mr. Edward Budd, the intelligent agent of the Havod Copper Works (one of the largest establishments), speaking of the health of the men observes —" They are generally very healthy, seldom or never attacked by epidemics or agues ; many live to a great age, some above ninety ; and the deaths among the workmen in this establishment, in the last four years, did not exceed 1¼ per cent. per annum ; not one died during the raging cholera in 1832, although many were attacked ; those dwelling close to the works are generally the most healthy ; and the doctor attends our people at one-third less per month than the colliers pay ;"—which statement is borne out by the evidence of Mr. W. P. Evans, the surgeon of the works, and of G. G. Bird, Esq., M.D., of Swansea, who has extensively practised in the immediate neighbourhood of copper-works for the last fifteen years" (R. W. Jones, Esq., Report, §§ 9, 10 : App. Pt. II., p. 679).

*Employment in
Smelting Places of
minor Importance.*

North Wales.

8.—*Employment of Children and Young Persons in Copper Works in the less important Smelting Places.*

1150. NORTH WALES.—The copper works in this district are chiefly in the neighbourhood of Holywell, and it appears from the evidence that both night-work and working over time is very general in these works.   For example in the copper manufactories of Pascoe Grenfell and Co., and Newton, Lyon, and Co., they work in night and day sets in alternate weeks, and frequently make overtime beside.   Referring to the evidence, pp. 436—444, for the details of this system, we may state briefly, in the words of the Sub-Commissioner, that he " examined a great many of the boys and men employed in these works, and they all confirm the previous evidence as to the frequency of working over-hours, and of continuing at times to work for twenty-four and thirty-six hours successively; but they are all looking healthy and well, and agreed together in opinion, that though frequently tired, weary, and exhausted by the work, yet that their health is not affected ; they agreed that the boys are well treated when at work, and wages well paid ; and that any measure to prevent night-work, and to shorten the hours of work, would be unfavourably received by parents, and even the boys themselves. The boys in this work, with but few exceptions, can read and write, but are notwithstanding very ignorant: their only opportunity for cultivating the understanding is in the Sunday-school" (H. H. Jones, Esq., Evidence, No. 168: App. Pt. II., p. 444, l. 69).

1151. CHEADLE.—The evidence taken by Mr. Scriven concerning the Cheadle Brass and Copper Foundry is in every respect favourable, (Evidence, App. Pt. II., p. 142, ll. 19, 32, 43).

LABOUR IN WORKS FOR SMELTING ORES OF TIN, COPPER, LEAD, AND ZINC.

Employment in Smelting Places of minor Importance.

Cheadle.

From the whole of the Evidence which has been collected, and of which we have thus endeavoured to give a digest, we find,—

In regard to COAL MINES—

1. That instances occur in which Children are taken into these mines to work as early as four years of age, sometimes at five, and between five and six, not unfrequently between six and seven, and often from seven to eight, while from eight to nine is the ordinary age at which employment in these mines commences.

2. That a very large proportion of the persons employed in carrying on the work of these mines is under thirteen years of age; and a still larger proportion between thirteen and eighteen.

3. That in several districts female Children begin to work in these mines at the same early ages as the males.

4. That the great body of the Children and Young Persons employed in these mines are of the families of the adult workpeople engaged in the pits, or belong to the poorest population in the neighbourhood, and are hired and paid in some districts by the workpeople, but in others by the proprietors or contractors.

5. That there are in some districts also a small number of parish apprentices, who are bound to serve their masters until twenty-one years of age, in an employment in which there is nothing deserving the name of skill to be acquired, under circumstances of frequent ill-treatment, and under the oppressive condition that they shall receive only food and clothing, while their free companions may be obtaining a man's wages.

6. That in many instances much that skill and capital can effect to render the place of work unoppressive, healthy, and safe, is done, often with complete success, as far as regards the healthfulness and comfort of the mines; but that to render them perfectly safe does not appear to be practicable by any means yet known; while in great numbers of instances their condition in regard both to ventilation and drainage is lamentably defective.

7. That the nature of the employment which is assigned to the youngest Children, generally that of "trapping," requires that they should be in the pit as soon as the work of the day commences, and, according to the present system, that they should not leave the pit before the work of the day is at an end.

8. That although this employment scarcely deserves the name of labour, yet, as the Children engaged in it are commonly excluded from light and

CONCLUSIONS.

are always without companions, it would, were it not for the passing and repassing of the coal carriages, amount to solitary confinement of the worst order.

9. That in those districts in which the seams of coal are so thick that horses go direct to the workings, or in which the side passages from the workings to the horseways are not of any great length, the lights in the main ways render the situation of these Children comparatively less cheerless, dull, and stupifying; but that in some districts they remain in solitude and darkness during the whole time they are in the pit, and, according to their own account, many of them never see the light of day for weeks together during the greater part of the winter season, excepting on those days in the week when work is not going on, and on the Sundays.

10. That at different ages, from six years old and upwards, the hard work of pushing and dragging the carriages of coal from the workings to the main ways, or to the foot of the shaft, begins; a labour which all classes of witnesses concur in stating requires the unremitting exertion of all the physical power which the young workers possess.

11. That, in the districts in which females are taken down into the coa. mines, both sexes are employed together in precisely the same kind of labour, and work for the same number of hours; that the girls and boys, and the young men and young women, and even married women and women with child, commonly work almost naked, and the men, in many mines, quite naked; and that all classes of witnesses bear testimony to the demoralizing influence of the employment of females underground.

12. That, in the East of Scotland, a much larger proportion of Children and Young Persons are employed in these mines than in other districts, many of whom are girls; and that the chief part of their labour consists in carrying the coals on their backs up steep ladders.

13. That when the workpeople are in full employment, the regular hours of work for Children and Young Persons are rarely less than eleven; more often they are twelve; in some districts they are thirteen; and in one district they are generally fourteen and upwards.

14. That in the great majority of these mines night-work is a part of the ordinary system of labour, more or less regularly carried on according to the demand for coals, and one which the whole body of evidence shows to act most injuriously both on the physical and moral condition of the workpeople, and more especially on that of the Children and Young Persons.

15. That the labour performed daily for this number of hours, though it cannot strictly be said to be continuous, because, from the nature of the employment, intervals of a few minutes necessarily occur during which the muscles are not in active exertion, is nevertheless generally uninterrupted by any regular time set apart for rest and refreshment; what food is taken in the pit being eaten as best it may while the labour continues.

16. That in well-regulated mines, in which in general the hours of work are the shortest, and in some few of which from half an hour to an hour is

regularly set apart for meals, little or no fatigue is complained of after an ordinary day's work, when the Children are ten years old and upwards; but in other instances great complaint is made of the feeling of fatigue, and the workpeople are never without this feeling, often in an extremely painful degree.

17. That in many cases the Children and Young Persons have little cause of complaint in regard to the treatment they receive from the persons in authority in the mine, or from the colliers; but that in general the younger Children are roughly used by their older companions; while in many mines the conduct of the adult colliers to the Children and Young Persons who assist them is harsh and cruel; the persons in authority in these mines, who must be cognizant of this ill-usage, never interfering to prevent it, and some of them distinctly stating that they do not conceive that they have any right to do so.

18. That, with some exceptions, little interest is taken by the coal owners in the Children and Young Persons employed in their works after the daily labour is over; at least little is done to afford them the means of enjoying innocent amusement and healthful recreation.

19. That in all the coal-fields accidents of a fearful nature are extremely frequent; and that the returns made to our own queries, as well as the registry tables, prove that of the workpeople who perish by such accidents, the proportion of Children and Young Persons sometimes equals and rarely falls much below that of adults.

20. That one of the most frequent causes of accidents in these mines is the want of superintendence by overlookers or otherwise to see to the security of the machinery for letting down and bringing up the work-people, the restriction of the number of persons that ascend and descend at a time, the state of the mine as to the quantity of noxious gas in it, the efficiency of the ventilation, the exactness with which the air-door keepers perform their duty, the places into which it is safe or unsafe to go with a naked lighted candle, and the security of the proppings to uphold the roof, &c.

21. That another frequent cause of fatal accidents in coal mines is the almost universal practice of intrusting the closing of the air-doors to very young Children.

22. That there are many mines in which the most ordinary precautions to guard against accidents are neglected, and in which no money appears to be expended with a view to secure the safety, much less the comfort, of the workpeople.

23. That there are moreover two practices peculiar to a few districts which deserve the highest reprobation, namely,—first, the practice not unknown in some of the smaller mines in Yorkshire, and common in Lancashire, of employing ropes that are unsafe for letting down and drawing up the workpeople; and second, the practice, occasionally met with in Yorkshire, and common in Derbyshire and Lancashire, of employing boys at the steam-engines for letting down and drawing up the workpeople.

2 L

24. That in general the Children and Young Persons who work in these mines have sufficient food, and, when above ground, decent and comfortable clothing, their usually high rate of wages securing to them these advantages; but in many cases, more especially in some parts of Yorkshire, in Derbyshire, in South Gloucestershire, and very generally in the East of Scotland, the food is poor in quality, and insufficient in quantity; the Children themselves say that they have not enough to eat; and the Sub-Commissioners describe them as covered with rags, and state that the common excuse they make for confining themselves to their homes on the Sundays, instead of taking recreation in the fresh air, or attending a place of worship, is that they have no clothes to go in; so that in these cases, notwithstanding the intense labour performed by these Children, they do not procure even sufficient food and raiment: in general, however, the Children who are in this unhappy case are the Children of idle and dissolute parents, who spend the hard-earned wages of their offspring at the public house.

25. That the employment in these mines commonly produces in the first instance an extraordinary degree of muscular development accompanied by a corresponding degree of muscular strength; this preternatural development and strength being acquired at the expense of the other organs, as is shown by the general stunted growth of the body.

26. That partly by the severity of the labour and the long hours of work, and partly through the unhealthy state of the place of work, this employment, as at present carried on in all the districts, deteriorates the physical constitution; in the thin-seam mines, more especially, the limbs become crippled and the body distorted; and in general the muscular powers give way, and the workpeople are incapable of following their occupation, at an earlier period of life than is common in other branches of industry.

27. That by the same causes the seeds of painful and mortal diseases are very often sown in childhood and youth; these, slowly but steadily developing themselves, assume a formidable character between the ages of thirty and forty; and each generation of this class of the population is commonly extinct soon after fifty.

When we consider the extent of this branch of industry, the vast amount of capital embarked in it, and the intimate connexion in which it stands with almost all the other great branches of trade and manufacture, as a main source of our national wealth and greatness, it is satisfactory to have established, by indubitable evidence, the two following conclusions :—

1. That the coal mine, when properly ventilated and drained, and when both the main and the side passages are of tolerable height, is not only not unhealthy, but, the temperature being moderate and very uniform, it is, considered as a place of work, more salubrious and even agreeable than that in which many kinds of labour are carried on above ground.

2. That the labour in which Children and Young Persons are chiefly employed in coal mines, namely, in pushing the loaded carriages of coals

from the workings to the mainways or to the foot of the shaft, so far
from being in itself an unhealthy employment, is a description of exercise
which, while it greatly develops the muscles of the arms, shoulders, chest,
back, and legs, without confining any part of the body in an unnatural
and constrained posture, might, but for the abuse of it, afford an equally
healthful excitement to all the other organs ; the physical injuries produced by it, as it is at present carried on, independently of those which
are caused by imperfect ventilation and drainage, being chiefly attributable to the early age at which it commences, and to the length of time
during which it is continued.

There is, however, one case of peculiar difficulty, viz. that in which all
the subterranean roadways, and especially the side passages, are below a certain
height: by the Evidence collected under this Commission, it is proved that there
are coal mines at present in work in which these passages are so small, that even
the youngest Children cannot move along them without crawling on their hands
and feet, in which unnatural and constrained posture they drag the loaded carriages after them; and yet, as it is impossible, by any outlay compatible with a
profitable return, to render such coal mines, happily not numerous nor of great
extent, fit for human beings to work in, they never will be placed in such a
condition, and consequently they never can be worked without inflicting great
and irreparable injury on the health of the Children.

In regard to IRONSTONE MINES, we find—

> That on account of the greater weight of the material to be removed, the
> labour in these mines, which are worked on a system similar to that of
> the coal mines, is still more severe than that in the latter, and renders
> the employment of older and stronger Children a matter of absolute
> necessity; while the ironstone pits are in general less perfectly ventilated
> and drained than the coal mines, and are, therefore, still more unhealthy,
> producing the same physical deterioration and the same diseases, but in
> a more intense degree.

In regard to BLAST FURNACES, for reducing the ores of iron, we find—

> That the operations connected with these works involve the absolute neces-
> sity of night work; that Children and Young Persons invariably work
> at night with the adults; that the universal practice is for one set of
> workpeople to work one week during the day, and the same set to work
> the following week during the night; and that there is, moreover, in
> addition to the evil of alternate weeks of night work, a custom bearing
> with extreme hardship upon Children and Young Persons, namely, that
> of continuing the work without any interruption whatever during the
> Sunday, and thus rendering every alternate Sunday the day during which
> the labour of one set of workpeople is continued for twenty-four hours in
> succession ; a custom which still prevails, notwithstanding that a consider-
> able proportion of the proprietors have dispensed with the attendance of
> the workpeople during a certain number of hours on the Sunday,
> without disadvantage to their works.

In regard to UNDERGROUND LABOUR IN TIN, COPPER, LEAD, AND ZINC MINES, we find—

1. That very few Children are employed in any kind of underground work in these mines before they are twelve years old, and that in many cases even the young men do not commence underground work until they are eighteen years of age and upwards.

2. That there is no instance in the whole kingdom of any girl or woman being employed in underground work in these mines.

3. That it is in the Cornish district alone that Children and Young Persons of any age are constantly employed under ground in considerable numbers.

4. That, in general, the Children and Young Persons employed in these mines have sufficient food, and decent and comfortable clothing.

5. That employment in these mines does not, in general, produce any apparent injury to the young worker during the period of boyhood and adolescence, but that his employment is essentially, and in every mode in which it has hitherto been carried on, necessarily injurious in after life.

6. That the very general and early deterioration and failure of the health and strength of those who have followed this occupation from boyhood and youth, is increased by certain circumstances which are not necessarily connected with the nature of the employment; among these may be reckoned the practice, almost universal in these mines, of associating the Young Persons in partnership with the adult miners, by which the former are stimulated to exertions greatly beyond their age and powers; and though these Young People, thus excited, work with spirit and without apparent injury for some time, yet in a few years it is proved by experience that they have expended the whole capital of their constitution.

7. That this result is materially hastened by the fatigue of climbing the ladders; these being, with few exceptions, the only means by which the miners can go to and return from their places of work.

8. That these, however, are only the accessory causes of the general and rapid deterioration of the health and strength of the miners; since the primary and ever active agent which principally produces this result is the noxious air of the places in which the work is carried on; the difficulties connected with the purification and renovation of this air, and with the whole subject of ventilation, being incomparably greater in the mines in question than in coal mines.

9. That the ultimate effect of the disadvantageous circumstances under which the miner is obliged to pursue his laborious occupation, is the production of certain diseases (seated chiefly in the organs of respiration), by which he is rendered incapable of following his work, and by which his existence is terminated at an earlier period than is common in other branches of industry, not excepting even that of the collier.

With regard to the surface employments connected with DRESSING THE ORES OF TIN, COPPER, LEAD, AND ZINC, we find—

That these employments, though entered into at very early ages, and in the Cornish district by great numbers of girls as well as boys, are wholly free from the evils connected with underground work; that, with the exception of a very injurious exposure to the inclemency of the weather, which might be obviated by a small expenditure in providing shelter, and with the exception of two or three occupations, such as those of "bucking" and "jigging," for the manual labour of which the substitution of machinery is gradually taking place, there is nothing in this branch of mining industry injurious, oppressive, or incompatible with the maintenance even of robust health, which indeed is described as the general condition of the workpeople; the Children and Young Persons thus employed having commonly sufficient food, and warm and decent clothing, being subjected to no harsh or tyrannical treatment, and enjoying an almost complete immunity from any serious danger.

With regard to the works for SMELTING ORES OF TIN, COPPER, LEAD, AND ZINC, we find—

That in smelting the ores of lead, near the places at which they are raised, no Children and very few Young Persons are engaged, while those employed in the tin works will require a separate notice in treating of manufactures; but that in the copper works of South Wales, in which the Cornish ores are smelted, and in those of North Wales, which reduce the ores raised in their vicinity, a number of Children and Young Persons are employed, from nine years of age and upwards (in South Wales girls as well as boys), of whom those engaged at the calcining furnaces regularly work with the men twenty-four hours consecutively, on alternate days, without excepting the Sunday; a term of work which is sometimes extended to thirty-six hours, and even to forty-eight hours, when, as in South Wales, the "long watch" includes the Sunday.

We have thus endeavoured to present a faithful account of the "actual state, condition, and treatment" of the Children and Young Persons employed in the "Collieries and Mines" of the United Kingdom, and "of the effects of such employment on their Bodily Health:" the effects of this employment on their "Morals," it appears to us, will best be shown by bringing them into view in our next Report, in connexion with the intellectual, moral, and religious state of the whole of that portion of the working population which is included under the terms of our Commission.

All which we humbly certify to Your Majesty.

THOˢ. TOOKE.
T. SOUTHWOOD SMITH.
LEONARD HORNER.
ROBT. J. SAUNDERS.

Westminster, April 21, 1842.

APPENDIX.

INSTRUCTIONS

From the Central Board of the Children's Employment Commission to the Sub-Commissioners.

GENTLEMEN,

THE object of the present Commission is to inquire into the employment and condition of all Children of the poorer classes, not under the protection of the Factories' Regulation Act, who are employed in any description of mining and manufacturing labour whatsoever, in which they work together in numbers.

By the term Children is to be understood those who have not completed the Thirteenth year of their age.—(See " Supplemental Instructions," p. 7.)

The investigation being instituted for the purpose of obtaining correct and complete information as to how far the present well-being of the Children who are its object, and their future health, usefulness, and happiness, are promoted, injured, or endangered, by the course of labour to which they are subjected during the period of Childhood, you will endeavour, by all the means at your command, to ascertain fully their actual condition, which you will faithfully describe; and you will endeavour to discriminate as accurately as possible how far that condition is directly or indirectly the consequence of their employment.

A slight consideration is sufficient to show that in the wide field of inquiry opened by the terms of this Commission are included very dissimilar employments, and that there must exist a great diversity in the condition of the Children engaged in them. The main duty which you have undertaken to perform is, to collect the most full and complete evidence which it is practicable to obtain, as to the number and nature of those employments, the distinguishing peculiarities of each, and the nature and extent of the evils which may result to the Children, whether from the tenderness of their age, the peculiarities of sex, the severity or duration of their labour, the insufficiency of their food and clothing, the inadequate time allowed for their meals, or the absence of any opportunity during the twenty-four hours for healthful recreation, and for religious, moral, and intellectual culture.

The principal subjects which will demand your careful investigation are the following:—

1.—AGES AND NUMBER OF CHILDREN.

You will ascertain the number of the Children employed in each of the Establishments which you may visit; the youngest age at which any Child is employed; and the number in each year of age, from the youngest to those who have completed their Thirteenth year.

It is of great importance that you should see the Children at their work; and if among those at work you observe any persons whom you consider from their appearance not to have completed the Thirteenth year of their age, you will examine whether they have been included in the Lists to be returned to the Commissioners in the tabular form, of which a copy is annexed; and if not, you will endeavour to ascertain their real age, and correct the Return accordingly.

The determination of the *real* age of the Children must be an object of your special attention. You will find many who do not know their own age; and a large proportion will be unable to prove their age by a baptismal certificate. In any case of doubt you will of course adopt the best means which circumstances admit to obtain the nearest approximation to the real age.

2.—HOURS OF WORK.

You will ascertain the regular hours during which the Children work, namely, at what hour they commence in the morning, and at what hour they leave off at night, and whether these hours vary at different seasons.

You will also report—

[margin note:] APPENDIX.
Instructions to the Sub-Commissioners.

Whether they work over-time; if so, the greatest number of hours they work over-time, and the frequency with which they are forced or induced so to work.

Whether any and what proportion of their work is night-work; that is, between nine o'clock at night and five o'clock in the morning.

Whether there are any and what circumstances of *occasional* occurrence in relation to their work which render their labour more oppressive at one time than at another; the nature and extent of the pressure at those periods; and whether such pressure is to any and what degree absolutely unavoidable, or how far it might be prevented or diminished by greater care and forethought on the part of those by whom they are employed.

3.—Meals.

You will ascertain the time allowed to the Children for meals; whether it is uniformly the same in summer and winter; whether the Children, or any of them, and what proportion, leave the place of work and go to their own houses to take their meals; and whether there is any accommodation in the building for the workpeople to wash, change their clothes, &c., on going to their meals.

You will inquire also whether the work and machinery are stopped during each meal; whether any persons are employed at meal-times to clean machinery, and if so, the age of the persons thus employed; whether this is an essential arrangement, and why; and whether, if the persons engaged in this office be Children, time is allowed them from their work to make up the regular meal-times taken by the adults.

4.—Nature of Employment.

You will, in each case, give a particular description of the different kinds of Work in which the Children are employed, specifying the numbers and ages of the Children so employed.

You will carefully inquire whether any branch of manufacture carried on in the Establishment is unfavourable to health, and why; and if any Children are employed in it, at what ages, and for what number of hours daily.

5.—State of the Place of Work.

You will examine whether the state of the place in which the labour of the Children is carried on is healthy or unhealthy; whether the air which they usually respire while at their work is rendered offensive by the situation or neglected state of drains, privies, &c.; and, as materially influencing the condition of the Children, the state of the neighbourhood as to dampness or uncleanliness.

You will also inquire what are the effects upon the Children of their exclusion from daylight and the open air when employed in mines, and their exposure to subterraneous damp

6.—Accidents.

You will endeavour to ascertain the number of Accidents that have happened, in the place in which the work is carried on, each year during the last three years, and what proportion they bear to the number of persons employed; the nature of each accident, and the probable cause; whether any and what proportion was owing to the crowded state of the machinery, to inadequate boxing or fencing off its dangerous parts, or to other neglect of precautions for safety.

You will also specially inquire whether the Children are ever employed in cleaning the machinery while it is in motion.

7.—Holidays.

You will learn whether any and what time is allowed to the Children for daily recreation and play: and also the number of Holidays and Half-holidays allowed them in the year.

8.—Hiring and Wages.

You will inquire whether the Children are hired by the master or by the adult whom they assist; whether the terms upon which they are hired are determined by the master or by the adult whom they assist; whether the Children make their own contracts, or whether they are made by the parents; whether the contracts made either by the Children or the parents are in any mode disadvantageous to the Children; whether, for example, there exists the practice, and to what extent, of masters lending money to parents to be repaid out of the labour of their Children.

You will also ascertain the amount of the Wages earned by the Children; whether the wages are paid by the master or by the adult whom they assist; whether the payment is made to themselves or to their parents or guardians; and whether by the piece or by weekly wages.

9. —TREATMENT AND CARE.

You will examine by what means the exertions of the Children at their work are encouraged or enforced; if encouraged by rewards, what they are, and how apportioned; if enforced by punishments, their nature and extent, by whom inflicted, and for what offences. You will also particularly inquire whether any, and what, care is taken of the Children when they have finished their daily labour.

10.—PHYSICAL CONDITION.

You will carefully examine the actual Physical Condition of the Children; whether that condition is better or worse than that of other Children in the same neighbourhood; if better, in what respects, and from what cause; if worse, whether the inferiority is wholly or partially the result of the nature of their labour, the early age at which it is enforced, or the number of hours during which it is continued; or whether there are any and what contributing causes for it in the state of their domestic habits; and whether their physical condition is worse than that of other Children in the same neighbourhood not so employed.

More especially you will report—

Whether, in *external appearance,* the Children you inspect are healthy or sickly, robust or delicate, well-formed or ill-formed. If you detect anything bad in the conformation, you will endeavour to ascertain the proportionate number of such cases, and in each instance endeavour to ascertain the probable cause.

Whether, in *stature,* there is an appreciable difference at any age, and what age, and in either sex, between Children early and constantly employed in the description of labour in question, and Children of the same age and station in the same neighbourhood not put to any such labour; and whether the physical deterioration of the Child employed in such labour is, in any case which you have an opportunity of examining, still visible in the adult.

Whether, as to *food,* the number of meals, the quantity and quality of food at each meal, and the time allowed for taking it, are adequate to maintain the health and strength of Children employed in constant labour, Whether the Children employed in labour are better or worse off in regard to the quantity and quality of their food than Children of their station and neighbourhood who do no work.

Whether, as to *clothing,* the Children are well or ill clothed, and whether any, and what, difference is made in their clothing in summer and winter.

Whether, as to *cleanliness,* the Children are encouraged to be neat and cleanly in their persons and clothing, or the contrary.

Whether the *amount of sickness* to which the Children within the terms of this Commission are subject is greater than that among the Children of the poorer classes employed at home or remaining unemployed. You are requested particularly to collect, as fully and correctly as possible, from medical men attached to the works, or practising in the neighbourhood, information as to what are the prevalent surgical diseases among the Children in question; whether, for example, hernia, distortion of the spine, swelling of the ankles, distortion of the joints from relaxation of the ligaments owing to long standing, mal-formation of the pelvis, or any other maladies which are usually the result of early and excessive work, or of an unfavourable posture of the body during a large portion of the day, are remarkably prevalent, or not more prevalent among these Children than among the Children of other classes of the people; also, whether among the acute medical diseases, fever, and among the chronic ailments, consumption, scrofula, and atrophy, or wasting, are peculiarly prevalent; and whether any other malady that may be supposed to be directly or indirectly connected with labour enforced at a tender age is of frequent occurrence.

11.—MORAL CONDITION.

You will carefully examine into the moral condition of the Children; whether any, and what, provisions are made for their religious instruction and moral training; how many attend Sunday-schools; and whether any, and what, secular instruction is given in such Schools, distinguishing those in which it is *not* the practice to conduct the Children to any place of public worship.

You will inquire in what numbers, at what ages, and for how many hours per week, the Children attend Day-schools; and endeavour to obtain from the teachers an account of the methods of instruction pursued, the books used, and whether the girls are instructed in needle and other household work in these schools. You will learn whether any, and what, provisions are made in them for training the Children in moral habits, for affording them religious knowledge, and for exercising them in the practice of religious duties. You will also inquire whether the religious instruction in the Day-schools is under any other superintendence than that of the teacher.

You will inquire whether any of the Children attend Industrial schools, in which it is attempted to communicate to them some knowledge of the principles of the machinery and implements employed in manufacturing processes, or in their own particular trade; or which tend to fit the Children for any other and what employments.

You will ascertain the expense of school attendance; by whom the money is paid; and the degree in which the attendance of the Child is interrupted by ignorance, poverty, negligence, or selfishness on the part of the parents; and, by a personal examination of the Children in the several Establishments which you visit, you will learn the extent to which they appear to have profited by their attendance at school.

You will collect information as to the station, salaries, knowledge, and qualifications of the teachers, and especially whether they have themselves received any training for their office; if so, where, and with what methods of instruction they are acquainted.

You will in every instance inquire whether any school is connected with the Works you visit; what interest is taken in the education of the Children by the employers and parents, or their indifference to it; and the capacity or inaptitude of the Children for receiving instruction after their hours of labour.

In regard to female workers, you will inquire how far their employment during Childhood has prevented them from forming the domestic habits usually acquired by women in their station, and has rendered them less fit than those whose early years have not been spent in labour for performing the duties of wives and mothers.

12.—COMPARATIVE CONDITION.

In examining into the condition of Children employed together in numbers, you will, throughout this Inquiry, endeavour to keep in view the *comparative* state of the Children of the poorer classes in the same neighbourhood, employed at home, or remaining unemployed.

With a view to ascertain how far the employment of the Children included in the terms of this Commission is beneficial or injurious to them in after-life, you will inquire into the positive and comparative condition of those whose term of infant labour has ceased; whether they usually experience greater or less difficulty than persons whose Childhood has not been spent in labour, in finding profitable employment in after-life; in what numbers, and at what ages, they continue in the employment in which they have worked during Childhood; and what are the trades, as far as can be ascertained, to which they generally have recourse, and the character they acquire as workpeople.

You will also examine how far the unlimited power to employ Children at any age, and for any number of hours, possessed both by parents and masters in all Trades and Works which are exempt from legislative restriction, operates injuriously on those branches of manufacturing industry which arc now subject to legislative restriction; and you will show, as far as practicable, the nature and extent of the evils which result from this partial legislation both to the employers and to the employed.

THE preceding heads of Inquiry indicate the kind of information which is sought, but are not intended as a complete enumeration of all the subjects which require investigation. In the outset of an Inquiry like the present, it is not possible to make an enumeration that shall be complete; and new points of inquiry, interesting and important, will probably arise as the investigation proceeds.

It is hoped that it will be possible, from the whole of the evidence which you collect, to arrive at a just conclusion as to the actual state and condition of the

Children who are the object of the present Inquiry, and to discriminate between the evils, physical, social, and moral, that may be peculiar to this class, and those that are common to this and to the other classes of the community.

It is deemed of great importance that you should in every instance acquire as intimate an acquaintance as may be practicable with the nature of the processes in which the Children are employed.

You will, however, carefully abstain from inquiring at the Works you visit into any of the processes of manufacture that are not necessarily connected with the object of your investigation, and from divulging anything connected with such processes which may either, directly or indirectly, come to your knowledge.

On arriving in any town or district, you will, as a general rule, seek an interview with the chief magistrate, the parochial clergy and other ministers of religion, the town-clerk, the relieving officers, and other public functionaries whose duties bring them into constant intercourse with the working classes.

You will inquire of the magistrates whether any, and what, complaints have been made before them, arising out of the hours of labour, or the treatment of the Children employed in mines, collieries, and the various branches of trade and manufacture within their districts. You will endeavour to see any Minutes of Evidence that may have been taken on those occasions, and to procure copies of any portion of them which may appear to you to be of importance.

You will also inquire, from the magistrates and clergy, and from the officers mentioned above, as to any facts, within their knowledge, illustrative of the comparative moral character of the Children employed in the several branches of mining and manufacturing industry in question, and that of those who are not so employed. In this, as in other instances, where any general allegations are made with respect to the character or conduct of parties, you will take care to ascertain how far those general allegations are justified by the number and the frequency of the instances; you will guard against any precipitate conclusions from extraordinary or anomalous cases; you will ascertain and show how far any irregularities of conduct are within the proper control of the employers or the parents of the Children, or whether any other, or what, control is available for their repression.

In order to guard against the risk of losing any evidence which might promote the objects of this Commission, you will take care to make your arrival in any place generally known, so as to give to all persons who are desirous of affording information ample opportunity of communicating with you, either verbally or by writing; and for the convenience of the workpeople, and of all persons who are engaged in labour during the day, you will probably find that a very convenient hour for personal communications will be between eight and ten o'clock in the evening.

You will be careful to examine the Children by themselves, and not in the presence of their parents or employers; and to take every precaution you can to diminish the chances of inaccuracy of statement, from timidity, or from the confusion to which Children are subject when spoken to by a stranger.

You will also carefully examine the parents of the Children employed, particularly with a view to ascertain how far the account given by the Children may agree or disagree with that given by the parents.

In examining the persons in each Establishment you visit, you will ascertain from them whether any, and what, alterations have been made in the mode of conducting the Works since the commencement of the year 1840; and whether, if the alterations made are substantial improvements, any measures may be taken to secure their permanence and their general adoption.

You will inquire into the general character of the parents of the Children, the influence of that character on their offspring, and the extent to which any legislative securities would probably be seconded by the exertions of the parents; whether they have complained of the treatment of their Children; and, if there be ground for supposing that the Children have been subjected to ill treatment, and no complaint has been made, then you will endeavour to ascertain how the absence of complaint is to be accounted for.

If testimony which you deem important be positively refused, or if any obstructions be wilfully placed in the way of an important course of inquiry, you will immediately transmit to the Commissioners an account of the circumstances of the case, in order that steps may be taken to meet the exigency.

With relation to the workmen, the parents, and the Children, whom you may examine, you will endeavour to secure for them such protection as may induce them to give their evidence freely; by preventing, when required, and when practicable or expedient, their names from being made public, or by requiring from the masters some public assurance or pledge that the witnesses shall in no way be prejudiced by any evidence which they may give.

It is desirable that the *smaller*, as well as the larger, Works in which Children are employed should be carefully examined; and that the Children or workmen who have been successively employed in large and small Works should be questioned as to the comparative treatment in the former and the latter. It may be well, as a general rule, in visiting any Work, that you should inquire whether any persons are there who have been employed in other mines, collieries, or manufactories, and examine them as to the general treatment of the Children in the several places of work where they were previously employed.

Whatever information you obtain under this Commission you will consider as strictly confidential, and communicate it only to the Board of Commissioners.

You will transmit to the Board of Commissioners the minutes of your own proceedings, and of the evidence you take at every place or district previously to your quitting it; and you will make your full and complete report as soon as possible.

Throughout the whole of this Inquiry you cannot too constantly bear in mind, nor will you lose any opportunity of impressing upon the minds of those with whom your investigations may bring you into communication,—

That Childhood is essentially the period of activity of the nutritive processes necessary to the growth and maturity of the body; that if at this period the kind and quantity of food necessary to afford the material for these processes be not supplied—if, instead of the pure air which is indispensable to convert the aliment into nutriment, the air which is constantly respired be loaded with noxious matters,—if the comparatively tender and feeble frame be now taxed by toil beyond its strength, and at unseasonable and unnatural periods,—and if the day be consumed in labour, and no time during the twenty-four hours be allowed for healthful recreation,—the organs will not be developed, their functions will be enfeeble and disordered, and the whole system will sustain an injury which cannot be repaired at any subsequent stage of human life;—and above all, that Childhood is no less essentially the period of the development of the mental faculties, on the culture and direction of which, at this tender age, the intellectual, moral, and religious qualities and habits of the future being almost wholly depend.

Experience having shown that certain kinds of labour, if moderate in degree, are not incompatible with health and vigour of body and mind at this period, while they may afford the means of improving the condition of both, it will be incumbent on you to inquire, whether, on the one hand, that portion of the infant population of the poorer classes of this country which is the object of the present investigation be subject only to such moderate and beneficial labour,—whether, taking together all the circumstances of their condition, these Children are better off, physically and mentally, than those of the same station who are employed at home, or who remain unemployed;—or, on the other hand, whether, instead of deriving any real advantage from their toil, their physical health and strength be not deteriorated, and their opportunities of intellectual, moral, and religious culture diminished; in short, whether they are not only constrained to pass their Childhood in privation and suffering, but, as the necessary result of such privation and suffering, whether their state in adolescence, manhood, and womanhood, will not probably be worse than it would have been but for the constraint and labour of their Childhood.

You have undertaken the task of collecting, from the various sources which will be pointed out to you, the information necessary to arrive at a just conclusion on these deeply interesting and important subjects; and you will feel that your responsibility is not diminished, when you consider that the number whose welfare is involved in the Inquiry is so large that in a few years it will constitute a very considerable proportion of the adult working population of the country; and that, upon the religious, moral, and physical culture and improvement of this portion of the population, the well-being of the whole community will in a great degree depend.

We are, Gentlemen,
Your faithful Servants,

THOS. TOOKE.
T. SOUTHWOOD SMITH.
LEONARD HORNER.
ROB. J. SAUNDERS.

*Children's Employment Commission,
3, Trafalgar Square, Westminster,
November 16th, 1840.*

SUPPLEMENTAL INSTRUCTIONS

To the Sub-Commissioners.

GENTLEMEN,

WE have to inform you that the Marquess of Normanby has signified to us, that the Queen has been pleased to comply with the prayer of an humble address presented to Her Majesty, in pursuance of a Resolution of the House of Commons, dated the 4th of February, 1841 :—

" That Her Majesty will be graciously pleased to direct that the Commission " appointed, in answer to an Address of this House on August 4, 1840, for the " investigation of certain branches of Infant Labour, do include within its inquiry " the Labour also of Young Persons designated as such by the provisions of the " Factory Act."

The Commissioners therefore desire that you will consider the preceding Instructions as applying equally to " Young Persons."

By the term " Young Persons" is to be understood Person between Thirteen and Eighteen years of age.

It does not appear to the Commissioners that this extension of the inquiry calls for any additional Instructions from them—all the subjects of investigation which relate to Children under Thirteen years of age being equally applicable to Young Persons between Thirteen and Eighteen years of age.

The Commissioners take this opportunity of stating to you—

That it is deemed essential that, before leaving any district, you should transmit to the Central Board as complete a List as it may be in your power to form of the Employers of Children and Young Persons in *each description* of work, together with the date on which the Tabular Forms and Queries were sent to them.

That you should on no account neglect personally to visit several of the mines and workshops of *each description* of employment.

That you should take measures for ascertaining, with as much correctness and completeness as possible, the AGGREGATE NUMBERS of Children and Young Persons employed in *each description* of work in the districts assigned to you.

APPENDIX.

Instructions to the Sub-Commissioners.

We are, Gentlemen,

Your faithful Servants,

THOˢ. TOOKE.
T. SOUTHWOOD SMITH.
LEONARD HORNER.
ROB. J. SAUNDERS.

Children's Employment Commission,
3, Trafalgar Square, Westminster,
February 15th, 1841.

LONDON:
Printed by WILLIAM CLOWES & SONS, Stamford Street,
For Her Majesty s Stationery Office.